KISSING THE ROD

KISSING THE ROD:

AN ANTHOLOGY OF SEVENTEENTH-CENTURY WOMEN'S VERSE

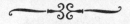

EDITED BY

GERMAINE GREER
SUSAN HASTINGS
JESLYN MEDOFF
MELINDA SANSONE

But why do I complain of thee?
'Cause thou'rt the Rod that scourgeth mee?
But if a good child I will bee,
I'le kiss the Rod, and honour thee.
                                    'Eliza', 1652

Published by VIRAGO PRESS Limited 1988
20-23 Mandela Street, Camden Town, London NW1 0HQ

British Library Cataloguing in Publication Data

Kissing the rod : an anthology of Seventeenth-
    century British women's verse.
    1. English poetry — Early modern, 1500-
    1700
    I. Greer, Germaine
    821'.4'08   PR1209

    ISBN 0-86068-851-8

1000346140

Photoset in North Wales by
Derek Doyle & Associates, Mold, Clwyd
Printed in Great Britain by
Mackays of Chatham PLC, Chatham, Kent

For our four mothers, Bess, Marjorie, Mary and Peg

CONTENTS

CONTENTS

CONTENTS

ACKNOWLEDGMENTS

Grateful acknowledgment is here made to: the Bodleian Library, University of Oxford, for permission to quote Bodleian MSS Locke c. 32, Ashmole 226, Don. e. 17, Rawl. d. 1308, Rawl. d. 360, Rawl. poet. 16, Rawl. poet. 154:50, Rawl. poet. 155, Rawl. poet. e. 173, Rawl. poet. 196, Rawl. poet. 173, Fairfax 40, Eng. Misc. C. 116, Eng. poet. e. 87, and also Wood 517, Pamphlet 6; to the British Library, for permission to quote from Harl. MS 1052, Add. MSS 4162, 4264, 4265, 4279, 19,333, 21,621, 28,693, Egerton MS 607; to Christ Church College Library (Oxford) and the Trustees of the Will of Major Peter George Evelyn, for permission to quote MS 92, Mary Evelyn's 'Miscellaneous Book of Meditations'; to Dame Alix Meynell, for selections from Mary Carey's MS book of 'meditations and poetry' in her possession; to the Hertfordshire County Record Office, for permission to quote from the Ashridge MSS, AH 1074 and 1075; to the President and Fellows of Magdalen College, Oxford, for permission to quote from Magdalen MS 343, 'Poems on Several Occasions, in three parts' by Jane Barker; to the Keeper of the Manuscripts, Nottingham University Library, for permission to quote Portland MSS Pwl. 69, 84, 88, 118, 119, 367, 368, PwV. 19, 31, 40, 43, 89, 329; to the Lambeth Palace Library, for permission to quote from Court of Arches Records, Ee 8; to Louisiana State University Press, for permission to publish selections from *The Poems of Lady Mary Wroth* edited by Josephine A. Roberts (1983); to the Duke of Sutherland (and the Huntington Library), for permission to quote from the Ellesmere MSS 8353, 8367, 35/B/65; to Scholars' Facsimiles and Reprints, for permission to quote from *The Novels of Mary Delariviere Manley* ed. Patricia Koster (1971); to the Archives and Rare Books Department, University of Cincinnati Libraries, for permission to quote from the letterbook of Sir Edward Dering, Phillipps MS 14392; to the Curator of the James Marshall and Marie Louise Osborn Collection, at the Beinecke Rare Book and Manuscript Library, Yale University Library, for permission to quote the MS poem 'To the Queens Most Excellent Majestie' inscribed in their copy of *The Reply of the Most Illustrious Cardinall Of Perron* (Douay, 1630); to the National Library of Wales, for permission to quote from Orielton MSS Box 24, MSS 775 and 776; to the Institut für Englische Sprache und Literatur, Universität Salzburg, for permission to quote from *The Triumph of Death and Other Unpublished and Uncollected Poems by Mary Sidney, Countess of Pembroke (1561-1621),* ed. G. F. Waller (1977); to G. K. Hall and Co., for permission to quote from *The Complete Works of Anne Bradstreet,*

ed. Joseph R. McElrath, Jr., and Allen P. Robb (1981); to the Harry
Ransom Humanities Research Center, The University of Texas at
Austin, for permission to publish the text of 'On the Numerous
Accesse of the English to wait upon the King in Holland', 'On the
Death of the Queen of Bohemia' and 'To her royall highnesse the
Dutchesse of Yorke', as given in the copies made by Sir Edward
Dering now in their possession; to the Rev. Dr Patrick Thomas, for
permission to quote from his Ph. D. thesis 'An Edition of the Poems
and Letters of Katherine Philips 1632-1664' to be published in due
course, we understand, by the University of Wales Press; to the
Keeper of Public Records, Public Records Office, London, for
permission under Crown copyright to quote from SP 29/167, f.160,
SP 29/169, ff.38, 39; SP 29/170, f.75; SP 29/171, f.120; SP 29/172,
f.14, SP29/141, 81, 81I, 81II; SP 29/177, f.42; SP 29/182, f. 143; SP
29/251, ff.91, 91I, 92; to the Huntington Library, for permission to
quote from MSS HA 8799, EL 8353, EL 8367, EL 11143, EL
35/B/62, Bridgewater Trust Paper No. 8331, and the manuscript
poem inscribed in their copy of *Lachrymae Musarum* (1650); to the
Chapin Library, Williams College, Williamstown, Massachusetts, for
permission to publish the MS inscription in their copy of *Salve Deus
Rex Judaeorum* by Aemilia Lanyer (1611); to the Houghton Library,
Harvard University, for permission to quote *An Elegy Upon the Death
of Mrs. A. Behn*, *pEB65. A100. 689e3; to the Trustees of the
National Library of Scotland, for the text of Lady Melville's sonnet,
in Wodrow 4to MS 29, No.4; to the Augustan Reprint Society,
William Andrews Clark Memorial Library, University of California,
Los Angeles, for permission to publish poems from their edition of
Divine Songs and Meditacions Composed by An Collins (1653), No. 94; to
the Keepers of the Theater Collection, Harvard University, for
permission to quote from an uncatalogued autograph letter from
Katherine Philips to Dorothy Temple, 22 January 1663.

We would like also to express our warm appreciation to all the
librarians who have helped us, whether at the Bodleian, the British
Library, the Huntington Library, the Alexander Library of Rutgers
University, New Brunswick, or especially the Cambridge University
Library, where in the dark days of the English summer two of the
editors struggled to co-ordinate this vast mass of material. A special
thanks is due to Rita Winfield, who turned the vegetable garden
into wonderful meals and kept the house full of music and flowers,
while we raved and maddened in the 'room of blots'.

EDITORS' NOTE

In this book we have taken the rather unusual step of adopting a system of reference more usually encountered in scientific publications. Because of the intricacy of the combination of text, bibliographical commentary and elucidation, it was both undesirable and extremely difficult to include footnotes, or notes at the end of entries marked by superscript figures on the text, or a vast section of notes at the back of the book. By way of keeping the bulk of the apparatus to the minimum we decided to acknowledge sources as fully as possible in parentheses in the text.

Our copy texts are named in full at the end of the first selection from each in each entry, and these texts are not repeated in the list of works cited unless they are cited elsewhere in the book as well.

All manuscript sources are so identified in the text by the name of the library, usually abbreviated, the MS number, and the page or folio number. We have not included a separate list.

Printed sources are acknowledged by the last name of the author, and the page number; the interested reader is asked to check the full title, date and publisher of the book in the list included at page 452. Where we have cited more than one work by an author, we have identified the particular work in each case by its publication date, unless more than one work appeared in the year in question, in which case we resort to other indications, such as an abbreviated form of the title.

Works mentioned but not quoted are not generally listed with a fuller citation because the list would then become too unwieldy to be genuinely useful. Poems by better-known poets are referred to not by editor but by title; line numbers are given so that readers can find the relevant passages in whatever edition they have access to. We cite particular editions only when commentary or annotation has contained information not available elsewhere. Problems have arisen because we are four editors working in locations thousands of miles apart; it would be invidious to specify which of us has had to work without adequate library facilities, but heavy reliance on superseded nineteenth-century texts has been a problem for more than one of us at different times in the five years we have taken to put the book together. Readers requiring more detailed reading lists for our women poets are invited to write to us, and we will respond as soon as we can get access to the computer files, which are more comprehensive than the book can possibly be.

Our selections have been made with the best interests of our poets at heart, both individually and as a group; we are acutely aware that such selection is draconian and can be extremely distorting. Each selection was hotly debated, but our book is finite, and we hope possible to read on the train or in any other of the short intervals of time that are all most women get to themselves. Some readers will notice that we have not included Elizabeth Weston, author of *Parthenicon* (1602); our only excuse is that like most of our readers we are not competent to judge her Latin; others will wonder why we did not include Ann Finch, Countess of Winchilsea or Lady Chudleigh, who were both active in the 1690s. Both poets are much better known than all but a few of the poets we have included, and are usually associated with the eighteenth century.

One motive for selection was to illuminate the general lot of women in the seventeenth century, another to show how women trying to develop their creativity supported each other, another to illustrate how dubious and contradictory were the women's relations to the male establishment, whether in the persons of their husbands, their public or their publishers. Above all we wanted to convey in as lively a manner as possible, the individuality and the surprisingness of the women in whose company we have spent so much time. We all feel that all our women deserve less summary treatment; one motive for publishing this book at this time is that other women will join us in this work so that our poets will get the interest and respect that they deserve.

Before publication we were already hearing shock reaction to the title we have chosen. To kiss the rod, in the words of Torriano's *Proverbial Phrases* (1666), means 'not only to have patience, but also to thank those by whom one hath been chastis'd, and as it were to seem to be beholding to them for their correction; taken from Children, who when they do amiss, and are punish'd, they are made to vent their vexation no otherwise than by kissing that rod with which they were punish'd' (575). Whether the rod is wielded by paternal authority, the male establishment, a husband, the king, Cromwell or God himself, women have always been obliged for their own survival to humble themselves before it, and to flatter it. Such contradictions constitute the peculiarly insidious and destructive character of sex oppression.

ABBREVIATIONS

BL	British Library
Bod.	Bodleian Library
CSPD	*Calendar of State Papers Domestic*
DWB	*Dictionary of Welsh Biography*
DNB	*Dictionary of National Biography*
HL	Huntington Library
HMC	Historical Manuscripts Commission Reports
HRC	Harry Ransom Humanities Research Center, The University of Texas at Austin
HRO	Hertfordshire Record Office
LAO	Lincolnshire Archives Office
LC	Lord Chamberlain's Records (PRO)
N&Q	*Notes and Queries*
NLS	National Library of Scotland
NLW	National Library of Wales
NRO	Northamptonshire Record Office
OED	*Oxford English Dictionary*
PMLA	*Publications of the Modern Language Association*
PRO	Public Record Office
TLS	*The Times Literary Supplement*
UNott	University of Nottingham

INTRODUCTION

This book is about women and poetry, in particular about some of the women who tried to write poetry in the century of Donne, Milton, and Dryden. We have aimed to show who the women were who tried to storm the highest bastion of the cultural establishment, the citadel of 'sacred poetry'. They were all *guerrilleras*, untrained, ill-equipped, isolated and vulnerable. We have done our best to let them speak in their own voices; our commentary upon their performance reveals more about the English literary culture of which we ourselves are victims than it does about women's creativity. The book-selling trade has always made use of women, women as subjects, women as captive audience, women as amanuenses, as buyers of books, and occasionally as authors. If women had been totally excluded from literary life in the seventeenth century, their creativity might well have suffered less than it did through the demands of their incompatible ancillary roles as muses, interpreters, consumers and admiring audience of masculine literary achievement.

In seventeenth-century England literary activity was exclusively oriented to the concerns of the classically educated males who formed the ruling class. This is not to say that the mass of the people had no culture, but that popular culture was not expressed in literary forms. There were songs and sermons and plays for the delight and instruction of the masses, but books and writing were irrelevant to most people's daily lives. If poetry is 'making' then all women were poets, but they did not make primarily with words, and certainly not with characters inscribed upon a page.

An English household in the seventeenth century was not the dull and confined place it is today. The larger households were workplaces, more like a cross between a factory and an office building than the homes where we go to eat and sleep. Housework was not mechanical cooking and cleaning but highly skilled and demanding work. Even in small households the goodwife was responsible for raising poultry and keeping the kitchen garden as well as spinning, dressmaking, baking and brewing. More ambitious households added candying, preserving, pickling, smoking, cheesemaking, distilling, drying, salting, potting, pork-butchery and even the preparation of medicaments to that list (Hole, *passim*). As soon as it could be afforded householders acquired servants, from children to run messages to expert ladies' maids, with skills like those of present-day hairdressers and beauticians. Trained

1

laundresses and seamstresses could sell their services to the highest bidder; everyone who called herself a lady, from the queens downwards, had to have them, and starchers, midwives and wet and dry nurses as well, all skilled workers. At the beginning of the century the mistress of the house, no matter how grand, lived in this concrete active world. She had to take part in the training of staff and to be a good judge of a working woman's competence. After the Restoration the appeal to woman's capability and her responsibilities as manager and producer began to be made in more shamefaced fashion: in the list of female accomplishments *The Ladies Calling* (1673) mentions first 'ornamental improvements which become their quality as Writing, Needlework, Languages, Music or the like', and then goes on: 'If I should here insert the art of Oeconomy and Houshold Managery I should not think I affronted them in it, that being the most proper feminine business, from which neither wealth nor greatness can totally absolve them...' The Anglo-Saxon scholar Elizabeth Elstob (1683-1756) was justifiably proud that she could spin thread and knit her own stockings.

After the Restoration the lady of fashion, whose chief duty was vicarious leisure and titillating display, replaced the godly housewife as the most pervasive stereotype. With her came the cult of feminine delicacy, and a double standard which argued that as women were made of finer stuff, less was to be expected of them in the way of achievement and more in the way of passive virtue. Even so a Restoration lady spent less time with her husband than with her maidservants, chatting, working, going out with them to shop or visit other women. Although the middle-class women for whom books like *The Ladies Calling* were written might dream of marrying into the gentry, there was by the end of the century a marked surplus of never married females in London (Stone, 1977, Fig. 2). A provident parent had to ensure that daughters acquired some saleable skill, and were not idling away their time in poetical fantasies. A wife who knew how to brew good ale saved many a family from going to the wall (see, e.g., Richard Gough, *The History of Myddle, passim*) but no 'poetress' ever staved off destitution by her literary efforts, not even Aphra Behn.

It is a commonplace of feminist literary history that the seventeenth century reacted against the kind of humanist concern that produced a generation of Tudor noblewomen fully literate in classical languages, of whom Viscountess Falkland (see p.54ff.) is the last example, but the decline of interest in female prodigies was accompanied by a gradual if patchy improvement in basic education for women. Throughout the seventeenth century the proportion of women who could sign their names to legal documents remained low, in the region of 11 per cent. In London, where literate women who needed to make a living were likely to try their fortunes as 'governantesses' or traders, or servants to professional men, the

INTRODUCTION

proportion of women signing their own names gradually rises to about half at the end of the century. However, many who could not write could read, and that proportion gradually rises through the century (Cressy, 1980, 147).

Evidence of the extent and nature of elementary education in the seventeenth century is sketchy; much depended upon the attitude of local dignitaries and parish officials and the money available. A bequest specifying the providing of education to poor children, an impoverished scholar setting up a fee-paying school, a literate woman with time on her hands could all make a significant contribution. At some times, when the authorities were anxious that heresy and sedition might be taught by zealots in village schools, attempts were made at registration and control, but generally there was no attempt to set standards. Even where schools were competently run, the literacy of female pupils was never as important as their acquisition of manual skills. At the Free School at Great Marlow, Bucks, twenty-four girls were taught to knit, spin and make bone-lace while the boys were taught to read. The Red Maids at a school in Bristol set up by a merchant's bequest in 1627 were given the choice of reading or plain needlework. In other circumstances, girls might be admitted to a local school only when there were not enough boy pupils to pay the schoolmaster's wages (Houston, 1985, 106). It is probably safe to assume that most girls attended 'dame-schools' or the equivalent along with little boys, where a schoolmaster or cleric, or a woman who may well herself have been unable to write, taught them their 'book' (Cressy, 1980, 36-38; Spufford, 1979, 409-410, 434-435). By the age of seven when they could decipher their letters, most girls left school to work for the family, either at home or in service. Elizabeth Joceline, who knew Latin, did not wish her daughter to have the same education:

I desire her bringing up may be learning the Bible as my sisters doe, good houswifery, writing and good workes: other learning a woman needs not; though I admire it in those whom God hath blest with discretion, yet I desire it not much in my own, having seene that sometimes women have greater portions of learning than wisdome, which is no better use to them than a mainsail to a flye boat, which runs it under water. (1624, 35-36)

The anonymous author of *The Ten Pleasures of Marriage* (1682) tells us that 'the Daughter, which goes along with her mother is kindled with no small matter of jealousie to see that her Brother puts her parents to so much charge, gets what he pleases, and that their minds are never at rest about him. When she, on the contrary, being at home, is thrust by the mother into the drudgery of the house or kept close to her needle'(241).

Persons wishing their girls to acquire more genteel accomplishments could send them to private finishing schools, like the one run by Mr and Mrs Robert Perwick in Hackney (1637-1660) or the Ladies' Hall in Deptford, or Mr Bevens's Finishing School in Ashford. In such establishments they would certainly learn music

3

and dancing and 'curious work' and they might have the choice of learning handwriting from a scrivener and letter-writing modelled on 'Mr. Ford, Mr. Howell, Mr. Loveday and Monsieur Voiture' (Woolley, 1673, 13) and the art of 'conference' or conversation. Such girls' schools spread outwards from Chelsea and Hackney to most provincial commercial centres; as the number of upwardly mobile middle-class families increased, Manchester, Oxford, Exeter, Taunton, and Leicester all came to boast ladies' academies. D'Urfey's *Love for Money; or, the Boarding School* (1691) showed the pupils to be vulgar hoydens acquiring a gloss of spurious refinement through the kind offices of the French and the dancing masters.

By the end of the century there was in London a generation of semi-literate maidservants who read periodicals like *The Athenian Mercury*, but could not themselves write a connected sentence. Hannah Woolley, teenage schoolmistress, then secretary and upper servant and then school usher's wife, is the purported author of eight different manuals of instruction intended primarily not for the gentlewoman but for her companion, which went through dozens of editions in the sixties and seventies, along with many other manuals of household skills, most put together by male hacks. Though most women could read their Bibles, writing remained, in the phrase used by Dorothy Leigh in *The Mother's Blessing* (1616) 'a thing unusual among us'. *The English Scholemaster*, a primer originally published in 1596 by Edmund Coote, which offered a method of teaching oneself writing to men and women 'that now are ashamed to write to their best friends', was republished more than a hundred times in the seventeenth century. The anonymous female author of *Six Familiar Essays upon Marriage, Crosses in Love, Sickness, Death, Loyalty and Friendship* (1696) in an introductory epistle 'To the Bookseller' assures him that 'Gentlemen will kindly overlook a woman's Errors... false English being particularly intailed upon the Sex'.

It must not be forgotten that in the seventeenth century there was no cheap or easily available writing material; in an account book of 1651 we learn that six quire (144 sheets) of writing paper and a bottle of ink cost three shillings and sixpence, more than a labourer's weekly wage (HMC 78 Hastings Vol.4). The acquisition of paper and pens and ink involved a commitment to literacy which most working people could not afford, except in the case of exceptionally gifted boys, whose mothers were often responsible for securing educational opportunities for them, as Abraham Cowley's mother, a stationer's widow, did for him.

If the lower orders could not afford to learn to write, no one who was or aspired to be 'of the quality', that is, unsullied by commerce or manual labour, could write too seriously or too well. Handwriting itself was considered a manual occupation. The gentry and nobility for the most part scorned to write a 'clerk-like' hand

4

and usually had a clean copy made by a scribe for presentation to the intended recipient of their effusions. The Marquis of Halifax sent his famous letter to his daughter to a scrivener who had the wit to make an extra copy, knowing that what he had before him was booksellers' gold. The booksellers attempted to disarm the Marquis's wrath by claiming that when the copy was brought to them the bearer knew nothing of the provenance and therefore they were justified in securing a licence for it as the work of an unknown author (Savile, 1688). By such shifts the Marquis's elegant and merciless description of a well-bred woman's duty came to exercise malefic influence for the best part of a century.

When Dorothy Osborne asked William Temple to send her the Duchess of Newcastle's *Poems and Fancies* (1653) and went on 'Sure the poore woman is a litle distracted, she could never bee soe ridiculous else as to venture at writeing book's and in verse too' (Smith, 37), she was expressing the reaction of her peers to the Duchess's obsession with producing actual books with her name on the title-pages. The Duchess was flouting not principally the canons of sexual respectability, but the decorum of her class and the requirements of her position by exposing her lucubrations under her own name to the curiosity of the profane public.

Verse was a genteel accomplishment expected of both ladies and gentlemen of noble birth for the amusement and edification of their own kind. Ideally such occasional verse should be light and brief and apparently artless, but there must have been more than one lonely young woman who wrote for the reasons given by Hester Wyat in 'A Poem made by [a Frie]nd of mine in Answere to One who Askt w[hy s]he wrotte' (Bod. MS Rawl. d. 360, f.53).

> What makes me write my dearest Freind you aske
> For our Sex always thought too great a taske
> I grant you this yet 'tis no ill spent time
> And my thoughts natur'ly fall into Rime
> Rude and unpolish't from my pen they flow
> So artless I my native tongue scarce know
> Learning the Wit & judgment must improve
> Refine the verse and tender passion move
> Whilst me no muse assists nor God of Love
> Like those whose hearts with suden greife oprest
> No kind freind near on whose lov'd constant Breast
> Leening their drooping Heads they may complain
> To Groves which no return can make again
> They sigh their Woes to ease theyr killing pain
> So whilst in Solitude the days I pass
> Paper I make my Freind & minds true Glass
> To that my selfe unbosome free from fear
> Of a false womans tongue or Lissening eare
> Blessing their Fate who your dear Sight enjoye
> Pleasures their hours their happy hours imploy
> This to us Rurall Nimphs is now deny'd
> A life wch is you know my humble share
> Free from Ambition nor yet clog'd with care
> Nor need I tell you Freind this dismall truth

How vice & folly has possest our youth
So empty is our Sex, yet so vain grow'n
And more debauch't the other ne're were known
Out of such Company whats to be brought
Scandal or nonsense not one solid thought
With joy I from these noysy crouds retire
And from my thoughts of my owne Heart inquire
Shou'd we not to ourselves this great debt pay
The little time that fleeting Life does stay
Wear worthless if unthinking thrown away
Then I my secret thoughts colect & write
Cause this improves me, most does most delight
And whilst with innocence my time I spend
That soonest leads to the proposed end
No guilty blush my cheekes dye to impart
These lines my Freind chast as the Authors Heart
Happy if they can answere your desire
Tho they in flames bright as your eyes expire

Most of the poetry written by lonely women in the seventeenth century probably ended as Wyat expects hers to, in the fire, burned by their authors if not by the people they addressed. Certainly we have not found any more of the poetry that Wyat wrote, which, judging by her facility with iambic pentameter, must have been copious. The survival of this poem we owe to the fact that another of her friends thought it worth copying and keeping. Many women who versified in their youth destroyed the evidence when they came to riper years or lost their privacy by marrying. If a lady showed unusual talent, her works would be widely copied and circulated until they became famous among her own class, as was the case with Mary Herbert, Countess of Pembroke, Katherine Philips (see pp.186ff.) and Anne Wharton (see p.286ff.) A lively tutor or secretary could see his opportunity, make his fair copy and hawk it round the booksellers, who would pay him for it. (The author had no rights in the work.) Only a bookseller fearful of alienating a powerful family would hesitate before rushing into print.

Most of the poetry printed in the seventeenth century was not by professionals. Publication was usually a consequence of fame already achieved. The poems of Rochester, Denham, Carew, Herbert, Crashaw, Traherne, for example, were circulated not only in the author's autograph, but copied and re-copied, accurately and inaccurately, scribbled down from recollection or while listening. The copyist might go so far as to sign the work, specially if it was meant for a present to an absent friend, and so we have a body of suppositious works by women based on the superscription 'by the gracious hand of the Lady So-and-So' none of which we have included in this book. Such copies were eagerly sought, most eagerly of course by booksellers, only too happy to bandy about an imposing name archly concealed beneath initials. The more notorious a poet, the more likely he was to have inferior works published under his name or, more likely, his initials. Giles Fletcher's *Brittains Ida* was published as by 'that renowned poet

INTRODUCTION

E—— S——'. The corpus of the 'E of R——' included hundreds of verses by other hands.

After the Restoration, as the number of books printed increased exponentially, publishing began very gradually to gain in respectability. Careful editing was pioneered by Tonson, who invited well-born poets to contribute works for miscellanies, where they were printed accurately with full attribution. Katherine Philips's poems were registered under her full name for publication in 1664; some of 'Orinda's' rather unconvincing indignation at the appearance of the volume with her initials on the title-page may have been prompted by a desire to show that she was as genteel as her mentor, Sir Charles Cotterell, whose work was published anonymously. Perhaps she was incensed because the title-page did not identify her as a person of quality. Most of the work of 'persons of quality' continued to be published anonymously well after 1700, and the reason was not chiefly feminine modesty. Of forty-three elegies published on the death of Queen Mary (1694) twenty-two were by named poets; five authors are identified only by initials; five poems appear without any ascription at all; two are ascribed to a 'Person of Honour'; another to a 'Private Hand', three to gentlemen of various kinds and only two to women, one 'A Young Lady' and the other 'A Gentlewoman of Quality'.

A male relative might without prejudice publish the works of a gentlewoman under her own name after her death, for the edification of other women. Anne Killigrew's works were published by her father in 1685 after her untimely death from smallpox (see p.299); Mary Evelyn's *Mundus Muliebris* was published by her father in 1690, five years after her death (see p.324), with the difference that no author's name appears on the title-page. How much emendation, suppression and editorial tinkering was done in such cases is not now possible to determine. Living ladies were only too grateful when a properly educated male of their acquaintance agreed to correct their work. Katherine Philips submitted all of her work to Sir Charles Cotterell, enjoining him to 'put it in a better dress... if it be capable of improvement, if it be not, commit it to the flames' (*Letters from Orinda to Poliarchus*, IX). Fifty years later Elizabeth Thomas sent poetry by her friend Lady Chudleigh to Henry Cromwell begging him to 'condescend to bestow a few Plashes of Ink upon it', assuring him that her ladyship would 'think herself honoured' by his notice (*Pylades and Corinna*, I, 281-283).

Such readiness to accept correction was not displayed solely by women. No one in the seventeenth century would have chosen to publish his own words rather than a version improved by an abler hand; many poems now attributed to well-known poets are to be found in variant versions in various hands among the papers of other poets. A poem like 'I prithee send me back my heart' which exists in dozens of contemporary manuscript sources, may reflect a collective effort (see p.116). A similar case is the poem which appears in many anthologies of women's verse as by Anne Howard, Countess of Arundel.

> In sad and ashy weeds I sigh,
>   I grone, I pine, I mourne;
> My oten yellow reeds
>   I all to jet and ebon turne.
> My watrie eyes, lyke winter's skyes,
>   My furrowed cheekes o'erflowe.
> All heavens knowe why, men mourne as I,
>   And who can blame my woe.

The sole reason for the attribution to the Countess of Arundel is that a transcript of the first four stanzas of the poem appears on the back of a letter dated 25 July 1617, which used to be among the Harington MSS at Arundel Castle and is now lost. The handwriting was assumed by one scholar to be that of the Countess. In fact the full version of the poem had been published as a broadside (Rollins, *The Pepys Ballads*, I, 352-353) which was registered on 19 November 1612, under the name 'The Good Shepherds Sorrow for the death of his beloved Sonne'; the son was identified by a woodcut as Prince Henry, who died on 6 November. The persona of the poem is clearly King James; the author is still unidentified. Another case of a famous poem traditionally attributed to a woman, which exists in several versions, is 'Lines on seeing King James's Picture'.

> What Briton can survey that heavenly face
> And doubt his being of the Martyr's race?
> His every feature doth his birth declare;
> The monarch and the saint are shining there.
> That face must sure the boldest Whig convince
> Which speaks at once the Stuart and the prince.
> O lovely Youth, 'tis evidently plain
> By thy majestick look thou art born to reign.
> My heart bleeds as I view this noble shade
> And grieves it cannot bring thee better aid;
> I on no other terms a man would be
> But to defend thy glorious cause and thee.
>   O were my pen a sword that I in fight
>   Instead of verse might vindicate thy Right.

The argument of the sonnet makes clear that the picture is one of James Frances Edward, Prince of Wales, who was said by the Protestant opponents of James II to have been smuggled into the bed of Mary of Modena in a warming pan; the Jacobite poet argues for his legitimacy as James's son and heir to the throne of England. The poem, which can be found in various manuscript sources, is always attributed to a lady and in one case to a Lady W—; confusion has arisen because one surviving version of the poem includes twenty-five additional lines of satire against prominent Whigs written at a much later date (Bod. MS Rawl. poet. 155, 133). Our view is that the poem is by a woman and refers to a widely circulated engraved portrait of the Old Pretender as a child. It must therefore have been written in the 1690s, probably in the sonnet form we have conflated from Bod. MSS. Eng. Misc. c. 116, f.10 and Eng. poet. e. 87, p.120, and Rawl. poet. 173, f.2ᵛ. None of the MS sources is contemporary, which in part justifies the conflation of all of them, to produce the clearest and most concise version.

Elsewhere throughout this volume we have indulged a twentieth-century preference for authenticity and have sought to reproduce the exact language of each individual woman, however chaotic the spelling, grammar and punctuation. We are also concerned to convey the real situation of women vis-à-vis the means of expression and to provide materials for discussion of whether or not there is a female language and female prosody. The question is a vexed one, for women who want to write in metre are already accepting an externally imposed discipline (the rod of our title); even so we can discern some syntactic patterns, such as endless chains of clauses which may be related back and forwards with equal justification, rather than a hierarchy of main clauses with obvious subordinates, which other scholars may well make more of than we have. After our struggle to dig out autograph poems wherever possible, it is chastening to reflect that the poets themselves might not have thanked us for it.

The seventeenth century shared none of our post-romantic awe of poets. Until Dryden's fame reached its apogee, a professional writer in verse or prose was a mere artisan, with no higher status than, say, the advertising copy-writer has today. The poet's job was, not to express his own ideas or fantasies, but to write to order, celebrating the births, deaths, marriages and coronations of the ruling class, much today as an advertising copy-writer sings the praises of Guinness and Coca Cola. On the occasion of the death on the eve of his wedding of Henry Hastings, son and heir of Ferdinando, sixth Earl of Huntingdon, in 1649, ninety-eight elegies by different hands were accepted for the memorial volume entitled *Lachrymae Musarum*. Any professional poet wishing to display his skill could find such a volume extremely useful; Dryden contributed his first published poem as did a number of his schoolfellows at Westminster. The published volume did not include the poem said to be in the handwriting of Henry Hastings's mother, Lucy, daughter of Sir John Davies the poet and the mad mystic, Lady Eleanor Audeley, on the fly-leaf of the Huntington Library copy of *Lachrymae Musarum*:

> The Bowells of the Earth my bowells Slide
> Whilst these Dear relicks here interrd abide
> Thus I die Living, thus alass mine Eyes,
> My funerall see, since hee before me Dyes
> Whom I brought forth my Dear Son here he Lies.
> Clear up mine eyes hee Lies not here,
> His Soul is he, which when his Dear
> Redeemer had refin'd to a height
> Of Purity, and Solid Weight;
> No Longer would he Let it Stay,

With in this Crucible of Clay,
But meaning him a richer Case,
To raise his Luster, not imbase,
And knowing the infectious Dust
Might Canker the bright piece with Rust,
Hasted him hence; into his Treasure
Of Blessed Spirits, where till the Measure
Accomplish'd bee of the Elect;
They Rest and Joyfully expect
The image of our Lords perfection,
In the aproaching Resurection.

The poem is signed simply L.H. for Lucy Hastings or Lucy Huntingdon. The artificiality of the elaborate conceit of her son as a jewel in the heavenly treasury is not evidence that the Countess's feeling is not genuine. The apparent corruption of the first line may be an indication of the shortcomings of this kind of therapy for grief or the result of inept transcription, rendering the word 'Hide', perhaps, as 'Slide'; the authenticity of the poem is not yet proved to our satisfaction, for its central conceit is expressed in terms closely related to Thomas Pestel's 'For the Right Honourable Lucie Countess of Huntingdon' in *Lachrymae Musarum*, which is partly written in the Countess's persona.

Ladies were expected not only to write out their own heart-break in metrical form, but to contribute epitaphs and panegyrics on their friends: the Lady Carey sent such an 'elogy' to her neighbour Lord Thomas Fairfax on the death of his wife in 1665 (Bod. MS Fairfax 40, 596-597). Her couplets end:

Her Body deare her All thats out of Heaven
To Billbrough church as a riche Treasure's given
Bilbrough church-yeard daine me a little roome
That after death my grave waite on her Tombe.

The epitaph 'promised and made' by Margaret, Countess of Cumberland, for Richard Candish was actually engraved upon his monument in Hornsey church; it is a poised and impressive exercise in the genre:

Candish deriv'd from Noble Parentage
Adorn'd with Vertuous and heroicke partes
Most learned bountifull Devout and Sage
Grac'd with the graces Muses and the Artes
Deer to his Prince in English Court admird
Beloved of great & Honorable Peeres
Of all estemed embraced & desired
Till Death Cut of his well employed yeere.
Within this earth his earth entombed lies
Whose heavenly part Surmounted hath the skies. (*N&Q*, Ser.7, iv, 374)

The formality of such funerary verse was eventually superseded by a more straightforward language of bereavement, informed always by religious feeling. In an elegy 'On my Dearly beloved Husband Taken from me by y[e] hand of God January 17th 1661', an unknown lady lamented her husband in these terms:

> Oh Death that hath with thine impartiall stroak
> Cancell'd ye bond, and broake ye yoake –
>   soe firmly tyed my love & I
> That nought but thow, as Gods Decree
> Could alter ought in him or mee.
> And though as his, hee would me try,
> Yet I by it will Learne to Dye,
>   submitting to his will
> By whose meare mercy I doe live,
> And on it still I shall Rely,
>   from thee to bee Repriv'd.

A second poem in couplets celebrates the anniversary of her husband's death, praising him for

> Beeing A Patterne to all those,
> that with A wife would happier Live,
> And to thine owne deare ofspring shew,
> Much love & yet correction give:
> Thy servants all so happie were,
> that they with us doe beare a share:
> Of sorrowes cause, even they as wee
> noe more can here soe happie bee... (Huntington MSS)

Among the genres a literate gentlewoman might be expected to master was the farewell to her husband about to be widowed. Such a poem was intended to display deep love and fortitude, with control and resignation mimetically conveyed by lucid, balanced syntax uncontorted by demands of rhyme or metre. The best examples of this kind became famous in their own time; they served as incantations for frightened women embarking on the grim lottery of childbed, and mnemonics for female magnanimity. They are also one genre which is always everywhere female.

Another female genre was the 'mother's legacy'. At a time when perhaps 45 per cent of middle- and upper-class women died before reaching the age of fifty and more than half of them of complications of pregnancy (Dobbie, *passim*; Eccles, 125-130) it was only proper that pregnant women were encouraged by their spiritual advisers to be prepared for death. One way of preparing was to compile books of advice and guidance for the children who might have to grow up motherless. The most famous of these was the prose work by Elizabeth Joceline, *The Mothers Legacie To her unborne Childe* (1624) which went through three editions in two years and was still being quoted at the end of the century. Thomas Goad, her spiritual adviser, approved of the fact that Joceline ordered her winding-sheet within days of quickening and asked for it to be laid upon her as soon as she was delivered of her daughter, although she did not actually die for nine days, interpreting such disturbed behaviour as evidence of an exemplary degree of resignation. All Elizabeth Grymeston's son Bernye knew of his mother was the 'portrait of a mother's mind' left him in her *Miscelanea. Meditations. Memoratives* which were published in 1604 with such success that three augmented editions followed. The book was compiled between 1601 and Grymeston's death in 1602 or 1603; it is a patchwork of quotations, unacknowledged and often modified to suit her purpose, drawn from Robert Southwell and Richard Rowlands, whose *Odes in Imitation of the Seaven Penitential Psalms* (1601) she transcribes almost verbatim to make a chapter in her book (Hughey and Hereford, *passim*). Grymeston's failure to acknowledge her sources ought not to be interpreted as plagiarism; she confesses her borrowings:

the spiders webbe is neither the better because woven out of his own brest, nor the bees hony the woorse for that gathered out of many flowers: neither could I ever brooke to set down that haltingly in my broken stile, which I found better expressed by a graver author. (Sig.A4)

Another of these grim genres was the poem accepting child loss, in which broken-hearted exhausted women tried to justify the ways of God to themselves (see pp.156ff.). It has been argued by social historians that child loss was too common to have been regarded as a catastrophe, for perhaps as many as half the children born did not live beyond five years. Such an argument would have seemed curious, to say the least, to women who spent all their adult lives pregnant and had no living child. Patients mentally disturbed by bereavement were a significant proportion of the case load of Richard Napier, and of them the largest group (52 out of 134) were women crazed with grief by the death of a child (McDonald, 78). Napier assumed, conversely, that people who took no pleasure in their children were mentally disturbed.

The pious of both sexes were often required to keep a spiritual diary. Frances Lady Pelham put together her twenty-seven page book, 'An Expression of Faith' (UNott Portland MS PwV 89), in the mid-seventeenth century, dedicating it to her 'Dearly beloved Children'. She included with her own version of the Creed, a history of Christ, a history of the church militant, prayers, personal revelations, moral advice to her children and a poetic epitome of the Christian life:

First in white Innocence wee appeer,
Then our Actions Guiltless, cheer;
Time gives a dy, such as our strength can bear.
Our actions will try if virtue be the grain:
For then no soil of filth will take way the truth,
       virtue will prevail again
And length of time will change the youthful dy
      & give ye harmless colour once again.
Vertue will be seen in strength of Judgement, Knowledge and Grace:
On Earth a blessing to their dwelling Place,
In which they pass to heaven in the true ran Race. (26)

The attempt to versify on religious themes was a discipline intended to focus concentration on well-worn pious truisms. Anne Oakeley's couplets 'On a Future State' (UNott Portland MS PwV 329) are fairly typical. She begins with a rather derivative flourish:

Beyond the Grave stupendous Regions lye

12

INTRODUCTION

> The boundless Realms of vast Eternity...

only to founder in the eighth couplet:

> The way of dying is my Least concern:
> That will give no disturbance in my Urn...

All this writing was intended to remain private; most of the women who versified as part of a religious exercise had no interest in communicating their individual experience to outsiders; the poems, as in the case of those included in the diaries of Elizabeth, Viscountess Mordaunt (1632?-1679), are usually laborious and dull. As religious controversy heated up, such private spiritual exercise became public, to be used as ammunition in a veritable propaganda war, which produced more published books on religious matters than on all other subjects put together. The first such volume which is by a woman and in verse is Alice Sutcliffe's *Meditations of Man's Mortalitie* (1634, see p.175ff.); it was probably published on behalf of the Puritan cause and as a tacit condemnation of the court of Charles I. The point of adding commendatory poems contributed by such luminaries as Ben Jonson, Thomas May, George Withers and Peter Heywood, could well be to disarm suspicion, for the scriptural echoes in Sutcliffe's poetry are all from the Geneva Bible. Ben Jonson's commendatory poem is so contorted, being no more than a versification of her chapter headings, that we might suspect an element of parody:

> The comfort of weake Christians with their warning,
> From fearefull back-slides; And the debt we'are in,
> To follow Goodnesse, by our owne discerning
> Our great reward, th'aeternall crown to win.
> I sayd, who had supp'd so deepe of this sweet chalice,
> Must Celia bee, the Anagram of Alice.

The exception to the general rule, that the women who published religious works of any kind were not in control of the use made of their work, is Lady Eleanor Audeley, who paid for the printing of her prophecies herself (Hindle). She was Eleanor Touchet, daughter of Lord Audley, wife to Sir John Davies, whose sudden death in 1626 she foretold, and to Sir Archibald Douglas. Her addiction to prophesying incurred royal displeasure and, forbidden to publish, she betook herself to Holland in 1633 and evidently financed the printing of her works there, only to be fined £3,000 and imprisoned on her return. In 1649 she published *Strange and Wonderful Prophecies* 'which she Prophesied sixteen yeeres agoe, and had them Printed in Holland... for which she was imprisoned seven yeeres here in *England*, by the late King and his Majesties Councell; First she was put into the Gate-house, then into Bedlam, and afterwards into the Tower of London' (*Strange and Wonderful Prophecies,* 1649). As she had prophesied the execution of the King, using Belshazzar as a figure, this harsh treatment was not altogether surprising.

13

KISSING THE ROD

What came out of the mouths of the women who uttered incantations extempore, was almost invariably a stream of fourteeners, such as, from *Strange and Wonderful Prophecies*:

> Till walking at the twelve months end,
>   subject fill Tides do fall;
> Excellent Majesty how gon,
>   Court exchang'd for the Stall.
> The Grandsire on, as came to passe;
>   at all yet minded not,
> As if a feigned Story, but
>   his miserable lot.
>
> Expell'd was for the words escap'd,
>   memory can speak well,
> Hardened in pride, unheard of such,
>   the wild Ass as with did dwell:
> Sent to the Ox, its owner knows,
>   undreamt of this his doom:
> Fowls their appointed time observe,
>   wots not the night from noon. (Etc.)

Why the Holy Ghost should have favoured this form has not been revealed to us. Lady Eleanor is unique among the visionary women of the seventeenth century in that she was too grand to be manipulated by sectarian interests. Strangely although Lady Eleanor was not, we suppose, at the mercy of a male shorthand taker, her versification and syntax, if such they may be called, are especially chaotic. Anne Wentworth, publishing in 1677 after 'severe and cruel persecution... for the space of eighteen years from the unspeakable Tyrannies of a *Hard hearted Yoak Fellow*' is limpid by comparison:

> In coffee-house and Ale-House now
>   Why do you me defame?
> Why doth your Church a Heathen me,
>   And Publican proclaim...?
> But I commit my cause to him,
>   Who sees and sits above;
> And from his Sanctuary looks,
>   And roars out of Sion,
> To show my foes he is my God,
>   And I his little one...
> I give no other cause but in
>   The worship of my God;
> If clean from sin I'm in his sight,
>   My foes shall feel his Rod...etc.

Wentworth too may have financed the publication of her *Vindication* herself. Her work shows many points of similarity with that of Anna Trapnel (see p.175ff.) and we have not yet managed to exclude the possibility that she is the same person, although we consider it unlikely.

The editors of women's prophecies had no compunction in altering them to make a case more forcefully, or with more authority. Notes and interpolations were not usually differentiated with any degree of consistency or scrupulosity.

Jane Hawkins preached in verse for three days and nights to a huge audience against the Anglican bishops. The local vicar and curate, who had sat at her feet supposedly taking notes, later admitted that they were altering the text, which they planned to publish as popular songs. (Mack, 223)

Elinor Channel, who was awakened in the night by a blow on the heart from God and a conviction that she had to abandon her husband and their small children and set off for London with a message instructing the Lord Protector to restore the old religion, was used as a mouth-piece by fellow prophet Arise Evans who happened to be getting messages rather similar to hers. The non-conformist sects which preached a new role for women under their respective versions of theocracy were especially keen to publish women's work. However, the use made of women in religious controversy has often more to do with the idea that God speaks through the mouths of 'babes and sucklings', and idiots and others who would otherwise be dumb and of no account, than any conviction of the sexlessness of souls.

It was left to the Quakers seriously to develop the spirituality of women as of equal importance with that of men. Of the three hundred women who published spiritual testimonies during the Interregnum, 220 were Quakers. The success of Mary Mollineux's *Fruits of Retirement* (see p.236ff.) owes more to the Quaker policy of publishing and republishing spiritual writings by women than to the poems' intrinsic merit. Though there was an immediate reaction, the visibility of women during the Interregnum did produce a genuine change. Women emerged not only as possessors of a voice of their own, but as an audience with its own character and concerns.

When Samuel Woodford's wife died, he was encouraged to assuage his grief by completing his paraphrase of the Psalms by his wife's kinswoman, the painter Mary Beale (1633-1699). When *A Paraphrase upon the Psalms of David* appeared in 1667, it carried alternative versions of Psalms XIII, LII, LXX and CXXX, acknowledged simply as by *M.M.B.* which most people would have realised meant 'Mistress' M.B. The relative anonymity of the attribution could well have been requested by Beale herself; what is interesting and new is that Woodford acknowledged that the alternative versions were someone else's work, a female someone else at that. His intention could have been to make his own work more impressive by contrast, for Beale's versification is rather like that of the young bard of Japan, who always made the last line so long that it could not possibly scan, but it is equally a gesture to his female readership. Mary Beale was married to a Puritan who after the Restoration was having a hard time keeping his job in the Patents Office (Walsh and Jeffree, 11). Mary was a Cradock, whose own family loyalties had been split by the Restoration, leaving her on the losing side, so we are not surprised to find her choosing the

convention of paraphrasing the Psalms to express a violent reaction
to injustice.

> Monster of men, who canst such mischiefs act,
> And proudly triumph in the bloody fact,
>   Must this thy power declare,
> That they, who at Jehovahs Altar stood,
> The Priests themselves, stain'd with their own blood,
> The guiltless Victims of thy fury were?
> Yet not even this was able to asswage
> Thy own curst malice, or thy wicked Masters rage.
>
> But though my ruin thou didst most design,
> And that no blood should quench thy thirst but mine,
>   Know wretch that God is good,
> And has been so alwayes in Ages past,
> Nor shall Eternity His love exhaust;
> Wherefore 'tis not thy Force, though like a Flood,
> Nor all thy secret plots, which shall avayl,
> Unless thou canst against th'Almighty first prevail.
>
> Within thy heart lie hid those poysonous seeds
> Of treason, which thy tongue provokes to deeds:
>   So piercing are thy words
> They seem the Razours dulness to upbraid,
> As if unfit for action or afraid,
> And have more edge than all my Enemies Swords:
> By these thou dost the just ensnare and slay,
> And low as earth, their hopes and lives together lay.
>
> But who thinkst thou, these actions will admire,
> Since thou'rt inspir'd by an infernal fire?
>   A flame which strongly moves
> To lying mischiefs and unjust deceit,
> And all the false delights, which on them wait,
> Or sin presents to excite and raise new loves!
> Hence 'tis that Justice seems so mean and low,
> No longer fit for great men, then to make them so.
>
> Devouring words do thy best love command,
> And to them thou hast joined a bloody hand:
>   But the Almighty God
> In thy destruction shall His Power make known,
> Which in eternall torments thou shalt own,
> When he makes bare His Arm and shakes His Rod,
> Removing thee from thy beloved place,
> And from the Earth roots out thy trayterous name and race...(143-144)

At the Restoration the stage was set for the incorporation of
female experience in the mainstream of literature, after many
co-options and false starts. To the end of the century and long after,
religion remained the only area in which female wit could safely
exercise itself in print but some impetuous young women failed to
grasp the fact.

Professional poets were in the main unusually talented
middle-class males who like Cowley and Dryden had secured a
classical education and put their talents to work for the interests of

INTRODUCTION

their patrons. Among those patrons at the beginning of the century there were great ladies. Mary Herbert, Countess of Pembroke (1561-1621), gave poets employment, support and accommodation at Wilton; at least thirty books were hopefully dedicated to her and earned their two guineas for the writers. After her, Margaret Clifford, Countess of Cumberland, employed the poet Daniel as tutor for her daughter Anne, later Countess of Dorset, in whose huge retinue no poet was ever numbered. Thirty-seven books were dedicated to Lucy Russell, Countess of Bedford (d.1627), to whom Donne, Drayton, Jonson, Daniel and Chapman all held themselves beholden. After Lucy's death, there are no great patronesses in England, until at the end of the century the Countess of Coventry and her friends tried self-consciously to revive Tudor values ('the antient education of gentlewomen'), and were dissuaded by the ubiquitous Bishop Burnet (see p.333).

As trendsetters the queens influenced women away from intellectual pursuits and towards fashionable frivolity and display. In a sense this very activity was creative, as the Duchess of Newcastle, herself passionately interested in clothes, pointed out:

Our sex takes so much delight in dressing and adorning themselves, as we for the most part make our gowns our books, our laces our lines, our imbroideries our letters, and our dressings are the time of our studie; and instead of turning over solid leaves, we turn our hair into curles, and our Sex is as ambitious to shew themselves to the eyes of the world when finely drest, as Scholers do (*sic*) to express their learning to the ears of the world, when fully fraught with authors... (*The Philosophical and Physical Opinions*, 1655, Sig.B2)

Women repelled by the apparent empty-headedness of women of fashion turned back towards the great Tudor women for role models, particularly Elizabeth I, so much greater than her male successors. In 1612, this little sonnet appeared in the collection called *A Crowne-Garland of Goulden Roses*, 'made by one of the maides of honor upon the death of Queene Elizabeth, which she sowed uppon a sampler in red silke'. This intriguing detail is rather devalued by the information that the poem may be sung 'To a new tune or to Phillida flouts me'.

> Gone is *Elizabeth*,
>   whome we have lov'd so deare:
> She our kind mistris was,
>   full foure and forty yeare.
> England she governd well
>   not to be blamed:
> Flanders she succord still,
>   and Ireland tamed.
> France she befrended,
>   Spaine shee hath foiled:
> Papists rejected,
>   and the Pope spoyled.
> To princes powerfull,
>   to the world vertuous:
> To her foes mercifull,
>   to subjects gracious.

17

Her soule is in heaven,
  the world keepes her glory:
Subjects her good deeds,
  and so ends my story. (Sig.C4)

The metre, an unusual combination of dactyls with occasional spondees, is clearly based upon the song form of 'Phillida flouts me'. The attribution to the maid of honour's sampler is probably a fiction; few needlewomen would bother to work the number of supernumerary words that plump out the lyric. Nevertheless we are not entirely convinced that the poem is by Richard Johnson, the anonymous compiler of the collection. Praise of Elizabeth was one of the few safe ways of criticising her successors in print; both Diana Primrose (see p.83) and Anne Bradstreet (see pp.126-7) chose this way of expressing implicit condemnation of the status quo. Next in importance as a female heroine was Elizabeth Stuart, Queen of Bohemia (see pp.39ff.), who was perceived as Elizabeth Tudor's successor in guarding the Protestant faith, ill-served by the Stuart kings. At least fifty volumes were dedicated to her even though she lived almost all of her life in exile in Holland. Some of her poetry is preserved in the library of Heidelberg, but our resources did not stretch quite so far as to allow any of our editors actually to see it or to investigate other possible locations on the continent.

Henrietta Maria, wife of Charles I, had a more limited appeal. She brought with her the sophisticated manners of the French court, and drew the wrath of the Puritans not merely because of her Catholicism, but because of her interest in the courtly amusements of dancing and masking and Platonic love games. She has been called illiterate but it seems that at Christmas in 1626 she played in a pastoral of her own composition before a very small audience of selected grandees (HMC, xvi, 11th Report, App. Pt.1, 47). She set the enduring fashion for feminine accomplishments, rather than a high level of education or culture, among the nobility and all those who sought to ape them. Ladies were expected to be able to read English and French and write them tolerably well, to dance, to sing and do 'curious work' with the needle. Henrietta Maria's daughters, Mary, Princess of Orange, and Henriette, Duchess of Orleans, continued in the fashion she had set. Their niece, who was to become Mary II of England, was taught to read and write by a French tutor, dancing by a French master and drawing by Richard Gibson and his wife. When she was twelve she played the lead in Crowne's 'Masque of Calisto' (1674).

Although these royal trend-setters gave little boost to female ambition for solider achievements, they were an antidote to notions that women should be invisible. As Queen of England (1688-1694) Mary gained a reputation for genuine piety, attested by her written meditations, prayers and memoirs, and wrote in English, French and Dutch; she was a connoisseur of architecture and gardening; much of the beauty we associate with William and Mary is a direct result of her enterprise. Mary succeeded her step-mother, Mary of Modena, whose influence was also significant for women. Unable to share her husband's overriding interest in profligacy, she created a kind of secular nunnery with her ladies in waiting, where serious subjects were discussed, and poetry and other accomplishments earnestly practised. Mary wrote in English, French and Italian and could read Latin. All the foreign consorts of the English kings brought with them continental notions about the nature of women, and made their impact on British chauvinism. Madame Mazarin, who came to England in 1675, set up her own version of the French *ruelle* which provided the blueprint for English women who aspired to elegance and cultural refinement, as well as a refuge for women sickened by the monarchs' invincible predilection for low life.

Few later Stuart noblewomen had any sympathy with female literary pretensions. In 1651 Anna Weamys tried to turn the clock back sixty years by choosing the daughters of the Marquis of Dorchester to play the Countess of Pembroke's role for her *Continuation of Sir Philip Sidney's Arcadia*. The little book is heavily encrusted with encomia, one of which at least is rather ungracious. It seems that this gentlewoman, who was probably Scottish, had no real ambition to contribute to the stock of novels which remained young ladies' preferred reading matter until well into the next century, and did indeed publish only because she had 'received commands from those that cannot be disobeyed'.

By Weamys's time the bookseller was well on the way to replacing the flattered patron as the arbiter of a writer's fate. An interesting transitional work is *Fames Roule: or, the Names of our dread Soveraigne Lord King Charles, his Royall Queen Mary and his most hopefull Posterity: together with, The names of the Dukes, Marquesses, Earls, Viscounts, Bishops, Barons, Privie Counsellors, Knights of the Garter, and Judges. Of his three renowned Kingdomes, England, Scotland and Ireland: Anagrammatiz'd and expressed by acrosticke lines on their names. By Mistris Mary Fage, wife of Robert Fage the younger* (1637). Only three of Fage's offerings in this versified *Who's Who* were addressed to female subjects, to King Charles's three daughters, six-year-old Mary, four-year-old Elizabeth, and newborn Anne. 'To the High and Mighty... Anna Stuarte' may be considered representative:

Anagramma. A NU NEAT STAR.

A STAR remain you in our Firmament,
N ewly sprung forth, having the luster lent,
N EATLY wherewith your excellence doth shine,
(A h still increase you) from that SOL of thine.

S TAR doth your birth denote you, and your youth
T ruly averreth you NU STAR in truth:
V ery much likewise doth your little brow
A ctively set forth you A NEAT STAR now;
R eflecting then upon your Excellence,
T hat shews your radiant and sweet influence,
E ach one doth grant you A NU NEATE STAR hence. (9)

The new star (which Mrs Fage confuses with a planet) did not shine long; within weeks of her birth this 'high and mighty' princess was dead. The preface to the book is signed Mary Fage, but it is very doubtful that she could truthfully have written, in persuading the mighty to tolerate her tedious flattery: 'I remember Virgill, *Cum canerem Regibus, Cynthius aurem vellit*' [Sig.A3^v]. The use of her name on the book probably represents an attempt to excuse the lameness of the performance; one hopes rather than fears that Robert Fage did not leave all the drudgery to his wife. The book was printed by Richard Oulton, probably at the Fages' expense. History does not record how many of the anagrammatised functionaries responded with a gift of money.

The rise of the bookseller who paid for both writing and printing and in return owned all the rights in a work freed writers in some measure from the duty of servility, but the law of *noblesse oblige* did not apply to this purely commercial arrangement. The bookseller was not expected to keep the furnishers of his raw material from starving when their productivity declined. Until Dryden, the most successful professional writers did not earn enough to acquire security or property; in their old age they relied on pensions or grace and favour accommodation. Women trying to turn their fragile accomplishments to account were completely at the booksellers' mercy. Those who ventured though less than half-educated, to 'be inrolled among the Poetick Tribe', were paraded by the booksellers before a public that mauled them. Their self-esteem was called vanity and their courage impertinence, while their desire to communicate was interpreted as exhibitionism. The booksellers pushed them into notoriety that ruined their lives, and then dumped them.

Not a single woman survived unscathed, not even when she was hidden behind a coterie name, not even when her work was published without her knowledge or consent. If 'Mrs. *Philips's* sense and Mrs. *Behn's* wit (Joyned with her assurance) was not sufficient to protect them from the Critick's strokes' no woman writer could expect a tolerant reception (*Six Familiar Essays... by a Lady*, 1696, Sig.A2). The satiric account given by Rochester in 'A Letter from Artemisia in the Town to Cloe in the Country' (published as a broadside in 1679) contains a good deal of truth; his heroine apostrophises herself:

> Dear *Artemisia*! Poetry's a Snare:
> *Bedlam* has many Mansions: have a care:
> Your Muse diverts you, makes the Reader sad:
> You think your self inspir'd; He thinks you mad.
> Consider too, 'twill be discreetly done,
> To make your self the Fiddle of the Town.
> To find th'ill-humour'd pleasure at their need:
> Curst when you fail, and scorn'd when you succeed.

Rochester's poem goes on to give a masterful portrait of the

INTRODUCTION

destitute Corinna, whose name implies that she is a poet, in the tone of tragic satire, in this case not without compassion. The facts of her case resemble those of 'Ephelia's' autobiography (see pp.271-3); we have not discounted the possibility that 'Ephelia's' drama was played out some years before the publication of her *Female Poems* in 1679.

It was not only men who sneered at poetic women. Maria Burghope, daughter of the Earl of Bridgewater's chaplain at Ashridge, dedicating her manuscript celebration of the grandeur and beauty of the estate, called 'A Vision', to Lady Mary Egerton in 1699 complains that

the Illiterate part of our Sex (because they are proud & loth others Intellectualls should be better dress'd up then their Own) joyne with [men] in the comon cry. These latter are a sort of Ignorants that I both pitty & Scorne; & (notwithstanding their other Embelishments) are little better then the Brutes. Only they are proud & envious, (which Beast are not) They know not the use, & value of Learneing, & like brute Beast speak evill of that which they understand not.

Burghope excused her preference for spending time with the muses, as 'sure as lawfull & laudable, as our ordinary Chatt, telling of news, & Backbiteing, Dressing up, Patching, Painting, Putting ourselves into a Posture of Talking Nonsence in the Mode, & other the admired Qualifications of our Sex' (Huntington Library, Papers of the Bridgewater Trust, 35/B/62).

Women who put themselves in the power of booksellers were running a real risk, for the booksellers made money out of them any way they could, to an extent which can be called literary pimping. Prurient interest in the high life supplies us with the phantom female author 'E.G.', a 'Lady of Honour'. Her first appearance can be dated in about 1678 when a ballad appeared called *Portsmouth's Lamentation Or, a Dialogue between Two Amorous Ladies, E.G. and D.P.* In this case E.G. was clearly Eleanor or Nell Gwyn and D.P. her rival for the king's affections, the Duchess of Portsmouth. It was not long before E.G. made her debut as an author; *Four of the Choicest New Songs, as they are sung at Court, Written by a person of Quality, named E.G.* (s.d.) was published as a broadside by R. Chamberlain (BL Broadside 1876.f.1 [25]). All four poems are suggestive, the first grossly so, and there is no reason beside Chamberlain's ascription to connect any of them with Nell Gwyn, who in writing her own letters always used an amanuensis. In 1684, Absalom Chamberlain published *Strephon's Complaint for the Death of his Daphne* as a broadside, claiming that it was 'an Excellent new Copy of Verses Sung at Winchester the 24th day of September, 1684. by a Lady of Honour, named E.G.' (BL Broadside 1876. f. 1 [26]). The likeliest explanation of 'E.G.', pornographic authoress and lady of quality, is that she is a figment of a bookseller's venal imagination. However a real female author was just as likely to find her name tacked on to any greasy doggerel the booksellers had on their hands. So the name of 'Ephelia' was soiled by James Courtney (see p.272) in 1682.

21

KISSING THE ROD

The number of satiric or burlesque poems attributed to women increased steadily over the last decades of the century; by attributing a scurrilous lampoon to a lady of quality the bookseller appealed to the voyeurism of the public and at the same time disarmed any serious attempt at suppression. 'A Lady of Quality' is credited with two of the four parts of the serial ballad *Upon the Popish Plot* (1678); her description of the pamphleteer Henry Care is a fair indication of her sexless style:

> Then comes a crack'd Merchant with his shallow Brain,
> Who first did lead up this stigmatiz'd Train:
> He since is grown useless, his Skill being small,
> Yet at a dead list, he's still at their call.
>   He has pester'd the Press,
>   In ridiculous dress,
> In this scribbling Age he could not do less:
> But to so little purpose as plainly appears,
> With Pen he had as good fate picking his Ears.

We see no reason other than chaotic grammar to accuse any female of writing any part of this ballad, which was to be sung by the populace up and down the streets to the old tune of 'Packington's Pound' which dictates the stanzaic form. The pretence was maintained that such ballads were spontaneously engendered, but in truth they were the equivalent of advertising jingles, to be used in the struggle between Whigs and Tories. It has been suggested that the lady in this case was the Countess Powys, wife of a Catholic Privy Councillor and co-conspirator with Elizabeth Cellier in the Meal-tub Plot, which is probably what the printer of the ballad wanted people to think. An answer to the ballad makes reference to 'Counterfeit Ladies' using the press to air their views.

Ladies of high birth are known to have participated in the production of scurrilous lampoons on affairs of court and state, but this was one genre which had to be genuinely anonymous, for such utterances were dangerous to their authors. Katherine Sedley, only daughter of the playwright and for many years mistress to James II, is known to have exercised her wit upon her royal lover but no body of work attributable to her has survived. 'A Letter to the Lady Osbourne' (1688) is in some MS sources said to be 'By a Lady' and begs Lady Osbourne to

>   ...pity and forbear
> To tell the nauseous follies that you hear;
> Let each man sin without prescribing rules;
> We must have madmen, and we must have fools.
> (Huntington Library, Papers of the Bridgewater Trust, No.8331)

The work of Alicia Danvers (see pp.376ff.) illustrates that women were not disqualified by sex from publishing burlesque; some no doubt managed to vie with the men in obscene descriptions of their political enemies. Aphra Behn claimed that she had been used in writing Tory doggerel, of which there is no lack. Jane Barker called one of her early efforts a 'borlesk'. When women gathered together to mock men's 'py-work' they probably devised their own versions of the lampoons and epigrams that male poets collected with such assiduity, but there is now no separating them from the heap. Diligent sifting of the polemic poetry of the 1690s to arrive at a clear picture of women's participation must await other hands than ours.

The Loyal Englishman's Wish by Anne Morcott (1692), about whom we know nothing but her name, 'furnished the tune for almost innumerable other ballads' (Rollins, vi, 161) which means that it was the equivalent of top of the pops in its day and for twenty years after. The bald use of her name implies that Anne came from the lower orders, which renders her unique amongst our female writers. The words, it must be said, are what one might expect of a pop song:

> Let Mary Live long,
> She's Vertuous and witty,
> All Charmingly pritty,
> Let Mary Live long,
>   And Reign many Years.
>   Now the Clouds is gon o're,
> That troubled us sore:
>   Since the Sun-shine apears,
> We shall be Deliver'd,
> We shall be Deliver'd,
>   From Fury and Fears.

Strange to relate, after her initial success, song-writer Morcott wrote no more.

If the broadside ballad market was the seventeenth-century equivalent of the twentieth-century pop industry, the theatre provided the equivalent of television as a consumer of literary work. Plays ran only for a matter of days, although they might be (as television serials and plays are) repeated later in the season, or in the next season, by popular demand. There was more money to be made in the theatre than in publishing, for the proceeds of the third day of any run went to the author; further earnings could be expected when the script was sold to a bookseller. Elizabeth Cary, Viscountess Falkland (see pp.54ff.) and Margaret Cavendish, Duchess of Newcastle (see pp.163ff.), both wrote closet dramas on the classical model, never performed as far as we know. Katherine Philips's public literary career was launched by the Earl of Orrery's interest in staging her translation of Corneille's *Pompey*, in Dublin and London in 1663; her unfinished version of *Horace* was performed after her death, in 1668. Frances Boothby (see pp.233ff.) was successful in having her tragicomedy, *Marcelia*, performed by the King's Company in 1669, a year before Aphra Behn's tragicomedy, *The Forc'd Marriage* was played by the Duke's Company. However, despite Behn's eighteen plays, her female successors still entered the theatre at a grave disadvantage.

While male writers picked up no taint from their association with the theatre and were accepted in respectable society despite obvious profligacy, women were inevitably soiled by association with the prostitution that was practised not only by the punks in the pit but by some of the actresses on the stage. The use made by the professional troupes of the deluded young women who furnished pretentious or desperately sprightly works for the stage was almost certainly completely cynical. One trembles for the unknown Elizabeth Polwhele, described in the manuscript of her comedy *The Frolicks* as 'an unfortunate younge woman... haunted by poetick divills', who dared to dedicate her work to Prince Rupert (Milhous and Hume, pl. facing p.57). Hers was the first comedy written by a woman for the professional English stage; it shows too accurate a knowledge of the haunts of London gallants for Polwhele's respectability to have survived its performance. The manuscript copy sent to Prince Rupert was apparently never sent to the printer, but passed to his mistress, the actress Margaret Hughes. Polwhele's comedy was not her first attempt, for she refers in the manuscript to a play called 'faythfull virgins' (probably Bod. MS Rawl. Poet. 195, ff.49-78) which had evidently been played already by the Duke's Company, but was never published.

It seems hardly possible for a woman to write for the theatre and retain her anonymity. In 1696, a play given as 'written by a Young Lady' was played by the King's Servants at the New Theatre in Little Lincoln's Inn Fields. The Preface to the printed play, *She Ventures and He Wins*, which is signed 'Ariadne', claims that 'when our Island enjoyed the Blessing of the Incomparable Mrs. Behn, even then I had much ado to keep my Muse from showing her Impertinence' which implies that the young lady was not as young as all that, Mrs Behn having been dead seven years. The prologue spoken in the theatre by 'Mrs. *Bowman*, in Man's Cloaths' might give rise to the suspicion that Ariadne is not only not young but not female either.

> This is a Woman's Treat, y'are like to find;
> Ladies, for Pity; Men, for Love be kind.

The same suspicion arises about the 'young lady' who is supposed to have written *The Unnatural Mother,* published in 1698, after having been played by the King's Servants at Lincoln's Inn Fields. The prologue, spoken by Mr Verbruggen, combines the worst of gallantry and special pleading.

> A Woman now comes to reform the Stage,
> Who once has stood the Brunt of this unthinking Age;
> Yet shou'd her pen, her Beauty cannot fail,
> But Oh! she vows she'll not her Charms unvail,
> Nor shall you know, harsh Men, at whom you rail.
> Then how you censure this her Play beware,
> Lest thro' the Poetess you wound the Fair...

The effect of this kind of promotion of women is to alienate genuine writers from competition on such terms. In the 1685 *Miscellany* edited by Aphra Behn the following poem is described as 'The Female Wits. A Song by a Lady of Quality'.

INTRODUCTION

Men with much Toil, and Time, and Pain,
   At length at Fame arrive,
While we a nearer way obtain
   The Palms for which they strive.

We scorn to climb by Reason's Rules
   To the loud name of Wit,
And count them silly modest Fools,
   Who to that Test submit.

Our Sparkling way a Method knows,
   More Airy and refin'd,
And shou'd dull Reason interpose,
   Our lofty flight 'twould bind.

Then let us on --- and still believe;
   A good bold Faith will do,
If we our selves can well deceive,
   The World will follow too.

What matter tho the Witty few,
   Our emptiness do find,
They for their int'rest will be true,
   'Cause we are brisk and kind. (8)

The poem seems at first sight to be repulsively anti-feminist, but it does describe the way literary pimping works. We might conclude from the bitterness of the tone that the female persona hides a male writer, but a talented woman passed over for a younger or prettier or more complaisant female writer might well feel this kind of anger and disgust. Women's relation to the stage in the closing years of the seventeenth century is coquettish and self-conscious and the evaluation of their contribution problematic, because they are caught up in a tissue of sensationalism and innuendo, which even as energetic and forthright a character as Behn herself would have found invidious and enervating.

Delariviere Manley, who eventually capitulated to scandal, gossip and exhibitionism, wrote with unusual soberness in the Preface to *The Lost Lover* (1696):

I am now convinc'd Writing for the Stage is no way proper for a Woman, to whom all Advantages, but meer Nature, are refused; If we happen to have a Genius to Poetry, it presently shoots to a fond desire of Imitation. Tho' to be lamely ridiculous, mine was indulged by my Flatterers, who said, nothing could come from me unentertaining; like a Hero not contented with Applause from lesser Conquests, I find my self not only disappointed of my hopes of greater, but even to have lost all the glory of the former; Had I confin'd my Sense, as before, to some short Song of *Phyllis*, a Tender Billet, and the freedom of agreeable Conversation, I had still preserved the Character of a Witty Woman.

In Behn's hey-day the only censorship was political; female eroticism was a proper subject for writing and discussion and Behn was an acknowledged mistress of the theme and the manner. She capitulated to what was in fact a very sophisticated interest in a light and sophisticated way. Censoriousness was for the time being in abeyance, but during the closing years of the reign of Charles II the

25

brilliance of his favourites dimmed. Recklessness became poverty, illness and premature old age. The much publicised conversion and death of Rochester in 1680 at the age of thirty-three marked the turning-point. Behn never repented of her Toryism, her irreligion and her interest in eroticism. The only concession she made to respectability was to turn unofficial laureate for the Stuarts in decline. By that time the tide of hypocrisy was running strong; none but the most determined or deranged of women could have wished to follow in Astraea's footsteps. Curiously the rediscovery of Sappho, which roughly coincided with Behn's career, followed the same declining curve from recognition into obloquy.

There was great confusion about who Sappho in fact was and what she might have written; John Shirley gave this account in *The Illustrious History of Women* (1686):

> Sappho for her poetry was famous, and was as *Elianus* affirmeth, the daughter of *Scamandronius*, as Plato of Aristan, Suidas, and other Greek writers say, there were two of that name, the one called Erixa, a much celebrated Poetess, who flourish'd in the time of Tarquinius Priscus, and by many is imagin'd to be the inventeress of lyrick verses. The other was Sappho Mitelaena, who publish'd many poems among the *Greeks*, though somewhat extravagant *Yet* for her Ingenuity had the honour to be styled the Tenth *Muse* and of her Antipater Sidonus thus writes 'When Sappho's verse he did admiring read, Demanded whence the Tenth *Muse* did proceed'.

Shirley did not involve himself in speculations about Sappho and Phaon, although the myth of Sappho's suicide for love had been current for as long as Ovid's *Tristia* and *Heroides* had been studied. The chief source of the Sappho myth for Behn's contemporaries was Boileau's translation of Longinus 'On the Sublime' in which the Ode to Venus attributed to Sappho had been paraphrased (1674); in the 1685 *Miscellany*, Behn had included 'Verses made by Sapho done from the Greek by Boyleau, And from the French by a Lady of Quality'. The poem could be construed as an adaptation of the 'Anactoria' to apply to Behn herself.

> Happy who hears you sigh, for you alone,
> Who hears you speak, or whom you smile upon:
> You well for this might scorn a starry Throne.

The male establishment can tolerate only one woman at a time; if 'Orinda's' star was to rise, Behn's had to set. 'Astraea' or 'Sappho', Behn had been praised by her cronies for both equalling and excelling 'Orinda' Philips (see p.269) but her own view is less competitive. In one of the last things she wrote, the address of 'The Translatress in her own Person', in her version of Cowley's sixth book 'Of Plants' (1689), she asks Daphne, now the laurel tree:

> Let me with *Sappho* and *Orinda* Be
> Oh ever sacred Nymph, adorn'd by thee;
> And give my Verses Immortality. (143)

Already the name Sappho was used principally pejoratively: 'Sappho addrest to his Grace the Duke of Buckingham', much collected and published first under that title in Gildon's *Chorus*

26

INTRODUCTION

Poetarum (1694), is neither by Sappho nor by Behn, but by W. Bowles, to whom it was attributed in *Poems by Several Hands and on Several Occasions*, printed for J. Hindmarsh in 1685 (M. O'Donnell, 317, 323). The piquancy of republishing it in the edition of Buckingham (1715) as addressed by Aphra Behn to Dryden's Zimri, portrayed in scurrilous literature of the period as Priapus, is that the poem then becomes an obscene description of female orgasm.

> Then my Tongue fails, and from my Brow,
> The liquid Drops in Silence flow;
> Then wand'ring Fires run thro my Blood,
> Then Cold binds up the languid Flood;
> All Pale and Breathless then I lie,
> I sigh, I tremble, and I die.

Bowles's distortion of Boileau's paraphrase was inadvertent; the foisting of this stuff on to Aphra Behn reflects the utter obloquy into which both Sappho and Behn had fallen. Excited panting by females or pseudo-females was the chief stock in trade of John Dunton, editor, publisher and principal writer of *The Athenian Mercury* in the 1690s. It is typical of his kind of hypocrisy that *The Athenian Mercury* for 27 November 1694 separates Behn and Sappho from the blessed presence of 'Orinda', whose respectability is made a rod to beat them with. To a love-sick correspondent the paper replied:

> Thus *Afra*, thus despairing *Sappho* mourn'd;
> Sure both their Souls are to your *Breast* return'd.
> By the same Tyrant-Passion all enslav'd,
> Like you they wrote, like you they lov'd and rav'd.
> But ah! the *Vertue vanish'd*, what remain'd?
> Their *Verse* as spotted as their *Glory* stain'd?
> They lost that Gem with which *Orinda* shin'd,
> And left a sully'd Name and Works behind.

Elsewhere in an answer to the question 'Whether Sappho or Mrs. Behn was the better poet' Dunton gave an unusually sensible reply, 'Sappho writ too little & Mrs Behn too much for us to give 'em any just or equal character', but he could not resist a smear. Behn's 'soft strain' in 'The Lover's Watch' and the 'Voyage to the Isle of Love' 'proves her a great proficient both in the theory and practice of that passion' (V, No. 13, Q.8). Dunton was the archetypical literary pimp. The extent to which 'Philomela', Dunton's 'Pindarical Lady', was Dunton's invention rather than the authentic voice of Elizabeth Singer (see pp.383ff.), cannot now be known; certainly some of the torridness of her breathy enthusiasms can be attributed to Dunton's flatteries and promptings. None of the secular poems published during the period of Dunton's influence over her was acknowledged by her as her work in later life.

The stock in trade of a literate woman became more negotiable as the century drew to a close, but its value was inseparable from her readiness to exhibit herself. Every professional female author was touted as young and fair, even when she was fat and fifty; the discrepancy between the fiction and the fact was always laid to her charge. Foolhardy young women were only too easily flattered and egged on to make exhibitions of what more judicious judges called their impertinences. The principal theme of women's secular writing was, of course, love. Cultivated men and women, like Rochester and his wife (see pp.230ff.), exchanged sonnets, songs, pastorals and pasquils, that were eagerly sought by booksellers. Aphra Behn imitated these games of gallantry amid her own literary cabal, beating the leisured nobility at their own game, without their safety net to uphold her if she fell. Even during the most permissive phase of the Restoration she was taking a calculated risk, but the signs seem to be that, although she was subjected to bitter and wounding attack as a fraud and a whore because she was a Tory, Behn was also respected for her literary ability until her last years, when Bishop Burnet would reprove Anne Wharton (see p.290) for being flattered by the praise of such a woman. The immediate effect of the Behn phenomenon was negative; few women could contemplate having their names bandied about in Grub Street without a shudder. The women who did were a fairly desperate bunch.

Many sentimental, semi-pornographic and downright obscene effusions were attributed to unnamed female writers in the nineties and we have made no attempt to disentangle them, or to include them in our volume. The cases of Dunton, and his rival pimp, Charles Gildon, await the attentions of feminist literary historians, who must be grateful in this instance for the unforgivingness of Pope.

The Sappho stereotype dogged the ambitious writers of the nineties. Writing to Sarah Fyge on the occasion of the publication of her *Poems on Several Occasions* in 1703, S. C., probably Susannah Carroll or Centlivre, praised this 'champion' of the female sex at the expense of another dead for a thousand years:

> *Sappho* the Great, whom by report we know,
> Would yield her laurels were she living now,
> And strait turn Chast, to gain a Friend of you.

Chaste or otherwise, Fyge did not manage to maintain her respectability.

The early seventeenth century had not lumbered itself with a pseudo-scientific theory of sex differences. There was no a priori reason why women should not be poets. The teaching of the Church was still based on Genesis 2 as interpreted by Augustine; when God created Adam he breathed into the clay and gave it both life and a soul made in his own likeness. For the rib he fashioned to be alive, the process would have to have been repeated. Therefore the soul is like the angels sexless, and, in view of the doctrine of the resurrection of the body, cannot be considered male. Difficulties

28

arose when the doctrine of the resurrection of the body was denied; then it could be argued that the soul was in essence male, but even then no one could deny that women had souls. Francis Vaughan put the traditional case on behalf of Anna Weamys:

> Lay by your needles Ladies, take the Pen,
> The onely difference 'twixt you and Men.
> 'Tis tyrannie to keep your Sex in aw,
> And make wit suffer by a Salick law,
> Good Wine does need no Bush, pure Wit no Beard:
> Since all Souls equal are, let all be heard.

Vaughan's argument is supported by Galatians 3:28, Luke 20:34-36, Matthew 22:30, and Mark 12:25; in heaven 'There is neither Jew nor Greek, there is neither bond nor free, there is neither male or female: for ye are all one in Christ Jesus'. Frances, Lady Pelham spelled out the doctrine in the commonplace book that she compiled at about the same time as Weamys was working on her romance: 'Woman is not a help to Man as body to ye Soul; she brings wth her from God a part Divine ye wch is onely subdued to him by reason of her Sex: a punishment yt lasts but in this life... In heaven her part shall be as free as his.' Lady Pelham might have heard of *De Nobilitate et Praecellentia Foeminei Sexus* written by Cornelius Agrippa at the command of the Emperor Maximilian's daughter, Margaret of Austria (1580-1630), the *'gente demoiselle, qui eut deux maris et si mourut pucelle'*. Agrippa was translated for the 'Vertuous and Beautiful Female Sex of the Commonwealth of England' by Edward Fleetwood as *The Glory of Women; or, a Treatise declaring the excellency and preheminence of Women above Men*... and published in 1652, about the time Lady Pelham was making her book. Fleetwood's version of Agrippa on the soul is quite uncompromising:

certain it is [God] gave one and the same indifferent soule to Male and Female, in which undoubtedly there in [*sic*] no distinction of Sex; The woman is endued with the same rationall power, and Speech with the man... they rising againe it [*sic*] their proper Sex, doe not perform the function of Sexes, but become like unto the Angells. (Sig.A4)

Lady Pelham might have known the versification of Fleetwood's translation which appeared the same year, by H.C. Gent. who said that the traducers of women 'bark like a dog at moonlight'. Most of Agrippa's proofs of female superiority are self-conscious triumphs of ingenuity, flattering with ironic hyperbole. Defences of women were not primarily arguments for women's rights but occasions for displays of wit and gallantry; what emerged were the double standard of morality and the cult of fragile femininity. The gallantry intensified after the Restoration, resulting in deliberately preposterous flattery and unpleasant *doubles entendres*. Poulain de la Barre's theory of female eloquence is of a kind that has hurt women ever since:

Women, on the contrary, express neatly and in order what they conceive. Their words cost them nothing; they begin and go on at their pleasure, and when they have their liberty, their fancy supplies them alwayes with inexhaustible liberality. (31)

What is most extraordinary about this kind of drivel is that some twentieth-century feminists still mistake it for sense. James Norris's *Haec et Hic* (1683) cannot be so mistaken; his motives for spelling out Malebranche's position on sex differences, 'Women are made of purer plastical ingredients' (63), are clearly dishonest. His pious disclaimer gives the game away: ''Tis not good thus to play the butcher with the Naked Sex who have no Arms but for Embraces' (3). Nathaniel Crouch, who made a speciality of publishing shilling chap-books for the semi-literate written by himself as 'Richard Burton', published a condensed version of Agrippa in 1670 as *Female Excellency, or the Ladies Glory* and in a bid for the uneducated female reader's shilling tried to establish nine female worthies to counterbalance the nine male worthies of popular literature.

The doctrine of the sexlessness of souls has never been seriously challenged; however, the effect of Cartesian inquiry into the duality of body and soul was to begin to suggest distinctions between self and soul, mind and spirit, which undermined the confidence of those who argued that equality of souls entailed equality of intellectual capacity. The process of tabulating psychological sex differences was well advanced by the end of the century, and women were net losers by it.

The proliferation of pro-feminist titles in the second half of the seventeenth century is not evidence of a serious interest in women's emancipation: it testifies rather to the emergence of a distinct female readership which booksellers were anxious to exploit. Equally, many misogynist tracts were simply cynical exercises in drumming up profitable controversy, and many pro-feminist answers were penned with equal cynicism by professional (male) hacks. We are not surprised to find John Dunton in *The Athenian Mercury* 28 April, 1691, trotting out the old maxim: 'Souls have no Sexes, nor while those only are concerned can any thing that's criminal intrude,' by way of reassuring his semi-literate readers that blameless intimacy between male and female was possible. This is the background against which the educationalists, especially Locke and Mary Astell, sought vainly to stimulate a desire for dignity, moral worth and intellectual rigour in women themselves.

Anything written by an 'interesting' or 'ingenious' young member of the 'fair sex' was a saleable rarity, if such a creature could be found to write it. She needed sufficient education to be able to write reasonably coherently and correctly, and at the same time to have little or nothing to lose by public exposure in the literary market place. This means in effect that she would have to be poor, middle-class, to have lost all hope of an honourable or advantageous marriage, and therefore to need to turn her genteel accomplishment into a way of earning her living. When it is said that Aphra Behn was the first professional woman writer, this is what is meant. There is no evidence that she chose the profession of writing; there is every sign that she was reduced to making a living by her wits. We may honour her for refusing the other obvious alternative, prostitution, if only we could be sure that she did not, as other women did, mingle the role of kept woman with her literary activity. Given the common image of women who performed in public, whether on stage or in print, a woman writer had little to lose and everything to gain by accepting financial support from an influential or well-connected man, and our judgment of Behn ought not to be materially altered if we eventually find out that she did. Our responsibility to Behn is first to find out the truth about her; empty triumphalism is no substitute for understanding. Although Behn lived publicly she remains utterly mysterious, unlike that clamorously private person, 'Orinda' Philips.

If our book should be considered as comprehensive we shall have failed of our objective, which is to introduce a fascinating group of women to a sympathetic and respectful public. We are at the beginning of the long process of literary archaeology rather than the end. We know far too little about all the women in this book, if indeed they are all women and not some of them male hacks in drag. We have not found Ephelia, who is a better poet (or group of poets) than she is currently being given credit for. Nor have we found all the women of the 'Chorus Vatum Anglicanorum' (BL Add. MS 24,492), the three Grey women, Ann, Penelope and Mary, who is supposed to have married Michael Drayton, or Julia Palmer who made a book of religious poems in about 1672, which used to be in the library of Sir Thomas Phillips. We did not find Lady Anne Southwell's 'Meditations on the Decalogue' although we did find a poem in her autograph, in BL MS Lansdowne 740 (f.142). The book made by the family of the Earl of Westmoreland in 1640 or thereabouts, containing poems by Mary Mildmay, Lady Fane, slipped through our hands at auction in London in 1975 and disappeared.

Conscious of our inadequacies and the thousand faults escaped in the printing, we offer this book to the gentle reader as women have always done, hoping against hope for tolerance and constructive response, from our sisters above all, who will best understand the struggle to find the time and the money for work of this kind. We shall be best pleased if within the space of a few years our book is superseded by a hundred studies of more depth and discrimination, prompted in part by our efforts.

ELIZABETH MELVILLE, LADY CULROSS

Elizabeth Melville, daughter of Sir James Melville, Laird of Halhill, and Christina Boswell, was by 1598 married to John Colville, then holding the ecclesiastical office of Commendator of Culross, later to succeed to the title of Lord Culross. Though her father had been a successful diplomat for Mary Queen of Scots, Henry II of France, and Queen Elizabeth, and had been invited to accompany King James to London, Elizabeth Melville identified with the Presbyterian sympathies of her in-laws, to which she remained loyal after James's breach with the independent Scottish clergy.

In 1598 Alexander Hume, Rector of Logie, dedicated his *Hymns, or Sacred Songs* to Elizabeth Melville, praising the pious verses of 'a Ladye, a tender youth, sad, solitare and sanctified, oft sighing & weeping through the conscience of sinne'.

Melville's poem, *Ane Godlie Dreame*, is a Calvinist tract, dealing with her vision of the hell that awaits all but God's anointed, calling upon God to relieve the suffering of his 'saints' and upon the elect to resist the earthly tyrant's persecution. First person accounts of journeys through a Christian hell began with the 'Vision of St. Paul' of third-century Greece; the tradition was sustained in Scottish literature and provided Calvinists especially with the opportunity for personal Biblical exegesis. In 1598 James Melville, the Scottish reformer, known to Lady Culross but not as far as we can tell any near relation, published the dream poem, 'A Morning Vision' in *A Spiritual Propine*. In it the heavenly guide is replaced with allegorical figures. Much closer to *Ane Godlie Dream* is James Melville's 'Black Bastell' (Laing, 1826, IV, ii), which was probably written about 1611, but never printed in full.

Lady Culross's *Godlie Dreame* first appeared under the initials 'M.M.' in 1603 when Presbyterian ministers were pleading with James to repeal the laws forbidding 'prophesyings', when, on special days of fasting, prayer, open-air preaching and feasting, 'all pairts' of the congregation were encouraged to interpret Biblical texts. References as in John Armstrong's *Miscellanies* (1770, ii, 254) to the 'dreadful, wild expressions' of *Ane Godlie Dreame* may relate to the way it was transmitted through performance at such events. In 1606 the original printer produced an anglicised version of the *Dreame* with the name 'Eliz. Melville, Ladie Culros yonger'; it appeared again in 1620, 1644, 1680, 1692, 1698, 1718 and 1727, always in Scotland. Melville, who was alive in 1631, may have been directly responsible for both published versions of her poem, or for neither.

In 1630, Melville was present at a prophesying in Lanarkshire, when five hundred people were stirred by the preaching of John Livingstone, who had been closely connected with her since the beginning of his ministry (Tweedie, 350-369). In *Memorable Characters and Remarkable Passages of Divine Providence* Livingstone describes her as 'famous for her piety and for her dream concerning her spiritual condition which she put in verse and was afterwards published'.

Of all the christians I was ever acquainted with she was the most unwearied in religious exercise, and the greater her access to God in duty, the more was her hungring after more; when at communion of the *Shots anno* 1630. the Sabbath night was spent by a great many christians at prayer in her room, and they had retired to their private devotion in the morning, she also retired to a corner of the room for that purpose, and was known to continue at prayer with wonderful assistance from the holy Spirit and motion on her spirit for above three hours space. (92)

A Sonnet sent to Blackness to Mr. John Welsch, by the Lady Culross

My dear Brother, wt courage bear the crosse
Joy shall be joyned with all thy sorrow here
High is thy hope disdain this earthly drosse!
Once shall you see the wished day appear

Now it is dark thy sky cannot be clear,
After the clouds it shall be calm anone,
Wait on his will whoes blood hath bo't ye dear
Extoll his name tho' outward joyes be gone.
Look to the Lord thou art not left alone,
Since he is thine quhat pleasures canst thou take
He is at hand, and hears thy heavy groan
End out thy faught, and suffer for his sake
    A sight most bright thy soul shall shortly see
    When shew of C's love thy rich reward shall be:

From NLS MS Wodrow 4to MS 29, No. 4 among the documents collected by Robert Wodrow, historian of the Scottish Church. John Welsch was the son-in-law of John Knox. In 1605 he was imprisoned in Blackness Castle for refusing to give information about the Assembly at Aberdeen, and condemned to death for treason. His sentence was commuted to banishment which duly ensued in October, 1606. A version of this poem appears in David Laing's *Early Metrical Tales* (London, 1826) citing the Wodrow MS as its source but fully punctuated and incorporating peculiar changes. David Irving, in his *History of Scottish Poetry* (483), claims that a poem of this title was published in 1720 'in a publication of half a sheet' with other poems. It seems from a comparison of the sonnet with Lady Culross's extant letters (Tweedie, i) that she was capable of writing in both Scots and English.

10 thine / there Laing   11 groan / moan Laing   14 shew of C[hrist]'s love / store of glore (*sic*) Laing

From *Ane Godlie Dream*

Upon ane day as I did mourne full soir,
With sindrie things quhairwith my saull was greifit
My greif increasit & grew moir & moir
My comfort fled and could not be releifit,
5   With heavines my heart was sa mischeifit,
I loathit my lyfe, I could not eit nor drink,
I micht not speik nor luik to nane that leifit,
Bot musit alone and divers things did think.

The wrechit warld did sa molest my mynde,
10 I thocht upon this false and Iron age.
And how our harts war sa to vice inclynde,
That Sathan seimit maist feirfullie to rage.
Nathing in earth my sorrow could asswage,
I felt my sin maist stranglie to incres,
15 I greifit my Spreit that wont to be my pledge,
My saull was drownit into maist deip distres.

All merynes did aggravate my paine,
And earthlie joyes did still incres my wo:
In companie I na wayes could remaine,
20 Bot fled resort and so alone did go.
My sillie saull was tossit to and fro,
With sindrie thochts quhilk troublit me full soir:
I preisit to pray, bot sichs overset me so,
I could do nocht bot sich and say no moir.

25 The twinkling teares aboundantlie ran down,
My heart was easit quhen I had mournit my fill:
Than I began my lamentatioun,
And said, O Lord, how lang it is thy will,
That thy puir Sancts sall be afflictit still?

30   Allace, how lang sall subtill Sathan rage?
     Mak haist O Lord, thy promeis to fulfill,
     Mak haist to end our painefull pilgramage.

     Thy sillie Sancts ar tostit to and fro,
     Awaik, O Lord, quhy sleipist thou sa lang?
35   We have na strenth agains our cruell fo,
     In sichs and sobbes now chaingit is our sang.
     The warld prevails, our enemies ar strang,
     The wickit rage, bot wee ar puir and waik:
     O shaw thy self, with speid revenge our wrang,
40   Mak short thir days, even for thy chosens saik....

Worn out with prayer and repentance, the narrator retires to bed
where she is vouchsafed a dream in which an 'angel' appears, who,
after revealing himself as God and instructing her to hold fast
around his neck, takes her through mountains and deserts and
thorny wilderness and over 'great pricks of iron' to where she has
sight of heaven. When she starts to run up the stairs towards her
goal, he holds her back:

     This godlie way althocht it seime sa fair,
     It is to hie tho cannot clim to stay:
255   Bot luik belaw beneath that statlie stair,
     And thou sall sie ane other kynde of way.

     I luikit down and saw ane pit most black,
     Most full of smuke and flaming fyre most fell:
     That uglie sicht maid mee to flie aback,
260   I feirit to heir so manie shout and yell:
     I him besocht that hee the treuth wald tell,
     Is this said I, the Papists purging place?
     Quhair thay affirme that sillie saulles do dwell,
     To purge thair sin, befoir thay rest in peace?

265   The braine of man maist warlie did invent
     That Purging place, he answerit me againe:
     For gredines together thay consent,
     To say that saulles in torment mon remaine,
     Till gold and gudes releif them of thair paine,
270   O spytfull spreits that did the same begin:
     O blindit beists your thochts ar all in vaine,
     My blude alone did saif thy saull from sin.

This Pit is Hell, quhairthrow thou now mon go.
Thair is thy way that leids the to the land:
275 Now play the man thou neids not trimbill so,
For I sall help and hald thee be the hand.
Allace said I, I have na force to stand,
For feir I faint to sie that uglie sicht:
How can I cum among that bailfull band,
280 Oh help mee now, I have na force nor micht.

Oft have I heard, that thay that enters thair,
In this greit golfe, sall never cum againe:
Curage said hee, have I not bocht thee deir,
My precious blude it was nocht shed in vaine.
285 I saw this place, my saull did taist this paine,
Or ever I went into my fathers gloir:
Throw mon thou go, bot thou sall not remaine,
Thow neids not feir for I sall go befoir.

I am content to do thy haill command,
290 Said I againe, and did him fast imbrace:
Then lovinglie he held mee be the hand,
And in wee went into that feirfull place.
Hald fast thy grip said hee, in anie cace,
Let mee not slip, quhat ever thou sall sie:
295 Dreid not the deith, bot stoutlie forwart preis,
For Deith nor Hell sall never vanquish thee.

His words sa sweit did cheir my heavie hairt,
Incontinent I cuist my cair asyde:
Curage said hee, play not ane cowarts pairt,
300 Thocht thou be waik, yit in my strenth confyde.
I thocht me blist to have sa gude ane guyde,
Thocht I was waik, I knew that he was strang:
Under his wings I thocht mee for to hyde,
Gif anie thair sould preis to do me wrang.

305 Into that Pit, quhen I did enter in,
I saw ane sicht, quhilk maid my heart agast:
Puir dammit saullis, tormentit sair for sin,
In flaming fyre, war frying wonder fast:
And uglie spreits, and as wee thocht them past,
310 My heart grew faint, and I begouth to tyre:

Or I was war ane gripit mee at last,
And held me heich above ane flaming fyre:

The fyre was greit, the heit did peirs me sair,
My faith grew waik, my grip was wonderous smal,
315 I trimbellit fast, my feir grew mair and mair,
My hands did shaik, that I him held withall.
At lenth thay lousit, then thay begouth to fall,
I cryit O Lord, and caucht him fast againe:
Lord Jesus cum, and red mee out of thrall,
320 Curage said he, now thou art past the paine.

With this greit feir, I stackerit and awoke
Crying O Lord, Lord Jesus cum againe:
Bot efter this, no kynde of rest I tuke,
I preisit to sleip, bot that was all in vaine.
325 I wald have dreamit, of pleasour after paine,
Becaus I knaw, I sall it finde at last:
God grant my guyde may still with me remaine,
It is to cum that I beleifit was past.

From *Ane Godlie Dreame, Compylit in Scottish Meter be M.M. Gentelwoman in Culros, at the requeist of her freindis*. Edinburgh: Robert Charteris, l603. The M. M. is assumed to stand for Mistress Melville. Most of the hundreds of variants between the 1603 edition and the 1606 and 1620 editions are simply matters of orthography; we have therefore listed only those which seem to indicate substantive changes and authorial or other intervention.

24 sich / grone 1606   25 twinkling / trickling 1620   272 saif / cleanse 1620
321 stackerit / started 1606   322 Crying O Lord / Crying aloud 1606

15 Ephesians 4:30

28 Psalm 6:3: Melville's scriptural source is the Bassandynde Bible of 1579, a Scottish reprint of the second (1561) edition of the Geneva Bible, and from 1579 to 1636 required property of every household worth £500 in Scotland. In 1604 King James gave the Geneva Bible's 'very partial, untrue, seditious' marginalia as reason to authorise a new Bible.

258 *fell*: cruel

262 *the Papists purging place*: the Catholic doctrine of purgatory was anathema to reformed religion.

272 Hebrews 1:3

275 *Now play the man*: II Esdras 10:33: 'Then said he unto me, Stand up manly and I wil give thee exhortation.' This chapter of the aprocrypha is a dream vision with the angel Uriel as guide. 'Play the

man, Master Ridley' was a rallying cry of sixteenth-century Protestants, being the last words of Hugh Latimer before he was burnt at the stake in Oxford, 1555.

282 Luke 16:26

285-286 The Harrowing of Hell, the story of Christ's retrieval of virtuous souls after his crucifixion, based on Matthew 27: 52-53, was one of the most popular visions of medieval literature.

287 The Geneva Bible gloss on Psalm 9:15 ('The heathen are sunken down in the pit that they made...') reads: 'The mercy of God towards his Saints must be declared, & the fall of the wicked must always be considered. God promiseth not to help us before we have felt the cross.'

307-309 Revelation 16: 9-13

318 *I cryit O Lord*: cf. 1606: *And cried aloud*. A sign of verbal transmission, bearing out the comment of John Armstrong who found the poem 'almost too dreadful to the ear'. David Laing (1826) and David Irving suggest that the poem was either 'sung to some plaintive air' or 'chanted rather than sung'.

ELIZABETH STUART,
QUEEN OF BOHEMIA

Elizabeth (1596-1660) was the eldest daughter of King James VI of Scotland and Anne of Denmark. When her father came to the throne as James I of England in 1603, she was sent to Coombe Abbey, near Coventry, to be brought up by Lord and Lady Harington of Exton. Together with Anne Dudley, Harington's niece, she was instructed in French, Italian, music and dancing. Elegantly penned letters to her brother Henry in English, French and Italian (BL MS Harl. 6986) bear witness to the proficiency she achieved. Although King James was opposed to classical studies for women and Elizabeth did not learn Latin and Greek as her godmother Queen Elizabeth had, in many ways her education followed the programme the King had outlined for his son in the *Basilikon Doron* (1599) which included writing in verse in one's own language, and 'hunting, specially with running hounds' (Steeholm, 497), an exercise she loved all her life.

As a royal princess her function was to marry one of her father's allies; the first offers for her hand were made in 1607. By 1611 negotiations for her marriage were well advanced. Queen Anne favoured the Catholic Prince Philip of Spain, despite the Princess's earnest Protestantism, but in 1612 she was formally promised to the Protestant Elector Palatine, Frederick V. Their magnificent wedding on St Valentine's Day 1613 was followed by a triumphant nuptial progress to the Elector's residence in Heidelberg, where Elizabeth learned German and Dutch, and produced a translation of the Psalms and several hymns in her own hand (Heidelberg Library MSS 661, 690, 694). In 1619 Frederick was elected King of Bohemia by the Protestant Union, and Elizabeth, pregnant with their fourth child, was crowned Queen. Sir Francis Nethersole was appointed her secretary, but Elizabeth continued to write her own letters. Many of the nearly four hundred still extant plead for aid for her children and her new country.

As neither her father nor her brother, Charles I, would support the Protestant cause in Germany, Elizabeth was obliged to go into exile at the outbreak of the Thirty Years' War, living at the Hague and Rhenen, and bearing another nine children before her husband's death in 1632. Unable to return to England during the

Civil War or the Interregnum, she saw her eldest surviving son, Charles Louis, defect to Cromwell while her favourite, Prince Rupert, became a Royalist hero. Her first two daughters left her in the 1650s: Princess Elizabeth (1618-1680), famous for her learning and her intellectual patronage, became abbess of the Protestant nunnery at Herford in Westphalia shortly after the death of her friend Descartes; Louise (1623-1709) converted to Catholicism in 1657 and became abbess of a convent at Maubuisson where she was free to practise her painting. In 1660, the year of the Stuart Restoration, Elizabeth's youngest daughter Princess Sophia (1630-1714) gave birth to the child who would become George I of England. During her exile, Elizabeth was a tragic heroine to the English who called her 'The Winter Queen' and the 'Queen of Hearts' and to poets like 'Eliza' (see pp.133-4) who found in her trials a correlative of their own religious persecution. Queen Elizabeth finally returned to London in 1661 through the kindness of Lord Craven who paid the debts she had accumulated during her exile. She died on 13 February 1662 (see Katherine Philips 'On the death of the Queen of Bohemia', pp.198-200).

Verses by the Princess Elizabeth, given to Lord Harington, of Exton, her preceptor.

I

This is joye, this is true pleasure,
If we best things make our treasure,
And enjoy them at full leasure,
Evermore in richest measure.

II

God is only excellent,
Let up to him our love be sent,
Whose desires are set or bent
On ought else, shall much repent.

III

Theirs is a most wretched case,
Who themselves so far disgrace,
That they their affections place
Upon things nam'd vile and base.

IV

Let us love of heaven receave,
These are joyes our harts will heave
Higher then we can conceave,
And shall us not fayle or leave.

V

Earthly things do fade, decay,

Constant to us not one day;
Suddenly they pass away,
And we can not make them stay.

VI

All the vast world doth conteyne,
To content mans heart, are vayne,
That still justly will complayne,
And unsatisfyde remaine.

VII

God, most holy, high, and greate,
Our delight doth make compleate;
When in us he takes his seate,
Only then we are repleat.

VIII

Why should vain joyes us transport,
Earthly pleasures are but shorte,
And are mingled in such sorte,
Greifs are greater then the sporte.

IX

And regard of this yet have,
Nothing can from death us save,
Then we must unto our grave,
When we most are pleasure's slave.

X

By long use our soules will cleave
To the earth: then it we leave;
Then will cruell death bereave,
All the joyes that we receive.

XI

Thence they goe to hellish flame,
Ever tortur'd in the same,
With perpetuall blott of name,
Flowt, reproach, and endless shame.

XII

Torment not to be exprest,
But, O then! how greatly blest,
Whose desires are whole addrest
To the heavenly thinges and best.

XIII

Thy affections shall increase,
Growing forward without cease,
Even untill thou dyest in peace,

And injoyest eternall ease.

XIV

When thy hart is fullest fraught
With heavens love, it shall be caught
To the place it loved and sought,
Which Christs precious bloud hath bought.

XV

Joyes of those which there shall dwell,
No hearte thinke, no tounge can tell;
Wonderfully they excell,
Those thy soule will fully swell...

XXVII

O my soule of heavenly birth,
Doe thou scorn this basest earth,
Place not here thy joy and mirth,
Where of bliss is greatest dearth.

XXVIII

From below thy mind remove,
And affect the things above:
Sett thy heart and fix thy love
Where thou truest joyes shalt prove.

XXIX

If I do love things on high,
Doubtless them enjoy shall I,
Earthly pleasures if I try,
They pursued faster fly.

XXX

O Lord, glorious, yet most kind,
Thou hast these thoughts put in my mind,
Let me grace increasing find,
Me to thee more firmly bind.

XXXI

To God glory, thanks, and praise,
I will render all my dayes,
Who hath blest me many wayes,
Shedding on me gratious rayes.

XXXII

To me grace, O Father, send,
On thee wholly to depend,
That all may to thy glory tend;
Soe let me live, soe let me end.

XXXIII

Now to the true Eternal King,
Not seen with human eye,
The immortall, only wise, true God,
Be praise perpetually!

From *Nugae Antiquae: Being a Miscellaneous Collection of Original Papers, in Prose and Verse; Written During the Reigns of Henry VIII. Edward VI. Queen Mary, Elizabeth, and King James: By Sir John Harington, Knt. and by Others who lived in those Times. Selected from Authentic Remains.* Edited by Henry Harington. Vol. II. London, 1769, 1779, 1792. Re-edited by Thomas Park. London, 1804. Harington includes Princess Elizabeth's 'Verses' as the last of the 'Poems by Various Authors. (Written between 1540 and 1612)'. Sophia Benger, *Memoirs of Elizabeth Stuart, Queen of Bohemia*, 1825 (II, 226) believed that the poem was written when Elizabeth was thirteen; S. C. Lomas, in her 1909 revision of Mary Anne Everett Green's *Lives of the Princesses of England* (1854), noted that R.S. Rait, editor of *Five Stuart Princesses* (1902), claimed to have access to a copy of the poem headed 'This was written by Elizabeth daughter of James, 1609'; the whereabouts of this copy is unknown.

The poem is in the tradition of the *De Contemptu Mundi* exercise commonly assigned to young men studying Latin and sometimes practised by women (e.g. Anne Bradstreet's 'The Flesh and the Spirit', and 'The Vanity of All Worldly Things'). Elizabeth's monorhymed tetrameter quatrains are unusual in English. Thomas Tusser, who had translated the twelfth-century *De Contemptu Mundi* poems of St Bernard of Clairvaux, had used the repetitive rhyme scheme in several of his popular mnemonic verses in *Five Hundreth Pointes of Good Husbandry* (1573), and Sir Walter Raleigh, to whom the young Princess Elizabeth wrote letters, experimented with sustaining rhyme in longer stanzas. In the structure of her poem, Princess Elizabeth seems to be challenging King James's advice to Prince Henry, 'if ye write in verse, remember that it is not the principal part of a poem to rhyme rite' (*Basilikon Doron*, Steeholm, 497).

AEMILIA LANYER

On the evidence of the entry for 17 May 1597 in the case-book of Simon Forman, Renaissance astrologer and medical practitioner, Aemilia Lanyer was 'filia 2 Baptista Bassane' and 'Margarete Jhonson' (Bod. MS Ashmole 226). Baptista Bassani was an Italian musician at the Tudor court, one of five brothers of Jewish descent from Bassano, near Venice, who came to England in the sixteenth century and became members of the King's Musick (Prior, 253-265). The first appearance at court of Baptista Bassani was at the coronation of Edward VI, 20 February 1547, and the last performances for which payment was recorded took place before Michaelmas 1564 (De Lafontaine, *passim*). Margaret Bassani's burial at St Botolph's, Bishopsgate in 1587 has been noted by A.L.Rowse (1978, 14), but nothing else is known about Lanyer's mother.

Aemilia Bassani was christened at St Botolph's on 27 January 1569 (Rowse, 1978, 13), thus Simon Forman was more or less accurate in recording that Lanyer was 'of 27 years' on 17 May 1597. She had at least one sister, Angela, four years younger, who is mentioned along with Aemilia in their father's will; at his death in 1576, he left Aemilia a dowry of £100 to be paid when she was twenty-one (Rowse, 1976, 113).

The only information we have about Aemilia Lanyer's earlier years comes from her poems. In a poem dedicated 'To the Ladie Susan, Countesse Dowager of Kent, and daughter to the Duchesse of Suffolke', she speaks of the Duchess of Kent as 'the Mistris of my youth, / The noble guide of my ungovern'd dayes', which suggests Lanyer may have been a member of the Duchess's household. She compares the Duchess to 'the Sunnes virtue' and herself to 'that faire greene grasse, / That flourisht fresh by your cleere virtues taught'.

In the second column of Simon Forman's entry for 17 May 1597 he writes that Lanyer 'was p'amour to my old L. of HunsDean that was L. Chamberline and was maintained in great pride and y^t seams that being with child she was for collour maried to A minstrell'. Henry Carey, first Lord Hunsdon (1524?-1596) was forty-five years older than Lanyer. Forman claims in notes he made between 1597 and 1600 that Lanyer was in financial difficulties and came to him for advice regarding her future. In exchange for this advice she agreed to 'be a good fellow' and permitted Forman some sort of familiarity, although less than Rowse implies (Rowse, 1976, 101-102). Rowse's transcriptions of Forman are selective and surprisingly inaccurate; he also connects Lanyer with several entries of Forman's that may refer to any of his numerous female clients. (Forman's casebooks are an invaluable source for the feminist historian, as by far the greater proportion of his caseload was female, and have never been examined systematically.)

The 'minstrell' Aemilia married was Alfonso Lanyer, also from a family of musicians ('Lanier, Nicholas', *DNB*); the marriage was recorded at St Botolph's on 18 October 1592. Rowse has discovered a letter from Bishop Bancroft to Robert Cecil, Lord Cranborne, dated 24 August 1604, which mentions that

Captain Alfonso Lanier, the late Queen's and now his Majesty's servant, mine old fellow and loving friend, has obtained a suit of his Highness for the weighing of hay and straw about London. He was put in hope of your favour by the Earl of Southampton... He did her Majesty good service in Ireland and in some other employments, whereby he has decayed his estate; and we served both together the Lord Chancellor... (Rowse,1978, 19)

An Elizabethan civil servant might be well paid but he had no guarantee of regular employment or security. Alfonso Lanyer had the benefit of his straw-weighing privilege until he died in 1613. The publication of Aemilia Lanyer's only known volume of poems, *Salve Deus Rex Judaeorum* (1611), was evidently an effort to win support from patrons. M. C. Bradbrook has suggested that the nine dedications to the volume may have been written in expectation of the usual £2 per dedication (92). Desperation may have induced the direct plea to the Countess of Dorset: 'Gods Stewards must for all the poore provide... To you, as to Gods Steward I doe write.'

Alfonso Lanyer evidently promoted his wife's work. On the title-page of the Chapin Library's copy of *Salve Deus Rex Judaeorum* is the inscription 'The guift of Mr Alfonso Lanyer 8 No:1610 / Tho: Jones'. The gift was made only a month after the entry in the Stationers' Register (2 October 1610). Thomas Jones was Lord Chancellor of Ireland and Archbishop of Dublin from 1605, active in Irish politics from twenty years before. Alfonso Lanyer would have known of him from his service in Ireland.

The nine surviving copies of *Salve Deus Rex Judaeorum* fall into two groups, showing two typesettings, and with different dedicatory poems bound in with the main sheets. The two groups overlap, because old and new sheets were bound together. A thorough collation of all copies has not yet been done, but it seems that Lanyer reissued her book in different formats, for different patrons and dedicatees.

In financial difficulty with a school for educating 'noblemen and gentlemen's children of great worth' between 1617 and 1619, Lanyer went to court against her landlord claiming repairs against rent (Rowse, 1978, 34). Between 1635 and 1638 she made repeated applications for Alfonso Lanyer's monopoly of weighing hay, apparently without success. Aemilia Lanyer was buried at Clerkenwell on 3 April 1645, having survived her husband thirty-two years and brought up at least two children and two grandchildren.

There is no hard evidence to connect her in any way with William Shakespeare, A.L. Rowse's contentions notwithstanding.

The Description of Cooke-ham

Farewell (sweet *Cooke-ham*) where I first obtain'd
Grace from that Grace where perfit Grace remain'd;
And where the Muses gave their full consent,
I should have powre the virtuous to content:
5   Where princely Palace will'd me to indite,
The sacred Storie of the Soules delight.
Farewell (sweet Place) where Virtue then did rest,
And all delights did harbour in her breast:
Never shall my sad eies againe behold
10   Those pleasures which my thoughts did then unfold:
Yet you (great Lady) Mistris of that Place,
From whose desires did spring this work of Grace;
Vouchsafe to thinke upon those pleasures past,
As fleeting worldly Joyes that could not last:
15   Or, as dimme shadowes of celestiall pleasures,
Which are desir'd above all earthly treasures.
Oh how (me thought) against you thither came,
Each part did seeme some new delight to frame!
The House receiv'd all ornaments to grace it,
20   And would indure no foulenesse to deface it.
The Walkes put on their summer Liveries,
And all things else did hold like similies:
The Trees with leaves, with fruits, with flowers clad,
Embrac'd each other, seeming to be glad,
25   Turning themselves to beauteous Canopies,
To shade the bright Sunne from your brighter eies:
The cristall Streames with silver spangles graced,
While by the glorious Sunne they were embraced:
The little Birds in chirping notes did sing,
30   To entertaine both You and that sweet Spring.
And *Philomela* with her sundry layes,
Both You and that delightfull Place did praise.
Oh how me thought each plant, each floure, each tree
Set forth their beauties then to welcome thee!

46

35 The very Hills right humbly did descend,
    When you to tread upon them did intend.
    And as you set your feete, they still did rise,
    Glad that they could receive so rich a prise.
    The gentle Windes did take delight to bee
40 Among those woods that were so grac'd by thee.
    And in sad murmure utterd pleasing sound,
    That Pleasure in that place might more abound:
    The swelling Bankes deliver'd all their pride,
    When such a *Phoenix* once they had espide.
45 Each Arbor, Banke, each Seate, each stately Tree,
    Thought themselves honor'd in supporting thee.
    The pretty Birds would oft come to attend thee,
    Yet flie away for feare they should offend thee:
    The little creatures in the Burrough by
50 Would come abroad to sport them in your eye;
    Yet fearfull of the Bowe in your faire Hand,
    Would runne away when you did make a stand.
    Now let me come unto that stately Tree,
    Wherein such goodly Prospects you did see;
55 That Oake that did in height his fellowes passe,
    As much as lofty trees, low growing grasse:
    Much like a comely Cedar streight and tall,
    Whose beauteous stature farre exceeded all:
    How often did you visite this faire tree,
60 Which seeming joyfull in receiving thee,
    Would like a Palme tree spread his armes abroad,
    Desirous that you there should make abode:
    Whose faire greene leaves much like a comely vaile,
    Defended *Phebus* when he would assaile:
65 Whose pleasing boughes did yeeld a coole fresh ayre,
    Joying his happinesse when you were there.
    Where beeing seated, you might plainely see,
    Hills, vales, and woods, as if on bended knee
    They had appeard, your honour to salute,
70 Or to preferre some strange unlook'd for sute:
    All interlac'd with brookes and christall springs,
    A Prospect fit to please the eyes of Kings:
    And thirteene shires appear'd all in your sight,
    Europe could not affoard much more delight.
75 What was there then but gave you all content,
    While you the time in meditation spent,

Of their Creators powre, which there you saw,
In all his Creatures held a perfit Law;
And in their beauties did you plaine descrie,
His beauty, wisdome, grace, love, majestie.
In these sweet woods how often did you walke,
With Christ and his Apostles there to talke;
Placing his holy Writ in some faire tree,
To meditate what you therein did see:
With *Moyses* you did mount his holy Hill,
To know his pleasure, and performe his Will.
With lovely *David* you did often sing,
His holy Hymnes to Heavens Eternall King.
And in sweet musicke did your soule delight,
To sound his prayses, morning, noone, and night.
With blessed *Joseph* you did often feed
Your pined brethren, when they stood in need.
And that sweet Lady sprung from *Cliffords* race,
Of noble *Bedfords* blood, faire steame of Grace;
To honourable *Dorset* now espows'd,
In whose faire breast true virtue then was hous'd:
Oh what delight did my weake spirits find
In those pure parts of her well framed mind:
And yet it grieves me that I cannot be
Neere unto her, whose virtues did agree
With those faire ornaments of outward beauty,
Which did enforce from all both love and dutie.
Unconstant Fortune, thou art most too blame,
Who casts us downe into so lowe a frame:
Where our great friends we cannot dayly see,
So great a diffrence is there in degree.
Many are placed in those Orbes of state,
Parters in honour, so ordain'd by Fate;
Neerer in show, yet farther off in love,
In which, the lowest alwayes are above.
But whither am I carried in conceit?
My Wit too weake to conster of the great.
Why not? although we are but borne of earth,
We may behold the Heavens, despising death;
And loving heaven that is so farre above,
May in the end vouchsafe us entire love.
Therefore sweet Memorie doe thou retaine
Those pleasures past, which will not turne againe;

Remember beauteous *Dorsets* former sports,
120 So farre from beeing toucht by ill reports;
Wherein my selfe did alwaies beare a part,
While reverend Love presented my true heart:
Those recreations let me beare in mind,
Which her sweet youth and noble thoughts did finde:
125 Whereof depriv'd, I evermore must grieve,
Hating blind Fortune, carelesse to relieve.
And you sweet Cooke-ham, whom these Ladies leave,
I now must tell the griefe you did conceave
At their departure; when they went away,
130 How every thing retaind a sad dismay:
Nay long before, when once an inkeling came,
Me thought each thing did unto sorrow frame:
The trees that were so glorious in our view,
Forsooke both flowres and fruit, when once they
knew
135 Of your depart, their very leaves did wither,
Changing their colours as they grewe together.
But when they saw this had no powre to stay you,
They often wept, though speechlesse, could not pray
you;
Letting their teares in your faire bosoms fall,
140 As if they said, Why will ye leave us all?
This being vaine, they cast their leaves away,
Hoping that pitie would have made you stay:
Their frozen tops, like Ages hoarie haires,
Showes their disasters, languishing in feares:
145 A swarthy riveld ryne all over spread,
Their dying bodies halfe alive, halfe dead.
But your occasions call'd you so away,
That nothing there had power to make you stay:
Yet did I see a noble gratefull minde,
150 Requiting each according to their kind;
Forgetting not to turne and take your leave
Of these sad creatures, powrelesse to receive
Your favour, when with griefe you did depart,
Placing their former pleasures in your heart;
155 Giving great charge to noble Memory,
There to preserve their love continually:
But specially the love of that faire tree,
That first and last you did vouchsafe to see:

In which it pleas'd you oft to take the ayre,
160 With noble *Dorset*, then a virgin faire:
Where many a learned Booke was read and skand
To this faire tree, taking me by the hand,
You did repeat the pleasures which had past,
Seeming to grieve they could no longer last.
165 And with a chaste, yet loving kisse took leave,
Of which sweet kisse I did it soone bereave:
Scorning a sencelesse creature should possesse
So rare a favour, so great happinesse.
No other kisse it could receive from me,
170 For feare to give backe what it tooke of thee:
So I ingratefull Creature did deceive it,
Of that which you vouchsaft in love to leave it.
And though it oft had giv'n me much content,
Yet this great wrong I never could repent:
175 But of the happiest made it most forlorne,
To shew that nothing's free from Fortunes scorne,
While all the rest with this most beauteous tree,
Made their sad consort Sorrowes harmony.
The Floures that on the banks and walkes did grow,
180 Crept in the ground, the Grasse did weepe for woe.
The Windes and Waters seem'd to chide together,
Because you went away they knew not whither:
And those sweet Brookes that ranne so faire and
cleare,
With griefe and trouble wrinckled did appeare.
185 Those pretty Birds that wonted were to sing,
Now neither sing, nor chirp, nor use their wing;
But with their tender feet on some bare spray,
Warble forth sorrow, and their owne dismay.
Faire *Philomela* leaves her mournefull Ditty,
190 Drownd in dead sleepe, yet can procure no pittie:
Each arboure, banke, each seate, each stately tree,
Lookes bare and desolate now for want of thee;
Turning greene tresses into frostie gray,
While in cold griefe they wither all away.
195 The Sunne grew weake, his beames no comfort gave,
While all greene things did make the earth their
grave:
Each brier, each bramble, when you went away,
Caught fast your clothes, thinking to make you stay:

50

Delightfull Eccho wonted to reply
200   To our last words, did now for sorrow die:
The house cast off each garment that might grace it,
Putting on Dust and Cobwebs to deface it.
All desolation then there did appeare,
When you were going whom they held so deare.
205   This last farewell to *Cooke-ham* here I give,
When I am dead thy name in this may live,
Wherein I have perform'd her noble hest,
Whose virtues lodge in my unworthy breast,
And ever shall, so long as life remaines,
210   Tying my heart to her by those rich chaines.

From *Salve Deus Rex Judaeorum. Containing, 1 The Passion of Christ. 2 Eves Apologie in defence of Women. 3 The Teares of the Daughters of Jerusalem. 4 The Salutation and Sorrow of the Virgine Marie. With divers other things not unfit to be read.* Written by Mistris *Aemilia Lanyer*, Wife to Captaine *Alfonso Lanyer*, Servant to the Kings Majestie. London: Printed by *Valentine Simmes* for *Richard Bonian...* 1611. 'The Description of Cooke-ham' was, like the title poem, written in honour of Margaret Clifford, Countess of Cumberland (1560?-1616). Margaret Clifford's brother, Lord William Russell of Thornhaugh, was Lord-Deputy of Ireland from 1594 to 1597 when Alfonso was likely to have been in service there. We learn from the diary of the Countess's daughter, Lady Anne Clifford, that Lord Russell sometimes stayed at the royal manor of Cookham:

Not long before Michaelmas [1603], myself, my Coz. *Frances Bouchier*, Mrs *Goodwin* and Mrs *Howbridge* waiting on us, [went?] in my mother's coach from *Barton* to *Cookham* where my Uncle *Russell* his wife and son then lay. (Sackville-West, 15n)

The manor of Cookham, near Maidenhead, belonged to the Crown until 1818. On the occasion described by Lady Clifford, members of her family were following the progress of Queen Anne and Prince Henry, staying for a week at Nonsuch with the royal party. Nothing is recorded of Lanyer as a member of their household at any time. The Countess may have stayed at Cookham under a lease in her brother's or her own name. Lanyer's poem must have been completed after Lady Anne Clifford's marriage to the Earl of Dorset in February 1609 and before the Stationers' Register entry of October 1610, perhaps before Jonson's 'To Penshurst' which is considered to be the first poem in the English country house tradition (Lewalski, 1985, 220-224). The farewell-to-a-place topos is developed in Virgil's Eclogue I to which Lanyer's poem has some points of resemblance, in Meliboeus' sense of unfairness at his exile, and in the active sympathy of trees and streams who cry out at parting. The poem is similar in tone to Veronica Franco's '*In lode di Fumano*' (*Terze Rime*, 1575), and there

51

may well be a more immediate Italian source.

2 *that Grace*: her Grace, the Countess of Cumberland

6 *sacred Storie*: *Salve Deus Rex Judaeorum*

11 *great Lady*: Margaret Clifford, Countess of Cumberland (1560?-1616), wife of the third Earl, youngest daughter of Francis Russell, third Earl of Bedford, estranged from her husband on account of his adultery.

22-74 Lanyer's conceit of nature as a court and the Countess as its sovereign is influenced by Spenser's figure of Dame Nature in the Mutabilitie Cantos (*Faerie Queene*, 7.7.8-13). Lanyer would have been aware that Spenser dedicated his *Fowre Hymnes* (1596) to the Countess of Cumberland and her sister the Countess of Warwick.

31 *Philomela*: the nightingale

43 *swelling Bankes*: cf. Donne's conceit in 'The Extasie':

> Where, like a pillow on a bed,
> A Pregnant banke swel'd up, to rest
> The violets reclining head,
> Sat we two, one anothers best.

44 *Phoenix*: the mythical bird who rises from its own ashes, but used commonly at the time to signify a person of rare excellence and frequently during the reign of Elizabeth I as a figure of the Queen. Lanyer refers to Elizabeth I as 'The *Phoenix* of her age' in a dedicatory poem 'To the Lady Elizabeths Grace' (i.e. Elizabeth Stuart, Princess Royal, later Queen of Bohemia, see p.39). Lanyer applies the figure also to Lady Arabella Stuart in an invocation: 'Rare *Phoenix*, whose faire feathers are your owne' ('To the Ladie Arabella').

49 *Burrough*: burrow

51-52 *Bowe... stand*: Elizabethan women occasionally engaged in hunting and falconry (C. Camden, 162). See the woodcuts of Elizabeth in George Turberville, *The Booke of Faulconrie* (1575).

64 *Defended*: warded off

73 *thirteene shires*: in sixteenth-century usage the word shire could apply to a city, or other district.

76 *meditation*: Lady Anne Clifford describes her mother as 'truly religious and virtuous... the death of her two sonnes did so much afflict her as that ever after the booke of Jobe was her dayly companion' (Sackville-West, 18).

87 *With lovely David*: the portrait of the Countess at Appleby Castle shows her holding a book of the Psalms.

91 *Joseph*: Genesis 47:12

92 *pined*: afflicted

93 *that sweet Lady*: Anne Clifford (1590-1676), only surviving child of the Countess of Cumberland, tutored by Samuel Daniel.

94 *steame*: stem, meaning the main line or stock of a family tree, as in *Faerie Queene*, 7.6.2: 'Yet many of their stemme long after did survive.'

95 *Dorset now espows'd*: on 25 February 1609, Anne Clifford married

Richard Sackville, Lord Buckhurst, third Earl of Dorset, to whom she bore three sons all dead at an early age, and two daughters.

108 *parters*: dividers, separators

112 *conster*: construe

119 *beauteous Dorsets former sports*: the sports may have included dancing and card-playing as well as outdoor games like shuttlecock (C. Camden, 158-171; Sackville-West, 45). Lady Anne performed in at least two masques at the court of James I, the *Masque of Beauty* (1609) and the *Masque of Queens* (1610) both by Ben Jonson (Herford & Simpson, vii, 191, 317; x, 441). Sir Dudley Carleton criticised the behaviour of aristocratic women in these masques as 'too light and courtesan-like for such great ones' (Traill, IV, 222).

126 Cf. Wroth, 'After long trouble', 5-12 (see p.65).

145 *swarthy riveld ryne*: 'ryne' ('rine', 'rind') can mean both the bark of a tree and a frost, thus the conceit that the dark, wrinkled bark of the trees is a kind of frost on the tree-trunks that coincides with the white frost or snow, the 'hoarie haires', of the frozen tree-tops.

161 *skand*: scanned

178 *consort*: concert

179-204 Sympathetic Nature in Spenser's November eclogue, *The Shepheardes Calender* (1579) and Dame Nature's susceptibility to Time and Change in *The Faerie Queene*, Book 7, Canto 7 are notable antecedents of Lanyer's wintry, mourning landscape. See also Shakespeare's Sonnets 12 and 73.

ELIZABETH CARY,
VISCOUNTESS FALKLAND

Elizabeth, wife of Henry Cary, Lord Falkland, is generally assumed to be the 'learned, vertuous, and truly noble Ladie, E. C.' mentioned on the title-page of *The Tragedie of Mariam* (1613).

Lady Cary's life, written by her daughter and corrected by her son, mentions among her works a translation of Seneca's *Epistles*, a 'Life of Tamurlaine' and lives of St Mary Magdalene, St Agnes the Martyr and St Elizabeth of Portugal, all in verse and all lost, as well as a translation of *The Reply of Most Illustrious Cardinall of Perron* (Simpson, 9, 38) which was dedicated to Queen Henrietta Maria and printed in Douay in 1630. Unless the unnamed work that was 'stolen out of [her] sister-in-law's chamber, and printed, but by her procurement called in' (Simpson, 9) was the play *Mariam*, Lady Cary's daughter makes no reference to what would have been her mother's major achievement. Modern critical opinion also attributes to Lady Falkland a translation of Ortelius' *Miroir du Monde* to be found in MS at Burford Church in Oxfordshire, an 'Epitaph on Buckingham' (BL MS Egerton 2725, f.60), and the blank verse *History of the Life, Reign, and Death of Edward II* (London, 1680, from a MS dated 1627), none of which is mentioned in the biography (see Stauffer, Shapiro, Crawford).

Lady Cary was born Elizabeth Tanfield, only child of a prosperous lawyer. She learned French, Spanish, Italian, Hebrew and 'Transylvanian' before she was married at fifteen to Henry Cary, whose mother removed all her books. At the age of nineteen she secretly converted to Catholicism. Although Lord Falkland was passionately anti-Catholic, she continued to be a loyal wife, bearing eleven children between 1609 and 1624 and accompanying her husband to Ireland where he was Lord Deputy from 1622 to 1629.

In 1625 Lady Falkland announced her conversion, separated from her husband, and was formally received into the Catholic Church in 1626. In defiance of a royal command, Lord Falkland refused to support her and she was obliged to live separated from her children in a cottage by the Thames. Even so she mortgaged her jointure lands to pay the debts for which Lord Falkland was imprisoned in 1629, and was disinherited by her father as a result, her fortune passing to her son Lucius. After a brief period of reconciliation with her husband, she died of consumption in 1639, impoverished and alone.

Lady Falkland's claim to be authoress of *Mariam* rests in part upon dedicatory verses in John Davies of Hereford's *Muses' Sacrifice* (1612) in which he clearly identifies Elizabeth 'Wife of Sr Henry Cary' who makes her 'Muse to mete the scenes of Syracuse and Palestine' (Grosart, 1878, II, 4-5). Some of the surviving copies of *Mariam* contain a dedicatory sonnet addressed to 'my worthy Sister, Mistres Elizabeth Carye' signed 'E. C.' The sonnet calls the dedicatee 'Dianaes earthlie deputresse', and refers to an earlier work, dedicated to her husband, set in Sicily. (No work set in Syracuse has ever been traced to Lady Falkland or any other Elizabeth Cary.) Elizabeth, wife of Henry's younger brother Philip Cary, is probably the 'worthy sister'; the title 'Mistres' would have been appropriate before Philip Carey was knighted in 1605.

The Tragedie of Mariam is based upon the story told by Josephus in the *Wars of the Jews* and again in *Antiquities*, which seems to have been the source used by 'E. C.' There are significant departures from Thomas Lodge's translation, *The Famous and Memorable Works of Josephus*, published in 1602. While Lodge's Mariam is a shrew, railing at her infatuated husband for the deaths of her kinsmen, and quarrelling incessantly with her mother, her mother-in-law and her sister-in-law, 'E.C.' turns her into a tragic heroine. The historic events are compressed into a single day and 'A company of Jewes' functions as the Chorus. There are important parallels with Lady Cary's life as a blameless and constant wife separated from her husband by his intolerance of her religion; the emotional complexities of Mariam's divided allegiance provide the meat of the play.

Actus Primus. Scoena prima.
Mariam sola.

How oft have I with publike voyce runne on?
To censure *Romes* last *Hero* for deceit:
5   Because he wept when *Pompeis* life was gone,
Yet when he liv'd, hee thought his Name too great.
But now I doe recant, and *Roman* Lord
Excuse too rash a judgement in a woman:
My Sexe pleads pardon, pardon then afford,
10 Mistaking is with us, but too too common.
Now doe I finde by selfe Experience taught,
One Object yeelds both griefe and joy:
You wept indeed, when on his worth you thought,
But joyd that slaughter did your Foe destroy.

15 So at his death your Eyes true droppes did raine,
    Whom dead, you did not wish alive againe.
    When *Herod* liv'd, that now is done to death,
    Oft have I wisht that I from him were free:
    Oft have I wisht that he might lose his breath,
20 Oft have I wisht his Carkas dead to see.
    Then Rage and Scorne had put my love to flight,
    That Love which once on him was firmely set:
    Hate hid his true affection from my sight,
    And kept my heart from paying him his debt.
25 And blame me not, for *Herods* Jealousie
    Had power even constancie it selfe to change:
    For hee by barring me from libertie,
    To shunne my ranging, taught me first to range.
    But yet too chast a Scholler was my hart,
30 To learne to love another then my Lord:
    To leave his Love, my lessons former part,
    I quickly learn'd, the other I abhord.
    But now his death to memorie doth call,
    The tender love, that he to *Mariam* bare:
35 And mine to him, this makes those rivers fall,
    Which by an other thought unmoistned are.

From *The Tragedie of Mariam, the Faire Queene of Jewry. Written by that learned, vertuous, and truly noble Ladie, E. C.* London: Printed by Thomas Creede, for Richard Hawkins, and are to be solde at his shoppe in Chancery Lane, neere unto Sargeants Inne. 1613. Licensed December 17, 1612, Sig. A3-A3ᵛ.
Act I, Sc.i. Herod, the son of Antipater, having ingratiated himself with the Romans, has become king of the Jews, and, putting away Doris, his former wife and mother of his children, has married Mariam, granddaughter of the deposed ruler (niece, according to Lodge's *Josephus*, 589). Her kinsmen, who stood between him and the rightful succession, have been murdered. Accused of this crime to the emperor, Herod has to travel to Rome, leaving his wife in the protection of Josephus, whom out of extreme possessiveness he instructs to kill Mariam if he is killed by his enemies. Because Josephus tells Mariam of this, and is therefore guilty not only of disloyalty to Herod but affection for Mariam, he is executed and replaced by Sohemus. Once again Herod leaves for Rome, and again the news arrives that he is dead. Mariam despite their enmity grieves for him.
4-5 *Romes last hero... Pompeis life was gone*: Pompey was defeated by Julius Caesar at Pharsalus and then murdered by Ptolemy in Egypt

in 48 BC. The only source for Caesar's weeping is Plutarch's *Lives*. Many of the closet dramatists of the Countess of Pembroke's circle, following the example of Garnier, found their stories in Plutarch. The Countess's *Tragedie of Antonie* (1595), based on Garnier's *Marc-Antonie* (1578), was the first of the English plays to follow her brother Sir Philip Sidney's dictum to make 'the best of the *Historian...* subject to the *Poet*' (*Defence of Poesy*, 1595, Feuillerat, III, 17).

Chorus.

    Those mindes that wholy dote upon delight,
    Except they onely joy in inward good:
510 Still hope at last to hop upon the right,
    And so from Sand they leape in loathsome mud.
    Fond wretches, seeking what they cannot finde,
    For no content attends a wavering minde.

    If wealth they doe desire, and wealth attaine,
515 Then wondrous faine would they to honor lep:
    Of meane degree they doe in honor gaine,
    They would but wish a little higher step.
      Thus step to step, and wealth to wealth they ad,
      Yet cannot all their plenty make them glad.

520 Yet oft we see that some in humble state,
    Are chreefull [*sic*], pleasant, happy, and content:
    When those indeed that are of higher state,
    With vaine additions do their thoughts torment.
      Th'one would to his minde his fortune binde,
525   T'hother to his fortune frames his minde.

    To wish varietie is signe of griefe,
    For if you like your state as now it is,
    Why should an alteration bring reliefe?
    Nay change would then be fear'd as losse of blis.
530   That man is onely happy in his Fate,
      That is delighted in a setled state.

    Still *Mariam* wisht she from her Lord were free,
    For expectation of varietie:
    Yet now she sees her wishes prosperous bee,
535 She grieves, because her Lord so soone did die.

Who can those vast imaginations feede,
Where in a propertie, contempt doth breede?

Were *Herod* now perchance to live againe,
She would againe as much be grieved at that:
540 All that she may, she ever doth disdaine,
Her wishes guide her to she knowes not what.
And sad must be their lookes, their honor sower,
That care for nothing being in their power.

From *The Tragedy of Mariam*, 1612, Sig. C^v-C2. Salome, Mariam's sister-in-law and Josephus' widow, wishes to reverse the Hebrew law and divorce her husband Constabarus so that she can marry Sillius. Her restless search for self-gratification and the conflict in Mariam's heart are commented on by the Chorus.

There is no division between ll. 513 and 514 of the printed text. Other signs of hasty typesetting occur throughout the play (e.g. l. 521 in the same Chorus), suggesting that *Mariam* may have been piratically printed and could be the work stolen from Lady Cary's chamber.

[*Her.*]   But have you heard her speake?
                              Sal. You know I have.
Her. And were you not amaz'd?
                              Sal. No, not a whit.
Her. Then t'was not her you heard, her life Ile save,
1700 For *Mariam* hath a world amazing wit,
Salo. She speaks a beautious language, but within
Her heart is false as powder: and her tongue
Doth but allure the auditors to sinne,
And is the instrument to doe you wrong.
1705 *Herod.* It may be so: nay, tis so: shee's unchaste,
Her mouth will ope to ev'ry strangers eare:
Then let the executioner make haste,
Lest she inchant him, if her words he heare.
Let him be deafe, lest she do him surprise
1710 That shall to free her spirit be assignde:
Yet what boots deafenes if he have his eyes,
Her murtherer must be both deafe and blinde.
For if he see, he needs must see the starres
That shine on eyther side of *Mariams* face:
1715 Whose sweet aspect will terminate the warres,
Wherewith he should a soule so precious chase.

58

Her eyes can speake, and in their speaking move,
Oft did my heart with reverence receive
The worlds mandates. Pretty tales of love
1720 They utter, which can humane bondage weave.
But shall I let this heavens modell dye?
Which for a small selfe-portraiture she drew:
Her eyes like starres, her forehead like the skie,
She is like Heaven, and must be heavenly true.
1725 *Salom.* Your thoughts do rave with doating on the
Queen,
Her eyes are ebon hewde, and you'll confesse:
A sable starre hath beene but seldom seene,
Then speake of reason more, of *Mariam* lesse.
Herod. Your selfe are held a goodly creature heere,
1730 Yet so unlike my *Mariam* in your shape:
That when to her you have approached neere,
My selfe hath often tane you for an Ape.
And yet you prate of beautie: goe your waies,
You are to her a Sun-burnt Blackamore:

From *The Tragedy of Mariam* (1612), Sig. G2-G2ᵛ. Act IV. Sc vii.
Herod returns and Mariam's dutiful grief turns to loathing. The
conspiracies and machinations begun during his absence collapse,
and their perpetrators rush to inculpate each other. Herod turns on
Sohemus, who like Josephus has betrayed his trust, and on Mariam,
whom he suspects of seducing Sohemus. In this dialogue he rants of
his passion and Mariam's beauty. Lady Cary's alternately rhyming
quatrains, which appear in all the non-choral scenes of the play,
prolong the dialogue and create an effect that is more lyric than
dramatically intense. The quatrain form was popular with the
neo-Senecan closet dramatists and was used by Samuel Daniel in
The Tragedy of Cleopatra (1594) and *Philotas* (1595), by Samuel
Brandon in *The Virtuous Octavia* (1598), and by William Alexander
in the four plays of *Monarchicke Tragedies* (1603-1607).

To the Queenes most Excellent Majestie

'Tis not your faire out-side (though famous Greece
Whose beauties ruin'd kingdomes never sawe
A face that could like yours affections drawe)
Fittes you for the protection of this peice
It is your heart (your pious zealous heart)
That by attractive force, brings great Perroone

To leave his *Seyne*, his *Loyre*, and his *Garroone*;
    And to your handmaide *Thames* his guiftes imparte:
But staie: you have a brother, his kinge borne,
    (Whose worth drawes men from the remotest
                        partes,
To offer up themselves to his desartes.)
    To whom he hath his due allegiance sworne
    Yet for your sake he proves ubiquitarie
    And comes to England, though in France he
                        tarrie.

Written in Lady Cary's hand on a leaf in the Beinecke Library copy of *The Reply of the Most Illustrious Cardinall of Perron*. Douay: Martin Bogart, 1630. Rpt. in Arlene Iris Shapiro, 'Elizabeth Cary: Her Life, Letters and Art', Diss. State University of New York at Stony Brook, 1984.
Title *the Queene*: Henrietta Maria (1609-1669)
6 *great Perroone*: Cardinal Jacques Davy Perron (1556-1616). Between 1611 and 1612 James I and the French cleric corresponded on the nature of the true church. In 1628 Perron published his *Replique a la response du serenisme roy de la Grande Bretagne*. Lady Cary's 486-page translation, accomplished in thirty days, was suppressed in England and 'most of the copies were seized and burned' (Shapiro, 78).
7 *Garroone*: Garonne
9 *a brother*: Louis XIII (1601-1643)

LADY MARY WROTH

Lady Mary was the eldest child of Sir Robert Sidney, younger brother of Sir Philip; she was born the year after the poet died of an old war wound, whereupon Lady Mary's father took his place as governor of Flushing in the Netherlands. Her childhood was spent both in the Netherlands and at Penshurst, surrounded by poets and poetry. Mary Herbert, Countess of Pembroke, famous both as poet and patron of poets, was her aunt; her mother was first cousin to Sir Walter Raleigh; her family and their household were immortalised by Ben Jonson in 'To Penshurst'. Her father whiled away his loneliness in the Netherlands by writing poetry, which he gathered in a little book addressed to his sister. We know from his daughter's poetry that she knew her father's well. The editor of Sir Robert's poems speculates that his second daughter Katherine may also have written poetry while at Penshurst, possibly some of the anonymous poems in BL MS Add. 15232 (Croft, 6).

By the time Lady Mary was twelve, negotiations for her marriage had already begun; she was eventually married to Sir Robert Wroth, the sporting son of a rich landowner, with whom she can have had little in common. In a letter to his wife Sir Robert Sidney described a meeting with his new son-in-law in which he learned that Wroth 'had some what that doth discontent him' though he said that he could find no cause to quarrel with Lady Mary 'nor her carriage towards him' (Roberts, 1983, 11-12). It seems likely that Lady Mary was already in love with her cousin, William Herbert, third Earl of Pembroke (1580-1630), at whose London house, Baynard's Castle, the Sidney family often stayed.

Herbert, one of the dedicatees of the Shakespeare First Folio, was not only a poet-patron after the Sidney model, but an incorrigible womaniser. In 1601 he was imprisoned by order of the old queen for getting one of her ladies-in-waiting with child and refusing to marry her. This in itself is rather odd behaviour, for Mary Fitton was a desirable match; perhaps at bottom lies an idealistic emotional commitment to Lady Mary, whom, as his first cousin, and probably his mother's godchild, he could not marry. When Sir Robert Sidney was short of a dowry for Lady Mary, the earl contributed a thousand pounds towards it. He too was to marry for money in the same year as Lady Mary; his wife had no child by him.

In Ben Jonson's *Conversations with Drummond* he describes Lady

Mary, to whom he dedicated *The Alchemist*, as 'unworthily maried on a Jealous husband' (Herford and Simpson, I, 142). In the epistle 'To Sir Robert Wroth' Jonson limits his observations to a passing reference to his 'noblest spouse' while he might be said to overdo his praise of the chastity of Lady Mary's mother in 'To Penshurst':

> His children thy great lord may call his owne:
> A fortune, in this age, but rarely knowne. (91-92)

While Wroth impoverished his estate to provide King James with the best hunting, Lady Mary rebuilt their house, Loughton Hall, and cultivated the company of poets. By 1613, among the proliferating references to her as a model of wit and beauty, we begin to find references to her achievements as poet.

In February 1614, Lady Mary bore a son, James; the Earl of Pembroke was one of his godparents. A month later, her husband died, leaving an estate much encumbered with debts. Two years and five months later, James died and the estate reverted to Sir Robert's uncle. For the rest of her life, Lady Mary had to struggle to settle her debts, frequently requesting protection from creditors.

In a manuscript history of the Herbert family, compiled by one of the Earl of Pembroke's cousins, we learn that William Herbert 'had two naturall children by the Lady Mary Wroth... William who was a captain under Sir Hen Herbert... and dyed unmarried and Catherine the wife of Mr. Lovel near Oxford' (Roberts, 1982, 46). While it was not rare for noblemen to father illegitimate children, it was extremely rare for them to do so on the bodies of women of equal rank. Somehow, perhaps during the retirement from the court necessitated by her widowhood, Lady Mary Wroth's love for William Herbert was consummated. The products of this union were probably put out to nurse and the expense of their rearing borne by the Herberts. Lady Mary continued to appear at court, although less brilliantly than formerly.

In 1621, in a handsome folio edition with an engraved frontispiece by Simon Pass, appeared *The Countess of Montgomeries Urania Written by the right honorable the Lady Mary Wroath*, in imitation of *The Countess of Pembrokes Arcadia*. We do not know how long this huge pastoral romance had been circulating in Lady Mary's circle or why she decided to defy custom and publish it under her own name. It was roundly condemned as a malicious *roman à clef*. Lady Mary took refuge in the usual excuse that it was published without her permission, and claimed that she had stopped the sale of it. An unfinished 'Second Part' is now at the Newberry Library.

Appended to the *Urania* is a sonnet sequence constructed on the same lines as *Astrophil and Stella*, called *Pamphilia to Amphilanthus*, which had been in circulation long before 1621. It is the love poetry of a constant woman, Pamphilia, the all-loving, for Amphilanthus, the equivocator in love. Constancy is the unifying theme of the *Urania* as it seems to have been of Lady Mary's entire life. Seen in this way, constancy is not simply an aspect of personality, but a Platonic ideal, existing above and beyond behaviour, in the realm of spiritual commitment. It is obvious that Lady Mary was unlikely to have taken the same ironic view of adulterous passion as her uncle: in *Pamphilia to Amphilanthus* we find not only one of the earliest, but also one of the most intense expressions of an archetypal theme of women's poetry. The irony that reverberates in this sonnet sequence is tragic irony; the reality of women's love is here the relentless discipline of enforced passivity and endless waiting, complicated by fear of abandonment and of allowing love to be corrupted by hatred and jealousy. Lady Mary's prosody is often complex, but her diction tends to austerity; the intensity of her poetry comes from its casting and recasting of several key concepts, as if it were writhing in the bonds of the rigid forms she chooses, obsessively working and reworking the overwhelming idea.

Besides the *Urania* Lady Mary Wroth has left a pastoral entertainment, *Love's Victorie*, in two versions, one in the Huntington Library and another in private hands in England. Notices of her later life are scant and mostly connected with her financial difficulties. The exact date of her death, c.1652, is unknown.

From *Pamphilia to Amphilanthus*

Griefe, killing griefe: have nott my torments binn
    Allreddy great, and strong enough: butt still
    Thou dost increase, nay glory in mine ill,
    And woes new past affresh new woes beeginn!

Am I the only purchase thou canst winn?
    Was I ordain'd to give dispaire her fill
    Or fittest I should mounte misfortunes hill
    Who in the plaine of joy can-nott live in?

If itt bee soe: Griefe come as wellcome ghest
    Since I must suffer, for an others rest:
    Yett this good griefe, lett mee intreat of thee,

Use still thy force, butt nott from those I love
    Lett mee all paines and lasting torments prove
    Soe I miss thes, lay all thy waits on mee.

Roberts, 103 [P32]

This and all the succeeding texts are taken from the Folger MS in Lady Mary's hand of *Pamphilia to Amphilanthus* (V.a.104) as edited by Josephine A. Roberts, *The Poems of Lady Mary Wroth* (Louisiana

State University Press, 1983) incorporating authorial revisions and following the order adopted in the 1621 edition of *The Countess of Montgomeries Urania*, together with some modification of orthography and regularisation of punctuation, hereinafter referred to simply as Roberts, and giving page number and Roberts's identification number: 103 [P32].

3 mine 1621 / my MS   5 thou canst 1621 / you can MS

Fly hence O! joy noe longer heere abide
  Too great thy pleasures ar for my dispaire
  To looke on, losses now must prove my fare
  Who nott long since, on better foode relide;

Butt foole, how oft had I heavns changing spide
  Beefore of my owne fate I could have care,
  Yett now past time, I can too late beeware
  When nothing's left butt sorrowes faster tyde;

While I injoy'd that sunn whose sight did lend
  Mee joy, I thought, that day, could have noe end
  Butt soone a night came cloth'd in absence darke,

Absence more sad, more bitter then is gall
  Or death, when on true lovers itt doth fall
  Whose fires of love, disdaine rests poorer sparke.

                                        Roberts, 103 [P33]

2 Too 1621 / to MS   3 must 1621 / unjust MS
6 mine 1621 / my MS; have 1621 / take MS
7 I can too late 1621 / too late I can MS   8 When 1621 / now MS
11 soone 1621 / O! MS   14 Whose fires of love disdaineth reasts poore sparke MS

You blessed shades, which give mee silent rest,
  Wittnes butt this when death hath clos'd mine eyes,
  And separated mee from earthly ties,
  Beeing from hence to higher place adrest;

How oft in you I have laine heere oprest,
  And have my miseries in woefull cries
  Deliver'd forth, mounting up to the skies
  Yett helples back returnd to wound my brest,

Which wounds did butt strive how, to breed more
                                                harme

To mee, who, can bee cur'de by noe one charme
Butt that of love, which yett may mee releeve;

If nott, lett death my former paines redeeme,
  My trusty freinds, my faith untouch'd esteeme
And wittnes I could love, who soe could greeve.

Roberts, 103-4 [P34]

13 And you my, trusty freinds, my faith esteeme MS 14 I could 1621/I {well} could MS

12-14 Roberts compares the last stanza of Song 19 by Sir Robert
Sidney:

> Mortal in love are joye and pleasure
> The fading frame, wherein love moves
> But greef and anguish are the measure
> That do immortalyze owr loves.

After long trouble in a taedious way
  Of loves unrest, lay'd downe to ease my paine
  Hopeing for rest, new torments I did gaine
  Possessing mee as if I ought t'obay:

When Fortune came, though blinded, yett did stay,
  And in her blesse'd armes did mee inchaine;
  I, colde with griefe, thought noe warmth to obtaine
  Or to dissolve that ice of joyes decay;

Till, 'rise sayd she, Reward to thee doth send
  By mee the servante of true lovers, joy:
  Bannish all clowds of doubt, all feares destroy,
  And now on fortune, and on Love depend.

I, her obay'd, and rising felt that love
Indeed was best, when I did least itt move.

Roberts, 105 [P36]

9 Reward 1621/Venus MS

Faulce hope which feeds butt to destroy, and spill
  What itt first breeds; unaturall to the birth
  Of thine owne wombe; conceaving butt to kill,
  And plenty gives to make the greater dearth,

Soe Tirants doe who faulsly ruling earth
  Outwardly grace them, and with profitts fill

KISSING THE ROD

Advance those who appointed are to death
To make theyr greater falle to please theyr will.

Thus shadow they theyr wicked vile intent
　　Coulering evill with a show of good
　　While in faire showes theyr malice soe is spent;
　　Hope kills the hart, and tirants shed the blood.

For hope deluding brings us to the pride
Of our desires the farder downe to slide.

Roberts, 107 [P40]

8 theyr greater 1621 / the greater MS   10 a show 1621 / the mask MS   12 kill's 1621 / kills MS

I, that ame of all most crost
Having, and that had, have lost,
May with reason thus complaine
Since love breeds love, and lovs paine;

That which I did most desire
To allay my loving fire
I may have, yett now must miss
Since an other ruler is:

Would that I noe ruler had,
Or the service nott soe badd,
Then might I, with blis injoy
That which now my hopes destroy;

And thatt wicked pleasure gott
Brings with itt the sweetest lott:
I, that must nott taste the best
Fed must sterve, and restles rest.

Roberts, 117 [P59]

13 wicked 1621 / wished MS

Love a child is ever criing,
　　Please him, and hee straite is flying,
　　Give him hee the more is craving
　　Never satisfi'd with having;

His desires have noe measure,
　　Endles folly is his treasure,

LADY MARY WROTH

What hee promiseth hee breaketh
Trust nott one word that he speaketh;

Hee vowes nothing butt faulce matter,
    And to cousen you hee'l flatter,
    Lett him gaine the hand hee'll leave you,
    And still glory to deseave you;

Hee will triumph in your wayling,
    And yett cause bee of your fayling,
    Thes his vertus ar, and slighter
    Ar his guiftes, his favours lighter,

Feathers ar as firme in staying
    Woulves noe fiercer in theyr praying.
    As a child then leave him crying
    Nor seeke him soe giv'n to flying.

Roberts, 125 [P74]

17 Fathers 1621 / Feathers MS

Late in the Forest I did Cupid see
    Colde, wett, and crying hee had lost his way,
    And beeing blind was farder like to stray:
    Which sight a kind compassion bred in mee,

I kindly tooke, and dride him, while that hee
    Poore child complain'd hee sterved was with stay,
    And pin'de for want of his accustom'd pray,
    For non in that wilde place his hoste would bee,

I glad was of his finding, thinking sure
    This service should my freedome still procure,
    And in my armes I tooke him then unharmde,

Carrying him safe unto a Mirtle bowre
    Butt in the way hee made mee feele his powre,
    Burning my hart who had him kindly warmd.

Roberts, 139 [P96]

12 safe 1621 / omitted in MS

9-10 Roberts notes that the motif of Cupid as a beggar is drawn from *Anacreontea*, 33. Cf. *Astrophil and Stella*, 65; Barnes, *Parthenophil*, 93; Constable, *Diana*, Dec. II, 6 and 7; Drayton, *Idea*, 33, 48; Greville, *Caelica*, 12.1-4.

RACHEL SPEGHT

Rachel, born in 1597, was the daughter of James Speght, who was of a Yorkshire family and rector of the London churches of St Mary Magdalene, Milk Street (1592-1637) and St Clement in Eastcheap (1611-1637). In 1613 James published *A briefe demonstration who have, and of their certainity of their salvation that have the spirit of Jesus Christ* and in 1616 *The Christian's Comfort. A Sermon preached before the Lord Maior and Aldermen of London.* Thomas Speght, the editor of Chaucer (1598 and 1602), may have been a kinsman.

In 1617 Joseph Swetnam published *An Arraignment of Women*, provoking a storm of replies of which Rachel Speght's was the first. *A Mouzell for Melastomus, the Cynical Bayter of, and foule mouthed Barker against Evahs sex* was published in 1617: four years later the dedication of *Mortalities Memorandum, with a Dreame Prefixed* shows Speght to be still deeply embroiled in the accusations brought on by her first book:

having bin toucht with the censures of [critical Readers] by occasion of my *mouzeling Melastomus*, I am now, as by a strong motive induced (for my rights sake) to produce and divulge this of spring of my indeavor, to prove them further futurely who have formerly deprived me of my due, imposing my abortive upon the father of me, but not of it. Their variety of verdicts have verified the adagie *quot homines, tot sententiae* [there are as many opinions as there are men], and made my experience confirme that apothegme which doth affirme Censure to be inevitable to a publique act.

On 2 August 1621, seven months after *Mortalities Memorandum* was entered in the Stationers' Register, 'Rachel Speight, spinster, 24', was married to William Procter, 'gent., bachelor, 29' at St Mary Woolchurch in London. According to a note in *London Marriage Licenses, 1521-1869* (Foster, col. 1098), Procter was described 'in the Vicar-general's book' as a clerk; he may be the William Procter *pleb.* who matriculated at Oriel College in 1609 aged sixteen (*Athenae Oxoniensis*) who for some reason also went under the name Matthews. Although the marriage did not take place at James Speght's church, it was performed with his 'consent'; this legal term usually implied that the couple had obtained a special licence in order to dispense with the three-week reading of the banns. Nothing is known of Rachel Speght's life after her marriage.

RACHEL SPEGHT

From 'The Dreame'

My griefe, quoth I, is called *Ignorance*,
Which makes me differ little from a brute:
45   For animals are led by natures lore,
Their seeming science is but customes fruit;
When they are hurt they have a sense of paine;
But want the sense to cure themselves again.

And ever since this griefe did me oppresse,
50   Instinct of nature is my chiefest guide;
I feele disease, yet know not what I ayle,
I finde a sore, but can no salve provide;
I hungry am, yet cannot seeke for foode;
Because I know not what is bad or good.

55   And sometimes when I seeke the golden meane,
My weaknesse makes me faile of mine intent,
That suddenly I fall into extremes,
Nor can I see a mischiefe to prevent;
But feele the paine when I the perill finde,
60   Because my maladie doth make me blinde.

What is without the compasse of my braine,
My Sicknesse makes me say it cannot bee;
What I conceive not, cannot come to passe;
Because for it I can no reason see.
65   I measure all mens feet by mine own shooe,
And count all well, which I appoint or doe.

The pestilent effects of my disease
Exceed report, their number is so great;
The evils, which through it I doe incur,
70   Are more then I am able to repeat.
Wherefore, good *Thought*, I sue to thee againe,
To tell me how my cure I may obtaine.

Quoth she, I wish I could prescribe your helpe;
Your state I pitie much, and doe bewaile;
75   But for my part, though I am much imploy'd,
Yet in my judgement I doe often faile.

And therefore I'le commend unto your triall
Experience, of whom take no deniall.

For she can best direct you, what is meet
80 To worke your cure, and satisfie your minde;
I thank't her for her love, and took my leave,
Demanding where I might *Experience* finde.
She told me if I did abroad enquire,
'Twas likely *Age* could answer my desire.

85 I sought, I found, she ask't me what I would;
Quoth I, your best direction I implore:
For I am troubled with an irkesome griefe,
Which when I nam'd, quoth she declare no more:
For I can tell as much, as you can say,
90 And for your cure I'le helpe you what I may.

The onely medicine for your maladie,
By which, and nothing else your helpe is wrought,
Is *Knowledge*, of the which there is two sorts,
The one is good, the other bad and nought;
95 The former sort by labour is attain'd,
The latter may without much toyle be gaine'd.

But 'tis the good, which must effect your cure,
I pray'd her then, that she would further show,
Where I might hav it, that I will, quoth shee,
100 In *Eruditions* garden it doth grow:
And in compassion of your woefull case,
Industrie shall conduct you to the place.

Disswasion hearing her assigne my helpe,
(And seeing that consent I did detect)
105 Did many remoraes to me propose,
As dulnesse, and my memories defect;
The difficultie of attaining lore,
My time, and sex, with many others more.

Which when I heard, my minde was much perplext,
110 And as a horse new come into the field,
Who with a Harquebuz at first doth start,
So did this shot make me recoyle and yeeld.

70

But of my feare when some did notice take,
In my behalfe, they this reply did make,

115 First quoth *Desire, Disswassion*, hold thy peace,
These oppositions come not from above:
Quoth *Truth*, they cannot spring from reasons roote,
And therefore now thou shalt no victor prove.
No, quoth *Industrie*, be assured this,
120 Her friends shall make thee of thy purpose misse.

For with my sickle I will cut away
All obstacles, that in her way can grow,
And by the issue of her owne attempt,
I'le make thee *labor omnia vincet* know.
125 Quoth *Truth*, and sith her sex thou do'st object,
Thy folly I by reason will detect.

Both man and woman of three parts consist,
Which *Paul* doth bodie, soule, and spirit call:
And from the soule three faculties arise,   1.Thess.5.23
130 The mind, the will, the power; then wherefore shall
A woman have her intellect in vaine,
Or not endeavor *Knowledge* to attaine.

The talent, God doth give, must be imploy'd, Luke 19. 23
His owne with vantage he must have againe:
135 All parts and faculties were made for use;   I Sam. 2. 3
The God of *Knowledge* nothing gave in vaine.
'Twas *Maries* choyce our Savior did approve,   Luke 10. 42
Because that she the better part did love.

Cleobulina, and *Demophila*,
140 With *Telesilla*, as Historians tell,
(Whose fame doth live, though they have long bin
dead)
Did all of them in Poetrie excell.
A Roman matron that *Cornelia* hight,
An eloquent and learned style did write.

145 *Hypatia* in Astronomie had skill,
Aspatia was in Rheth'ricke so expert,
As that Duke *Pericles* of her did learne;

Areta did devote her selfe to art:
And by consent (which shewes she was no foole)
150 She did succeed her father in his schoole...

If thou didst know the pleasure of the place,
170 Where *Knowledge* growes, and where thou mayst it
gaine;
Or rather knew the vertue of the plant,
Thou would'st not grudge at any cost, or paine,
Thou canst bestow, to purchase for thy cure
This plant, by which of helpe thou shalt be sure.

175 Let not *Disswasion* alter thy intent;
'Tis sinne to nippe good motions in the head;
Take courage, and be constant in thy course,
Though irksome be the path, which thou must tread.
Sick folkes drinke bitter medicines to be well,
180 And to injoy the nut men cracke the shell.

When *Truth* had ended what shee meant to say,
Desire did move me to obey her will,
Whereto consenting I did soone proceede,
Her counsell, and my purpose to fulfille;
185 And by the helpe of *Industrie* my friend,
I quickly did attaine my journeyes end.

Where being come, *Instructions* pleasant ayre
Refresht my senses, which were almost dead,
And fragrant flowers of sage and fruitfull plants,
190 Did send sweete savours up into my head;
And taste of science appetite did move,
To augment *Theorie* of things above.

There did the harmonie of those sweete birds,
(Which higher soare with Contemplations wings,
195 Then barely with a superficiall view,
Denote the value of created things.)
Yeeld such delight as made me to implore,
That I might reape this pleasure more and more.

And as I walked wandring with *Desire*,
200 To gather that, for which I thither came;

72

(Which by the helpe of *Industrie* I found)
I met my old acquaintance, *Truth* by name;
Whom I requested briefly to declare,
The vertue of that plant I found so rare...

Great *Alexander* made so great account,
Of *Knowledge*, that he oftentimes would say,
225   That he to *Aristotle* was more bound
For *Knowledge*, upon which *Death* could not pray,
Then to his Father *Phillip* for his life,
Which was uncertaine, irkesome, full of strife.

This true report put edge unto *Desire*,
230   Who did incite me to increase my store,
And told me 'twas a lawfull avarice,
To covet *Knowledge* daily more and more.
This counsell I did willingly obey,
Till some occurrence called me away.

235   And made me rest content with what I had,
Which was but little, as effect doth show;
And quenched hope for gaining any more,
For I my time must other-wayes bestow.
I therefore to that place return'd againe,
240   From whence I came, and where I must remaine.

But by the way I saw a full fed Beast,
Which roared like some monster, or a Devill,
And on *Eves* sex he foamed filthie froth,
As if that he had had the falling evill;
245   To whom I went to free them from mishaps,
And with a *Mouzel* sought to binde his chaps.

But, as it seemes, my moode out-run my might,
Which when a self-conceited Creature saw,
Shee past her censure on my weake exployt,
250   And gave the beast a harder bone to gnaw;
Haman shee hangs, 'tis past he cannot shun it;
For *Ester* in the Pretertense hath done it.

And yet her enterprize had some defect,
The monster surely was not hanged quite:

255   For as the childe of *Prudence* did conceive,
     His throat not stop't he still had power to bite.
     She therefore gave to *Cerberus* a soppe,
     Which is of force his beastly breath to stoppe.

     But yet if he doe swallow downe that bit,
260   Shee other-wayes hath bound him to the peace,
     And like an Artist takes away the cause,
     That the effect by consequence may cease.
     This franticke dogge, whose rage did women wrong,
     Hath Constance worm'd to make him hold his
                                     tongue.
265   Thus leaving them I passed on my way,
     But ere that I had little further gone,
     I saw a fierce insatiable foe,
     Depopulating Countries, sparing none;
     Without respect of age, sex, or degree,
270   It did devoure, and could not daunted be.

     Some fear'd this foe, some lov'd it as a friend;
     For though none could the force of it withstand,
     Yet some by it were sent to *Tophets* flames,
     But others led to heavenly *Canaan* land.
275   On some it seazed with a gentle power,
     And others furiously it did devoure.

     The name of this impartiall foe was *Death*,
     Whose rigour whil'st I furiosly did view.
     Upon a sodeyne, ere I was aware;
280   With pearcing dart my mother deare it slew;
     Which when I saw it made me so to weepe,
     That tears and sobs did rouze me from my sleepe.

     But, when wak't, I found my dreame was true;
     For *Death* had ta'ne my mothers breath away,
285   Though of her life it could not her bereave,
     Sith shee in glorie lives with Christ for aye;
     Which makes me glad, and thankefull for her blisse,
     Though still bewayle her absence, whom I misse.

     A sodeine sorrow peirceth to the quicke,
290   Speedie encounters fortitude doth try;

RACHEL SPEGHT

Unarmed men receive the deepest wound,
Expected perils time doth lenifie;
Her sodeine losse hath cut my feeble heart,
So deepe, that daily I indure the smarte.

295   The roote is kil'd, how can the boughs but fade?
But sith that Death this cruell deed hath done,
I'le blaze the nature of this mortall foe,
And shew how it to tyranize begun.
The sequell then with judgement view aright,
300   The profit may and will the paines requite.
        Esto Memor Mortis

From *Mortalities Memorandum, with a Dreame Prefixed, imaginarie in manner; reall in matter. By Rachel Speght.* London, Jacob Bloom, 1621. *Mortalities Memorandum* is dedicated to 'The Worshipfull and Vertuous Gentlewoman, her most respected Godmother Mrs. Marie Moundford, wife unto the worshipfull Doctour Moundford Physitian'. The Moundefords were parishioners of James Speght's church; Thomas Moundeford was the author of *Vir Bonus* (1622).

The allegorical dream vision, one of the oldest conventions in European literature, is a courtly refinement of the apocalyptic vision and from the thirteenth century had often served as a framework for debating the woman question. Thomas Speght's *Chaucer* had included the translation of the genre's prototype, Guilliame de Lorris and Jean de Meun's *Roman de la Rose*, as well as three authentic Chaucerian examples, *The House of Fame*, *The Book of the Duchess*, *The Legend of Good Women* and three spurious ones, 'Chaucer's Dreame' (elsewhere called 'The Isle of Ladies'), *The Flower and the Leaf*, and *The Assembly of Ladies*. Speght also may have had access to the English translation of Christine de Pizan's dream vision, published as *The Boke of the Cyte of Ladyes* by Bryan Anslye in 1521. Speght's dream, like its medieval predecessors, follows the structure laid down by Macrobius in the fourth century, beginning with the *insomnium*; the troubled sleeper comes 'into a place most pleasant to the eye', the *locus amoenus*, and is guided by the female figures of Thought, Experience, Industrie, Desire and Truth. Speght uses the convention to allegorise her plea for the education of women, personifying the abstract values she wishes to invoke, and enlivening her argument by the constant use of prosopopoeia. (The first six stanzas of her poem have been omitted.)
43 *quoth*: like 'hight' (143) and 'sith' (125, 286, 296) a deliberate archaism.
55 *the golden meane*: the Aristotelian ideal of moderation in all things.

75

105 *remoraes*: literally, sucking fishes; Speght's figurative usage to mean 'obstacles' is contemporary.

111 *Harquebuz*: arquebus, a muzzle-loading gun

124 *labor omnia vincit*: labour overcomes all obstacles. Virgil, *Georgics*, I.145.

127 Cf. Philo-philippa, 43-54 (see p.205).

129 I Thess.5.23: Speght's scriptural source here and throughout the poem appears to be the Geneva Bible favoured by Puritans. The epigraph to *A Mouzell* is verbatim from its Proverbs 26:5: 'Answer a foole according to his foolishness, lest he bee wise in his own conceit.'

135 Cf. *Hamlet* IV, iv, 36-39

137 Cf. Astell, 'In Emulation of... the Motto', 29-32 (see p.336).

139 *Cleobulina*: (fl. 570 BC) the daughter of Cleobis of Lindus, also called Eumetis, who wrote riddles in hexameter verse. Catalogues of worthy and imperfect women from the Bible and antiquity were common to all works of the *querelle des femmes*; in *Mouzell* Speght attacks Swetnam for mixing heathen and Christian, 'Good and Badde' women, and concentrates her argument on her own selection of Biblical figures (Woodbridge, 89-90). Likewise she makes her own list of classical *exempla* in 'The Dreame'. The most likely sources for the poem are Plutarch's *Vitae* (translated into English by Thomas North in 1579 as *The Lives of the Noble Grecians and Romanes, Compared*), his *Moralia* (englished by Philemon Holland in 1603 as *The Philosophie, commonly called the Morals*), and Diogenes Laertius's *Vitae*, published several times in Latin during the sixteenth century, but untranslated until 1688. Plutarch in *Septem Sapientium Convivum* (*Moralia*, II, according to the division of Xylander, 1570) attributes to Cleobulina the riddle which Aristotle had quoted in the *Rhetoric*, Book 3; he also writes of Cleobulina in *Mulierum Virtutes* (*Moralia*, III), *Conjugalia Praecepta* (*Moralia*, II) and *De Pythiae Oraculis* (*Moralia*, V). Christine de Pizan mentions her in *L'Avision* (1405). Juan Luis de Vives, in his *Institutione Feminae Christiana* (1524, tr. by Richard Hyrd as *Instruction of a Christian Woman*, 1540) counts Cleobulina as a member of the 'hundred good' women of 'the old world' (Watson, 50; 206), probably deriving his biography from Plutarch, who was among the classical authors he recommended to women in the 'Plan of Studies for Girls' (1523), composed for the education of Princess Mary.

Demophila: or Damophyle, lyric poet of Pamphylia, pupil and companion of Sappho and composer of erotic poems and hymns, seventh century BC. Her name occurs in the *Life of Apollonius*, I, by Philostratus (AD 170-245), but not in Plutarch or Diogenes Laertius.

140 *Telesilla*: poet and heroine of Argos in the sixth century BC, she was of noble birth but affected by disease. According to Plutarch (*Mulerium Virtutes*), she consulted the Muses, was healed and became 'the mirror of women in the art of poetry', inspiring the women of Argos to arm and repulse the Spartan invaders.

143 *Cornelia*: daughter of Scipio Africanus (second century BC), married to Gracchus, mother of the Gracchi, Tiberius and Gaius. Her letters were models of composition and her eloquence was famous. With Aspasia, she is among the most commonly cited classic *exempla* of intellectual women. In Plutarch's 'Parallel Lives' her story is told with her sons'; Plutarch also includes her in *Mulierum Virtutes* and *Conjugalia Praecepta*. She is mentioned by Agrippa, by Castiglione (*Il Cortegiano*, 1528) and by Vives, as 'an example of all goodness and chastity, [who] taught her children herself' (Watson, 50). Cf. Philo-philippa, 99-102 (see p.206).

145 *Hypatia*: daughter of Theon of Alexandria, fifth century AD, and reputed author of commentaries on Diophantes's *Canon of Astronomy* and the *Conics of Invention* (Suidas, *Lexicon*, vol. 117). Diogenes Laertius includes her in *The Lives*.

146 *Aspatia*: daughter of Axiochus of Milesia, fifth century BC, mistress, then wife, to Pericles, who taught rhetoric to Socrates and founded a school in Athens. She is mentioned by Plato in *Menexenus* and maligned by Aristophanes in *The Acharnians*; Plutarch in the 'Life of Pericles' defends her against charges of harlotry and irreligion.

148 *Areta*: daughter of Aristippus, founder of the Cyrenaic school of philosophy which taught contentment and moderation (fifth century BC).

223 *Alexander*, etc.: Alexander the Great (356-323 BC), son of Philip of Macedonia, conqueror of Persia and Egypt. Speght repeats the story told by Plutarch in 'The Life of Alexander' of Alexander's education under Aristotle.

241 *a full fed Beast*: Joseph Swetnam, keeper of a fencing school and author of *The Arraignment of Lewd, idle, froward and unconstant Women; Or the Vanitie of them, choose you whether. With a Commendacion of wise, vertuous and honest Women*, 1615. This anti-feminist tract was reprinted in 1619, 1628, 1634, 1645 and 1690, as well as several times in the eighteenth century, and appeared twice in Dutch. Besides the rejoinders mentioned by Speght, it provoked Daniel Tuvil's *Asylum Veneris; or, a Sanctuary for Ladies, Justly Protecting Them, their virtues and sufficiencies, from the foule aspersions and forged imputations of traducing Spirits*, 1616, and a comedy, *Swetnam, the Womanhater, arraigned by Women* which was played at the Red Bull by 'the late Queen's Servants', 1620.

244 *the falling evill*: epilepsy

246 *chaps*: jaw

248 *a self-conceited Creature*: 'Ester Sowernam', author of *Ester hath hang'd Haman; Or, An Answer to a lewd Pamphlet... With the arraignment of lewd, idle, froward and unconstant men, and husbands* (1617). The answers to Swetnam form a curious group and seem mostly to have been undertaken in a more or less facetious vein, either eulogising women and exalting the double standard, or implicitly condemning most women by praising a few. The pseudonymous writer of *Ester*

hath hang'd Haman uses 'her' dedicatory epistle to sneer at 'a Minister's daughter', i.e. Speght.

> I stayed my pen, being as glad to be eased on my entended labour; as I did expect some filling performance of what was undertaken: At last the Maidens Booke was brought me, which when I had likewise runne over, I did observe, that wheras the Maide doth many times excuse her tendernesse of yeares, I found it to be true in the slendernesse of her answer, for she undertaking to defend women, doth rather charge and condemne women... (sig. A2)

251-252 Esther 5-7

255 *childe of Prudence*: the author of *The Worming of a mad Dogge: or a Soppe for Cerberus the Jaylor of Hell. No Confutation But a sharpe Redargution of the bayter of Women. By Constantia Munda*, 1617. This tract is dedicated to 'Lady Prudentia Munda', the author's mother; the tone of pseudo-chivalrous panegyric alternating with coarse abuse is difficult to associate with women's writing in any period:

> Woman the Crowne, perfection & the meanes
> Of all men's being, and this well-being, whence
> Is the propagation of all humane kinde,
> Wherein the bodies frame, th'intellect and mind
> With all their operations doe first finde
> Their essence and beginning, where doth lie
> The mortall meanes of our eternity,
> Whose vertues, worthinesse, resplendent rayes
> Of perfect beauty have alwaies had the praise
> And admiration of such glorious wits...
> Without exceptions hath your spungie pate
> (Voyd in itselfe of all things but of hate)
> Suckt up the dregs of folly, and the lees
> Of mercenary Pasquils, which doe squeeze
> The glaunders of abuses in the face
> Of them that are the cause that humane race
> Keeps his continuance... etc.

273 *Tophet*: hell

274 *Canaan*: the promised land, i.e. heaven

280 *pearcing*: emended from errata slip; the original reads 'perceiving'.

my mother: the date of Rachel Speght's mother's death is not known. James Speght married his second wife, Elizabeth Smith, less than a month after the registration of *Mortalities Memorandum* (12 January 1621).

MARY OXLIE OF MORPETH

Mary Oxlie, of Morpeth in Northumberland, is the author of a commendatory verse prefixed to the posthumous edition of the *Poems* of William Drummond of Hawthornden (1656), put together by Edward Phillips from manuscript papers brought to him by Sir John Scot of Scotstarvet, Drummond's brother-in-law. Phillips later wrote in his *Theatrum Poetarum* (1675) that 'Mary Morpeth' was 'a friend of the Poet Drummond, of whom, besides many other things in Poetry, she hath a large *Encomium* in Verse' (259), but no other work has been found. Oxlie's poem was probably written after Drummond had had his poems printed for circulation among his friends in 1614; it amplifies the argument of a prefatory sonnet which appeared both in that edition and the second impression of 1616, signed simply 'Parthenius'.

To William Drummond of Hawthornden.

I Never rested on the Muses bed,
Nor dipt my Quill in the *Thessalian* Fountaine,
My rustick Muse was rudely fostered,
And flies too low to reach the double mountaine.

5 Then do not sparkes with your bright Suns compare,
Perfection in a Woman's worke is rare;
From an untroubled mind should Verses flow;
My discontents makes mine too muddy show;
And hoarse encumbrances of houshold care
10 Where these remaine, the Muses ne're repaire.

If thou dost extoll her Haire,
Or her Ivory Forehead faire,
Or those Stars whose bright reflection
Thrals my heart in sweet subjection:
15 Or when to display thou seeks
The snow-mixt Roses on her Cheekes,
Or those Rubies soft and sweet,

Over those pretty Rows that meet.
The *Chian* painter as asham'd,
20 Hides his Picture so far fam'd;
And the Queen he carv'd it by,
With a blush her face doth dye,
Since those Lines do limne a Creature
That so far surpast her Feature.
25 When thou show'st how fairest *Flora*
Prankt with pride the banks of *Ora*,
So thy Verse her streames doth honour,
Strangers grow enamour'd on her,
All the Swans that swim in Po
30 Would their native brooks forgo,
And as loathing *Phoebus* beames,
Long to bath in cooler streames,
Tree-turn'd *Daphne* would be seen
In her Groves to flourish green,
35 And her Boughs would gladly spare.
To frame a garland for thy haire,
   That fairest Nymphs with finest fingers
   May thee crown the best of singers.

But when thy Muse dissolv'd in show'rs,
40 Wailes that peerlesse Prince of ours,
Cropt by too untimely Fate,
Her mourning doth exasperate
Senselesse things to see theé moane,
Stones do weep, and Trees do groane,
45 Birds in aire, Fishes in flood,
Beasts in field forsake their food,
The Nymphs forgoing all their Bow'rs
Teare their Chaplets deckt with Flow'rs;
Sol himselfe with misty vapor,
50 Hides from earth his glorious Tapor,
   And as mov'd to heare thee plaine
   Shews his griefe in show'rs of raine.
           Mary Oxlie of Morpet.

From *Poems By That most Famous Wit, William Drummond of Hawthornden...* London: Printed by W. H. and are to be sold in the Company of Stationers, 1656.
William Drummond (1585-1649), second laird of Hawthornden, is

known today for his *Conversations with Jonson*. He was a friend of
Michael Drayton, and advised James I on his metrical translations
of the Psalms. Drummond and Jonson are the first poets personally
to supervise the editing and printing of their work.

2 *Thessalian Fountaine*: probably mistaken for the Castalian spring
on Mt Parnassus.

4 *double mountaine*: the mountain of Parnassus was sometimes
referred to as having two summits, one sacred to Apollo and the
other to Dionysus.

9-10 Cf. 'The Emulation', 12-17 (see p. 310), about women's
confinement to a 'Kitchin or a Field'. Also, Mrs Evelyn: 'I find the
slight cares of a family are great hindrances to the study of
philosophy' (see p. 325); and Lady Masham: 'Tis in Vain that you
bid me Preserve my Poetry; Household Affairs are the Opium of
the Soul' (see p. 317).

11 *her Haire*: i.e. Auristella's, the mistress celebrated in Drummond's sonnet sequence. The sonnet by Parthenius 'To the Author'
in the 1614 and 1616 edition of *Poems by William Drummond, of
Hawthorn-denne* begins:

> While thou dost praise the Roses, Lillies, Gold,
> Which in a dangling Tresse and Face appeare...

13-14 Drummond makes much of Auristella's green eyes, e.g. in
'Song' and 'Madrigal', Sig. [C4ᵛ]; Oxlie claims that his description
has the same effect on her as the eyes have on him.

16-17 Oxlie's recollection is exact; Drummond praises

> That living Snow, those crimson Roses bright
> Those Pearles, those Rubies, which did breed Desire... (1614, Sig. [G2ᵛ])

19 *Chian painter*: Homer, who was from Chios, specifically perhaps
the Homer of the *Hymn to Venus*, as in Spenser's sonnet *To all the
gratious and beautifull Ladies in the Court* and his *Hymne of Heavenly
Beautie* (211).

25 *Flora*: goddess of flowers; 'the personification of nature's power
in producing flowers' (*OED*).

26 *Prankt*: decked or adorned. *Ora*: the river Ore in Fife near
Drummond's home in Scotland. Cf. Drummond: 'It was the time
when to our Northerne Pole...' The poet

> By Ora's flowrie Bancks alone did wander,
> Ora that sports her like to old *Meander*,...
> Into whose mooving Glasse the milk-white Lillies
> Doe dresse their Tresses & the Daffadillies. (Sig. B2)

29 *Swans that swim in Po*: The river Po in northern Italy. The *OED*
cites 'Swan-clad Po' in George Daniels's *Works* (1646).

33 *Daphne*: the nymph who became a laurel tree to escape Apollo's
pursuit; cf. 'To the Author' by 'Parthenius':

> And hence it is, that that once *Nymphe*, now Tree,
> Who did th'*Amphrisian Shepheards* Sighes disdaine,
> And scorn'd his Layes, mov'd by a sweeter Veine,

Is become pittifull, and followes Thee:
  Thee loves, and vanteth that shee hath the Grace,
  A Garland for thy Lockes to enterlace.

40 *peerlesse Prince*: Drummond's first publication was *Tears on the Death of Moeliades* (1613), a lamentation on the death of Henry, Prince of Wales, who died aged eighteen on 6 November 1612.

DIANA PRIMROSE

The only evidence for the existence of this poet is the title page of *A Chaine of Pearle. Or a memoriall of the peerles Graces, and Heroick Vertues of Queene Elizabeth of Glorious Memory. Composed by the Noble Lady, Diana Primrose*. London, 1630.

It is unlikely that her name is merely a poetic sobriquet, because she shares it with a distinguished family, including Gilbert Primrose (c.1580-1641) head of the reformed church in France and later chaplain in ordinary to James I; he had connections with Culross, and aided Elizabeth Melville's exiled friend, John Welsch, in France. Although her name does not appear in genealogical records, Diana may have been one of the twelve daughters (or wife to one of the twelve sons) of Gilbert's cousin James (d. 1641), clerk of the privy council of Scotland and an Edinburgh printer. Her book contains a commendatory poem by Dorothy Berry, but no further information about either woman can be gleaned from it.

The account of historical events used in *A Chaine of Pearle* is almost certainly the first part of William Camden's *Annals of Queen Elizabeth*, published in London in Latin in 1615, in French in 1624, and in an English translation from the French in 1625. As in Part I of the *Annals*, the earliest event referred to is Elizabeth's accession to the throne in 1559 and the latest her deliverance of Europe from the Spanish tyrant in 1588.

Diana Primrose's purpose in writing a panegyric on a queen dead twenty-seven years is clearly to criticise Charles I by implication. Elizabeth's ten ornaments, 'true Religion', chastity, prudence, temperance, clemency, justice, fortitude, science, patience and bounty, may have all been considered lacking in Charles. By 1630 his imprudence in trusting to Buckingham and allying himself with papist interests combined with his lack of concern for Protestant feeling had begun seriously to alienate him from a large proportion of his subjects.

John Nichols in the third volume of *The Progresses and Public Processions of Queen Elizabeth* includes 'A Chaine of Pearle' (1823, 640ff.) with the date of 1603 and enters it in his index under the name Pembroke, Anne Clifford, Countess of Dorset: 'the author of a Chain of Pearl (by Diana Primrose)'. Thomas Park, editor of *The Harleian Miscellany*, reprints the entire poem, citing Nichols (first edition, 1805) as his source, but giving the correct date (1813, 10, 72 ff.).

Robert Herrick's poem 'To His Booke' (one of several of the same title in *Hesperides*, 1648) concludes with lines which, while proving nothing, contribute to the mystery surrounding Diana Primrose's identity:

Say, if there be 'mongst many jems here; one
Deserveless of the name of *Paragon*:
Blush not at all for that; since we have set
Some *Pearls* on *Queens*, that have been counterfet. (Patrick, 109)

The first Pearle. *Religion.*

  The goodliest Pearle in faire *Eliza's* Chaine;
Is true Religion, which did chiefly gaine
A Royall Lustre to the rest, and ti'de
The Hearts of *All* to her when *Mary* di'de.
5 And though Shee found the Realme infected much
With Superstition, and Abuses, such
As (in all humane Judgement) could not be
Reform'd without domesticke Mutiny,
And great Hostility from Spaine and France;
10 Yet *Shee* undaunted, bravely did advance
Christs Glorious Ensigne, maugre all the Feares
Or Dangers which appear'd: and for ten yeares
Shee swaid the Scepter with a Ladies hand,
Not urging any Romist in the Land,
15 By sharpe Edicts the Temple to frequent,
Or to partake the holy Sacrament.
But factious Romanists not thus content,
Their Agents to their holy Father sent,
Desiring him. by sollemne Bull, proclaime
20 Elizabeth an Heretike, and name
Some other Soveraigne, which might erect
Their masking Masse, and hence forthwith eject
The Evangelicall Profession,
Which flourisht under her Protection.
25 The Pope to this petition condescends,
And soone his Leaden Bull to England sends,
By which one *Felton*, on the Bishops Gate
Of London was affixed; But the *State*
For that high Treason punisht him with death,
30 That would dethrone his Queene, *Elizabeth.*
Yet was this Ball of Wild-fire working still,
In many Romanists which had a will,

The present State and Governement to change;
That they in all Idolatrie might range.
35 And hence it came that Great *Northumberland*,
Associate with Earle of *Westmerland*,
And many moe, their Banners did display
In open Field; hoping to win the Day.
Against these Rebells, Noble *Sussex* went;
40 And soone their bloudy Purpose did prevent.
Westmerland fled, *Northumberland* did die,
For that foule Crime, and deepe disloyalty;
Having engaged Thousands in that Cause.
After which time, the *Queene* made stricter Lawes.
45 Against Recusants; and with Lyons heart,
Shee bang'd the *Pope*, and tooke the Gospells part.
The *Pope* perceiving that his Bull was baited
In such rude sort, and all his hopes defeated:
Cries out to Spaine for helpe; who takes occasion
50 Thereby t'attempt the Conquest of this Nation.
But such Sage Counsellers *Eliza* had;
As, though both Spaine* and Rome were almost mad
For griefe and anger, yet they still did faile,
And against England never could prevaile.

* In ultimam rabiem furoremq; conversi.

From *A Chaine of Pearle. Or, a Memoriall of the peerles Graces, and Heroick Vertues of Queen Elizabeth of Glorious Memory. Composed by the Noble Lady, Diana Primrose / Dat Rosa mel apibus, qua sugit Aranea virus.* London: Printed for Thomas Paine, and are to be sold by Philip Waterhouse at his shop at the signe of St. Paul's-head in Canning Street neare London-stone, 1630, 1-3.

2 Cf. Elizabeth's letter to Parliament (1586) quoted in the *Annals of Queen Elizabeth*, 1625: 'I begun my Raign in... the Religion wherein I was born and have beene brought up and I hope shall die...' (III, 175).

4 *Mary*: Elizabeth's half sister, Mary I, who re-established the Catholic Church during her reign (1553-1558).

20 On 25 February 1570 Pope Pius V issued the Bull *Regnans in Excelsis* excommunicating Elizabeth and absolving her subjects from the duty of allegiance.

27 *By which*: perhaps an accidental inversion by the printer; to make sense the line should begin 'Which by...' Signs of hurried typesetting occur throughout the text (e.g. in l.19). John Felton nailed a copy of the Bull to the Bishop of London's palace gate on 15 May 1570. He was soon apprehended and hanged.

31 *Ball of Wild-fire*: the gathering of the rebellion in the north.
35 *Northumberland*: Thomas Percy, seventh Earl of Northumberland (1528-1585) tried to free Mary Queen of Scots by force with the help of the Spanish and restore the Catholic religion.
36 *Westmerland*: Charles Neville (1543-1601), sixth Earl of Westmorland together with Northumberland led a force of 1,700 horse and 4,000 foot against the Queen.
39 *Sussex*: Thomas Radcliffe, third Earl of Sussex (1526-1583), commander of the Queen's forces in the north who forced the rebels back into Scotland.
46 *bang'd the Pope*: in 1571 an act was passed making it punishable by death for any Catholic priest to give absolution or for anyone to receive absolution, thus beginning the era of Catholic martyrdom under Elizabeth.
49 *Spaine*: from 1586 to 1588 the Spanish made repeated attempts to invade England.
52 *In ultimam rabiem furoremq; conversi*: Turned into the greatest rage and fury.

The fourth Pearle. Temperance.

The Golden Bridle of *Bellerophon*
Is Temperance, by which our Passion,
And Appetite we conquer and subdue
To Reasons Regiment: else may we rue
5   Our yeelding to Mens *Syren*-blandishments,
Which are attended with so foule Events.
   This Pearle in *Her* was so conspicuous,
As that the *King Her Brother still did use * Edward
To stile *Her* His sweete Sister Temperance;
10   By which Her much-admir'd Selfe-governance,
Her Passions still *Shee* checkt, and still *Shee* made
The World astonisht, that so undismaid
Shee did with equall Tenor still proceede
In one faire course, not shaken as a reed:
15   But built upon the Rocke of Temperance: * Semper eadem
Not daz'd with feare, not maz'd with any Chance;
Not wiih (*sic*) vaine Hope (as with an emptie Spoone)
Fed or allur'd to cast beyond the Moone:
Not with rash Anger to precipitate,
20   Not fond to love, nor too too prone to hate:
Not charm'd with Parasites, or *Syren* Songs,
Whose hearts are poison'd, though their sugred
                        Tongues

Sweare, vow, and promise all Fidelity,
When they are bruing deepest Villany.
25 Not led to vaine or too profuse Expence,
Pretending thereby State Magnificence:
Not spending on these momentany pleasures
Her precious Time: but deeming her best Treasures
Her Subjects Love, which *Shee* so well preserv'd,
30 By sweete and milde Deameanour, as it serv'd
To guard *Her* surer, then an Armie Royall;
So true their Loves were to Her, and so Loyall:
O Golden Age! O blest and happie Yeares!
O Musicke sweeter then that of the Spheares!
35 When Prince and people mutually agree
In sacred Concord, and sweete Symphonie!

* Omnibus incutiens blandum per pectora amorem

From *A Chaine of Pearle*, 6-7.
1 *The Golden Bridle*: a gift from Athena to Bellerophon, messenger of Proteus, enabling him to subdue Pegasus and slay the Chimera.
8 Edward VI, Elizabeth's half-brother, who ruled from 1547 to his death in 1553. Camden's *Apparatus* tells us that Edward never called Elizabeth anything but '*dulcis sororis Temperantiae*' (*Annales*, 1615, 9). De Bellegent alters the syntax to read 'Edouard, son frère ne la salüa jamais qu'en l'appelant de ce doulx nom, Soeur Temperance' (*Annales*, 1624, 9) but Darcie's 1625 translation of de Bellegent into English makes no mention of 'Temperance' saying merely that Edward called Elizabeth his '*sweet Sister*' (Sig. A1). *A Chaine of Pearle* was registered on 15 January 1630, so it is unlikely that Primrose had seen the translation of Camden's *Annals* by R[obert] N[orton] published in 1630, which tells us Edward 'called her by no other name than his sweet Sister *Temperance*' (6).
Given the Latin tags and mottoes with which Primrose's book is sprinkled it seems likely that her source was Camden's Latin original: nevertheless there are some striking correspondences between Norton's work and *A Chaine of Pearle*. Where Camden lists the four cardinal virtues as particular attributes of the Queen, Norton in his 'To the Reader' lists ten:

In this worthy Queene, many rare Vertues concurred... *Wisedom, Clemency, Learning, Knowledge of Tongues, Constancy, Temperance, Chastity, Magnanimity,* and (which Crowned all the rest,) *Zeale to Piety,* and true *Religion*... Hence it was that like Religious Josias she applied her first Cares in the entrance of her Reigne to the Purging of the Church of England from the dregges of Popery and Superstition. (Sig.A3)

15 *Semper eadem*: the Phoenix motto meaning 'always the same' often incorporated into emblematic portraits of the Queen (W. Camden, 1615, 40).
19 *Omnibus incutiens blandum per pectora amorem*: from the invocation

to Venus of Lucretius's *De Rerum Natura* (I, 19). Lucy Hutchinson's unpublished translation (see pp.216ff.) interprets this line as: 'Instilling wanton love into each mind' (BL Add. MS 19, 333, f.6). Spenser loosely paraphrased the entire hymn in Book IV, Canto 10, stanzas 44-46 of *The Fairie Queene* (1595), which he dedicated to Queen Elizabeth.

The sixt Pearle; *Justice*.

Her *Justice* next appeares, which did support
Her Crowne, and was her Kingdomes strongest Fort.
For should not Lawes be executed well,
And Malefactors curb'd, a very Hell
5   Of all Confusion and disorder would
Among all States ensue. Here to unfold
The exemplary Penalties of those,
Which to the Realme were knowne, and mortall Foes:
And as some putrid members par'd away,
10 Least their transcendent Villany should sway
Others to like Disloyalty; would aske
A larger Volume, and would be a Taske
Unfit for Feminine hands, which rather love
To write of pleasing subjects, then approve
15 The most deserved slaughtering of any;
Which justly cannot argue Tyranny.
For though the *Pope* have lately sent from Rome,
Strange Bookes and pictures painting out the Doome
Of his pretended Martyrs: as that they
20 Were baited in Beares skins, and made a prey
To wilde Beasts, and had Bootes with boiling Lead
Drawn on their Legges, and Hornes nail'd to their
                       head;
Yet all our British world knowes these are fables,
Chimaera's, Phantasm's, Dreames, and very Bables
25 For Fooles to play with: and right Goblin-Sprights,
Wherewith our Nurses oft their Babes affrights.
His Holinesse these Martyrdomes may adde
To the *Golden Legend*; for they are as madde,
    That first invented them, as *he that write * Vappa Voraginesa
30 That branelesse Booke: and yet some credit it.
For Cruelty and fond Credulity,
Are the maine Pillers of Romes Hierarchy.

DIANA PRIMROSE

From *A Chaine of Pearle*, 8-9.

17-22 In 1630 Pope Urban VIII issued a revised edition of Pope Gregory XIII's 1584 *Roman Martyrology*, a list of saints and martyrs arranged in the order of the feast days of the new (1582) calendar of the Church. The official martyrology existed side-by-side with 'legendaries or passionaries' (H.C.White, 24), printed abroad and distributed in England less for liturgical use than for popular entertainment and propaganda. Cardinal William Allen's *Briefe Historie of the Glorious Martyrdom of xii Reverend Priests* (n.p., n.d.; translated into Italian in 1583, 1584 and 1595; Latin in 1583, 1588, and 1594, and Spanish in 1599) was subject to attack by loyal Protestants like Camden. Only the first Italian edition, *Historia del glorioso martirio di Sedici Sacerdoti, martyrizati per la confessione & defesa della fide Catholica* (1583), included six engravings depicting the arrest, imprisonment, torture, hanging, and quartering of the English martyrs at Tyburn. The engravings are said to have inspired Niccolo Circiniani's frescoes at the Church of the English Martyrs in Rome which, in turn, were engraved by Giovani Battista Cavalieri, and published as *Ecclesia Anglicanae Trophaea* (Rome, 1584). Richard Verstegan's *Theatrum Crudelitatis Haereticorum nostri temporis* (Antwerp, 1592) borrows from both Allen and Circiniani (Pollen, 121-122).

By the beginning of the seventeenth century the extravagant Catholic legendaries were gradually being replaced by 'scientific hagiographies' (H.C.White, 321), especially those produced by the Bollandists, Belgian Jesuits. Since Jesuit priests were mainly responsible for Gilbert Primrose's expulsion from France, Primrose here may be attacking them through their work. Recusant exiles throughout the reigns of Elizabeth and James continued to smuggle martyrologies of both sorts into England. Curiously, these works may have influenced the success of expanded editions of the famous Protestant legendary, Foxe's *Actes and Martyrs* (1563, sixth edition 1610) which had provided the outline for Camden's *Annals* (Haller, 230).

28 *Golden Legend*: The *Legenda Aurea* of Jacobus de Voragine (written 1258-1270). William Caxton's illustrated English translation was printed 156 times between 1483 and 1527; no other English editions appeared until William Morris's 1892 edition of the Caxton text.

29 *Vappa Voraginesa*: O worthless Voragine

ALICE SUTCLIFFE

Alice Sutcliffe was the daughter of Luke Woodhows (Wodehouse, Woodhouse) of Kimberly, Norfolk, of the family of Sir Thomas Woodhouse, attendant to Prince Henry, son of James I (BL Harl MS 1052, f.147ᵛ-148; BL Add. MS 24,492, 320; Blomefield, II, 552-556; Collins, I, 223). By 1624 she was married to John Sutcliffe, an 'Esquire of the Body to King James', son of Salomon Sutcliff of Milroy, Yorkshire and nephew of Matthew Sutcliffe (1550?-1629), Dean of Exeter, prominent anti-Catholic polemicist and one of the royal chaplains ('Sutcliffe, Matthew', *DNB*). She had by him at least one daughter, Susan. On 30 January 1633 her *Meditations of Man's Mortalitie or, A Way to True Blessednesse* was entered in the Stationers' Register. A 'second edition, enlarged' appeared in 1634, with commendatory poems by Ben Jonson, Thomas May, a poet and translator favoured by Charles I, George Withers, the emblematist, and Francis Lenton, 'the Queen's poet'. Lenton and Withers knew her only through her husband, who was then Groom of Charles I's Privy Chamber, and through her book.

The work is dedicated to Catherine Villiers, widow of George Villiers, first Duke of Buckingham, and to George Villiers's sister, Susan, wife of William Feilding, Earl of Denbigh and Master of the Great Wardrobe. Sutcliffe expresses deep attachment to the Duchess:

you have beene more then a *Mother* to mee, I having onely from her received life, but next under God from your Grace, & your honorable *Sister* the being both of mee and mine.

John Sutcliffe had been a servant to Buckingham (*CSPD* 1627-28, p. 491).

Besides the formal dedication, she includes a flattering acrostic on the name of Philip, Earl of Pembroke and Montgomery, joint dedicatee of Shakespeare's first folio and, as Lord Chamberlain of the Household, her husband's superior.

The prose *Meditations* are written in a combination of Biblical and pagan images, reminding humanity of its mortality, admonishing against sin, and emphasising the day of judgment:

O then! be thinke thy selfe in time, before that gloomy day comes, that day of cloudes and thicke darknesse, that day of desolation and confusion approach: when all the Inhabitants of the Earth shall mourne and lament, and all faces shall gather blacknesse. Because the time of their Judgement is come; alas! with what a fearefull hart and weeping eyes, and sorrowful countenance, & tembling loynes, wilt thou at that last and great assize looke upon Christ Jesus,... when he shall most gloriously appeare, with innumerable Angels, in flaming fire, to render vengeance on them that know him not? (9-10)

From 'Of our losse by Adam, and our gayne by Christ;
The first *Adam* was made a living Soule,
the second *Adam* a quickning Spirit;
For as in Adam wee all dye, so in Christ, shall all be made alive.
I. *Corinth. 15.*'

25 Of all the Trees that in the Garden grew,
He onely was forbidden that alone,
His Wife from that obedience soone him drew,
And taste thereof he did although but one:
O wretched man! what hast thou lost hereby
30 Wicked woman to cause thy husband dye.

T'is not saying, the Serpent thee deceiv'd,
That can excuse the fault thou didst commit;
For of all Joyes thou hast thy selfe bereav'd,
And by thy Conscience thou dost stand convict.
35 Thy husband not alone the fault must rue,
A punishment for sinne to thee is due.

For as thou now conceives thy seed in sinne,
So in great sorrow thou must bring it foorth,
The game which thou by that same fruit didst winne,
40 Thou now dost find to bee but little worth:
Obedience to thy Husband yeeld thou must,
And both must Dye and turned be to Dust.

From *Meditations of Man's Mortalitie. Or, A Way to True Blessednesse. Written by M^rs. Alice Sutcliffe wife of John Sutcliffe, Esquire, Groome of his Majesties most Honourable Privie Chamber, The Second Edition, enlarged.* Rom. 6. The wages of Sinne is Death, but the guift of God, is Eternall life, through Jesus Christ our Lord. London: Printed by B.A. and T.F. for Henry Seyle at the Tygers Head in St. Paul's Church-yard. 1634, 144-146. The 528-line poem (pp. 141-200) is not mentioned in the table of contents, which lists only the six prose chapters.
Title: 1 Corinthians 15:22
30 This indictment of Eve is repeated in milder terms at ll.169-180:

'Twas Pride, that Author was of all mans evill:
'Twas Pride, made Eve desire still to excell;
When Sathan said, as Gods, you then shall be;
Incontinent, she tasted of that Tree.
This Lep'rous sinne, infected so the bloud,
That through her off-spring, it hath wholly runne;
Before the child can know, the bad from good,
It straight is proud, Nature, this hurt hath done.
A female sinne, it counted was to be,
But now Hermaphrodite, proved is shee.

Sutcliffe's adherence to the traditional view of Eve as the primary sinner can be compared with Anna Trapnel in her thousand-page untitled book (Bod. 1. 42. Th., p.211); it is to be contrasted with the apologies for 'our Mother Eve' commonly found in defences of women and in many women's works, e.g. Aemilia Lanyer, *Salve Deus Rex Judaeorum* (1611), 761-832; Joane Sharpe, 'A Defence of Women, Against the Author of the Arraignment of Women', 11-44, appended to Esther Sowernam's *Ester hath hang'd Haman* (1617); Rachel Speght, *A Mouzell for Melastomus* (1617), *passim*; Jane Barker, 'She begining to study phisick, takes her leave of poetry', 31-37 (see p. 364); and Sarah Fyge, *The Female Advocate* (1687), 9-55. Bathsua Makin's *An Essay to Revive the Antient Education of Gentlewomen* (1673) argues for women's education as a preventive against the 'Evil... propagated by [Eve's] Daughters' (7), for '*Heresiacks* creep into Houses, and lead silly Women captive, then they lead their Husbands, both their Children, as the Devil did *Eve*, she her husband, they their Posterity'(25).

38 Genesis 3:16. 'Unto the woman he said, I will greatly increase thy sorrows, and thy conceptions. In sorrow shalt thou bring forth children, and thy desire shall be subject to thine husband, and he shall rule over thee' (Geneva Bible). Cf. Bradstreet, 'Childhood', 64 (see p. 121).

39 *game*: From the thirteenth to the early seventeenth century, used to mean amorous sport or play; cf. *Troilus and Cressida*, IV.v.63.

> *Bacchus* that drunken God from Hell comes forth,
> And reeling here and there few scapes his knockes,
> Who shunnes his blowes esteem'd are of no worth,
> One Drunkard at anothers weaknesse mockes:
> What Isaiah saith, thereon they never thinke;
> Woe bee to them! are strong to pw'r in drinke.

125

> God, in his love form'd all things for mans use,
> That for his Comfort they might daily be,
> But they prove poyson through mans vilde abuse,
> Sinne changeth all into deformity:
> Paul for mans health, to drinke Wine doth advise.

130

But through excesse, both Soule and Body dyes.

Man, by this Sinne more vile is, than a Beast;
For but sufficient, they will never take,
135 Mans sences fayles him sinnes are still increast,
He tracing vices, doth all good forsake:
In Drunkennesse, Lot doth to Incest fall,
Noah in his Wine, his secrets shewes to all
Then Lust, and Murther hands together take,
140 Like full fed Beasts, they neigh at neighbours wife,
Stolne bread is sweet, hidwater theyr thirsts slake,
They fall to Murther, through discord and strife.
For when mans reason fayles, to guide his will;
He into mischiefe, runneth headlong still.

From *Meditations of Man's Mortalitie*, 155-157.
126 *strong to pow'r in drinke*: verbatim from the Geneva Bible: 'Woe
unto them that are mighty to drink wine, and to them that are
strong to power in drink' (Isaiah 5:22).
129 *vilde:* vile
131 *Paul:* 1 Timothy 5:23
137 Genesis 19:30-38
138 Genesis 9:20-29
140 *full fed Beasts*: cf. Speght, 'The Dreame', 241 (see p. 73).
141 Proverbs 9:17 'Stolen waters are sweet, and hid bread is
pleasant' (Geneva Bible). In the fifth chapter of her prose
meditations, 'Comforts for the weake Christian; and to beware of
Backesliding', Sutcliffe employs the same quotation, again reversing
'waters' and 'bread':

the Adulterer hee draweth on more easily, by the delightsomenesse of the sinne,
telling him that stolne bread is sweet, and hid waters pleasant... (101)

ELIZABETH MIDDLETON

In 1937 the Bodleian Library acquired a manuscript volume (Bod. Don. e.17) bearing the date 1637. Inside, all 'written in [the same] very clear and good cursive book-hand of Italian type' (Sotheby's Catalogue, 1 August 1934) and decorated with elaborately penned floral motifs, are an eighteen-page Calvinist prose tract, unsigned and unattributed, entitled 'A Soveraign Antidote agayst (*sic*) Despayre fitt to be taken of all those who are afflicted eyther outwardlye in Boddy or Inwardly in Mynde, or both' and an incomplete ninety-line version of William Austin's 'Ecce Homo'. (Austin's poem is unattributed; it had been widely circulated in manuscript as early as 1628 and printed as 'Paraseve for Good Friday' in Anne Austin's posthumous editions of her husband's work, *Devotiones Augustiniae Flammae, or Certayne Devout, Godly and Learned Meditations*, in 1635 and 1637.) Between the two is a 173-stanza poem, 'The Death and Passion of our Lord Jesus Christ; As it was Acted by the Bloodye Jewes, And Registred by The Blessed Evangelists', dedicated to Mrs Sara Edmondes by an Elizabeth Middleton.

At least one part of Elizabeth Middleton's poem is an obvious pastiche. Stanzas 145-147 are nearly identical to 11. 49-54, 61-67 and 163-168 of 'Saint Peter's Complaint' by the martyred Jesuit priest and poet Robert Southwell. The 'Complaint', along with fifty-two short lyrics, was circulated in manuscript copies among Catholics immediately after Southwell's arrest in 1592; after his execution in 1595, English publishers, quick to anticipate the commercial appeal of the poetry and 'careful to select poems that did not express specifically Catholic doctrine' (McDonald and Brown, lxii), rushed 'The Complaint' into print; by 1636 ten more enlarged English editions and two Scottish editions had been issued.

The curiously ecumenical nature of the manuscript volume may provide a clue to the identity of Elizabeth Middleton. The Middletons (or 'Myddeltons') of Denbighshire in Wales, devout Anglicans (*DWB*) who allied themselves politically with the Puritans and Parliamentarians, had nevertheless close contacts with the English Catholic community in exile on the Continent. They had interests in London finance and law, and a continuing literary association with the Salusbury (or 'Salisbury') family of Denbighshire, linked to Southwell through the part Thomas Salusbury

(1564-1586) played in the Babington plot, and to the poets Shakespeare, Marston, Chapman and Jonson through the involvement of Thomas's brother, the poet John (1566?-1612), with the publication of Robert Chester's *Love's Martyr* (1601). Sir Thomas Myddelton (1550-1631), a London financier and Lord Mayor in 1613, was a patron of the publisher, Thomas Salisbury (1567?-1620) who in 1603 published his cousin William Myddelton's (1556?-1621) translation of the Psalms into Welsh. In 1636 Thomas Salusbury (1612-1643), grandson of the poet John Salusbury, published *The History of Joseph: A Poem* and dedicated it to his maternal grandmother, the Lord Mayor's 'late' second wife Elizabeth Davers, with the intention of restoring among their Welsh friends the reputation, tarnished by Puritan associations, of the Myddeltons.

The number of Elizabeths in each of the three generations of Myddeltons beginning with the Lord Mayor (see Myddelton), makes an exact identification of the Elizabeth who compiled 'The Death and Passion' conjectural at best. She may be the daughter of Sir Thomas Myddelton (1586-1666), the Lord Mayor's oldest son, and his wife Mary Napier (d. 1675). Sir Thomas, educated at Gray's Inn, took part in local government in North Wales, and during the first Civil War was a leader of the Parliamentary forces which fought William Salusbury (d. 1660) in 1643 at Denbigh Castle and forced the surrender of Lord Herbert of Cherbury at Montgomery Castle in 1644. Sir Thomas's opposition to the trial of King Charles finally led to an alienation from the Parliamentarians. His interest in the Jesuits is evident from an entry in the Chirk Castle account books of 1664 that records the payment to 'Mr. Cupper what he paid for one booke called the mistery of Jesuitisme' (Myddelton, 24); in 1666 he composed a twelve-stanza poem, 'The Consolatary Soliloquies of Sr. Thomas Myddelton in His Solitude & Sickness before his death', written, like Southwell's *Complaint* and 'The Death and Passion', in sixains (Myddelton, 132).

Sir Thomas's daughter Mary, married in 1638 to Sir John Wittewrong and dead the next year of smallpox, was said to be 'a person, who, for her many excellent virtues, more particularly her singular piety and learning, her judiciousness in and studiousness about the best thinges... left not many equalls behind her' (Myddelton, 20). Another daughter, Anne, married the third Lord Herbert of Cherbury, Lord Edward's favourite grandson and heir to what remained at Montgomery Castle. Elizabeth, born in 1619, married George Warburton of Arley in Chester who was created a baronet at the Restoration. By him she had four daughters and two sons. Although no poetry can be traced to an 'Elizabeth Warburton', Sir George's second wife, Dianna Bisshop, wrote an elegy on his death in 1676 that begins 'Dearest of husbands he whose life records...' (Bod. MS Rawl. D. 682, f. 10).

KISSING THE ROD

Elizabeth Middleton's 'Death and Passion' has the form of an oratorio; the narration of each event of the passion, taken from the Gospel accounts, is followed by the equivalent of an aria developing the speaker's emotional response to the event; in such a context her borrowing from *Saint Peters Complaint* does not seem out of place, for she does preface her paraphrase with the words 'Quoth he' (1. 853). Austin's 'Ecce Homo', in turn, acts as a kind of threnody, or closing chorale, to the poem. The guilt of the Jews is a theme common to Southwell, Austin and Middleton herself, but principally she celebrates the magnificent myth of the redemption in simple and forceful imagery.

S – uche Is the Love I beare thy Honest Hart
A – s makes me this free guifte to thee Impart
R – eade theise Ensuing lynes, and thowe shalt see
A – Rare Effect of Divine Charitye:
E – v'n Christ his Passion; who for Love of Thee
D – eingd to forsake his Seate of Majestye
M – aking himselfe A Man; A skorne of Men,
O – nly to purdge our Synfull soules; And when
N – owe that He had full Thirty three yeares space
D – onne Good where ere he came, in Every place,
E – nradged w^{t}h spight ye Jewes contemptuouslye
S – end him to Death, and nayle him to A Tree.
    Reade with affection, laye it up in store;
    For here's a Soveraigne Salve for Every Sore.

From Bodleian MS Don. e.17, f. 13. This acrostic follows Middleton's dedication, 'To Mrs. Sara Edmondes. Elizabeth Middleton wisheth all Health and Happyness'.

Sara Edmondes may be the sister of Sir John Harington of Exton, tutor to the Princess Elizabeth (see p. 39). In 1626, at the age of sixty, Sara married Sir Thomas Edmondes who had helped to arrange the Princess's marriage and had served as an occasional ambassador to the French court, despite his open hostility to Catholicism. Both Edmondes and Thomas Myddelton, the Lord Mayor, had houses in Essex.

Enradged w^{t}h spight: The indictment of the Jews is a theological and literary convention, cf. Aemilia Lanyer, *Salve Deus Rex Judaeorum* (1611):

High Priests and Scribes, and Elders of the Land,
Seeking by force to have their wicked Wils,...
How void of Pitie, and how full of Spight,
Gainst him that was the Lord of Light and Truth... (490-510)

ELIZABETH MIDDLETON

a Soveraigne Salve: Middleton here appears to be attempting to make a transition from the 'Antidote' to the 'Death and Passion'.

From 'The Death and Passion'

23

Unhappy merchant, Thus t'expose thy Lord
  Our Saviour, and Redeemer to his foes
Thy price was small; And yet Thowe took'st theyr
                                        word
  Whiche very well to all men might Disclose
Howe basely Thowe vile Creature didst esteeme
Of Him, who Came, this sicke worlde to Redeeme.

24

Oh blessed virgin, Hadst thowe present bene
  When Thus Thy Sonne by Thievish handes was
                                        sould
To bloody Merchauntes: It had soone bene seene
  Howe deere true Owners well gott pearles doe
                                        hould
Thy Tender Love had pitcht yᵉ price soe high
That Juryes wealth, on hayre should never buy.

25

But Thowe true patterne of pure Pyety
  Resigndst to Heav'ns decree thy propper Right
Suffring A Damned wretche Contemptuously
  To make a Market of Thy Deere Delight.
Then Hye thee, Hye thee, Since yᵉ Case so standes
Goe buy thyne owne from those Preistes murth'ring
                                        handes.

26

And Judas ô yf Greedy hope of Gayne
  Entice thee Thus Thy Saviour to forgoe
Why dost Thowe shewe thy selfe so fondly vayne
  As t'offer him to Those, that hate him soe?
His freindes I wisse, would geve more mony for him
Then Scornefull foes, whose spight and Pyde abhorre
                                        him.

27

Oh what would Lazarus new brought to live
  From Grave, thee payd to keepe his Lord from
                                        Death?

97

What Price would Magdalen Refuse to geve?
   That lov'd her Master deerer Then her breath?
Or Martha, And Virgin Mother too
Who lov'd him more then all ye World Can doe.
28

Yea Leave the Earth, and aske the Angells bright
   What Thay would geve thee for theyre king divyne
Doubtles to gett him home theyre chiefe Delight
   Thay would have chaunged theyre Heavnly state
                    for Thyne
Oh hadst Thow Thus made Sale of Christ before
Thy guilt had bene the lesse, Thy Gayne The more.
29

But Synne, wth selfe Conceit It selfe doth blynde
   Daring w^thout Respect of what It may
Wittnes false Judas, who wth Desp'rat mynde
   Tells prowdly to the Preistes He will betray
As yf The maker of Heav'n Earth, and Seas
Weare in His pow'r, to use him, as he please.

From 'The Death and Passion of our Lord Jesus Christ, As it was Acted by the Bloodye Jewes, And Registred by the Blessed Evangelists'. Bod. MS Don. e. 17, 16^v-17^v.

    The response follows the account of Judas's selling Christ to the 'Priests and Scribes' for thirty pieces of silver, cf. Matthew 26:14, Mark 14:10-11, Luke 22:2-6. Middleton's source appears to be the English Catholic Rheims New Testament which uses the ecclesiastical term 'scandalised' in Matthew 26:31 and Mark 14:27; the Geneva and Authorised Bibles use the word 'offended'. Her version of Jesus' speech after the Last Supper reads, 'All yee this Night/Shall in great scandall Runne, because of me' (Stanza 78). Verbal echoes indicate that she may also have been working from a Catholic publication of Southwell's poetry. In the 1616 edition of *Saint Peters Complaint* issued by the Jesuits at St Omer, a poem about the Eucharist is entitled 'The Christians Manna'; in other editions and in surviving manuscript copies it is called 'Of the Blessed Sacrament of the Aulter'. Middleton uses the term 'True Manna' in stanza 50, as well as such other terms as 'Cates' and the theological 'Type' that occur in the Southwell poem. Access to the Catholic books may have come through the Roman Catholic William Myddelton who, though 'sheltered' and supported by his elder brother the Lord Mayor, lived in Flanders with his Flemish wife and was an associate of the Catholic conspirator, Hugh Owen (*DWB*, 676).
Stanza 23 *Unhappy Merchant*: Judas. Commercial terms occur

98

throughout 'The Death and Passion'; cf. Stanza 37: 'Judas ye Merchant; Jewes the Chapmen fitt/For such A merchandise, to be Enrould/In Hells blacke booke.' The Myddelton family fortune was based on entrepreneurial commerce. Thomas, the Lord Mayor, was a fourth son who began his career apprenticed to a London grocer; he became an important banker and moneylender, an original shareholder in the East India Company, and a partner in the Virginia Company. His younger brother Hugh, apprenticed to a goldsmith, later used the profits from his trade to lease and operate coal mines and form the New River Company that brought fresh water to London. Another brother, Robert, originally a glover, served in Parliament as an expert on commercial affairs.

Stanza 24 *well gott pearles*: Matthew 13:45-46

Stanza 26 *I wisse*: used as an adverb, 'certainly' or 'truly'; *Scornefull foes*: cf. 'Ecce Homo...', 46-47 (f. 24): 'He tooke this fleshe of oures./And walk't despised. Hated. Humble, Poore,/With weeping, fasting, praying Evermore.'

Stanza 27 *Magdalen*: cf. Southwell's 'Mary Magdalen's complaint at Christs death', published in all editions of *Saint Peters Complaint*: 'One that lives by others breath,/Dieth also by his death' (11-12).

ANNA HUME

Anna Hume was the daughter of the Scots historian, poet and essayist, David Hume of Godscroft, author of the Latin poems *Daphn-Amaryllis* (1605) and *Lusus Poetici* (1605). Her brother James was a mathematician and doctor of medicine who, besides scientific treatises in Latin and French, published a Latin romance and Latin poems. Next to nothing is known of Anna. She may have been the 'gentlewoman' referred to in a letter of William Drummond of Hawthornden (NLS MS 2061 No. 30) in which case she is responsible for the editing and publication of her father's *History of the Houses of Douglas and Angus*, which the Douglas family had long obstructed. She is usually given credit for the English translations of the Latin verses in her father's history, published by the same printer who issued her translation of three of Petrarch's *Trionfi* in the same year, 1644.

Of Petrarch's works the *Trionfi* were the most read in Britain. Henry Parker, Lord Morley, published the first English version of all six triumphs in about 1554 (Carnicelli, 10); Queen Elizabeth, perhaps as an exercise for her tutor, translated the first ninety lines of the 'Triumph of Eternity' (Hughey, 1960, I, 360-363); a translation of 1585, made by William Fowler, uncle of Drummond of Hawthornden, was dedicated to Queen Anne of Scotland and widely read in manuscript; the Countess of Pembroke's translation of 'The Triumph of Death' (made some time before 1599) was famous. Anna Hume, publishing nearly a half century later, is at pains however to convince her readers that she never saw the 'Triumphs', 'nor any part of them in any other language but *Italian*' (99).

She dedicated *Triumphs of Love: Chastitie: Death*: to Elizabeth, eldest daughter of the Queen of Bohemia, famous for her intellectual friendships with, among others, the feminist Anna Maria van Schurman and Descartes who dedicated the *Principes de la Philosophie* to her in 1644. In the second of her dedicatory poems, Hume explains her motive:

> Nor is it gratitude, because y'have been
> Pleas'd to approve some others you have seen:
> Since retribution so farre below
> Proportion, would be worse then still to owe:
> Nor vanity, that thus I may have leave

100

ANNA HUME

To tell the world the honour I receive,
In that my name hath reacht your sacred eare... (Sig. A3)

Nothing is known of when or how Anna Hume came to the notice of the Princess, then in exile at the Hague. By translating a work so imbued with ceremony and ritual iconography and by seeking the approval of King Charles's niece, Hume made clear her anti-Presbyterian sympathies in one of the bloodiest years of the Civil War.

Hume's book did not meet with the success she hoped for; she never published the promised 'other three Triumphs of *Fame, Time* and *Divinitie* or *Heaven*' (100). The Countess of Pembroke's version keeps Petrarch's *terza rima* as Hume's does not, and although more concrete and dramatic than the original is much closer to its singing tone than Hume's.

> The Argument, *Lauretta* meeting cruell Death,
>   Mildely resignes her noble Breath.

The glorious Maid, whose soule to Heaven is gone
And left the rest cold earth, she who was growne
A pillar of true vallour, and had gain'd
Much honour by her victory, and chain'd
5   That God which doth the world with terrour binde,
Using no armour but her own chaste minde:
A faire aspect, coy thoughts, and words well weigh'd,
Sweet modestie to these gave friendly aid.
It was a miracle on earth to see
10   The bow and arrowes of the Deitie,
And all his armour broke, who erst had slain
Such numbers, and so many captive tain:
The faire Dame from the noble fight withdrew
With her choise company, they were but few,
15   And made a little troup, true vertu's rare,
Yet each of them did by her selfe appeare
A theame for Poems, and might well incite
The best Historian: they bore a white
Unspotted Ermine, in a field of green,
20   About whose neck a Topas chain was seen
Set in pure gold; their heavenly words and gate
Exprest them blest were borne for such a fate.
Bright stars they seem'd, she did a Sun appeare,
Who darkned not the rest, but made more cleare
25   Their splendour; honour in brave minds is found:

101

This troup with Violets and Roses crown'd,
Chearfully march't, when lo, I might espie
Another ensigne dreadfull to mine eye,
A Ladie cloth'd in blacke, whose stern looks were
30 With horrour fill'd, and did like hell appeare,
Advanc't, and said, You who are proud to be
So fair and young, yet have no eyes to see
How neare you are your end, behold, I am
She, whom they, fierce, and blinde, and cruell name,
35 Who meet untimely deaths; 'twas I did make
Greece subject, and the Romane Empire shake;
My piercing sword sack't Troy, how many rude
And barbarous people are by me subdu'd?
Many ambitious, vaine, and amarous thought
40 My unwisht presence hath to nothing brought:
Now am I come to you, whiles yet your state
Is happy, ere you feel a harder fate.
On these you have no power, she then replide,
Who had more worth then all the world beside,
45 And little over me; but there is one
Who will be deeply griev'd when I am gone,
His happinesse doth on my life depend,
I shall finde freedome in a peacefull end.
As one who glancing with a sudden eye
50 Some unexpected object doth espie;
Then lookes again, and doth his owne haste blame:
So in a doubting pause, this cruell dame
A little staid, and said, The rest I call
To minde, and know I have o'recome them all:
55 Then with lesse fierce aspect, she said, Thou guide
Of this faire crew, hast not my strength assaid,
Let her advise, who may command, prevent
Decrepit age, 'tis but a punishment;
From me this honour thou alone shalt have,
60 Without or feare or paine, to finde thy grave,
As he shall please, who dwelleth in the Heaven
And rules on earth, such portion must be given
To me, as others from thy hand receive:
She answered then; a farre we might perceave
65 Millions of dead heapt on th'adjacent plain,
No verse nor prose may comprehend the slain
Did on deaths Triumph wait, from India,

From Spain, and from Morocco, from Cathai,
And all the skirts of th'earth they gathred were,
70 Who had most happy liv'd, attended there;
Popes, Emperours, nor Kings, no ensignes wore
Of their past height, but naked shew'd and poore.
Where be their riches, where their precious jems,
Their Miters, Scepters, Roabs and Diadems?...

The fatall houre of her short life drew neare,
That doubtfull passage which the world doth feare;
95 Another company, who had not beene
Freed from their earthy burden there were seene,
To try if prayers could appease the wrath,
Or stay th' inexorable hand of death.
That beauteous croude conveen'd to see the end
100 Which all must taste, each neighbor, every friend
Stood by, when grim death with her hand tooke hold,
And pull'd away one onely haire of gold.
Thus from the world this fairest flower is tane
To make her shine more bright, not out of spleen:
105 How many moaning plaints, what store of cries
Were uttered there, when fate shut those faire eyes
For which so oft I sung; whose beautie burn'd
My tortur'd heart so long; whiles others mourn'd
She pleas'd, and quiet did the fruit enjoy
110 Of her blest life, farewell, without annoy,
True Saint on earth, said they; so might she be
Esteem'd, but nothing bates deaths crueltie.
What shall become of others, since so pure
A body did such heats and colds endure,
115 And chang'd so often in so little space?
Ah wordly hopes, how blinde you be, how base?
If since I bathe the ground with flowing teares
For that milde soule, who sees it witnesse bears;
And thou who read'st maist judge she fetter'd me.
120 The sixt of April, and did set me free
On the same day and moneth: O! how the way
Of fortune is unsure, none hates the day
Of slavery, or of death, so much as I
Abhorre the time which wrought my liberty,
125 And my too-lasting life; it had been just

103

My greater age had first been turn'd to dust,
And paid to time, and to the world the debt
I ow'd, then earth had kept her glorious state:
Now at what rate I should the sorrow prise
130 I know not, nor have Art that can suffise
The sad affliction, to relate in verse
Of these fair Dames, that wept about her herse;
Courtesie, Vertue, Beautie, all are lost,
What shall become of us? none else can boast
135 Such high perfection, no more we shall
Heare her wise words, nor the Angelicall
Sweet musick of her voyce; whiles thus they cride
The parting spirit doth it selfe divide
With every vertue from the noble brest,
140 As some grave Hermite, seeks a lonely rest:
The Heav'ns were cleare, and all the ambient Aire
Without a threatning Cloud, no adversaire
Durst once appeare, or her calme minde affright;
Death singly did her selfe conclude the fight;
145 After, when feare, and the extreamest plaint
Were ceast, th'attentive eyes of all were bent
On that faire face, and by despaire became
Secure; she who was spent, not like a flame
By force extinguisht, but as lights decay,
150 And undiscerned waste themselves away:
Thus went the soule in peace, so lamps are spent,
As the oyle fails which gave them nourishment;
In summe, her countenance you still might know
The same it was, not pale, but white as snow,
155 Which on the tops of hills in gentle fleakes
Fals in a calme, or as a man that takes
Desired rest, as if her lovely sight
Were clos'd with sweetest sleep, after the spright
Was gone. If this be that fooles call to die,
160 Death seem'd in her exceeding faire to be.

From 'The Triumph of Death. Chap. I.' *The Triumphs Of Love:
Chastitie: Death: Translated Out Of Petrarch By M^{ris} Anna Hume*.
Edinburgh: Evan Tyler, Printer to the King's most Excellent
Majestie. 1644, 75-94. Hume's version is thirty lines longer than
Petrarch but the shortest of the English translations: Morley's is 219
lines, Fowler's 216 and the Countess of Pembroke's 172.
Triumph: in ancient Rome, the march through the city of a

victorious general displaying the spoils of war, extended in painting and literature during the Renaissance to signify the emblematic parade of a deity or personification amid conquered enemies and rejoicing partisans.

5 *that God*: Cupid

7 *coy*: quiet, still

13 *noble fight*: Hume's own annotations, appearing here in bold face, are placed at the end of each chapter; she explains this reference as **Her fight with Cupid: See above in the Triumph of Chastitie.**

14 *choise company*: **The Ladies that had been vertuous before her time, and now waited on her Triumph, *Lucrece, Penelope, &c.***

19-21 *Ermine, etc.*: **Their ensigne; a white Ermine in a greene field, with a chain of Topasses set in pure gold: the white Ermine was an Embleme of innocencie: The Topasses of Chastity: and the pure gold of tride Vertue.** Nicholas Hilliard's famous 'Ermine Portrait' (1585) of Queen Elizabeth is based on Petrarchan emblems. For further exampes of Renaissance artists adopting the iconography of the *Trionfi* see Yates, 1975.

29-30 Hume's version omits many of Petrarch's Platonic extravagances and witty ambiguities. Here a literal translation would read 'a woman wrapped in black garments with a fury the like of which I doubt existed even in the time of the giants at Phlegra, advanced and said...'

43 *On these*: **Meaning the other Ladies that waited on her because they were all dead long before.**

45 *there is one*: **Petrarch, whom she thought would be more hurt by her death then her self, in regard of his extreme affection.**

95 **The former Company who were dead, could not bee sory for her death; because she would be nearer them, but another company of Ladies, her friends and neighbours, came to pray that death would let her stay longer amongst them.**

102 *one onely haire*: **Alluding to the purple haire on the head of *Nisus*, which his daughter stole, because he could not die whiles he wore it, as if *Lauretta* had had such another: or as if every body had one: See above in the *Triumph of Love, 2. Chap. 155 line*.** This note does not appear in contemporary commentaries on Petrarch, and appears to be original with Hume.

113-114 The original reads, '*Che fia de l'altre se questa arse ed alse...*' (l.127) rendered by the Countess of Pembroke:

> What confidence for others if that she
> Could frye and freese... (Waller, 1977, 127-128)

Hume is generally at pains to smooth out all such kinks of style.

120 Laura died on 6 April 1348 (*Rime* 3, 211).

140 This image is not to be found in Petrarch.

142 *no adversaire*: **No wicked spirit, meaning, that she was troubled with no apparitions at her death.**

LADY JANE CAVENDISH
AND LADY ELIZABETH BRACKLEY

Jane (1621-1669) and Elizabeth (1626-1663) were two of the five
children of William Cavendish, first Duke of Newcastle, by his first
wife, the heiress, Elizabeth Bassett, widow of Henry Howard, son of
the Earl of Suffolk. At the age of fifteen, though her family
considered her 'too young to be bedded' (Firth, 74), Elizabeth
Cavendish became Lady Brackley upon her marriage to John
Egerton, Viscount Brackley (1622-1686), later second Earl of
Bridgewater. She continued living with her sister at Welbeck Abbey,
judging from lines in the pastoral they wrote together in about
1644:

> You owne yourselfe to bee a wife
> And yet you practice not that life.

The then Earl of Newcastle was perhaps the wealthiest man in the
north of England; he raised money, arms, and troops for the King,
was General of the King's northern forces, and fortified his family
estates at Welbeck Abbey and Bolsover Castle. In 1643, while their
father and brothers were serving with the Royalists, the girls'
mother died. Until 1644, Jane, Frances (a younger sister), and
probably Elizabeth lived at the estate at Welbeck with its garrison of
Royalist soldiers. We have record of Jane sending military
information to the King's councillors at Oxford during this time,
(*CSPD 1644*, Vol.42, 131; HMC 78 Hastings II, 125, 129). By
midsummer, 1644, the Duke had been defeated in the field and had
fled to the Continent with his sons. In Paris in 1645 he met and
married Margaret Lucas who became the famous Duchess of
Newcastle, poet (see pp.163ff.). On 2 August 1644 Welbeck was
captured by the Parliamentarians under the Earl of Manchester
who promised to see that Newcastle's daughters were maintained
safely there (*CSPD 1644*, Vol.42, 404-405), but hints in the girls'
verse suggest that the men of the garrison behaved no better than
soldiers usually do.

During these turbulent months, Jane and Elizabeth diverted
themselves by writing; a play (*The Concealed Fansyes*), a masque and
occasional poems were collected and written out in a fair hand,
possibly for presentation to their father (Bod. Rawl. MS Poet. 16;
the Duke's initials are on the binding of the manuscript volume).

106

JANE CAVENDISH AND ELIZABETH BRACKLEY

The earliest poem that can be dated is 'On the 30th of June to God', which refers to the Royalist victory of Adwalton Moor, 30 June 1643.

The noblewomen of Welbeck struggled to preserve the lightness and sophistication that characterised the culture of their class, at a time when this civilisation itself was under threat. Their models were probably the court masques that had been played during the visits of Charles and Henrietta Maria to Welbeck in the 1630s, as well as the poems and plays of their father. Their literacy is of none too high an order: punctuation is chaotic and spelling indifferent, though at times evocative of the soft burr of their Northern speech (e.g. 'darr' for 'dare'); grammar is not much attended to. The contrast of the elaborate play of wit and ironic social insight with gaucheries of style provides the special character of the work of two brave young women, who cannot conceal their desperate longing for their father's return or their distrust of the unknown woman he married. The character of 'Lady Tranquility' in *The Concealed Fansyes* is their amusing portrait of the young Margaret Lucas: she spends a day keeping her bed 'to plumpe upp' her face for a meeting with the witty daughters of 'Monsieur Calsendos' (the Duke), anxious for their approval of her impending 'marryage to their ffather'. The Cavendish brothers, Charles and Henry, had been sent back to England to be married (Firth, 46) and must have teased their sisters with exaggerated anecdotes of the notorious courtship then in progress.

The Royalists re-captured Welbeck for four months in 1645, but it was finally given up to Parliamentarian forces in November and disgarrisoned by mutual agreement. Only Jane and Frances were there; before they left the remains of the household furnishings to be plundered, the sisters paid the Royalist Major Jammot £200 and agreed to pay £600 more if he safely delivered the 'plate of my Lord of Newcastles' that was 'putt into two hogsheads & plac'd & layd deep in the grownd within the Brewhowse att Welbeck' (UNott Portland MSS Pw1.367 and Pw1.368). Jane was also responsible for saving some of her father's Van Dyck paintings out of Bolsover Castle. When her father's enthusiastic support of the Royalist cause got him into difficulties abroad, Jane sent him £1,000 of the fortune she inherited from her mother's side of the family (Firth, 69-70).

An entry of 1655 in Lady Jane's account book lists '2 pare of holland sheets which I used to lie in at Welbeck, I brought with mee to Ashridge, & from thens to Chellsey' (Ellesmere MS 11143, Huntington Library). In 1654 Jane had married Charles Cheyne (1624?-1698), who was from an old family in Northamptonshire and had served as Captain Cheyne for the Royalists (*CSPD 1646*, Vol.44, 456). By 1655 they were renting the manor house at Chelsea which her husband finally purchased in 1657 with the large dowry she brought him, as he recorded on her monument inscription (Faulkner, 93). Elizabeth's dowry of £12,000 seems not to have covered the debts on the Egerton estate (see her husband's letter, HRO AH 1075), though probably it was for this purpose that she was early contracted in marriage.

Jane had three children: Elizabeth, born in 1656, William, born in 1657, and Catherine, born in 1658. In *The Concealed Fansyes*, Luceny says that her 'distruction' in a marriage would be to 'bee condemn'd to looke upon my Nose, whenever I walk and when I sett at meate confin'd by his grave winke to looke upon the Salt, and if it bee but the paireing of his Nales to admire him'. Her happiness 'when I am in the condition of his Wife, is still to ymagin him Courtley and I M^ris Luceny', scorning those who think 'Husbands are the Rodd of authority'; Courtley agrees:

> I would not have hir thinke of wife
> Nor mee as Husband to make strife
> But justly have hir fraught with witt
> Soe by me, pritty man, may sitt. (Starr, 807)

Marriage turned out better than Jane expected; in a letter to her brother in 1656 she describes her husband's fondness: 'did I not know my self Maried, I should think by what hee writs, that hee was still a woer, which puts mee in mind of your woords, for you tould mee it would bee allwayes so, beeing the nature of the person' (UNott Portland MS Pw1.88). Charles Cheyne, later Viscount Newhaven, became Tory MP for Amersham and Great Marlow and had a reputation as a chess player. Jane's account book notes purchasing 'a ches bord & men to it, of Evory which I gave my deare husband' on New Years Day, 1659.

So far only one more poem by Lady Elizabeth Brackley has been identified, in the 'Loose Papers left by y. Right ho^bl Elizabeth Countesse of Bridgewater', which her husband had copied into several identical volumes for her children. Many of the prose meditations in the volume are prayers for strength during her pregnancies and childbed which echo the service for the Churching of Women in the Book of Common Prayer. In one she prays:

O Lord, I knowe thou mightest have smothered this my Babe in the wombe, but thou art ever mercyfull, and hast at this time brought us both from greate dangers, and me from the greate torture of childbirth. (BL MS Egerton 607, f.30)

Elizabeth died in premature labour in 1663, after having joined her husband in prison where he was confined on a duelling charge. Jane was at her sister's deathbed and expressed her grief in a poem which we include below. John Egerton was so affected by his wife's death that were it not for his children, he writes, 'I should be very Carelesse w^t became of me; but for their sakes... I do endeavour to live' (HRO AH 1074). The Earl of Bridgewater's eloquent eulogy on his wife was inscribed on her monument and later printed by George Ballard in his *Memoirs of Learned Ladies* (1755).

Jane suffered a series of epileptiform seizures in 1668, and died on 8 October 1669. We know from a poem on her death by Thomas

JANE CAVENDISH AND ELIZABETH BRACKLEY

Lawrence saying that poetry was 'An Art she knew and Practised so well / Her Modesty alone could it excell' (UNott Portand MS PwV.19) that she must have continued writing, but only the poem on her sister's death is known.

A Pastorall
The Antemasque.
Witches the nomber beinge five.

JC

	Bell	Come let us burne our severall horrid peeces.
45	Hag	Thus is our Mischiefe drawne in yeares of Leases
	Pre	If you a Prentice doe call mee
		Pray, let mee know of thee
		What you intend soe hollyly to burne
	Hag	To sacrafice unto Loves Devills urne
50	Pre	What's the ingrediece of your Perfume
	Bell	All horrid things to burne i'th Roome
	Hag	As Childrens heads
	Bell	Mens leggs
	Hag	Weomens Armes
55	Bell	And little Barnes
	Hag	And these wee will you show
	Pre	Noe thanke you, I will take my leggs to goe.
	Bell	Noe stay we will not you soe fright
	Hag	That you the better may us like
60	Bell	For wee're resolv'd that us you shall not slight
	Hag	For with us you shall oynt and make a flight
	Pre	And must all this bee done to night
	Bell	But wee've forgot our Songe
	Hag	Let's singe, but let's not bee too longe.

From Bod. Rawl. MS Poet. 16, 53-54.
The initials 'JC' and 'EB' in the manuscript designate Jane's or Elizabeth's authorship. The first antemasque is by Jane and the second by Elizabeth; in the pastoral proper, authorship alternates between the sisters. We have printed the initials as they appear in the text. Earlier in the antemasque the witches Hag and Bell boast of causing the Civil War, making ladies captives, and tying their tongues. Prentice disagrees, 'wee are but the people that's taulked on, to serve others designes'. In this passage the witches perform a magic ritual just before their departure on 'distaffs' to cause more mischief and 'see great Lucyfer to night'.

Antemasque: introduction to the masque.
43 *Witches the number beinge five*: only four witches, one unnamed, actually speak.
44 *Bell*: beldam
46 *Pre*: Prentice, the apprentice witch
55 *Barnes*: bairns, children
61 *oynt*: cf. 'aroynt' or 'aroint' (*Macbeth*, I.iii.6; *King Lear*, III.iv.121); a dialect word in all three contexts connected with witches, meaning begone.
64 *Let's singe*: Hag, Bell, Prentice and another witch then sing to the Devil.

The 2 Antemasque.
Two Countrye Wives.
The Songe.

EB

   He. I have lost my melch Cow.
   Pr   And I have lost my Sow
   Ry And for my Corne I cannot keepe,
   Ha Nether can I my pritty sheepe.
5 He And I have lost fowre dozen of Eggs
   Pr   My Pigs are gone, & all their Heads
   Ry Come let us wishe for Health
   Ha For wee can have noe wealth
   He Now I will hope for Joy
10 Pr   And in meane tyme let's bee a Toy
   Ry Since that wee have noe plenty
   Ha And our Purses, they are empty
   He Since that wee have noe plenty
   Pr. And our Purses they are empty.

From Rawl. MS Poet. 16, 61.
A second antemasque, beginning with 'Two Countrye Wives', follows the witch scene. Gossip Pratt tells Naunt Hen about visiting her 'Lord & Maisters' house to present a pig to his children, 'the Ladies', with instructions to 'looke into my Pigs Tale, & there they would fynd... My Pigg fatt'. (The word 'fat' as a noun meant vessel or container.) She seems to be speaking enigmatically about passing a message on as a spy: 'that word would have beene held uncivill, for such a word to have beene sent, or sayd to any one... I sayd it, & I repented not.' Two countrymen join the women, Goodman Rye and Goodman Hay, and after a discussion on the relative merits of having their 'Kine & sheepe' taken by Witches or by Satyrs, the four 'singe a songe of all our losses'.

1 *He*: Naunt Hen, i.e. aunt Hen; hen is a low colloquial way of designating a female.
2 *Pr*: Gossip Pratt, i.e. prat, meaning trick, prank, or fraud. It can also mean the buttocks.
3 *Ry*: Goodman Rye
4 *Ha*: Goodman Hay
10 *Toy*: used in the sense of a person of little or no value, frivolous, as in *The Merry Wives of Windsor*, V.v.46, and Jonson's *The Devil is an Ass*, IV.vii.
13 *noe plenty*: scarcity of food and water more than once forced an otherwise impregnable country house to surrender to opposing forces during the Civil War. Evidence of starving non-combatants under siege is reported at Colchester in 1648 where

this day the Women & Children were at the Lord Goring's Door for Bread; That he told them, They must eat their Children if they wanted; the Women Reviled his Lordship, told him, They would pull out his Eyes rather than starve, and were in a High Discontent.

> The three sad Sheppardesses, goe to a little
> Table, where they singe this Songe in parts.
> The Sheppards sadly sitt on the grownd,
> and the Jearer wench apart from them.
5   The Shee Preist begins.

Songs Anthome

EB

Cha When once the presence of a freind is gone
      Not knoweing when hee'le come or stay how
                               longe
      Then griefe doth fill it selfe wth a reward
10   That is when passion flowes without regard.
JC   Inn   His absence makes a Chaos sure of mee
      And when each one doth lookeing looke to see
      They speakeing say, That I'm not I
      Alas doe not name mee for I desire to dye
15   Ver   And I your Sister can noe way goe lesse
      As by my Face of palenes you may gesse
      Then let us singe in Choros Anthome, pray,
      To see our loved freinds, doth make our day.

> The 3 Sheppardesses Sisters speakes
20   this in severall lines in answeare to one
> another.

The Shee Priest begins.

Cha: The univers mee thinks I see
Inn: In little moddle is just wee
25 Ver For wee're as constant to our way
Cha: As it can bee of night and day
Inn Our mallencholly that's the night
Ver And when Joyes hope then 'tis day light
Cha: Our Winter is sad thoughts dispare
30 Inn Soe mallencholly sighes makes Ayre
Ver Which wth feares conflicts makes a wind
Cha And after doth raine showers of kind
Inn Our couler hopes of what wee wishe
Ver Can water freize to Ices Dysh,
35 Cha: And passion thoughts of what wee feare
Inn: Can thaw Ice Dyshe, though nea're soe deare
Ver Our Springe is onely Joyes of thinke
Cha: Yet frosty feare doth make us shrinke
Inn Our Summer is, if that could bee
40 Ver Father, Brothers, for to see.
Cha: God of our love happines to say,
Your welcome, when wee owne him as our
day.

1 *three sad Sheppardesses*: Cha(stity), the 'Shee Preist', Inn(ocence?),
and Ver(tue?); otherwise, Jane, Elizabeth and Frances. The maiden
shepherdesses are pursued by shepherds called Careless, Freedom,
Persistent and Constant(?), but so sad are they at the absence of
their father and brothers, they will admit no suit.
4 *the Jearer wench*: the jeerer, evidently an Arcadian of a satiric bent,
perhaps a mask assumed by another of the players.
17 *Choros Anthome*: chorus anthem
23-40 This poem, entitled 'Loves Universe', is one of a number
preceding the pastoral in Rawl. MS Poet. 16 (20):

> The universe mee thinkes I see
> In little moddle is just mee
> For I'm as constant to my way
> As it can bee of night and day...

In the pastoral's version Jane changes the single speaker to a group.
24 *moddle*: model

EB   The 3^d Sheppard speakes this to the rest
      whose name is Careles

45   Now what's here a Hee cave, as was a Shee

Or are you a could Groto for to bee.

The 3 sad Sheppards sings this in parts
And the two last lynes in Choros.

	Per	Since that our Deares wee cannot have,
50		Wee're bueryed in loves cruell Grave,
	Con:	Noe wee're tortred upon the rack of griefe,
		As soe to love wee make our selves a Theife.
	Per	When steale a looke it is a Plunder,
	Con	If bar'd sight, our hearts doe breake assunder
55	Car	This to mee is a great wonder.

The 4ᵗʰ Sheppard whose name is
Freedome sings this as hee comes
in, to the sad Lovers.

	Fre:	Fy, fy, what a coyle is here,
60		To make love chyme to feare.

JC		Freedome then speakes this to the three
		sad Sisters Sheppardesses

	Fre:	You three Devinities of sad, pray tell
		What kind of way you would like well
65		Could I but any of you please
		I'de runn into Loves high disease
		But your most cruell, gentle flame
		Will make mee tell my courtshipp dreame
		For otherwaies I darr not speake to you
70		Doubting you'l judge mee of a looser crue
		But now I begg to freely heare
		What one you'l harber in your Eare
		If this noe word of you can sure begett
		Tell mee how I, my Mistris would besett.

JC		
75	Cha:	Tell hir noe more your fancyes dreame
		Nor in your Cupps hir health inflame
		But if you speake let it bee witt
		Soe by you shee, may darr to sitt.

I would not have you hir prophane

80 With formall speeches which proves lame
For in loue sure it is a sinn
If not by sword your Mistris winn

Your courage should soe well bee known
As thoughts of you protected hir alone
85 And if by chaunce, each speake your publique
fame
Then should shee blush, at nameing but your
name

And when you meete your carrage should be
such
As you should speake, but yet not speake too
much
But gentle lookes, and after then
90 Give hir your gentle language of the Penn.

Fre: This is good Counsaile, & I'le follow it,
That is, that if I can, I will have witt.

EB   The 4th Sheppard speakes this to the three
sad Sheppards.

95 Fre: Now to you my Country wench I'le bringe
Whose very face sweares shee's right the
Spring
Thus I'le bring you every one a lass
Whose skinne's as smooth as Cristall ball or
Glass
Per Noe by Cupid they shall not bee our Loves
100 Con: For wee will bee as true as Turkle Doves
Fre: Come promise mee with them you'l dance
And then your Eye to them must glance.

JC   Freedome speakes this to the three
sad Sheppardesses.

105 Fre: If you will dance, wee'le have an Ayre
Shall chyme as chast as devine care
Ch: Our vow will admitt noe such Toye

114

For absent freinds gives us noe joy
Car.   Come Jearer wee will have you in
110   Though I doe vow, good nature you'l ne're
                                             winn
Fre: How like you now my Country Lasces,
       That in love lookes, will bee your Glasses

JC

Car.   Now could wee Ladies have but such a dance
       That would but fetch your freinds, now
       out of Fraunce
115   You then would well approve of this our mirth
       But since not soe, you doe appeare sad Earth.
Fre: Come Musicke let's have now a Rownd,
       To prove my Country Wenches rightly sound.

[Envoi]

JC   My Lord it is your absence makes each see
       For want of you, what I'm reduc'd to bee
       Captive or Sheppardesses life
       Gives envy leave to make noe strife
       Soe what becomes mee better then
125   But to bee your Daughter in your Penn
       If you're now pleased I care not what
       Becomes of mee, or what's my lott
       Now if you like, I then doe knowe
       I am a Witt, but then pray' whisper't low.

EB   My Lord your absence makes I cannot owne,
       My selfe to thinke I am alone
       Yet Sheppardesses can see to read
       And soe upon your stock of wit I feede
       Soe beggs your blesseing to like this
135   Then I am crown'd wth hight of bliss.

From Rawlinson MS poet. 16, 53-54; 61; 77-84.
45 *a Hee cave*: earlier in the pastoral Chastity has described the setting as 'this our Grotto... a sad Shee Hermits Cave'.
59 *coyle*: fuss
70 *crue*: crew
107 *Toye*: amorous dallying

An answeare to my Lady Alice Edgertons Songe

Of I prethy send mee back my Hart

I cannot send you back my hart
   For I have but my owne
And that as Centry stands apart
   Soe watchman is alone

5   Now I doe leave you for to spy
     Where I my Campe will place
   And if your Scouts, doe bringe alye
     May bee your selfe will face

   Then if you challenge mee the feild
10   And would mee batle sett
   I then as Maister of the feild
     Perhaps may prove your nett

From Rawlinson MS poet. 16, 16. By Lady Jane Cavendish. All the
occasional poems in the manuscript are hers.
Title *Lady Alice Egerton* (1619-1689), later Countess of Carbery, was
the daughter of John Egerton, first Earl of Bridgewater, and
Frances Stanley, daughter of the Earl of Derby. She was the sister of
John Egerton, Elizabeth's husband, and is known for having acted
the part of 'The Lady' in the original presentation of Milton's
'Comus' at Ludlow Castle in 1634; her brother John played the
'Eldest Brother'. The poem to which this title refers appears set to
music in Henry Lawes' *Ayres, and Dialogues, For One, Two, and Three
Voyces: The Third Book* (1658), ascribed to Dr Henry Hughes:

> I prethee send me back my heart,
>   Since I cannot have thine:
> For if from yours you will not part,
>   Why then should you keep mine?
>
> Yet now I think 'n't, let it lie,
>   To send it me were vain,
> For th'hast a thief in either eye
>   Will steal it back again.
>
> Why should two hearts in one breast lie,
>   And yet not lodge together?
> Oh Love, where is thy sympathie
>   If thus our hearts thou sever?

Lawes was Alice Egerton's music teacher; he dedicated his first book
of *Ayres and Dialogues* (1653) to her and her sister Mary, Lady

Herbert of Cherbury. In *The Works of Sir John Suckling* (1971), Clayton prints 'I prethee send me back my heart' and includes the above poem of Lady Jane Cavendish in an appendix (187), granting that its title gives some ground for ascribing 'I prethee send me back my heart' to Alice Egerton rather than to Henry Hughes. The connection with Sir John Suckling is based on a mistaken identification of Lady Elizabeth Brackley, co-author of Rawlinson MS poet. 16, as Lady Elizabeth Brackley, née Cranfield, the daughter-in-law of our poet, and a relative of Suckling.
12 *prove*: test

On my Boy Henry

    Here lyes a Boy ye finest child from me
    Which makes my Heart & Soule sigh for to see
    Nor can I think of any thought, but greeve,
    For joy or pleasure could me not releeve,
5   It lived dayes as many as my years,
    No more; wch caused my greeved teares;
    Twenty and Nine was the number;
    And death hath parted us asunder,
    But y^u art happy, Sweet'st on High,
10 I mourne not for thy Birth, nor Cry.

From BL Egerton MS 607, f.119. By Elizabeth Egerton, Countess of Bridgewater.
On 2 June 1656, Elizabeth bore a son, Henry, who died twenty-nine days later. Over a period of seventeen years from 1646 when her first child was christened, she gave birth to nine children, six of whom survived her. In the same manuscript volume are the Countess's prose meditations on the illnesses and deaths of the three children who died in infancy, Frances, Henry, and Catherine. Several of the few surviving family letters record details of both sisters' pregnancies in 1656, Jane being delivered of her first child on 18 May 1656, though Elizabeth had predicted 'there will bee but a weeke difference beetweene my Sister Cheyne and I' (29 April 1656, UNott Portland MS Pw1.119). Elizabeth earlier wrote to her brother Charles that she believed she would give birth before her 'Sister Jane', for Jane is not 'neere so bige as I am: she Breeds the best that Ever I knewe: ffor she makes noething of a great Belly' (26 March 1656, UNott Portland MS Pw1.118). Their sister Frances, by then Lady Bolingbroke, writes on 7 June of her 'Deare Sister Bridgwaters ill Labor... as yet she is far from well', though her 'sister Cheny thanks bee to God is so well that I saw her walk in her

Chamber pritty strongly' (UNott Portland MS Pw1.69). Charles Cheyne wrote an hour-by-hour account of Lady Jane's labour pains to her brother, noting 'signes of neare Labour', 'hard paines', and 'chearfull intermissions' (UNott Portland MS Pw1.84).

On the death of my Deare Sister the Countesse of Bridgewater dying in Childbed, Delivered of a dead Infant a Son, the 14:th day of June 1663.

O God thy Judgments unto sinfull eye
Were greate, when I did see my Sister dye,
Her last look was to heaven, from whence she came,
And thither going, she was still the same,
5   No Discomposure in her life or Death,
She lived to pray, prayer was her last Breath:
And when Deaths heavy hand had closed her eyes,
Me thought the World gave up it's Ghost in Cryes:
What ere relations choyce, or nature made
10   Lost their best light, and being in that Shade;
For none can give Example like her life,
To Friendship, Kindred, Family, or wife.
A greater Saint the Earth did never beare,
She lived to love, and her last thought was care;
15   Her new borne Child she asked for, which n'ere
                                 cryed,
Fearing to know its end she Bowed, and Dyed:
And her last Vale to Heaven appeared to all,
How much she knew her Glory in the call.

From Ellesmere MS 8353, Huntington Library. Written in a fair copy hand with the inscription 'By yᵉ Lady Jane Cheyne' in Lady Jane's hand at the top.
7 *Deaths heavy hand*: the image is a stock one, however see Damaris Lady Masham (see pp.318ff.), 'When death's cold hand shall close my eyes...'
17 *Vale*: farewell

ANNE BRADSTREET

Anne Bradstreet is the best known of all the English women poets of the seventeenth century, for the simple reason that she is one of the earliest poets of either sex to be writing in 'America'. She was born in Northamptonshire in about 1613, the second child of Thomas Dudley and Dorothy Yorke. Little is known of Anne's mother other than that she was the daughter of Edmund Yorke, and a 'Gentlewoman whose extraction and estate were considerable' (Mather, 121); Thomas Dudley was probably a descendant of the noble family of the Suttons, Lords of Dudley, an ancestry that may account for his education and his continued use of the heraldic shield of the Dudleys. At the time of Anne's birth Dudley was clerk to Judge Augustine Nicholls and a follower of the Puritan preacher John Dod. Anne may have been baptised by Dod at Canons Ashby House, the home of Dod's protector, Sir Erasmus Dryden (E.W.White, 49).

In 1619 Anne's father was engaged as steward to the fourth Earl of Lincoln and the family went to live at Sempringham Manor in Lincolnshire. According to her own memoir, at the age of six or seven Anne 'found much comfort in reading ye Scriptures' (McElrath and Robb, 215). Staunch Puritans, the Dudleys became, through the Earl and his connections with Emmanuel College in Cambridge where the Earl and Anne's brother both studied, prominent among the leading Puritans. Anne's education in the devout household was rigorous, but along with conventionally pious works she read the poems of Edmund Spenser and Sir Philip Sidney, who had once written, 'My chiefest honour is to be a *Dudley*' (E.W.White, 12).

In 1622, Simon Bradstreet, a graduate of Emmanuel, took up the position of assistant to Thomas Dudley. When Dudley moved his family to nearby Boston (Lincolnshire), presumably to be near the preacher John Cotton and carry on his activites in the Puritan cause, Bradstreet took over management of the Earl's estates; within a year or so, however, he too left to become steward to the Puritan Countess of Warwick, widow of Lord Rich.

In 1627, Lord Lincoln was arrested for leading opposition to Charles I's attempt to raise money by forced loan; soon afterwards three other members of the Sempringham household were arrested and for a while the threat of a similar fate hung over Thomas

Dudley. Amidst this anxiety, Anne was stricken by smallpox and loss of faith. Nevertheless, she wrote in her memoir, 'After a short time I changed my Condition and was marryed' (McElrath and Robb, 216). She and Simon remained for less than a year at the Countess's estate, for the Puritans were already planning to emigrate to a godlier world; in 1629 Thomas Dudley and Simon Bradstreet were signatories to the application for a charter under the Great Seal for the Massachusetts Bay Company. Barely a year later, on 23 March 1630, the Dudleys and the Bradstreets boarded the *Arbella* to bid farewell to their 'Jerusalem at home' (Haraszati, 14); they landed at Salem on 12 June 1630.

In the first nine months, two hundred of the seven hundred settlers who made the journey with them died; a hundred returned to England and Ireland, preferring to face persecution rather than the hardships of the New World. Anne herself fell ill, and upon her recovery, she began, rather haltingly, to write poetry. In 1634, the same year her father became governor of the colony, the first of her eight children was born. Five or six years later the Dudley family moved from what is now Cambridge forty miles north to Ipswich and the Bradstreets followed. Despite the ruggedness of life in an isolated settlement Anne Bradstreet continued working on her poetry; she did not limit herself to occasional verse, but broached public poetry on epic themes, including a metrical commentary on the Civil War.

After her mother's death in 1644 and her father's remarriage less than four months later, the Bradstreet household moved again, this time to the outpost settlement of Andover. Anne was pregnant with her sixth child, and writing her major poem 'The Four Monarchies'. On 1 July 1650, 'a book called *The tenth muse lately sprung up in America*, written by Ann Bradstreet' was entered in the Stationers' Register. The book carried an introductory letter from I.W., probably John Woodbridge, who had married Bradstreet's sister Mercy, explaining:

I feare the displeasure of no person in the publishing of these Poems but the Authors, without whose knowledge and contrary to her expectation, I have presumed to bring to publick view what she resolved should never in such a manner see the Sun; but I found that divers had gotten some scattered papers, affected them wel, were likely to have sent forth broken peices to the Authors prejudice, which I sought to prevent, as well as to pleasure those that earnestly desired the view of the whole.

Woodbridge was put in contact with the London publisher Stephen Bowtell by his brother Benjamin and Nathaniel Ward, author of *The Simple Cobbler of Aggawam in America*, published by Bowtell in 1647.

On 22 July 1652 Bradstreet bore her eighth and last child and a year later her father died. Her own health was uncertain, but she continued writing poetry of a more personal, inward, contemplative cast than her first ambitious efforts which may have been modelled on Thomas Dudley's work; it is for these later poems she is nowadays best known. She died on 16 September 1672, and was buried in Andover. Simon Bradstreet remarried and returned to Salem to become governor of the colony during its 'troublesome time' (Mather, 128); he died and was buried there in 1697.

In July 1678 a second edition of Anne Bradstreet's poems was published in Boston. The title-page claimed that the reprinted works had been 'corrected by the Author'; certainly many changes had been incorporated in the intervening twenty-eight years. Bradstreet is usually considered responsible for these herself on the evidence of 'The Author to her Book' where she claims to have been deeply embarrassed by the appearance of *The Tenth Muse*:

> Yet being mine own, at length affection would
> Thy blemishes amend, if so I could:
> I wash'd thy face, but more defects I saw,
> And rubbing off a spot, still made a flaw.
> I stretcht thy joynts to make thee even feet,
> Yet still thou run'st more hobling then is meet...

The only poem we have in her own hand is forty-four lines at the end of a manuscript volume of prose meditations compiled for her son Simon on the eve of his taking up his ministry in New London in 1664. A book she made for her children in the 'mother's legacy' tradition is known to us only in copies made by two of the children.

From 'The Four Ages of Man.'

Childhood.

Ah me! conceiv'd in sin, and born in sorrow,
65   A nothing, here to day, but gone to morrow.
Whose mean beginning, blushing cann't reveale,
But night and darkenesse, must with shame conceal.
My mothers breeding sicknes, I will spare;
Her nine months weary burden not declare.
70   To shew her bearing pangs, I should do wrong,
To tel that paine, which cann't be told by tongue;
With tears into this world I did arrive;
My mother stil did waste, as I did thrive:
Who yet with love, and all alacrity,
75   Spending was willing, to be spent for me;
With wayward cryes, I did disturbe her rest;
Who sought stil to appease me, with her brest,
With weary armes, she danc'd, and *By, By*, sung,
When wretched I (ungrate) had done the wrong.
80   When Infancy was past, my Childishnesse,
Did act al folly, that it could expresse.
My sillinesse did only take delight,

In that which riper age did scorn, and slight:
In Rattles, Bables, and such toyish stuffe.
85 My then ambitious thoughts, were low enough.
My high-borne soule, so straitly was confin'd:
That its own worth, it did not know, nor mind.
This little house of flesh, did spacious count:
Through ignorance, all troubles did surmount.
90 Yet this advantage, had mine ignorance,
Freedome from Envy, and from Arrogance...

120 But yet let me relate, before I go,
The sins, and dangers I am subject to.
From birth stayned, with *Adams* sinfull fact;
From thence I 'gan to sin, as soon as act.
A perverse will, a love to what's forbid:
125 A serpents sting in pleasing face lay hid.
A lying tongue as soon as it could speak,
And fift Commandement do daily break.
Oft stubborn, peevish, sullen, pout, and cry:
Then nought can please, and yet I know not why.
130 As many was my sins, so dangers too:
For sin brings sorrow, sicknesse, death, and woe.
And though I misse, the tossings of the mind:
Yet griefs, in my fraile flesh, I still do find.
What gripes of wind, mine infancy did pain?
135 What tortures I, in breeding teeth sustain?
What crudities my cold stomach hath bred?
Whence vomits, wormes, and flux have issued?
What breaches, knocks, and falls I daily have?
And some perhaps, I carry to my grave.
140 Some times in fire, sometimes in waters fall:
Strangely preserv'd, yet mind it not at all.
At home, abroad, my danger's manifold.
That wonder tis, my glasse till not doth hold.
I've done, unto my elders I give way.
145 For 'tis but little, that a childe can say.

From *The Tenth Muse Lately sprung up in America. Or Severall Poems, compiled with great variety of Wit and Learning, full of delight. Wherein especially is contained a compleat discourse and description of The Four Elements, Constitutions, Ages of Man, Seasons of the Year. Together with an Exact Epitomie of The Four Monarchies, viz. The Assyrian, Persian,*

Grecian, Roman. Also a Dialogue between Old England and New, concerning the late troubles. With divers other pleasant and serious Poems. By a Gentlewoman in those parts. London, Stephen Bowtell, 1650, 43-45.

The version of the poem published in 1678 contains many variants. We have listed only those which indicate possible authorial revision, taking them from McElrath and Robb, *The Complete Works of Anne Bradstreet.*

64 in sorrow/with sorrow 1678	65 but gone/and gone 1678
71 that paine/those pangs 1678	77 her brest/the breast 1678
84 Bables/Baubles 1678	122 From birth stayned/ Stained from birth 1678
123 From thence I'gan/ Thence I began 1678	130 was my sins/are my sins 1678

64 *conceiv'd in sin*: Psalms 5:15: 'Behold, I was born in iniquity, and in sin hath my mother conceived me' (Geneva Bible); cf. *The Whole Book of Psalmes Faithfully Translated into English Metre*, known as the Bay Psalm Book (1640), the first book published in America, and used by New England Puritan congregations:

> Behold, how in iniquity
> I did my shape receive:
> also my mother *that mee bare*
> in sin did mee conceive.

and the Countess of Pembroke's lines in her version of the Fourth Penitential Psalm, 'Miserere mei Deus':

> My mother, loe! when I began to be,
> conceaving me, with me did sinne conseave:
> and as with living heate shee cherist me
> corruption did like cherishing receave. (Waller, 1979, 231)

Dorothy Leigh's *The Mother's Blessing. Or the godly counsaile of a Gentle-woman not long since deceased, left behind for her Children* (1616; at least twenty editions through the seventeenth century) accepts women's traditional role as conveyors of sin to their progeny and entreats them to 'bee carefull of their children', defining one of the 'causes' that moved her to the unwomanly act of writing:

> to encourage women (who, I feare, will blush at my boldnesse) not to bee ashamed to shew their infirmities, but to give men the first and chiefe place: yet let us labour to come in the second; and because wee must needs confesse, that sin entred by us into posterity, let us shew how carefull we are to seeke to Christ to cast it out of us, and our posterity, and how fearefull we are that our sinne should sinke any of them to the lowest part of the earth...(16-17)

born in sorrow: Genesis 3:16 and Jeremiah 20:18; cf. Alice Sutcliffe, 'Of our losse by Adam' (see p.91), note to l. 30 and ll. 37-42.

65 *here to day, but gone to morrow*: recorded as a proverb by 1549 in John Calvin, *Life and Conversion of a Christian man*: 'This proverbe that man is here to-day and gone to morow'.

66 *mean beginning*: sexual intercourse: *inter faecem et urinam nascimur.*

75 Cf. Shakespeare, Sonnet 76: 'Spending again what is already spent'/

76 *I did disturbe her rest*: While Bradstreet was living at Sempringham

Manor the earl's mother, Elizabeth Knyvet, was responsible for the publication of a plea to women of rank to breast-feed their own children. *The Countesse of Lincolnes Nurserie* (1622) replies to those who would say that nursing is 'troublesome... noisome to one's clothes, makes one look old, endangers health' (Fraser, 79).

82 *sillinesse*: innocence

122 *Adams sinfull fact*: original sin

127 *fift Commandement*: in the Geneva Bible, 'Honour thy father and thy mother'.

134 *gripes of wind*: colic pains

136 *crudities*: undigested matter in the stomach; *cold stomach*: in Bradstreet's 'Of the foure humours', 'Choler' claims,

> Nay, th'stomach, magazeen to all the rest,
> Without my boiling heat cannot digest. (*The Tenth Muse*, ll.150-151)

137 *wormes*: internal parasites; *flux*: liquid bowels, diarrhoea

From 'The Foure Monarchies, the *Assyrian* being the first, beginning under *Nimrod*, 131. yeares after the Floud.'

Semiramis.

70　This great oppressing *Ninus* dead, and gone,
　　His wife, *Semiramis*, usurp'd the throne,
　　She like a brave Virago, play'd the rex,
　　And was both shame, and glory of her sex;
　　Her birth-place was *Philistrius Ascalon*,
75　Her Mother *Docreta,* a Curtezan;
　　Others report, she was a vestal Nun,
　　Adjudged to be drown'd, for what she'd done;
　　Transform'd into a fish, by *Venus* will,
　　Her beautious face (they feign) retaining still.
80　Sure from this fiction, Dagon first began,
　　Changing his womans face, into a man.
　　But all agree, that from no lawfull bed;
　　This great renowned Empresse, issued.
　　For which, she was obscurely nourished.
85　Whence rose that fable, she by birds was fed.
　　This gallant dame, unto the *Bactrian* war;
　　Accompaning her husband *Menon* far,
　　Taking a towne, such valour she did show,
　　That *Ninus* of her, amorous soon did grow;
90　And thought her fit, to make a Monarch's wife,

Which was the cause, poor *Menon* lost his life,
She flourishing with *Ninus,* long did reigne;
Till her ambition, caus'd him to be slaine:
That having no compeer, she might rule all,
95 Or else she sought, revenge for *Menons* fall:
Some think the *Greeks,* this slander on her cast,
As of her life, licentious, and unchast.
And that her worth, deserved no such blame,
As their aspersions, cast upon the same.
100 But were her vertues, more, or lesse, or none,
She for her potency, must go alone.
Her wealth she shew'd, in building *Babylon*;
Admir'd of all, but equaliz'd of none.
The walls so strong, and curiously were wrought;
105 That after ages, skil, by them were taught.
With Towers, and Bulwarks made of costly stone
Quadrangle was the forme, it stood upon:
Each Square, was fifteen thousand paces long,
An hundred gates, it had, of mettall strong;
110 Three hundred sixty foot, the walls in heighth:
Almost incredible, they were in breadth.
Most writers say, six chariots might a front,
With great facility, march safe upon't.
About the wall, a ditch so deep and wide,
115 That like a river, long it did abide.
Three hundred thousand men, here day, by day;
Bestow'd their labour, and receiv'd their pay,
But that which did, all cost, and art excell,
The wondrous Temple was, she rear'd to *Bell*;
120 Which in the midst, of this brave Town was plac'd,
(Continuing, till *Xerxes* it defac'd)
Whose stately top, beyond the clouds did rise;
From whence, Astrologers, oft view'd the skies.
This to discribe, in each particular,
125 A structure rare, I should but rudely marre,
Her gardens, bridges, arches, mounts, and spires;
All eyes that saw, or ears that hears, admires.
On *Shinar* plain, by the *Euphratan* flood,
This wonder of the world, this *Babell* stood.
130 An expedition to the East she made.
Great King *Staurobates*, for to invade.
Her Army of four Millions did consist,

(Each man beleive it, as his fancy list)
Her Camells, Chariots, Gallyes in such number,
135 As puzzells best hystorians to remember:
But this is marvelous, of all those men,
(They say) but twenty, ere came back agen.
The River *Indus* swept them half away,
The rest *Staurobates* in fight did slay.
140 This was last progresse of this mighty Queen,
Who in her Country never more was seen.
The Poets feign her turn'd into a Dove,
Leaving the world, to *Venus,* soar'd above,
Which made the *Assyrians* many a day,
145 A Dove within their Ensigne to display.
Forty two years she reign'd, and then she dy'd,
But by what means, we are not certifi'd.

From *The Tenth Muse* (1650), 67-70. The four monarchies are traditionally Assyria (sometimes called Babylon), Persia, Greece and Rome, from the visions of Daniel, chapters 7 and 8; the fall of the fourth kingdom presages the Second Coming of Christ and his kingdom on earth. The source of Bradstreet's histories is *The History of the World* by Sir Walter Raleigh who sent the first fleet of English colonists to Virginia in 1585-1586. Raleigh's *History* was published anonymously in London in 1614, and many times thereafter; according to Hill (1966, 204) it was 'the most popular of all histories by an Englishman in America'.

74 *Philistrius Ascalon* / Philistines *Ascolan* 1678   75 *Docreta* / *Dorceta* 1678
77 what / the crime 1678   81 his / the 1678
89 of her, amorous / amorous of her 1678
97 As of her life, / As on her life 1678
98 And that her worth, deserved no such blame, / That undeserv'd, they blur'd her name and fame 1678
99 As their/ By their 1678   112 Most writers/ Some writers 1678
122 beyond the Clouds / above the clouds 1678
131 Great King *Staurobates*, for to invade./ *Staurobates*, his Country to invade: 1678
136 marvelous/ wonderful 1678   138 *Indus/ Judas* 1678

Title *Semiramis*: Greek name for Sammu-ramat, legendary Assyrian queen who, according to Diodorus Siculus, Raleigh's chief source, succeeded her husband Ninus.
70 *Ninus*: husband of Semiramis, King of Nineveh and 'all those Regions betweene [Bactria] and the *Mediterran Sea*, and *Hellespont*', c. 2071-2019 BC.
72 *She like a brave Virago, play'd the rex*: cf. Bradstreet's 'In honour of that High and Mighty Princess, Queen Elizabeth, of most happy memory':

She hath wip'd off th' aspersion of her Sex,
That women wisdome lack to play the Rex;...

126

ANNE BRADSTREET

She their Protectrix was, they well doe know,
Unto our dread Virago, what they owe... (*The Tenth Muse*, ll.29-52)

Later in the poem to Elizabeth, Bradstreet writes, '*Semiramis* to her is but obscure' (67). James I tried to suppress Raleigh's *History* 'specially for beeing too sawcie in censuring princes' (John Chamberlain in Patrides, 11). Bradstreet's condemnation of Ninias in the section which follows 'Semiramis' may be a commentary on the policies of Charles I, who was forced by Parliament in 1641 to promise 'to reduce all matters of religion and government to what they were in the purest time of Queen Elizabeth's days' (Kenyon, 124).

72 *Virago*: a man-like, vigorous, and heroic woman; a female warrior; an amazon.

74 *Philistrius Ascalon*: Ascalon, a city of the Philistines, on the Mediterranean Sea near Gaza.

75 *Docreta*: a Syrian goddess, the equivalent of the Phoenician goddess Astarte. Raleigh writes, 'Some writers... report [Semiramis] to be the daughter of *Derceta*, a *Curtizan* of *Ascalon*, exceeding beautifull. Others say that this *Derceta* or *Dercetis*, the mother of *Semiramis*, was sometimes a Recluse, and had profest a holy and a religious life' (182). Docreta, ashamed of her indiscretion with a Syrian youth, hid her daughter in the reeds; there Semiramis was fed by doves until she was rescued by shepherds and raised by Simmas, chief shepherd of the royal herds. Docreta was cast into a lake and 'changed by *Venus* into a fish, all but her face, which stil held the same beauty & humane shape' (182). Raleigh suggests that 'from this *Derceta* the invention of that Idoll of the *Philistims* (called *Dagon*) was taken' (182).

76 Bradstreet often notes that information conflicts in different sources; her father's library contained other histories besides Raleigh's, for example, Knolles, *Generall Historie of the Turkes* (D. D., 355-356; Stanford, 1974, 137-138).

80 *Dagon*: see Judges 16:23, I Samuel 5:3,4, and I Chronicles 3:24.

86 *Bactrian war... her husband Menon*: Semiramis was first married to the Syrian general Menon who called her to accompany him to the seige of Bactra (now Balkh in northern Afghanistan). Semiramis planned the attack on the citadel and took the city, charming Ninus with her beauty and courage, causing Menon to drown himself 'for her sake' (Bradstreet, 'Ninus', 60).

93 *caus'd him to be slaine*: after the birth of Ninias, his father Ninus granted Semiramis supreme power for five days according to Diodorus (one day, according to Plutarch) during which time she had Ninus imprisoned and executed.

96 *Some think the Greeks*: cf. Raleigh:

for her vitious life, I ascribe the report thereof to the envious and lying *Grecians*. For delicacy and ease doe more often accompany licentiousnesse in men and women, than labour and hazzard doe. (183)

127

102 *building Babylon*: cf. Raleigh:

[Semiramis] sought to exceed her husband by far... living in that Age, when Ambition was in strong youth: and purposing to follow the conquest which her husband had undertaken, gave that beauty and strength to *Babylon* which it had. (181-182)

119 *Bell*: Bel, also called Baal, or Belus. The historical figure of Belus (or Bellus), son of Nimrod and father of Ninus, Semiramis's husband, is sometimes taken as the original of the pagan god Baal, for whom Semiramis erected her famous temple. In the section on 'Bellus' Bradstreet states that his

> acts, and power, is not for certainty,
> Left to the world, by any History;
> But yet this blot for ever on him lyes,
> He taught the people first to Idolize; (*The Tenth Muse*, ll. 25-28)

Following Raleigh, she identifies Belus with the Bell of the Chaldees and Israelites, '*Belzebub*, god of *Ekronites*', and the Moabites' Bal-peor. In 'Ninus' she writes, 'This *Ninus* for a god, his father canoniz'd, / To whom the sottish people sacrific'd' (48-49).

121 *Xerxes*: King in Persia in the fifth century BC; according to Bradstreet in 'The Second Monarchy', 'full of pride and cruelty'.

122-123 Cf. Raleigh:

Among all her other memorable & more than magnificent works (besides the wall of the City of *Babylon*) was the Temple of Bel, erected in the middle of this City,... upon the top whereof the *Chaldæan* Priests made the observation of the stars; because this Tower over-topped the ordinary clouds. (183)

Raleigh notes that the ruins of Semiramis's towering Temple of Bel were often mistaken for the ruins of Nimrod's Tower (the Tower of Babel). According to Raleigh, Semiramis's edifice was 'founded on that of *Nimrod*' (184).

128 *Shinar plain*: in Babylonia, now southern Iraq, the location of the Tower of Babel (Genesis 11:1-9).

129 *Babell*: here not the Tower of Babel, but the city of Babylon.

131 *Staurobates*: Stabrobates, an Indian king. Raleigh cites '*Strabo* and *Arianus*' as the source of his story of Semiramis's last campaign, and Diodorus as the source of these 'incredible and impossible numbers' (183).

134 *Gallyes*: low flat-built ships with one or more banks of oars worked by slaves.

136-139 Cf. Raleigh: 'of all her most powerfull Army there survived but onely twenty persons: the rest being drowned in the River of *Indus*, dead of the famine, or slaine by the sword of *Staurobates*' (183).

138 *Indus*: the change to 'Judas' in the 1678 edition is a compositor's error.

142-145 Cf. Raleigh: '(As Antiquity hath fained) [she] was changed by the gods into a Dove, (the bird of Venus) whence it came that the *Babylonians* have a Dove in their ensignes'(183).

ANNE BRADSTREET

The *Roman* Monarchy,
being the Fourth, and last,
beginning, *Anno Mundi*,
3213.

An Apology.

To finish what's begun, was my intent,
My thoughts and my endeavours thereto bent;
3555 Essays I many made but still gave out,
The more I mus'd, the more I was in doubt:
The subject large my mind and body weak,
With many moe discouragements did speak.
All thoughts of further progress laid aside,
3560 Though oft perswaded, I as oft deny'd,
At length resolv'd, when many years had past,
To prosecute my story to the last;
And for the same, I hours not few did spend,
And weary lines (though lanke) I many pen'd:
3565 But 'fore I could accomplish my desire,
My papers fell a prey to th' raging fire.
And thus my pains (with better things) I lost,
Which none had cause to wail, nor I to boast.
No more I'le do sith I have suffer'd wrack,
3570 Although my Monarchies their legs do lack:
Nor matter is't this last, the world now sees,
Hath many Ages been upon his knees.

First printed in *Several Poems Compiled with great variety of Wit and Learning, full of Delight; Wherein especially is contained a compleat Discourse, and Description of The Four Elements, Constitutions, Ages of Man, Seasons of the Year. Together with an exact Epitome of the three first* Monarchyes, Viz. *The Assyrian, Persian, Grecian.* And the beginning of the *Romane Common-wealth to the end of their last King: with diverse other pleasant and serious Poems* By a Gentlewoman in *New-England.* The second Edition, Corrected by the Author, and enlarged by an Addition of several other Poems found amongst her Papers after her death. Boston: Printed by John Foster, 1678, 191.
An Apology: only 108 lines on the Roman monarchy appeared in *The Tenth Muse* in disproportion to the more than 3,000 lines written on each of the first three. Toward the end of the section on the Grecian monarchy Bradstreet wrote,

> With these three Monarchies, now have I done,
> But how the fourth, their Kingdoms from them won;
> And how from small beginnings it did grow,

> To fill the world with terrour, and with woe:
> My tired braine, leaves to a better pen,
> This taske befits not women, like to men:... (*The Tenth Muse*, 174)

Raleigh also abandoned his *History* after only a few pages about the Roman Empire, the death of Prince Henry 'besides many other discouragements, perswading [his] silence' (669). In a ten-line coda to the section on the Grecian monarchy Bradstreet indicated her willingness to continue where Raleigh left off:

> *After some dayes of rest, my restlesse heart,*
> * To finish what begun, new thoughts impart*
> *And maugre all resolves, my fancy wrought*
> *This fourth to th'other three, now might be brought.* (*The Tenth Muse*, 174)

but the 'Apology' indicates that true weariness with the project finally caused her to give it up.

3557 *The subject large... body weak*: in 'The Prologue', the poem some scholars believe is a special preface to 'The Foure Monarchies', Bradstreet ironically echoes the first line of the *Aeneid*:

> To sing of Wars, of Captaines, and of Kings,
> Of Cities founded, Common-wealths begun,
> For my mean Pen, are too superiour things,
> And how they all, or each, their dates have run:
> Let Poets, and Historians set these forth,
> My obscure Verse, shal not so dim their worth. (*The Tenth Muse*, 3)

3565-3566 Sometime after the publication of *The Tenth Muse* (1650) and before the fire that destroyed her house in Andover in 1666, Bradstreet attempted to expand the account of the Roman monarchy. Her father, for whom the poems were originally written, died in 1653.

3566 By an unhappy coincidence Raleigh 'cast Part Two [of the *History*] into the fire' after Prince Henry's death (Patrides, 24-25).

3571-3572 *this last... upon his knees*: this last, the Roman monarchy, i.e. Popery, whose adherents pray on their knees, for Bradstreet a maimed deformed religion, here taken as an apt figure for her maimed legless poem. Cf. 'A Dialogue between Old *England* and New', l.227.

From 'A Dialogue between Old *England* and New, concerning their present troubles. Anno 1642.'

Old England.

Well, to the matter then, there's grown of late,
'Twixt King and Peeres a question of state,
170 Which is the chief, the law, or else the King,
One saith its he, the other no such thing.
My better part in Court of Parliament,

To ease my groaning land shew their intent,
To crush the proud, and right to each man deal.
175 To help the Church, and stay the Common-Weal,
So many obstacles comes in their way,
As puts me to a stand what I should say,
Old customes, new Prerogatives stood on,
Had they not held law fast, all had been gone,
180 Which by their prudence stood them in such stead,
They took high *Strafford* lower by the head,
And to their *Laud* be't spoke, they held i'th' Tower,
All *Englands* Metropolitane that houre,
This done, an Act they would have passed fain,
185 No prelate should his Bishoprick retain;
Here tugg'd they hard indeed, for all men saw,
This must be done by Gospel, not by law.
Next the *Militia* they urged sore,
This was deny'd, I need not say wherefore.
190 The King displeas'd, at *York* himself absents,
They humbly beg return, shew their intents,
The writing, printing, posting to and fro,
Shews all was done, I'll therefore let it go.
But now I come to speak of my disaster,
195 Contention's grown 'twixt Subjects and their Master:
They worded it so long, they fell to blows,
That thousands lay on heaps, here bleeds my woes.
I that no warres, so many yeares have known,
Am now destroy'd, and slaughter'd by mine own,
200 But could the field alone this cause decide,
One battell, two or three *I* might abide,
But these may be beginnings of more woe,
Who knows, the worst, the best may overthrow;
Religion, Gospell, here lies at the stake,
205 Pray now dear child, for sacred *Zions* sake,
Oh pity me, in this sad perturbation,
My plundered Townes, my houses devastation,
My ravisht virgins, and my young men slain,
My wealthy trading faln, my dearth of grain,
210 The seed time's come, but Ploughman hath no hope,
Because he knows not, who shall inn his crop:
The poore they want their pay, their children bread,
Their wofull mother's tears unpitied.
If any pity in thy heart remain,

215 Or any child-like love thou dost retain,
For my relief now use thy utmost skill,
And recompence me good, for all my ill.

New England.
Dear mother cease complaints, and wipe your eyes,
220 Shake off your dust, chear up, and now arise,
You are my mother, nurse, I once your flesh,
Your sunken bowels gladly would refresh:
Your griefs I pity much, but should do wrong,
To weep for that we both have pray'd for long,
225 To see these latter dayes of hop'd for good,
That Right may have its right, though't be with blood;
After dark Popery the day did clear,
But now the Sun in's brightnesse shall appear,
Blest be the Nobles of thy Noble Land,
230 With (ventur'd lives) for truths defence that stand,
Blest be thy Commons, who for Common good,
And thine infringed Lawes have boldly stood.
Blest be thy Counties which do aid thee still
With hearts and states, to testifie their will.
235 Blest be thy Preachers, who do chear thee on,
O cry: the sword of God, and *Gideon*:
And shall I not on those with *Mero's* curse,
That help thee not with prayers, arms, and purse,
And for my self, let miseries abound,
240 If mindlesse of thy state I e'r be found.
These are the dayes, the Churches foes to crush,
To root out Prelates, head, tail, branch, and rush.
Let's bring *Baals* vestments out, to make a fire,
Their Myters, Surplices, and all their tire,
245 Copes, Rochets, Crossiers, and such trash,
And let their names consume, but let the flash
Light Christendome, and all the world to see,
We hate *Romes* Whore, with all her trumperie...

From *The Tenth Muse* (1650), 186-188. Although this poem appears after 'The Foure Monarchies' in *The Tenth Muse*, Stanford places the date of completion of 'A Dialogue' at 1642-1643, before 'The Foure Monarchies' (Stanford, 1974, 126). Bradstreet's account of the 'deluge of new woes' follows a 127-line history of English troubles beginning with the invasions of the Saxons. The poem continues in fifty-eight more lines, praising the third Earl of Essex, Commander of the Parliamentary Army from 1642 to 1645, and celebrating the fall of 'High Commissions... Pursevants and Catchpoles'.

171 One saith its / One said, it's 1678   172 My better part in Court of Parliament, /
'Tis said, my better part in Parliament 1678   176 comes / came 1678
200 cause / strife 1678   203 Who knows, the worst, the best may overthrow;/
Who knows, but this may be my overthrow. 1678   204-205 [deleted] 1678
208 ravisht virgins / weeping Virgins 1678
216 relief now use thy utmost skill, / relief, do what there lyes in thee, 1678
217 me good, for all my ill. / that good I've done to thee. 1678
221 I once your / and I your 1678   223 pity much, but should do wrong, /
pity, but soon hope to see, 1678
224 To weep for that we both have pray'd for long, / Out of your troubles much good
fruit to be; 1678
225 these / those 1678   226 That Right may have its right, though't be with blood;
/ Though now beclouded all with tears and blood: 1678
233 which do / who did 1678

Title *present troubles*: with the outbreak of civil war, the migration of Puritans to New England was halted. Thomas Shepard and John Allin's *Defense of the Answer* (London, 1648) pleaded that the American Puritans were not 'rash, weak-spirited, inconsiderate of what they left behinde', but instead that they were moved by 'bowells of compassion [for] our deare Countrey... heart-breaking affections, [for] our deare relations and Christian friends' (Miller and Johnson, 121). The General Court of the Massachusetts Bay Colony instituted days of public prayer and fasting for the Commonwealth cause.

172 *Court of Parliament*: after Charles's dissolution of the Parliaments of 1625 and 1626, both Houses of Parliament reassembled for three weeks in April 1640 and again on 3 November 1640 for the Long Parliament which would continue until the Restoration (1660).

178 *Old customes, new Prerogatives*: among the immediate causes of the Civil War was the King's abuse of royal prerogative; in 1637, hard pressed to finance the war on the Continent, Charles devised a new tax on land and property, known as 'ship-money' which was bitterly resented.

180 *their prudence*: Parliament's wisdom is contrasted with Charles's unfortunate choice of counsellors (181-182); cf. Diana Primrose (see pp.83ff.), 'The third Pearle. Prudence' on Queen Elizabeth:

> Her choice of Famous Councellors did show,
> That *Shee* did all the Rules of Prudence know:
> For though her Wit and Spirit were divine; . . .
> Counsels (*Shee* knew) were best, where more combine: (*A Chaine of Pearle*, 5)

181 *Strafford*: Thomas Wentworth, first Earl of Strafford (1593-1641), impeached and executed in 1641.

182 *Laud*: a punning reference to William Laud, Archbishop of Canterbury (1573-1645), impeached in 1640, beheaded in 1645.

183 *Metropolitane*: principal bishop

184 *an Act*: a reference to the 'Root and Branch Petition', presented by the citizens of London to the House of Commons on 11

December 1640 with 15,000 signatures. The petition called for the abolition of episcopal church rule in order that 'the government according to God's Word may be rightly placed among us' (Hughes, 69).

188 *the Militia*: in March 1642 Parliament passed the Militia Ordinance which would have put Lords Lieutenant sympathetic to Parliament in charge of county militias.

190 *at York*: Charles went to Yorkshire in March 1642 to gather support for an attack on Hull, one of the chief trading centres of the Puritans.

192 Among the documents of the propaganda war which preceded the first military action was the *Grand Remonstrance*, a 204-paragraph list of grievances against the King, debated in Parliament during the autumn of 1641. Its publication in December opened the way for a stream of petitions from all parts of the country protesting Catholic influence on the King.

209 The 'Root and Branch Petition' of 1640 took particular notice of the wrongs suffered by 'clothiers, merchants and others', but also noted that 'the whole land is much impoverished'. By 1642 there were riots over Parliament's enclosure acts in many counties, including Bradstreet's own Lincolnshire. In London on 31 January 'the poor artificers... presented a petition to Parliament calling simply for bread; next day their wives picketed the Commons, pleading that their children were starving' (Lockyer, 141).

210 *The seed time's come*: E. W. White claims that this line is evidence that the 'Dialogue' was composed early in 1643 (164).

211 *inn*: to harvest or gather

236 *the sword of God, and Gideon*: Judges 5:23

237 *Mero's curse*: Meroz was the town cursed for failing to join the Israelites' battle against Sisera.

242 *head, tail, branch, and rush*: cf. the 'Root and Branch Petition' (Hughes, 69).

243 *Baal's vestments*: see Bradstreet, 'Semiramis' note to l.119 (p.128). The Puritans extended the analogy of the Church of Rome as the whore of Babylon to the Church of England hierarchy.

244-245 *Myters... Crossiers*: the headgear and staves of bishops and archbishops.

Before the Birth of one of her Children.

All things within this fading world hath end,
Adversity doth still our joyes attend;
No tyes so strong no friends so clear and sweet,
But with deaths parting blow is sure to meet.
5 The sentence past is most irrevocable,
A common thing, yet oh inevitable;

How soon, my Dear death may my steps attend,
How soon't may be thy Lot to lose thy friend,
We both are ignorant, yet love bids me
10 These farewell lines to recommend to thee,
That when that knots untyd that made us one,
I may seem thine, who in effect am none.
And if I see not half my dayes that's due,
What nature would, God grant to yours and you;
15 The many faults that well you know I have,
Let be interr'd in my oblivious grave;
If any worth or virtue were in me,
Let that live freshly in thy memory
And when thou feel'st no grief, as I no harms,
20 Yet love thy dead, who long lay in thine arms:
And when thy loss shall be repaid with gains
Look to my little babes my dear remains.
And if thou love thy self, or loved'st me
These O protect from step Dames injury.
25 And if chance to thine eyes shall bring this verse,
With some sad sighs honour my absent Herse;
And kiss this paper for thy loves dear sake,
Who with salt tears this last Farewel did take.

A.B.

From *Several Poems* (1678), 239. This poem, along with twelve other personal lyrics, appears under the heading, 'Several other Poems made by the Author upon Diverse Occasions, were found among her Papers after her Death, which she never meant should come to publick view; amongst which, these following (at the desire of some friends that knew her well) are here inserted' (237).

Title *Before the Birth*: cf. Elizabeth Joceline's dedication of *The Mothers Legacie To her unborne Childe* (1624) to her 'Truly loving, and most dearly loved Husband':

But I know thou wondrest by this time what the cause should be that we two continually unclasping our hearts one to the other, I should reserve this to writing. When thou thinkest thus, deare, remember how grievous it was to thee but to heare me say, I may die, and you wilt confesse this would have been an unpleasant discourse to thee, & thou knowest I never durst displease thee willingly, so much I love thee. All I now desire is, that the unexpectednes of it make it not more grievous to thee... Thus humbly desiring God to give thee all comfort in this life, and happinesse in the life to come, I leave thee and thine to his most gracious protection. (B-Bᵛ; [B9-B10]; [B11-B11ᵛ])

For other poems in which an author imagines her own death, see Damaris Masham, 'When deaths cold hand shall close my eyes', (p.318) and 'Eliza', 'To my Husband', (p.144).

13 *half my dayes that's due*: see Psalm 90:10 (Geneva Bible): 'The time of our life is threescore years and ten, and if they be of strength four score years: yet their strength is but labour and sorrow: for it is cut off quickly, and we flee away.' The last of Bradstreet's children, John, was born when she was about forty.

16 *oblivious*: an errata leaf that survives only in the Prince copy (Boston Public Library) of *Several Poems* corrects the 'oblivions' of the printed text to 'oblivious' (E.W. White, 200).

24 *step Dames injury*: Alice Thornton expressed a similar concern for the welfare of her children should her husband remarry:

> I was the most conserned for my poore children, who might peradventure want some helps from their weake mother, and haveing noe relation or friend of my owne that might take caire of them, if theire father should see cause to marry againe, according as I had bin tould that it would be necessary for him for his health. I was indeed the more solicitous for my three young children, casting in my mind what friend of my owne to desire to intrust with theire education, if he did soe. (*Autobiography*, 145)

as did Mrs Margaret Godolphin:

> Pray, my deare, be kind to that poore Child I leave behind, for my sake, who lov's you soe well; butt I need not bidd you, I know you will be soe. If you should think fitt to marry againe, I humbly begg that little fortune I brought, may be first settled upon my Child, and that as long as any of your Sisters live, you will lett it (if they permitt) live with them, for it may be, tho' you will love itt, my successor will not be soe fond of itt, as they I am sure will be. (Evelyn, *Life of Mrs. Godolphin*, 156)

To my Dear and loving Husband.

    If ever two were one, then surely we.
    If ever man were lov'd by wife, then thee;
    If ever wife was happy in a man,
    Compare with me ye women if you can.
5   I prize thy love more then whole Mines of gold,
    Or all the riches that the East doth hold.
    My love is such that Rivers cannot quench,
    Nor ought but love from thee, give recompence.
    Thy love is such I can no way repay,
10   The heavens reward thee manifold I pray.
    Then while we live, in love lets so persever,
    That when we live no more, we may live ever.

From *Several Poems* (1678), 240.

1 *If ever*: Bradstreet's use of the device of anaphora harks back to Tudor poetry; cf. Joshua Sylvester, 'An Epitaph, on ever-blessed Queene Elizabeth' in his translation of Du Bartas (Grosart, 1880, II, 339).

ANNE BRADSTREET

A Letter to her Husband, absent upon
Publick employment.

My head, my heart, mine Eyes, my life, nay more,
My joy, my Magazine of earthly store,
If two be one, as surely thou and I,
How stayest thou there, whilst I at *Ipswich* lye?
5 So many steps, head from the heart to sever
If but a neck, soon should we be together:
I like the earth this season, mourn in black,
My Sun is gone so far in's Zodiack,
Whom whilst I 'joy'd, nor storms, nor frosts I felt,
10 His warmth such frigid colds did cause to melt.
My chilled limbs now nummed lye forlorn;
Return, return sweet *Sol* from *Capricorn*;
In this dead time, alas, what can I more
Then view those fruits which through thy heat I
                                         bore?
15 Which sweet contentment yield me for a space,
True living Pictures of their Fathers face.
O strange effect! now thou art *Southward* gone,
I weary grow, the tedious day so long;
But when thou *Northward* to me shalt return,
20 I wish my Sun may never set, but burn
Within the Cancer of my glowing breast,
The welcome house of him my dearest guest.
Where ever, ever stay, and go not thence,
Till natures sad decree shall call thee hence;
25 Flesh of thy flesh, bone of thy bone,
I here, thou there, yet both but one.

                                      A.B.

From *Several Poems* (1678), 240-241.
Title *Publick Employment*: Simon was a member of the General Court
in Boston which was trying to combine the individual colonies of
Massachusetts Bay, Plymouth, Connecticut and New Haven as the
United Colonies of New England.
4 *I at Ipswich lye*: the Bradstreets in 1635 or 1636 followed the
Dudleys from Newtown (Cambridge) to Agawam, or Ipswich, about
forty miles north of Boston, then the most remote plantation in the
Bay Colony. In 1646 the Bradstreets moved fifteen miles inland to
Quichíchuick, or Andover, where John Woodbridge was pastor of
the church.

8 *my Sun is gone:* see Sylvester's note on Du Bartas... 'The sun is in Heaven as the heart in man's body' (Grosart, 1880, I, 56).

12 *Sol from Capricorn*: the sun, or Sol, is in the house of Capricorn in December and January. Sylvester says, 'Capricornus in mid-Decmber beginneth winter' (Grosart, 1880, I, 54).

14 *those fruits*: when Anne and Simon lived at Ipswich there were five children in the household: Samuel (b. 1633), Dorothy (b. 1635 or 1636), Sarah (b. 1638), Simon (b. 1640), and Hannah (b. 1652). Mercy (b. 1646), Dudley (b. 1648) and John (b. 1652) were born at Andover.

17 *Southward*: towards Boston

21 *Cancer*: beginning with Capricorn, the fourth ascending zodiacal sign, and the first sign of summer. In Bradstreet's 'The four Seasons of the Yeare', Summer speaks:

> Bright *June, July,* and *August,* hot are mine,
> I'th' first, *Sol* doth in crabed *Cancer* shine.
> His progresse to the North; now's fully done,
> And retrograde, now is my burning Sun. (*The Tenth Muse*, ll.95-98)

25 *Flesh of thy flesh, bone of thy bone*: Genesis 2:23

On my dear Grand-child Simon Bradstreet, Who dyed on 16. Novemb. 1669. being but a moneth, and one day old.

No sooner come, but gone, and fal'n asleep,
Acquaintance short, yet parting caus'd us weep,
Three flours, two scarcely blown, the last i'th bud,
Cropt by th'Almighties hand; yet is he good,
5 With dreadful awe before him let's be mute,
Such was his will, but why, let's not dispute,
With humble hearts and mouths put in the dust,
Let's say he's merciful, as well as just.
He will return, and make up all our losses,
10 And smile again, after our bitter crosses.
Go pretty babe go rest with Sisters twain
Among the blest in endless joyes remain.

A.B.

From *Several Poems* (1678), 250.

Title *On my dear Grand-child Simon Bradstreet*: the son of Samuel, Anne's oldest child (1633-1682), and his wife Mercy Tyng (see below). Samuel's departure for England to study medicine in 1657 and his safe return in 1661 occasioned two poems included in the book óf meditations Anne dedicated to her second son, Simon, in 1664 (Andover Manuscript Book; first published in Ellis, 1867).

While Samuel practised medicine in Boston, Mercy and her children probably lived with Anne at Andover (E.W. White, 349).
3 *Three flours*: of the five children of Samuel and Mercy Bradstreet, only one, Mercy, survived infancy; *the last i'th bud*: cf. 'In memory of... Elizabeth Bradstreet':

> But plants new set to be eradicate,
> And buds new blown, to have so short a date,
> Is by his hand alone that guides nature and fate. (*Several Poems*, ll.12-14)

Bradstreet also composed an elegy on the death of a granddaughter, her namesake, who died at the age of three.
4-10 Cf. Mary Carey, 'Upon ye Sight of my abortive Birth', verses 27-43 (see p.160).

To the memory of my dear Daughter in Law, Mrs. Mercy Bradstreet, who deceased Sept. 6. 1669. in the 28. year of her Age.

And live I still to see Relations gone,
And yet survive to sound this wailing tone;
Ah, woe is me, to write thy Funeral Song,
Who might in reason yet have lived long,
5   I saw the branches lopt the Tree now fall,
I stood so nigh, it crusht me down withal;
My bruised heart lies sobbing at the Root,
That thou dear Son has lost both Tree and fruit:
Thou then on Seas sailing to forreign Coast;
10   Was ignorant what riches thou hadst lost.
But ah too soon those heavy tydings fly,
To strike thee with amazing misery;
Oh how I simpathize with thy sad heart,
And in thy griefs still bear a second part:
15   I lost a daughter dear, but thou a wife,
Who lov'd thee more (it seem'd) then her own life.
Thou being gone, she longer could not be,
Because her Soul she'd sent along with thee.
One week she only past in pain and woe,
20   And then her sorrows all at once did go;
A Babe she left before, she soar'd above,
The fifth and last pledge of her dying love,
E're nature would, it hither did arrive,
No wonder it no longer did survive.
25   So with her Children four, she's now at rest,
All freed from grief (I trust) among the blest;

She one hath left, a joy to thee and me,
The Heavens vouchsafe she may so ever be.
Chear up (dear Son) thy fainting bleeding heart,
30   In him alone, that caused all this smart;
What though, thy strokes full sad & grievous be,
He knows it is the best for thee and me.

A.B.

From *Several Poems* (1678), 250-251.

Title *Sept. 6, 1669*: the date is obviously a misprint. An entry in the diary of Anne's son Simon for September 1670 reads, 'My B^r Samuel Bradstreet his wife dyed, wch was a soar affliction to him, and all his friends' (Ellis, 407). On 3 September 1670, Mercy had given birth to a daughter, a second 'Anne', who died soon after her mother.

5 *the branches lopt*: cf. Job 14: 7-9, which begins 'For there is hope of a tre, if it be cut downe, that it wil yet sproute, and the branches thereof wil not cease...' Bradstreet's poem does not become hopeful until line 26.

9 *forreign Coast*: Samuel was going to Jamaica where he eventually settled and remarried; he died in 1682, leaving the three children of his second marriage to the charge of his father.

27 *she one hath left*: Mercy Bradstreet, born 20 November 1667, who remained behind with Anne and Simon Bradstreet in Andover. Governor Bradstreet's will, signed 20 February 1688, calls her one 'whom I have been forced to educate and maintain at considerable charge ever since September 1670' (Ellis, 408). Mercy married Dr James Oliver and was an ancestor of Oliver Wendell Holmes and Wendell Phillips.

'ELIZA'

During the Interregnum the Puritan emphasis upon personal testimony of the action of grace often acted as an encouragement to women who wished to publish. The author of *Eliza's Babes: or The Virgins-Offering* (London, 1652) was one of the few to take advantage of the situation who chose to write in verse. Her book was issued, she says, because 'my desires were not given me, to be kept in private to my self, but for the good of others' (Sig. A2).

Although *Eliza's Babes* is a spiritual autobiography 'Eliza' remains anonymous throughout her poems and prose meditations. She is described on the title-page as 'a Lady, who onely desires to advance the glory of God, and not her own'. Her book is dedicated simply 'To my Sisters', and poems are addressed to individual sisters only by initials as 'S.G.' (9) and 'S.S.' (27). Three poems refer to a 'Brother' who was ill and who died. Like other religious women poets of the century (e.g. Elizabeth Major and Elizabeth Tipper; see pp.183 and 422), 'Eliza' claims to have a secret sin in her past. A 'Mr. C.' (47) was evidently her spiritual adviser.

Throughout her book, 'Eliza' writes as the bride of Christ: in 'The Bride' (31) she says,

> Sith you me ask, why borne was I?
> I'le tell you; twas to heaven to fly,
> Not here to live a slavish life,
> By being to the world a wife.

She contrasts the lot of an earthly spouse with that of the heavenly one; in the prose meditation 'My Contract' (67) she announces, 'When I consider any creature, I can finde in it little to be belov'd, but a great deal of inconvenience with it to be dislik't,' concluding,

> I being wedded to Heavens King
> As his blest Spouse must his praise sing.

The biblical justification for 'Eliza's' rejection of carnal marriage is to be found in Isaiah 54 which begins 'Sing, O barren, thou that didst not bear, break forth into singing and cry aloud, thou that didst not travail with child: for more are the children of the desolate than the children of the married wife, saith the Lord' (Authorised version).

'Eliza' retains the title's imagery of virgin birth in her address 'To the Reader' and in her poems; she is not ashamed of her offspring for, she says, 'before I knew it, the Prince of eternall glory had affianced mee to himselfe... (Sig. A2) my Babes... were obtained by vertue, borne with ease and pleasure' (Sig. A3-A3ᵛ). Within a few years of the publication of *Eliza's Babes* at least two other religious women poets would adopt the metaphor of literary babies to excuse their pride in their work: An Collins writes of 'the offspring of my mind' (see p.148, 78 ff.); Elizabeth Major (see p.183), in her address to the 'Courteous Reader', says: 'For though I was not ambitious of a beautiful babe, yet I confess I would gladly have had it appear comely'. Margaret Cavendish Duchess of Newcastle (see p.163) who like all these women did not bear a child of flesh and bloud, also presented her poems as her children.

The Dart

Shoot from above
Thou God of Love,
And with heavn's dart
Wound my blest heart.

5   Descend sweet life,
And end this strife:
Earth would me stay,
But I'le away.

I'le dye for love
10   Of thee above,
Then should I bee
Made one with thee.

And let be sed
Eliza's dead,
15   And of love dy'd,
That love defi'd.

By a bright beam, shot from above,
She did ascend to her great Love,
And was content of love to dye,
20   Shot with a dart of Heavens bright eye.

From *Eliza's Babes: or the Virgins-Offering. Being Divine Poems, and Meditations. Written by a Lady, who onely desires to advance the glory of God, qnd not her own.* London: Printed by M.S. for Laurence Blaiklock, and are to be sold at his Shop neer the Middle-Temple Gate, 1652, 22.

3 *heavn's dart*: 'Eliza' uses the well-worn imagery of Cupid or Eros, the god of Love, but transfers it to the Christian God of love. The same switch can be seen in the emblem books of the period. Francis Quarles's *Emblemes* appeared for the first time in 1635 and found immediate popularity among those who could 'see the allusion to our blessed Saviour figured in these types' (*Emblemes*, 1643, Sig. A3); most of the emblems illustrated by the engravings were earlier images adapted to their new purpose. Quarles's poetic meditation for Isaiah 10:3 begins:

> Is this that jolly God, whose Cyprian bowe
> Has shot so many flaming darts,
> And made so many wounded Beauties go
> Sadly perplext with whimp'ring hearts? (97)

Other poets, both Catholic and Protestant, were influenced by what Barbara Lewalski (1979, 193) calls 'the school of the heart, in which a heart figure is represented undergoing progressive purgation from sin and spiritual renovation'. Richard Crashaw's 'Hymn to St. Teresa' also speaks of God's Dart,

> thrice dip't in that rich flame
> Which writes thy spouse's radiant Name
> Upon the roof of Heav'n. (81-83)

John Saltmarsh in 'A Meditation upon the Song of Songs, or, a request to Solomon', *Poemata Sacra* (1636), spells it out:

> There is a *Cupid* more divine I finde
> Then that same wanton wandring boy that's blinde:
> I see there's arrows too, but yet I spie
> That they are pointed with more sanctitie: (23-26)

To the Queen of Bohemiah.

Long since, it was by me desir'd,
To see that Queen so much admir'd;
But well I knew, t'was not for mee,
Great Princesses to goe to see.
5   But thraldomes key, did let me out,
And trouble brought my wish about,
By thraldome then I freedome gain'd,
By trouble my desire obtain'd.
I then did see her so admir'd,
10   And thy rich graces Lord inspir'd.
A minde so great and bravely beare,
What in the most breeds care and feare.
A spirit high so humble bee,
To deigne her sweet regards to me.

15   Her I admire, and for her pray
     On earth she may live many a day:
     And when this earth she shall forsake,
     That into heaven, thou wouldst her take,
     Where on a Throne she may be Crown'd,
20   And with bright Angels compast round.

From *Eliza's Babes*, 23-24.
This poem follows 'To the King. Writ 1644' but is probably of a later date. In 1649, after the end of the Thirty Years' War, Elizabeth, Queen of Bohemia (see p.39), was making plans to return to England when her brother King Charles was executed. The widowed queen then broke all contact with her old Puritan friends in Parliament and vowed never to return home again, though she did in 1662.
5 *thraldomes ke*y: perhaps 'Eliza' was among those who fled to Holland to escape persecution, and so saw Elizabeth. A poem addressed to 'Generall Cromwell' (54) calls him 'the rod that scourgeth me' and begs him to deal with lawyers who separate people from their rightful possessions, implying that, despite her Calvinist sentiments, 'Eliza' may have come from a dispossessed Royalist family. 'Eliza's' intolerance of Catholicism ('the contrary religion', 74) makes it improbable that she was one of those who accompanied Henrietta Maria to The Hague in 1642.
9 *so admir'd*: cf. 'To the Queene of Bohemia' (BL Harl. MS 3910, 121-122):

> O what a poore thing 't is to be a Queene,
> When scepters, state, Attendants are the screene
> Betwixt us and the people!
>   ...but that face
> Whose native beauty needs not dresse or lace
> To serve it forth, and being stript of all
> Is self-sufficient to bee the thrall
> Of thousand harts, that face doth figure thee
> And show thy undivided Majestye;

13-14 Cf. Philips, 'On the Death of the Queen of Bohemia' 40 (see p.199).

To my Husband

    When from the world, I shall be tane,
    And from earths necessary paine,
    Then let no blacks be worne for me,
    Not in a Ring my dear by thee.
5   But this bright Diamond, let it be
    Worn in rememberance of me.

And when it sparkles in your eye,
Think 'tis my shadow passeth by.
For why, more bright you shall me see,
10   Then that or any Gem can bee.
Dress not the house with sable weed,
As if there were some dismal deed
Acted to be when I am gone,
There is no cause for me to mourn.
15   And let no badge of Herald be
The sign of my Antiquity.
It was my glory I did spring
From heavens eternall powerful King:
To his bright Palace heir am I.
20   It is his promise, hee'l not lye.
By my dear Brother pray lay me,
It was a promise made by thee,
And now I must bid thee adieu,
For I'me a parting now from you.

From *Eliza's Babes*, 46-47.
This poem could be a set piece but it seems that, despite her low opinion of earthly marriage and cohabitation, 'Eliza' was married.
3 *Then let no blacks be worne for me*: Luke 23:28, 'But Jesus turning unto them said Daughters of Jerusalem, weep not for me...'; cf. Anne Bradstreet, 'Before the Birth of one of her Children', 26 (see p.135).
4 *Ring*: mourning ring
15 *badge of herald*: coat of arms
20-23 Cf. ll.3-4 of 'Upon the losse of my Brother' (38): 'My love must not divided be, / 'Twixt Earth and Heaven, thou'lt have me see.'

To a Friend for her Naked Breasts

Madam I praise you, 'cause you'r free,
And you doe not conceal from me
What hidden in your heart doth lye,
If I can through your breasts spy.

5   Some Ladies will not show their breasts,
For feare men think they are undrest,
Or by't their hearts they should discover,
They do't to tempt some wanton Lover.

They are afraid tempters to be,
10   Because a Curse impos'd they see,
Upon the tempter that was first,
By an all-seeing God that's just.

But though I praise you have a care
Of that al-seeing eye, and feare,
15   Lest he through your bare breasts see sin,
And punish you for what's within.

From *Eliza's Babes*, 56.
10 *a Curse*: in Genesis 3, after the temptation and fall, God cursed
the serpent; Adam and Eve expelled from the Garden, made 'coats
of skins' to hide their nakedness.
13 'Eliza's' ironic praise may refer indirectly to the kind of
devotional poetry that uses sex as a metaphor for communion with
God, e.g. Francis Quarles's 'Bridegroom's Sonet' XII, Verse 5
where the conceits aligning divine love and sexual love become so
contorted they have to be annotated in order to avoid appearing
'loose and lascivious' to the 'wanton Reader':

> The dear-bought fruit of that forbidden Tree,
> Was not so daintie as thy Apples bee,
> These curious Apples of thy snowy *breasts
> Wherein a Paradise of pleasure rests;
> They breathe such life into the ravisht Eye
> That the inflam'd Beholder, cannot die. (36-41)

In this case, the '*breasts' are identified in a note as 'The Old and
New Testaments' (*Sions Sonnets*, 1625).

The Lover

Come let us now to each discover,
Who is our friend, and who our Lover,
What? art thou now asham'd of thine,
I tell thee true, Ime not of mine.

5   And you will say when you him see,
That none but he, desir'd can bee,
He is the onely pleasing wight,
Whose presence can content my sight.

For He's the purest red and white,
10   In whom my soule takes her delight:
He to the flowrs their beauty gives,
In him the Rose and Lilly lives,

146

'ELIZA'

His pleasant haire with seemly grace,
Hangs by his faire sweet lovely face,
15 And from his pleasing eyes do dart
Their arrows which do pierce my heart.

These beauties all are richly grac'st,
For on his head, a crown is plac'st,
Of glory, which doth shine so bright,
20 As mortall eye can see this light,

This lovely Lord's, the Prince of Peace,
In him, my joyes will full increase;
For he's the true, and constant friend,
Whose love begun, will never end.

25 From Heaven he came with me to dwell,
And sav'd my soul from direfull hell,
'Tis he alone my heart doth gaine,
That keeps me from eternall pain.

While here I live, here he will bee;
30 Death cannot separate him from me:
And when I dye, he will me place,
Where I shall ever see his face.

Into his glory, hee'l take mee,
This doe I know, this shall you see
35 And now you know my loved friend,
My loves begun, it will not end.

From *Eliza's Babes*, 24-25. 'Eliza's' inspiration is Canticles 5.

AN COLLINS

All we know of An Collins are the stray autobiographical details that can be gleaned from *Divine Songs and Meditacions Composed By An Collins* published in London by R. Bishop in 1653. From 'To the Reader', the 'Preface' and 'The Discourse' we learn that, when she sent her book to the printer, the poet was childless and entering on middle age, having been chronically ill since childhood. Prose meditations included in the volume reiterate the theme of resignation to the will of God in order to overcome mental and physical suffering. Unable to participate in normal female employments she turned first to 'prophane Histories' and then to 'Theological employments' in the form of poetry. From her devotional reading, and her 'Song composed in time of Civill Warr, when the wicked did much insult over the godly' we believe that if not actually a Catholic, she was devoutly anti-Calvinist.

The Preface to *Divine Songs and Meditacions*

Being through weakness to the house confin'd,
My mentall powers seeming long to sleep,
Were summond up, by want of wakeing mind
Their wonted course of exercise to keep,
5 And not to waste themselves in slumber deep;
Though no work can bee so from error kept
But some against it boldly will except:

Yet sith it was my morning exercise
The fruit of intellectuals to vent,
10 In Songs or counterfets of Poesies,
And haveing therein found no small content,
To keep that course my thoughts are therefore bent
And rather former works to vindicate
Than any new concepcion to relate...

Now touching that I hasten to expresse
Concerning these, the offspring of my mind,

148

80 Who though they here appeare in homly dresse
   And as they are my works, I do not find
   But ranked with others, they may go behind,
   Yet for theyr matter, I suppose they bee
   Not worthlesse quite, whilst they with Truth agree.

85 Indeed I grant that sounder judgments may
   (Directed by a greater Light) declare
   The ground of Truth more in a Gospel-way,
   But who time past with present will compare
   Shall find more mysteries unfolded are,
90 So that they may who have right informacion
   More plainly shew the path-way to Salvacion.

   Yet this cannot prevayl to hinder me
   From publishing those Truths I do intend,
   As strong perfumes will not concealed be,
95 And who esteemes the favours of a Freind,
   So little, as in silence let them end,
   Nor will I therfore only keep in thought,
   But tell what God still for my Soule hath wrought.

   When Clouds of Melancholy over-cast
100 My heart, sustaining heavinesse therby,
   But long that sad condicion would not last
   For soon the Spring of Light would blessedly
   Send forth a beam, for helps discovery,
   Then dark discomforts would give place to joy,
105 Which not the World could give or quite destroy.

   So sorrow serv'd but as springing raine
   To ripen fruits, indowments of the minde,
   Who thereby did abillitie attaine
   To send forth flowers, of so rare a kinde,
110 Which wither not by force of Sun or Winde:
   Retaining vertue in their operacions,
   Which are the matter of those Meditacions.

   From whence if evill matter be extracted
   Tis only by a spider generacion,
115 Whose natures are of vennom so compacted,
   As that their touch occasions depravacion

149

Though lighting in the fragrantest plantacion:
Let such conceale the evill hence they pluck
And not disgorg themselves of what they sucke.

120 So shall they not the humble sort offend
Who like the Bee, by natures secret act
Convert to sweetnesse, fit for some good end
That which they from small things of worth extract;
Wisely supplying every place that lackt,
125 By helping to discover what was meant
Where they perceive there is a good intent.

So trusting that the only Sov'rain Power
Which in this work alwaies assisted mee,
Will still remain its firme defensive Tower,
130 From spite of enemies the same to free
And make it usefu[l]l in some sort to bee,
That Rock I trust on whom I doe depend,
Will his and all their works for him defend.

From 'The Preface' to *Divine Songs and Meditacions Composed by An Collins.* London: Printed by R. Bishop. Anno Dom. 1653. Rpt. in Stanley N. Stewart, ed., Augustan Reprint Society Publication No. 94, San Marino, California, 1961. Stewart uses Thomas Park's copy now held by the Huntington Library.

The poem is written in rime royal, so named after James I of Scotland had used it in *The Kingis Quair.* The form was not often used in the seventeenth century; examples by contemporaries include Milton's 'On the Morning of Christ's Nativity' and 'The Passion', and *The Penitent Publican*, 1610, by a Thomas Collins whose relationship, if any, to An is unknown. Like many of the religious poets of her time, Collins experiments with a wide variety of verse forms in her book; in her address to the '*Christian Reader*' she states, 'To be breif, I became affected to Poetry, insomuch that I proceeded to practise the same; and though the helps I had therein were small, yet the thing it self appeared unto me so amiable, as that it enflamed my faculties, to put forth themselves, in a practise so pleasing' (Sig. A1).

8 *morning exercise*: Collins appears to be following the 'Short Method for Meditation' outlined by the Catholic Bishop of Geneva, Francis de Sales, in his *Introduction a la vie devote* (1609). Originally written as a guide to virtue for a French Catholic woman, Madame de Charmoisy, the *Introduction to a Devout Life* achieved great popularity in England with three English editions by 1614; James I is said to have 'always carried it on his person' (Lelen, 438). De

Sales's 'Method' includes 'morning exercises' to prepare the heart 'to pray mentally, for it is a thing which few in our age are so happy to be acquainted' (Lelen, 87); cf. Anne Douglas, Countess of Morton, *The Countess of Mortons Daily Exercise* (1666).

9 *intellectual*s: mental powers

87 The suppositious Milton, *A Necessary Representation of the Present Evils and imminent dangers to religion, laws and liberties arising from the late and present practices of the Sectarian Party in England* (1649) condemns 'Such as... invent damnable errors under specious pretence of a gospel way and new light' (Millar, ed., *The Works of Milton. Historical, Political and Miscellaneous*, 1753, 387).

114 *a spider generacion*: cf. the motto to *A Chaine of Pearle* by Diana Primrose, *Dat rosa mel apibus qua sugit aranea virus*, 'The rose gives honey to the bee whereas the spider sucks poison.' The origin of the mistaken notion that spiders use the same nutrients to manufacture poison as bees do to make honey has so far escaped us. The conceit was commonly used at least since 1542 (by Wyatt) to disarm malicious interpretation.

121 *like the Bee*: cf. I. Y. (trans.), *Introduction to the Devoute Life Composed in Frenche by the R. Father in God Francis Sales* (1637): 'The Bee (saith the Philosopher) sucketh honey from hearbes and flowers, without hurting or endamaging them, but leaving them as whole and as freshe, as before she found them: but true devotion doth more then so: for it not onely hurteth no state, vocation, or affaire, but contrary-Wise bettereth and adorneth it' (18).

Another Song

The Winter of my infancy being over-past
When supposed, suddenly the Spring would hast
Which useth everything to cheare
Which invitacion to recreacion
5   This time of yeare,

The Sun sends forth his radient beames to warm the
        ground
The drops distil, between the gleams delights
        abound,
Ver brings her mate the flowery Queen,
The Groves shee dresses, her Art expresses
10   On every Green.

But in my Spring it was not so, but contrary,
For no delightfull flowers grew to please the eye,
No hopefull bud, nor fruitfull bough,

15 No moderat showers which causeth flowers
    To spring and grow.

    My Aprill was exceeding dry, therfore unkind;
    Whence tis that small utility I look to find,
    For when that Aprill is so dry,
    (As hath been spoken) it doth betoken
20 Much scarcity.

    Thus is my Spring now almost past in heavinesse
    The Sky of pleasure's over-cast with sad distresse
    For by a comfortlesse Eclips,
    Disconsolacion and sore vexacion,
25 My blossom nips.

    Yet as a garden is my mind enclosed fast
    Being to safety so confind from storm and blast
    Apt to produce a fruit most rare,
    That is not common with every woman
30 That fruitfull are.

    A Love of goodnesse is the cheifest plant therin
    The second is, (for to be briefe) Dislike to sin.
    These grow in spight of misery,
    Which Grace doth nourish and ease to flourish
35 Continually.

    But evill mocions, currupt seeds, fall here also
    When[c]e springs prophanesse as do weeds where
                                        flowers grow
    Which must supplanted be with speed
    These weeds of Error, Distrust and Terror,
40 Lest woe succeed

    So shall they not molest, the plants before exprest
    Which countervails these outward wants, & purchase
                                        rest
    Which more commodious is for me
    Then outward pleasures or earthly treasures
45 Enjoyd would be.

    My little Hopes of wordly gain I fret not at,
    As yet I do this Hope retain; though Spring be lat

Perhaps my Sommer-age may be,
Not prejudiciall, but beneficiall
50 Enough for me.

Admit the worst it be not so, but stormy too,
Ile learn my selfe to undergo more than I doe
And still content my self with this
Sweet Meditacion and Contemplacion
55 Of heavenly blis,

Which for the Saints reserved is who persevere
In Piety and Holynesse, and godly Feare,
The pleasures of which blis divine
Neither Logician nor Rhetorician
(Last line missing from copy text).

From *Divine Songs and Meditacions*, 56-58. This song follows 'A Song shewing the Mercies of God to his people...' (33-35), and 'Another Song exciting to spiritual Mirth' (50-52) with similar opening lines. The Biblical source for the lines may be Canticles 2, but there are recurring echoes of Spenser's *Shepheards Calender* (1579) throughout the poem, indicating that his works were perhaps among those 'prophane Histories' of An Collins's youth. Imitations of the psalms were often carried out in complex song forms, in this case a variant on a ballad form, each stanza consisting of two rhymed lines of six iambs, a line of four iambs, a line of four dactyls internally rhyming, and a line of two iambs rhyming with the last but one; we have found no other example of the form.
1-2 Cf. Sidney, *Astrophil and Stella*, 67, 7-8: 'Gone is the winter of my miserie, / My spring appeares, O see what here doth grow.'
8 *Ver*: spring; *her mate the flowery Queen*: Flora
11 An Collins's contrast of the 'springtime of youth' and the springtime of spirit is a traditional device of the meditative poets (Stewart, 1966, 106-108); cf. Elizabeth Major (see p.184).
16 *My Aprill was exceeding dry*: this may be a reference to sinfulness or a lack of good works leading to withholding of grace, often expressed as rain, as in line 34.
26 *as a garden is my mind enclosed*: Canticles 4:12: 'A garden inclosed is my sister, my spouse; a spring shut up, a fountaine sealed' (Authorised version). According to contemporary Catholic and Protestant exegesis the figure of the enclosed garden represented the Church, also symbolized as 'the Spouse'; the spouse analogy is also extended to the individual soul, especially in the religious verse of women. Luis de la Puente (*Meditations upon the Mysteries of our Holie Faith*, St. Omers, 1619) wrote that Solomon

twice calleth her [the Spouse] an inclosed garden, for that shee was perfectly chaste both in soule, and in body, confirming it with a perpetuall vowe, which served as a locke for her greater security; adding for gardes, humility, modesty, silence, and abstinence, by reason whereof hee also calleth her a garden: to give us to understand, that her virginity was not barren, but accompanied with many flowers of vertues. (Stewart, 1966, 37)

The garden emblems of George Wither's *A Collection of Emblemes, Ancient and Moderne...* London, 1635, may have influenced Collins's imagery as they did that of George Herbert in 'Grace' and 'Vanitie' (*The Temple*, 1633) and Henry Vaughan in 'The Showre' (*Silex Scintillans*, 1655).

28 The 'Glosse' for the December emblem in the *Shepheardes Calender* reads, 'The meaning wherof is that all thinges perish and come to theyr last end, but workes of learned wits and monuments of Poetry abide for ever'.

31 Collins's belief in the innate attraction of the soul to goodness places her squarely in opposition to the Calvinists; her view is rather that of Vives, in likening the Christian virgin to Christ's spouse, in *The Instruction of a Christian Woman* (tr. Richard Hyrde, 1540).

36 *currupt seeds*: cf. *Instruction of a Christian Woman*:

Stoic philosophers say there be certain fires or seeds bred by nature in us of the same justice which the first father of mankind was made by almighty God;... Fathers and mothers, nurses, schoolmasters,... common people, all these do what they can to pluck up those seeds of virtue by the roots, and to over-whelm that little fire as soon as it beginneth to appear. (Watson, 128)

60 The last line is missing from the copy text. 'Can e'er define' completes the sense.

MARY CAREY

Mary Carey, the author of 'my Lady Carey's Meditation, & Poetry' was the daughter of Sir John Jackson of Berwick. She married Pelham Carey, son of Henry, fourth Lord Hunsdon, who was knighted in 1633 (*N&Q*, third series, VII, 203-206). Carey says in typically laconic fashion, 'I had good husbands, the last is so, & good it was for me that I was wife to the first' who came of a 'frivolous set'. In her 'Meditation' Carey regrets her early life, when she spent her time 'in Carding, Dice, Dancing, Masquing, Dressing, vaine Companye, going to Plays, following Fashions, & yᵉ like' (Autograph, 15).

Her second husband, George Payler, was paymaster of the Parliamentary forces in garrison at Berwick where in 1642, according to the 'certificate of Sir Michael Eames... he often procured money on his own credit, whereby he hath given good satisfaction to his soldiers, who were otherwise likely to mutiny; and he hath frequently, at his own cost, made journeys to London to solicit the Parliament for money to pay the soldiers' (HMC, *Fifth Report*, 40). In August of 1646 Payler was in London writing to the guild of Berwick about Parliamentary concessions he had gained for the town (HMC, *Various Collections*, I, 15). He may be the George Payler, naval commissioner from 1654-1660, mentioned in Pepys's diary (Latham and Matthews, 3, 197; 11, 206).

Their marriage took place at least a year before Mary (who never used her second husband's name) wrote to her uncle by her first marriage, Sir Thomas Pelham, on 4 July 1644; the letter (BL Add. MS 33,084, f.51) refers to a recent confinement which evidently took place at her parents' house in Berwick, for it purports to be sent from 'Bar:' or Barwick in Mary's spelling. She often praises her loving parents in her 'Meditation' and tells her uncle that they are so tender of her that it is a 'torment' to mention parting from them. She concludes by presenting her humble service to her uncle and his lady and 'your little servant my sonne also'. It was common for the nobility to send their children to be brought up as pages in the houses of their more affluent or powerful relatives, but it seems unlikely that the child referred to can have been a Payler; he may have been the child of her first marriage, or a godchild.

In a 'Meditation' written when she was forty-five, Mary Carey says: 'I have liv'd in Barwick; London; Kent; Hunsden; Edenbroughe; Thistleworth; Hackney; Tottrige; Grenwicke; Bednell-grene; Claphame; York; Mountaine; James's; Newington; Coven-garden; and deare Katherine's.' The Paylers came from Nun Monkton ('Mountaine') in Yorkshire. Carey's wanderings took her from garrison to garrison with her husband, from whom she was loth to be separated in these 'dividing times'. 'In all thes warres,' she writes, 'I was safe in Garrisons, & was not straitned; nor plundred; nor separated from my deare Relations'. Other women, as her words imply, were not so fortunate.

Of the first marriage, one child survived; of the second, two. Carey writes, 'I want not that desired Mercy of Children; but have now more than ever; One was my greatest number formerly and all my Children were only Children; each Child when it died; was all I had alive: Now great, & tender Mercy gives, & continues me two, a Son, & a Daughter, all my former were sickly, weake, pained, not likely to live; but these have been, & are healthfull, strong, enjoying Ease, hopefull; blessed be God for Bethia and Nathaniel...' (Autograph, 122).

In 1680, 'Dame Mary Cary, alias Payler, late of Nun Monkton' acted as executor of the estates of her husband George and her son Nathaniel, both of whom had pre-deceased her (*N&Q*, third series, VII, 259). It is curious that Mary never assumed the name of Payler; a baronetcy of that name was created in 1642; the title became extinct in 1706 (Burke, *Extinct Baronetcies*, 404). The marriage of a Maria Anna Payler, daughter of Nathaniel Payler of Nun Monkton, to a George Cressner of London who died in 1722 is recorded in the Harleian Society's *Visitation of Essex* (Part II, Appendix, 721).

> Wretten by me att the same tyme; on the death
> of my 4th, & only Child, Robert Payler; – – –
>
> My lord hath called for my sonne
> my hart breth's forth; thy will be done:
>
> my all; that mercy hath made mine
> frely's surendered to be thine:
>
> But if I give my all to the
> lett me not pyne for poverty:
>
> Change wth me; doe, as I have done
> give me thy all; Even thy deare sonne:
>
> Tis Jesus Christ; lord I would have;
> he's thine, mine all; 'tis him I crave:

MARY CAREY

Give him to me; and I'le reply
   Enoughe my lord; now lett me dye.

covengarden, decemb: 8th: 1650
     Mary Carey

From p.149 of Carey's autograph MS book in the possession of the
Meynell family, which begins 'To my Most loving, and dearly
beloved Husband George Payler, Esq., My deare, the occation of my
writing this following dialogue; was my apprehending I should dye
on my fourth child...' The dedication is dated 17 October 1653, the
day on which Mary Carey began putting together her prayers,
poems and meditations in this form. The 'dialogue' is dated 11
February 1649 (old style). (A copy of this little book made by
Charles Hutton in 1681 is in the Bodleian Library, Rawl. MS
D.1308, 'Herein is contained my Lady Carey's Meditation, & Poetry,
from ye first to ye 222th Page...') The confinement Mary Carey
feared produced Robert Payler, who died soon after, leaving the
Paylers once again childless.
Title *att the same tyme*: Mary Carey's poem follows 'Written by my
dear Husband at ye Death of our 4th (at that time) only Child,
Robert Payler':

   1. Dear wife, let's learne to get that Skill,
      Of free Submission to God's holy Will;
   2. He like a Potter is; & we like Clay,
      Shall not ye Potter mould us his own Way?
   3. Sometimes it is his Pleasure that we stand
      With pretty lovely Baby's in our hand:
   4. Then he in wisedome turnes ye Wheel about,
      And drawes ye Posture of those Comforts out;
   5. Into another Forme; either this, or that
      As pleases him; & 'tis no matter what:
   6. If by such Changes, God shall bring us in
      To love Christ Jesus, & to loath our Sin.

Wretten by me at the death of my 4th sonne
   and 5th Child Perigrene Payler:

I thought my all was given before
   but mercy ordred me one more:

A Perigrene; my God me sent
   him back againe I doe present

as a love token; 'mongst my others,
   One Daughter; and hir 4 deare Brothers:

To my Lord Christ; my only bless;
　　is, he is mine; and I am his

My Dearest Lord; hast thou fulfill'd thy will,
　　thy hand maid's pleas'd, Compleatly happy still:

Grovestreat May
12th, 1652:　　　　　　　　　　Mary Carey

From her autograph, 150. On 14 May 1652, the Paylers buried their fifth child, Peregrine. Mary wrote, 'I have now buried fower sonnes & a daughter.　God hath my all of Children; I have his all (belov'd Christ) a sweet change: in greatest sorrowes Content & happy' (Autograph, 153).

Upon ye Sight of my abortive Birth
ye 31th: of December 1657

1. What birth is this; a poore despised creature?
　　A little Embrio; voyd of life, and feature:

2. Seven tymes I went my tyme; when mercy giving
　　deliverance unto me; & mine all living:

3. Stronge, right-proportioned, lovely Girles, & boyes
　　There fathers; Mother's present hope't for Joyes:

4. That was great wisedome, goodnesse, power love
　　　　　　　　　　　　　　　　　　　　　praise
　　to my deare lord; lovely in all his wayes:

5. This is no lesse; ye same God hath it donne;
　　submits my hart, thats better than a sonne:

6. In giveing; taking; stroking; striking still;
　　his Glorie & my good; is. his. my will:

7. In that then; this now; both good God most mild,
　　his will's more deare to me; then any Child:

8. I also joy, that God hath gain'd one more;
　　To Praise him in the heavens; then was before:

9.   And that this babe (as well as all the rest,)
       since 't had a soule, shalbe for ever blest:

10.   That I'm made Instrumentall; to both thes;
       God's praise, babes blesse; it highly doth me please:

11.   May be the Lord lookes for more thankfulnesse,
       and highe esteeme for [of] those I doe posesse:

12.   As limners drawe dead shadds for to sett forth;
       ther lively coullers, & theyr picturs worth;

13.   So doth my God; in this, as all things; wise;
       by my dead formlesse babe; teach me to prise:

14.   My living prety payre; Nat: & Bethia;
       the Childrene deare, (God yett lends to Maria:)   Psal:119.65

15.   Praisd be his name; thes tow's full Compensation:
       For all thats gone; & y^t in Expectation:

16.   And if heere in God hath fulfill'd his Will,
       his hand-maides pleassed, Compleatly happy still:

17.   I only now desire of my sweet God
       the reason why he tooke in hand his rodd?

18.   What he doth spy; what is the thinge amisse   Mica: 6. 9
       I faine would learne; whilst I ye rod do kisse:

19.   Methinkes I heare Gods voyce, this is thy [the] sinne;
       And Conscience justifies ye same within:

20.   Thou often dost present me wth dead frute;
       Why should not my returns, thy presents sute:

21.   Dead dutys; prayers; praises thou dost bring,   Rev. 3. 1.
       affections dead; dead hart in every thinge:

22.   In hearing; reading; Conference; Meditation;
       in acting graces & in Conversation:

23. Whose taught or better'd by ye no Relation;
     thou'rt Cause of Mourning, not of Immitation:

24. Thou doest not answere that great meanes I give;
     my word, and ordinances do teache to live:

25. Lively: o do't, thy mercyes are most sweet;   Psal:25.10.
     Chastisements sharpe; & all ye meanes that's meet: Heb:12.6.

26. Mend now my Child, & lively frute bring me;   Psal:119.71.65.
     so thou advantag'd much by this wilt be;

27. My dearest Lord; thy Charge, & more is true;
     I see't; am humbled, & for pardon sue;   Psal:25.7.11.

28. In Christ forgive; & henceforth I will be   Mat:3.17.
     what, Nothing Lord; but what thou makest mee;   Dan:9.17.   Phil:2.13.

29. I am nought, have nought, can doe nought but sinne;
     as my Experience saith, for I'ave ben in: Rom:7.18.19.24.

30. Severall Condissions, tryalls great and many;
     in all I find my nothingnesse; not any

31. Thing doe I owne but sinne; Christ is my all;   Col:3.11   Heb.7.25.
     that I doe want, can crave; or ever shall: I.John.2.1.2.

32. That good that suteth all my whole desires;
     and for me unto God, all he requires;

33. It is in Christ; he's mine, and I am his;   Cant: 2.16. & 6.3. & 7.10.
     this union is my only happynesse:

34. But lord since I'm a Child by mercy free;
     Lett me by filiall frutes much honnor thee;   John.15.8.

35. I'm a branch of the vine; purge me therfore;   John.15.2.
     father, more frute to bring, then heertofore;

36. A plant in God's house; O that I may be;   Psal: 92.13.14.
     more florishing in age; a grouing tree:

37.   Lett not my hart, (as doth my wombe) miscarrie;
        but precious meanes received, lett it tarie;

38.   Till it be form'd; of Gosple shape,& sute;   Phil.1.27 Col:1.6.1(
        my meanes, my mercyes, & be pleasant frute:

39.   In my whole Life; lively doe thou make me: Isa:4.1.
        for thy praise. And name's sake, O quicken mee;   Psal:143.11.

40.   Lord I begg quikning grace; that grace aford;
        quicken mee lord according to thy word: Psal: 119. 15(

41.   It is a lovely bonne I make to thee.   Psal: 119. 88. 37.
        after thy loving Kindnesse quicken mee: Psal: 119. 159.

42.   Thy quickning Spirit unto me convey;
        and therby Quicken me; in thine owne way: Psal: 119. 37.

43.   And let the Presence of thy spirit deare,
        be wittnessd by his fruts; lett them appeare;

44.   To, & for the; Love; Joy; peace; Gentlenesse;
        longsuffering;   goodnesse;   faith;   &   much
                                                        meeknesse,   Gal

45.   And lett my walking in the Spirit say,
        I live in't; & desire it to Obey: Gal: 5. 25.

46.   And since my hart thou'st lifted up to the;
        amend it Lord; & keepe it still with thee:

Januarie: 12: 1657   Saith Maria Carey
                                        always in Christ happy:

From her autograph, 195-201. Verbal correspondences show that
Carey used the Geneva Bible; its glosses on the texts she cites are the
best indication of the figurative meaning of her poem.
1 *voyd of life, and feature*: cf. Mary Sidney's paraphrase of Psalm 58,
Si Vere Utique, ll.26-30:

> O let them so decay
> As the dishous'd snail doth melt away
> Or as the embryo, which formless yett
> Dyes ere it lives, and cannot get
> Though born to see sun rise or sett. (Waller, 1977, 110)

5 *submits my hart*: the point of poems on child loss was not to complain but to demonstrate acceptance of the will of God, as in the diary entries of Elizabeth Walker, beginning on 12 July 1651 and ending on 1 May 1665, annotated and published by her husband, the vicar of Fyfield in Essex in 1690. Mrs Walker's reaction to the death of her six-year-old daughter, Mary, in 1669, is remarkably like Mary Carey's:

Lord I bless thee that of Eleven, for whom I praise thee, thou hast yet spared me two; I beseech thee, if it may consist with thy good Pleasure, continue them in this World, keeping them from the Evil of it, to a good Old-Age, choice Instruments of thy Glory... (*The Holy Life*, 99-100)

Cf. Bradstreet, 'Before the Birth of one of her Children' (see p.134).
9 The poet believes with other Calvinists that baptism is not necessary for salvation.
10 *blesse*: bliss
12 *as limners draw dead shadds*: as painters make sketches of their work in chalk or pen and ink and wash for the information of prospective clients.
20-24 The speaker in these verses is God, and again in verse 26.
22 Carey lists the principal spiritual exercises of Calvinism.
33 Cf. 'Eliza' (see p. 141) and 'The Lover' (see p. 146).
39 *quicken mee*: Carey asks for actual grace, but the ordinary meaning of the verb 'to quicken' is to conceive.
41 *bonne*: boon
43 *thy spirit deare*: the Holy Ghost

MARGARET CAVENDISH, DUCHESS OF NEWCASTLE

The youngest of eight children, Margaret Lucas was born c.1624 to Sir Thomas Lucas, Earl of Colchester, and Elizabeth, daughter of John Leighton. Her father died in her infancy, and she was brought up by her mother at St John's near Colchester in Essex. Her autobiographical sketch, 'A True Relation of my Birth, Breeding and Life', appended to the first edition of *Natures Pictures drawn by Fancies Pencil to the Life* (1656), describes Margaret's childhood as a happy one. Surrounded by a loving family, she was 'reasoned with' rather than beaten, and encouraged to gratify her taste for 'inventing fashions', reading, and writing.

After the outbreak of the Civil War, Margaret became Maid of Honour to Henrietta Maria. At court, she was 'so bashful' that she was unable to speak and was regarded by the court as 'a natural fool' (Firth, 161) but she remained with Henrietta Maria, accompanying her into exile in Paris in 1644. There, in April 1645, she met William Cavendish, Marquis (later Duke) of Newcastle, a widower at least thirty years her senior and friend of her brother, Lord Lucas; they married later that year. According to the Duchess, her husband chose her for 'such a wife as he might bring to his own humours, and not such a one... that had been tempered to the humours of another'. The Marquis was a poet, playwright and philosopher; he courted Margaret by writing her verse (first published in 1956). As an author in his own time he was best known for his studies of horsemanship. The Duchess made the distinction that theirs was not 'amorous love' but love that was 'honest and honourable' (Firth, 162).

They remained in exile for fifteen years, in Paris, Rotterdam and Antwerp. Because Cavendish was regarded by the Commonwealth as one of the chief delinquents of the Civil War, his estates were sequestered, their lavish furnishings plundered (see p.107). The Cavendishes subsisted by pawning Margaret's jewels and receiving money from the Queen and other friends. When those resources were exhausted, Margaret went to England with William's brother, Charles, to apply for money from the sequestration committee (petition dated 10 December 1651). Margaret was unsuccessful in her suit, but Sir Charles sent some of the money he obtained to his brother.

In England she visited Henry Lawes's house and Hyde Park 'to take the air'; during this visit she claims that 'seldom did I dress myself, as taking no delight to adorn myself, since he I only desired to please was absent, although report did dress me in a hundred several fashions' (Firth, 170). While in England she 'writ a book of poems', which she had published in 1653 as *Poems, and Fancies: Written by the Right Honourable, the Lady Margaret Countesse of Newcastle.* 'They say tis ten times more Extravagant then her dresse,' wrote Dorothy Osborne of the Duchess's book in April, 1653, but begged William Temple, 'for God sake if you meet with it send it mee' (Smith, 1968, 37). After she had seen it, she wrote that 'there are many soberer People in Bedlam' (7 May 1653, Smith, 1968, 41).

In a dedicatory 'Epistle to Mistris Toppe' the Duchess writes:

in this Action of setting out of a Booke, I am not clear without fault, because I have not asked leave of any Freind thereto; for the *feare* of being denied, made me silent: and there is an *Old saying*; That it is easier to aske *Pardon*, then *Leave*.

'Mistris Toppe', formerly Elizabeth Chaplain, was the Duchess's maid and good friend since childhood, who replied to her mistress's dedication with a letter of her own: 'Madam, You are not onely the first *English Poet* of your *Sex*, but the first that ever wrote this way.'

The prefatory material also includes a congratulatory poem by the Duke: '*I* Saw your *Poems,* and then wish'd them mine, / Reading the *Richer Dressings* of each Line.' The Duchess later thanked her husband in a dedication, 'you have always encouraged me in my harmless pastime of Writing' (*Philosophical Letters*, Sig. a1). A note at the end of *Poems, and Fancies* states, 'Reader, I have a little *Tract* of *Philosophicall Fancies* in *Prose*, which will not be long before it appear in the *world*'; her *Philosophicall Fancies* appeared later that year.

The Duchess returned to Antwerp where she and her husband lived lavishly on credit until the Restoration. When the Duke returned to England, Margaret was left behind as a pledge against their debts. After she joined him, they retired from the court in order to piece together the remnants of the Newcastle estate. Though they were able to retrieve some of it, Margaret calculated that their losses came to about £940,000. In 1665 Charles II restored to the Marquis the offices he held before the war and made him Duke of Newcastle.

In retirement at Welbeck Abbey, the Duke replenished his stables with thoroughbreds and Margaret Cavendish continued in her favourite occupation, writing. She produced at an astonishing rate philosophical studies, orations, discourses, letters, poems, plays, and a biography of her husband. Margaret claimed that she never corrected her work, 'for there was more pleasure in making than mending' (Cavendish, *The World's Olio*, Sig. A3ᵛ), yet there are changes in the 1664 edition of her poems that suggest careful authorial revision.

On 26 April 1667 Pepys caught sight of the Duchess

going with her coaches and footmen all in velvet; herself... as I have heard her often described (for all the town-talk is nowadays of her extravagancies) with her velvet-cap, her hair about her ears, many black patches because of pimples about her mouth, naked necked, without anything about it, and a black juste-au-corps; she seemed to me a very comely woman. (Latham and Matthews, VIII, 186-187)

Pepys saw the Duchess ahead of him in her coach again on 10 May, 'with 100 boys and girls running looking upon her' (209). After reading her life of the Duke, he decided that she was 'a mad, conceited ridiculous woman and he an ass to suffer [her] to write what she writes to him and of him' (IX, 123). Apparently the Duke's family found her embarrassing. The Duke's granddaughter wrote the following poem to her mother, the Countess of Bridgewater (see pp.106ff.), seeking approval for her own verse-making:

> Madam I dedicate these lines to you
> To whom, I doe confesse, Volumes are due;
> Hoping your wonted Goodness will excuse
> The errours of an Infant Female Muse.
> Mongst Ladyes let Newcastle weare ye Bayes,
> I onely sue for Pardon, not for Praise.   (HL MS EL 8367)

Not everyone found her ridiculous. Hobbes was one of many contributors of encomiastic poems.

The Duchess of Newcastle died in London, and was buried in Westminster Abbey on 7 January 1674. A monument was erected in the north transept by her husband, who died three years after her. Shortly after her death appeared *Letters and Poems in Honour of the incomparable Princess Margaret, Dutchess of Newcastle* (1676), to which Glanville, Etherege and Shadwell contributed. Her most eloquent epitaph was written by Virginia Woolf 250 years later:

although 'they', those terrible critics who had sneered and jeered at her... continued to mock, few of her critics, after all, had the wit to trouble about the nature of the universe, or cared a straw for the sufferings of the hunted hare, or longed, as she did, to talk to some one 'of Shakespeare's fools'. Now, at any rate, the laugh is not all on their side. (*Collected Essays*, III, 58)

The *Poetresses* hasty Resolution.

Reading my Verses, I like't them so well,
Selfe-love did make my *Judgement* to rebell.
Thinking them so good, I thought more to write;
Considering not how others would them like.
5   I writ so fast, I thought, if I liv'd long,
A *Pyramid* of *Fame* to build thereon.
Reason observing which way I was bent,
Did stay my hand, and ask't me what I meant;
Will you, said shee, thus waste your time in vaine,
10   On that which in the World small praise shall gaine?
For shame leave off, sayd shee, the *Printer* spare,

Hee'le loose by your *ill Poetry*, I feare
Besides the World hath already such a *weight*
Of uselesse Bookes, as it is over fraught.
15 Then pitty take, doe the World a good turne,
And all you write cast in the fire, and burne.
Angry I was, and *Reason* strook away,
When I did heare, what shee to me did say.
Then all in haste I to the *Presse* it sent,
20 Fearing *Perswasion* might my *Book* prevent:
But now 'tis done, with greife repent doe I,
Hang down my *head* with *shame, blush, sigh,* and *cry.*
Take pitty, and my drooping *Spirits* raise,
Wipe off my *teares* with *Handkerchiefes* of *Praise.*

From *Poems, and Fancies: Written by the Right Honourable, the Lady Margaret Countesse of Newcastle.* London: T.R. for J. Martin and J. Allestrye, 1653, Sig. [A8]. In 1664 a new edition appeared, *Poems, and Phancies, Written By the Thrice Noble, Illustrious, And Excellent Princess The Lady Marchioness of Newcastle.* The Second Impression, much Altered and Corrected. London: William Wilson, 1664. Given the Duchess's personal involvement in the production of her books of poetry, many of the variants in the second edition must represent direct authorial intervention; we here print a selection:

3 And thinking them so Good, thought more to make, 1664
4 them like./them take. 1664
5 fast, I thought, if I liv'd long, / fast, thought, Liv'd I many a Year, 1664
6 to build thereon / thereon to Rear; 1664   9 shee / He 1664
11 off, sayd shee, the *Printer* spare, / off, and do the Printer spare, 1664
13 World hath already such a *weight* / World already hath great store 1664
14 Bookes, as it is over fraught. / Books, wherefore do Write no more, 1664
15 Then / But 1664   18 shee / he 1664

6 *Pyramid*: at this time the name given to any pinnacle, often to an obelisk; cf. Milton, 'On Shakespeare' (1630):

What needs my *Shakespeare* for his honor'd Bones,
The labor of an age in piled Stones,
Or that his hallow'd relics should be bed
Under a Star-ypointing *pyramid*?

The *Poetresses* Petition.

Like to a *Feavers pulse* my *heart* doth beat,
For fear my *Book* some great repulse should meet.
If it be naught, let her in silence lye,
Disturbe her not, let her in quiet dye;
5 Let not the *Bells* of your *dispraise* ring loud,

But wrap her up in *silence* as a *Shrowd*;
Cause *black oblivion* on her *Hearse* to hang,
Instead of *Tapers*, let darke night there stand;
Instead of *Flowers* to the grave her strow
10 Before her *Hearse, sleepy, dull Poppy* throw;
Instead of *Scutcheons*, let my *Teares* be hung,
Which *greife* and *sorrow* from my eyes out wrung:
Let those that beare her *Corps*, no *Jesters* be,
But *sad,* and *sober, grave Mortality*:
15 No *Satyr Poets* to her *Funerall* come;
No *Altars* rays'd to write *Inscriptions* on:
Let dust of all *forgetfulnesse* be cast
Upon her *Corps*, there let them lye and waste:
Nor let her rise againe; unlesse some know,
20 At *Judgements* some good *Merits* shee can shew;
Then shee shall live in *Heavens* of high *praise*:
And for her glory, *Garlands* of fresh *Bayes*.

From *Poems, and Fancies* (1653), Sig. [A8]

3 her / it 1664   4 her... her / it... it 1664   6 her / it 1664   7 hang, / lye 1664
8 there stand; / stand by; 1664   9 to the grave her strow / on its Grave to strow, 1664
10 her / its 1664   13 her / its 1664   15 to her *Funerall* come/by its *Grave* appear, 1664
16 on:/ there: 1664   19 her/ it 1664   20 shee/it 1664   21 she shall/shall it 1664
22 her glory, *Garlands* of fresh *Bayes*. / its glory, *Garlands* have of *Bays*. 1664

11 *Scutcheons*: funeral escutcheons or hatchments, which were
square or lozenge-shaped tablets exhibiting the armorial bearings
of the deceased over the entrance to the house or on the hearse.

An excuse for so much writ upon my Verses.

Condemne me not for making such a coyle
About my *Book*, alas it is my *Childe*.
Just like a *Bird*, when her *Young* are in Nest,
Goes in, and out, and hops, and takes no Rest;
5 But when their *Young* are fledg'd, their heads out
peep,
Lord what a chirping does the *Old* one keep.
So I, for feare my *Strengthlesse Childe* should fall
Against a doore, or stoole, aloud I call,
Bid have a care of such a dangerous place:
10 Thus write I much, to hinder all *disgrace*.

KISSING THE ROD

From *Poems, and Fancies* (1653), Sig. [A8ᵛ]

Title: An Apology for Writing so much upon this Book. 1664
1-2 Condemne me not, I make so much ado / About this *Book*, it is my *Child*, you know; 1664

1 *coyle*: fuss or bother

The Hunting *of the Hare*.

Betwixt two *Ridges* of *Plowd-land*, lay *Wat*,
Pressing his *Body* close to *Earth* lay squat.
His *Nose* upon his two *Fore-feet* close lies,
Glaring obliquely with his *great gray Eyes*.
5 His *Head* he alwaies sets against the *Wind;*
If turne his *Taile*, his *Haires* blow up behind:
Which *he* too cold will grow, but *he* is wise,
And keepes his *Coat* still downe, so warm *he* lies.
Thus resting all the *day*, till *Sun* doth set,
10 Then riseth up, his *Reliefe* for to get.
Walking about untill the *Sun* doth rise,
Then back returnes, downe in his *Forme he* lyes.
At last, *Poore Wat* was found, as *he* there lay,
By *Hunts-men*, with their *Dogs* which came that way.
15 Seeing, gets up, and fast begins to run,
Hoping some waies the *Cruell Dogs* to shun.
But they by *Nature* have so quick a *Sent*,
That by their *Nose* they trace what way *he* went.
And with their deep, wide *Mouths* set forth a *Cry*,
20 Which answer'd was by *Ecchoes* in the *Skie*.
Then *Wat* was struck with *Terrour*, and with *Feare*,
Thinkes every *Shadow* still the *Dogs* they were.
And running out some distance from the *noise*,
To hide himselfe, his *Thoughts* he new imploies.
25 Under a *Clod* of *Earth* in *Sand-pit* wide,
Poore *Wat* sat close, hoping himselfe to hide.
There long he had not sat, but strait his *Eares*
The *Winding Hornes*, and crying *Dogs* he heares:
Starting with *Feare*, up leapes, then doth he run,
30 And with such speed, the *Ground* scarce treades upon.
Into a great thick *Wood he* strait way gets,
Where underneath a *broken Bough he* sits.
At every *Leafe* that with the *wind* did shake,
Did bring such *Terrour*, made his *Heart* to ake.

35 That *Place he* left, to *Champian Plaines he* went,
    Winding about, for to deceive their *Sent.*
    And while they *snuffling* were, to find his *Track,*
    Poore Wat, being weary, his swift pace did slack.
    On his two *hinder legs* for ease did sit,
40 His *Fore-feet* rub'd his *Face* from *Dust,* and *Sweat.*
    Licking his *Feet, he* wip'd his *Eares* so cleane,
    That none could tell that *Wat* had hunted been.
    But casting round about his *faire great Eyes,*
    The *Hounds* in full *Careere* he neere him 'spies:
45 To *Wat* it was so terrible a *Sight,*
    Feare gave him *Wings,* and made his *Body* light.
    Though weary was before, by running long,
    Yet now his *Breath* he never felt more strong.
    Like those that *dying* are, think *Health* returnes,
50 When tis but a *faint Blast,* which *Life* out burnes.
    For *Spirits* seek to guard the *Heart* about,
    Striving with *Death,* but *Death* doth quench them out.
    Thus they so fast came on, with such loud *Cries,*
    That *he* no hopes hath left, nor *help* espies.
55 With that the *Winds* did pity *poore Wats* case,
    And with their *Breath* the *Sent* blew from the *Place.*
    Then every *Nose* is busily imployed,
    And every *Nostrill* is set open, wide:
    And every *Head* doth seek a severall way,
60 To find what *Grasse,* or *Track,* the *Sent* on lay.
    Thus quick Industry, that is not slack,
    Is like to Witchery, brings lost things back.
    For though the *Wind* had tied the *Sent* up close,
    A *Busie Dog* thrust in his *Snuffling Nose:*
65 And drew it out, with it did foremost run,
    Then *Hornes* blew loud, for th' *rest* to follow on.
    The *great slow-Hounds,* their throats did set a *Base,*
    The *Fleet Swift Hounds,* as *Tenours* next in place;
    The little *Beagles* they a *Trebble* sing,
70 And through the *Aire* their *Voice* a round did ring?
    Which made a *Consort,* as they ran along;
    If they but *words* could speak, might sing a *Song,*
    The *Hornes* kept time, the *Hunters* shout for *Joy,*
    And valiant seeme, *poore Wat* for to destroy:
75 Spurring their *Horses* to a full *Careere,*
    Swim Rivers deep, leap Ditches without feare;

Indanger *Life*, and *Limbes*, so fast will ride,
Onely to see how patiently *Wat* died.
For why, the *Dogs* so neere his *Heeles* did get,
80 That they their sharp *Teeth* in his *Breech* did set.
Then tumbling downe, did fall with *weeping Eyes*,
Gives up his *Ghost*, and thus poore *Wat he* dies.
Men hooping loud, such *Acclamations* make,
As if the *Devill* they did *Prisoner* take.
85 When they do but a *shiftlesse Creature* kill;
To hunt, there needs no *Valiant Souldiers* skill.
But *Man* doth think that *Exercise*, and *Toile*,
To keep their *Health*, is best, which makes most spoile.
Thinking that *Food*, and *Nourishment* so good,
90 And *Appetite*, that feeds on *Flesh*, and *Blood*.
When they do *Lions, Wolves, Beares, Tigers* see,
To kill poore *Sheep*, strait say, they cruell be.
But for themselves all *Creatures* think too few,
For *Luxury*, wish *God* would make them new.
95 As if that *God* made *Creatures* for *Mans meat*,
To give them *Life*, and *Sense*, for *Man* to eat;
Or else for *Sport*, or *Recreations* sake,
Destroy those *Lifes* that *God* saw good to make:
Making their *Stomacks, Graves*, which full they fill
100 With *Murther'd Bodies*, that in sport they kill.
Yet *Man* doth think himselfe so gentle, mild,
When *he* of *Creatures* is most cruell wild.
And is so *Proud*, thinks onely he shall live,
That *God* a *God*-like *Nature* did him give.
105 And that all *Creatures* for his sake alone,
Was made for him, to *Tyrannize* upon.

From *Poems, and Fancies* (1653), 110-113.

1 lay / sat 1664;   2 Whose body press'd to th'Earth lay close, and squat 1664;
3 close lies / did lye 1664;   4 With his gray Eyes he glared Obliquely; 1664
5 sets/set 1664;
6-7 His Tail when turn'd, His Hair blew up / And made him to get Cold; but he being Wise, 1664
8 And keepes/doth keepe 1664   9-10 Thus rests he all the Day, till th'Sun doth set/ Then up he riseth his Relief to get, 1664   11 Walking about/ And walks about 1664
12 Then coming back in's former Posture lies, 1664
14-15 By Huntsmen, which came with their Dogs that way   17 have / had 1664
    Whom seeing, he got up, and fast did run, 1664   18 trace / Trac'd 1664
22 Seeing each Shadow, thought the Dogs were there, 1664
23 the noise / their Cry, 1664   24 new imploies / did employ; 1664
27 sat / been; his / in's 1664   29-30 then starting up with fear, he Leap'd, and such/ Swift speed he made, the Ground he scarce did touch; 1664

31 he strait way gets/strait way he got 1664
32 Where / and; sets. / Sat, 1664   33 At/Where 1664
34 Brought him such Terrour, that his Heart did Ake 1664
39 did set,/ he Sat, 1664   43 great / gray 1664
47 weary was before/he was Tyr'd before 1664
53 The Hounds so fast came on, and with such Cry 1664
54 espies / could'spy 1664   57 is / was 1664
58 is / was 1664   60 To find the Grass, or Track where the Sent lay; 1664
61-62 For *Witty Industry is never Slack,*
        'Tis like to Witchcraft, and brings lost things back: 1664
63 For / But 1664   65 it / that 1664   66 th'rest / the rest 1664
69 they / did 1664   70 Voice a round / Voices round 1664
71 a / such 1664   72 That, had they Spoken words, t'had been a Song 1664
73 the Hunters/the men did 1664
74 And seem'd most Valiant, *poor Wat* to destroy 1664
76 Swim / Swam; leap / Leap'd 1664   77 Indanger / indanger'd; will/they'ld 1664
79 For why / At last 1664   80 That their sharp Teeth they in his Breech did set. 1664
81 Then tumbling down he fell, with weeping Eyes, 1664   82 Gives / gave 1664
84 did Prisoner take/Imprison'd had 1664   85 do but/but did 1664 87 Man/men 1664
90 Which doth proceed from others Flesh and Blood 1664
92 poore Sheep, strait say,/ kill silly sheep, they say 1664
94 them / more 1664   95 that God made / God did make 1664
96 To give / And gave 1664   98 For to Destroy those Lives that God did make 1664
100 that / which 1664   101 gentle, mild, / Gentle and Mild, 1664
102-103 When of all Creatures he's most cruell wild   104 did him / him did 1664
        Nay, so Proud, that he only thinks to Live 1664   106 Was / Were 1664

Poems describing the hunt from the point of view of the quarry are not common; the Duchess has Shakespeare's *Venus and Adonis*, ll.679-708 in mind; in Denham's *Cooper's Hill* (1642) the stag hunt is principally an occasion for political allegory. Poems against blood sports tend to be a female genre. For example, Anne Bradstreet identifies her children with hunted birds, 'In Reference to Her Children, 23 June 1656':

> Whilst pecking corn, and void of care,
> They fall un'wares in fowler's snare.

See also Mary Jones, 'To Mrs Clayton with a Hare' (c.1740) and Laetitia Pilkington, 'The Petition of the Birds to Mr Pilkington on his return from Shooting' (c.1740).

1 *Wat*: a familar name for the hare, e.g. Drayton, 'the nimble wat', *Poly-Olbion* (1622).
12 *Forme*: the hollow in which a hare sleeps
19-20 Cf. *Venus and Adonis*, ll.695-696:

> Then they do spend their mouths: echo replies,
> As if another chase were in the skies.

21-22 Cf. *Venus and Adonis*, l.706: 'Each shadow makes him stop, each murmur stay.'
28 *Winding*: blowing
35 *Champian*: level and open; unenclosed. Gervase Markham recommends beating the shrubs near the woods, and driving the hares into the 'champaigne'.
36 Cf. *Venus and Adonis*, l.704: 'Turn, and return, indenting with the

way' ('indenting' is zigzagging) and also ll.685-686:

> Sometime he runs among a flock of sheep,
> To make the cunning hounds mistake their smell;

and Gervase Markham, *Country Contentments* (first published in 1615, reprinted in 1631, and after as part of *A Way to Get Wealth* in 1638, 1648, 1653 and six more times before 1684):

> The next thing you observe must be the shifts and sleights of the *hare*, when she is wearily hunted, as her dubblings and windings and at every default give the *Hounds* leasure enough and compasse enough in the casting about of your rings for the unwinding of the same; then you shall observe her leapes and skippes before she squat... (34-35)

38-39 Cf. *Venus and Adonis*, ll.697-698:

> By this, poor Wat, far off upon a hill,
> Stands on his hinder-legs with list'ning ear...

67-72 The Duchess's description of the barking pack of hounds as a harmonious 'Consort' could have been taken from Markham:

> some large dogges, that have deepe solemne mouthes, and are swift in spending, which must as it were beare the base in the consort, then a double number of roaring, and loud ringing mouthes, which must beare the countertenor, then some hollow plaine sweete mouthes, which must beare the meane or middle part: and soe with these three parts of musicke you shall make your cry perfect... amongst these you cast in a couple or two of small singing Beagles, which as small trebles may warble amongst them: the cry will be a great deale the more sweeter. (8)

83-106 In Cavendish's 'True Relation' she describes herself as 'tender-natured, for it troubles my conscience to kill a fly, and the groans of a dying beast strike my soul' and earlier had written, 'neither have I the *courage* to looke on the cruell assaults, that *Mankind* (as I have heard) will make at each other; but according to the constitution of my *Sex*, I am as fearefull as a Hare' (Cavendish, *Philosophical and Physical Opinions*, 167). An old English folk song called 'The Hares on the Mountain' begins,

> Young women they'll run like hares on the mountain (twice)
> If I was but a young man I'd soon go a-hunting... (Cole, 32)

90 *Flesh, and Blood*: Markham recommends the hare's flesh as 'good for all manner of Fluxes' and 'the Braines good to make children breed their teeth with ease' (33).

103-106 An almost direct rebuttal of Markham's claim that the country landowner 'should not be deprived of any comfort, or felicity, which the earth, or the creatures of the earth can affoord to him, being indeed the right Lord and Master (next under God) of them both...'(2).

> I *Language* want, to dresse my *Fancies* in,
> The *Haire's* uncurl'd, the *Garments* loose, and thin;
> Had they but *Silver Lace* to make them gay,
> Would be more courted then in *poore array*.

5   Or had they *Art*, might make a *better show*;
But *they are plaine*, yet cleanly doe they goe.
The world in *Bravery* doth take delight,
And *glistering Shews* doe more attract the *sight*;
And every one doth honour a rich Hood,
10   As if the *outside* made the *inside* good.
And every one doth bow, and give the place,
Not for the *Mans sake*, but the *Silver Lace*.
Let me intreat in my Poore Bookes behalfe,
That all may not adore the Golden Calf.
15   Consider pray, *Gold* hath no life therein,
And *Life* in *Nature* is the richest thing.
So *Fancy* is the *Soul* in *Poetrie*,
And if not *good*, a *Poem* ill must be.
Be just, let Fancy have the upper place.
20   And then my *Verses* may perchance finde grace.
If *flattering Language* all the *Passions* rule,
Then *Sense*, I feare, will be a meere dull Foole.

From *Poems, and Fancies* (1653), 212.

[UNTITLED] / *Of the Style of this Book.* 1664   4 Would / They'ld 1664
5 might / would 1664   9 And / For 1664   12 Not for the *Mans Sake*, / Not to the
Person 1664   13 intreat in / intreat ye'in 1664
15 Consider pray, that Gold no Life doth bring, 1664

12 *Silver Lace*: lace made out of silver thread, appliquéed to coats
and petticoats, worn by fashionable men and women in the 1660s,
see Pepys, *Diary* (Latham and Mathews, I, 38, 225; V, 188, 239, 325;
VIII, 242).
14 *the Golden Calf*: Exodus 32

A *Poet* I am neither *borne*, nor bred,
But to a *witty Poet* married:
Whose Braine is *Fresh*, and *Pleasant,* as the Spring,
Where *Fancies* grow, and where the *Muses* sing.
5   There oft I leane my Head, and *list'ning* harke,
To heare *his words*, and all his *Fancies* mark;
And from that *Garden Flowers* of *Fancies* take,
Whereof a *Posie* up in *Verse* I make.
Thus I, that have no *Garden* of mine owne,
10   There gather *Flowers* that are *newly-blowne*.

From *Poems, and Fancies* (1653), 214.

6 To heare *his words*, / T'observe his Words 1664

2 *witty Poet married*: the Duke of Newcastle's poetry to Margaret during their courtship shows an interest in natural philosophy and a fondness for tortured conceits that may have influenced the Duchess. For example, see his abstruse simile in 'Love's Snake':

> To say wee'r like one Snake, not Us disgrases,
> That winds, delights it selfe, with selfe Imbrases,
> Lappinge, Involvinge, in a thousand rings,
> It selfe thus tieinge by love's phansy'd winges;
> And so do wee. (Grant, 42)

9-10 *no Garden of mine owne*: the Duke's daughters also claim that their creativity comes from the Duke; Jane Cavendish signs herself 'your Daughter in your Penn' while Elizabeth tells the Duke, 'upon your stock of wit I feede' (see pp.106ff.).

ANNA TRAPNEL

In January 1654, Vavasour Powell, one of the leaders of the Fifth Monarchists, was summoned to Whitehall to account for his announcement in a sermon that the Protectorate would be short-lived. Among the supporters who waited outside the council chamber was a woman who was seized by the spirit so that she burst out singing and praying, and continued to do so throughout twelve days. Hundreds came to hear her at lodgings just outside Whitehall. Though much of what she uttered was incomprehensible, her words were taken down as they were uttered and published as *The Cry of a Stone or a Relation of Something spoken in Whitehall, by Anna Trapnel... uttered in Prayers and Spiritual Songs, by an Inspiration extraordinary, and full of wonder* (London, 1654).

Anna was the daughter of William Trapnel, a shipwright in Poplar. On New Year's Day 1642, the day after the death of her mother, while she was listening to a sermon by John Simpson, at St Botolph's Church in Aldgate, she was seized with the spirit of the Lord. Her spiritual rebirth may have been suggested by her aunt's exhortation, 'Cosen, the Lord hath taken your mother from you, now labour to be married to Christ' (*Legacy*, 10). From the time of her 'glorious sealing' with the Lord she was frequently transported by religious rapture, seeing visions, uttering endless streams of prophecy, and falling to the ground.

She was 'about twenty years' at her mother's death and had been 'trained up to [her] book and writing' (*Report*, 50; *Cry*, Sig. A2). Her father was dead, and she 'kept house' with means her mother left her, but soon contributed most of her worldly possessions to the godly Parliamentarian army: 'I sold my Plate and Rings, and gave the mony to the Publick use;... the sum of mony my Mother left me, I freely gave for the Armies use, and I wrought many nights to get mony... so I might minister towards the relief of the Nation.' She writes that she then went to live with a succession of women friends and a kinswoman, Mrs Wythe, 'a Merchants wife'. When in 1654 she was harassed by Cromwell's government because of her part in Fifth Monarchy agitation, she was 'rejected of [her] kinswoman for the Rulers sake', and apparently lived on her own, claiming to have 'a settled habitation, and pay assessments' (*Report*, 50-51).

The Fifth Monarchists interpreted Revelations 20:1-5 to mean that Christ would return to earth in person to reign for a thousand years; his reign was called 'The Fifth Monarchy' from the vision in Daniel 8:20-22 prophesying that a succession of four kingdoms (Assyria, Persia, Greece, and Rome) would be followed by the fifth

monarchy of Christ (see pp.124ff., Anne Bradstreet's 'The Foure
Monarchies'). The preachers and the discontented faction in the
army (some of whom were also members of the Rump Parliament)
who formed the Fifth Monarchy alliance, met regularly 'at one Mr
Squibb's house' throughout 1653; they discussed tactics to control
Parliamentary decisions and propaganda campaigns using
pamphlets and 'the publicity-making machine of the London
pulpits' (Trevor-Roper, 367). The moderates in Parliament,
pressured by the 'crescendo of Fifth Monarchist and army prayer
meetings' (Capp, 61), gave up their power into the hands of the
'Lord Protector' in December 1653 rather than see a takeover by
radicals leading to 'blood and confusion'. Denied participation in
the legislative process, the Fifth Monarchist alliance was forced to
use the word or take up arms. Trapnel may have become a Fifth
Monarchist through the Baptist minister at her parish church of St
Botolph's, John Simpson, who had been a prominent leader in the
movement from 1652 and a major in the Parliamentarian army
(Capp, 262).

Trapnel's inspired verses accuse Cromwell of betraying the
Lord's plan for the kingdom of saints by setting himself up as Lord
Protector. The woman who sold her plate and rings for the army
may have suffered another kind of disillusionment as well:

> Yea Lord thou knowst thy servant did,
> Lord let her life go for
> The life of that deare one abroad,
> who is a man of War. (*Cry*, 55)

From Trapnel's own ingenuous account we may infer that the
'friends' who directed her after her performance at Whitehall were
part of the army conspiracy, taking advantage of her disenchant-
ment with Cromwell, whom by this time she was calling the 'little
horn' on the head of the Beast. In *Anna Trapnel's Report* she records
her invitation from 'friends': '*Pray go down with us to Cornwal; there
you may do good to poor souls*' (1). The Fifth Monarchists were
strongest in the west of England from where they hoped to spread
fear and restlessness throughout England by a propaganda
campaign in which Trapnel's electrifying performances were to
play an important part. Trapnel's 'sister', Ursula Adman, herself a
Fifth Monarchist (see Capp, 239) was 'much against' going to
Cornwall, and Trapnel admits that she wanted so much not to go
that 'when I went up a pair of stairs, I was tempted that I should fall
from the top to the bottom of the stairs and break my limbes, so that
I should in such a way be hindered my journey' (*Report*, 6). When
she became convinced that the Lord did want her to go, she left in a
coach with her 'friends for the journey': Colonel Bennet, Captain
Langden, Bennet's daughter, and Langden's wife. Captain Francis
Langden, MP for Cornwall in the Rump, and active Fifth
Monarchist agent, is listed, along with Bennett and several other
army officers, among those who witnessed Trapnel's collapse into

prophecy at Whitehall (*Cry*, Sig. A1). Her *Legacy for Saints* was written under Langden's auspices: it is directed 'To the Church sometimes meeting at Al-Hollows' from 'Tregasow *at Captain Langdons*, near Trurow, *this* 15, of the 2 moneth [April], 1654', signed 'Anna Trapnel' (49, 52).

In Cornwall she was arrested and accused of being a vagabond. She writes that, at the hearing in Plymouth,

they questioned me about the book pen'd at *London*, which they tendered to me, and asked me whether I would own that book as mine; I answered, I was not carefull to answer them to that matter: they then caused the Vision which mentions the horns, and Cows, and Oxen, to be read, and asked me what I would say to that? was that mine... I would not answer them touching the book. I saying that they were not to question me in this County, concerning what was spoken at *White-hall*... Farther they came to question me where I had dwelt? and from what part of *London* I came? and what moved me to come hither? did none ask me to come? this they asked me often... (*Legacy*, 56)

She spent fifteen weeks in a men's prison, was committed to Bridewell on 2 June 1654, and released after eight weeks, though she refused to promise to stop her public prophecies. She was in Cornwall again in the following year. In 1657 she evidently prophesied in verse for hours at a time in the presence of a religious congregation, which included on one or more occasions some doubting Quakers whom she roundly attacked. Bod. S. 42. I. Th. appears to be a printed transcript of more than a thousand pages of these rhapsodic utterances, part of which were again published in 1658 as *Voice for the King of Saints and Nations*. The last mention of her is in the *Bibliotheca Fanatica* (1660): '*A. T.* is as good for a Sow as a Pancake' (4).

From *The Cry of a Stone*

Therefore *John* read how that thou wouldst
    the earth again restore.
None shall hinder them from those thrones
    w^{ch} *John* there did declare
5 Oh a Sea of glasse there chrystal was
    which none could it compare:
But oh your standing on the earth,
    on glasse that brittle is,
Which shall crumble under your feet
10   when that there comes forth this,
This Sea of glasse which is indeed,
    that where thine thee behold:
Oh they may look up unto thee,
    and thorow it extoll
15 Thy love that did a book write sweet,

and many things there in store
Of Royalties which should come out,
   and be given more and more,
Unto those that deny thy foes,
20   and Antichrist also,
They that go forth to strike at him,
   thou wilt upon them blow,
Thy spirit upon them shall come forth
   and Antichrist shall fall
25   Both in person, and also too,
   in his coming principall.
Oh it is Lord, then sweet surely,
   to read of such things here,
And *John* he mourn'd abundantly,
30   that th' mystery might draw near,
That new Jerusalem above,
   might come down here below,
And that they might see their High,
   when that forth he doth go.

From *The Cry of a Stone or a Relation of Something spoken in Whitehall*, by Anna Trapnel, being in the Visions of God. Relating To the Governors, Army, Churches, Ministry, Universities: And the whole Nation. Uttered in Prayers and Spiritual Songs, by an Inspiration extraordinary, and full of wonder. London: 1654, 61.
The title comes from Habakkuk 2:11-12: 'For the stone shall cry out of the wall,... Woe to him that buildeth a town with blood, and stablisheth a city by iniquity.' *The Cry of a Stone* consists of a narration describing Trapnel's visionary behaviour, interspersed with transcriptions of her ravings, taken down as she uttered them extempore, hundreds of lines at a time, as far as one can gather without drawing breath; her visions and prophecies are given in prose, culminating in songs of which the above is a representative fragment. The metre of the songs is a kind of Poulter's measure, with split lines of fourteen, thirteen, twelve or eleven syllables; some of the irregularities are doubtless the result of the circumstances of the transcription.

    After speaking the words in the text above, the 'Relator' of Trapnel's words describes her as falling silent for two or three hours. When only a few people remained of the 'press of people crowding and darkening the Chamber', she coughed, responded to questions about her welfare in a few words, and began singing and praying again.

    Trapnel's publications were almost certainly guided into print by her Fifth Monarchy 'friends'; the *Cry* appeared about a month after her appearance at Whitehall, judging from Thomason's manuscript note 'ffeb; ye th/20' on the title-page of the British Library copy (E.730 [3]). *A Legacy for Saints; Being Several Experiences of the Dealings of God with Anna Trapnel* was said on the title-page to have been 'written some years since in her own hand'. *Anna Trapnel's Report and Plea, or a Narrative of her Journey from London into Cornwal* seems likely to be her own work. As both bear stylistic resemblances to the utterance transmitted by the shorthand takers at Whitehall, it is reasonable to assume that while the circumstances of transmission have caused distortion, the result is recognisably Trapnel's voice. The fourth book published under her name in 1654, *Strange and Wonderful Newes from White-Hall*, is merely an attempt to capitalise on her notoriety by reiterating the story told in *The Cry of a Stone*. When Arise Evans published Elinor Channell's *A Message from God, [By a Dumb woman]* (1654; MS note 'July 20', BL E. 1471. [3]), a tract advising, but sympathetic to Cromwell, he added, 'you will find more truth and substance in it, than in all *Hana Trampenels* songs or sayings, whom some account of as the *Diana* of the English, *Acts* 19.34,' meaning that her prophecies enriched those who marketed them, as Diana's oracles created the wealth of Ephesus.

1 *John*: Revelations
3 *thrones*: Revelations 20:4
5 *Sea of glasse*: Revelations 4:6
15 *a book*: Revelations 5-10
17 *Royalties*: royal prerogatives granted by a sovereign to an individual or corporation. The Fifth Monarchists commonly characterised the kingdom of Christ to come in terms of universal wealth and privilege.
24-25 *Antichrist... in person*: Revelations 20:1-3. Cromwell. Earlier in the poem she calls for 'pens' to 'make known' that 'Protectors shall go, / And into graves there lye'.
26 *his coming principall*: Satan
31 *New Jerusalem*: Revelations 21

ANNE KING

Last-born child of John King, Bishop of London, and Joan Freeman, Anne King was only five weeks old at the time of her father's death in 1621. She is the sister of Henry King (1592-1669), Bishop of Chichester, poet and friend of Ben Jonson, John Donne and Izaak Walton. In 1651 Henry King sought refuge at Richings, near Langley in Buckinghamshire, the house of Lady Salter, widowed niece of Brian Duppa, Bishop of Salisbury and King's predecessor at Chichester. His sister Anne was one of the company that formed around him and John Hales of Eton, Lady Salter's chaplain.

Since 1648 Anne had been married to John Dutton, twenty-eight years older than she, a member for Gloucestershire in the Long Parliament and one of the richest men in England, until he was massively fined for his adherence to the Royalist cause. In 1657 Dutton died, leaving her £500 'with all the plate and household goods she brought when he married her – and all his coaches and coach-horses and two saddle nags' (Hannah, ciii).

In the same year the occasional poems of Henry King were collected and published without King's authorisation. *Poems, Elegies, Paradoxes, and Sonnets* includes poems by other people, among which may be some, not yet identified, written by his sister. One poem entitled 'To my sister Anne King, who chid me in verse for being angry', is a sincere and generous compliment expressed in twenty lines both vigorous and urbane.

> Well I am charm'd, and promise to redresse
> What, without Shrift, my follyes doe confesse
> Against my self. Wherefore let mee intreat,
> When I fly out in that distemper'd heat,
> Which fretts mee into Fasts, Thou wilt reprove
> That froward Spleene in Poetry and Love:
> So though I loose my Reason in such fitts,
> Thou'lt Rime mee back againe into my witts. (13-20)

Anne may be the 'noble lady' for whom Henry King wrote 'Upon a Table-Book Presented to a Lady'. Jasper Mayne, archdeacon of Chichester and dramatist, praised her talents in 'On Mrs. Anne King's Table-Book of Pictures' (BL Harl. MS 6931). In 1637, inspired by an epitaph and an anagram of Anne King's 'own composure', James Howell (1594?-1666) wrote a poem entitled 'For the admitting Mistress Anne King to be the Tenth Muse'. He later called her a 'great Minion of the Muse' (*Epistolae Ho-Elianae*, 311-312, 324).

ANNE KING

When Henry died in 1669 he left Anne 'one guilt cup and cover of Noremberg the fashion of a Chalice and alsoe my great french Bible with prints which once belonged to my honoured Friend, Doctor Donne, Dean of Saint Paules', because he says, after the sequestration of all his goods at Chichester he had received from Anne 'speciall signification of her love' (Hannah, cxii). We know from her nephew's will dated 1671, where she is called 'the Lady How' that she was by then wife of Sir Richard Grobham Howe (1621-1703) of Great Wishford, near Salisbury in Wiltshire, by whom she had no issue, and with whom she is buried at Great Wishford.

Under Mr. Hales Picture

    Though by a sodaine and unfeard surprise,
thou lately taken wast from thy friends eies:
Even in that instant, when they had design'd
to keipe thee, by thy picture still in minde:
5   least thou like others lost in deths dark night
shouldst stealing hence vanish quite out of sight;
I did contend with greater zeale then Art,
This shadow of my phancie to impart:
which all shood pardon, when they understand
10 the lines were figur'd by a womans hand,
who had noe copy to be guided by
but Hales imprinted on her memory.
     Thus ill cut Brasses serve uppon a grave,
     Which less resemblance of the persons have.

From Reverend J. Hannah, ed., *Poems and Psalms by Henry King*. London and Oxford, 1843, 175, text taken from Bod MS 306, Isaac Walton's letter to Fulman October 20 1673. Printed also in Butt and Crum.

John Hales (1584-1656), well-known for his learning and quiet common sense, was a fellow at Eton from 1613 until 1649, when he was formally dispossessed of his fellowship. He had been ejected from his canonry at Windsor in 1642, and gone into hiding for a time in 1644 when the Parliament seized the college rents. Declining an offer of assistance from his successor at Eton, he retreated to the 'sort of college' set up by Henry King at Richings, acting as chaplain to the group and tutor to Lady Salter's son. He insisted on leaving Richings after the 'order against harbouring malignants', and returned to Eton where he died six months later on 19 May 1656 at the home of an old servant ('Hales, John', *DNB*). Izaak Walton describes the circumstances of the writing of the poem:

About the time he was forc't from the Lady Salt^{rs} that ffamily or collage broke vp, or desolu'd, a littel before wch time, they were resolud to haue m^r Ha picture taken, and to that end, a picture maker had promis'd to atend at Richking^s to take it, but faild of his time; and m^r Ha being gone thence dyed not long after. The not hauing his picture, was lamented very much, by the sotietie, in wch nomber the Bish^s sister (once m^{rs} Anne king now the lady How) vndertooke boeth for theirs and her owne satisfaction to draw it, and did so, in black and white boeth exilently well as to the curiousnes, and as well as to the likenes. – but before she wood shew it to any that knew ether him or her selfe, she writ vnderneth it, this which she ment to be an Apologie for her vndertaking it... Yo^u may take notice that she is a most generose and ingenious lady. (Butt, 271)

Anne King's portrait drawing of Hales has apparently not survived. She is named in Izaak Walton's will as the recipient of a ring.

Inscription on monument of Dorothy, Lady Hubert at Langley, Buckinghamshire
M.S.

Reader upon this field of Marble see
How Death and Love Contend for masterie
Vaunting her spoils Death warn's Thee, Here lies
one of her Choice peeces of destruction
5   For Wit, Forme, Sweetness, So sublime that higher
Her Dart nor Malice ever did aspire.
Love from a Friend (scarse willing to surviue
But to preserve the Other's Fame alive
A Sister so endeer'd in Blood and Heart
10   She felt the stroke and still weep's for ye smart)
Inform's thee (if Thou'lt help) these Virtues, Fate
Cannot consume, or time obliterate,
But by Thine Eyes embalmed She will lie
Living and fresh till Death Herself must die
15   Then lend some Tears for mine must need's be spent
Being both the Dead's, and Living's Monument.

From Hannah, 176. Dorothy, third daughter of Bishop John King and Joan Freeman, married Sir Richard Hubert, of Langley, Buckinghamshire, Groom Porter to Charles I. Henry King took refuge with her in 1643 and stayed in their house until 1651, when he went to Richings. Dorothy died in 1658, twenty-six years before Anne erected this monument.

M. S. : *memoriae sacrum*, sacred to the memory of

ELIZABETH MAJOR

Joseph Caryl (1602-1673), leading non-conformist divine and examiner of candidates for the ministry under the Protectorate (*DNB*), says in an introduction to *Honey on the Rod: Or a comfortable Contemplation for one in Affliction* (London, 1656), that Elizabeth Major was an 'afflicted Gentlewoman' with both 'heart and hand long exercised under a heavy cross... as Christ hath dropt honey into her soul from the Rod, her pen drops honey into thy soul...' The reader is exhorted to taste it 'as Jonathan did the honey on the end of the rod that was in his hand (1 Sam. 14)'. It is probable that Major was one of Caryl's parishioners at St Magnus's church near London Bridge, and that her book was put together under his tutelage.

Honey on the Rod carries Caryl's *imprimatur*; fifteen years before, Milton had characterised the *imprimatur* as permission obtained from 'the shallow hand of some mercenary, narrow Soul'd, and illiterate Chaplain' (*Animadversions on the Remonstrants' Defence*, 1641), but by 1656 the spirit of *Areopagitica* was dead. Major's book was issued only a year after Cromwell's Order of Suppression was enacted; Caryl's name may have appeared on it as much to demonstrate his support of the cause of censorship as to promote his protegee.

In her address to the reader, Major provides us with a brief story of her life:

> I was, till the fifteenth or sixteenth year of my age, brought up by a godly and careful father (my Mother being taken from me in my infancy) from whom I went to a great and honorable Family, where no vice I think was tolerated; and under a wise and vertuous Governess I lived nere ten years, 'til God was pleased to visit me with lameness... Then I was forc't to repair home to my Father again, where I was pursued with an inordinate desire of recovery, and having some money in my own hands, I endeavoured the accomplishing of that desire. (Sig. h2)

Because Major sinned by not consulting the will of God in the matter, he 'blasted her' so that she 'spent all, and was much worse'.

Elizabeth may have been a member of the distinguished Hampshire family that furnished the Protector's son, Richard Cromwell, with his wife Dorothy in 1649. *The Visitation of London, 1634* (Harleian Society, 1883, II, 73) identifies another apparently wealthy family of Majors living in Blackfriars; Elizabeth could have been the daughter of John 'Maior' and Mary Allton.

The main part of *Honey on the Rod* is a collection of biblical paraphrases, sermon-like essays and dialogues between *Soul* and *Consolation*, followed by forty pages of verse, with a separate title-page, 'Sin and Mercy Briefly discovered; or The vail taken a little from before both. Together with the author's accusation, confession and belief...' The whole book, prose and verse, reiterates the theme of acceptance of suffering, first simply because it is God's will (which Major sometimes renders as God's pleasure) and secondly because no suffering, however intense and prolonged, is punishment too great for sin that displeases God.

From *The Authors Confession.*

Old age... The eternal son of God for sin did die:
Observe his passion, he run a weary race,
70 In steps of love, my soul, thy Saviour trace:
His Throne he quits, the humane nature he
Upon him takes, lays by his Majesty,
Descends on earth, where he's revil'd with scorn,
He's smote, he's scourged, he's stript, he's crown'd
                                            with thorn:
75 His agony was such, that a sweat of blood
Did him possess, 'cause in mans room he stood:
Witness is sought, though false, and can't agree,
For he's pronounced innocent to be:
Yet he must die, nay even a cursed death,
80 Justice for sin bereaves my Lord of breath;
Yet all this love did not unglue my heart
From earthen pleasures, until I felt the smart
Of a Fathers rod, my strength was seized, and I
In prime arrested, here I in prison lie,
85 Where Lord, thou knowest much sorrow I have seen,
Some prentiships I have close Prisoner been;
My Spring and Summer been so Winter like,
That I with comfort scarce bring day to night.
And to conclude, had he a poysoned dart
90 Sent, I confess I had but my desert;
(But here mistake me not, to think I am far,
That here corrections satisfactions are
I'th'least degree, or for the least offence,
For God's corrections bear another sense.)
95 *Eccho.* Now I beseech thee for cure and clothing
                                                    haste,
O let not any intice thee time to waste.

From *Honey on the Rod: Or a comfortable Contemplation For One in*

ELIZABETH MAJOR

Affliction; With sundry Poems on several Subjects. By the unworthiest of the servants of the Lord Jesus Christ, Elizabeth Major. London: Printed by Tho: Maxey, Thames-Street, near Baynards-Castle, 1656, 196.

68 *Old age*: Major's confession follows almost the same schema as Jacques's speech in *As You Like It*, II.vii.139-67. 'Old Age' follows 'Infancy', 'Youth', and 'Man-hood' as they discuss sin with 'Soul' and 'Eccho'. 'Infancy' is quoting either Shakespeare or their common source, Boaistuau's *Theatrum Mundi*:

> My infant eyes being open, sure I spy'd
> More then the standers by could in me see,
> They but Spectators, mine's the Tragedy:
> This world the Stage is, where some years I pass'd
> Of infancy, then to wilde youth I haste. (16-20)

80 *Justice for sin*: Job 8:3-6

84 In her address to the reader, Major uses the same expressions: 'know that [God] was pleased in the prime of my years to take me, as it were, from a Palace to a Prison, from liberty to bondage, where I have served some *Apprentiships*...'

85 *sorrow I have seen*: see Anne Bradstreet (p.119) on the 'adversities' of 'Old Age' in 'The Four Ages of Man', 355-456.

87-88 Cf. An Collins, 'Another Song', 11-25 (see p. 151).

91-94 The afterthought was probably included at her mentor's insistence. Major describes her torments as divine discipline and bondage, inflicted in order to correct her, as in her address to the reader: '[God] was pleased to own me as one of the poor Scholars in the School, of the lowest Form, and according to my weakness he dealt with me: He was likewise pleased for some years to exercise me with much trouble...'

95 *cure and clothing*: the healing action of grace, and the garment of blessedness, according to Major in the 'Authors Belief' which follows.

KATHERINE PHILIPS

Philips was born Katherine Fowler in London on New Year's Day, 1632, daughter of an influential merchant and his second wife, Katharine Oxenbridge (Souers, 5-6). When she was eight years old she was sent to Mrs Salmon's school in Hackney where she became friends with Mary Aubrey, the 'Rosania' of her poems, and with Mary Harvey who later married Sir Edward Dering, 'Silvander'. Fowler died in 1639; seven years later his widow married a wealthy Welsh baronet to whose castle in Pembrokeshire, newly liberated from Cavalier forces, Katherine went to live. A husband was found for her, James Philips, a widowed kinsman of her mother's new husband, thirty-eight years older than Katherine, who was not seventeen at the time of their marriage in August 1648.

For the next twelve years Katherine lived quietly in the small town of Cardigan, while her husband's affairs prospered and he became a powerful figure in local and national politics. She may have accompanied him to London for the Parliamentary terms but her significant relationships were with other young wives dwelling in the comparative wilderness of Wales. Philips was first noticed as a poet in 1651, when Henry Vaughan praised her work in his *Olor Iscanus* (28-29) and her poem in memory of the playwright, William Cartwright, appeared in the edition of his *Comedies, Tragi-Comedies*.

She bore two children, Hector in April 1655, who lived less than two weeks and, a year later, Katherine, who lived to become Mrs Lewis Wogan and bear sixteen children of whom only one survived (P. Thomas, vi). When Philips's old friend Mary Aubrey married William Montagu, 'Orinda', as she called herself for poetic purposes, was obliged to seek a new Platonic friend and chose Anne Owen, 'Lucasia'.

Although she had grown up in a Puritan family and married into the Puritan ruling class, Philips's sympathies were Royalist. She joined in the panegyrics of the returning Stuarts and grieved eloquently over the death of Prince Henry, but her poetic allegiance could hardly hope to ward off the reversal of her husband's fortunes. He narrowly escaped prosecution as a regicide and summary ejection from his parliamentary seat for Cardiganshire only to be found guilty of an electoral irregularity and ejected anyway. His enjoyment of estates sequestered under the Commonwealth was likewise terminated.

Help was at hand in the form of the new Master of Ceremonies at the Court of Charles II, Sir Charles Cotterell, who may have made the acquaintance of Katherine Philips at the same time as his eye fell on the widowed Anne Owen, in whom he saw a likely candidate for the second Lady Cotterell. By 1661 Cotterell and Philips were on intimate terms as evinced by the *Letters from Orinda to Poliarchus* (1705), and it seems that by way of furthering his courtship of Anne Owen, Cotterell took up the case of James Philips. In recompense, the Philipses took it upon themselves to get Cotterell elected MP for Cardigan, after a difficult contest and without his prior consent. Anne rejected Philips's choice, and in 1662 married an Irish military man in whom 'Orinda' could find nothing to admire.

Nevertheless, a month later 'Orinda' accompanied 'Lucasia' to her husband's home in Ireland, where Philips investigated the possibility of redeeming one of her father's investments in confiscated Royalist property. Unsuccessful in this enterprise and virtually ignored by 'Lucasia', who was apparently besotted with her new husband, she concentrated on writing her translation of *La Mort de Pompée* by Corneille which was staged in Dublin in the second week of February 1663, through the kind offices of Lord Orrery. An Irish bookseller rushed it into print and brought out a London edition a few weeks later. Although only her initials were on the title-page Philips was now famous.

In November 1663, the Stationers' Register announced a book of poems by 'Mrs Katherine Phillips'; on 14 January 1664 *Poems. By the Incomparable, Mrs. K. P.* duly appeared only to be suppressed within four days on the grounds that the printer did not have the author's permission and the texts were corrupt. Philips protested mightily about this publication, but in fact the poems follow the same order as the authorised version was later to do, and exhibit very few significant textual inaccuracies; pirated though it undoubtedly was, the 1664 version is based on something unusually close to the poet's autograph.

'Orinda' returned from Ireland in July 1663 and was gratified that the husband she had left almost suicidal had recovered his spirits, but she pined for London. She almost immediately set about arranging a visit which materialised at the end of March 1664. There, at the height of her fame, in the midst of the refined and cosmopolitan society she had always dreamed of, she got smallpox. Twelve days after penning her last poem she was dead.

Her friend, Sir Charles Cotterell, prepared her poems for an authorised edition which appeared in 1667; another edition appeared in 1669, another in 1678 and another in 1710. She was the best known female poet not only of her generation but of succeeding generations, who often held up her refined and sensitive persona as the corrective to Aphra Behn's undeniable coarseness. She was born in the same year as Dryden, who was proud to have met her and even boasted of a distant connection to her. Like him she was initially attracted to the extravagant conceits of Cowley, but, because her best poetry was invariably written under the peremptory pressure of strong feeling, such twists were early ironed out and the result is a clear and unforced diction in simple and elegant cadences. It would be vain to argue that Philips's refinement was more influential than Dryden's stronger line, but it was attractive to imitators. Her meticulous and skilful translation of Corneille was a veritable eye-opener to the public that had lived through the Philistinism of the Interregnum. To modern feminists she is chiefly important for her exaltation of Platonic friendship between women; some of her champions choose to ignore her own stipulation that such friendship be free from carnal interest. When the dust settles perhaps we shall see that 'Orinda' should be counted amongst those who purified the language of the tribe.

> No blooming youth shall ever make me err
> I will the beauty of the mind prefer
> If himans rites shall call me hence
> It shall be with some man of sence
> 5 Nott with the great butt with a good estate
> Not too well read nor yet illiterate
> In all his actions moderate grave & wise
> Redyer to bear than offer injuries
> And in good works a constant doer
> 10 Faithfull in promise & liberall to the poor
> He thus being quallified is allways seen
> Ready to serve his friend his country & his king
> Such men as these youl say there are but few
> Their hard to find & I must grant it too
> 15 Butt if I ever hap to change my life
> It's only such a man shall call me wife
>   Humbly dedicated too Mrs Anne Barlow
>   C Fowler

This poem and the one following are on two sides of a single sheet in Orielton MSS Box 24 at the National Library of Wales. The poem has been published in Lockley, 19-20. The signature 'C. Fowler' indicates that they were written before Philips's marriage in 1648. She probably made the acquaintance of Anne Barlow, eldest daughter of John and Dorothy Barlow of Slebech, after the move to Pembrokeshire in 1646. Barlow's first husband was Nicholas Lewis of Hean Castle, Pembrokeshire. She later married a Mr Wogan of Wiston, a kinsman of Philips's mother-in-law, and died sometime before August 1676.

> · A marry^d state affords but little Ease
> The best of husbands are so hard to please

188

This in wifes Carefull faces you may spell
Tho they desemble their misfortunes well
5 A virgin state is crown'd with much content
Its allways happy as its inocent
No Blustering husbands to create yr fears
No pangs of child birth to extort yr tears
No childrens crys for to offend your ears
10 Few wordly crosses to distract yr prayers
Thus are you freed from all the cares that do
Attend on matrymony & a husband too
Therefore Mad^m be advised by me
Turn turn apostate to loves Levity
15 Supress wild nature if she dare rebell
Theres no such thing as leading Apes in hell

Praise of the single life is a commonplace of women's poetry. See
Jane Barker's 'A Virgin Life' (p.360 and note).
16 *leading Apes in hell*: proverbially, the fate of spinsters, e.g. *Much
Ado About Nothing*, II.i.35, *The Taming of the Shrew*, II.i.34 and these
lines of Rebecca Salisbury (1731-1811), an American:

> Lead apes in hell – 'tis no such thing –
>   The story's told to fool us.
> But better there to hold a string,
>   Than here let monkeys lead us. (Kuhl, 453)

6^t Aprill 1651 L'Amitie: To Mrs M. Awbrey.

Soule of my soule! my Joy, my crown, my friend!
A name which all the rest doth comprehend;
How happy are we now, whose souls are grown,
By an incomparable mixture, One:
5 Whose well acquainted minds are now as neare
As Love, or vows, or secrets can endeare.
I have no thought but what's to thee reveal'd,
Nor thou desire that is from me conceal'd.
Thy heart locks up my secrets richly set,
10 And my brest is thy private cabinet.
Thou shedst no teare but what my moisture lent,
And if I sigh, it is thy breath is spent.
United thus, what horrour can appeare
Worthy our sorrow, anger, or our feare?
15 Let the dull world alone to talk and fight,
And with their vast ambitions nature fright;

Let them despise so inocent a flame,
While Envy, pride, and faction play their game:
But we by Love sublim'd so high shall rise,
20 To pitty Kings, and Conquerours despise,
Since we that sacred union have engrost,
Which they and all the sullen world have lost.

From National Library of Wales MS 775, an autograph volume of fifty-three of Philips's poems or fragments of poems. For the copy text of this poem and the subsequent poems we have used Rev. Patrick Thomas's 'An Edition of the Poems and Letters of Katherine Philips 1632-1664', Ph. D. thesis, The University College of Wales, Aberystwyth, 1982 from which we have taken information for variant and contextual notes.

This poem also appears in an uncatalogued manuscript in the hand of Philips's friend Sir Edward Dering at the Harry Ransom Humanities Research Center, the University of Texas at Austin, and in NLW MS 776, the most complete manuscript collection of Philips's poems, prepared for presentation to Mary Aubrey after Philips's death.

The poem was first published in the unauthorised edition of 1664, where it carries the title 'L'Amitie. *To Mrs.* Mary Awbrey'; in 1667 it was called simply *'To Mrs.* Mary Awbrey'. This is not the only case where the 1664 edition is closer to the poet's autograph than the authorised edition. In the 1667 and all subsequent editions 'sullen' in the last line is altered to the directly antithetical 'factious'.

Title *Mrs M. Awbrey*: Mary Aubrey (1631-1700), the cousin of the diarist and Philips's schoolfriend, was called 'Rosania' after a character in James Shirley's *The Doubtful Heir* (1652). In her formation of a society and in her detailed poetic study of the subject, Philips gave new meaning to the concept of Platonic friendship. Her connections with the Cavalier circle of Lawes, Cartwright and Vaughan would have brought 'Orinda' into contact with the continental notions Henrietta Maria had brought from France. The pastoral sobriquets that her courtiers took from French romances became for Philips coterie names borrowed from English plays. Though the Platonic love concept was considered by more robust spirits, such as Thomas Killigrew, to be mere 'spiritual Non-sense' (*The Parson's Wedding*, I,iii), 'Orinda's' circle took the idea seriously. *Friendship* by Francis Finch ('Palaemon' in 'Orinda's' coterie), privately published in 1654, Robert Mead's comedy *The Combat of Love and Friendship* (1654), Abraham Cowley's 'Friendship in Absence' in *Poems* (1656), Jeremy Taylor's *A Discourse of the Nature and Offices of Friendship* (1657), and Robert Boyle's *Seraphick Love* (composed 1648, published 1659) all contributed to the modishness of idealistic friendship. Philips set forth the conditions of true friendship, employing themes often used by lovers, Platonic or otherwise: the exchanging or uniting of souls and hearts, the immortal flame of love, the exclusion of an outside world, which Philips often terms 'dull', the superiority of the fortunate pair. The flame is always pure, the relationship strictly Platonic, a meeting of souls, never the flesh.

19-20 Cf. Shakespeare's Sonnet 29: 'For thy sweet love remember'd such wealth brings / That then I scorn to change my state with kings' and 'Eliza's' 'To a friend at Court': 'This blessing sweet retirednesse brings, / We envy none, but pity Kings.' Sarah Fyge's 'On Friendship' takes a more realistic view:

> Sometimes a fond good Nature lights upon
> A soft and civil temper like its own;
> Strait they resolve to be those happy things,
> Which when combin'd, pity contending Kings:
> Yet e'er they reach these sublimated Joys,
> They'r poorly lost, in Treachery or Toys.
> The mighty Notions of the exalted State,
> Sink to a vulgar Commerce, or Debate:... (*Poems on Several Occasions*, 1-2)

After Philips's death her good friend Sir Edward Dering ('Silvander') expressed a different kind of disillusionment to Lady Roscommon, one of Philips's Dublin friends:

I entertain nothing with delight, even the satisfactions of sincere & virtuous friendship, which among humane joyes I did esteeme the most, have not the sweetnesse which they had, and it seems allmost as reasonable now, to lay the foundation of our happiness in earth or aire in money or titles, as in that societie & entercourse of soules, which we so much prizd, alas! in vain we call it eternall and divine, when every irregular humour, & every accident of our life, every mistake in nature, and every mistake in art, hath power to deprive us of it... (Sir Edward Dering's letter book, University of Cincinnati, Phillipps MS 14392, f. 50, quoted in Thomas, xi-xii)

Mary Astell's 'Enemies' claims to value critics over friends for their 'spurs' which 'correct and mend' her faults:

> But a Friend's loving eyes are sometimes blind,
>   And will not any blemish find,
> Or if a secret ulcer they espie,
> They'l sooner Balsom than sharp Wine apply. (Bod. MS Rawl. poet. 154, f.7)

To the Excellent Mrs A. O. upon her receiving the name of Lucasia, and adoption into our society. 29 Decemb 1651.

> We are compleat; and fate hath now
> No greater blessing to bestow:
> Nay, the dull World must now confess
> We have all worth, all happiness.
> 5 Annalls of State are triffles to our fame,
> Now 'tis made sacred by Lucasia's name.

But as though through a burning glasse
The sun more vigorous doth passe,
It still with generall freedom shines;
10   For that contracts, but not confines:
So though by this her beams are fixed here,
Yet she diffuses glorys every where.

Her mind is so entirely bright,
The splendour would but wound our sight,
15   And must to some disguise submit,
Or we could never worship it.
And we by this relation are allow'd
Lustre enough to be Lucasia's cloud.

Nations will own us now to be
20   A Temple of divinity;
And Pilgrims shall Ten ages hence
Approach our Tombs with reverence.
May then that time, which did such blisse convey,
Be kept with us perpetuall Holy day!

From NLW MS 775; also in HRC MS and NLW MS 776. First published in 1664.

Title 29/28 1664, 1667 and NLW 776   A. O./Anne Owen 1664 and 1667
9 It / Yet 1664, 1667 and NLW 776   24 with/by 1664, 1667 and NLW 776

Title *Mrs. A. O.*: Anne Owen (1633-1692), to whom 'Orinda' addressed a number of her poems, was originally Anne Lewis of Anglesea. Her first husband was John Owen of Orielton, Pembrokeshire (d. 1655), called 'Charistus' by 'Orinda'. In May 1662 she married Colonel Marcus Trevor, who later that year became Viscount Dungannon. Philips greatly disapproved of the second marriage; she dubbed Trevor 'Memnon', the protagonist in Beaumont and Fletcher's play *The Mad Lover* (1647).
Lucasia: the name of a character in *The Lady Errant* by William Cartwright to the posthumous edition of whose works Philips contributed a commendatory poem.
our society: several months after Philips's death, Sir Edward Dering wrote to 'Lucasia':

Orinda had conceived the most generous designe, that in my opinion ever entered into any breast, which was to unite all those of us of her acquaintance, which she found worthy, or desired to make so, (among which later number she was pleased to give me a place) into one societie, and by the bands of friendship to make an alliance more firm then what nature, our countrey or equall education can produce: and this would in time have spread very farr, & have been improved with great and yet unimagind advantage to the world: for it would have been of great use sure, to shew the world that there were satisfactions in vertuous friendship farre transcending all those dull delights, which the most specious follyes can tempt us with... (Sir Edward Dering's letter book, f.65, quoted in Thomas, xxi-xxii)

7 *burning glasse:* magnifying glass. Jeremy Taylor (1613-1667) in *A Discourse of the Nature and Offices of Friendship. In a Letter to the Most Ingenious and Excellent M[istress] K[atherine] P[hilips]* (1657) employs the image of a burning glass and the sun to depict the concentrations and diffusions of friendship, or what he calls 'Christian charity':

Christian charity is friendship to all the world; and when friendships were the noblest things in the world, charity was little, like the sun drawn in at a chink, or his beams drawn into the centre of a burning-glass; but Christian charity is friendship, expanded like the face of the sun when it mounts above the eastern hills. (Heber, I, 72)

Friendship's Mysterys, to my dearest Lucasia.
(set by Mr. H. Lawes.)
1

Come, my Lucasia, since we see
   That miracles men's faith do move
By wonder and by Prodigy
   To the dull, angry world let's prove
5   There's a religion in our Love.
2

For though we were design'd t'agree,
   That fate no liberty destroys,
But our election is as free
   As Angells, who with greedy choice
10   Are yet determin'd to their Joys.
3

Our hearts are doubled by their loss,
   Here mixture is addition grown;
We both diffuse, and both engrosse:
   And we, whose minds are so much one,
15   Never, yet ever, are alone.
4

We court our own captivity,
   Then Thrones more great and innocent:
'Twere banishment to be set free,
   Since we weare fetters whose intent
20   Not bondage is, but Ornament.
5

Divided Joys are tedious found,
   And griefs united easyer grow:
We are our selves but by rebound,

193

And all our titles shuffled so,
25   Both Princes, and both subjects too.
6
Our hearts are mutuall victims lay'd,
    While they (such power in friendship ly's)
Are Altars, Priests, and off'rings made,
    And each heart which thus kindly dy's,
30   Grows deathless by the sacrifise.

From NLW MS 775. This poem was printed as 'Mutuall Affection betweene *Orinda* and *Lucatia*' in *The Second Book of Ayres and Dialogues* of Henry Lawes in 1655, with a number of gross inaccuracies.

Title (set by Mr. Lawes) omitted in 1667   4 dull / fierce 1655   16 court / count 1664
17 Then greatest thrones more innocent: 27 while / which 1655   30 Grows /
Graces 1655

Title *(set by Mr. H. Lawes)*: a number of Philips's poems are described in manuscripts as set by Henry Lawes (1596-1662), but the music for only this poem has survived. Philips's friend, Lady Dering, was Lawes's pupil; his *Second Book of Ayres and Dialogues* is dedicated to her. It includes commendatory poems by Philips and Mary Knight, another pupil, who later became one of Charles II's many mistresses. The most celebrated singer of her day, Knight is briefly mentioned in a letter from Philips to Cotterell (10 January 1663). Lawes was at the centre of the Cavalier social life that managed to survive in London during the Interregnum. He gave concerts of profane music in his house and his song books are a principal source for Cavalier poetry.

On *Rosania*'s Apostasy, and *Lucasia*'s Friendship

Great Soul of Friendship whither art thou fled,
Where dost thou now chuse to repose thy head?
Or art thou nothing but voice, air and name,
Found out to put Souls in pursuit of fame?
5   Thy flames being thought Immortal, we may doubt
Whether they e're did burn that see them out.

Go weary'd Soul, find out thy wonted rest,
In the safe Harbour of *Orinda*'s brest;
There all unknown Adventures thou hast found
10   In thy late transmigrations expound;
That so *Rosania*'s darkness may be known
To be her want of Lustre, not thy own.

194

Then to the Great *Lucasia* have recourse,
There gather up new excellence and force,
15   Till by a free unbyass'd clear Commerce,
Endearments which no Tongue can e're rehearse,
Lucasia and *Orinda* shall thee give
Eternity, and make even Friendship live.

Hail Great *Lucasia*, thou shalt doubly shine,
20   What was *Rosania*'s own is now twice thine;
Thou saw'st *Rosania*'s Chariot and her flight,
And so the double portion is thy right:
Though 'twas *Rosania*'s Spirit be content,
Since 'twas at first from thy *Orinda* sent.

This poem was first printed in Cotterell's 1667 edition, 106. There
are no manuscript versions.
Title *Rosania's apostasy*: in 1652 Mary Aubrey privately married Sir
William Montagu (1619?-1706), an influential lawyer, later
appointed Attorney General to the Queen and Chief Baron of the
Exchequer, and went to live with him in London.
10 *transmigrations*: according to Pythagoras, the soul after death
passed into another living body. In the tradition of Platonic
friendship as understood by Philips, friends exchanged souls.
Philips here calls the soul of Friendship back from 'Rosania' to her
own 'brest', and then sends it on to 'Lucasia'.
21 *Rosania's Chariot*: 2 Kings 3:9-ll. 'Lucasia' takes up the soul of
friendship as Elisha did Elijah's mantle when he was taken up to
heaven.

EPITAPH. On her Son *H.P.* at St. Syth's Church
where her body also lies Interred

What on Earth deserves our Trust?
Youth and Beauty both are dust.
Long we gathering are with pain,
What one Moment calls again.
5   Seaven years Childless Marriage past,
A Son, A Son is born at last;
So exactly limm'd and Fair,
Full of good Spirits, Meen, and Aire,
As a long life promised;
10   Yet, in less than six weeks, dead.
Too promising, too great a Mind

In so small room to be confin'd:
Therfore, fit in Heav'n to dwell,
He quickly broke the Prison shell.
15 So the Subtle Alchymist,
Can't with Hermes=seal resist
The Powerfull Spirit's subtler flight,
But 'twill bid him long good night.
So the Sun, if it arise
20 Half so Glorious as his Ey's,
Like this Infant, takes a shroud,
Bury'd in a morning Cloud.

From NLW MS 776, the fair copy of Philips's works made soon after her death for presentation to Mary Aubrey. The poem was first published in 1667 in an oddly inaccurate version.

5 Childless Marriage / childless, marriage 1667   10 weeks, dead / weeks dead 1667
13 Therfore fit / Therefore, as fit 1667   19 So/And so 1667
Title *St. Syth's Church*: the church of St Bene't Sherehog at the end of Syth's lane. It was burned down in the fire of London (1666).
16 *Hermes=seal*: Hermetic seal, the air-tight closure of a vessel by fusion or welding.

On the death of my first and dearest childe,
Hector Philipps,
borne the 23ᵈ of Aprill, and dy'd the 2ᵈ
of May 1655. set by Mr Lawes.

I

Twice Forty moneths in wedlock I did stay,
    Then had my vows crown'd with a lovely boy.
And yet in forty days he dropt away;
    O! swift vicissitude of humane joy!

II

5 I did but see him, and he disappear'd,
    I did but touch the Rose=bud, and it fell;
A sorrow unfore=seen and scarcely fear'd,
    Soe ill can mortalls their afflictions spell.

III

And now (sweet Babe) what can my trembling heart
10   Suggest to right my doleful fate or thee?
Tears are my Muse, and sorrow all my Art,
    So piercing groans must be thy Elogy.

IV

Thus whilst no eye is witness of my mone,
    I grieve thy loss (Ah boy too dear to live)

196

15   And let the unconcerned World alone,
     Who neither will, nor can refreshment give.
                         V
     An Off'ring too for thy sad Tomb I have,
     Too just a tribute to thy early Herse,
     Receive these gasping numbers to thy grave,
20   The last of thy unhappy Mothers Verse.

The poet's autograph (NLW MS 775) contains only the first two
stanzas of this poem; the rest appeared in Cotterell's edition in
1667. We have used the autograph version for the first two stanzas,
which were significantly altered in the published version.

1 in/of 1667   6 touch/pluck 1667 Cotterell's emendation here destroys the sense.
8 Soe/ For 1667 The sense is here weakened.

1 Philips was married in August 1648.
3 *forty days*: according to the title Hector lived barely ten days.
20 Philips's poetic career was of course far from ended.

     On the numerous accesse of the English to waite
              upon the King in Holland.

     Hasten (great prince) unto thy British Isles,
     Or all thy subjects will become exiles;
     To thee they flock, Thy presence is their home,
     As Pompey's residence made Afrique Rome.
5   They that asserted thy just cause go hence,
     There to expresse their joy and reverence;
     And they that did not, now, by wonder taught,
     Go to confesse and expiate their fault;
     So that if thou dost stay, thy gasping land
10   Will it selfe empty on the Belgique strand,
     Where the affrighted Dutchman doth professe
     He thinkes it an invasion, not addresse.
     As we unmonarch'd were for want of thee,
     So till thou com'st we shall unpeopled be.
15   None but the close Fanatique will remaine,
     Who by our Loyaltie his ends will gaine:
     And he the exhausted land will quickly find
     As desolate a place as he design'd.
     For England (though growne old with woes) will see
20   Her long deny'd and soveraigne remedy.

So when Old Jacob could but credit give
That his prodigious Joseph still did live,
(Joseph that was preserved to restore
Their lives, who would have taken his before)
25   It is enough (sayes he), to Egypt I
Will go, and see him once before I dye.

From an uncatalogued MS at the Harry Ransom Humanities Research Center, University of Texas at Austin in the hand of Sir Edward Dering; cf. Bod. Tanner MS 306 and NLW MS 776. First published in 1664.

Title: Holland/Flanders 1664 & 1667
4 As Pompey's Camp, where e're it mov'd, was Rome. 1667
6 There to expresse / To testifie 1664 & 1667   7 they/those 1664 & 1667
10 will it selfe / it self will 1667; strand/sand 1664 & 1667   22 That his so long lost Joseph did still live 1664

Charles left Brussels for Holland on 30 March 1660 on his way back to England. Pepys, who accompanied his employer to meet the King at The Hague, described the town as 'very full of Englishmen' (Latham and Matthews, I, 138). Bishop Brian Duppa in a letter dated 8 May 1660 wrote, 'All countries have of late emptied themselves into London and now London is as busy to empty itself into Holland' (G. Isham, 183).
4 *Pompey*: until defeated by Julius Caesar in AD 48 Pompey and his governors represented Roman rule in Africa. Corneille's *La Mort de Pompée* which Philips translated deals with Pompey's murder in Egypt.
21 Genesis 45:25-28

On the death of the Queen of Bohemia

Allthough the most do with officious heat
Only adore the living and the great;
Yet this Queene's merit fame so far hath spread,
That she rules still, though dispossesst and dead.
5   For loosing one, two other crownes remain'd:
Over all hearts and her own griefes she reign'd.
Two thrones so splendid, as to none are lesse,
But to that third which she doth now possesse.
Her birth and heart fortune so well did know,
10   That seeking her owne fame in such a foe,
She dress'd the spacious theatre for the fight,
And the admiring world call'd to the sight:
An army then of mighty sorrowes brought,

Who all against this single vertue fought;
15 And sometimes stratagems, and sometimes blowes,
To her heroique soule they did oppose;
But at her feet their vaine attempts did fall,
And she discover'd and subdu'd them all.
Till fortune weary of her malice grew,
20 Became her captive and her trophy too;
And by too late a tribute, beg'd to have been
Admitted subject to so brave a Queen.
But as some Hero who a field hath won,
Viewing the things he had so greatly done,
25 When by his spirit's flight he finds that he
With his owne life must buy the victory,
He makes the slaughter'd heape that next him lyes
His funerall pile, and there in triumph dies:
So fell the royall dame, with conquering spent,
30 And left in every brest her monument;
Wherein so high an Epitaph is writt,
As I must never dare to coppy it;
But that bright angel which did on her waite,
In fifty yeares contention with her fate,
35 And in that office did with wonder see
How great her troubles, how much greater she;
How she maintain'd her best prerogative,
In keeping still the power to forgive;
How high she did in her devotions go,
40 And how her condescensions stoopt as low; ·
With how much glory she had ever been
A daughter, sister, mother, wife, and Queen;
Will sure employ some deathlesse Muse to tell
Our children this instructive miracle,
45 Who may her sad illustrious life recite,
And after all her wrongs, may do her right.

From the HRC MS; also in NLW 776. First published in 1664.

3 so far hath / hath so far 1664   5 remain'd / she gain'd NLW MS 776
9 birth and heart / Heart and Birth 1664 & 1667
14 who / which NLW MS 776   16 soule / Brest NLW MS 776
21 Tribute / suit NLW 776 & 1664   24 greatly / bravely 1664
26 the / his NLW MS 776, 1664 & 1667   27 next / near NLW MS 776
28 there / then 1664 & 1667   29 the / this 1664 & 1667
39 devotions / Directions 1664; devotion 1667

Elizabeth, Queen of Bohemia (see p.39) died on 13 February 1662.

Sir Charles Cotterell was on her staff from 1650 to 1655. In a letter dated 3 May 1662, Philips wrote to Cotterell, 'I have been told that when her Highness [the Duchess of York] saw my Elegy on the Queen of Bohemia, she graciously said, it surpriz'd her!' (*Letters from Orinda to Poliarchus*, 38).

5 *loosing one* [crown]: Elizabeth and her husband Frederick were exiled from Germany in 1620, when the Thirty Years' War began.

8 *that third* [crown]: a saint's or martyr's crown, cf. 'Eliza', 'To the Queen of Bohemiah', 15-20, (p.144).

13 *an army then of mighty sorrowes*: Elizabeth's sorrows include fifty years of exile, the death of her favourite brother, Prince Henry, in 1612, her flight from Prague in 1620, during which she gave birth to her fifth child, the beheading of her brother, Charles I, the death by drowning of her eldest son in 1629, the death of a three-year-old daughter two years later, and her husband's death a year after that, as well as the constant vexations of raising a large family in a household infested with rats and creditors.

To my Antenor, March 16, 1661/2

My dear *Antenor* now give ore,
For my sake talk of graves no more,
Death is not in our power to gain,
And is both wish'd and fear'd in vain.
5 Let's be as angry as wee will,
Grief sooner may distract then kill,
And the unhappy often prove
Death is as coy a thing as Love.
Those whose own sword their death did give,
10 Afraid were or a sham'd to Live;
And by an act so desperate,
Did poorly run away from fate;
'Tis braver much t'out-ride the storm,
Endure its rage, and shun his harm;
15 Affliction nobly undergone,
More Greatness shews then having none.
But yet the wheel in turning round,
At last may lift us from the ground,
And when our fortune's most severe,
20 The less we have, the less we fear.
And why should we that grief permit,
Which can nor mend nor shorten it?
Let's wait for a succeeding good,
Woes have their Ebb as well as flood:

25   And since the Parliament have rescu'd you,
     Believe that Providence will do so too.

From *Poems By the most deservedly Admired Mrs. Katherine Philips the matchless Orinda. To which is added Monsieur Corneille's Pompey & Horace, Tragedies. With Several other Translations out of French.* London: Printed by *J. M.* for *H. Herringman* at the Sign of the *Blew Anchor* in the Lower Walk of the New Exchange. 1667, 145-146.
'Antenor' was the coterie name of James Philips, 'Orinda's' husband. He had just been cleared of the charge that while sitting as a member of the High Court of Justice during the Interregnum, he had sentenced Col. John Gerard to death. If the charge had been proved he would have lost his parliamentary seat and perhaps his life. He was also in financial difficulties owing to his investments in properties confiscated during the Interregnum which were now to be restored to their Royalist owners.

To her royall highnesse the Dutchesse of Yorke, on her command to send her some things I had wrote

     To you, whose dignitie strikes us with awe,
     And whose far greater judgment gives us law,
     Your mind being more transcendent then your state,
     (For while but knees to this, hearts bow to that)
5   These humble papers never durst come neare,
     Had not your powerfull word bid them appeare;
     In which such majestie, such sweetnesse dwells,
     As in one Act obligeth and compells.
     None can dispute commands vouschafd by you;
10   What shall my feares then, and confusions do?
     They must resigne, and by their just pretence
     Some value set on my obedience;
     For in religious dutyes, 'tis confest,
     The most implicite are accepted best.
15   If on that score your highnesse will excuse
     This blushing tribute of an artlesse muse,
     She may (encourag'd by your least regard,
     Which first doth worth create, and then reward)
     At modest distance, with improved straines,
20   That mercy celebrate which now she gaines.
     But should you that severer justice use,
     Which these too prompt approaches may produce,
     As the swift Doe, that hath escaped long,

Believes a vulgar shot would be a wrong;
25 But wounded by a prince, falls without shame,
And what in life she looseth gains in fame:
So if a ray from you chance to be sent,
Which too consume, and not to warme, is meant
The trembling muse at least more nobly dyes,
30 And falls by that a truer sacrifice.

From the HRC MS. The poem is also to be found with minor variants in NLW MS 776, and in Bodleian MS Locke e. 17, a miscellany of poems partially in John Locke's hand, containing three of Philips's poems in an unknown hand. First published in 1664.

15 will / can NLW MS 776 & MS Locke e.17
18 first doth worth / first doe's worth NLW MS 776 /
worth do's first Bod MS Locke e.17/ first did worth 1664
23 Doe that hath / Hinde 1664   24 shot / hand 1664   29 The / my 1664 & 1667

The Duchess of York was Anne Hyde (1637-1671), eldest daughter of the Earl of Clarendon, who had been secretly married to the Duke in September 1660. Philips submitted the poem to Cotterell on 3 May 1662, with a letter written from Landshipping, Anne Owen's house in Pembrokeshire:

You see, most generous Poliarchus, that your repeated Commands have at length compell'd a very melancholy Muse to appear in a more chearful Dress than she usually wears; and tho' you will find by the Unhappiness of the Expressions in the enclos'd Copy of Verses, that the Muses have been as unkind to me, as the Committee of Privileges were to Antenor; yet I am resolv'd to give you this testimony, that I can deny you nothing in my Power, since I thus expose my frailties to you. I confess much of the Gallantry of that Action is abated by the Knowledge I have to whom I send this Poem, and that you are so much my Friend, that it shall not be seen at Court, till you have first put it in a better Dress, which I know you will do, if it be capable of Improvement, if it be not, commit it to the Flames, with this assurance, That 'twas want of Power not of Will, that prevented you from being better regal'd. If it passes your Judgement in any degree, let me have your Remarks upon it and I will correct it by them and send the Dutchess another Copy, in obedience to the Commands she was pleas'd to lay upon me, that I should let her see all my Trifles of this nature . . .(*Letters from Orinda to Poliarchus*, 37-38)

Cotterell did not scruple to edit the letters as freely as he edited the poems. 'Ephelia's' 'To the Honoured *Eugenia*' (see p.284) emulates this poem in subject and style.

Lucasia, Rosania, and Orinda parting at a Fountain.
July 1663.
I
Here, here are our enjoyments done,
And since the Love and grief we weare
Forbids us either word or teare,
And Art wants here expression,
5 See Nature furnish us with one.

II

The kind and mournfull Nimph which here
   Inhabits in her humble Cells,
   No longer her own Sorrow tells,
Nor for it now concern'd appears,
10   But for our parting sheds these tears.

III

Unless she may afflicted be,
   Least we should doubt her Innocence;
   Since she hath lost her best pretence
Unto a matchless purity;
15   Our love being clearer far than she.

IV

Cold as the streams that from her flow,
   Or (if her privater recess
   A greater coldness can express)
Then cold as those dark beds of snow
20   Our hearts are at this parting blow.

V

But Time, that has both wings and feet,
   Our suffering Minutes being Spent,
   Will visit us with new content;
And sure, if kindness be so sweet
25   'Tis harder to forget then meet.

VI

Then though the sad Adieu we say,
   Yet as the wine we hither bring,
   Revives, and then exalts the Spring;
So let our hopes to meet allay,
30   The fears and Sorrows of this day.

From NLW MS 776. First published in 1667. Thomas considers this scene to be fictitious. 'Orinda' returned to Wales from Ireland on 15 July 1663, leaving 'Lucasia' behind, while 'Rosania' seems never to have left England. The date may be a misprint for 1662, for it was in late June or early July of that year that 'Orinda' and 'Lucasia' left England for Ireland, shortly after 'Lucasia's' marriage. The tone of the poem is much like that of Philips's Letter XIII to Cotterell from Dublin, 30 July 1662:

we may generally conclude the Marriage of a Friend to be the Funeral of a Friendship; for then all former Endearments run naturally into the Gulf of that new and strict Relation, and there, like Rivers in the Sea, they lose themselves for ever. (*Letters from Orinda to Poliarchus*, 58)

'PHILO-PHILIPPA'

Among the eulogies included in the 1667 edition of the works of
Katherine Philips, appears this offering by an Irishwoman,
evidently inspired by Philips's version of Corneille's *La Mort de
Pompée* which was played in Dublin in February 1663. In Letter
XXVI of the *Letters from Orinda to Poliarchus*, dated 8 April 1663,
Philips wrote from Ireland, 'I have had many Letters and Copies of
Verses sent me, some from Acquaintance, and some from
Strangers, to compliment me upon Pompey, which were I capable
of Vanity, would even surfeit me with it; for they are so full of
Flattery, that I have not the Confidence to send them to you. One of
them, who pretends to be a Woman, writes very well, but I cannot
imagine who the Author is, nor by any Inquiry I can make, have
hitherto been able to discover' (124). The poem is extraordinary,
both in the violence of its conceits and the degree of radical
feminism it expresses.

To the Excellent *Orinda*

Let the male Poets their male *Phoebus* chuse,
Thee I invoke, *Orinda*, for my Muse;
He could but force a Branch, *Daphne* her Tree
Most freely offers to her Sex and thee,
5   And says to Verse, so unconstrain'd as yours,
Her Laurel freely comes, your fame secures:
And men no longer shall with ravish'd Bays
Crown their forc'd Poems by as forc'd a praise.
   Thou glory of our Sex, envy of men,
10 Who are both pleas'd and vex'd with thy bright Pen:
Its lustre doth intice their eyes to gaze,
But mens sore eyes cannot endure its rays;
It dazles and surprises so with light,
To find a noon where they expected night:
15 A Woman Translate *Pompey*! which the fam'd
Corneille with such art and labour fram'd!
To whose close version the Wits club their sence,
And a new Lay poetick SMEC springs thence!
Yes, that bold work a Woman dares Translate,

20 Not to provoke, nor yet to fear mens hate.
   Nature doth find that she hath err'd too long,
   And now resolves to recompence that wrong:
   Phoebus to *Cynthia* must his beams resigne,
   The rule of Day, and Wit's now Feminine.
25   That Sex, which heretofore was not allow'd
   To understand more than a beast, or crowd;
   Of which Problems were made, whether or no
   Women had Souls; but to be damn'd, if so;
   Whose highest Contemplation could not pass,
30 In men's esteem, no higher than the Glass;
   And all the painful labours of their Brain,
   Was only how to Dress and Entertain:
   Or, if they ventur'd to speak sense, the wise
   Made that, and speaking Oxe, like Prodigies.
35 From these thy more than masculine Pen hath rear'd
   Our Sex; first to be prais'd, next to be feard.
   And by the same Pen forc'd, men now confess,
   To keep their greatness, was to make us less.
      Men know of how refin'd and rich a mould
40 Our Sex is fram'd, what Sun is in our Gold:
   They know in Lead no Diamonds are set,
   And Jewels only fill the Cabinet.
   Our Spirits purer far than theirs, they see;
   By which even Men from Men distinguish'd be:
45 By which the Soul is judg'd, and does appear
   Fit or unfit for action, as they are.
      When in an Organ various sounds do stroak,
   Or grate the ear, as Birds sing, or Toads Croak;
   The Breath, that voyces every Pipe, 's the same,
50 But the bad mettal doth the sound defame.
   So, if our Souls by sweeter Organs speak,
   And theirs with harsh, false notes the air do break;
   The Soul's the same, alike in both doth dwell,
   'Tis from her instruments that we excel.
55 Ask me not then, why jealous men debar
   Our Sex from Books in Peace, from Arms in War;
   It is because our Parts will soon demand
   Tribunals for our Persons, and Command.
      Shall it be our reproach, that we are weak,
60 And cannot fight, nor as the School-men speak?
   Even men themselves are neither strong nor wise,

If Limbs and Parts they do not exercise,
 Train'd up to arms, we *Amazons* have been,
And *Spartan* Virgins strong as *Spartan* Men:
65 Breed Women but as Men, and they are these;
Whilst *Sybarit* Men are Women by their ease.
Why should not brave *Semiramis* break a Lance,
And why should not soft *Ninyas* curle and dance?
Ovid in vain Bodies with change did vex,
70 Changing her form of life, *Iphis* chang'd Sex.
Nature to Females freely doth impart
That, which the Males usurp, a stout, bold heart.
Thus Hunters female Beasts fear to assail:
And female Hawks more mettal'd than the male:
75 Men ought not then Courage and Wit ingross,
Whilst the Fox lives, the Lyon, or the Horse.
Much less ought men both to themselves confine,
Whilst Women, such as you, *Orinda*, shine.
 That noble friendship brought thee to our Coast,
80 We thank *Lucasia*, and thy courage boast.
Death in each Wave could not *Orinda* fright,
Fearless she acts that friendship she did write:
Which manly Vertue to their Sex confin'd,
Thou rescuest to confirm our softer mind;
85 For there's requir'd (to do that Virtue right)
Courage, as much in Friendship as in Fight.
The dangers we despise, doth this truth prove,
Though boldly we not fight, we boldly love.
 Ingage us unto Books, *Sappho* comes forth,
90 Though not of *Hesiod*'s age, of *Hesiod*'s worth.
If Souls no Sexes have, as 'tis confest,
'Tis not the he or she makes Poems best:
Nor can men call these Verses Feminine,
Be the sense vigorous and Masculine.
95 'Tis true, *Apollo* sits as Judge of Wit,
But the nine Female learned Troop are it:
Those Laws for which *Numa* did wise appear,
Wiser *AEgeria* whisper'd in his ear.
The *Gracchi*'s Mother taught them Eloquence,
100 From her Breasts courage flow'd, from her Brain
             sence;
And the grave Beards, who heard her speak in Rome,
Blush'd not to be instructed, but o'recome.

Your speech, as hers, commands respect from all,
Your very Looks, as hers, Rhetorical:
105   Something of grandeur in your Verse men see,
That they rise up to it as Majesty.
The wise and noble *Orrery*'s regard,
Was much observ'd, when he your Poem heard:
All said, a fitter match was never seen,
110   Had *Pompey*'s widow been *Arsamnes* Queen.
     Pompey, who greater than himself 's become,
Now in your Poem, than before in *Rome*;
And much more lasting in the Poets Pen,
Great Princes live, than the proud Towers of Men.
115   He thanks false *Egypt* for its Treachery,
Since that his Ruine is so sung by thee;
And so again would perish, if withall,
Orinda would but celebrate his Fall.
Thus pleasingly the Bee delights to die,
120   Foreseeing, he in Amber Tomb shall lie.
If that all *AEgypt*, for to purge its crime,
Were built into one Pyramid o're him,
Pompey would lie less stately in that Herse,
Than he doth now, *Orinda*, in thy Verse:
125   This makes *Cornelia* for her *Pompey* vow,
Her hand shall plant his Laurel on thy brow:
So equal in their merits were both found,
That the same Wreath Poets and Princes Crown'd:
And what on that great Captains Brow was dead,
130   She Joies to see re-flourish'd on thy head.
     In the French Rock *Cornelia* first did shine,
But shin'd not like herself till she was thine:
Poems, like Gems, translated from the place
Where they first grew, receive another grace.
135   Drest by thy hand, and polish'd by thy Pen,
She glitters now a Star, but a Jewel then:
No flaw remains, no cloud, all now is light,
Transparent as the day, bright parts more bright.
Corneille, now made English, so doth thrive,
140   As Trees transplanted do much lustier live.
Thus Oar digg'd forth, and by such hands as thine
Refin'd and stamp'd, is richer than the Mine.
Liquors from Vessel into Vessel pour'd,
Must lose some Spirits, which are scarce restor'd:

145 But the French wines, in their own Vessel rare,
Pour'd into ours, by thy hand, Spirits are;
So high in taste, and so delicious,
Before his own *Corneille* thine would chuse.
He finds himself inlightned here, where shade
150 Of dark expression his own words had made:
There what he would have said, he sees so writ,
As generously to just decorum fit.
When in more words than his you please to flow,
Like a spread Floud, inriching all below,
155 To the advantage of his well meant sence,
He gains by you another excellence.
To render word for word, at the old rate,
Is only but to Construe, not Translate:
In your own fancy free, to his sense true,
160 We read *Corneille*, and *Orinda* too:
And yet ye both are so the very same,
As when two Tapers join'd make one bright flame.
And sure the Copier's honour is not small,
When Artists doubt which is Original.
165 But if your fetter'd Muse thus praised be,
What great things do you write when it is free?
When it is free to choose both sence and words,
Or any subject the vast World affords?
A gliding Sea of Chrystal doth best show
170 How smooth, clear, full and rich your Verse doth
flow:
Your words are chosen, cull'd, not by chance writ,
To make the sence as Anagrams do hit.
Your rich becoming words on the sence wait,
As Maids of Honour on a Queen of State.
175 'Tis not White Satin makes a Verse more white,
Or soft; Iron is both, write you on it.
Your Poems come forth cast, no File you need,
At one brave Heat both shap'd and polished.
But why all these Encomiums of you,
180 Who either doubts, or will not take as due?
Renown how little you regard, or need,
Who like the Bee, on your own sweets doth feed?
There are, who like weak Fowl with shouts fall
down,
Doz'd with an Army's Acclamation:

185   Not able to indure applause, they fall,
      Giddy with praise, their praises Funeral.
      But you, *Orinda*, are so unconcern'd,
      As if when you, another we commend.
      Thus, as the Sun, you in your Course shine on,
190   Unmov'd with all our admiration:
        Flying above the praise you shun, we see
        Wit is still higher by humility.

From *Poems by the most deservedly Admired Mrs Katherine Philips The Matchless Orinda. To which is added Monsieur Corneille's Pompey & Horace, Tragedies. With several other Translations out of French.* London: Printed by J.M. for H.Herringman, at the Sign of the Blew Anchor in the Lower Walk of the New Exchange. 1667.

1-8 *Phoebus... Daphne*: Ovid's *Metamorphoses*, I, 452-567. Daphne, sworn to a life of virginity, changed into a laurel tree to escape Apollo's pursuit. He tore off a branch and placed it on his head, thereafter the laurel became a symbol for Apollo and for poetry. Relying on a tactic often employed by women writers, the author relates a traditional myth from the female's point of view. 'Force' in ll. 3 and 8 means both to bring a plant to fruition by artificial means and to ravish (l.7) or rape. Apollo and all male writers are presented as usurpers, if not rapists, and women as rightful poets.

15 *Pompey*: *La Mort de Pompée* by Corneille (Paris, 1644)

17 Another translation of Corneille's play, produced by Sir William Davenant just before Philips's version was brought out, was the collaborative effort of 'the Wits', Waller, Sedley, Lord Buckhurst, Sir Edward Filmer and Sidney Godolphin. An autograph letter from Philips to Dorothy Temple, dated 22 January 1663, records Philips's reaction to the reported performance of the play:

I believe ere this you have seen the new Pompey either acted or written, and then will repent your partiallity to the other; but I wonder what preparations for it could prejudice Will D'avenant, when I heare they acted in English habits, and that so a propos, that Cesar was sent in with his feather and staff, till he was hiss'd off the Stage, and for the Scenes, I see not where they could place any that are very extra=ordinary; but if this play hath not diverted the Cittizens wives enough Sir W: D: will make them amends, for they say Harry the 8th. and some later ones are little better then Puppett=plays... (uncatalogued MS in Harvard Theater Collection, Thomas, 782-783)

18 *Lay poetick SMEC*: 'Smectymnuus' was a participating 'author' in the pamphlet war of 1641 over the episcopacy; the name was composed of the initials of the joint authors, Stephen Marshal, Edmund Calamy, Thomas Young, Matthew Newcomen and William Spurstow, five Puritan divines.

23 *Phoebus* to *Cynthia*: the sun (male) must give way to the moon (female).

25-28 See also Sarah Fyge, *The Female Advocate* (1687):

> Unless she [Woman] will believe without controul,
> Those that did hold a Woman had no Soul;
> And then doth think no obligation lies
> On her to act what may be just or wise:
> And only strive to please her Appetite,
> And to imbrace that which doth most delight.
> And when she doth this Paradox believe,
> Whatever Faith doth please she may receive.
> She may be Turk, Jew, Atheist, Infidel,
> Or any thing, 'cause she need fear no Hell;
> For if she hath no Soul, what need she fear?
> Something, she knows not what, or when, or where.(192-203)

and Mary Astell, 'Ambition', p.334, 7-8.

34 *Made that, and speaking Oxe, like Prodigies*: thought it as extraordinary as an ox talking.

40 *What Sun is in our Gold*: the ancients believed that the sun generated threads of gold in the earth as it travelled around the planet, and matured the ore with its rays, as in Cowley's *Davideis*:

> Beneath the silent chambers of the earth,
> Where the *Suns* fruitful beams give *metals* birth,
> Where he the growth of *fatal Gold* does see,
> *Gold* which above more *Influence* has then *Hee*. (I, 74-77)

and Pope's 'Windsor Forest': 'And *Phoebus* warm the ripening Ore to Gold' (396).

42 *Cabinet*: a case for storing jewels and valuables, often used figuratively to designate the physical body, which houses or stores the soul. 'Orinda' employs the image in 'To Mr *Henry Vaughn, Silurist, on his Poems*': 'What Savage breast would not be rap'd to find / Such Jewels in such Cabinets enshrin'd?' (23-24) and in 'To Mrs Mary Aubrey': 'Thy Heart locks up my Secrets richly set, / And my Breast is thy private Cabinet' (9-10). See also 'On Rosania's Apostasy and Lucasia's Friendship', p.194, 7-8.

43 In declaring women's 'Spirits' to be 'purer' than men's, the author is referring to the three components of mankind as given in I Thessalonians 5:23, body, soul and spirit. She may refer to the animal, natural, and vital spirits, substances believed to permeate the human body (cf. Barker, 'She begining to study phisick, takes her leave of poetry', p.365, 77), or the particular dispositions that characterise women. Possibly the alchemical conceit is continued here, since alchemists ascribed moral qualities such as 'base' and 'noble' to metals and considered them too to be composed of body, soul, and spirit.

47 *Organ*: a pipe

50 *mettal*: the substance of which an object is made. Also, the character of an individual.

51-52 Poulain de la Barre's *De l'égalité des deux sexes* (Paris, 1673, 1676, 1679 and 1690), translated as *The Woman As Good As The Man* (London, 1677) similarly but rather patronisingly contrasts the 'sweetness' with which women express their ideas with the harshness of the educated male discourse:

Women... express neatly, and in order, what they conceive: Their words cost them nothing; they begin, and go on at their pleasure, and when they have their liberty, their fancy supplies them alwayes with inexhautible [*sic*] liberality. They have the gift of proposing their thoughts, with a sweetness, and complacency that insinuates as strongly as Reason: When men on the other hand, do it in a manner rough and dry. (31)

53-54 *The Soul's the same*: the argument that souls have no sex is a commonplace of the seventeenth century, (see Introduction, pp.28ff.). In Cornelius Agrippa's *De nobilitate et praecellentia foeminei sexus* (Cologne, 1532), translated by Edward Fleetwood as *The Glory of Women. Or, A Treatise declaring the excellency and Preheminence of Women above Men* in 1652, the argument is put in these terms:

God the Creator of all things, in whom the plenitude of both Sexes dwels, both made Man like himselfe: *Male and Female Created he them*: It is manifest that the difference of the Sexes consists only in the different Scituation of the parts of the Body, which the office of generation did necessarily require. But certain it is, he gave one and the same indifferent Soule to Male and Female, in which undoubtedly there is no distinction of Sex: The woman is endued with the same rationall power, and Speech with the man, and indeavoreth to the same end of blessednesse; where there is no exception against Sex, for according to Evangelicall truth, they rising againe it [*sic*] their proper Sex, doe not perform the function of Sexes, but become like unto the Angells. Therefore there is no preheminence of Nobility (between man and woman, by the essence of the soule) of one above the other, but an equal in bred dignity to both. But as for the exercise and operation of the soule, the illustrious Sex of women, infinitely almost excells the rough and unpolished generation of men. (1-2)

Like Agrippa, but perhaps with more conviction and less hyperbole, 'Philo-philippa' argues that since souls are equal, women surpass men in the soul's 'instruments', their 'mettal' or character, and their 'Spirits', attributing women's 'sweetness' not, as Poulain de la Barre does, to their uneducated naïveté, but to their natural superiority. An argument for the equality of souls appears in 'Eliza' (see pp.141ff.), 'The Royal Priesthood':

Peace! Present now no more to me (to take my spirit from the height of felicity) that I am a creature of a weaker sex, a woman. For my God!... thou hast said by thy servant... thou wilt make all thy people as Kings and Priests, Kings are men, and men are Kings; and Souls have no sex; the hidden man of the heart makes us capable of as great a dignity as any mortal man. (*Eliza's Babes*, 100)

See also l.91 of this poem, Masham, 'When deaths cold hand shall close my eyes', p.321, 136-138, and Speght, 'The Dreame', p.71, 127-132.

63 *Amazons*: Henry Cogan's translation of *The History of Diodorus Siculus* (1653) provides a description of the warrior women:

The *Amazons*... like unto men excelled in feats of Arms and strength of body. Their Queen in the beginning leavyed an Army of women, whom she trained up in military exercises, and with them invaded certain of the neighbouring Nations...(100).

66 *Sybarit*: of Sybaris, a town in Magna Grecia whose inhabitants were famed for their epicureanism.

67 *Semiramis*: Assyrian queen who upon the death of her husband Ninus, assumed the throne and became a legendary conqueror. See

Anne Bradstreet, 'Semiramis' (p.124).

68 *soft Ninyas*: the weak son of Semiramis, according to Bradstreet 'A Prince wedded to ease, and to delight' ('The Four Monarchies', l.150).

70 *Iphis*: in Ovid's *Metamorphoses*, 9, 666-797, an impoverished couple pray for a son, but have a daughter instead. The child is given a masculine name, Iphis, and dressed as boy for thirteen years, until betrothed to a young maid. Iphis' mother prays to Isis, and in the nick of time, she is transformed into a young man.

74 *female Hawks more mettaled than the male*: in falconry, the female hawk is considered more aggressive and high-mettled than the male.

80 *Lucasia*: the coterie name of Philips's friend, Anne Owen, with whom she had travelled to Ireland

90 *not of Hesiod's age*: Hesiod fl. c. 700 BC; Sappho's birthdate is usually given as 612 BC.

91 *Souls no Sexes have*: see note to l.53; cf. Philips, 'A Friend':

> If Souls no Sexes have, for Men t'exclude
>   Women from Friendship's vast capacity,
> Is a Design injurious or rude,
>   Onely maintain'd by partial tyranny.
> Love is allow'd to us and Innocence,
> And noblest Friendships do proceed from thence. (19-24)

96 *the nine Female learned Troop*: the nine muses, cf. Sarah Fyge Egerton, 'The Emulation' *(Poems on Several Occasions* [1703]): 'There's ten celestial Females govern Wit, / And but two Gods that dare pretend to it' (35-36).

97 *Numa*: second king of Rome, who established priestly colleges and the twelve month calendar

98 *AEgeria*: the nymph who Numa claimed advised him *(Metamorphoses*, XV, 482-551)

99 *Gracchi's mother*: Cornelia; see Speght, 'The Dreame', p.71, 143.

107 *Orrery*: Roger Boyle, first Earl of Orrery (1621-1679), Lord President of Munster, who drew up the Act of Settlement for Ireland. The author of a romance, *Parthenissa* (1665), and a number of plays, he was instrumental in the production of Philips's play at Dublin's Smock-Alley theatre in February 1663.

110 *Pompey's widow*: Cornelia, daughter of Metellus Scipio, the heroine of Corneille's play, in which the eponymous hero features only as a ghost.

115 *Egypt's treachery*: Pompey was murdered in Egypt by the young King Ptolemy's advisors.

119 *the Bee delights to die*: Martial, *Epigrams*, IV, 32; cf. Philips, 'To Lucasia', 31-34:

> Thus the poor Bee unmark'd doth hum and flye,
> And droan'd with age would unregarded dye,
> Unless some lucky drop of precious Gum,
> Do bless the Insect with an Amber-tomb.

141 *Oar*: ore

143-147 A rather bibulous image drawn from the business of racking off wines

175 *'Tis not White Satin*: the subject matter does not make the poem.

177 *Your Poems*: if she is indeed the woman referred to in Philips's letter, 'Philo-philippa' would have read 'Orinda's' poems before April 1663. She may have read them in a collection of poems published in Dublin mentioned in Letter **XXX** of *Orinda to Poliarchus*, dated 15 May 1663, from Ireland:

I intend to send you by the first Opportunity a Miscellaneous Collection of Poems, printed here; among which, to fill up the Number of his Sheets, and as a Foil to the others, the Printer has thought fit, tho' without Consent or Privity, to publish two or three Poems of mine, that had been stollen from me; but the others are worth your reading. (148)

According to Thomas no copy of the book in question, *Poems by Several Persons of Quality and Refined Wits*, has survived.

183 *weak Fowl, with shouts fall down*: Jane Barker employs the same image in 'To Mr C. B. On his Incomparable Singing' in *Poetical Recreations* (1688): '*Birds* have been said to fall down dead / At th' shouting of a throng' (I, 76).

184 *doz'd*: stupefied

LUCY HUTCHINSON

Lucy Apsley was born in the Tower of London on 29 January 1620, the daughter of Sir Allen Apsley, Lieutenant of the Tower and his third wife, Lucy, daughter of Sir John St John of Lidiard Tregoz, Wiltshire. According to her autobiography, Lucy read English perfectly at four years old and, by the time she was seven, had eight tutors in languages, music, dancing, writing and needlework. At her father's express wish she was tutored in Latin. Her mother helped finance Raleigh's chemistry experiments in the Tower and probably handed down some of her knowledge of herbs and the healing arts to her daughter.

Lucy described her courtship by Colonel John Hutchinson as 'a true history of a more handsome management of love then the best romances describe' (*Memoirs*, 10-11). Listening to 'a lady's' song one night, Hutchinson, 'fancying something of rationallity in the sonnett, beyond the customary reach of a she-witt', inquired about its author. He was told that Lucy Apsley 'shuns the converse of men as the plague, she only lives in the injoyment of herself, and has not the humanitie to communicate that happinesse to any of our sex'. Undaunted, he replied, 'but I will be acquainted with her'. Upon hearing false rumours that Lucy was to be married, Hutchinson became ill, but recovered when he learned she was still free. Though Lucy caught smallpox before her marriage on 3 July 1638 and was badly scarred, Hutchinson 'lov'd her soule and her honor more than her outside, and yet he had even for her person a constant indulgence, exceeding the common temporary passions of the most uxorious fooles' *(Memoirs*, 12). After miscarrying twins in the early months of her marriage, she was successfully delivered of twin boys in September, 1639. She bore two more sons and four daughters, the last in 1662.

Memoirs of the Life of Colonel Hutchinson, a book intended for her children's eyes only and unpublished until 1806, narrates her husband's military career and governorship of Nottingham for Parliament during the Civil War. The *Memoirs*, like the Duchess of Newcastle's life of her husband, is a well-informed and lively, if partisan, account of the Civil War, and is considered by historians a valuable source document on those years. Colonel Hutchinson took over his father's former seat in Parliament as a member for Nottingham in 1646 and in 1649 signed Charles I's death sentence. At odds with Cromwell, Hutchinson retired to his country seat at Owthorpe after the Long Parliament ended in 1653 and only briefly engaged in national politics during the Protectorate. After the

Restoration, Lucy Hutchinson 'made it her businesse to sollicite all her friends for his safety', disobeying the Colonel's wishes. Colonel Hutchinson escaped execution for regicide, but died in 1664 at Sandowne Castle of a fever contracted in prison.

Lucy Hutchinson subsisted partly on the equity in property she retained (in a letter of 11 February 1670, BL Add. MS 6672, f.248, she complains sharply to a Mr Bateman for bungling the sale of one of her properties) and probably partly on the assistance of relatives and patrons like the Earl of Anglesea whose 'benigne favour to me, I have so many wayes experienced', she writes in 1675. The date of her death is not known.

While her children were growing up, Lucy wrote poetry in their schoolroom, according to her own account in the dedication to her translation of Lucretius' *De rerum natura* (BL Add. MS 19,333): 'I turned it into English in a roome where my children practizd the severall quallities they were taught, with their Tutors, & I numbred the sillables of my translation by the threds of the canvas I wrought in, & sett them downe with a pen & inke that stood by me' (f.3). Her translation was apparently circulated in manuscript among her friends: she speaks of 'the little glory I had among some few of my intimate friends, for understanding this crabbed poet' (f.4ᵛ). In the autobiographical fragment published with the *Memoirs* she writes that she was not averse to 'wittie songs and amorous sonnetts or poems' in her youth. Julius Hutchinson mentions finding 'several short copies of verses, some finished, some unfinished, many of which are above mediocrity' when editing her papers, but these have not surfaced. Her translation of part of the *Aeneid* was in the possession of the Rev. F. E. Hutchinson, vicar of Tisbury, Wiltshire at the end of the nineteenth century (*DNB*) but has since disappeared. Besides poetry and biography, she wrote theological treatises; 'On the Principles of the Christian Religion', written for her daughter, Mrs Orgill, was published in 1817.

Though Lucy Hutchinson was one of the most learned women of her time, she is sceptical of the merits of educating the young in 'Pagan Poets & Philosphers', calling it 'one greate means of debauching the learned world'; they 'puddle all the streames of Truth, that flow downe to them from devine Grace, with this Pagan mud' (BL Add. MS 19,333, f.3ᵛ). When presenting the manuscript of *De rerum natura* to Arthur Annesley, Earl of Anglesea in 1675 at his request, she decries her knowledge of Lucretius as her 'shame', claiming to have 'translated it only out of youthfull curiositie, to understand things I heard so much discourse of at second hand, but without the least inclination to propagate any of the wicked pernitious doctrines in it' (f.2ᵛ). If the translation had not 'gone out of her hands in one lost copie' even the Earl's command 'should not have redeemd it from the fire'. For Hutchinson, the conventional posture of authorial modesty was accompanied by a sense of transgression. She doubted whether her 'sex (whose more

becoming vertue is silence) [could] derive honor from writing'.
Although her translation is elegant and learned, she insisted that
the book was 'not worthy either of review or correction, the whole
work being one fault' (f.3). Whatever pride Hutchinson took in her
accomplishment is hidden behind her disclaimer: 'I did attempt
things out of my owne Sphere' (f.2ᵛ).

From Lucretius, *de Rerum natura, Liber primus*

Why only in the spring are roses borne?
Why ripens summer fruite, and Autumne corne?
But that all creatures are, at times disposd
By the due confluence of their seeds, disclosd
180 In fitting seasons, when the quickning earth
May give her tender ofspring a safe birth;
Which if they were of nothing made, would be
Suddaine productions, sprung uncerteinely
In seasons not their owne, for if there were
185 No principles, which by geniall councells are
Kept back from killing seasons, there would need
No space for growth, or junctures of the seed.
If creatures out of nothing sprung; for soe
Men sudenly would from small infants grow
190 Young shoots would trees become, but that all these
    Are otherwise we know for by degrees
From certeine seeds they grow, & still reteine
Their owne kind in their growth, which makes it
                                              plaine
That all the creatures in this manner bred,
195 By their owne matter are encreast and fed.
To this, even as without due showers the ground
Cannot with new and happie births abound,
Soe without food no creatures nature can
Encrease their kind, or their owne lives susteine.
200 Wherefore of things, it rather may be sayd
As words are out of many letters made,
That common bodies doe their beings give
Then that ought without principles can live.
Lastly why should not nature frame a race
205 Of mighty men, outliving mortall space
Who on their feete could travell through the deepe,

And with their hands could levell mountains steepe,
But that a proper matter is assignd
To all things, which distinguisheth their kind.

From BL Add. MS 19,333, f.9.

The first published English translation of all six books of Lucretius'
De Rerum natura was that of Thomas Creech in 1682. In her
dedication, Lucy Hutchinson distinguishes her lack of ambition
from that of 'a masculine Witt [who] hath thought it worth printing
his head in a lawrell crowne for the version of one of these bookes',
by whom she means John Evelyn, whose *Essay on the First Book of
T.Lucretius Carus De Rerum Natura* was published in 1656.

Warburg (1937) identifies Hutchinson's source as the edition by
Daniel Pareus, published in Frankfurt in 1631 (66). The quality of
Hutchinson's version can best be gauged by comparison with John
Evelyn's attempt:

> Whence is't we see the *Rose* in *Spring*, the *Corn*
> In *Summer*, and ripe *Grapes* in *Autumn* born?
> But that of every thing the constant seed
> Concurring with the time in which they breed,
> What ere's engendred in due season grows,
> When the quick Earth her tender ofspring shows:
> Things made of nothing, would *at once* appear
> In doubtful space, and unfit times o'th year... (Sig.C4)

and Thomas Creech's:

> Besides why is ripe Corn in Summer found?
> Why not *bald* Winter with fresh Roses crown'd?
> .Why not his Cups o'reflow with new-prest Wine?
> But sweaty Autumn only treads the Vine?
> But because Seeds to vital union cast
> Spring and appear but whilst the Seasons last;
> Whilst Mother Earth hath warmth and strength to bear,
> And can safely trust her infant-fruits to the mild Air. (Sig.A4)

Hutchinson called the doctrines of Lucretius and 'his masters'
'ridiculous, impious, execrable' and sees the philosophy that would
revive their 'foppish casuall dance of attoms' as 'denying the
Soveraigne Wisedome of God in the greate Designe of the whole
Universe' (f.4). Lucretius' poem was seen by Creech, among others,
as a source for Hobbes:

Hence also the admirers of Mr. *Hobbes* may easily discern that his *Politicks* are but
Lucretius enlarg'd; His state of *Nature* is sung by our *Poet*; the rise of *Laws*; the
beginning of *Societies*; the *Criteria* of *Just* and *Unjust* exactly the same, and natural
Consequents of the Epicurean Origine of Man; no new Adventures. (Sig.b3ᵛ)

Creech, known to the coterie as 'Daphnis', was a good friend of
Aphra Behn and John Hoyle (see p.242). Behn wrote a
commendatory poem for the second edition of his translation of
Lucretius (1683) in the kind of language which was later
interpreted as evidence of her irreligion:

... Reason over all unfetter'd plays,
Wanton and undisturb'd as Summers breeze. (Sig.d4)

The Argument of the fourth booke

The Poet first his owne high prayses sings
For having tracd out such mysterious things
Then treats of image, species which be
From Bodies passing of perpetually
5   Or formd by chance in the superiour ayre
With swiftest motion ever wandring there
Who often stooping in their agile flight
And touching th'eies are there the cause of sight,
Why images beyond the glasse wee see
10   Why in't, reverst, & unreverst they be
Why there they walke he next proceeds to explaine
Then doth the certeinty of Sence maintaine.
Confuting their bold ignorance who owne
A fallabillity in all that's knowne
15   Next treats the cause of hearing, tast, & smell
How various soules in various sence excell
The secret touch whence thoughts & dreams arise,
That Organs for the Sence were made, denies
Shewes why all natures food require, the cause
20   Which vigorous Members into motion drawes
Whence Sleepe proceeds, & the varietie
Of visions which then represented be
By th'active fancy, chiefly among these
How Love, the waking dreame, our souls doth seize,
25   The vanity of that ill hatch't desire;
And how th'entangled wisely may retire.
Last doth of Wedlocks fruite & its want treate
Advizing weomen to be cleane & neate
And well behavd, that so they may
30   Retaine mens love, when beauty fades away.

BL Add. MS. 19,333, f.76ᵛ.
In the translation each book is preceded by an original poem
summarising its 'argument'. In the MS the first five books are
transcribed in a fair copy hand, but the arguments and all of Book
VI are in Lucy Hutchinson's autograph. It is possible that she wrote
the argument poems specifically for the Earl of Anglesea's copy.

1-2 Hutchinson remarks in the dedication:

this poet therefore sings high applause to his owne wisedome, for having explord such deepe misteries of Nature, though even these discoveries of his, are so silly, foolish, and false, that nothing but his Lunacy can extenuate the crime of his arrogant ignorance. (f.4)

28-30 Hutchinson's translation of this passage in Book IV brings the Puritan ideology of marriage to her Latin original:

Wives also should take heed that they be neate
Nor need our husbands care to be in love,
Sometimes unhandsome weomen good wives proove;
Her modest carriage, and her cleanely dresse,
Her wise behaviour, and her gentlenesse
Will yeild her husband a contented life,
And custome will encline him to his wife. (f.99ᵛ)

In the Latin, Lucretius writes to convince men that a plain girl with gentle ways might be worth loving, for really it is only custom that makes love; Hutchinson seems rather to be subtly advising women what behaviour to adopt to make a good marriage. Creech makes no mention of wives in his translation.

From Liber Quartus

Nor will ingenious women, free from pride
1265 Humane defects from honest lovers hide.
Nor doe the female sex their sighs still feigne
Sometimes their brests a reall love conteine.
One fire, them and their lovers doth enflame,
Their joyes are equall, their desires the same.
1270 Nor could all birds, beasts, heards and flocks
encrease,
Unless desires the females did possesse.
Both sexes must all generations make,
In which some ofsprings more the sire pertake,
Some more the dam, and soe we find
1275 Even in the generations of menkind,
Their fathers images some children beare,
Some like their mothers, and their grandsires are.
For in their parents bodies are mixt seeds
Which this varietie of figures breeds;
1280 Wherein the litle ofspring doe arise
With their forefathers countenance, shape, hayre,
voyce.

Sometimes in girles the fathers face we see,
The mothers in the boyes, sometimes they be
Made up of both, and soe we in one face

219

1285 Lines both of father and of mother trace.
And whom the children do most represent
That parents nature is most prevalent.

From BL Add. MS 19,333, ff.98ᵛ-99ᵛ.
1266-71 Hutchinson remains moderately faithful to the Latin in this passage about female desire, but leaves out Lucretius' description of women manifesting their equal flame with burning kisses. She does not translate Lucretius' misgivings about equal desires which he says can sometimes chain lovers together like two dogs unable to separate during coition. Creech, on the other hand, completely rewrites this passage, finding no usefulness in women's desire at all. His entire translation of the passage is:

> Nay if she's *free*, if not designs to vex
> Nor cross thy Courtship, or thy thought perplex,
> She'l show the *common* failures of her Sex... (136)

Verses Written By Mrs. Hutchinson
In the small Book containing her own Life, and most probably composed by her during her Husband's retirement from public business to his Seat at Owthorpe.

All sorts of men through various labours presse
To the same end, contented quietnesse;
Great princes vex their labouring thoughts to be
Possesst of an unbounded soveraignetie;
5 The hardie souldier doth all toyles susteine
That he may conquer first, and after raigne;
Th' industrious merchant ploughs the angrie seas
That he may bring home wealth, and live at ease,
Which none of them attaine; for sweete repose
10 But seldome to the splendid pallace goes;
A troope of restlesse passions wander there,
And private lives are only free from care.
Sleep to the cottage bringeth happie nights,
But to the court, hung round with flaring lights,
15 Which th' office of the vanisht day supplie,
His image only comes to close the eie,
But gives the troubled mind no ease of care;
While countrie slumbers undisturbed are;
Where, if the active fancie dreames present,
20 They bring no horrors to the innocent.

Ambition doth incessantly aspire,
And each advance leads on to new desire;
Nor yet can riches av'rice satisfie,
For want and wealth together multiplie:
25   Nor can voluptuous men more fullnesse find,
For enjoy'd pleasures leave their stings behind.
He's only rich who knows no want; he raignes
Whose will no severe tiranny constreins;
And he alone possesseth true delight
30   Whose spotlesse soule no guiltie feares affright.
This freedome in the countrie life is found,
Where innocence and safe delights abound:
Here man's a prince; his subjects ne'er repine
When on his back their wealthy fleeces shine:
35   If for his appetite the fattest die,
Those who survive will rayse no mutinie:
His table is with home-gott dainties crown'd,
With friends, not flatterers, encompast round;
No spies nor traitors on his trencher waite,
40   Nor is his mirth confin'd to rules of state;
An armed guard he neither hath nor needs,
Nor fears a poyson'd morsell when he feeds;
Bright constellations hang above his head,
Beneath his feete are flourie carpetts spred;
45   The merrie birds delight him with their songs,
And healthfull ayre his happie life prolongs.
Att harvest merrily his flocks he sheares,
And in cold weather their warme fleeces weares;
Unto his ease he fashions all his clothes;
50   His cup with uninfected liquor flows:
The vulgar breath doth not his thoughts elate,
Nor can he be o'erwhelmed by their hate;
Yet, if ambitiously he seeks for fame,
One village feast shall gaine a greater name
55   Then his who weares th' imperiall diadem,
Whom the rude multitude doe still condemne.
Sweete peace and joy his blest companions are;
Feare, sorrow, envie, lust, revenge, and care,
And all that troope which breeds the world's offence,
60   With pomp and majestie, are banisht thence.
What court then can such libertie afford?
Or where is man soe uncontroul'd a lord?

From *Memoirs of the Life of Colonel Hutchinson, Governor of Nottingham Castle and Town... Written By His Widow Lucy*, edited from original MS by the Rev. Julius Hutchinson. London, 1806, 445-446. This poem was appended to the *Memoirs* by Julius Hutchinson who published no other of her poems; the manuscript of the *Memoirs* has been lost, though some pages of a draft in Lucy Hutchinson's hand are at the British Library (Add. MSS 25,901; 39,779; 46,172).

The poem was written after the Restoration (see l.55) and before Colonel Hutchinson's imprisonment in October 1663. Lucy writes in the *Memoirs* that after his reprieve under the Act of Indemnity in 1660,

the colonell liv'd with all imaginable retiredness att home, and, because his active spirit could not be idle nor very sordidly employ'd, tooke up his time in opening springs, and planting trees, and dressing his plantation; and these were his recreations, wherein he reliev'd many poore labourers when they wanted worke... not envying the glories and honors of the court, nor the prosperity of the wicked. (386)

Lucy's poem was evidently written to console 'his active spirit'.

The classical poem recognised as the prototype for this genre of retirement poem is Horace's Epode II, 'Beatus ille', in Ben Jonson's translation, 'The praises of a Countrie life' (*The Underwood*, 1640). Hutchinson draws on more sober classical conventions than those favoured by the 'Sons of Ben'. Hutchinson's poem differs from the retirement poems written by her contemporary, Katherine Philips, in that her argument for retirement as an honourable choice is part of a tradition of writing to console the man of action, while Philips, in such poems as 'A Country Life' and 'A Resvery' [*sic*], writes to defend her own pleasure in that life.

1-24 Cf. Horace, Ode II. xvi.

13-20 Cf. Martial, Epigram I. xlix and Epigram X. xlvii, also Horace, Ode II. xvi and Ode III. i.

21-22 *Ambition... desire*: cf. the *Memoirs*: 'now had the poyson of ambition so ulcerated Cromwell's heart, that the effects of it became more apparent than before' (309).

27 *He's only rich who knows no want*: cf. Horace, Ode II. xvi.

28 *no severe tiranny constreins*: probably a barbed reference to Cromwell; Lucy Hutchinson apparently never forgave him for transforming their hard-won republic into the Protectorate.

37 *home-gott dainties*: cf. Jonson's 'unbought viands' ('The praises of a Countrie life') and 'with un-bought provision blest' ('To Sir Robert Wroth').

39 *trencher*: a serving plate for meat

49 *Unto his ease... clothes*: in the *Memoirs* Lucy writes that the Colonel 'would rather weare clothes absolutely plaine, then pretending to gallantry' yet 'in his plainest negligent habitt appear'd very much a gentleman' (5, 15); the convention is found also in Martial.

50 *uninfected liquor*: 'His whole life was the rule of temperance in meate, drinke, apparell, pleasure' (*Memoirs*, 16); the Colonel was strongly opposed to drunkenness, closing down public houses in his

neighbourhood if he heard that any patrons had been disorderly. Martial praises 'nox non ebria' (Epigram X. xlvii), translated by Jonson as 'Thy night not dronken'. Wine flows plentifully in most of the poems in this genre, e.g. Jonson's 'jolly wassail' ('To Sir Robert Wroth').

55-56 *imperiall diadem... condemne*: a reference to Charles II's restored title, not yet accepted by the people according to Hutchinson.

BATHSUA MAKIN

Bathsua Makin was the daughter of John Pell, rector of Southwick, Sussex and Mary Holland of Halden, Kent. The eminent mathematician and fellow of the Royal Society, John Pell (1611-1685), and Thomas Pell (c.1610-1669), gentleman of the bedchamber to Charles I and early settler of Westchester County, New York, were her brothers. Her father died in 1616 and her mother in 1617. Nothing is known of her early life. By the 1640s she was one of the most learned women in England; her letters in Greek to Anna Maria van Schurman, the famous European scholar, appear in van Schurman's *Opuscula*. The letters are undated, but the two women were apparently acquainted by 1645: Van Schurman's letter to Sir Simonds D'Ewes dated 'Nov. 1645' published in *The Learned Maid; or, Whether a Maid may be a Scholar?* (1659), the English translation of her *Dissertatio, De ingenii muliebris*, claims that the high commendation he was given of her by 'the most Learned Matron, Madame *Bathsua Metkins*' was prompted by 'her undeserved affection toward me' (48). Some scholars speculate that John Pell, who was Professor of Mathematics at Amsterdam and Breda from 1643 to 1652, brought the two women together. The one letter catalogued in the British Library from Makin to her brother suggests he was an intellectual mentor of sorts. Makin writes:

Most learned Brother, I pray send me a few lines of the position of the late Comet, out of the 3 papers you shewed me, that were sent you from beyond sea, and your owne observation if you please: if it shalbe too much trouble for you to transcribe out of those papers, if you send them to me, I will write it out and returne your papers very safe. Your loving sister Bathsua Makin. (Add. MS 4279, f.103)

The postscript adds:

I send you some raisons which are the best breakfast you can eat, if you spit out the stones.

Makin served as tutor for some time to the second daughter of Charles I, the frail Princess Elizabeth (1635-1650), who was placed under the supervision of Parliament after her mother and sister Mary fled to Holland without her in 1642. The princess did not live to develop the proficiency which Makin later claimed she had at the age of nine in 'Latin, Greek, Hebrew, French and Italian', for she died in 1650, a week after her transfer to Carisbrook Castle, where her father had been imprisoned.

An anonymous pamphlet entitled *The Malady and Remedy of Vexation and Unjust Arrests and Actions* (1646) has been ascribed to

Makin (P. Barbour, 1980, iii; Mahl & Koon, 117; Mulvihill, 208), but no grounds for the attribution are given. She has been suggested as the mistress of a school for young gentlewomen in Putney visited by John Evelyn in 1649 (*DNB*), but again there is no real evidence for this identification.

John Pell was employed in confidential missions by Cromwell, and was generally friendly to the parliamentary cause. Makin's well-known *Essay to Revive the Antient Education of Gentlewomen, in Religion, Manners, Arts & Tongues*, published anonymously in 1673, harks back to a soberer age, ostensibly to classical and Tudor times, but plausibly to the Interregnum. Its call for women to take their lives seriously is expressed in language with Puritan associations. In the male voice of the essay she qualifies her position: 'Let not your Ladyships be offended, I do not (as some have wittily done) plead for female pre-eminence.' She is here dissociating herself from Henry Care's 1670 English translation of Cornelius Agrippa entitled *Female Pre-eminence: or the Dignity and Excellency of that Sex, above the Male*. While some may feel it is only canny on her part to explain, 'To ask too much is the way to be denied all,' she sincerely believes that 'God hath made man the head'.

She had been promised a yearly pension of £40 in recognition of her services to the crown, but in 1655 a suit to obtain it from the council of state was finally rejected. In three letters held by the Huntington Library dated 1664 and 1668 she seeks the patronage of Lucy Hastings, Countess Dowager of Huntingdon, widow of Ferdinando, sixth Earl of Huntingdon and daughter of the notorious Lady Eleanor Audley (MS H.A. 8799). Makin's three extant poems were written for Lucy Hastings; two are elegies for the Countess's children, Lady Elizabeth Langham (d.1664) and Lord Henry Hastings (d.1649).

Makin's 1673 *Essay* is followed by the prospectus for a school she established at Tottenham High Cross, four miles from London, where young gentlewomen were to spend half their time acquiring the usual accomplishments, 'Work [needlework] of all Sorts, Dancing, Musick, Singing, Writing, Keeping Accompts', and the other half learning Latin and French, at a cost of £20 a year.

Who her husband was, what part he played in her life and when he died are unknown; from her *Essay* it appears that she relied on someone else to take care of the public business of her school. She instructs those interested in 'further account' of the school to talk to 'some Person whom Mris. Makin shall appoint' on '*Thursdayes* at the Bolt and Tun in *Fleetstreet*, between the hours of three and six' (43). This 'Person' may be Mark Lewis, author of *An essay to facilitate the education of youth, by bringing down the rudiments of grammar to the sense of seeing* [1670], who she earlier mentioned would answer questions about his new method of teaching grammar at the same time at the same Bolt and Tun (41).

It is likely that Makin wrote more poetry than has been

preserved, for her *Essay* argues that poetry is the epitome of all learning:

If I do make this appear, that Women have been good Poets, it will confirm all I have said before: for, besides natural Endowments, there is required a general and universal improvement in all kinds of Learning. A good Poet, must know things Divine, things Natural, things Moral, things Historical, and things Artificial; together with the several terms belonging to all Faculties, to which they must allude. Good Poets must be universal Scholars, able to use a pleasing Phrase, and to express themselves with moving Eloquence. (16)

Upon the much lamented death of the Right Honourable, the Lady Elizabeth Langham

Pass not, but wonder, and amazed stand
At this sad tomb; for here enclosed lie
Such rare perfections that no tongue or hand
Can speak them or portray them to the eye;
5   Such was her body, such her soul divine!
Which now ascended, here hath left this shrine.
To tell her princely birth, her high descent
And what by noble Huntingdon is meant,
Transcends the herald's art, beyond the rules
10   Of Or, or Argent, Azure, or of Gules;
To that nobility her birth had given
A second added was, derived from heaven;
Thence her habitual goodness, solid worth,
Her piety; her virtues blazon forth;
15   Her for a pattern unto after ages,
To be admired by all, expressed by sages,
Who when they write of her, will sadly sorrow
That she did not survive to see their morrow.
So good in all relations, so sweet
20   A daughter, such a lovely wife, discreet
A mother; though not hers, not partial
She loved, as if they had been natural.
To th' Earl and Ladies she a sister rare,
A friend where she professed, beyond compare.
25   Her hours were all precisely kept, and spent
In her devotions; and her studies meant
To share some for her languages, which she
In Latin, French, Italian happily
Advanced in with pleasure; what do I

226

30   Recount her parts? her memory speaks more
      Than what can be, or hath been said before:
      It asks a volume, rather than a verse,
      Which is confined only to her hearse.
      But now blessed soul, she is arriv'd at heaven,
35   Where with a crown of life to her is given
      A new transcendent Name, to th' world unknowne,
      Not writ in marble, but the saint's white stone:
      Inthron'd above the stars, with glory crown'd,
      Installed with bliss, and Hallelejahs sound.

From Huntington Library MS H.A. 8799, dated 'May 2, 1664'.
Elizabeth Hastings married on 18 November 1662 as his second wife, Sir James Langham (1620-1699), second baronet, Fellow of the Royal Society, MP for Northamptonshire 1656-1662, named Sheriff of Northampton in 1664. She died childless on 28 March 1664.

10 *Or, Argent, Azure, Gules*: in heraldry, the colours gold, silver, blue, red.

21 *though not hers*: Elizabeth was stepmother to at least one child by her husband's first wife, Mary Alston (d. 1660). A daughter, Mary, who lived to adulthood, was born in 1652.

32 *a volume, rather than a verse*: the death of Lady Langham's brother in 1649 occasioned a volume of verses, *Lachrymae Musarum; The Tears of the Muses: Exprest in Elegies... Upon the death of the most hopefull, Henry Lord Hastings*, with poems by Robert Herrick, Sir John Denham, Andrew Marvell and 'Johannes Dryden', whose poem was his first publication. Makin's Latin poem, 'In Mortem Clarissimi Domini Henrici Hastings', is among the Huntingdon papers at the Huntington Library, but was not included in *Lachrymae Musarum*. Makin may here be specifically calling for a volume of poems on Lady Langham's death and not simply using the hyperbolic rhetoric typical of elegies. Possibly she hoped that this time her poem would be included, or perhaps she merely felt that a daughter was as important as a son. Such a volume was never made.

34-37 See Revelations 2:17 and elsewhere in Revelations for this view of heaven; an emphasis on Revelations is more common in Puritan writers. The white stone is given to the elect in heaven 'and in the stone a new name written, which no man knoweth saving he that receiveth it', a greater piece of writing than verses inscribed on a marble tomb; cf. the last two lines of Anne Bradstreet's 'Contemplations':

> But he whose name is grav'd in the white stone
> Shall last and shine when all of these are gone.

Makin could not have seen 'Contemplations', which first appeared in 1678, but she did commend *The Tenth Muse* in her *Essay*, saying, 'How excellent a Poet Mrs. Broadstreet is (now in America) her works do testify.'

To the Countess Dowager of Huntingdon

Illustrious Lady, where shall I begin
To speak your praises? or your merit in
Such rare perfections of both sexes joind,
And here epitomiz'd? Where shall we finde
5   Your paralel? for learning humane & divine?
For vertues where true piety doth shine?
A president for Ladies of this age,
So noble, humble, modest & so sage;
For French, Italian, Hebrue, Latin, Greek
10 The ornament of our sex; where may we seek
Another like her self? it is not here,
England affords not such another Peer.
The Muses are divided and contend
Who shall your splendid rarities commend,
15 Minerva she comes in among the throng
And chides them all for their poor empty song,
that reaches not above the hemisphare
Of our Meridian, for her race whose yeares
are by extraction of most noble birth,
20 Transcending chief nobility on earth;
Be silent then & let seraphick laies
Speak out the rest, you cannot reach Her praise.

HMC *78 Hastings,* IV, 348, from a signed holograph in the Hastings MSS, dated provisionally 1656-1679, i.e. the period of Lucy Hastings's widowhood. This manuscript is not with the Hastings MSS at the Huntington Library. Its current location is unknown.
In the *Essay*, Makin says the Countess was 'instructed sometimes by Mrs. *Makin*' (9).
5 Though Makin conventionally claims that the Countess is without 'paralel' for 'learning humane & divine' when flattering her as a patron, in the *Essay* she is placed among a group of equally learned women, including Lady Jane Gray, Queen Elizabeth of Bohemia and the Duchess of Newcastle, among others.
7 *president*: precedent
17-18 *hemisphare / Of our Meridian*: the idea that the earth was enclosed in a number of spheres was still current at this time.

BATHSUA MAKIN

Minerva mocks earthly celebration of the Countess which can reach no higher than the first sphere of which the sun is the meridian. The outer sphere was traditionally the region of the angels who alone are fit to praise the Countess's perfections.

ELIZABETH WILMOT,
COUNTESS OF ROCHESTER

Elizabeth was the daughter of Elizabeth Hawley and John Mallet of Somersetshire, an heiress Pepys described as 'the great beauty and fortune of the North' (Latham & Matthews, VI, 110). Among her many suitors when she went to London in 1665, was the poet and young favourite of King Charles, John Wilmot, second Earl of Rochester. On 29 January 1667, nearly two years after a spectacular kidnapping attempt by Rochester, she married him, against the wishes of her family. Living in his house at Adderbury in Oxfordshire, she was often in the company of her own mother Lady Warre, her mother-in-law Anne Wilmot and Rochester's nieces Eleanor and Anne Lee (see p.286). She died in 1681, only a year after her husband; their son Charles died a few months later. Of her three daughters, the eldest Anne, who married Henry Baynton and then Francis Greville, was also a poet, and Elizabeth, married to Edward Montagu, was famous for her learning and her satiric wit.

Lady Rochester's manuscript works, now held by the University of Nottingham (Portland Ms PwV 31), consist of four complete poems, two fragments, a couplet and a heavily revised 70-line fragment of a pastoral dialogue. Three of the shorter poems also show marks of authorial revision, indicating that Lady Rochester was not serving as an amanuensis for her husband. The language of her poetry is, however, so similar to that of the poems Rochester wrote to her in the days of their courtship and early in their marriage that some sort of literary collaboration cannot be ruled out.

Song

Nothing ades to Loves fond fire
More then scorn and cold disdain
I to cherish your desire
kindness used but twas in vain
5   you insulted on your Slave
To be mine you soon refused
Hope hope [sic] not then the power to have
Which ingloriously you used

Thinke not Thersis I will ere
10 By my love my Empire loose
you grow Constant through dispare
kindness you would soon abuse
Though you still possess my hart
Scorn and rigor I must fain
15 there remaines noe other art
your Love fond fugitive to gain

From Portland MS PwV 31, f.12. A 24-line version of this poem appeared in the Antwerp edition of *Poems on Several Occasions. By the Right Honourable, the E. of R– – –* (1680), in *Female Poems on Several Occasions. Written by Ephelia* (London, 1682), in *Poems on Several Occasions. Written by a late Person of Honour* (London, 1685), in *Poems, &c. on Several Occasions: With Valentinian, a Tragedy. Written by the Right Honourable John Late Earl of Rochester* (London, 1691), and in Tonson's editions of Rochester's works in 1696, 1705 and 1714. The poem as printed here appears on one side of a small sheet of paper, in Lady Rochester's hand, with the following corrections also in her hand:
3 *cherish*: 'lighten' struck out
11 *growe*: 'grewe' struck out
12 *kindness*: 'My' struck out
15 *there*: 'since' struck out
When published the poem was usually ascribed to Rochester, a companion piece to his 'Song' beginning 'Give me leave to rail at you'. As 'The Answer' it appeared with full punctuation and substantive changes; the expanded version published in 1680 reads:

Nothing adds to your fond Fire,
More than scorn and, cold disdain,
I to cherish your desire,
Kindness us'd, but 'twas in vain.
You insulted on your *Slave*,
Humble love you soon refus'd,
Hope not then a pow'r to have,
Which ingloriously you us'd.

Think not *Thirsis*, I will e're,
By my love my *Empire* loose;
You grow constant through despair,
Love return'd, you wou'd abuse.
Though you still possess my *Heart*,
Scorne, and rigor, I must feign.
Ah! forgive that only Art,
Love has left, your love to gain,

You that cou'd my *Heart* subdue,
To new *Conquests* ne're pretend,
Let your example make me true,
And of a Conquer'd *Foe*, a *Friend*:
Then if e're I shou'd complain,

Of your *Empire*, or my *Chain*,
Summon all your pow'rful Charmes,
And fell the *Rebel*, in your Armes.

Song

Cloris misfortunes that can be exprest
Admit sume gentle howers of peace and rest
But from Loves Empire I hope noe release
for though despairing still my flames increase
5   And dull complaint can never ease a care
Thats caused by absence norished by despaire

Such conquering charmes contribute to my chain
And ade fresh torments to my lingering pain
That could blind Love juge of my faithfull flame
10   He would return the fugitive with Shame
For having bin insenceble to love
That does by constancy it merritt prove

But I that can thus slavishly complain
of tedious absence and unjust disdain
15   Merit the Scorn with which I am repayd
for She that calls not reason to her aid
Deserves the punishmentt Thersis hate
The utmost rigor of relentless fate.

From Portland MS PwV 31, f.15. This poem appears twice in Lady
Rochester's hand in the Portland MS; in both the lady is addressed
as Phillis, but in the version we have chosen Phillis is crossed out,
and Cloris substituted. The other version (f.14) differs in
orthography only, and that slightly.
1 *Cloris*: a name used by Rochester in a bawdy song and in another
poem in Lady Rochester's hand (ff.16-17), 'Cloris to love without
return'.

FRANCES BOOTHBY

Frances Boothby's tragicomedy, *Marcelia: or The Treacherous Friend*, was acted in 1669 at the Theatre Royal, shortly after the production of Katherine Philips's *Horace* at the same theatre. The play was licensed for publication in October 1669, and published in 1670, with her name on the title page as 'Mrs. F. Boothby'. Though the prologue has the line, 'With Ballading I think she mad is grown', *Marcelia* is Boothby's only known literary work. The play is first noticed in Langbaine's *Momus Triumphans: Or the Plagiaries of the English Stage* (1688), where she is identified as 'Frances', but the source of Boothby's plot is not given. Other theatre annals add nothing to the information provided by the title-page of the printed play.

Boothby dedicated her play to a 'kinswoman', 'Lady Yate of Harvington in Worcestershire', asking her to 'appose the Censuring World, upon this uncommon action in my Sex' (A2^v). Lady Mary Yate (1610-1696), daughter of Abigail Sacheverell, originally from Derbyshire, and Humphrey Pakington of Worcestershire, the wife of Sir John Yate, lived at the manor house of Harvington Hall near Chaddesly Corbett, from 1658 until her death. The name Boothby is prominent in Derbyshire; the two women may have been related through the Sacheverells. It has been said, though never proved, that Lady Yate, an influential Roman Catholic, harboured a priest, Father John Wall, at Harvington Hall until he was arrested and hanged in 1679 (Camm, 23-24; Hodgetts, 123-132). A year later, she asked permission to leave England temporarily for reasons of her health, and was given special leave by the Secretary of State, on the conditions that she not 'enter into any plot or conspiracy', or 'repair to the city of Rome', and that the Secretary of State be notified in advance of her return to England (Noake, 61). In her dedication to Lady Yate, Boothby compares herself to 'Sinners' who 'look not upon their own weak merits, but Heavens Bounty, when they implore Benefits'.

Early in 1669 Elizabeth Cottington, a member of the prominent Catholic Thimelby family wrote to her uncle, Herbert Aston:

you must know Cousin [Walter] Aston is this day gone to a new play, which was never acted but by the lady Castlemaine [Katherine Philips's *Horace*]. Wee ar in expectation still of Mr. Draidens play [*Tyrannic Love*, produced in June, 1669]. Ther is a bowld woman hath oferd one: my cosen Aston can give you a better account of her then I can. Some verses I have seen that ar not ill: that is commentation enouf: she will think so too, I believe, when it comes upon the stage. I shall tremble for the poor wooman exposed among the critticks. She stands need to be strongly fortified agenst them. (Clifford, II, 60)

233

Scholars have suggested that Mrs Cottington was referring to Aphra Behn's first play, *The Forc'd Marriage*, not produced until September, 1670. It is more likely that *Marcelia* was meant.

From *Marcelia*, IV.ii.

Marc. What strange effects of Fortune do I prove!
How variously she in my life doth move!
A Prince so brave, and in his Power so great,
Forc'd to beg favors humbly at my feet:
She never for thy glory more could do,
10   Then she in that, *Marcelia*, did for you.
Pride could not raise, nor swell my hopes more high,
Then she has given me Power to satisfie:
Nor can she bring my heart to more distress,
Then she has done in all my happiness:
15   Then bribes me with a Crown to be content,
And makes Ambition prove Loves Monument.
But love, if true, did never Power know,
That greater, then it self, could ever grow;
But that of Heaven; when it within the Soul
20   Does monstrous prove, and Virtue would controul.
No, no, I still must love whilst I have breath;
Nothing can give my passion date, but death.
But that *Lotharicus* mayn't pleasure take,
To think that his doth sleep, and mine doth wake;
25   I'le force my courage, give me to thee King,
Though I shall be a heartless offering:
And on a Throne in secret mourn that Fate
Destroy'd his Love, and rais'd me to such State.
As Princes ought, I then will act my part,
30   Not make my face prospective to my heart;
Nor give the Kings contentment cause to doubt,
When his confin'd, my Love does wander out:
My griefs and passions all shall inward burn;
The brave, their bodies, makes their troubles Urn.

From *Marcelia: Or The Treacherous Friend. A Tragicomedy. As it is Acted at the Theatre-Royal, by His Majesties Servants. Written by Mrs. F. Boothby*. Licenc'd, October 9, 1669. Roger L'Estrange. London: William Cademon and Giles Widdowes, 1670, Sig. H-H^v.
Sigismund, the King of France, wishes to forsake his mistress Calinda for the virtuous Marcelia, cousin of the King's favourite

Melinet and beloved of Lotharicus, a nobleman. Through the
machinations of Melinet, Marcelia is made to believe that her
beloved Lotharicus has abandoned her for another. In this speech,
she decides to give herself to the king. At the end of the play, the
King returns to Calinda, and Marcelia, still virtuous, is reunited
with Lotharicus.

Song from Marcelia, IV.v.
1

Eric. Oh, you powerful Gods, if I must be,
An injur'd Off'ring to Love's Deity,
Grant my revenge, this Plague on men,
85   That Women ne're may love agen:
    Then I'le with joy submit unto my Fate,
    Which by your Justice gives their Empire date.

2

Depose that proud insulting Boy,
Who most is pleas'd when he can most destroy:
90   O! let the world no longer govern'd be,
By such a Blind and Childish Deity;
    For if you Gods be in your Power severe,
    We shall adore you not from love but fear.

3

But if you'l his Divinity maintain
95   O're men, false men, confine his tort'ring raign:
And when their Hearts Love's greatest torments
prove,
Let that not pity, but our laughter move.
    Thus scorn'd and lost to all their wishes aim;
    Let Rage, Despair, and Death, then end their
flame.

From *Marcelia*, Sig.I^v-I2. Reprinted in Arber, 1899, 37.
Calinda, forsaken for Marcelia, 'sits down, and leans melancholly
upon her arm', to be comforted by her friend, Ericina, with a song.
88 *proud insulting Boy*: Cupid

MARY MOLLINEUX

Mary Mollineux was born Mary Southworth in 1651, the date of her birth computed from her marriage date of 10 February 1685, when she is said to have been thirty-four years old. According to the Preface to her *Fruits of Retirement or Miscellaneous Poems Moral and Divine*, written by her cousin, Frances Owen, she was an only child, afflicted with weak eyesight. This did not hinder her from studying Latin, Greek, arithmetic, 'Physick and Chyrurgy', and the natural sciences. She began writing pious exhortations in verse to members of her family when she was twelve.

In 1684 Mary was imprisoned at Lancaster Castle for taking part in a Quaker assembly, and in the next year, married a fellow prisoner, Henry Mollineux, at Penketh, near Warrington. From this time her poetic output gradually ceases, judging by the dates affixed to each poem in *Fruits of Retirement*, except for the Latin poems she sent her husband while he was in prison. In December 1690, Henry Mollineux was arrested again for non-payment of tithes. When the Bishop of Cheshire and Lancashire visited Ormskirk, near the Mollineux home at Lydiate, in June 1691, Mary Mollineux pleaded her husband's case so well that 'the Bishop, his Chaplain, and the Chaplain's Brother, a Lawyer, were all put to silence'. Although Henry Mollineux was then released, he was almost immediately re-arrested.

Despite their frequent long separations and Mary's delicate health, she bore two sons who survived her. The manner of her death on 3 November 1695, in Liverpool, is recounted in affecting detail by her husband, including the odd circumstance that she spoke to him in Latin whenever there were others present. Mary Mollineux refused to publish her work; 'she chose rather to appear little to Men'. *Fruits of Retirement* was first published in 1702, seven years after her death, going through at least six editions in England and four in Philadelphia before 1783. Henry claimed that he published Mary's work to establish her as an edifying example to her readers; he follows the tradition of publishing Friends' spiritual autobiographies five to ten years after the writer's death. Friends accumulated written testimonies to such an extent that in 1698 'more than 200 Quaker books and Pamphlets' were found among the possessions of a Quaker widow 'whose substance was not £10' at her death (Vann, 214).

Mary Mollineux has been dismissed as a 'facile writer of pious verse': the truth is rather that her verse is crude and often clumsy while her utter lack of exhibitionism leads her into diction not so

236

much plain as positively gaunt. Mollineux's muted style is rooted in
Quaker ideology of the late seventeenth century and is justified in
her poem 'Of Modesty' where she writes that modesty 'refines the
language', intimating that one should

> Be swift to hear, but never over-bold
> To speak, tho' Eloquent; and then take heed,
> Lest Words extravagantly may exceed
> A mild and civil Tone; for spoken loud,
> They seem to Summons-in the list'ning Crowd... (126-130)

Many Quaker tracts analysed what manner of utterance was
proper for those 'in the spirit'; George Fox's *The Woman learning in
Silence* (1656) and Margaret Fell's *Women's Speaking Justified* (1666)
defended a woman's right to speak when the spirit moved her.
Towards the end of the century, Friends began to censor their own
writings in pursuit of a respectable public image, rejecting the
prophetic and mystical; a Women's Meeting of London Friends in
1697 decided that older women should instruct the younger to
control the gift of prophecy (Mack, 224).

From 'Of Modesty'

45   Thus Modesty, and Spotless Innocence,
      Is often to its self a sure Defence.
      This is the Virgin's Ornament, whereby
      Beauty's adorned; for this doth Beautify,
      Where fading Colours flourish not, and may
50   Be term'd a *Dow'r*, whose Worth shall ne'er decay.
      Sure Men, as Men, cannot forget to prize it;
      Tho' some, as Bruits, not minding it, despise it...

      Nor let it seem to any sober Mind
      A Paradox, that Modesty should find
      A place in either Sex, altho' it be
90   Ascribed to the one peculiarly.
      Reason, that honours Mankind more than Beast,
      Gives forth its Laws and Dictates in each Breast;
      Vertue should therefore in both Sexes dwell;
      Some may in these, and some in those excel:
95   Yet this, with many more, are not confin'd
      To either solely; but the prudent Mind
      In both embrace it; for it Regulates
      Deportment both in high and low Estates:
      For where she dwells, insulting Arrogance,

100　Or any unbecoming Confidence,
　　　Must not remain, lest these defile and stain
　　　The Heart, where Vertue should prevail and reign.
　　　　　　　　　　　　　　　　　　　　　1679

From *Fruits of Retirement: Or, Miscellaneous Poems, Moral and Divine. Being Some Contemplations, Letters, &c.* Written on Variety of Subjects and Occasions. By Mary Mollineux, Late of *Leverpool*, Deceased. London: T. Sowle, 1702. New editions appeared about once a generation in the eighteenth century; in 1739 a duodecimo pocket edition appeared. Mollineux's works strongly defend the tenets of Quakerism and were evidently kept in print for succeeding generations of Friends in order to encourage similar loyalty to their religion.

An Epistle

　　　Is Friends fled, or Love grown cold?
　　　Do frozen Walls of Ice with-hold
　　　Its Pearly Streams? O let the Sun,
　　　That gave it being, shine upon
5　　The brittle Fence! Or is some Skreen
　　　Injuriously set up between
　　　The gentle Spring, and that bright Ray
　　　Which, conqu'ring Night, brings joyful Day?
　　　Remove that Obstacle away:
10　Then, tho' with Grief I may confess,
　　　In Winter-time th' Effects be less,
　　　Because of Distance, or cold Air
　　　Prevailing in our Hemisphere,
　　　And interposing (For Sol's Pow'r
15　Is still the same each Day and Hour)
　　　It will dissolve the Frost in time,
　　　If its warm Ray there-on may shine;
　　　Tho' vacant Clouds do interpose
　　　Its pure refulgent Beam, and those
20　Inferiour Concrets that have Birth
　　　From the gross Element of Earth.
　　　But stay! Methinks a Spring should be
　　　From Winters chilling force, more free
　　　Than to be Frozen! Inbred Heat
25　Is then, with purest Springs, more great;
　　　And with its Current soon doth glide

Through Ice besetting either side.
Let Love spring up, that we may see
The same Effects, *dear Friend*, in thee.   1682.

From *Fruits of Retirement: or, Miscellaneous Poems, Moral and Divine*,
1702, 107.
1 *Friends*: members of the Society of Friends, but also loved ones;
Quaker thought held both to be the same.
Love grown cold: Quaker writing emphasised 'love' as the principle
aspect of divinity; in loving another, one acts as a conduit for divine
love on earth.
2 *Walls of Ice*: cf. Emblem 4, 'Divine Love', from *Emblems with elegant
Figures newly published. By J[ohn] H[all] Esq.*, (1648), Sig.A9:

> Should'st thou not (Lord!) dispence
>   Thy powerfull influence,
>   We all should freez
>   Like Scythian seas
> Bound up in flinty ice, and all
> The suns kind warmth in vain should fall.

7 *gentle Spring*: for Katherine Philips's use of a spring as an emblem
of friendship, see p. 203.
14 *Sol's Pow'r*: i.e. God's love, which is the light of the spirit. The
Friends first name for themselves in the mid-seventeenth century
was 'Children of the Light' (Braithwaite, I, 131).
20 *Inferiour Concrets*: carnal elements. See John Sergeant: 'The sun
is a concrete of combustible matter' (1656, *OED*).

APHRA BEHN

Behn's given name, date of birth, marital status, nationality, class, and religion have all been questioned (M. O'Donnell, 364-483). Probably the only unquestionable attribute of the talented writer who published as 'A. Behn' or 'Mrs A. Behn' between 1670 and 1689 is her sex. The main source of Behn's romantic biographical legend is 'The Life and Memoirs of Mrs. Behn. Written by One of the Fair Sex' who claims to be 'a Gentlewoman of her Acquaintance', which appears in *The Histories and Novels of the Late Ingenious Mrs Behn* (1696). It expands on a short version published in the introduction to her play *The Younger Brother* in 1696, and was further amplified for successive editions of *The Histories and Novels*. The 'gentlewoman' was probably Charles Gildon, who tried to exploit Behn's literary estate after her death; the additional material is all fictionalised and sensational.

Despite extensive research in Kent parish registers, shipping records, and London marriage licences, biographers have produced only fragile hypotheses which illuminate nothing. Thomas Culpeper claimed in a note to his 'Adversaria' (BL Harl. MS 7588, f.426b) that Behn was the daughter of his wet-nurse; Anne, Countess of Winchilsea, tells us in the 'Circuit of Apollo' that she was the daughter of a barber in Wye (Reynolds, 92). The only hard fact to be gleaned from both is that Behn's background was then, as it continues to be, a matter of speculation. We do not know how she learned to write with such style and vigour or to read French. One possibility is that she grew up outside England, either in the Europe of Royalist exiles or in America.

Critics have tried to prove that because Behn's account of Surinam resembles published reports her stay in Surinam is a fiction; if her description had differed from the published ones, doubtless they would have decided with equal certainty that she was making it all up. In fact there can be no doubt that Behn did live for a time in Surinam; although the villain of her novel *Oroonoko*, William Byam, deputy-governor of the colony, was known by report in London, other characters, all actual members of the English community in the colony, were not. A letter from William Byam to Sir Robert Harley (14.3.1664, Harlow, 191) speaks of an amour between 'Astrea' and 'Celadon', or William Scot, son of Thomas Scot, the regicide, one of whose brothers had a plantation in Surinam to which he fled at the Restoration. He was watched by Byam for he was expected to lead a Roundhead revolt from the Colonies, but when the colony was to be exchanged for New York in

1665, he left and went to Holland where he was prepared to inform upon rebels in exile.

On her return to England, Behn presented some 'rare flies' to the King's Antiquary and lent an Indian feather costume to be worn in Howard's *Indian Queen* (*Oroonoko*, 1688, 4-5); she had already written a play (Summers, II, 103) but before she was successful in having it produced she went to Holland to spy for the crown, her contact William Scot. She sailed on the *Castel Rodrigo* in July 1666, and kept in regular contact with the office of the Secretary of State, Lord Arlington (PRO SP 29/169, Nos. 38, 117; SP 29/172, No. 81, I; SP 29/167, No. 160). She was obliged to borrow money to cover her expenses in Holland but her repeated pleas for payment for services to the crown after her return in 1667 were disregarded. In this connection she wrote in surprisingly familiar terms to Thomas Killigrew, Groom of the Royal Bedchamber, (PRO SP 29/169, No. 118; SP 29/170, No. 75; SP 29/172, No. 14) and finally to Lord Arlington (PRO SP 29/182, No. 143). In 1668 she was still unsuccessfully petitioning for payment and evidently in danger of being imprisoned at the instance of her creditor, Edward Butler. 'I will send my mother to the King with a Pitition... if I have not the money to night you must send me som thing to keepe me in Prison for I will not starve,' she wrote to Killigrew (PRO SP 29/251, No.91, I).

Her first play, *The Forc'd Marriage*, was produced at the Duke of York's theatre in September 1670 and thereafter seventeen more plays by her were produced and printed. Behn was evidently accepted into the confraternity of professional writers, for we find her supplying prologues and epilogues and commendatory verses for Creech, Stafford, Dryden, Ravenscroft, and Howard, and receiving them from Ravenscroft and Otway, Charles Cotton, Nahum Tate, Richard Ferrar, Daniel Kendrick and George Jenkins.

Recognition as a poet as well as playwright was remarkably swift. Behn is mentioned in *Bristol Drollery* (1674) and called a modern poetess in Edward Phillips's *Theatrum Poetarum* of 1675. 'Ephelia's' poem 'To Madam Bhen' was published in 1679, five years before Behn published her *Poems upon Several Occasions* (1684). Lines, stanzas, and versions of songs from her plays are to be found in miscellaneous collections and broadsides without attribution of authorship. Three noteworthy publications of her poems occur before 1684, linking her with important contemporary writers: in *Ovid's Epistles, Translated by Several Hands* (1680) is Behn's paraphrase of the epistle of Oenone to Paris, explained by Dryden in the second edition to be 'in Mr. Cowleys way of Imitation only' by one of the 'Fair Sex' who 'understood not Latine', yet commended since 'if she does not, I am afraid she has given us occasion to be asham'd who do'; in *Poems on Several Occasions By the Right Honourable, The E. of R---* (1680), three major poems, 'The

Disappointment', 'On a Giniper Tree', 'On the Death of Mr. Greenhill', were included as if Rochester's work; and in the second edition of *Female Poems on Several Occasions. Written by Ephelia* (1682), three short poems by Behn were included.

Her reputation was no sooner made than gossip set about destroying it. Alexander Radcliffe in *The Ramble* (1682) claimed that it was thought

> The Plays she vends she never made.
> But that a *Greys Inn* Lawyer does 'em,
> Who unto her was Friend in Bosom. (6)

The Gray's Inn lawyer was presumably John Hoyle, who was admitted in 1660, and graduated to the Inner Temple in 1679, in Behn's own words 'A Wit uncommon, and Facetious, / A great admirer of *Lucretius*' (*Miscellany*, 1685, 75), to whom and of whom Behn wrote under the names of 'Lysidas' and 'Amyntas'. *Covent Garden Drolery*, an anthology edited by Behn in 1672 contains 'I led my Sylvia to a Grove', one of the more risqué Amyntas poems. Hoyle was a spectacular libertine and the association proved harmful for Behn in many ways. In 1687 he was arraigned before a Grand Jury on a charge of sodomy with a poulterer, which resulted in a verdict of *Ignoramus*. Behn did not live to know of his death in a tavern brawl in 1692.

Behn's friendship with Otway, whose tragedy *Iphigenia* she tried to promote when he was in desperate need, was also held against her. Shadwell attacked her in *The 'Tory-Poets'* (1682).

> Such stupid humours now the Gallants seize
> Women and Boys may write and yet may please.
> Poetess *Afra* though she's damned to day
> Tomorrow will put up another Play;
> And *Ot--y* must be pimp to set her off,
> Lest the enraged Bully scoul and scoff,
> And hiss and laugh, and give not such applause
> To th'*Citie-Heresie* as the *Good Old Cause*. (8)

Some of the hostility towards Behn may be explained by her loyalty to the good old Stuart cause. As the debauchery of fashionable Restoration society took its toll, and the King's policies became more reactionary, the hacks turned their allegiance to the rising Whigs and triumphed over staunch Royalists like Behn. One of her few letters, written around the end of 1683, shows her begging Jacob Tonson to pay her £5 more than the £25 he was offering for her *Poems*; 'I have been without getting so long that I am just on the poynt of breaking... I want extreamly or I would not urge this' (*Gentleman's Magazine*, May 1836, 481).

After 1683, instead of trusting entirely to the lottery of the stage now under serious attack from the city, Behn tried more sedentary forms of writing, but the earnings from writing novels, translating and collecting poems were small. On 1 August 1685 we find her borrowing money from a Zachary Baggs (holograph letter, Folger)

with Jacob Tonson standing as surety. When Charles died she
turned her hand to celebratory Pindarics, with some success, for
John Dunton thought her ode on the King's death the best, but no
recognition was forthcoming from Charles's successors. There is
probably an element of truth in the disgusting lampoon sent to
'Capt' Robert Julian, a year or two after the death of Charles II (BL
Harl. MS 7317 f.58*).

> Doth that lewd harlot, that poetic queen
> Fam'd through Whitefriars, you know who I mean
> Mend for reproof, others set up in spight
> To flux, take glisters, vomits, purge and write.
> Long with a sciatica, she's beside lame,
> Her limbs distortur'd, nerves shrunk up with pain,
> And therefore I'll all sharp reflections shun,
> Poverty, poetry, pox, are plagues enough for one.

After the death of Edward Waller in October 1687, Behn wrote a
letter (holograph now in the Pierpont Morgan Library) to his
daughter-in-law, presenting her with a fair copy of a poem 'On the
Death of E. Waller, Esq.', and telling her, 'I am very ill & have been
dying this twelve month.' On 16 April 1689 she died and was
accorded the honour of burial in the cloisters of Westminster Abbey
as Astrea Behn.

On *a* Juniper-Tree, *cut down to make* Busks.

    Whilst happy I Triumphant stood,
    The Pride and Glory of the Wood;
    My Aromatick Boughs and Fruit,
    Did with all other Trees dispute.
5   Had right by Nature to excel,
    In pleasing both the tast and smell:
    But to the touch I must confess,
    Bore an ungrateful Sullenness.
    My Wealth, like bashful Virgins, I
10 Yielded with some Reluctancy;
    For which my vallue should be more,
    Not giving easily my store.
    My verdant Branches all the year
    Did an Eternal Beauty wear;
15 Did ever young and gay appear.
    Nor needed any tribute pay,
    For bounties from the God of Day:
    Nor do I hold Supremacy,
    (In all the Wood) o'er every Tree.
20 But even those too of my own Race,

That grow not in this happy place.
But that in which I glory most,
And do my self with Reason boast,
Beneath my shade the other day,
25 Young *Philocles* and *Cloris* lay,
Upon my Root she lean'd her head,
And where I grew, he made their Bed:
Whilst I the Canopy more largely spread.
Their trembling Limbs did gently press,
30 The kind supporting yielding Grass:
Ne'er half so blest as now, to bear
A Swain so Young, a Nimph so fair:
My Grateful Shade I kindly lent,
And every aiding Bough I bent.
35 So low, as sometimes had the blisse,
To rob the Shepherd of a kiss,
Whilst he in Pleasures far above
The Sence of that degree of Love:
Permitted every stealth I made,
40 Unjealous of his Rival Shade.
I saw 'em kindle to desire,
Whilst with soft sighs they blew the fire:
Saw the approaches of their joy,
He growing more fierce, and she less Coy,
45 Saw how they mingled melting Rays,
Exchanging Love a thousand ways.
Kind was the force on every side,
Her new desire she could not hide:
Nor wou'd the Shepherd be deny'd.
50 Impatient he waits no consent
But what she gave by Languishment,
The blessed Minute he pursu'd;
And now transported in his Arms,
Yeilds to the Conqueror all her Charmes,
55 His panting Breast, to hers now join'd,
They feast on Raptures unconfin'd;
Vast and Luxuriant, such as prove
The Immortality of Love.
For who but a Divinitie,
60 Could mingle Souls to that Degree;
And melt 'em into Extasie.
Now like the *Phenix*, both Expire,

244

While from the Ashes of their fire,
Sprung up a new, and soft desire.
65 Like Charmers, thrice they did invoke,
The God! and thrice new vigor took.
Nor had the Mysterie ended there,
But *Cloris* reassum'd her fear,
And chid the Swain, for having prest,
70 What she alas wou'd not resist:
Whilst he in whom Loves sacred flame,
Before and after was the same,
Fondly implor'd she wou'd forget
A fault, which he wou'd yet repeat.
75 From Active Joyes with some they hast,
To a Reflexion on the past;
A thousand times my Covert bless,
That did secure their Happiness:
Their Gratitude to every Tree
80 They pay, but most to happy me;
The Shepherdess my Bark carest,
Whilst he my Root, Love's Pillow, kist;
And did with sighs, their Fate deplore,
Since I must shelter them no more;
85 And if before my Joyes were such,
In having heard, and seen too much,
My Grief must be as great and high,
When all abandon'd I shall be,
Doom'd to a silent Destinie.
90 No more the Charming strife to hear,
The Shepherds Vows, the Virgins fear:
No more a joyful looker on,
Whilst Loves soft Battel's lost and won.
   With grief I bow'd my murmering Head,
95 And all my Christal Dew I shed.
Which did in *Cloris* Pity move,
(*Cloris* whose Soul is made of Love;)
She cut me down, and did translate,
My being to a happier state.
100 No Martyr for Religion di'd
With half that Unconsidering Pride;
My top was on that Altar laid,
Where Love his softest Offerings paid:
And was as fragrant Incense burn'd,

105   My body into Busks was turn'd:
      Where I still guard the Sacred Store,
      And of Loves Temple keep the Door.

From *Poems upon Several Occasions: With a Voyage to the Island of Love.
By Mrs. A. Behn*. London: Printed for R. Tonson and J. Tonson...
1684, 19-24. This poem was first published without attribution as
'*On a* Giniper Tree *now cut down to make Busks*' in the collection which
appeared shortly after the Earl of Rochester's death, *Poems on
Several Occasions* By the Right Honourable, The E. of R---. Printed
at Antwerp, 1680. Though Behn published it in her collection of
her own poems in 1684, along with 'The Disappointment' and 'On
the Death of Mr. Greenhill', the other two poems of Behn's in the
1680 Rochester, the three poems appeared without attribution
again in the edition of Rochester published by A. Thorncome in
1685, *Poems on Several Occasions, Written by a late Person of Honour*.
The three poems reappear in *The Works of the Earls of Rochester,
Roscommon, Dorset* in 1712, 1718, 1731, 1739, 1752, and 1800. 'On a
Juniper-Tree' was circulated in manuscript; a fair copy among the
Portland MSS (UNott PwV40) was made from the same version of
the poem that appeared in print in 1680. The 1684 version of 'On a
Juniper-Tree' clearly reflects authorial changes to the earlier
printed text. The caesural commas of the 1680 version are mostly
eliminated in favour of the 'equal pace' and 'airy path' that Behn
recommends in 'To Henry Higden, Esq.; On his Translation of the
Tenth Satyr of Juvenal' (1687). Subtle changes in wording give the
woman a less passive role. Although Behn compiled *Poems upon
Several Occasions* because she needed the money, she took pride in it.
    It is a curious coincidence that at the end of her career Behn was
to write of the juniper again, in her versification of the translation
of the Sixth Book of Cowley's Latin poem 'Of Plants', published in
the year of her death. Cowley's Latin condemns the juniper as the
source of savin, much used as an abortifacient, and Behn follows:

    Fatal Sabina Nymph of Infamy.
    For this the *Cypress* thee Companion calls,
    Who piously attends at Funerals:
    But thou more barbarous, dost thy pow'r employ,
    And even the unborn Innocent destroy.
    Like Fate destructive thou, without remorse,
    While she the death of ev'n the Ag'd deplores. (142)

8 ungrateful Sullenness./ unwilling sullenness: 1680
26 Root she lean'd her head,/Root, he plac'd her *Head*, 1680
27 their Bed: / her *Bed*; 1680   28 [missing] 1680
30 supporting yielding Grass: / supporting, yeelding *Moss*; 1680
48 desire...hide: / desires,...hide, 1680
61 In Harvard's copy of Rochester's 1680 *Poems* l.60 ends with a question mark and
this line is missing (deleted?).
62 Now like the *Phenix*, / Where like the *Phoenix* 1680
67 2 lines inserted: And had the *Nymph*, been half so kind, / As was the *Shepherd*, well
inclin'd; 1680

APHRA BEHN

67 The Myst'ry had not ended there 1680
73 Fondly implor'd / Humbly implores 1680
75 Joyes with some / joys, with shame 1680
86 In having seen, and heard so much; 1680
87 Grief...great / griefs,...great, 1680
88 I shall be, / I must lye, 1680

70 alas wou'd / (alas) cou'd 1680
74 A fault, / That fault, 1680
77 my *Covert* / the *Covert* 1680

90 Charming strife / Am'rous strife 1680

Title: according to John Evelyn (*Sylva,* 1664):

Of *Juniper* we have two Sorts, whereof one is much taller and more fit for improvement. The wood is *yellow* and as *sweet* as cedar whereof it is accounted a dwarfish sort... My *Brother* having cut of one only *Tree* an *Arbour* capable for three to fit in... If it arrive to full growth it is Timber for many curious works; the very *chips* render a wholesome perfume within doors... (67)

A busk is 'a strong peece of Wood, or Whalebone thrust down the middle of the Stomacker' or in modern parlance, corset (1688, *OED*). Juniper wood was used in making musical instruments; we have found no other mention of its use in corset-making.

3 *Aromatick Boughs and Fruit*: when crushed, juniper leaves give off the scent of apples. Juniper berries were used in seasoning, especially before black pepper was available, and to flavour (and give the name to) gin.

7-8 *touch... Sullenness*: juniper leaves are narrow and sharp-pointed.

10 *Yielded with some Reluctancy*: juniper berries are firmly attached to the stem, and well guarded by the leaves, cf. Behn's Cowley:

> Thy Aromatick shade, whose verdant Arms
> Even thy own useful fruits secures from harms... (141)

13 *all the year*: the juniper is an evergreen.

16-19 Behn's description plays on the fact that junipers are low-growing trees frequently overshadowed by other trees and unexposed to direct sunlight.

28 *Canopy*: *Juniperus communis*, the only tall species growing in Britain at this time, does not usually have a spreading crown; the tree may have been clipped to a shape.

38 *that degree of Love*: i.e. love without the goal of sexual intercourse. The tree's interest is voyeuristic and inferior in Behn's estimation.

40 *Rival Shade*: the male partner's shadow

45 *mingled melting Rays*: cf. Donne, 'The Extasie', 7, 'Our eye-beams twisted...'

57-58 Cf. Donne, 'The Canonization' (26-27):

> Wee dye and rise the same, and prove
> Mysterious by this love.

62 *Phenix*: the phoenix which was reputed to rise reborn from its own ashes is a frequent figure of sexual passion, here used specifically to signify repeated sequences of tumescence and detumescence.

65 *Charmers*: necromancers

67 *Mysterie*: ritual, cf. Donne, 'The Extasie', 71

82 *Love's Pillow*: cf. 'The Extasie', 1. In *The Athenian Mercury*, 24 October 1693, John Dunton includes Donne among seventeen

non-religious poets whom he advises Elizabeth Singer (see p.383) to read.

In Imitation of Horace

I

What mean those Amorous Curles of Jet?
    For what heart-Ravisht Maid
Dost thou thy Hair in order set,
    Thy Wanton Tresses Braid?
5   And thy vast Store of Beauties open lay,
That the deluded Fancy leads astray.

II

For pitty hide thy Starry eyes,
    Whose Languishments destroy:
And look not on the Slave that dyes
10   With an Excess of Joy.
Defend thy Coral Lips, thy Amber Breath;
To taste these Sweets lets in a Certain Death.

III

Forbear, fond Charming Youth, forbear,
    Thy words of Melting Love:
15 Thy Eyes thy Language well may spare,
    One Dart enough can move.
And she that hears thy voice and sees thy Eyes
With too much Pleasure, too much Softness dies.

IV

Cease, Cease, with Sighs to warm my Soul,
20   Or press me with thy Hand:
Who can the kindling fire controul,
    The tender force withstand?
Thy Sighs and Touches like wing'd Lightning fly,
And are the Gods of Loves Artillery.

From *Poems upon Several Occasions*... 1684, 98-100.
In his edition of Behn's work Montague Summers calls this poem an expansion of Horace's Ode I.v (VI, 426); Milton's translation of the ode is well known. Horace addresses a woman, Pyrrha, and scolds her for her vain seductions of beautiful youths and her fickleness. Although two English versions of the ode were published in 1684, one by Thomas Creech and one by 'J. H., Esq.', both are fairly strict translations and very unlike Behn's poem; e.g. see Creech (1684):

What tender Youth upon a Rosy bed
  With Odours flowing round his head

Shall ruffle Thee, and loose a heart?
For what fond Youth wilt Thou prepare
The lovely Mazes of thy Hair,
And spread Charms neat without the help of Art?

Behn's first stanza contains verbal echoes of Abraham Cowley's version, 'In Imitation of *Horaces* Ode' (1656):

In whom now *Pyrrha*, art thou kind?
To what heart-ravisht Lover,
Dost thou thy golden locks unbind,
Thy hidden sweets discover,
And with large bounty open set
All the bright stores of thy rich *Cabinet*?

The resemblances do not extend beyond the first stanza however. In reversing the sex roles, Behn changed the emphasis and tone, using only Horace's initial idea to construct a new kind of erotic poem. The woman writes not from a position of scornful superiority but emphasises her own vulnerability. It has been noted that Behn similarly made a new species of 'imperfect enjoyment' poem by taking the woman's point of view in 'The Disappointment' (Quaintance, 199). Less sensitive critics have accused Behn of taking a male view of sex.

To Mrs.W. On her Excellent Verses (Writ in Praise of some I had made on the Earl of Rochester) Written in a Fit of Sickness.

Enough kind Heaven! to purpose I have liv'd,
And all my Sighs & Languishments surviv'd.
My Stars in vain their sullen influence have shed,
    Round my till now Unlucky Head:
5   I pardon all the Silent Hours I've griev'd,
    My Weary Nights, and Melancholy Days;
        When no Kind Power my Pain Reliev'd,
    I lose you all, you sad Remembrancers,
    I lose you all in New-born Joys,
10   Joys that will dissipate my Falling Tears.
    The Mighty Soul of *Rochester's* reviv'd,
    Enough Kind Heaven to purpose I have liv'd.
    I saw the Lovely *Phantom*, no Disguise,
    Veil'd the blest Vision from my Eyes,
15   Twas all o're *Rochester* that pleas'd and did surprize.
Sad as the Grave I sat by Glimmering Light,
Such as attends Departing Souls by Night.
Pensive as absent Lovers left alone,
Or my poor Dove, when his Fond Mate was gone.

20 Silent as Groves when only Whispering Gales,
         Sigh through the Rushing Leaves,
As softly as a Bashful Shepherd Breaths,
         To his Lov'd Nymph his Amorous Tales.
So dull I was, scarce Thought a Subject found,
25 Dull as the Light that gloom'd around;
         When lo the Mighty Spirit appear'd,
         All Gay, all Charming to my sight;
         My Drooping Soul it Rais'd and Cheer'd,
         And cast about a Dazling Light.
30   In every part there did appear,
         The Great, the God-like *Rochester*,
His Softness all, his Sweetness everywhere.
It did advance, and with a Generous Look,
To me Addrest, to worthless me it spoke:
35 With the same wonted Grace my Muse it prais'd,
With the same Goodness did my Faults Correct:
And Careful of the Fame himself first rais'd,
Obligingly it School'd my loose Neglect.
The soft, the moving Accents soon I knew
40 The gentle Voice made up of Harmony;
Through the Known Paths of my glad Soul it flew;
I knew it straight, it could no others be,
'Twas not Alied but very very he.
         So the All-Ravisht Swain that hears
45 The wondrous Musick of the Sphears,
For ever does the grateful Sound retain,
         Whilst all his Oaten Pipes and Reeds.
The Rural Musick of the Groves and Meads,
Strive to divert him from the Heavenly Song in vain.
50   He hates their harsh and Untun'd Lays,
Which now no more his Soul and Fancy raise.
         But if one Note of the remembred Air
              He chance again to hear,
         He starts, and in a transport cries, — *'Tis there!*
55   He knows it all by that one little taste,
         And by that grateful Hint remembers all the rest.
Great, Good, and Excellent, by what new way
         Shall I my humble Tribute pay,
         For this vast Glory you my Muse have done,
60   For this great Condescention shown!
         So Gods of old sometimes laid by

Their Awful Trains of Majesty,
And chang'd ev'n Heav'n a while for Groves and
Plains,
And to their Fellow-Gods preferr'd the lowly Swains.
65 And Beds of Flow'rs would oft compare
To those of Downey Clouds, or yielding Air;
At Purling Streams would drink in homely Shells,
Put off the God, to Revel it in Woods and Shepherds
Cells;
Would listen to their Rustick Songs, and show
70 Such Divine Goodness in Commending too,
Whilst the transported Swain the Honour pays
With humble Adoration, humble Praise.

From *Poems upon Several Occasions...* 1684, 57-60.
Title *Mrs. W.*: Anne Wharton, Rochester's niece (see p.286)
Excellent Verses: 'To Mrs. A. Behn, On what she Writ of the Earl of
Rochester', first published in *A Collection of Poems by Several Hands*,
1693:

> In pleasing Transport rap't, my Thoughts aspire
> With humble Verse to Praise what you Admire:
> Few living Poets may the Laurel claim,
> Most pass thro' Death to reach at Living Fame.
> Fame, Phoenix like, still rises from a Tomb;
> But bravely you this Custom have o'ercome.
> You force an Homage from each Generous Heart,
> Such as you always pay to just Desert.
> You prais'd him Living, whom you Dead bemoan,
> And now your Tears afresh his Laurel crown.
> It is this Flight of yours excites my Art,
> Weak as it is, to take your Muse's part,
> And pay loud Thanks back from my bleeding Heart.
> May you in every pleasing Grace excel,
> May bright *Apollo* in your Bosome dwell;
> May yours excel the Matchless *Sappho's* Name;
> May you have all her Wit, without her Shame:
> Tho' she to Honour gave a fatal Wound,
> Employ your Hand to raise it from the ground.
> Right its wrong'd Cause with your Inticing Strain,
> Its ruin'd Temples try to build again.
> Scorn meaner Theams, declining low desire,
> And bid your Muse maintain a Vestal Fire.
> If you do this, what Glory will insue,
> To all our Sex, to Poesie, and you?
> Write on, and may your Numbers ever flow,
> Soft as the Wishes that I make for you.

some I had made on the Earl of Rochester: Rochester died on 26 July
1680. Behn's 'Elegy on the Death of the Late Earl of Rochester' was
not printed until 1685 in her *Miscellany*.
Fit of Sickness: the descriptions of Behn's ailment in 'An Epistle to

KISSING THE ROD

Julian' (1686-1687), 'her limbs distortur'd, nerves [i.e. sinews] shrunk up with pain' and later in *A Satyrical Epistle to the Female Author of a Poem call'd Silvia's Revenge &c* (1691), indicate that Behn suffered from a degenerative arthritis which may well have attacked her as early as 1680.

1 *to purpose I have liv'd*: it is unlikely that the extravagance of this flattery implies sarcasm, but the editors have debated the point. Although Wharton's poem takes a superior tone, it is still extraordinary that a woman of her class should condescend to notice Behn, whose answer was required by decorum to demonstrate her consciousness of the gulf between them.

15 *Twas all o're Rochester*: embodied Rochester, seemed to speak in his voice. Behn is using the same kind of conceit as Edmund Waller in 'Of an Elegy made by Mrs. Wharton on the Earl of Rochester' (published in *Examen Miscellaneum* in 1702): '*Chloris* [Wharton] in lines so like his own, / ...Shews that still in her he lives'. The device does become strained.

37 *Fame himself first rais'd*: Behn is here implying that Rochester promoted her work in the beginning.

43 *'Twas not Alied but very very he*: allied, joined, by kindred or affinity, with a possible play on 'allayed' or 'alloyed', mixed with impurities or inferior substance, not the genuine article; cf. Waller, 'Ally'd in Genius, as in Blood' ('Of an Elegy made by Mrs. Wharton...').

67 *Purling*: rippling; also, murmuring

Silvio's Complaint: A Song, *To a Fine Scotch Tune.*

I

In the Blooming Time o'th' year,
In the Royal Month of *May*:
Au the Heaves were glad and clear,
Au the Earth was Fresh and Gay.
5   A Noble Youth but all Forlorn,
Lig'd Sighing by a Spring:
'Twere better I's was nere Born,
Ere wisht to be a King.

II

Then from his Starry Eyne,
10   Muckle Showers of Christal Fell:
To bedew the Roses Fine,
That on his Cheeks did dwell.
And ever 'twixt his Sighs he'd cry,

252

How Bonny a Lad I'd been,
15   Had I, weys me, nere Aim'd high,
    Or wisht to be a King.

III

With Dying Clowdy Looks,
Au the Fields and Groves he kens:
Au the Gleeding Murmuring Brooks,
20   (Noo his Unambitious Friends)
Tol which he eance with Mickle Cheer
His Bleating Flocks woud bring:
And crys, woud God I'd dy'd here,
    Ere wisht to be a King.

IV

25   How oft in Yonder Mead,
Cover'd ore with Painted Flowers:
Au the Dancing Youth I've led,
Where we past our Blether Hours.
In Yonder Shade, in Yonder Grove,
30   How Blest the *Nymphs* have been:
Ere I for Pow'r Debaucht Love,
    Or wisht to be a King.

V

Not add the *Arcadian Swains*,
In their Pride and Glory Clad:
35   Not au the Spacious Plains,
Ere coud Boast a Bleether Lad.
When ere I Pip'd, or Danc'd, or Ran,
Or leapt, or whirl'd the Sling:
The Flowry Wreaths I still won,
40   And wisht to be a King,

VI

But Curst be yon Tall Oak,
And Old *Thirsis* be accurst:
There I first my peace forsook,
There I learnt Ambition first.
45   Such Glorious Songs of *Hero's* Crown'd,
The Restless Swain woud Sing:
My Soul unknown desires found,
    And Languisht to be King.

VII

Ye Garlands wither now,
50 Fickle Glories vanish all:
Ye Wreaths that deckt my Brow,
To the ground neglected fall.
No more my sweet Repose molest,
Nor to my Fancies bring
55 The Golden Dreams of being Blest
    With Titles of a King.

VIII

Ye Noble Youths beware,
Shun Ambitious powerful Tales:
Distructive, False, and Fair,
60 Like the Oceans Flattering Gales.
See how my Youth and Glories lye,
Like Blasted Flowers i'th' Spring:
My Fame Renown and all dye,
    For wishing to be King.

From *Poems upon Several Occasions*... 1684, 95-98.
This poem is usually taken to be about Monmouth, Charles II's illegitimate son by Lucy Walters, given the grace titles of Duke of Monmouth and Buccleugh. In 1683, he was banished for his continuing attempts to secure the right of succession, and in particular his involvement in the plotting of Shaftesbury to kill the king and his brother, the rightful heir to the throne. Frequent anti-Monmouth ballads and broadsides appeared, often in a pseudo-Scots dialect in ironic reference to his Scottish titles and his famous Scottish campaign. Behn's poem 'When Jemmy first began to love' (*Poems upon Several Occasions*, 1684), which is clearly about Monmouth, appeared in *Covent Garden Drolery* (1672) as 'Song to a Schotish tune'. A warrant for Behn's arrest was issued in 1682 for the attack on Monmouth in her epilogue to the anonymous play *Romulus and Hersilia* (LC 5/191; 5/16, 118).

In 1684 when this poem appeared Monmouth was living in Flanders. He had yet to be involved in the abortive rebellion against the accession of James II for which he was beheaded on 15 July 1685; it is not clear why Behn should have attacked him at this time. Another possibility is that 'Silvio's Complaint' is written about John Sheffield, third Earl of Mulgrave, who was made the subject of lampoons and satires by members of the Rochester circle as early as 1677. He is the 'Bajazet' of the poem 'Ephelia to Bajazet' first printed in *Female Poems* (1679) by 'Ephelia' (see p.277) and the 'Lord All-Pride' and 'King John' of the linked satires that followed (Vieth,

1963, 338). Mulgrave was an attractive, ambitious womaniser satirised for his pride, lust and avarice. In 1682, he attempted to court the Princess Anne surreptitiously, evidently wishing 'to be a King'. The poem 'Bajazet to Gloriana', a dramatic epistle in which the persona excuses his presumption thus –

> ... my haughty Soul cou'd ne'er have bow'd
> To any Beauty, of the common Crowd.
> None but the Brow, that did expect a Crown
> Cou'd Charm or Awe me with a Smile, or Frown

– is clearly about Mulgrave and was almost certainly written by Behn (Harris, 92); the same poem with minor variants appears as 'Ovid to Julia' in Behn's *Miscellany* (1685). When the Princess's infatuation was discovered, Charles banished Mulgrave from England and took his offices from him.

31 *I for Pow'r Debaucht Love*: this line seems quite inappropriate to Monmouth. In 'Bajazet to Gloriana' ('Ovid to Julia'), Bajazet protests:

> Yet witness all ye spightful Powers above,
> If my ambition did not spring from love! (*Miscellany*, 265)

25-40 Cf. *Miscellany*, 266:

> I had the Envy of th'*Arcadian* Plains,
> Sought by the Nymphs, and bow'd to by the Swains;
> Where I pass'd, I swept the Fields along,
> And gather'd round me all the gazing throng:
> And when I spread my wanton wishes round,
> They wanted nothing but my being Crown'd.'

41 *yon Tall Oak*: a symbol of stability and order that became particularly associated with Charles II and the restored monarchy.

A Letter to a Brother of the Pen in Tribulation.

Poor *Damon*! Art thou caught? Is't ev'n so?
Art thou become a **Tabernacler* too?
Where sure thou dost not mean to Preach or Pray,
Unless it be the clean contrary way:
5   This holy (a) time I little thought thy sin
Deserv'd a *Tub* to do its Pennance in.
O how you'll for th'*Aegyptian Flesh-pots* wish,
When you'r half-famish'd with your Lenten-dish,
Your *Almonds, Currans, Biskets* hard and dry,
10 Food that will Soul and Body mortifie:
Damn'd Penetential Drink, that will infuse
Dull Principles into thy Grateful Muse.
– Pox on't that you must needs be fooling now,
Just when the Wits had greatest (b) need of you.

15 Was Summer then so long a coming on,
   That you must make an Artificial one?
   Much good may't do thee; but 'tis thought thy Brain
   E'er long will wish for cooler Days again.
   For Honesty no more will I engage:
20 I durst have sworn thou'dst had thy Pusillage.
   Thy Looks the whole Cabal have cheated too;
   But thou wilt say, most of the Wits do so.
   Is this thy writing (c) Plays? who thought thy Wit
   An Interlude of Whoring would admit?
25 To Poetry no more thou'lt be inclin'd,
   Unless in Verse to damn all Woman-kind:
   And 'tis but Just thou shouldst in Rancor grow
   Against that Sex that has Confin'd thee so.
       All things in Nature now are Brisk and Gay
30 At the Approaches of the *Blooming May*:
   The new-fletch'd Birds do in our Arbors sing
   A Thousand Airs to welcome in the Spring;
   Whilst ev'ry Swain is like a Bridegroom drest,
   And ev'ry Nymph as going to a Feast:
35 The Meadows now their flowry Garments wear,
   And ev'ry Grove does in its Pride appear:
   Whilst thou poor *Damon* in close Rooms art pent,
   Where hardly thy own Breath can find a vent.
   Yet that too is a Heaven, compar'd to th' Task
40 Of Codling every Morning in a Cask.
       Now I could curse this Female, but I know,
   She needs it not, that thus cou'd handle you.
   Besides, that Vengeance does to thee belong,
   And 'twere Injustice to disarm thy Tongue.
45 Curse then, dear Swain, that all the Youth may hear,
   And from thy dire Mishap be taught to fear.
   Curse till thou hast undone the Race, and all
   That did contribute to thy Spring and Fall.

   *So he called a Sweating-Tub.
   (a) Lent. (b) I wanted a Prologue to a Play.
   (c) He pretended to Retire to Write.

From *Poems upon Several Occasions...* 1684, 80-82.
1 *Damon*: thought by some commentators to be the playwright
Edward Ravenscroft.

2 *Tabernacler*: one who has withdrawn into an enclosed space, used of Christ in the wilderness, also applied to non-conformist worshippers; Behn's note claims that Damon himself made the irreverent connection between a sweating-tub and a tabernacle.

6 *Tub*: a sweating-tub 'without a bottom, a shut at the top to be locked, and a hole to put one's head out at' (George Etherege, *The Comical Revenge, or Love in a Tub*, 1664, IV.vi.15) in which sufferers from syphilis underwent treatment. The treatment included 'Abstinence, Fumigations, Sudorificks, and drying Decoctions, for to consume the Phlegmatick humour, to which they pretend the Venereal Matter doth particularly adhere...' (De Blegny, 125).

7 *Aegyptian Flesh-pots*: Exodus 16:3

8 *Lenten-dish*: during the forty days before Easter, Christians were required to eschew meat and eggs and to limit food intake to two meals of four ounces and one of half a pound.

9 *Almonds, Currans, Biskets*: 'Physitians appoint bisket-bread for such as are troubled with rheumes,' (Gervase Markham, ed., *The Country Farm*, 1616, 583). Syphilitics were encouraged to eat dry foods; biscuit was dry, unleavened bread.

11 *Penetential Drink*: a drink meant to cool the blood, cf. 'diet-drink' in Etherege, *The Comical Revenge*, IV.vi.11, and a 'Diet-drink effectual in Venereal Accidents' as described in *Dr. Lower's and Several Other Eminent Physicians Receipts* (1700):

Take of China, Sassafras, and Sarsparilla Root, of each 2 Ounces, Guaiacum one Ounce and a half, Crude Antimony, made into a Nodulus, 2 Ounces, boil them in a Gallon of Water, and two Quarts about the latter end, add of Coriander-seeds half an Ounce, of Raisins and liquorish sliced, of each 2 Ounces, strain and drink instead of Beer.

20 *Pusillage*: littleness, smallness, insignificance. (Behn seems to be confusing this word with 'pucellage', virginity.)

21 *Cabal*: a group of people engaged in secret machinations; applied by a pamphleteer to the five powerful ministers who signed the Treaty of Alliance with France in 1672, Clifford, Arlington, Buckingham, Ashley and Lauderdale. Behn uses the modish word to refer to her circle, which included Ravenscroft, Nahum Tate, Thomas Otway among others. In her poem 'Our Cabal', the members of the cabal include 'Amoret', probably Elizabeth Barry (1658-1713) in love with 'Philocles' or N. R. V., Mr. Je. B., probably Jeffrey Boys of Gray's Inn (Gray, 1930, 456), another 'Amintas', J. C[ooper?], 'Damon', G[eorge?] V[illiers?], 'Alexis', E[dward] B[utler], beloved of Mrs F[rances] M[asters], and J[ames?] B[oys?], 'Thyrsis', among others.

40 *Codling*: coddling, i.e. stewing

Epitaph On the Tombstone of a Child, the last of
Seven that died before.

This Little, Silent, Gloomy Monument,
Contains all that was sweet and innocent;
The softest pratler that e'er found a Tongue,
His Voice was Musick and his Words a Song;
5   Which now each List'ning Angel smiling hears,
Such pretty Harmonies compose the Spheres;
Wanton as unfledg'd Cupids, ere their Charms
Had learn'd the little arts of doing harms;
Fair as young Cherubins, as soft and kind,
10   And tho translated could not be refin'd;
The Seventh dear pledge the Nuptial Joys had given,
Toil'd here on Earth, retir'd to rest in Heaven;
Where they the shining Host of Angels fill,
Spread their gay wings before the Throne, and smile.

From *Miscellany, Being A Collection of Poems by several Hands. Together with Reflections on Morality or Seneca Unmasqued.* [ed. Aphra Behn] London: J.Hindmarsh, 1685, 257-258.
10 *translated*: conveyed to Heaven, originally without death, then applied to the deaths of the righteous. Behn's meaning turns on using the word in two senses; the child has been translated to a heavenly state, but being innocent cannot be translated in another sense, i.e. refined.

To Alexis *in Answer to his Poem against Fruition.*
Ode. *by Mrs.* B.

Ah hapless sex! who bear no charms,
But what like lightning flash and are no more,
   False fires sent down for baneful harms,
Fires which the fleeting Lover feebly warms
5   And given like past Beboches o're,
   Like Songs that please, (thô bad,) when new,
   But learn'd by heart neglected grew.

In vain did Heav'n adorn the shape and face
With Beautyes which by Angels forms it drew:
10   In vain the mind with brighter Glories Grace,
While all our joys are stinted to the space

APHRA BEHN

Of one betraying enterview,
With one surrender to the eager will
We're short-liv'd nothing, or a real ill.

15 Since Man with that inconstancy was born,
To love the absent, and the present scorn.
Why do we deck, why do we dress
For such a short-liv'd happiness?
Why do we put Attraction on,
20 Since either way tis we must be undon?

They fly if Honour take our part,
Our Virtue drives 'em o're the field.
We lose 'em by too much desert,
And Oh! they fly us if we yeild.
25 Ye Gods! is there no charm in all the fair
To fix this wild, this faithless, wanderer.

Man! our great business and our aim,
For whom we spread our fruitless snares,
No sooner kindles the designing flame,
30 But to the next bright object bears
The Trophies of his conquest and our shame:
Inconstancy's the good supream
The rest is airy Notion, empty Dream!

Then, heedless Nymph, be rul'd by me
35 If e're your Swain the bliss desire;
Think like *Alexis* he may be
Whose wisht Possession damps his fire;
The roving youth in every shade
Has left some sighing and abandon'd Maid,
40 For tis a fatal lesson he has learn'd,
After fruition ne're to be concern'd.

From *Lycidus: or the Lover in Fashion... From the French. By the same author of the Voyage to the Isle of Love. Together with a Miscellany of New Poems. By several Hands*. London: Joseph Knight and Francis Saunders, 1688, 129-131.
Title *Alexis*: one 'G.V.', a member of Behn's cabal. Another poem addressed to him, 'To *Alexis*, On his saying, I lov'd a Man that talk'd much', was also published in *Lycidus*. One possibility for 'G.V.' is of course George Villiers, Duke of Buckingham.
his Poem against Fruition: 'A Poem against fruition written on the

reading in Mountains Essay: by Alexis' which precedes Behn's poem in *Lycidus*. A new translation of Montaigne's *Essais* was published in 1685-1686 by Charles Cotton, author of *Scarronides* and a prefatory poem addressed to 'the admir'd Astraea' in Behn's *La Montre* (1686). The essay in question is 'That our Desires are augmented by difficulty' (II, xv). 'Alexis' adopts Cotton's use of 'fruition' for Montaigne's *jouyssance*. Montaigne accepts a cyclical process of desire and satiation as natural; Alexis argues against 'fruition' on the grounds that the moment of detumescence is too disappointing to endure again and again, using the well-known argument of Petronius, *Foeda est in coitu et brevis voluptas*. The woman's point of view has been put also in 'The Platonick Lady', a poem to be found in Bod. Add MS A 301, 24, where it carries a side-note 'By the Lord Rochester'. 'The Platonick Lady' declares:

> I hate the thing is call'd Injoyment,
> Besydes it is a dull imployment,
> It cutts of al that's Life and fier,
> From that which may be term'd Desire.
> Just (like the Be) whose sting is gon,
> Converts the owner to a Droane.

Ode: the poem by 'Alexis' is in heroic couplets; Behn chooses an irregular and more difficult form.

1 *Ah hapless sex!*: the female sex, cf. Alexis, 'Ah, wretched Man'! (1)

5 *Beboches*: possibly a misprint for 'deboches', debauches or perhaps a version of the old word 'bobaunces', vanities.

8-20 These stanzas echo and counter Alexis's description of male disillusionment with the object of desire:

> Far from our Eyes th'inchanting objects set
> Advantage by the friendly distance get.
> Fruition shews the cheat, and views 'em near,
> Then all their borrow'd splendours plain appear,
> And we what with much care we gain and skill
> An empty nothing find, or real ill.
> Thus disappointed, our mistaken thought,
> Not finding satisfaction which it sought
> Renews its search, and with much toil and pain
> Most wisely strives to be declin'd again. (5-14)

12 *enterview*: interview; meeting (here, sexual encounter)

16 Cf. Alexis: 'We loath the present, absent things admire' (16).

23 *desert*: worthiness, merit

32-33 Cf. Alexis:

> Philosophers and Poets strove in vain
> The restless anxious Progress to restrain,
> And to their loss soon found their Good supream
> An Airy notion and a pleasing Dream. (23-26)

APHRA BEHN'S CIRCLE

A Pindarick To Mrs. Behn *on her Poem on the*
Coronation. Written by a Lady.

Hail, thou sole Empress of the Land of wit,
To whom all conquer'd Authors must submit,
And at thy feet their fading Laurels lay,
The utmost tribute that a Muse can pay,
5   To thy unlabour'd Song o'th' Coronation day.
The subject was Divine we all confess,
Nor was that flame, thy mighty fancy, less.
That cloth'd thy thought in such a pleasing dress,
As did at once a Masculine wit express,
10   And all the softness of a Femal tenderness.
No more shall men their fancy'd Empire hold,
Since thou *Astrea* form'd of finer mould,
By nature temper'd more with humid cold,
Doth man excel –
15   Not in soft strokes alone, but even in the bold.
And as thy purer Blood,
Thrô more transparent vessels is convey'd
Thy spirits more fine and subtil do thy brain invade.
And nimbler come uncall'd unto thy aide;
20   So the gay thought –
Which thy still flowing fancy does inspire
New, uncontroul'd and warm, as young desire,
Have more of kindling heat and fiercer fire;
Not to be reach't, or prays'd, unless by such
25   As the same happy temperament possess;
Since none with equal numbers can reward thy Lays,
May the just Monarch, which you praise,
        Daine to acknowledg this.
Not with a short applause of crackling Bays
30   But a return that may revive thy days;
And thy well-meaning grateful loyal Muse
Cherisht by that blest theam its zeale did chuse.

Maist thou be blest with such a sweet retreat,
That with contempt thou maist behold the great;
35   Such as the mighty *Cowlys* well-known seat.
Whose lofty Elms I wou'd have all thy own,
And in the mid'st a spacious shady Throne,
Rais'd on a Mount that shou'd Parnassus be,
And every Muse included all in thee.
40   On whose coole top alone thou shoud'st dispense
The Laws of Wit, Love, Loyalty and Sense:
The new *Arcadia* shou'd the Grove be nam'd
And for the guift our grateful Monarch fam'd.

Amidst the shade, I'd wish a well built House,
45   Like *Sidneys* Noble Kalendar shou'd stand,
Raising its head and all the rest command.
Its out-side gay, its inside clean and neat
With all of lifes conveniencies replete,
Where all the Elements at once conspire
50   To give what mans necessities require,
Rich soyle, pure Aire, streams coole, and useful fire.
The fertil spot with pleasure shou'd abound
And with *Elizium*-Spring be ever crown'd.
When thou thy mind unbend'st from thoughtful
                                  hours,
55   Then shou'dst thou be refresht with Fruits and
                                    Flowrs,
The Gods and Nymphs of Woods and Springs
Shall Dance in Antique Rural Rings:
While scaly Trytons and grim Satyrs play
Such Tunes, as Birds compose, to welcome day.
60   Till the glad noyse to distant shores resound,
And flying Birds joyn in th'Harmonious sound
Which listning Echo's catch at the rebound.
Here without toyle, or pining want perplext
Thy Body easy and thy mind at rest,
65   With all Lifes valu'd pleasures blest,
Thy largest wishes still thou shou'st enjoy
Inviron'd with delights that ne're can cloy.

Accept, thou much lov'd *Sappho* of our Isle,
This hearty wish, and grace it with a smile,
70   When thou shalt know that thy Harmonious Lire

262

Did me, the meanest of thy sex, inspire.
And that thy own inimitable lays
Are cause alone that I attempt thy praise.
Which in unequal measure I rehearse
75 Because unskill'd in numbers Grace, or Verse;
Great Pindars flights are fit alone for thee,
The witty *Horace*'s Iambicks be
Like *Virgils* lofty strains, alas too hard for me.
And if enough this do not plead excuse,
80 Pity the failings of a Virgin Muse.
That never in this kind before essai'd,
Her Muse till now was, like her self, – a Maid.
Whose Blooming labours thus she dedicates to you,
A Tribute justly to your merits due;
85 At least her part of gratitude to pay
For that best Song o'th' Coronation day.
How bad wou'd the Ill-natur'd World requite
Thy noble labours if they do not write,
Who have, perhaps, been happy in this kind
90 To own thou'st now out-done all that they e're
                                          design'd.
Sure none with malice e're was so accurst,
This to deny but will with envy burst,
Since even thy own more envious sex agree
The glorious theam had right alone from thee;
95 The femal Writers thou hast all excell'd,
Since the first mother of mankind rebell'd.

From *Lycidus: or the Lover in Fashion... From the French. By the same
author of the Voyage to the Isle of Love. Together with a Miscellany of New
Poems. By several hands*. London: J. Knight and F. Saunders, 1688,
89-94.
Title *A Pindarick*: the popularity of exuberantly irregular odes of
this kind was initiated by Cowley with his *Pindarique Odes* (1656),
which have little resemblance to the form of the Greek pindarics.
See Dryden's preface to *Sylvae* (1685): 'Every one knows [Pindaric
verse] was introduced into our language, in this age, by the happy
genius of Mr. Cowley.'
her Poem on the Coronation: *A Pindarick Poem on the Happy Coronation
of His Most Sacred Majesty James II and his Illustrious Consort, Queen
Mary*. London: J. Playford for Henry Playford, 1685. In 1685, poor
and ill, Behn began a series of futile bids for royal patronage by
celebrating royal occasions in pindaric odes which were published
as broadsides, of which the first is *A Pindarick On The Death Of Our*

Late Sovereign: With An Ancient Prophecy On His Present Majesty, followed by *A Poem Humbly Dedicated To the Great Pattern of Piety and Virtue Catherine Queen Dowager on the Death of her Dear Lord and Husband King Charles II.* Printed by J. Playford for Henry Playford, 1685. All are omitted from Summers's edition of Behn's works.

12 *Astrea*: in classical mythology the constellation Virgo, or 'Starry Maid', associated with justice; the name was first given to Behn by William Byam, in ironic reference, one supposes, to D'Urfé's *L'Astrée*, for it was coupled with 'Celadon'; the implication is that Behn played the same role as D'Urfé's *Astrée* and schooled the Surinam colonials in the arts of refined love and gallantry. Evidently Behn accepted the sobriquet, which was her code name in Antwerp (1666-1667). Edward Phillips listed 'Astrea' Behn under 'Modern Poetesses' in *Theatrum Poetarum* (1675), but only in the 1680s do references to Behn as Astraea proliferate, predominantly in poems addressed to her, as in 'the Lovely, Witty Astraea', 'the Incomparable Astraea', 'the Excellent Astraea' in Behn's *Poems upon Several Occasions*, 1684; 'the Admir'd Astrea', 'the Most Ingenious Astraea', 'the Divine Astraea' in Behn's *La Montre*, 1686. She was buried finally as Astrea Behn.

13 *humid cold*: in women the cold, damp humours were thought to dominate; in *The Way to Health, Long Life and Happiness* (1683), a volume to which Behn contributed a commendatory poem, Thomas Tryon writes:

For the Creator in the beginning hath implanted *Modesty*, and given the *Bridle of Chastity unto Women*, and indeed unto the *Females* of all Creatures, by enduing them with a cold meek Temper, derived from the *Element of Water*, which doth allay and cool them, and therefore they are naturally more moderate, and not so hot and *desirous of Copulation as Men.* (276)

16-18 *purer Blood... more transparent vessels... spirits more fine and subtil...*: according to Tryon women are:

of a *finer, softer, yielding Temper* then Men, and their *Love* doth exceed that of the other Sex, and indeed all kind of Passions do both *sooner* and *deeper* wound their Spirits. (273)

The ideas expressed by Tryon were commonplace; see for example 'Philo-philippa', 'To the excellent Orinda', 43, p.205).

26-28 Although in 1688, on the occasion of the birth of the Prince of Wales, Behn made two more attempts to win royal patronage and again in 1689 with *A Congratulatory Poem To Her Sacred Majesty Queen Mary, Upon Her Arrival in England,* this wish never came true.

35 *Cowlys well-known seat*: Abraham Cowley's influential friends, the Earl of St Albans and the Duke of Buckingham, secured for him a favourable lease of the queen's lands at Barn Elms where he lived in the closing years of his life, cf. Cowley's poem 'The Wish':

> Ah, yet, e're I descend to th'Grave
> May I a *small House*, and *large Garden* have!

42 *new Arcadia*: not only a reference to a new Golden Age, but also

to Sidney's *Arcadia*.

45 *Sidneys Noble Kalendar*: the country house owned by Kalendar, in Book I, Chapter 2 of the *Arcadia*.

47-50 Cf. the description of Kalendar's house:

The lightes, doores and staires, rather directed to the use of the guest, then to the eye of the Artificer: and yet as the one cheefly heeded, so the other not neglected; each place handsome without curiositie, and homely without lothsomnes: not so daintie as not to be trode on, nor yet slubberd up with good felowshippe: all more lasting then beautifull, but that the consideration of the exceeding lastingnesse made the eye beleeve it was exceeding beautifull. (Feuillerat, I, 15)

51 Cf. Jonson, 'To Penshurst', 7-8.

53 *Elizium-Spring*: there is no spring specifically associated with the abode of the blest, Elysium, in classical literature, except perhaps the river in *Aeneid*, VI, 656-659.

56-57 and 62 Cf. Spenser, *Faerie Queene*, 6.10.10-18.

68 *Sappho*: for Behn's contemporaries Sappho was best known as the heroine of 'Sappho to Phaon', in Ovid's *Heroides*, and therefore as the victim of uncontrolled heterosexual passion (see Introduction, p.26). Behn may have known the translation from the Greek of Anacreon and Sappho published in 1681 by Madame Dacier. In *Theatrum Poetarum* (1675), Edward Phillips gives an account of Sappho:

(the Daughter of *Scamandarus*, and Wife of *Cercilas*, a Rich Man of *Andros*, by whom she had a Daughter nam'd *Clio*) not inferiour in fame to the best of Lyric Poets, and said to be the first Composer of that sort of Lyric Verse, which from her is call'd *Sapphic*; in which some are extant under her name, besides which she is said to have writen [*sic*] Epigrams, Elegies, Iambics and Monodies, and to have flourisht in the 42ᵈ *Olympiad*, and invented the *Plectrum*. Moreover, being a Poetess her self, she is likewise the subject of Poetical Tradition, if at least it were the same *Sappho* (for there have been imagin'd others of the same name) who falling in love with *Phao* the Ferry Man, and finding her self slighted, was possest with a worse than Poetic madness to throw her self headlong from the rock *Leucus* into the Sea. *Ovid*, *Statius*, and others of the Latin Poets ackowledge [*sic*] but one *Sappho*. (247)

Sir Carr Scrope translated 'Sappho to Phaon' for *Ovid's Epistles translated by Several Hands* (1680) in which Behn's version of 'Oenone to Paris' appeared. Anne Wharton, writing to Behn in about 1682, wished her all Sappho's fame 'without her Shame', probably the shame of being overcome by sexual passion. Behn was attacked under the name of Sappho in 'The Play-house. A Satyr' (1689) by Robert Gould, and *A Satyrical Epistle to the Female Author of a Poem call'd Sylvia's Revenge &c.* (1691). In the seventeenth century licentiousness was the same sin whether principally concerned with one's own sex or another; 'guilty love' as in Pope's version of the Ovidian 'Sapho to Phaon' (1712), l.18, was the same whether with a ferryman or 'the Lesbian Dames'. Most of the great Restoration rakes were what we would nowadays call 'bisexual', promiscuous and omnivorous in their sexual appetites.

John Adams in a commendatory poem in Behn's *Poems on Several Occasions* (1684) claims that Behn had surpassed Sappho as a poet;

by the time Behn died it was barely possible to use the sobriquet unmaliciously, as in this case.

70-76 After Behn's death, her Pindaric odes were criticised as 'unskill'd in numbers Grace'. The *Muses Mercury*, October 1707, noted:

...Mrs. *Behn* had no Notion of a Pindarick Poem, any farther than it consisted of irregular Numbers, and sav'd the Writer the Trouble of even Measure; which indeed is all our common Pindarick poets know of the Matter. (quoted in Summers, VI, 427)

See Swift, *The Battle of the Books* (1710), 'Then Pindar slew... Afra the Amazon, light of foot' (Davis, I, 158).

93-96 These anti-feminist observations rather tarnish the appeal of a generous and elegant tribute.

96 *first mother of mankind*: Eve, cf. Alice Sutcliffe, 'Of our losse by Adam', l.30, and note (see p.91).

To Mrs. B. from a Lady who had a desire to see her,
and who complains on the ingratitude of her fugitive Lover.

Send me your pity bounteous Shepherdess;
That I the face of grief no more may know,
If I deserve it that cou'd Love so low;
35 Consult not that, but charity and give
One tender pittying sigh that I may live:
(That I may thus make my complaint to you,)
Kind are my Stars indeed at last 'tis true;
Let not my rude and untam'd griefs destroy,
40 The early glimmerings of an infant joy:
And add not your neglect, for if you doe,
Cleone finds her desolation too!
Know this it yet remains in your fair breast,
To render me the happy or unblest.
45 You may act miracles if you'l be kind,
Make me true joys in real sorrows find;
And bless the hour I hither did pursue
A faithless Swain and found access to you:
Accept the heart I here to you present,
50 By the ingratitude of Strephon rent;
Till then gay, noble, full of brave disdain,
And unless yours prevent shall be again;
As once it was, if in your generous brest,
It may be Pensioner at my request
55 No more to Treasons subject as before
To be betray'd by a fair tale no more,

As large as once, as uncontroul'd and free,
But yet at your command shall always be.

From *Lycidus*... 1688, 172-175. The address to Behn is preceded by thirty-one lines in which 'Cleone' laments her abandonment by 'Strephon', who is her social inferior, cf. 'Ephelia' (see p.276).

An Elegy Upon The Death of Mrs. A. Behn;
The Incomparable Astrea.
By a Young Lady of Quality.

I

Summon the Earth (the fair *Astrea's* gone,)
　　And let through every Angle fly,
　　　　Till it has fill'd the mighty Round,
　　And thence arise to the expanded Sky,
5　　　　In Murmurs for the misery done,
To see if Heaven, Heaven will our Grief supply,
　　With Tears enough to mourn her Destiny.
　　　　Assemble all the Crowds below,
　　　　You that Obedience to the Muses owe,
10　　And teach the Sighing Maids to mourn,
　　　　With unbound Hair, and flowing Tears,
　　　　In Strains as moving as her Numbers were,
　　　　The mighty Desolation, mighty Woe.
　　　　　　Teach them in Charming accents, such as once
15　　She did the list'ning Crowds inform,
　　　　When high as Heaven her Praise was born,
　　　　　　And taught the Angels to rejoyce,
　　　　In sweeter, truer Numbers than before,
　　　　In all their bright Seraphick Store,
20　　　　Had ever tun'd their Heavenly Voice:
And thus prepar'd, let them the Loss deplore,
The charming wise *Astrea* is no more.

II

What have we done? What have our Crimes deserv'd?
　　Why this injurious Rape?
25　　　　The World is Widdow'd now,
And Desolation every where
With dismal Groans invades the Air;
　　　　My sullen Muse, that ne're before

The sacred Title wore,
30 Untaught, unpractis'd, has preferred
(For none from Mourning can escape)
In uneven Strains, and much below
All but my Grief,
To tell the World their Universal Woe,
35 Which ne're can hope Relief:
'Tis an implacable Decree,
That Languishments, Diseases, Death,
Must attend all that live on Earth...

IV

Who now, of all the inspired Race,
Shall take *Orinda's* Place?
70 Or who the Hero's fame shall raise?
Who now shall fill the Vacant Throne?
The bright *Astrea's* gone,...

VI

Let all our Hopes despair and dye,
90 Our Sex for ever shall neglected lye;
Aspiring Man has now regain'd the Sway,
To them we've lost the Dismal Day:
Astrea an equal Ballance held,
(Tho' she deserv'd it all;)
95 But now the rich Inheritance must fall;
To them with Grief we yeild
The Glorious envy'd Field.
Of her own Sex, not one is found
Who dares her Laurel wear,
100 Withheld by Impotence or Fear;
With her it withers on the Ground,
Untouch'd, and cold as she,
And Reverenc'd to that degree,
That none will dare to save
105 The Sacred Relick from the Grave;
Intomb'd with her, and never to return,
Fills up the narrow Urn,
Which more Presumption, or more Courage has than
we.

VII

In Love she had the softest sense;
110 And had her Virtue been as great,
In Heaven she'd fill'd the foremost Seat.

268

This failure, or she had Immortal been,
And free as Angels are from Sin;
'Twas pity that she practis'd what she taught;
115   Her Muse was of the bolder Sex;
Such Mysteries of Love she did dispence,
Such moving natural Eloquence,
As made her too much Wit her fault.
Her ever-loyal Muse took no pretext,
120   To discommend what once it prais'd;
And what has most her Glory rais'd,
Her Royal Master she has follow'd home,
Nor would endure the World when he had lost his
Throne...

From *An Elegy upon the Death of Mrs. A. Behn; The Incomparable Astrea. By a Young Lady of Quality*. London: Printed by E. J., 1689. Broadside. Houghton Library, Harvard University, shelf-mark *pEB65.A100.689e3. The Houghton Library owns the only known copy.

3 *it*: this floating pronoun has no antecedent nor is it subsequently identified; 'it' is perhaps the cry of 'the fair *Astrea*'s gone' here given in parentheses, but given the unrepeated rhyme of 'round' at the end of l.3 we assume that the text is corrupt.

Lines 39-67 and 73-88 have been omitted.

69 *Orinda's Place*: for at least a hundred years after her death in 1664 Katherine Philips (see pp.186-203) is invariably produced as the sole model for female poets. One dissenting voice is Daniel Kendrick in 'To Mrs. B. on her Poems' prefaced to *Lycidas* (1688):

> If we *Orinda* to your works compare,
> They uncouth, like her countrys soyle, appear,
> Mean as its Pesants, as its Mountains bare...(33-35)

71 *fill the Vacant Throne*: cf. Manley, 'To the Author of Agnes de Castro', ll.1-4 (see p.398). Verbal echoes of the elegy in Manley's poem suggest that she may in fact be the 'Young Lady of Quality' to whom the elegy is attributed; she was between seventeen and twenty-two when the 'Elegy' was published.

98 *Of her own Sex*: Anne Wharton, Mary Evelyn and Anne Killigrew were all dead when these lines were written; we suspect that the unknown 'Ephelia' too was dead. Jane Barker had followed the Stuarts to exile in France. Only Sarah Fyge, whose juvenile work *The Female Advocate* had been published in 1686 and 1687, and Delariviere Manley could have taken up the bays at this point.

110 *had her Virtue been as great*: the poet seems anxious to avoid guilt by association, so complete has been the reaction to Restoration permissiveness. In her lifetime, Behn made no claim to morality;

accusations of immorality do not stem from new libels spread about her, but from a change in attitude to her public *persona*.

114 *practis'd what she taught*: Behn wrote poetry of gallantry and flirtation, but she can hardly have been said to have 'taught' anything. None of her writing is actually prescriptive. This vulgar and inappropriate taunt suggests that our poet knew little of Behn but her reputation.

115-121 The poet justly observes a change in public mores in the closing years of the reign of Charles II and congratulates Behn for having remained loyal to the permissiveness of the Restoration.

122 *her Royal Master*: the poet must be referring to Charles II who employed Behn as a spy (who is dead and gone 'home' to Heaven presumably) and by extension his brother for whom she wrote, who lost his throne in 1688.

124 The poem continues for twenty-two lines, which, out of consideration for the reader, we have omitted.

'EPHELIA'

Whereas Katherine Philips's identity was known to all, despite her reiterated disgust at the very idea of publicity, 'Ephelia' remains unidentifiable. She seems to have been in public life, probably the theatre, possibly the court, but no woman who satisfies all the known circumstances of her career can be found. Apparent clues to her identity lead nowhere. The heraldic badge included in the frontispiece portrait of *Female Poems On several Occasions. Written by Ephelia.* (London, 1679) belongs to a family, the Tilleys of Dorset, which was extinct a century earlier. The names Anne Bury, Ann Gilbert (6), Venetia Cooke (47), and Rachel Powney (50) upon which 'Ephelia' makes acrostics cannot be traced in the historical record nor can an individual who fits all the details of her description of her faithless lover, 'J. G.', be identified.

'Ephelia' was certainly a follower of Aphra Behn; in *A Satyrical Epistle to the Author of a Poem Call'd Sylvia's Revenge* (1691), Robert Gould links 'poor Ephelia ragged jilt' with 'Sappho famous for her gout and guilt'. In the first edition of *Female Poems* there are suggestions, for example in the risqué songs on pp. 27-28 and 34-35, that 'Ephelia' was a lady of the town. If she was an actress, she may have been, as Elizabeth Barry was, partly dependent upon favours from the likes of Rochester and Etherege. The last poem in *Female Poems*, 1679, is addressed to a 'Madame G.' (111-112) who must be Nell Gwyn, given the lines,

> So bright your Beauty, so Sublime your Wit,
> None but a Prince to wear your Chaine is fit.

'Ephelia' also wrote a play, now lost, 'The Pair-Royal of Coxcombs' which was acted at a dancing school.

'Ephelia' often refers to hers as an 'Infant Muse', and in 'My Fate' (95-97) writes of having lost her parents in their 'tender Age', cursing the 'Easiness believ'd at first' which may mean that she lost her reputation when she was very young. Even in the 1670s, however, female poets might profitably exaggerate their youth. The central theme in *Female Poems* is 'Ephelia's' hopeless love for 'J. G.' or 'Strephon', who appears to have courted her until she returned his affection, then tired of her and gone to embarrassing lengths to avoid her. The poems that mark the stages in their four-year love affair are distinguished by a degree of psychological realism and good humoured self-deprecation. 'Ephelia' does not take herself or her infatuation particularly seriously, and seven pages after her 'To J. G. on the News of his Marriage' reveals that for two years she has 'sighed in private and in private wept' for 'Coridon' (94).

To provide 'Diversion in Company' 'Ephelia' creates her own coterie, composed of 'Eugenia', 'Marina', 'Damon', 'Clovis', 'Coridon' and 'Phylocles' whose stories run concurrently with the main love affair. The mock pastoral convention is adopted more in the playful spirit of Behn's cabal than that of 'Orinda' but the influence of Philips is evident in several of 'Ephelia's' poems. Like Philips, she wrote a poem about Gilbert Sheldon, the high Tory Archbishop of Canterbury, an elegy on his death in 1677.

Like Philips and Behn 'Ephelia' entered into political controversy. A broadside, *A Poem To His Sacred Majesty on the Plot. Written by a Gentlewoman* (Bod. Ash. G. 16 [45]) was published in November 1678 in the midst of Titus Oates's revelations of the details of the Popish Plot; less than a year later, this poem was credited to 'Ephelia' in *Female Poems*. Another broadside, *Advice to His Grace* warning the Duke of Monmouth against rebellion, bears the manuscript date '6. June. 1681' in the Bodleian copy (Bod. Ash. G.5[86]) and is signed 'Ephelia'. The name also appears in connection with the verse epistle from 'Ephelia to Bajazet'; what is not clear is whether 'Ephelia' is a sobriquet for another writer or group of writers besides the author of *Female Poems*.

Less than two months after the publication of *Female Poems*, Sir Thomas Isham, son of a prominent Tory, died in London; 'Ephelia's' name appears on an unpublished 'Funerall Elegie' (UNott Portland MS PwV 336); whether the poem was a commissioned piece or was, with its tried sentiments, a genuine expression of grief for a young man who loved the theatre is not known. Curiously, among his papers at his death was a note from Sir George Etherege, implying a degree of familiarity (T. Isham).

Despite the small measure of fame 'Ephelia' seems to have achieved, *Female Poems* did not sell well, for the sheets of the 1679 edition were reissued in 1682 together with five new gatherings containing a mixture of poems, some salacious and obviously by other hands. Most notable among the authors represented is Rochester, but the edition also presents the same poems by Lady Rochester, Thomas D'Urfey and Sir Carr Scrope that had appeared in *Poems on Several Occasions By the Right Honourable, the E. of R---*. (1680). The new edition also contains an unpublished song from *The Spanish Friar* (1681) by Dryden, and two songs from *The Rover* (1681) and a broadside ballad (1681) by Aphra Behn. The kindest explanation for the pirating of the work of others for the second edition is that an enlarged edition had been promised and 'Ephelia' was unable either to provide enough material to fill it out, or could not protest when other people's work was passed off as her own.

After the second publication of *Female Poems* 'Ephelia's' career seems to have ceased. It is unlikely that she was the 'Ephelia' (Frances Worsley, nee Thynne) addressed in a poem ('Ardelia's Answer to Ephelia') by Anne Finch, Countess of Winchelsea

(Reynolds, 38-46). Even less probable is that she was the 'Ephelia' who wrote Letter XXXIV in Dunton's *The Female War* (1697, 97-100), from whom Dunton promises a 'Defence of *Red Hair*' for a forthcoming volume. Dunton and the other Athenians would have known that the name 'Ephelia' is derived from the Greek word for freckles. Delariviere Manley uses the name for a red-headed woman in the *New Atalantis* II (1709, 247) identified by Patricia Koster as Elizabeth Mordaunt (II, 902).

At the end of the nineteenth century, Halkett and Laing identified 'Ephelia' as 'Joan Phillips' (*sic*); Edmund Gosse picked up the name, and 'not knowing whether I start too wild a Theorie' (Gosse, 227), made her the daughter of Katherine Philips on the sole ground of the similarity of her poems to those of the 'Matchless Orinda'. The identification has endured even though Philips's only daughter, born in 1655, was named after her mother and her mother's mother.

Love's first Approach.

    Strephon I saw, and started at the sight,
    And interchangably look'd red and white;
    I felt my Blood run swiftly to my heart,
    And a chill Trembling seize each outward part:
5   My Breath grew short, my Pulse did quicker beat,
    My Heart did heave, as it wou'd change its Seat:
    A faint cold Sweat o're all my Body spread,
    A giddy Megrim wheel'd about my head:
    When for the reason of this change I sought,
10   I found my Eyes had all the mischief wrought;
    For they my Soul to *Strephon* had betray'd,
    And my weak heart his willing Victim made:
    The Traytors, conscious of the Treason
    They had committed 'gainst my Reason,
15   Look'd down with such a bashful guilty Fear,
    As made their Fault to every Eye appear.
    Tho the first fatal Look too much had done,
    The lawless wanderers wou'd still gaze on,
    Kind Looks repeat, and Glances steal, till they
20   Had look'd my Liberty and Heart away:
    Great Love, I yield; send no more Darts in vain,
    I am already fond of my soft Chain;
    Proud of my Fetters, so pleas'd with my state,
    That I the very Thoughts of Freedom hate.
25   O Mighty Love! thy Art and Power joyn,

To make his Frozen breast as warm as mine;
But if thou try'st, and can'st not make him kind,
In Love such pleasant, real Sweets I find;
That though attended with Despair it be,
30 'Tis better still than a wild Liberty.

From *Female Poems On several Occasions. Written by Ephelia*. London: Printed by William Downing, for James Courtney, Anno Dom. 1679, 7-8.

1 *Strephon*: probably the commonest lover's sobriquet in pastoral poetry, used here by 'Ephelia' in describing the beginning of her affair. Later, in poems addressed to 'J. G.' and about him, we learn that he sails to 'Tangiere', is elected 'Steward of his Club', and is 'twice [her] age and more'. The poems to 'Strephon' offer less information and are often set pieces, 'Songs' and lamentations, paralleling, but occasionally contradicting the 'J. G.' story (as in the poem beginning 'Stay lovely youth!', 70). In 1693 a 'Mrs. L—ce', wrote in very similar terms of falling in love with yet another Strephon:

> How swiftly does the poison spread!
>   How soon't has seized each noble part!
> Wildly it rages in my head!
>   Like tides of fire, consumes my heart!
> Yet think not, that you conqu'ror are
> By the wise conduct of the war!
> There was a traitor took your part within;
> And gave you Strephon! what you could not win! (9-16, *Gentleman's Journal*, October 1693, rpt. Arber, 249)

Mrs L—ce could be Elizabeth Laurence, the red-haired daughter of Dr Thomas Laurence, Queen Anne's physician, later Elizabeth Mordaunt, Manley's 'Ephelia'; she is, however, too young to be our 'Ephelia'.

8 *Megrim*: vertigo. 'Ephelia's' use of this term is cited in the *OED*.

10 The betraying eye is a convention of love poetry: cf. Cowley, 'Love's Visibility', *The Mistress* (1647) and Anne Wharton, 'Song', from her unpublished play 'Love's Martyr':

> Whilst Strephon with much care suppress'd
> The too aspiring flame
> Which Love had kindled in his breast
> And durst not tell the pain
> His unexperienc'd eyes betray
> What he with care conceal'd
> His heart no sooner learnt 'obey'
> But they the pain reveal'd. (f.42)

'EPHELIA'

Prologue to the Pair-Royal of Coxcombs,
Acted at a Dancing-School.

Gallants,
If, as you say, you Love Varietie,
   We have some hopes, that you so kind will be
To the poor Play, to give it your Applause,
5   Though not for Wit, nor Worth, but yet because
A Woman wrote it; though it be not rare,
It is not common. Women seldom dare
To reach so high, to entertain your Ears,
Which strikes our Poets with a thousand fears
10 Of your displeasure; yet some little Ray
Of hope is left; for womens Pardons may
Be gain'd with ease surely from Gentlemen;
Be kind for once then to a Female Pen.
When you with women in discourse do sit,
15 Before their Faces you'l commend their wit,
Pray flatter now, the Poet heareth it:
She hopes too, the great Wits, who croud the Age,
Censure the Poets, and undo the Stage,
Won't undervalue so their mighty Wit,
20 To Criticize on what a Woman writ:
Yet if you'l have it so, it shall be Naught,
They that dislike, are welcome to find Fault;
For She protests, She had no other ends
In writing this, than to divert her Friends:
25 Like, or dislike, She's careless, bid me say,
That you shou'd Censure only when you Pay:
True, they must fawn, that write for a Third day.
She scornes such Baseness, therefore will not sue:
But yet, bright Ladies, does submit to you;
30 Your Smiles may cherish, what their Frowns wou'd
                                blast,
Then when they Hiss, be pleas'd to Clap more fast:
She knows your Judgments are too clear, and high
To be Deceiv'd, but knows no Reason why
You may not Pardon all the Faults you spy.
35 Be kind then Ladies to this trifling Play,
Her Wit is now i'th' Bud, when blown, She may
Present you with a better; till It come,
This, Ladies, humbly begs a gentle Doom.

KISSING THE ROD

From *Female Poems On several Occasions...*1679, 16-17. Two songs and the Epilogue from the play appear on succeeding pages. There is no other evidence for the performance of a play of this name in the late 1670s.

6 *though it be not rare*: by 1679 women playwrights were no longer a novelty as they were when Frances Boothby (see p.233) and Elizabeth Polwhele (fl. c.1670) were struggling to break into the professional theatre. Aphra Behn had eight plays produced and printed, *The Forc'd Marriage* (1671), *The Amorous Prince* (1671), *The Dutch Lover* (1673), *Abdelazar* (1677), *The Town-Fopp* (1677), *The Rover* (1677), *Sir Patient Fancy* (1678), and *The Feign'd Courtesan*, published March 1679, by the time 'Ephelia's' book appeared. It seems likely that 'Ephelia's' play was written some years earlier; her argument, that a woman's unambitious effort is not worth the attention of male critics and that all its faults can be pardoned on the basis of her sex, was actually disproved by the success of Aphra Behn who asked for no special consideration.

27 *Third day*: playwrights received the profits from every third performance in a play's run. 'Ephelia' is boasting of her amateur status and independence.

To J. G.

Tell me you Hate; and Flatter me no more:
By Heaven I do not wish you shou'd adore;
With humbler Blessings, I content can be,
I only beg, that you would pity me;
5 In as much Silence as I first design'd,
To bear the Raging Torture of my Mind;
For when your Eyes first made my Heart your Slave,
I thought t'have hid my Fetters in my Grave:
Heaven witness for me, that I strove to hide
10 My violent Love, and my fond Eyes did chide
For glancing at thee; and my Blushes hid,
With as much care as ever Virgin did,
And though I languish'd in the greatest pain
That e're despairing Lover did sustain;
15 I ne're in publick did let fall a Tear,
Nor breath'd a Sigh i'th' reach of any Ear:
Yet I in private, drew no Breath but Sighs,
And Showr's of Tears fell from my wretched Eyes:
The Lillies left my Front, the Rose my Cheeks,
20 My Nights were spent in Sobs and suddain Shreeks,
I felt my strength Insensibly decay'd,
And Death aproach; but ah! then you convey'd

276

Soft Am'rous tales into my listning Ears,
And gentle Vows, and well becoming Tears,
25   Then deeper Oaths, nor e're your Seige remov'd
'Till I confest my Flame, and own'd I lov'd:
Your kinder Smiles had rais'd my Flames so high,
That all at Distance might the Fire Discry,
I took no care my Passion to suppress,
30   Nor hide the Love I thought I did possess:
But ah! too late I find, your Love was such
As Gallants pay in course, or scarce so much:
You Shun my sight, you feed me with delays,
You slight, affront, a Thousand several ways
35   You doe Torment with Study'd Cruelty,
And yet alternately you Flatter me.
Oh! if you Love not, plainly say you hate,
And give my Miseries a shorter date,
'Tis kinder than to Linger out my Fate;
40   And yet I cou'd with less regret have Dy'd,
A Victime to your Coldness, than your Pride.

From *Female Poems On Several Occasions*... 1679, 32-34.
'Ephelia' takes the poetic convention of the lover asking the beloved to treat him with 'more love or more disdaine' and works a subtle change in it. The female lover, unlike a male lover, was under the necessity of concealing her infatuation, caused as usual by the beloved's eyes. The description of the effects of frustration and enforced silence is original. The beloved then begins a seduction merely for his own ego gratification, his 'Pride', but has hardly sufficient interest to keep up the pressure. 'Ephelia' protests that his ego-tripping at her expense is harder to bear than complete indifference or actual dislike would have been.

A similarly subtle play of feeling is to be found in an Ovidian epistle 'In the Person of a Lady to Bajazet, Her Unconstant Gallant', which first appears in print in *Female Poems*, 104-106.

> Let me not live in dull indiff'rency,
> But give me Rage enough to make me die:
> For if from you I needs must meet my Fate,
> Before your Pity, I would choose your Hate.

Following its appearance in *Female Poems* this poem appeared in *Poems on Several Occasions By the Right Honourable, the E. of R– – –.* (1680) as 'Ephelia to Bajazet', with Rochester's 'Very Heroicall Epistle in Answer to Ephelia,' first published as a broadside in 1679. The occasion is believed to be the affair of John Mulgrave, Earl of Sheffield, with Mall Kirke, Maid of Honour to the Duchess of York. 'Ephelia to Bajazet' is to be found in at least nine manuscript versions, the earliest of which is in a collection dated 1677 (Thorpe, 82). Although the version printed in 'Ephelia's' book is conflated and corrupt, the correspondence between the sentiments of the Ephelia-Bajazet exchanges and the poems of the J. G. / Strephon series is such that a connection between them cannot be ruled out. The poem is nowadays thought to be by Etherege on the evidence of two lines from the 'Epistle to Mr. Julian': 'Poor George grows old, his Muse worn out of fashion / Hoarsely he sings Ephelia's Lamentation' (Vieth, 1963, 323-352).

22-26 Cf. 'In the Person of a Lady to Bajazet...' 9-10:

> So kind he look'd, such tender Words he spoke,
> 'Twas past Belief such Vows shou'd e're be broke:

29 Cf. 'In the Person of a Lady to Bajazet...' 22-25:

> For him, my Duty to my Friends forgot;
> For him I lost – alas what lost I not?
> Fame, all the Valuable Things of Life,
> To meet his Love by less a Name than Wife.

Maidenhead: *Written at the Request of a Friend.*

At your Intreaty, I at last have writ
This whimsey, that has nigh nonplust my wit:
The Toy I've long enjoyed, if it may
Be call'd t'Enjoy, a thing we wish away;
5   But yet no more its Character can give,
Than tell the Minutes that I have to Live:
'Tis a fantastic Ill, a loath'd Disease,
That can no Sex, no Age, no Person please:
Men strive to gain it, but the way they chuse
10   T'obtain their Wish, that and the Wish doth lose;
Our Thoughts are still uneasie, till we know
What 'tis, and why it is desired so:
But th'first unhappy Knowledge that we boast,
Is that we know, the valu'd Trifle's lost:
15   Thou dull Companion of our active Years,
That chill'st our warm Blood with thy frozen Fears:
How is it likely thou shou'dst long endure,
When Thought it self thy Ruin may procure?
Thou short liv'd Tyrant, that Usurp'st a Sway
20   O're Woman-kind, though none thy Pow'r obey,
Except th' Ill-natur'd, Ugly, Peevish, Proud,
And these indeed, thy Praises Sing aloud:
But what's the Reason they Obey so well?
Because they want the Power to Rebell:

25   But I forget, or have my Subject lost:
Alas! thy Being's Fancy at the most:
Though much desired, 'tis but seldom Men
Court the vain Blessing from a Womans Pen.

From *Female Poems On several Occasions...* 1679, 40-41.
2 'Ephelia's' lighthearted treatment of her subject is perhaps in imitation of 'sweet Cowley's' (47) occasional poem, 'The Maiden-head', first published in *The Mistresse, or Severall Copies of Love Verses*, 1647; however the tone of this poem and others in the collection reinforces our suspicion that 'Ephelia' is a composite of unacknowledged male and female poets. In 1696 another anonymous woman poet addressed the subject from a different perspective in 'Innocence: Or the Inestimable Gemm. Written by a Young Lady':

> What's Innocence? – A brighter Gemm,
> Than e'er enricht a Diadem.
> A Gemm that bears a Price so high,
> As Crowns and Empires cannot Buy.
> Yet by the poorest Mortal's Brest
> This matchless Treasure is possest,
> A Treasure not like other Wealth,
> That's liable to Fraud or Stealth;
> No Soul of this can be bereft
> By open Force, or secret Theft;
> Safe in it's Cabinet 'twill stay,
> Till by the Owner thrown away.
>
> O dismal Bargain, when for Sin we fell
> This Gemm! 'Tis Life for Death, and Heav'n for Hell. (*Miscellanea Sacra*, 1696, I, 4)

To a Proud Beauty.

Imperious Fool! think not because you're Fair,
That you so much above my Converse are,
What though the Gallants sing your Praises loud,
And with false Plaudits make you vainly Proud?
5   Tho they may tell you all Adore your Eyes,
And every Heart's your willing Sacrifice;
O spin the Flatt'ry finer, and perswade
Your easie Vanity, that we were made
For Foyles to make your Lustre Shine more Bright,
10   And must pay Homage to your dazling Light;
Yet know what ever Stories they may tell,
All you can boast, is, to be pretty well:
Know too, you stately piece of Vanity,
That you are not Alone ador'd, for I

15   Fantastickly might mince, and smile, as well
     As you, if Airy Praise my mind cou'd swell:
     Nor are the loud Applauses that I have,
     For a fine Face, or things that Nature gave;
     But for acquired Parts, a gen'rous Mind,
20   A pleasing Converse, neither Nice nor Kind:
     When they that strive to Praise you most, can say
     No more, but that you're Handsome, brisk and gay:
     Since then my Fame's as great as yours is, why
     Should you behold me with a loathing Eye?
25   If you at me cast a disdainful Eye,
     In biting Satyr I will Rage so high,
     Thunder shall pleasant be to what I'le write,
     And you shall Tremble at my very Sight;
     Warn'd by your Danger, none shall dare again,
30   Provoke my Pen to write in such a strain.

From *Female Poems On several Occasions...* 1679, 54-55.

22 *brisk*: lively, forward, wanton. In 'To a Gentleman that had left a Vertuous Lady for a Miss' 'Ephelia' describes the seductress as 'very Witty, / Gay, Brisk, had Teeth; oh! infinitely Pretty' (76).

26 *biting Satyr*: scurrilous lampoons on identifiable women of court and town were the fashion in the 1670s; 'Colon' by the Earl of Dorset (1679) attacked the whole gamut of court beauties. In 'To my Rival' (36-37) 'Ephelia' has already treated another woman to a taste of her Pen:

> But when I heard he was so wretched Base
> To pay devotion to thy wrinkled Face
> I Banisht him my sight, and told the Slave,
> He had no Worth, but what my Fancy gave:...
> His Punishment shall be, the Loss of Me,
> And be Augmented, by his gaining Thee.

To one that asked me why I lov'd *J. G.*

Why do I Love? go, ask the Glorious Sun
Why every day it round the world doth Run:
Ask *Thames* and *Tyber,* why they Ebb and Flow:
Ask Damask Roses, why in *June* they blow:
5 Ask Ice and Hail, the reason, why they're Cold:
Decaying Beauties, why they will grow Old:
They'l tell thee, Fate, that every thing doth move,
Inforces them to this, and me to Love.
There is no Reason for our Love or Hate,

10 'Tis irresistable, as Death or Fate;
'Tis not his Face; I've sence enough to see,
That is not good, though doated on by me:
Nor is't his Tongue, that has this Conquest won;
For that at least is equall'd by my own:
15 His Carriage can to none obliging be,
'Tis Rude, Affected, full of Vanity:
Strangely Ill-natur'd, Peevish, and Unkind,
Unconstant, False, to Jealousie inclin'd;
His Temper cou'd not have so great a Pow'r,
20 'Tis mutable, and changes every hour:
Those vigorous Years that Women so Adore,
Are past in him: he's twice my Age and more;
And yet I love this false, this worthless Man,
With all the Passion that a Woman can;
25 Doat on his Imperfections, though I spy
Nothing to Love; I Love, and know not why.
Sure 'tis Decreed in the dark Book of Fate,
That I shou'd Love, and he shou'd be ingrate.

From *Female Poems On several Occasions*... 1679, 58-59.
11ff. The tradition of praising ugliness (as in Donne's 'The Anagram' and Suckling's 'The Deformed Mistress') was well established when 'Ephelia' wrote but was rarely, if ever, practised by women.
21-22 Another anti-Petrarchan sub-genre is praise of the old by the young, see for example the 'Song of Young Lady to her Ancient Lover' attributed to Rochester (*Poems on Several Occasions*, 1691).

To Madam *Bhen.*

Madam! permit a Muse, that has been long
Silent with wonder, now to find a Tongue:
Forgive that Zeal I can no longer hide,
And pardon a necessitated Pride.
5 When first your strenuous polite Lines I read,
At once it Wonder and Amazement bred,
To see such things flow from a Womans Pen,
As might be Envy'd by the wittiest Men:
You write so sweetly, that at once you move,
10 The Ladies Jealousies, and Gallant's Love;
Passions so gentle, and so well exprest,
As needs must be the same fill your own Breast;

Then Rough again, as your Inchanting Quill
Commanded Love, or Anger at your Will:
15 As in your Self, so in your Verses meet,
A rare connexion of Strong and Sweet:
This I admir'd at, and my Pride to show,
Have took the Vanity to tell you so
In humble Verse, that has the Luck to please
20 Some Rustick Swains, or silly Shepherdess:
But far unfit to reach your Sacred Ears,
Or stand your Judgment: Oh! my conscious Fears
Check my Presumption, yet I must go on,
And finish the rash Task I have begun.
25 Condemn it Madam, if you please, to th' Fire,
It gladly will your Sacrifice expire,
As sent by one, that rather chose to shew
Her want of Skill, than want of Zeal to you.

From *Female Poems On several Occasions*... 1679, 72-73.
5 *strenuous polite*: 'Ephelia' shows that she has mastered the new aesthetic which combined 'Strong and Sweet' (l.16), or vigour and significance with smoothness and refinement. Her use of the word 'strenuous' as the second half of the oxymoron is unusual; it is the correct opposite of polite in the sense that it applies to physical labour, and 'polite' society is that which need not exert itself physically. Her use of these terms implies that she has rejected the extravagance of Cowley for the controlled power and elegance of Dryden.
I read: 'Ephelia' is not here referring to Behn's writing heard in the theatre.
15-16 Although prologues, epilogues and songs had appeared in her published plays and individual verses had been printed in miscellanies before 1679, Aphra Behn's first volume of poetry, *Poems upon several Occasions*, was not issued until 1684.
19-20 'Ephelia' seems from these lines to have been a member of a coterie which amused itself by writing mock pastorals.
23 *Check my Presumption*: 'Ephelia' here offers Behn all the respect that was later denied to her.

To *Phylocles*, inviting him to Friendship.
1
Best of thy Sex! if Sacred Friendship can
Dwell in the Bosom of inconstant Man;
As cold, as clear as Ice, as Snow unstain'd,
With Love's loose Crimes unsully'd, unprophan'd.

2

5   Or you a Woman, with that Name dare trust,
And think to Friendship's Ties, we can be just;
In a strict League, together we'l combine,
And Friendship's bright Example shine.

3

We will forget the Difference of Sex,
10   Nor shall the World's rude Censure [us?] Perplex:
Think Me all Man: my Soul is Masculine,
And Capable of as great Things as Thine.

4

I can be Gen'rous, Just, and Brave,
Secret, and Silent, as the Grave;
15   And if I cannot yield Relief,
I'le Sympathize in all thy Grief.

5

I will not have a Thought from thee I'le hide,
In all my Actions, Thou shalt be my Guide;
In every Joy of mine, Thou shalt have share,
20   And I will bear a part in all thy Care.

6

Why do I vainly Talk of what we'l do?
We'l mix our Souls, you shall be Me, I you;
And both so one, it shall be hard to say,
Which is *Phylocles,* which *Ephelia.*

7

25   Our Ties shall be strong as the Chains of Fate,
Conquerors and Kings our Joys shall Emulate;
Forgotten Friendship, held at first Divine,
T'it's native Purity we will refine.

From *Female Poems upon several Occasions...* 1679, 85-86.
Title *Phylocle*s: In 'Our Cabal', *Poems upon Several Occasions* (1684),
85-86, Aphra Behn identifies her Philocles as 'Mr. N. R. V.' loved by
'Amoret, Mris. B[arry]'.
1 *Sacred Friendship*: 'Ephelia' is obviously writing in imitation of
Katherine Philips's famous Platonic friendship poems (see
pp.190-1).
3 *as cold, as clear as Ice, as Snow unstain'*d: a commonplace of erotic
poetry (cf. Suckling's 'Against Fruition': 'Shee's but an honest whore
that yields, although / She be as cold as ice, as pure as snow',
Clayton, 38) and totally contrary to Philips's image of the refining
'nobler flame' of friendship.

7 Cf. Aphra Behn, 'Absence', *Poems upon several Occasions* (1684):
'On a strict league of friendship we agree,...' (82, 1.28), and
Elizabeth Thomas, 'The Triple League' (see p.432).
26 *Conquerors and King*s: See Philips's 'To Mrs. Mary Awbrey', 20
(p.190).

To the Honoured *Eugenia*, commanding me to Write to Her.

<blockquote>

Fair Excellence! such strange Commands you lay,
I neither dare Dispute, nor can Obey:
Had I the sweet *Orinda's* happy Strain,
Yet every Line would Sacriledge contain:
5   Like to some awful Deity you sit,
At once the Terrour and Delight of Wit:
Your Soul appears in such a charming Dress
As I admire, but never can express:
Heav'n that to others had giv'n sev'ral Graces,
10 Some noble Souls, some Wit, some lovely Faces:
Finding the World did every one Admire,
Resolv'd to raise their Admiration higher:
And in one Piece, every Perfection croud,
So fram'd your Self, and of it's work grew Proud:
15 Each Rising Sun saw you more Good, more Fair;
As you alone took up all Heaven's Care:
Such awful Charms do in your Face appear,
As fill Man-kind at once with Love and Fear.
Who hear you Speak, must take your Tongue to be
20 The first Original of Harmony:
Your Meen hath such a Stately Charming Air,
As without Heralds doth your Birth declare:
Your Soul so Noble, yet from Pride so free,
That 'tis the Pattern of Humility.
25 Else I had never dar'd to give one Line
To your fair Hand, so Impolite as Mine.
Pardon, dear Madam, these untuned Lays,
That have Prophan'd what I design'd to Praise.
Nor is't possible, but I so must do,
30 All I can think falls so much short of you:
And Heaven as well with Man might angry be,
For not describing of the Deity,
In its full height of Excellence, as you
Quarrel with them that give you not your Due.

</blockquote>

'EPHELIA'

From *Female Poems upon several Occasions...* 1679, 87-88.
Title *the Honoured Eugenia*: 'Eugenia' means 'high-born'. This is the first of three poems tracing 'Ephelia's' friendship with the woman who appears to be the doyenne of the coterie and 'Ephelia's' patron. 3 *sweet Orinda*: 'Ephelia's' lavish praise is to be contrasted rather than compared with the 'modest distance' 'Orinda' achieves in 'To her royall highnesse the Dutchesse Of *Yorke*' (see p.201).

ANNE WHARTON

During her brief life and for a few years following her death, Anne
Wharton was one of the most highly esteemed women poets in
England, perhaps not entirely because of her influential
connections. Anne's father, Sir Henry Lee, died of the plague
several months before her birth; her mother, Anne Danvers, died in
childbirth. Anne was thus co-heiress with her sister, Dryden's
'Eleanora', to extensive properties in Oxfordshire and around
London. Anne Lee was baptised at Spelsbury on 24 July 1659 and
was brought up by her grandmother, Anne St John Lee Wilmot,
mother of the poet, John Wilmot, Earl of Rochester, mostly at
Ditchley in Oxfordshire, or at nearby Adderbury, where Rochester
lived after his marriage in 1667.

By the time she was twelve years old, Anne Lee was already in the
marriage market; against the wishes of her uncle Rochester, but
greatly to the satisfaction of his mother and the furtherance of the
political aims of her guardian, Sir Ralph Verney, she was married
on 16 September 1673 to Thomas Wharton, who was to become
leader of the Whig faction in Parliament and win himself an
unchallenged reputation as the greatest rake in England. Wharton
was more interested in the £10,000 and £2,500 a year that Anne
brought as her dowry than in his child-wife, and seems to have
divided his time between Parliament and the race track until 1679
when he began to take a serious interest in Whig politics.

Wharton's lack of interest in his rich wife was common
knowledge, yet Anne's devotion to him was for many years
unwavering. Sick, childless and too often alone, she still managed to
write playful letters to him (BL Add. MS 4162 ff. 232, 234), but
gradually melancholy began to pervade her life and thought. The
death of Rochester and his much publicised death-bed repentance
brought her into close contact with his spiritual mentor, Bishop
Gilbert Burnet, who took it upon himself to reprove her for the
religious doubts she expressed in her poetry, and may indeed have
prompted the suppression of much of it, for remarkably little has
survived.

Biblical paraphrases, an elegy on her cousin, a single political
poem, a handful of short poems about disillusionment and
loneliness and a paraphrase of one of Ovid's *Heroides* (predictably
perhaps, the epistle of Penelope to Ulysses) are virtually all we have.
Yet Wharton was a deliberate and self-conscious poet, correspond-
ing with Edmund Waller, Aphra Behn and Robert Wolseley. John
Grubham Howe, Bishop Burnet, Robert Gould and William

ANNE WHARTON

Atwood all wrote poems to her, sometimes under the name 'Urania'. Something of her uncle's bitterness can be found in an unpublished tragedy, 'Love's Martyr' (BL Add. MS 28,693), which refers ironically to the 'rudest untaught things' (i.e. women and fools) who despite discouragement 'will poets turn', and seems to be constructed on roughly autobiographical plot lines. Publicly, in several poems, Wharton eschewed scorn as unbecoming a Christian and a woman.

On 29 October 1685, Anne Wharton died in Rochester's house at Adderbury, attended as Rochester was by his mother and the Rev. Robert Parsons. Her will leaving her whole fortune to her husband was bitterly contested by her grandmother, who accused Thomas Wharton of giving his wife the pox and then deserting her. After her death her poems were much sought for publication in anthologies, including those edited by Aphra Behn, Nahum Tate and John Dryden. More appeared in the Wharton family anthology, *Whartoniana* (1727).

Elegy on the Earl of Rochester. By Mrs. Wh-----.

Deep waters silent roul, so Grief like mine
Tears never can relieve, nor Words define.
Stop then, stop your vain Source, weak springs of
                               Grief,
Let Tears flow from their Eyes whom Tears relieve.
5   They from their Heads shew the light Trouble there,
Could my Heart weep, its Sorrows 'twould declare:
Weep drops of Blood, my Heart, thou'st lost thy
                               Pride,
The Cause of all thy Hopes and Fears, thy Guide.
He would have led thee right in Wisdom's way,
10 And 'twas thy Fault whene'er thou went'st astray:
And since thou stray'dst when guided and led on,
Thou wilt be surely lost now left alone.
It is thy Elegy I write, not his,
He lives immortal and in highest Bliss.
15 But thou art dead, alas! my Heart, thou'rt dead,
He lives, that lovely Soul for ever fled,
But thou 'mongst Crowds on earth art buried.
Great was thy loss, which thou canst ne'er express,
Nor was th'insensible dull Nation's less;
20 He civiliz'd the rude and taught the young,
Made Fools grow wise; such artful magick hung
Upon his useful kind instructing Tongue.

His lively Wit was of himself a part,
Not as in other men, the Work of Art;
25 For, tho his Learning like his Wit was great,
Yet sure all Learning came below his Wit;
As God's immediate Gifts are better far
Than those we borrow from our Likeness here,
He was, – but I want words, and ne'er can tell,
30 Yet this I know, he did Mankind excell.
    He was what no Man ever was before,
Nor can indulgent Nature give us more,
For to make him she exhausted all her store.

From *Poems by Several Hands, And on Several Occasions*. Collected by N. Tate. London: J. Hindmarsh, 1685, 392-393. This is a shortened, corrected version of the poem published in *Examen Miscellaneum. Consisting of Verse and Prose*. London: B[ernard] L[intot], 1702.

Rochester died on 26 July 1680. In the same year, Bishop Burnet rushed into print an account of the poet's last days. Wharton clearly shares the popular belief in the sincerity of Rochester's death-bed conversion. Her poem occasioned effusive poetic responses from Waller and Howe in *Examen Miscellaneum* and from the unknown author of 'To Urania in Mourning' in Aphra Behn's *Lycidus* (1688). The passages deleted from the elegy's first publication cast light upon the relationship between Rochester and the younger poet.

3 Stop then your rainy Source, weak Springs of Grief, 1702.
5 the light Trouble/their light Sorrows 1702
17 10 lines deleted: according to the 1702 version the poem continues,

> He led thee up the steep and high Ascent
> To Poetry, the Sacred Way he went.
> He taught thy Infant Muse the Art betime,
> Tho' then the way was difficult to climb.
> Since *Daphne* prostituted has her Tree
> We well may scorn the *Chime* of Poetry:
> Then she was only his, Constant and Fair,
> And taught us all Desire, and all Despair.
> But now like other Beauties, oft enjoy'd,
> Her Charms are gone, and all her Lovers cloy'd:

31 He/ And 1702
33 37 lines deleted: in the 1702 version,

> His Childhood flam'd with that Poetic Rage,
> With which he since inform'd and blest the Age.
> Then, when his Limbs were weak, his Wit was strong,
> Good sense, before plain Words, adorn'd his Tongue.
> No wonder that he left the World so soon,
> The little time he had was all his own.
> No part of it in Childhood stole away,
> And yet this matchless Pattern went astray.

When such as he can Err, and Angels fall,
What hope have we ever to climb at all?
God saw this drooping Star, and cast him down,
That he might raise his Soul to be his own.
God saw and lov'd him, saw this chiefest Part
Of his Creation from his Precepts start,
Blest him with dying Pains, and gave him more
In that last mournful Gift, than all before.
Gave him a Penitence so fixt, so true,
A greater Penitence, no Saint e're knew.
Which done, the merciful Creator said,
This Creature of my own is perfect made;
No longer fit to dwell with Man below,
He'll be a Wonder amongst Angels now;
I'll strait to those exalted Spirits show
What stupid man cannot enough admire;
He stopt, and his best finish'd Work expir'd,
And the Triumphant Soul to Heav'n aspir'd.
To Heav'n, where everlasting Glories shine;
To Heav'n, where Cherubim with Angels join,
To welcome him, whom we'll no more deplore,
Since so well landed on that happy Shoar.
He who cou'd here below such wonders sing,
What will he now to Heav'ns eternal King?
And since our Joys in him were here so great,
What will they be, when we immortal meet.
With Extasie these Thoughts enflame my Mind,
Me thinks I leave this Case of Flesh behind,
And to him, wing'd with Joy out-flye the Wind.

Wit's Abuse

I ask not why *Astrea* fled away,
But wonder more, why any Vertues stay;
In such a World, where they are made a scorn,
Oppress'd by numerous Vice, mangled and torn,
5   Wounded by Laughter, and by wit forlorn.
I mean not here by Wit, what's truly so,
But that false Coin which does for Current go.
'Tis certain but a few can Judgment make
Of such a gift, which but a few partake.
10   Ignorant Judges may decide a Cause,
Sooner against than for Concealed Laws.
This is Wit's Pledge, but few those Precepts know,
Which many false Pretenders over-throw.
And yet amongst those very few there are
15   Some who betray that Glorious Character;
Whilst low-born Falshood goes for Heavenly Wit;
How many aim at what so few can hit?

The Trade of Hell was never hard to get.
Thus these Intruders double ends pursue,
20   Rooting out Wit, they root out Vertue too.
Soft Pity passes now for Servile Fear,
A generous scorn of Life for mean despair.
Truth and Sincerity the Fools proclaim,
Which witty falsehood always load with shame.
25   An Active Soul affected Notions prove,
Out-flying common Thoughts, or private Love.
Thus tho' each Vertue in itself they hate,
They love to make it add to a Deceit.
Undress'd 'tis scorned; but favour'd and allow'd,
30   When to the Neighbouring Vice it lends a Cloud.
Thus the Inconstant Empress of the Night,
Tho' foul, and spotted, cloaths her self with Light,
And can with borrow'd Beams be always bright.

From *A Collection of Poems by Several Hands Most of them Written by Persons of Eminent Quality*. London: F. Saunders, 1693, 248-250. 'Wit's Abuse', along with six other poems, also appeared in the re-issue, re-titled *The Temple of Death* (1695). This poem and four others were deleted in subsequent editions in 1701, 1702 and 1716.

1 *Astrea*: Astraea, daughter of Jupiter and Themis, fled the earth at the onset of the Iron Age, to dwell among the stars until the return of the Golden Age. Dryden used the myth for his celebration of the Restoration, *Astraea Redux*, in which Astraea stands for justice embodied in a strong secular power, i.e. the monarchy. Wharton also uses the myth, rather than the vaguer pastoral concept of D'Urfé's *L'Astrée*; it is difficult to apply the conceit to any but Aphra Behn. The women had been in contact since Rochester's death. In December 1682, Burnet chid Mrs Wharton for being gratified by Behn's flattery:

she is so abominably vile a woman, and rallies not only all Religion but all Virtue in so odious and obscene a manner, that I am heartily sorry she has writ any thing in your commendation... the praises of such as she are as great reproaches as yours are blessings. (Malcolm, 234)

In *The Idea of Christian Love* (1688), his paraphrase of Edmund Waller's 'Of Divine Love', William Atwood also counselled Wharton against the influence of Behn:

When counterfeit Astrea's lustful Rage
Joyns to Debauch the too Effem'nate Age;
Draws an Embroider'd Curtain over Sin,
And jilts with Promise of Bliss within:...
You best can tell the Charms of vertu'ous Joy;
Despising Venus with her Wanton Boy. (vii)

ANNE WHARTON

'Wit's Abuse' can be interpreted as a defence of witty women against Burnet's kind of censure. Wharton's awareness of her own vulnerability may be the reason that only her pious and melancholy poetry has survived.
1 *fled away*: On 12 August 1682 the Lord Chamberlain issued a warrant for the arrest of Aphra Behn and Lady Slingsby, the actress who had spoken Behn's epilogue against Monmouth in the anonymous play *Romulus and Hersilia*. It is thought by most commentators that Behn absented herself from London for a time after that, but this is not necessarily implied.

From Penelope to Ulysses

    Penelope this slow Epistle sends
    To him on whom her future hope depends;
    'Tis your *Penelope*, distress'd, forlorn,
    Who asks no Answer but your quick Return.
5   *Priam* and *Troy*, the *Grecian* Dames just Hate;
    Have long e're this, 'tis known, receiv'd their Fate.
    For which thy Absence pays too dear a Rate.
      O e're my Hopes and Joys had found their Graves,
    Why did not *Paris* perish by the Waves?
10 I should not then pass tedious Nights alone,
    Courting with fervent Breath the rising Sun;
    But all in vain, for Day is Night to me,
    Nor Day nor Night brings Comfort, only Thee.
    My tender Hands with weaving would not tire,
15 Nor my soft Thoughts with unobtain'd Desire.
      Still did my mind new fearful Forms present
    To kill my Hopes, and raise my Discontent.
    Love, Jealous Love, has more than Eagles Eyes
    To spy out Sorrows but o'er look our Joys;
20 I fancy'd furious *Trojans* still were nigh
    To slay my Lord, and all my Hopes destroy.
    As there the Arms of *Hector* still prevail,
    Here at his very Name my Cheeks grew pale;
    When told *Antilochus* by him was slain,
25 My Hopes decay'd, my Fears reviv'd again.
    I wept when young *Patroclus* was o'erthrown,
    To find how weak the Arts of Wit were grown.
    The Deeds of fierce *Tlepolemus* alarm'd
    My tender Soul, and all my Spirits charm'd.
30 Each fatal Scene Grief to my Heart did show,

Whate'er they felt, I suffer'd here for you.
But virtuous Love propitious Heav'n befriends,
My Husband's safe, on whom my life depends;
Troy is o'erthrown, and all our Sorrow ends.
35 The *Grecians* Triumph, they at large declare
The Fall of *Ilium*, and the Foes Despair.
Old men and tender Maids with Pleasure hear
The fatal end of all their Griefs and Fear.
The joyful Wife from soft Embraces now
40 Will hardly time to hear these Tales allow,
Forgets long Absence and renews her Vow.
     Some on the Tables their feign'd Combats draw,
With sparing Bowls the Victor speaks his Joy,
And with spilt Wine describes the famous *Troy*:
45 Here, says he, *Priam*'s Palace did appear,
The far-fam'd River *Simois* glided here;
Here 'twas *Achilles* fought, *Ulysses* too;
At that to guard my Heart my Spirits flew:
Achilles mighty Name pass'd carelss by,
50 But at this Name *Penelope* could dye.
One shows the Place where mangled *Hector* lay,
To fierce *Achilles*' Fury made a Prey,
Describes the horses which his Body drew,
Taught by an Instinct they before ne'er knew,
55 To fear the Man, who could no more pursue.
Breathless on Earth was laid the Soul of *Troy*,
The Army's Triumph and the City's Joy.
     This *Nestor* told your Son, whom my fond haste
Sent to enquire of Dangers which were past.
60 He told how *Resus* was with *Dolon* slain;
These tedious Tales did but augment my Pain,
I listen'd still to hear of you again.
How truly Valiant were you, tho' Unkind?
You little thought of what you left behind,
65 When in the Night you ventur'd to invade
The *Thracian* Camp, my Soul was fill'd with dread.
Assisted but by one their Strength you prove,
Too strong your Courage, but too weak your Love.
     But what remains to me for Conquests past,
70 If, like that City, still my Hopes lye waste?
Your Presence would my springing Joy renew;
Would *Troy* were glorious still, so I had you...

ANNE WHARTON

From 'Penelope to Ulysses. By the Honourable Mrs. Wharton' in *Ovid's Epistles Translated By Several Hands. The Eighth Edition. With a new Translation of Three Epistles and several Cuts never before Published.* London: Printed for Jacob Tonson, at Shakespeare's Head over-against Catherine Street in the Strand, 1712, 160-163.

Here and in the 1716 and 1725 editions, Wharton's Epistle follows 'Penelope to Ulysses. By Mr. Rymer' which had been included since Dryden inaugurated the popular series in 1680. Her 184-line poem is nearly twice as long as that of Rymer, a Latin translator and poet who, line for line, remained more true to the original. In addition to Rymer's poem, Wharton may have been familiar with any one of three other English versions, by George Turberville (*Heroicall Epistles*, 1567), by Wye Saltonstall (*Ovid's Heroicall Epistles*, 1636) and by John Sherburne (*Ovid's Heroical Epistles*, 1639). Anne Killigrew's fragment 'Penelope to Ulysses' was not published until 1686. The slow, dignified tone of Wharton's opening lines, meant to capture the monotonous tedium of Penelope's vigil, was attempted by the other poets, but nowhere else does it succeed with such Miltonic poise. Her skilful use of triplets, long and sonorous vowels, and complex syntax may give lie to Bishop Burnet's 1683 criticism, 'you have not yet the talent of correcting what you write, and therefore your composures must be considered but as first draughts' (Malcolm, 240) or may indicate that Wharton's poetry was indeed heavily edited by another hand.

2-4 The lines bespeaking a dependent love do not appear in the original or in English translations, and reflect, perhaps, Wharton's feelings about being separated from her husband. Her letter to Thomas Wharton from Paris 1 April 1681 begins: 'Forgive me for giveing you ye troble of a letter every post, but I am indeed grown so fond a foole that I cant help it; ye other day, in a fitt, I almost beat my branes out against ye pavements...' (BL Add. MS 4162, f.232).

28 *Tlepolemus*: Telephus, wounded in battle by Achilles, called Tlepolemus by Ovid.

30-40 Wharton here, and again at l.64, omits all the religious references to Altars and Gods of the original.

61 *tedious tales*: Wharton does not account for the causes of the deaths of Resus and Dolon as the original does.

70 In 'The Lamentations of Jeremiah' (the first chapter published in *A Collection of Poems by Several Hands*, 1693 and *The Temple of Death* 1695; the entire poem published in *Whartoniana* II, 1727 and *Poetical Works of Philip, late Duke of Wharton*, II, 1731), Wharton also compares a war-ruined city to a deserted wife. Her lamentation begins,

> How doth the Mournful Widow'd City bow?
> She that was once so great: Alas, how low?
> Once fill'd with Joy, with Desolation now.

293

ELIZABETH TAYLOR

The 'Mrs. Taylor' whose three poems appear in Aphra Behn's 1685 *Miscellany* has been hitherto unidentified. In the second volume of Delariviere Manley's *The New Atalantis* (1709) appears the story of one 'Olinda', including an ode she wrote 'so many years past that it's almost quite forgotten' (257-262). Thomas Hearne's contemporary keys to *The New Atalantis* identify 'Olinda' as Lady Withers, or Wythens (Doble, 292). Although as a young girl 'Olinda' was in love with a 'young Chevalier', identified as Sir Thomas Colepepper (c.1657-1723), third and last baronet of Preston Hall, Aylesford, she was married off to a man who was 'Old, Infirm, and Humourous'. In fact, Sir Francis Wythens (1634?-1704), a judge, married Elizabeth Taylor, the daughter of his contemporary, Sir Thomas Taylor (1630-1665), first baronet of Park House, Maidstone, Kent (*DNB*, 'Wythens, Sir Francis') in May 1685.

The ode, which begins 'Ah poor Olinda never boast', was published anonymously in at least two song-books of the 1680s, *A Collection of Twenty Four Songs* (1684) and *The Theater of Music: or, A Choice Collection of the newest and best Songs Sung at the Court, and Public Theaters* (1685). One of the three poems by the 'Mrs. Taylor' in Behn's *Miscellany*, 'Ye virgin powers defend my heart', appears in the 1685 *Theater of Music* with the Olinda ode (44, 60). It is likely then that Manley's 'Olinda', Elizabeth Taylor Wythens, and Behn's Mrs Taylor are the same person. The Olinda ode appears also in a manuscript collection of songs typical of the 1670s and 1680s in the Bodleian Library (Rawl. MS poet. 196, f.12) as 'the Answeare' to a song beginning 'Fly frome Olinda young and fair' (f.11ᵛ).

Elizabeth Taylor may have been living in London before her marriage; her mother, Lady Elizabeth Taylor, took as her second husband Percy Goring 'of London, esq., widower' in 1667 (Foster, col. 569; [G.E.C.] *The Complete Baronetage*, IV, 7). Lady Wythens left her husband soon after their marriage and was installed in a house not far from Colepepper's country villa where her husband, refusing to believe she had a lover, would visit her. Lady Wythens then moved into Colepepper's villa and Colepepper successfully sued Wythens for financial support for the children she brought with her. On Wythens's death in 1704, his widow and Colepepper married, although she was older than he and their mutual affection was cooling. She was buried at Aylesford in 1708 ([G.E.C.], *The Complete Baronetage*, II, 16).

Two of Mrs Taylor's poems from Behn's *Miscellany* appear in John Dunton's 'The Muses Magazine. or: Poeticall Miscellanies'

294

ELIZABETH TAYLOR

(1705, Bod. MS Rawl. poet. 173), a collection which he says was 'never design'd for publick view'. He lists Mrs Taylor's poems as 'by a timorous Lady'; the only other women represented are the ubiquitous 'Orinda' (see pp.186ff.) and Elizabeth Singer (see pp.383ff.). In Dunton's 'Conversation in Ireland' (1699), a friend tells him about a 'very celebrated *Female Poet*' in Ireland '(one Mrs. *Taylor*) who had writ her own life to a Wonder, when but *Ten Years of Age*' (333). Dunton's text of the two poems is so different from published versions as to suggest he copied them from another source.

Elizabeth Taylor continued writing poetry as Lady Wythens. 'A Drinking Song, made Extempore. By the Lady Withins' was collected in a 1720 miscellany by Anthony Hammond. Its brisk rhythm and ironic tone are like those of her earlier songs; the sentiment too is congenial, 'Tis safer for Ladies to Drink than to Love' (Hammond, 130).

ODE

I

Ah poor *Olinda* never boast
Of *Charms* that have thy *Freedom* cost,
They threw at *Hearts*, and thine was lost!

II

Yet let none thy *Ruin* blame,
His *Wit* first blew thee to a *Flame*,
And fann'd it with the Wings of *Fame!*

III

In vain I do his *Person* shun,
I cannot from his *Glory* run,
'Tis universal as the *Sun!*

IV

In *Crowds,* his *Praises* fill my Ear!
Alone, his *Genius* does appear!
He, like a *God,* is e'ry *where!*

From *Secret Memoirs and Manners of Several Persons of Quality, of Both Sexes, From the New Atalantis, an Island in the Mediterranean, Written Originally in Italian.* Vol.II. London, 1709, 257-258.

Manley introduces this ode by discussing 'the *witiest* Lady of the Age... She had also the *Face* of a *wit, much Sprightliness,* and but *little Beauty.* The *Muses* took up their Habitation in *Olinda's* lovely Breast: All she wrote was *Natural, Easy, Amorous* and *Sparkling!*' Cf. Bod. Rawl. MS poet. 196, f.12:

Ah Poor Olinda never bost of Charms that haith thy fredome Cost
Thou threu, at hearts and thine is Lost
Yet none thy rewin aught to blame

His Witt first blew me to a flame and fans it with the wings of fame
And fans it with the wings of fame
2
In vain do I his persone Shun, I cannot frome his Glowry Run
That's Universall as the Sun
In Crouds his praises fills my Ears
Alone his Genius doth Apear, he like a God is every where
he like a God is every where

The poem in manuscript was almost certainly copied down the way it was sung. According to Percy Simpson in a note inserted in the manuscript, many of the poems are to be found set to music in seventeenth-century song-books; the 'M.N.' or 'Mary N---' who signed one group of poems may have been a singer who copied and collected the songs. Manley's source is unknown.

Song, Made by Mrs. Taylor.

Ye Virgin Pow'rs defend my heart
   From Amorous looks and smiles,
From sawcy Love, or nicer Art
   Which most our Sex beguile;

5   For Sighs, and Vows, from awful fears
      That do to Pity move,
From speaking silence, and from Tears,
      Those Springs that Water Love,

But if through Passion I grow blind,
10   Let Honour be my guide.
And where frail Nature seems inclin'd,
      There fix a guard of Pride.

A heart whose Flames are seen tho pure,
      Needs every Vertues aid,
15   And those who think themselves secure,
      The soonest are betray'd.

From *Miscellany, Being a Collection of Poems By several Hands*. [ed. Aphra Behn]. London: J. Hindmarsh, 1685, 69-70. In Dunton's manuscript (Bod. Rawl. MS poet. 173, f.72), this poem is called 'A Song By a Lady, mistrustfull of her own strength'.
Dunton's version contains variants as listed:

3 or nicer Art / and nicer arts Dunton   4 beguile / beguiles Dunton
9 I grow blind / I am bold Dunton   12 fix / place Dunton
15 And those who think themselves / And she who thinks her self Dunton
16 are betrayed / is betray'd Dunton

ELIZABETH TAYLOR

To Mertill who desired her
to speak to Clorinda of his Love.
By Mrs. *Taylor*.

Mertill Though my heart should break,
    In granting thy desire,
To cold *Clorinda* I will speak,
    And warm her, with my fire.

5 To save thee from approaching harm,
    My Death I will obey.
To save thee, sinking in the Storm,
    I'll cast my self away.

May her Charms equal those of thine!
10   No words can e're express,
And let her Love be great as mine,
    Which thee wou'd only bless.

May you still prove her faithful slave,
    And she so kind and true,
15 She nothing may desire to have,
    Or fear to Lose,--but you.

From *Miscellany* (1685), 71-72. Not found in Dunton's manuscript.
Title: the poet in love with Mertill agrees to woo the woman of his
choice on his behalf, as Viola does for Orsino in *Twelfth Night*, but
this time she is not disguised as a boy.

Song.
by Mrs. *Taylor*

Strephon has Fashion, Wit and Youth,
    With all things else that please,
He nothing wants but Love and Truth,
    To ruine me with ease.
5 But he is flint, and bears the Art,
    To kindle strong desire,
His pow'r inflames anothers heart,
    Yet he ne'er feels the fire.
Alas, it does my Soul perplex,
10   When I his charms recall,

297

To think he should despise the Sex,
   Or what's worse, love 'em all;
My wearied heart, like *Noah*'s Dove,
   In vain may seek for rest,
15   Finding no hope to fix my Love,
   Returns into my Breast.

From *Miscellany* (1685), 72-73. In Dunton's manuscript (f.72ᵛ) this is called 'Another Song by a Lady. The Heart at rest at home' and divided into numbered quatrains.

1 has / hath Dunton   6 kindle strong / Kindle fierce Dunton
7 His / whose Dunton   8 yet / and Dunton
9 Alas, it does / Oh, how it do's Dunton   11 the Sex / my Sex Dunton
13 So that my Heart, like Noah's Dove Dunton
14 may seek / has sought Dunton   15 hope / hopes Dunton

1 *Strephon*: noted elsewhere as the commonest sobriquet for a faithless lover.

ANNE KILLIGREW

Anne Killigrew (1660-1685) was the daughter of Dr Henry Killigrew (1613-1700), chaplain to the Duke of York and later Master of the Savoy, and his wife Judith (d. 1683). The dramatists Thomas Killigrew, founder of the Theatre Royal (later known as Drury Lane), and Sir William Killigrew, were her uncles. She was born in 1660 in St Martin's Lane, London, just before the Restoration, and christened privately, since the offices of the common prayer were not then allowed. She served as Maid of Honour to Mary of Modena, second wife of the Duke of York (later James II), along with Catherine Sedley (later the Countess of Portmore), Sarah Jennings (later Lady Churchill), and Anne Kingsmill (later the Countess of Winchilsea). On 16 June 1685 Anne Killigrew died of smallpox in her father's lodgings within the cloister of Westminster Abbey, and was buried in the chapel of the Savoy Hospital.

Less than three months after her death Henry Killigrew had licensed for publication a volume of his daughter's verse, *Poems by Mrs. Anne Killigrew*. Though the book appears with the publication date of 1686, it was listed in the Term Catalogue for November 1685 and advertised early that month in *The Observator*. At Dr Killigrew's request Dryden composed a prefatory poem, 'To the Pious Memory of the Accomplisht Young Lady Mrs Anne Killigrew, Excellent in the two Sister-Arts of Poesie, and Painting'. According to Dryden's ode, Anne Killigrew painted pastoral scenes as well as portraits of James II (in possession of Her Majesty the Queen) and Mary of Modena; her own poetry refers to two paintings of the life of St John the Baptist and another 'representing two Nimphs of Diana's, one in a posture to Hunt, the other Batheing'. An engraving of her self-portrait was prefixed to the edition of her *Poems*. 'Venus and Adonis', 'Satyr Playing on a Pipe', 'Judith and Holofernes' and 'Venus Attired by the Graces' were listed in Admiral Killigrew's sale in 1717 (Vertue, BL Add. MS 23,070).

Both Dryden's ode and the inscription on her monument praise Anne Killigrew's modesty and piety above her talents. Dryden explained Killgrew's love poetry as 'Cupid bathing in Diana's Stream'. A translation of the Latin monumental inscription prefaced to the volume reads: 'Or if her Worth she rightly knew, / More to her Modesty was due'. Her admirers depicted Anne Killigrew as the quintessential virtuous virgin, immune to the seductions of Charles II's court.

KISSING THE ROD

To the Queen.

As those who pass the *Alps* do say,
The Rocks which first oppose their way,
And so amazing-High do show,
By fresh Ascents appear but low,
5   And when they come unto the last,
They scorn the dwarfish Hills th'ave past.

   So though my *Muse* at her first flight,
Thought she had chose the greatest height,
And (imp'd with *Alexander*'s Name)
10   Believ'd there was no further Fame:
Behold an Eye wholly Divine
Vouchsaf 'd upon my Verse to Shine!
And from that time I 'gan to treat
With Pitty him the World call'd *Great*;
15   To smile at his exalted Fate,
Unequal (though Gigantick) State.
I saw that Pitch was not sublime,
Compar'd with this which now I climb;
His Glories sunk, and were unseen,
20   When once appear'd the Heav'n-born Queen:
Victories, Laurels, Conquer'd Kings,
Took place among inferiour things.

   Now surely I shall reach the Clouds,
For none besides such Vertue shrouds:
25   Having scal'd this with holy Strains,
Nought higher but the Heaven remains!
No more I'll Praise on them bestow,
Who to ill Deeds their Glories owe;
Who build their *Babels* of Renown,
30   Upon the poor oppressed Crown,
Whole Kingdoms do depopulate,
To raise a Proud and short-Liv'd State:
I prize no more such Frantick Might,
Than his that did with Wind-Mills Fight:
35   No, give me Prowess, that with Charms
Of Grace and Goodness, not with Harms,
Erects a Throne i'th' inward Parts,
And Rules mens Wills, but with their Hearts;

Who with Piety and Vertue thus
40 Propitiates God, and Conquers us.
O that now like *Araunah* here,
Altars of Praises I could rear,
Suiting her worth, which might be seen
Like a Queens Present, to a Queen!

45 'Alone she stands for Vertues Cause,
'When all decry, upholds her Laws:
'When to Banish her is the Strife,
'Keeps her unexil'd in her Life;
'Guarding her matchless Innocence
50 'From Storms of boldest Impudence;
'In spight of all the Scoffs and Rage,
'And Persecutions of the Age,
'Owns Vertues Altar, feeds the Flame,
'Adores her much-derided Name;
55 'While impiously her hands they tie,
'Loves her in her Captivity;
'Like *Perseus* saves her, when she stands
'Expos'd to the *Leviathans*.
'So did bright Lamps once live in Urns,
60 'So Camphire in the water burns,
'So *Aetna*'s Flames do ne'er go out,
'Though Snows do freeze her head without.

How dares bold Vice unmasked walk,
And like a Giant proudly stalk?
65 When Vertue's so exalted seen,
Arm'd and Triumphant in the Queen?
How dares its Ulcerous Face appear,
When Heavenly Beauty is so near?
But so when God was close at hand,
70 And the bright Cloud did threatning stand
(*In sight of Israel*) on the Tent,
They on in their Rebellion went.

O that I once so happy were,
To find a nearer Shelter there!
75 Till then poor Dove, I wandering fly
Between the Deluge and the Skie:
Till then I Mourn, but do not sing,

And oft shall plunge my wearied wing:
If her bless'd hand vouchsafe the Grace,
80   I'th'Ark with her to give a place,
I safe from danger shall be found,
When Vice and Folly others drown'd.

From *Poems by Mrs Anne Killigrew*... Licensed to be Published, Sept. 30. 1685. London: Printed for Samuel Lowndes, 1686, 6-10. A facsimile edition has been published by Scholars' Facsimiles & Reprints, Gainesville, Florida (1967).

Title: the last stanza seems to indicate that this poem is a request to join the household of Mary of Modena, who became Queen four months before Anne's death. Court attendants would have been reappointed upon her accession to the throne, and Mary's Maid of Honour would desire assurance of a new place at Court.

9 *imp'd*: to imp in falconry is to engraft feathers in the wing of a bird, to restore the powers of flight. Hence, allusively, having enlarged one's powers, attempted flights.

Alexander's Name: the first of Anne Killigrew's verses in *Poems* is 'Alexandreis', which ambitiously echoes Virgil, 'I sing the Man that never Equal knew, / Whose Mighty Arms all *Asia* did subdue'. According to a note by her father the 'Alexandreis' 'was the first Essay of this young Lady in Poetry, but finding the Task she had undertaken hard, she laid it by till Practice and more time should make her equal to so great a Work'; cf. the opening lines of Anne Bradstreet's 'The Prologue':

> To sing of Wars, of Captaines, and of Kings,
> Of Cities founded, Common-wealths begun,
> For my Mean pen, are too superiour things.

34 *his*: Don Quixote's

41 *Araunah*: Araunah the Jebusite in Sam. 2:24 was the owner of the threshing-place where the Lord stopped a plague against Israel; David bought the threshing-place and reared an altar which became the site of the Temple of Jerusalem.

47 Part of the general outcry against James II's unpopular Catholic wife was a movement 'to Banish her'.

57 *Perseus*: Perseus saved Andromeda, chained to a rock as a sacrifice for her mother Cassiopeia's offence to the Nereids, by showing Medusa's head to the sea-monster guarding her.

58 *Leviathans*: Biblical sea-monsters as in Psalms 104:26.

59 Cf. Abraham Cowley, 'Dialogue', *The Mistress* (1656), 19-24:

> *He.* Never, my dear, was *Honour* yet undone,
>   By *Love*, but *Indiscretion.*
> To th' *wise* it all things does allow;
> And care not *What* we do; but *How.*
>   Like *Tapers* shut in ancient *Urns,*
> Unless it let in *air*, for ever *shines* and *burns.*

60 *Camphire*: camphor
70 *bright Cloud*: Exodus 24 and 32; while the people made an idol of
a golden calf, the Lord hovered in a cloud of fire over Moses on Mt
Sinai.
75 *poor Dove*: Noah's dove, Genesis 8:9

On Death.

Tell me thou safest End of all our Woe,
Why wreched Mortals do avoid thee so:
Thou gentle drier o'th'afflicteds Tears,
Thou noble ender of the Cowards Fears;
5   Thou sweet Repose to Lovers sad dispaire,
Thou Calm t'Ambitions rough Tempestuous Care.
If in regard of Bliss thou wert a Curse,
And then the Joys of Paradise art worse;
Yet after Man from his first Station fell,
10   And God from *Eden Adam* did expel,
Thou wert no more an Evil, but Relief;
The balm and Cure to ev'ry Humane Grief:
Through thee (what Man had forfeited before)
He now enjoys, and ne'r can loose it more.
15   No subtile Serpents in the Grave betray,
Worms on the Body there, not Soul do prey;
No Vice there Tempts, no Terrors there afright,
No Coz'ning Sin affords a false delight:
No vain Contentions do that Peace annoy,
20   No feirce Alarms break the lasting Joy.

Ah since from thee so many Blessings flow,
Such real Good as Life can never know;
Come when thou wilt, in thy afrighting'st Dress,
Thy Shape shall never make thy Welcome less.
25   Thou mayst to Joy, but ne'er to Fear give Birth,
Thou Best, as well as Certain'st thing on Earth.
Fly thee? May Travellers then fly their Rest,
And hungry Infants fly the profer'd Brest.
No, those that faint and tremble at thy Name,
30   Fly from their Good on a mistaken Fame.
Thus Childish fear did *Israel* of old
From Plenty and the Promis'd Land with-hold;
They fancy'd Giants, and refus'd to go,

KISSING THE ROD

When *Canaan* did with Milk and Honey flow.

From *Poems by Mrs Anne Killigrew...* 1686, 13-14.
Title: a similar philosophic approach to death appears in Lady Masham's poem, 'When deaths cold hand shall close my eyes' (see p.318). For Lady Masham's comments on the publication of Anne Killigrew's poetry, see p.317.
31-34 Numbers 13:27-33

On a Picture Painted by her self,
representing two Nimphs of Diana's, *one in a Posture to Hunt,*
the other Batheing.

    We are *Diana*'s Virgin-Train,
    Descended of no Mortal Strain;
    Our Bows and Arrows are our Goods,
    Our Pallaces, the lofty Woods,
5   The Hills and Dales, at early Morn,
    Resound and Eccho with our Horn;
    We chase the Hinde and Fallow-Deer,
    The Wolf and Boar both dread our Spear;
    In Swiftness we out-strip the Wind,
10 An Eye and Thought we leave behind;
    We *Fawns* and Shaggy *Satyrs* awe;
    To *Sylvan Pow'rs* we give the Law:
    Whatever does provoke our Hate,
    Our Javelins strike, as sure as *Fate*;
15 We Bathe in Springs, to cleanse the Soil,
    Contracted by our eager Toil;
    In which we shine like glittering Beams,
    Or Christal in the Christal Streams;
    Though *Venus* we transcend in Form,
20 No wanton Flames our Bosomes warm!
    If you ask where such Wights do dwell,
    In what Bless't Clime, that so excel?
    The Poets onely that can tell.

From *Poems by Mrs Anne Killigrew...* 1686, 28-29.

Upon the saying that my Verses *were made by another.*

    Next Heaven my Vows to thee (O Sacred *Muse!*)
    I offer'd up, nor didst thou them refuse.

O Queen of Verse, said I, if thou'lt inspire,
And warm my Soul with thy Poetique Fire,
5 No Love of Gold shall share with thee my Heart,
Or yet Ambition in my Brest have Part,
More Rich, more Noble I will ever hold
The *Muses* Laurel, than a Crown of Gold.
An Undivided Sacrifice I'le lay
10 Upon thine Altar, Soul and Body pay;
Thou shalt my Pleasure, my Employment be,
My All I'le make a Holocaust to thee.

The Deity that ever does attend
Prayers so sincere, to mine did condescend.
15 I writ, and the Judicious prais'd my Pen:
Could any doubt Insuing Glory then?
What pleasing Raptures fill'd my Ravisht Sense?
How strong, how Sweet, Fame, was thy Influence?
And thine, False Hope, that to my flatter'd sight
20 Didst Glories represent so Near, and Bright?
By thee deceiv'd, methought, each Verdant Tree,
Apollos transform'd *Daphne* seem'd to be;
And ev'ry fresher Branch, and ev'ry Bow
Appear'd as Garlands to empale my Brow.
25 The Learn'd in Love say, Thus the Winged Boy
Does first approach, drest up in welcome Joy;
At first he to the Cheated Lovers sight
Nought represents, but Rapture and Delight,
Alluring Hopes, Soft Fears, which stronger bind
30 Their Hearts, than when they more assurance find.

Embolden'd thus, to Fame I did commit,
(By some few hands) my most Unlucky Wit.
But, ah, the sad effects that from it came!
What ought t'have brought me Honour, brought me
shame!
35 Like *Esops* Painted Jay I seem'd to all,
Adorn'd in Plumes, I not my own could call:
Rifl'd like her, each one my Feathers tore,
And, as they thought, unto the Owner bore.
My Laurels thus an Others Brow adorn'd,
40 My Numbers they Admir'd, but Me they scorn'd:
An others Brow, that had so rich a store

305

Of Sacred Wreaths, that circled it before;
Where mine quite lost, (like a small stream that ran
Into a Vast and Boundless Ocean)
45   Was swallow'd up, with what it joyn'd and drown'd,
And that Abiss yet no Accession found.

    Orinda, (*Albions* and her Sexes Grace)
Ow'd not her Glory to a Beauteous Face,
It was her Radiant Soul that shon With-in,
50   Which struk a Lustre through her Outward Skin;
That did her Lips and Cheeks with Roses dy,
Advanc't her Height, and Sparkled in her Eye.
Nor did her Sex at all obstruct her Fame,
But higher 'mong the Stars it fixt her Name;
55   What she did write, not only all allow'd,
But ev'ry Laurel, to her Laurel, bow'd!

    Th'Envious Age, only to Me alone,
Will not allow, what I write, my Own,
But let 'em Rage, and 'gainst a Maide Conspire,
60   So Deathless Numbers from my Tuneful Lyre
Do ever flow; so *Phebus* I by thee
Divinely Inspired and possest may be;
I willingly accept *Cassandras* Fate,
To speak the Truth, although believ'd too late.

From *Poems by Mrs Anne Killigrew...* 1686, 44-47.
Title: a commonplace in women's writing; cf. Rachel Speght's defence of her work as 'of spring of my indeavor', others having formerly 'deprived me of my due, imposing my abortive upon the father of me, but not of it' (see p.68); Anne Bradstreet's poem 'The Prologue': 'If what I doe prove well, it wo'nt advance, / They'l say its stolne, or else, it was by chance'; and Aphra Behn's postscript to *The Rover* (1677): 'Therefore I will only say in English what the famous Virgil does in Latin; *I Make Verses, and others have the Fame.*'
12 *Holocaust*: burnt offering
22 *Daphne*: Daphne became a bay-tree to escape Apollo's pursuit; the poet mocks herself for having seen a laurel wreath in every tree.
35 *Esops Painted Jay*: in Roger L'Estrange's 1693 translation of Aesop, the jay is called a jackdaw who 'Trick'd himself up with all the *Gay-Feathers* he could Muster together: And upon the Credit of these Stoll'n, or Borrow'd Ornaments, he Valu'd himself above All the Birds in the Air Beside'; cf. Aphra Behn's translation in Francis Barlow's *Aesop's Fables* (1687):

306

The Jay would for a gawdy Peacock pass,
And with their borrowed plumes her tayle dos grace
But when from thence each had his feathers torne,
By her own Birds she is receiv'd with scorne.
                    Morall
Tis the gay Dress that makes the Lover doat,
Not the fine Soule, but the fine Petticoat. (95)

61 *Phebus*: Apollo, god of poetry
63 *Cassandras Fate*: because Cassandra rejected Apollo's advances,
he changed his gift of prophecy to a curse; he decreed that her
predictions, though true, would go unheeded.

To My Lord Colrane, *In Answer to his Complemental Verses sent me under the Name of* Cleanor.

Long my dull *Muse* in heavy slumbers lay,
Indulging Sloth, and to soft Ease gave way,
Her Fill of Rest resolving to enjoy,
Or fancying little worthy her employ.
5   When Noble *Cleanors* obliging Strains
Her, the neglected Lyre to tune, constrains.
Confus'd at first, she rais'd her drowsie Head,
Ponder'd a while, then pleas'd, forsook her Bed.
Survey'd each Line with Fancy richly fraught,
10 Re-read, and then revolv'd them in her Thought.

    And can it be? she said, and can it be?
That 'mong the Great Ones I a Poet see?
The Great Ones? who their Ill-spent time devide,
'Twixt dang'rous Politicks, and formal Pride,
15 Destructive Vice, expensive Vanity,
In worse Ways yet, if Worse there any be:
Leave to Inferiours the despised Arts,
Let their Retainers be the *Men of Parts*.
But here with Wonder and with Joy I find,
20 I'th'Noble Born, a no less Noble Mind;
One, who on Ancestors, does not rely
For Fame, in Merit, as in Title, high!

    The Severe Godess thus approv'd the Laies:
Yet too much pleas'd, alas, with her own Praise.
25 But to vain Pride, *My Muse*, cease to give place,
Virgils immortal Numbers once did grace

A *Smother'd Gnat*: by high Applause is shown,
If undeserv'd, the Praisers worth alone:
Nor that you should believ't, is't always meant,
30 'Tis often for Instruction only sent,
To praise men to Amendment, and display,
By its Perfection, where their Weakness lay.
This Use of these Applauding Numbers make
Them for Example, not Encomium, take.

From *Poems by Mrs Anne Killigrew*... 1686, 49-50.
Title: Henry Hare, second Baron Colraine (1636-1708) was an antiquary of Tottenham, Middlesex.
26-27 *Virgils*... *Smother'd Gnat*: the mock heroic Latin poem *Culex*, paraphrased by Spenser as *Virgil's Gnat*, is not actually by Virgil; Killigrew's reference is certainly to Spenser's poem.

'THE EMULATION'

All we know of the author or authors of 'The Emulation' can be found on the title-page of *Triumphs of Female Wit, in Some Pindarick Odes. Or the Emulation. Together With an Answer to an Objector against Female Ingenuity, and Capacity of Learning. Also, A Preface to the Masculine Sex, by a Young Lady*, published in London in 1683. The prose preface addressed to 'the Masculine Sex' is specifically ascribed to a female author, although in describing women's nights as devoted to 'the ungratifying Divertisement of an unperforming Husband', and in boasting of women's 'Ingenuity of Revenge' it displays a slant uncharacteristic of most women's writing.

'The Emulation' is the first of three pindaric odes, followed by 'The Answer to the Emulation', by 'Mr H.' which concludes:

> A Woman Fair, Wise, Learn'd, and Humble too,
>   Will be a *Species* alone,
>   A *Phoenix* true,
> Talk'd of by all but seen by none. (108-111)

In 'A Reply to the Answerer of the Emulation' a 'Mr F.' writes as a woman, ostensibly in defence of women's 'choicer Gifts', but actually limiting women's sphere once again:

> We only let our Reason go
> At things convenient fit to know:
> We act just as the Gods enjoyn,
> And on permitted Objects fix our aim... (110-113)

'The Emulation' is attributed by an end note, '*Written by a* Young Lady', but doubts persist. It is a competent catalogue of what had become commonplaces in the women's defence against misogynist attacks (see Speght, p.76): women's present benighted state; the equality of souls and parts in both sexes; women's confinement to the most sordid tasks of life and to frivolous activities; their function as ignorant foils to men; male fear of educated and therefore powerful women; reference to successful women of the past; the idea of the Muses favouring their own sex. However, stanzas three and four deviate slightly from the norm. Although the claim that women should be allowed education in the interests of morality and the social order is usual in polemics by reformers like Mary Astell and Bathsua Makin, the author of 'The Emulation' asks for only 'a part of learning, to assure men that women 'no nobler, braver, Conquest wish to gain'. The 'Young Lady' concedes too much.

309

KISSING THE ROD

The Emulation. A Pindarick Ode.

I

Ah! tell me why, deluded Sex, thus we
    Into the secret Beauty must not prye
    Of our great *Athenian* Deity.
Why do we *Minerva*'s Blessings slight,
5   And all her tuneful gifts despise;
    Shall none but the insulting Sex be wise?
    Shall they be blest with intellectual Light?
    Whilst we drudge on in Ignorances Night?
    We've Souls as noble, and as fine a Clay,
10 And Parts as well compos'd to please as they.
    Men think perhaps we best obey,
    And best their servile Business do,
    When nothing else we know
But what concerns a Kitchin or a Field,
15   With all the meaner things they yield.
As if a rational unbounded Mind
Were only for the sordid'st task of Life design'd.

II

    They let us learn to work, to dance, or sing,
    Or any such like trivial thing,
20 Which to their profit may Increase or Pleasure bring.
    But they refuse to let us know
    What sacred Sciences doth impart
    Or the mysteriousness of Art.
In Learning's pleasing Paths deny'd to go,
25   From Knowledge banish'd, and their Schools;
    We seem design'd alone for useful Fools,
    And foils for their ill shapen sense, condemn'd to
                   prise
    And think 'em truly wise,
    Being not allow'd their Follies to despise.
Thus we from Ignorance to Wonder run.
(For Admiration ceases when the Secret's known)
    Seem witty only in their praise
    And kind congratulating Lays.
Thus to the Repute of Sense they rise,
35 And thus through the applauder's Ignorance are
                   wise.
    For should we understand as much as they,
    They fear their Empire might decay.

310

For they know Women heretofore
Gain'd Victories, and envied Lawrels wore:
40   And now they fear we'll once again
    Ambitious be to reign
And to invade the Dominions of the Brain.
And as we did in those renowned days
Rob them of Lawrels, so we now will take their Bayes.

III

45   But we are peaceful and will not repine,
    They still may keep their Bays as well as Wine.
    We've now no *Amazonian* Hearts,
They need not therefore guard their *Magazine* of *Arts*.
    We will not on their treasure seise,
50 A part of it sufficiently will please:
    We'll only so much Knowledge have
    As may assist us to enslave
    Those Passions which we find
    Too potent for the Mind.
55   'Tis o're them only we desire to reign,
And we no nobler, braver, Conquest wish to gain.

IV

    We only so much will desire
    As may instruct us how to live above
    Those childish things which most admire,
60   And may instruct us what is fit to love.
We covet Learning for this only end,
That we our time may to the best advantage spend:
    Supposing 'tis below us to converse
    Always about our Business or our Dress;
65 As if to serve our Senses were our Happiness.
    We'll read the Stories of the Ancient Times,
To see, and then with horror hate their Crimes.
But all their Vertues with delight we'll view,
    Admir'd by Us, and imitated too.
70   But for rewarding Sciences and Arts,
    And all the curious Products which arise
    From the contrivance of the Wise,
We'll tune and cultivate our fruitful Hearts.
    And should Man's Envy still declare,
75   Our Business only to be fair;
    Without their leave we will be wise,
And Beauty, which they value, we'll despise.

Our Minds, and not our Faces, we'll adorn,
For that's the Employ to which we are born.
80   The *Muses* gladly will their aid bestow,
And to their *Sex* their charming Secrets show.
Whilst Man's brisk Notions owe their rise
To an inspiring Bottle, Wench, or Vice,
Must be debauch'd and damn'd to get
85   The Reputation of a Wit.
To Nature only, and our softer Muses, we
Will owe our Charms of Wit, of Parts, and Poetry.

From *Triumphs of Female Wit, in Some Pindarick Odes. Or the Emulation. Together With an Answer to an Objector against Female Ingenuity, and Capacity of Learning. Also, A Preface to the Masculine Sex, by a Young Lady.* London: T. Malthus and J. Waltho, 1683, 1-5.

Title *Emulation*: here meaning imitating in order to excel or surpass, in the same spirit as Henry Care used the term in his 'Translators Preface' to *Female Pre-eminence: or the Dignity and Excellency of that Sex, above the Male* (1670), his version of Cornelius Agrippa's *De nobilitate et praecellentia foeminei sexus*:

Yet is it no part of our Design to flatter Women, but to put some *check* to the rude, undeserv'd *reproaches, cast on them,* by the Men: To acquaint the *fair Sex* with its natural Dignity, that they may scorn to act anything unworthy of themselves: to treat them with variety of *real* (not *Romantick*) *Examples* of true *Piety*, exact *Chastity*, sincere unalterable *Affection*, and other rare, sublime *qualities*; whence inspir'd with a generous emulation they may strive to *out-vye* these ancient *Heroinae*, and transcend the excellent *Patterns* here recommended;... (Sig.A3)

A poem of the same name appears in Sarah Fyge, *Poems on Several Occasions* [1703], 108-109. Fyge (see pp.345ff.) makes a similar argument in heroic couplets, using some of the same commonplaces: 'Poor Womankind's in every State, a Slave'; '[Men] keep us Fools to raise their own Renown'; 'Wits Empire, now, shall know a Female Reign'. Fyge's poem does not attempt to justify women's education in order to control 'too potent' passions, nor is it concerned with 'what is fit to love'. It concludes: 'And shall these finite Males reverse their Rules, / No, we'll be Wits, and then Men must be Fools.' In the year following the publication of *Triumphs of Female Wit* she composed *The Female Advocate*, first published in 1686, a response to a misogynist poem by Robert Gould.

1-5 Bathsua Makin, in *An Essay to Revive the Antient Education of Gentlewomen* (1673) finds fault with the 'vain lives' of the 'deluded Sex':

persons of higher quality, for want of this Education, have nothing to employ themselves in, but are forced to Cards, Dice, Playes, and frothy Romances, meerly to drive away the time; whereas knowledge in Arts and Tongues would pleasantly employ them, and upon occasion benefit others.... God, that will take an account for every idle thought, will certainly reckon with those Persons that shall spend their whole lives in idle play and chat. Poor Women will make but a lame excuse at the last day for their vain lives; it will be something to say, that they were educated no better. (26)

4 *Minerva*: cf. *The Compleat Woman* (1639), a translation of Jacques Du Bosc's *L'honneste femme* (1632): '[A]s men have an *Apollo*, for the Author of Sciences, Women have their *Minerva*, who invented the best learnings, and who affords them a just right to pretend to it' (30).

9 *Souls as noble*: cf. 'Philo-philippa', 53-54 (see p.205). *Clay*: the material part of the human body, as distinguished from the soul.

17 *sordid'st task of Life*: the limitations of women's education and work are presented in *The women's sharpe revenge* (1640), a response to John Taylor's misogynist *Divers Crab Tree Lectures* (1639) and *A Juniper Lecture* (1639). Attributed to 'Mary Tattlewell' and 'Ioane Hit-Him-Home', the rejoinder may be by Taylor himself:

When we, who may stile by a name of weaker Vessells, though of a more delicate, fine, soft and more plyant flesh, and therefore of a temper most capable of the best Impression, have not that generous and liberall Educations, lest we should bee made able to vindicate our own injuries, we are set onely to the Needle, to pricke our fingers: or else to the Wheele to spinne a faire thread for our owne undoings, or perchance to some more durty and deboysed drudgery: If wee be taught to read, they then confine us within the compasse of our Mothers Tongue, and that limit wee are not suffered to passe; or if (which sometimes happeneth) wee be brought up to Musick, to singing, and to dancing, it is not for any benefit that thereby wee can ingrosse unto our selves, but for their own particular ends, the better to please and content their licentious appetites, when we come to our maturity and ripenesse; and thus if we be weake by Nature, they strive to makes us more weake by our nurture. And if in degree of place low, they strive by their policy to keepe us more under. (40-42)

18 *work*: needle-work
21-44 Cf. 'Philo-philippa', 25-58 (see p.205).
24 The Duchess of Newcastle's 'Address to Two Universities' warns of the results when women are barred from 'Learning's pleasing Paths':

in time we should grow irrational as idiots, by the dejectednesse of our spirits, through the carelesse neglects, and despisements of the masculine sex to the effeminate, thinking it impossible we should have either learning or understanding, wit or judgement, as if we had not rational souls as well as men, and we out of a custom of dejectednesse think so too, which makes us quit all all [sic] industry towards profitable knowledge being employed onely in looe, and pettye imployments, which takes away not onely our abilities towards arts, but higher capacities in speculations, so as we are become like worms, that onely live in the dull earth of ignorance... (*The Philosophical and Physical Opinions*, 1655, B2ᵛ)

27 *foils for their ill shapen sense*: cf. Barker, 'A Farewell to Poetry, With A Long Digression on Anatomy', *Poetical Recreations* (1688):

And because we *precipitated* first,
To Pains and Ignorance are most accurs'd;
Ev'n by our *Counter-parts*, who that they may
Exalt themselves, insultingly will say,
Women know little and they practise less;
But Pride and Sloth they glory to profess. (35-40)

36-37 Cf. Bathsua Makin, *Essay* (1673): 'Many men, silly enough, (God knows) think themselves wise, and will not dare to marry a wise Woman, lest they should be over-topt' (30) and Du Bosc, *The Compleat Woman* (1639):

They that distrust a Woman of Letters, are truely weake spirits, who deserve what they feare so much, and who ground their suspitions on the reasons which ought to afford them the most security. (24)

38-39 Aphra Behn's epilogue to *Sir Patient Fancy* (1677) criticises women's exclusion from the world of letters and cites accomplishments of women in the past:

> What has poor Woman done, that she must be
> Debar'd from Sense, and sacred Poetry?
> Why in this Age has Heaven allow'd you more,
> And Women less of Wit than heretofore?
> We once were fam'd in story, and could write
> Equal to Men; cou'd govern, nay, cou'd fight.
> We still have passive Valour, and can show,
> Wou'd Custom give us leave, the active too,
> Since we no Provocations want from you. (5-13)

Cf. also Rachel Speght, 'The Dreame', 127-150 (see pp.71-2).

48 *magazine*: storehouse

52-54 *enslave Those Passions... Too potent for the Mind*: Mary Astell's *A Serious Proposal for the Ladies,* I (1701 edition) observes,

the true end of all our Prayers and external observances is to work our minds into a truly Christian temper, to obtain for us the Empire of our Passions, and to reduce all irregular Inclinations... (10)

The Passions of the Soule in three Books (1650), a translation of Descartes, addresses itself to the control of the passions:

souls may be thought stronger or weaker according as they...resist the present Passions contrary to them... even those who have the weakest Souls, may acquire a most absolute Empire over all their Passions, if art, and industry be used to mannage, and govern them. (42-44)

77 *Beauty...we'll despise*: cf. Mary Astell, *Serious Proposal* I (1701):

Let us learn to pride our selves in something more excellent than the invention of a fashion, and not entertain such a degrading thought of our own *worth*, as to imagine that our Souls were given us only for the service of our Bodies, and that the best improvement we can make of these, is to attract the Eyes of Men. We value *them* too much, and our *selves* too little, if we place any part of our desert in their Opinion, and don't think our selves capable of Nobler Things than the pitiful Conquest of some worthless heart. She who has opportunities of making an interest in Heaven, of obtaining the love and admiration of GOD and Angels, is too prodigal of her Time, and injurious to her Charms, to throw them away on vain insignificant men. (10)

80-81 Cf. 'Philo-philippa', 95-96 (see p.206).

DAMARIS, LADY MASHAM

Born in Cambridge on 18 January 1659, Damaris was the daughter of Ralph Cudworth, Regius Professor of Hebrew, Master of Christ's College from 1654 and leader of the Cambridge Platonists. His major work, *The true Intellectual System of the Universe, wherein all the reason and philosophy of Atheism is confuted and its impossibility demonstrated* (1678) attempts to reconcile Cartesian and Platonic principles and develops the theory of 'plastic nature'. Damaris's mother, Damaris Cradock, came of a distinguished family which for generations had produced divines of differing persuasions, including Cudworth's pupil Zachary Cradock (1633-1695) chaplain in ordinary to Charles II and Provost of Eton. Mary Cradock, who became the painter Mary Beale (see pp.15-16) was a kinswoman. Ballard in his memoir of Lady Masham (1752) writes that her father took 'particular care in her tuition' (Perry, 1985, 332). Damaris gave a different account of her education in a letter to Locke (1688); when asked to evaluate the abridgement which was the first published version of his *Essay Concerning Human Understanding*, she replied:

I do not I confess think my self altogether Uncapable of Things of that Nature; And I am sure I have a Universal Love for All usefull Knowledge Beyond that Capacitie; But as I was Diverted from It when I was Young, first by the Commands of Others And Afterwards by that Weakness which Hapned in my Sight, The World through long Acquaintance begun almost to Claime All my Thoughts. (De Beer, 1976, III, 431-432)

Damaris became acquainted with John Locke sometime before 1681, possibly at the London home of Mary and Edward Clark, cousins of Locke and friends of Ralph Cudworth. For the next seven years Locke, then forty-nine, and Damaris, twenty-two, corresponded as 'Philander' and 'Philoclea'. Her letters lightly gossip about the latest works of philosophy and literature and complain about her health (she describes classic symptoms of severe migraine headaches), but the subtext is always a persistent metaphysical debate, she pushing him to define his position on such issues as 'the Souls Haveing no Actual Knowledge'. It is no overstatement to say that Locke refined his thinking through her prodding.

In 1685 Damaris married Sir Francis Masham (d.1723), third baronet, of Oates, Essex, a widower with nine children. In the following year she gave birth to her only child, Francis Cudworth Masham, who became accountant-general to the Court of Chancery. From several of her letters to Locke dated 1684, it appears that she was pressured to marry; how she then saw her relationship with Locke, who had gone into voluntary exile in Holland in 1683, is unclear. The poetry they had exchanged the previous year was in the nature of a debate on amorous vs. Platonic love. Damaris Cudworth wrote 'On Damons Loveing of Clora':

> Say wherefore is't that Damon flys,
> From the Weake Charms of Cloras Eyes?
> Weake Charms they surely needs must bee,
> Which till this Houre he could not see,
> Nor is she now more Faire, then when
> Theire first acquaintance they began,
> When the Gay shepherd Laugh'd at love,
> Swore it no Gen'rous Heart could move,
> Disease of Fools, Fond Lunacie,
> To Cloras Face oft would he Cry,
> on mee your Friendship but bestow,
> (Friendship, the onely Good below)
> Faire shepherdess Ile ask no more,
> Since more to give, exceeds your Pow'r.... (De Beer, 1976, II, 571)

Locke's poem responds,

> I freindship beg'd and did obteine
> And thought my self a happy swain
> But 'twas not ignorance nor pride
> Made me ask noe thing els besides
> He that asks freindship asks the heart
> Unlesse there be some better part... (De Beer, 1976, II, 574)

By the time Locke returned to England at the accession of William and Mary, their friendship had deepened to a settled affection. After repeated invitations Locke moved from London to Oates in 1691. Though he made the move ostensibly for his own health (he suffered from asthma), the arrangement was mutually beneficial, Damaris having complained of boredom induced by 'the Insipid Coxcombs of the Countrey'. In addition to encouraging Damaris in her studies of Latin, mathematics, philosophy, and theology, Locke looked after her business affairs, managed household accounts, tended her sick mother, and played with the youngest children.

Lady Masham continued to involve herself in philosophical debate. John Norris of Bemerton, the English Platonist, wrote his *Reflections upon the Conduct of Human Life... In a letter to the excellent lady, the Lady Masham* (1690). In *A Discourse Concerning the Love of God*, published anonymously in 1696 (translated into French in 1705), Masham criticised theories put forward by Norris and Mary Astell (see pp.333ff.) in *Letters Concerning the Love of God* (1695) as 'too Visionary to be likely to be received by many Intelligent Persons' (Sig.A2ᵛ). Astell in turn replied in *The Christian Religion as Professed by a Daughter of the Church of England* (1705). In 1705 Masham published, again anonymously, *Occasional Thoughts in Reference to a Vertuous or Christian Life*, urging women to reject the notion that 'the praise of Men ought to be the Supreme Object of their Desires, and the great Motive with them to Vertue' (21);

instead women should be encouraged to use reason as an internal guide to the Christian life.

Lady Masham and Locke maintained their happy domestic arrangement until his death in 1704. Locke left sizable legacies to Lady Masham and her son, whom he had nicknamed 'Totty', and was buried at his own request in the local parish church at High Laver. Lady Masham's biography of Locke was published in Jean Le Clerc's Amsterdam journal, *La Bibliothèque universelle*, shortly after his death. She died three years later, on 20 April 1708, and was buried at Bath Abbey.

Lady Masham's poems came to light in Locke's published correspondence. In August 1682, she writes that she has 'much Curiositie to know the Poetess you speake of ', and elsewhere quotes from Cowley and Katherine Philips. After her marriage she assured Locke: 'I cannot yet forget my Poetry upon occasion', but in another letter complained ' 'Tis in Vain that you bid me Preserve my Poetry; Household Affairs are the Opium of the Soul' (De Beer, 1976, II, 757). In a letter of 14 December 1685 she laments the lack of good company in the country and says she is

Forc'd now... to seeke my entertainment in Books Altogether; and that Principally in Poetry, to which the Present Fancie most inclines me, and Therefore know at this Time that it is out of pure Crosness that I send You none, since I Hardly write of Late to Any Body but your self in Prose.

She adds, however, referring to the just published collected *Poems* of Anne Killigrew (see pp.299ff.) who died in June 1685:

How ever perhaps you may see me in Print in a little While, and then need not be Beholden to me, it being growne much the Fasion of late for our sex, Though I confess it has not much of my Approbation because (Principally) the Mode is for one to Dye First; and at this time if I might Have my owne Choice I Have no Great Inclination That Way. (De Beer, 1976, II, 762)

The only poem of this period we would ascribe to Lady Masham appears in *A Collection of Miscellanies: Consisting of Poems, Essays, Discourses & Letters, Occasionally Written by John Norris* (1687). 'The Irreconcilable', the only one of a group of poems printed as the work of John Norris to use a female point of view, begins:

> I Little thought (*my Damon*) once, that *you*
> Could prove, and what is more, to *me, untrue*.
> Can I *forget* such *Treachery*, and *Live*?
> *Mercy* it self would not this Crime forgive.
> *Heaven*'s Gates refuse to let *Apostates* in,
> No, that's the *Great unpardonable Sin*. (31)

The rallying tone of the poem and its easy play between conventions of theology and love idolatry recall her other poems and letters. The following year Norris dedicated *The Theory and Regulation of Love* to Lady Masham, encouraging her to 'bequeath some Monument' of her 'extraordinary Genius' otherwise he doubts that 'the *Future* will ever *believe*' the extent of her accomplishments.

KISSING THE ROD

When deaths cold hand shall close my eyes
And my freed soule from earth is fled
Glad that at length she broke those ties
W^{ch} her soe long imprisoned
5   She'l leave the breathlesse trunk behinde
Sport in the aire & wanton in ye winde

Whilst those who heare my dying breath
And see my parting soule expire
call my release unhappy death
10   which robbs me of ye worlds desire
wth teares bewail my untimely fall
And thus lament my funeral

she's gone Awe me she's gone say they
hard fate in midst of youths fresh bloome
15   scarce out of childhood snatch'd away
Early Alas to finde a Tomb
who mightst have blest in Future Yeares
Thy parents age & joyd their cares

Inclosd now in some hallow Vault
20   Thou pale & Mould'ring Dust must ly
wth Teares & Mournfull Sighs, there brought
In thy dark Dungeon thou must lye
Till time has made thy name forgot
& none knows whom thou wert or what,

25   Ah Cruell Death are not ye old
ye weake diseasd & maimed Enow
To glut thy rage must thou lay hold
& to thy malice make them bow
whose Youth claimes many yeares in store
30   & puts far off its fatal houre.

Tis true they talk of Joye to come
in y^t new state to wch we pass
But who ere try'd y^t finall doome
came back & told what pleasure 't was
35   of present life ye Joye we know
but Future to o[ur]^e Faith must owe

Though grant if it were as they perswade
And y^t such bliss ye good attend
th'unknown pleasures were delayd
40 Till death by age us thither send
   were it not a much more happy fate
   T'enjoy ye best of either state.

Tis thus me thinks, I heare ye rout
of Vulgar Souls my death bemoane
45 I oft have smild shall then laugh out
At their ill placd empassion
   pitty their narrow childish minding
   movd but by w^t their Senses finding

whilst my deare freinds who shall survive
50 (Robing not nature of her due)
a Nobler judgment much will give
Their thoughts more generous & true
   Though funerall pomp surprize their teares
   Nought strange or sad in death appeares.

55 Ah weepe not long for me who then
Lifes dangerous Gulph haveing past
and all ye snares surround frail men
Rest & sure harbour, find at last
   midst ye blest spirits of ye just
60   who did their maker serve & trust

Strip'd then of Earth above it raisd
How Vaine will mortall life appeare
ye greatest actions men have praisd
or mightiest Heroes practisd ere
65   ye huge designe ye Vast desires
   Ambition in ye soul inspires,

The business then of life will show
as childrens play to men appeares
on wch some minuts they'l bestow
70 in smiling at their hopes & feares
   Anxious who shall ye gainer bee
   In some small childish Victory

319

So will ye grand affairs of life
To souls when once awakend seeme
75 Its great contests like this low strife
Its Joye imaginary dreame
were this ye only change in death
we gaine enough by loseing breath

But Oh! ye Joye of y^t blessd state
80 Freindship refind, & purest love
Softest delighte, Lasting yet great
Such as no mortall ere did prove
Converse y^{ts} innocent & free
Bles'd Unione sweetest Harmonie

85 No sullen peevish discord here
Disturbs their well establish'd Joy
nor opposite opinions ere
Their Mutual charitie destroy
Since all agree in ye great end
90 To wch theire different notions tend

[missing in MS] wth ye Nobles Wise of Old
whom natures glimring light did guide
wch ye inlightened shall behold
whom now no differences divide
95 Since both in th'object they adore
agree of in their lifes before

How would it make one smile to see
Some honest bigot enter here
whose well meant Zeal must surely bee
100 his only plea when he appeares
That without mercy has damn'd all
Hee of his party cannot call.

who when he comes ye names to heare
of Socrates & Pythagores
105 wth ye great Antonine I feare
he almost will advance no more
but hastily retreating say
your pardon I mistook my way.

Heavens self will seeme unsanctify'd
110 to him who did not know before
what's Infinite's not Limited
Nor God nor arbitrary power
  who like himself th'Almighty drew
  & thought ye loved Idea true

115 Sure to's Resemblance he'l be Kind
of man he took no farther care
but like his owne Gods love confind
nor would admit ye world a share
  but now ashamd he doth Implore
120 pardon for his mistake before.

All Harsh opinions here shall cease
products of ignorance & Pride
where charity good will & peace
no differences can ere divide.
125 All freely seeke each others good
  where pride, nor Envy's understood.

And our weake sex I hope will then
disdaine y^t stupid ignorance
wch was at first impos'd by men
130 their owne high merits to inhance
  & now pleads custome for pretence
  to banish knowledg witt & sence

Long have we here condemned been
to Folly & impertinence
135 but then it surely will be seene
There's in our Souls no difference
  when we no longer Fetterd are
  but like to them o[ur]^e selves appeare.

These great advantages are sure
140 a part of them we may propose
when we Eternall life insure
& doe this Momentarie lose
  Enough are these to let us know
  pitty on death we ill bestow.

321

145 Our Envy rather due does seeme
　　　but Oh! – who dares at fate repine
　　　or does not y^t ye fittest deeme
　　　wch God sees best him to assigne
　　　　nor life nor death my wish shal bee
150　　but humbly to submit to Thee.

From Locke MS c. 32, f.17, Bodleian Library, Oxford, dated 1682. Though no name is endorsed on the MS all sources ascribe the poem to Masham. It exists in a manuscript collection of poems from Locke's papers and is partly written in Locke's hand, partly in that of his amanuensis, Sylvester Brounower; preceding it is a poem beginning 'Who knows but w^t we call to live' and following one entitled 'Upon the former and present state of the Soule', transcribed also by Brounower and tentatively identified as Masham's (Crum, *First-Line Index*, II, 901; Long, 45). On f.19 is Lady Masham's poem, 'On Damons Loveing of Clora', in her own hand, printed in De Beer, 1976, II, 571-573 with Locke's poem in answer. De Beer suggests January 1683 as the date of this exchange (571). The wry tone of 'When deaths cold hand' is similar to that of Lady Masham's letters; she attempts to conciliate conflicting opinions about the relationship between the mind and body rather than resolve the issue, closing with resignation amid lingering tension. O'Donnell describes the poem as typical of Masham's writing before her marriage, disdaining domesticity and the material world, using the familiar tropes of Neoplatonic consolatory verse (O'Donnell, 1984, 36).
13-42 spoken in the person of 'ye rout / of Vulgar Souls', whose short-sighted view misrepresents death according to Lady Masham.
15 *scarce out of childhood*: in 1682 Damaris was twenty-three and unmarried.
18 *joyd*: enjoyed
26 *Enow*: enough
46 *empassion*: used here as a noun, unrecorded as such by the *OED*, probably used here for 'compassion'; but see Henry More's use of the verb (*OED* 'impassion').
48 According to the Platonists the information conveyed by the senses was inferior and misleading compared to the conclusions arrived at by reason.
50 *Robing not nature of her due*: i.e., not dying childless
80-84 See also John Norris, 'Damon and Pythias. Or, Friendship in Perfection', describing the friendship of souls in heaven:

> Pyth.　When I like you become all thought and mind
> 　　　　By what mark then shall we each other know?
> Da.　　With carer on your last hour I will attend,
> 　　　　And lest *like* Souls should me deceive
> 　　　　I closely will embrace my *new-born* friend,
> 　　　　And never after my dear *Pythias* leave. (Norris, 1687, 95)

DAMARIS, LADY MASHAM

97-120 Lady Masham's condemnation of bigotry and plea for tolerance are typical of the latitudinarian Christianity of the Cambridge Platonists among whom she spent the greater part of her life (De Beer, 1976, II, 493). In 1664 and 1670 the Acts of Conventicles were passed, preventing non-conformist gatherings; the Test Acts of 1673 and 1678 required denials under oath of the doctrine of transubstantiation from all holders of public office, thus excluding Catholics. At the time the poem was written, Shaftesbury and other prominent Whig dissenters were being threatened with prosecution for treason, and fled to Holland. After the accession of William and Mary (1688) the Act of Toleration granted Protestant dissenters the right to worship freely. John Locke's *Epistola de Tolerantia* (1689) argued for the disestablishment of religion.

104 *Socrates & Pythagores*: Socrates' philosophy as presented by Plato is central to Platonism; Cudworth speaks of 'an Admirable Correspondency betwixt the Platonick Philosophy and Christianity' (407). The pre-Socratic philosopher Pythagoras was considered by Cudworth 'to be representative of the ideal type of true philosophy' (Aspelin, 25), founder of a school in which 'they did Atomize, – but they did not Atheize' (Cudworth, 1678, 27).

105 *wth ye great Antonine*: Marcus Aelius Aurelius Antoninus, usually known as Marcus Aurelius, second-century Roman emperor and Stoic philosopher, author of the *Meditations*. Lady Masham wrote in a letter to Locke, 14 November 1685, that among the items 'Jumbled together' in her Closet were 'Receits and Account Books with Antoninus's his Meditations' (De Beer, 1976, II, 759).

136 See Introduction pp.28-30, p.211 and p.335, for accounts of the arguments for the sexlessness of souls.

MARY EVELYN

The burlesque poem *Mundus Muliebris* is attributed to Mary Evelyn on the grounds of the entry made by her father, John Evelyn, in his Diary when she died at the age of nineteen. He wrote that she could 'compose very happily, & put in her pretty Symbol, as in that of the *Mundus Muliebris*, wherein is an enumeration of the Modes & ornaments belonging to the Sex' (De Beer, 1955, IV, 423-424). The editors of the present volume are divided as to the meaning of the entry, which could signify that the poem is only hers in part; in this common seventeenth-century usage, 'symbol' means contribution, share, or portion (*OED*).

Born at her father's family home at Wotton in Surrey on 1 October 1665, Mary Evelyn was buried at Deptford in March 1685, having died of smallpox, according to her father, though her brother John blamed 'trash and sweetmeats which have chiefly been the cause of Mary's death. She eat those filthy things so constantly at my Lady Faulkland's that it was impossible to overcome the tough phlegm they had bred in her' (Hiscock, 137).

'My Lady Faulkland' was Rebecca (1662-1709), daughter of Sir Rowland Lytton, an heiress who married Evelyn's friend, Viscount Falkland, Treasurer of the Navy. Evelyn writes that 'My Lord Viscount Falklands Lady having ben our Neighbours... she tooke so greate an Affection to my Daughter, that when they went back in the Autumn [1684] to the Citty, nothing could pacifie their uncessant importunity, but the letting of my <daughter> accompany my Lady, & the staying some time with her' (De Beer, 1955, IV, 427). Lady Falkland was only three years older than Mary, who stayed with her until the following February.

According to her father in his 'little History, & Imperfect Character of my deare Child' (429), Mary was sought out for her charming conversation and sweet singing voice by 'severall persons of the first rank, especialy my Lord Treasurers Lady, my Lady Rochester, Sunderland, Burlington, Clarendon, Arlington, Dutchesse of Grafton; besides other Ladys & persons lovers of Musick'.

John Evelyn had many friends at Court and mentions that Mary spent a summer with the Court at Windsor with Lady Tuke, the widow of his cousin Sir Samuel Tuke (d. 1674), 'one of the dressers belonging to Queen Catherine' (*Athenae Oxon.* ii, 802). As a young girl Mary had already known the company of several of Queen Catherine's Maids of Honour, her father's friends Margaret Blagge (later Lady Godolphin) and Anne Howard, who came to Sayes Court to nurse her sister Elizabeth during an illness in 1673. Some

324

of Anne Howard's teasing verse to John Evelyn survives in a letter. She writes

> that Little Blagge as bright as day
> nor all the rest of the Court splendour
> Could make to playfellow your love less tender. (Hiscock, 87)

Mary's mother, Mary Browne, daughter of Sir Richard Browne, was a woman known for her probity and learning. Mrs Evelyn corresponded frequently with her son's tutor, the Rev. Ralph Bohun, about matters philosophical and literary. 'I find the slight cares of a family are great hindrances to the study of philosophy,' begins one such letter of Mrs Evelyn's (Bray, IX, 34). In another she wrote:

> Women were not born to read authors and censure the learned, to compare lives and judge of virtues, to give rules of morality, and sacrifice to the Muses. We are willing to acknowledge all time borrowed from family duties is misspent;... if sometimes it happens by accident that one of a thousand aspires a little higher, her fate commonly exposes her to wonder, but adds little of esteem. (Bray, IX, 31)

John Evelyn wrote that his daughter was 'curious of knowing every thing to some excesse' and had educated herself in his study reading 'aboundance of History, & all the best poets, even to Terence, Plautus, Homer, Vergil, Horace, Ovide, all the best Romances, & modern Poemes' (De Beer, 1955, IV, 423).

In her 'Miscellaneous Book of Meditations' found by John Evelyn after his daughter's death and now kept at Christ Church College Library, Oxford, she argues against delight in worldly things.

> when I have beene very talkativ & pert, I will for my punishment endeavor to be very silent & get some opportunitye to bee alone as much as I can & meditate on my Saviour... so y^t when I return to ye Company, if I have any Sence or Reason I shall not be apt to *Discourse with Men, or suffer them talk to me, much less delight to hear them upon a beastly or Censorious Lying & Prophane Subject*. And because I have been much addicted to Raillery, & Mimicking, I must reflect *upon my own defects*, without partiality & without reguard to ye Comendations I have receiv'd upon such occasions, for doing it Ingeniously, & all of it is but ye praise of vain Man, whose breath is uncertaine to me, & therefore I ought not Expose many Good deserving Persons for some unhappy Infirmitys that reach no further than ye outside, & which may befoe I Dye, either through Accident or Old Age, befall my own selfe... (Evelyn MSS 92, f.19)

From *Mundus Muliebris*

85   In Pin-up Ruffles now she flaunts,
     About her Sleeves are *Engageants*:
     Of Ribbon, various *Echelles*,
     Gloves trimm'd, and lac'd as fine as *Nell's*.
     Twelve dozen *Martial*, whole, and half,
90   Of *Jonquil, Tuberose*, don't laugh
     Frangipan, Orange, Violett,
     Narcissus, Jassemin, Ambrett:
     And some of *Chicken* skin for night,

To keep her Hands plump, soft, and white:
95 *Mouches* for pushes, to be sure,
From *Paris* the *tré-fine* procure,
And *Spanish* Paper, Lip, and Cheek,
With Spittle sweetly to belick:
Nor therefore spare in the next place,
100 The Pocket *Sprunking* Looking-Glass;
Calembuc Combs in *Pulvil* case,
To set, and trim the Hair and Face:
And that the Cheeks may both agree,
Plumpers to fill the Cavity.
105 The *Settée, Cupée* place aright,
Frelange, Fontange, Favorite;
Monté la haut, and *Palisade,*
Sorti, Flandan, (great helps to Trade)
Burgoigne, Jardiné, Cornett,
110 *Frilal* next upper Pinner set,
Round which it does our Ladies please
To spread the Hood call'd *Rayonnés:*
Behind the Noddle every Baggage
Wears bundle *Choux,* in *English* Cabbage.
115 Nor *Cruches* she, nor *Confidents,*
Nor *Passagers* nor *Bergers* wants;
And when this Grace Nature denies,
An Artificial *Tour* supplies;
All which with *Meurtriers* unite,
120 And *Creve-Coeurs* silly Fops to smite,
Or take in Toil at *Park* or *Play,*
Nor Holy *Church* is safe, they say,
Where decent Veil was wont to hide
The modest Sex Religious Pride;
125 Lest these yet prove too great a Load,
'Tis all compris'd in the *Commode;*
Pins tipt with Diamond Point, and head,
By which the Curls are fastened,
In radiant *Firmament* set out,
130 And over all the Hood *sur-tout:*
Thus Face that *Erst* near head was plac'd
Imagine now about the Wast,
For *Tour* on *Tour,* and *Tire* on *Tire,*
Like Steeple *Bow,* or *Grantham* Spire,
135 Or *Septizonium* once at *Rome,*

(But does not half so well become
Fair Ladies Head) you here behold
Beauty by Tyrant Mode controll'd.
The graceful *Oval*, and the *Round*,
140 This *Horse* Tire does quite confound;
And Ears like *Satyr*, Large and Raw,
And bony Face, and hollow Jaw;
This monstrous Dress does now reveal
Which well plac'd Curles did once conceal.
145 Besides all these, 'tis always meant
You furnish her Appartment,
With *Moreclack* Tapistry, Damask Bed,
Or Velvet richly embroidered:
Branches, *Brasero, Cassolets,*
150 A *Cofre-fort*, and Cabinets,
Vasas of Silver, *Porcelan*, store
To set, and range about the Floor:
The Chimney Furniture of Plate,
(For Iron's now quite out of date:)
155 *Tea*-Table, *Skreens*, Trunks, and Stand,
Large Looking-Glass richly *Japan'd*,
An hanging Shelf, to which belongs
Romances, Plays, and Amorous Songs;
Repeating Clocks, the hour to show
160 When to the Play 'tis time to go,
In Pompous Coach, or else Sedan'd
With Equipage along the *Strand*,
And with her new *Beau* Foppling mann'd.
A new Scene to us next presents,
165 The Dressing-Room, and Implements,
Of Toilet Plate Gilt, and Emboss'd,
And several other things of Cost:
The Table *Miroir*, one Glue Pot,
One for *Pomatum*, and what not?
170 Of *Washes, Unguents,* and *Cosmeticks,*
A pair of Silver Candlesticks;
Snuffers, and Snuff-dish, Boxes more,
For Powders, Patches, Waters store,
In silver Flasks, or Bottles, Cups
175 Cover'd, to open, to wash Chaps;
Nor may *Hungarian* Queen's be wanting,
Nor store of Spirits against fainting:

Of other waters rich, and sweet,
To sprinkle Handkerchief is meet;
180 *D'Ange, Orange, Mill-Fleur, Myrtle,*
Whole Quarts the Chamber to bequirtle:
Of Essence *rare, & le meilleure*
From *Rome,* from *Florence, Montpellier,*
In *Filgran Casset* to repel,
185 When Scent of *Gousset* does rebel,
Though powder'd *Allom* be as good
Well strew'd on, and well understood;...

Nor here omit the Bob of Gold
Which a *Pomander* Ball does hold,
This to her side she does attach
With Gold *Crochet,* or *French Pennache,*
215 More useful far then *Ferula,*
For any saucy Coxcombs Jaw:
A graceful Swing to this belongs,
Which he returns in Cringe, and Songs,
And languishings to kiss the hand,
220 That can Perfumed blows command...

240 Gold is her Toothpick, Gold her Watch is,
And Gold is every thing she touches
But tir'd with numbers I give o're,
Arithmetick can add no more,
Thus Rigg'd the Vessel, and Equipp'd,
245 She is for all Adventures Shipp'd,
And Portion e're the year goes round,
Does with her Vanity confound.

From *Mundus Muliebris: or, the Ladies Dressing-Room unlock'd, and her Toilette spread. In Burlesque. Together With the Fop-Dictionary, Compiled for the Use of the Fair Sex.* London: Printed for R. Bentley, 1690, 5-9, 11-12. A second issue and a second edition also appeared in 1690, and the second edition was issued again in 1700. The poem appeared anonymously five years after Mary Evelyn's death, prepared for publication by her father, according to Keynes (216), though John Evelyn records no information about its publication in the Diary. The Preface was presumably written at the time of publication by John Evelyn; J.L. Nevinson, in his 1977 edition of the poem for The Costume Society, finds John Evelyn's pen in the poem's mock-heroic frame, especially in the six-line translation from Plautus which precedes the poem, and in some of the more satirical verses.

Judging from her 'Miscellaneous Book of Meditations' and some lines of scribbled verse in her handwriting (Evelyn MSS 322), we find the entire poem and the 'Fop-Dictionary' well within the range of Mary's character and capabilities. Her desire to write a poem which indicts women's vanity may have been provoked by a personal experience she records:

I did Intend to pray for a poor Man (who was sick this Morning) (December ye 4th Monday 1682) and by that tyme My Body was Provided for with vain Clothing, his Wanted a shroud & a coffin to lay him in the Dust; so that doing that unnessecary part to my selfe, I have miss'd an opportunity of praying to God seasonably, & have Irrecoverably lost an occasion to do that poor Man Good;...This afflicts me very much. (Evelyn MSS 92, f.6)

The poem may have been known to Swift, and served as one of the sources for 'The Lady's Dressing-Room' (printed in 1732) but Evelyn does not share Swift's Juvenalian revulsion.

Notes given in bold are from the 'Fop-Dictionary', the glossary supplied with the printed editions of the poem.

85 *Ruffles*: **By our Fore-fathers call'd Cuffs.**

86 *Engageants*: **Deep double Ruffles, hanging down to the Wrists.**

87 *Echelles*: **A Pectoral or Stomacher lac'd with Ribbon, like the rounds of a Ladder.** A stomacher was 'an ornamental covering for the chest worn by women under the lacing of the bodice' (*OED*). 'Echelle' is French for ladder, but the *OED* records only this example of its use in English.

88 *Nell's*: Eleanor 'Nell' Gwyn (1650-1687), actress and mistress of Charles II.

89 *Martial*: **The Name of a famous *French* Perfumer, emulating the Frangipani of Rome.**

90 *Tuberose, don't laugh*: the essence of *Polyanthes tuberosa*; the name describes the root of the flower, a relatively new import from the East Indies, and means 'tuberous', i.e., like a potato. The first recorded uses of the name 'tuberose' in English are both in Evelyn's *Kalendarium Hortense* (1664); such a gardener's pun suggests either that he 'put in his symbol' here or that Mary Evelyn knew her father's writing.

95 *Mouches*: **Flies, or, Black Patches, by the Vulgar.** *pushes*: pimples

96 *tré-fine*: **Langage de beau. Extreamly fine, and delicate, *cum multis allis*.**

97 *Spanish Paper*: **A beautiful red Colour, which the Ladies, &c. in Spain paint their Faces withal.**

100 *Sprunking*: **A *Dutch* term for Pruning, Tiffing, Trimming, and setting out, by the Glass or Pocket *Miroir*.**

101 *Calembuc*: **A certain precious Wood, of an agreeable Scent, brought from the *Indies*.** Calambac, or the wood of *Aquilaria agallocha*, native of South East Asia.

Pulvil: **The *Portugal* term for the most exquisite Powders and**

Perfumes. The first recorded use of the term in the *OED* is 1690; clearly it is an anglicised form of the Italian *polviglio* meaning dusting powder.

104 *Plumpers*: **Certain very thin, round, and light Balls, to plump out, and fill up the Cavities of the Cheeks, much us'd by old Court-Countesses.** In the 1697 translation of the Countess d'Aunoy's *Travels*, 'two little Cork plumpers' fall out of a woman's mouth (*OED*).

105 *Settée*: **The double Pinner.** *Cupée*: **A kind of Pinner.** Pinner is the name given to the elaborate women's headdress of the period, which consisted of flaps of lace and ribbon hanging down on to the bosom and over the shoulders and back; cf. John Dunton's *Ladies Dictionary* (1694):

> Top Knot: you'd swear they were Conjuring, they sputter out such a confus'd Jargon of hard words.... Bring me my *Palisade* there, quoth Madam: You'd think she were going to encamp. Will it not be convenient to attack your *Flandan* first, says the Maid? More Anger yet? still Military Terms? Let me see; says Madam, where's my *Cornet*? Pray carine this *Favourite*: So, so, good words; now there's some hopes of Peace, till the blustering *Frilal* and *Burgoign* are called for, and then the old Catterwawling begins again? – There is a Clack of *Settees*, *Passes*, *Monte la hauts*, *Crotches*, and other Trinkums, would make a Man suspect they are raising the Devil...

106 *Frelange*: **Bonnet and Pinner together.** *Fontange*: **The Top-knot, so call'd from Mademoiselle de Fontange, one of the French King's Mistresses, who first wore it**, i.e. Marie-Angelique de Scorailles, created Duchesse de Fontange in April 1680, who became the mistress of Louis XIV in 1678 and died in July 1681 at the age of twenty. A story survives that the duchess lost her hat in the wind during a hunt and tied an impromptu hair knot which became the fashion (*Dictionnaire de Biographie Française*). This reference dates the poem to after April 1680. *Favorite*: **Locks dangling on the Temples.**

107 *Monté la haut*: **Certain degrees of Wire to raise the Dress.** *Palisade*: **A Wire sustaining the Hair next to the *Dutchess*, or first Knot.**

108 *Sorti*: **A little Knot of small Ribbon, peeping out between the Pinner and Bonnet.** *Flandan*: **A kind of Pinner joyning with the Bonnet.**

109 *Burgoigne*: **The first part of the Dress for the Head next the Hair.** *Jardiné*: **That single Pinner next the Bourgogne.** *Cornett*: **The upper Pinner, dangling about the Cheeks, like Hounds Ears**.

110 *Frilal*: 'a border of ornamental ribbon' (*OED*), derived from the context in this poem, the only usage of the word recorded.

112 *Rayonnés*: **Upper Hood, pinn'd in Circle, like the Sun-Beams**.

113 *Baggage*: a belittling term for a woman; in context the word could be used playfully, as here, or quite nastily.

114 *Choux*: **The great round Boss or Bundle, resembling a Cabbage, from whence the French so give it that name.**

115 *Cruches*: **Certain smaller Curles, placed on the Forehead.**

Confidents: **Smaller *Curles* near the Ears.**

116 *Passagers*: **A Curl'd Lock next the Temples.** *Bergers:* **A plain small Lock (a la Sheperdesse) turn'd up with a Puff.**

118 *Tour*: **An artificial Dress of Hair on the Forehead, &c.**

119 *Meurtriers*: **Murderers; a certain Knot in the Hair, which ties and unties the Curls.**

120 *Creve-Coeurs*: **Heart-breakers, the two small curl'd Locks at the Nape of the Neck.**

121 *take in Toil*: used figuratively as 'to entrap, entangle' (*OED*) from the lexicon of trapping game.

126 *Commode*: **A Frame of Wire, cover'd with Silk, on which the whole Head-Attire is adjusted at once upon a *Bust*, or property of Wood carved to the Breasts, like that which Perruque-makers set upon their Stalls.**

129 *Firmament*: **Diamonds, or other precious Stones heading the *Pins* which they stick in the *Tour*, and Hair, like Stars.**

130 *sur-tout*: **A Night-Hood covering the entire Dress.**

132 *Wast*: waist

133 *Tire*: attire, embellishment, in this case for the head

134 *Steeple Bow*: The steeple on St Mary-le-Bow in London completed by John Evelyn's good friend Sir Christopher Wren in 1680. *Grantham Spire*: According to Allen's *History of the County of Lincoln* (1834), the Grantham church had a 'quadrangular tower' of 135 feet on top of which were 'hexangular crocketted pinnacles' on each corner from which rose an 'octagonal spire' with three rows of encircling windows.

135 *Septizonium*: **A very high Tower in *Rome*, built by the Emperour *Severus*, of Seven Ranks of Pillars, set one upon the other, and diminishing to the Top, like the Ladies new Dress for their Heads, which was the mode among the *Roman* Dames, and is exactly describ'd by *Juvenal* in his 6th Satyr**; cf. Dunton: 'Do but regard her Rigging above Deck, and you'd swear she carries *Bow-Steeple* upon her Head, or the Famous Tower of *Severus* in *Rome*' (*Ladies Dictionary*, 425).

140 *Horse*: from nautical usage, a support structure, usually of ropes or beams on a ship.

141 *Ears like Satyr*: satyrs are often portrayed with large goat ears.

147 *Moreclack Tapistry*: a kind of tapestry woven in the Surrey town of Mortlake during the reigns of James I and Charles I (*OED*).

149 *Branches*: **Hanging Candlesticks, like those used in Churches.** *Brasero*: **A large Vessel, or moving-Hearth of Silver for Coals, transportable into any Room, much used in *Spain*.** *Cassolets*: Perfuming Pot or Censer.

150 *Cofre-fort*: **A strong Box of some precious or hard wood, &c. bound with gilded Ribs.**

151 *Vasas*: this form of the word is a peculiarity of John Evelyn's style: the *OED* cites four examples of his usage of the term between 1643 and 1700 and only one other.

156 *Japan'd*: **Any thing Varnish'd with *Laccar*, or *China* Polishing, or that is old or fantastical.**
168-175 Cf. Swift, 'The Lady's Dressing-Room', 33-36:

> Here Gallypots and Vials plac'd,
> Some fill'd with Washes, some with Paste,
> Some with Pomatum, Paints and Slops,
> And Ointments good for scabby Chops.

168 *Miroir*: **In general, any Looking Glass; but here, for the Table, Toilet, or Pocket *Sprunking*-Glass.**
169 *Pomatum*: pomade
170 *Cosmeticks:* **Here used for any Effeminate Ornament, also artificial Complections and Perfumes.**
175 *Chaps*: jaws or jowls
176 *Hungarian Queen's*: in his *Cyclopaedia* (1728), Chambers defines 'Hungary water' as 'a distilled water, denominated from a Queen of Hungary, for whose use it was first prepared;... made of rosemary flowers infused in rectified spirit of wine, and thus distilled' ('Hungary', *OED*).
182 *rare, & le meilleure*: **Best, and most Excellent,** in *Langage de beau* happily rhyming with *Montpellier*.
184 *Filgran*: **Dressing-Boxes, Baskets, or whatever else is made of Silver wire-work.** *Casset*: **A Dressing Box.**
185-186 *Scent of Gousset... Allom*: seventeenth-century tailoring involved the insertion of a gusset under the arms; the 'powder'd Allom' recommended instead of perfume is the mineral salt alum, or aluminum sulfate, in use since ancient times as an astringent and anti-sudorific; cf. Swift, 'The Lady's Dressing-Room', 27-28:

> Here Allum Flower to stop the Steams,
> Exhal'd from sour unsavoury Streams.

214 *Crochet*: **The Hook to which are chain'd the Ladies Watch, Seals, and other *Intaglias*, &c.** *Pennache:* **Any Bunch or Tassel of small Ribbon.**
215 *Ferula*: **An instrument of Wood us'd for Correction of lighter faults, more sensibly known to School-Boys than to Ladies.**

MARY ASTELL

Mary Astell (1666-1731) was the daughter of a Newcastle coal merchant, Peter Astell, and Mary Errington, of another prosperous Tyneside coal-mining family. Her uncle, Ralph Astell, who had studied under Lady Masham's father, Ralph Cudworth, instructed Mary in philosophy, logic and mathematics. In 1688 Astell went to London, where she found herself in financial difficulties, and was assisted by William Sancroft, Archbishop of Canterbury (Perry, 1986, 66). It was during this period that she compiled her manuscript collection of poems (Bod. Rawl. MS poet. 154:50), dedicated to Sancroft. By 1692 she had settled in Chelsea, where she began writing to John Norris of Bemerton, the last of the Cambridge Platonists, in response to his *Practical Discourses on Divine Subjects* (1691-1693). Their correspondence was published in 1695 as *Letters Concerning the Love of God*, dedicated to Astell's friend, Lady Catherine Jones.

In 1694 Astell published the work for which she is best known, *A Serious Proposal To the Ladies*, in which she suggested the establishment of women's 'seminaries' to provide education for upper-class women, and shelter for hunted heiresses and aging gentlewomen. George Ballard claimed that she was on the verge of receiving a massive donation of £10,000 from 'a certain great lady' (either Princess Anne or Astell's patron Lady Elizabeth Hastings), when Bishop Gilbert Burnet dissuaded the benefactor on the grounds that Astell's seminaries were too like Roman Catholic nunneries (Perry, 1985, 445-446). In spite of this defeat, *A Serious Proposal* was influential. Defoe used Astell's ideas in his *Essay on Projects* (1697); Steele incorporated over a hundred pages of it without acknowledgement in *The Ladies Library* (1714); Swift satirised Astell in *The Tatler*, Nos. 32 and 63, as 'Lady Platonne' and 'Madonella', a projector who proposes to educate young ladies in 'Antient and Modern Amazonian Tactics'.

The second part of *A Serious Proposal* (1697) was a distillation of Astell's readings in philosophy, intended to inspire women to exercise their minds in abstract reasoning. Although both parts were published anonymously, Astell's authorship was common knowledge. By the early eighteenth century, she was known and respected by many women intellectuals and writers; Elizabeth Thomas, Lady Chudleigh, Elizabeth Elstob and the young Lady Mary Wortley Montagu among them. *Some Reflections on Marriage* (1700) discussed the seriousness of marriage for women, who should be aware of the obedience required of a wife. (Astell chose never to marry.) Her preface to the 1706 edition describes a time when 'a Tyrannous Domination which Nature never meant, shall no longer render useless, if not hurtful, the Industry and Understandings of half Mankind' (Sig. [b3ᵛ]).

Although a reformer in her proposals for women's education, Astell was essentially conservative, supporting the Anglican church and the Tory party in opposition to Whiggish religious and political tolerance. After a spate of Anglican/Tory publications (1704-1709) Astell published no new work. With the help of her friends, she established a girls' charity school in Chelsea in 1729. She died two years later, after an operation for a breast tumour.

Mar 30. 1684   Ambition

I

What's this that with such vigour fills my brest?
    Like the first mover finds no rest,
    And with it's force dos all things draw,
Makes all submit to its imperial Law!
5 Sure 'tis a spark 'bove what Prometheus stole,
    Kindled by a heav'nly coal,
    Their sophistry I can controul,
Who falsely say that women have no Soul.

II

Vile Greatness! I disdain to bow to thee,
10   Thou art below ev'n lowly me,
    I wou'd no Fame, no Titles have,
And no more Land than what will make a grave.
I scorn to weep for Worlds, may I but reign
    And Empire o're my self obtain,
15   In Caesars throne I'de not sit down,
Nor wou'd I stoop for Alexanders Crown.

III

Let me obscured be, & never known.
    Or pointed at about the Town,
    Short winded Fame shall not transmit
20 My name, that the next Age may censure it:
If I write Sense no matter what they say,
    Whither they call it dull, or pay
    A rev'rence such as Virgil claims,
Their breath's infectious, I have higher aims.

IV

25 Mean spirited men! that bait at Honour, Praise,
    A Wreath of Laurel or of Baies,

334

MARY ASTELL

> How short's their Immortality!
> But Oh a Crown of Glory ne're will die!
> This I'me Ambitious of, no pains will spare
30   To have a higher Mansion there,
>   There all are Kings, here let me be,
> Great O my God, Great in Humilitie.

From 'A Collection of Poems humbly presented and Dedicated To the most Reverend Father in God William By Divine Providence Lord Archbishop of Canterbury &c 1689', Bod. MS Rawl poet. 154:50, ff.54^v-55.

Title *Mar 30. 1684*: Astell was eighteen when she composed this poem.

2 *the first mover*: the *primum mobile*, in medieval astronomy, the force that sets the planets in motion.

7-8 Cf. *A Serious Proposal* I:

Let such therefore as deny us the improvement of our Intellectuals, either take up *his* Paradox, who said that *Women have no Souls*, which at a time when the most contend to have them allow'd to Brutes, wou'd be as unphilosophical as it is unmannerly, or else let them permit us to cultivate and improve them. (67)

Cf. 'Philo-philippa', 25-28 (see p.205), and Sarah Fyge, *The Female Advocate* (1687), 192-203.

25-28 Cf. *A Serious Proposal* I:

Here will be no Rivalling but for the Love of God, no Ambition but to procure his Favour, to which nothing will more effectually recommend you, than a great and dear affection to each other... No Covetousness will gain admittance in this blest abode, but to amass huge Treasures of Good Works, and to procure one of the brightest Crowns of Glory. (55)

Astell's fourth stanza repeats the sentiments of the fourth stanza of Katherine Philips's ode, 'Upon Mr. Abraham Cowley's Retirement':

> No other wealth will I aspire,
>   But that of Nature to admire;
> Nor envy on a laurel will bestow,
> Whilst I have any in my garden grow.
>   And when I would be great,
>   'Tis but ascending to a seat
> Which Nature in a lofty rock hath built;
> A throne as free from trouble as from guilt. (47-54)

29-32 In *A Serious Proposal* I, Astell exhorts women to aspire to intellectual and spiritual heights, invoking the name of the much-admired 'Orinda' and envisioning the reward of 'higher Mansions':

Remember, I pray you, the famous Women of former Ages, the *Orinda*'s of late, and the more Modern Heroins, and blush to think how much is now, and will hereafter be said of them, when you your selves (as great a Figure as you make) must be buried in silence and forgetfulness! Shall your Emulation fail *there only* where 'tis commendable? Why are you so preposterously humble, as not to contend for one of the highest Mansions in the Court of Heav'n? (9-10)

In the poem and the proposal Astell refers to John 14:2, 'In my father's house are many mansions', 'mansions' meaning separate apartments.

Jan 7. 1687/8 In emulation of Mr Cowleys Poem
call'd the Motto

I

What shall I do? not to be Rich or Great,
   Not to be courted and admir'd,
   With Beauty blest, or Wit inspir'd,
Alas! these merit not my care and sweat,
5   These cannot my Ambition please,
My high born Soul shall never stoop to these;
But something I would be thats truly great
In'ts self, and not by vulgar estimate.

II

If this low World were always to remain,
10   If th' old Philosophers were in the right,
   Who wou'd not then, with all their might
Study and strive to get themselves a name?
   Who wou'd in soft repose lie down,
Or value ease like being ever known?
15 But since Fames trumpet has so short a breath,
Shall we be fond of that wch must submit to Death?

III

Nature permits not me the common way,
   By serving Court, or State, to gain
   That so much valu'd trifle, Fame;
20 Nor do I covet in Wits Realm to sway:
   But O ye bright illustrious few,
What shall I do to be like some of you?
Whom this misjudging World dos underprize,
Yet are most dear in Heav'ns all-righteous eyes!

IV

25 How shall I be a Peter or a Paul?
   That to the Turk and Infidel,
   I might the joyfull tydings tell,
And spare no labour to convert them all:
   But ah my Sex denies me this,
30 And Marys Priviledge I cannot wish;
Yet hark I hear my dearest Saviour say,
They are more blessed who his Word obey.

336

V

Up then my sluggard Soul, Labour and Pray,
    For if with Love enflam'd thou be,
35   Thy Jesus will be born in thee,
And by thy ardent Prayers thou can'st make way,
    For their Conversion whom thou may'st not teach,
Yet by a good Example always Preach:
And tho I want a Persecuting Fire,
40   I'le be at lest a Martyr in desire.

From Bod. MS Rawl. poet 154:50, ff.52^v-53.
Title: 'The Motto' was first published in Cowley's *Poems* (1656), with
the following title: 'Tentanda via est qua me quoque possim /
Tollere humo, victorque virum volitare per ora.' [I must attempt the
path whereby I may aspire to leave the earth, And soar a victor in
the mouths of men]. Virgil's *Georgics*, III, 8.
1-8 Astell's emulation of Cowley paraphrases his lines:

> What shall I do to be for ever known,
>   And make the *Age to come* my owne?
> I shall like *Beasts* or *Common People* dy,
>   Unlesse you write my *Elegy*;
> Whilst others *Great*, by being *Born* are grown,
>   Their *Mothers Labour*, not their own.
> In this Scale *Gold*, in th' other *Fame* does ly,
>   The *weight* of *that*, mounts this so *high*.
> These men are *Fortunes Jewels*, moulded bright;
>   Brought forth with their own fire and light.
> If I, her *vulgar stone* for either look;
>   Out of *my self* it must be strook. (1-12)

and goes one step further, rejecting even 'Wit'. In Cowley Astell
recognised a kindred spirit, a self-described 'vulgar stone' of
Fortune, delineating the obstacles of his position in the world.
15-16 Cf. Cowley:

> Yet I must on; what sound is't strikes mine ear?
>   Sure I *Fames Trumpet* hear.
> It sounds like the *last Trumpet*; for it can
>   Raise up the *buried Man*. (13-16)

17-32 While Cowley rejects the temptations of 'flattering Vanities',
'desire of Honour or Estate', and 'Love himselfe' in order to strive
for immortality through his poetry, Astell spurns 'Wit's Realm' in
favour of religious devotion and posits the Apostles as her models,
over Cowley's Aristotle, Cicero and Virgil.
25-28 In *A Serious Proposal* I, Astell suggests that the women in her
seminaries become active proselytisers:

such an Institution will much confirm us in Virtue and help us to persevere to the end,
and by that substantial Piety and solid Knowledge we shall here acquire, fit us to
propagate Religion when we return into the World... And then what a blessed World
shou'd we have, shining with so many stars of *Vertue*, who... would... diffuse their

benign Influences where-ever they come. Having gain'd an entrance into Paradise themselves, they wou'd both shew the way, and invite others to partake of their felicity. (115-118)

29-32 Cf. the preface to the third edition of *Some Reflections Upon Marriage* (1706):

For, as in the *Old*, so in the *New Testament*, Women make a considerable Figure;... And if it is a greater Blessing *to hear the Word of God and keep it*, who are more considerable for their Assiduity in this, than the Female Disciples of our Lord? *Mary* being Exemplary, and receiving a noble Encomium from Him, for her Choice of the better Part. (Sig. b^v)

In this passage and in 'Marys Priviledge' (l.30) Astell refers to Mary, the sister of Martha, who chooses 'the better part', to sit at the feet of Jesus and listen to his word, Luke 10:42. Astell quotes from Luke 11:27-28 in both the poem and the preface:

And it came to pass, as he spake these things, a certain woman of the company lifted up her voice, and said unto him, Blessed is the womb that bare thee, and the paps which thou hast sucked. But he said, Yea rather, blessed are they that hear the word of God, and keep it.

Cf. Speght, 'The Dreame', 137-138 (see p.71).

I

Awake my Lute, daughters of Musick come,
　　To Allalujah's tune my tongue,
My heart already hath the Canticle begun:
And leaps for Joy, because it's business is
5　　In a better world than this.
Blessed be God and evermore extoll'd,
Who wou'd not let me fetter'd be with Gold:
Nor to a dang'rous World expose weak me,
　　By giving oppertunitie
10　For ev'ry sin, which wanton appetite
　　Too easily can entertain,
　　Nor needs temptations to invite;
　　Did we but know the secret bane,
The perdue poyson, hidden aconite,
15　　Which Riches do infold,
Not all its charms, nor all its shining would
　　Persuade us to the Love of Gold.
Happy am I who out of danger sit,
Can see and pitty them who wade thro it;
20　Need take no thought my treasure to dispose,
What I ne're had I cannot fear to lose:
Nor am concern'd what I must wear or buy,
To shew my plenty and my vanity.

II

From my secure and humble seat,
25 I view the ruins of the Great.
And dare look back on my expired days,
To my low state there needs no shameful ways.
 O how uneasy shou'd I be,
 If tie'd to Custom and formalitie,
30 Those necessary evils of the Great,
Which bind their hands, and manacle their feet.
Nor Beauty, Parts, nor Portion me expose
My most beloved Liberty to lose.
And thanks to Heav'n my time is all my own,
35 I when I please can be alone;
Nor Company, nor Courtship steal away
 That treasure they can ne're repay.
 No Flatterers, no Sycophants,
  My dwelling haunts,
40 Nor am I troubl'd with impertinents.
Nor busy days, nor sleepless nights infest
My Quiet mind, nor interrupt my rest.
My Honour stand's not 'on such a ticklish term
That ev'ry puff of air can do it harm.
45 But these are blessings I had never known,
Had I been great, or seated near a Throne.
My God, forever blessed be thy Name!
That I'me no darling in the list of Fame;
While the large spreading Cedars of the wood,
50 Are by their eminence expos'd to storms,
I who beneath their observation stood,
 Am undisturb'd with such alarms.
None will at me their sharp detractions throw,
Or strive to make me less who am already low.

III

55 I thank thee Lord that I am Friendless too,
  Tho that alas be hard to do!
  Tho I have wearied Heav'n with Prayers,
  And fill'd it's bottles with my tears.
 Tho I always propos'd the noblest end,
60 Thy glory in a Friend.
And never any earthly thing requir'd,
  But this thats better part divine,
And for that reason was so much desir'd;

Yet humbly I submit,
65   To that most perfect will of thine,
And thank thee cause thou hast denied me it.
   Thrice blessed be thy Jealousie,
     Which would not part
   With one smal corner of my heart,
70   But has engross'd it all to Thee!
Thou woul'dst not let me ease my burthens here,
     Which none on Earth cou'd bear,
   Nor in anothers troubles share:
   O sweet exchange thy Joys are mine,
75   And thou hast made my sorrows thine.
   Now absence will not break my heart,
   Jesus and I can never part,
   By night, or day, by Land or sea,
His right hand shades, his left hand under me
80   Nor shall I need to shed a tear,
Because my Friend is dead or I must leave her here.

IV

If I can thank for this, what cannot I
Receive with chearful mind, and perfect joy?
No want so sharply doth affect the heart,
85 No loss nor sickness causeth such a smart,
No racks nor tortures so severely rend,
As the unkindness of a darling Friend.
Yet ev'n this bitter pil had done me good,
Without it I had hardly understood,
90   The baseness which attends
   On ev'ry sin, because it is
Ingratitude and black perfidiousness,
   To thee my God the best of Friends.
   Thus by th' assistance of thy grace,
95 Joyn'd with a lively Faith, and honest mind,
In most untastefull things I pleasure find,
And beauty in the darkest sorrows face.
   The eater brings forth meat, the strong affords
Like Sampson's Lion, sweetness to thy Servants
                                 boards.
100 Who has the true Elixir, may impart
Pleasure to all he touches, and convert
The most unlikely greif to Happiness.
   Vertue this true Elixir is,

'Tis only Vertue this can do,
105 And with this choicest Priviledge invest,
Can make us truly happy now,
And afterwards for ever blest.

From Bod. MS Rawl. poet. 154:50, ff.91-93.

1-5 Astell follows the teaching of Ephesians 15:19-20:

Speaking to yourselves in psalms and hymns and spiritual songs, singing and making melody in your heart to the lord; Giving thanks always for all things unto God and the Father in the name of Our Lord Jesus Christ.

14 *perdue*: French for lost, here meaning 'hidden away' (the first use cited by the *OED* is dated 1734); *aconite*: a poisonous extract made from the plant commonly known as Wolf's-bane or Monk's-hood.

24-25 Katherine Philips, in 'A Country Life', also found herself 'secure' in her humble position:

When all the stormy World doth roar
How unconcerned am I!
I cannot fear to tumble lower
Who neer could be high.
Secure in these unenvied walls
I think not on the State,
And pity no man's case that falls
From his Ambition's height. (41-48)

25 *ruins of the Great*: cf. Cowley's 'Of Obscurity':

Upon the slippery tops of humane State,
The guilded Pinnacles of Fate,
Let others proudly stand, and for a while
The giddy danger to beguile,
With Joy, and with disdain look down on all,
Till their Heads turn, and down they fall.
Me, O ye Gods, on Earth, or else so near
That I no fall to earth may fear,
And, O ye gods, at a good distance seat
From the long Ruines of the Great. (1-10)

55-87 In *A Serious Proposal* I, Astell describes her ideal of friendship as practised in her proposed institution:

we shall have opportunity of contracting the purest and noblest Friendship; a Blessing, the purchase of which were richly worth all the World besides! For she who possesses a worthy Person, has certainly obtain'd the richest Treasure... Probably one considerable cause of the degeneracy of the present Age, is the little true Friendship that is to be found in it... yet the Danger is great lest being deceiv'd in our choice, we suck in Poyson where we expected Health. And considering how apt we are to disguise our selves, how hard it is to know our own hearts much less anothers, it is not advisable to be too hasty in contracting so important a Relation; (81-82; 84-85)

Katherine Philips's 'Injuria Amicitiae' also expresses the pain of disappointment by an unkind 'darling Friend':

While glorious Friendship, whence your Honour springs,
Lies gasping in the Crowd of common things;
And I'm so odious, that for being kind
Doubled and studied Murthers are design'd. (25-28)

98-99 Judges 14:14

LADY GRISELL BAILLIE

Grisell Baillie was born on Christmas Day 1665, at Redbraes Castle in Berwickshire, the daughter of Sir Patrick Hume of Polwarth and Grisell Ker. Her father was a devout Presbyterian who was forced to flee Scotland for Utrecht when he came under suspicion of participating in the Ryehouse Plot to kill King Charles. The oldest girl in a family of eighteen children, Grisell heroically took on the responsibility of caring for her family in exile, managing the household and once making a secret voyage home to obtain desperately needed funds and rescue her sister Julian, who had been too ill to travel when the family left.

In 1688 she and her mother travelled back to Scotland with the Princess of Orange who invited Grisell to become a Maid of Honour. She refused, having fallen in love with George Baillie, the son of one of her father's martyred friends, and on 17 September 1692 she married him. She died on 6 December 1746, eight years after her husband, and was buried beside him at Mellerstain, near Polwarth.

Grisell Baillie was a meticulous keeper of records, and the Day Books which she began upon her marriage show her to have been an astute businesswoman as well as a hoarder of recipes, menus and travel itineraries. Lady Grisell Murray, one of her two daughters, in 1749 wrote a private account of Grisell Baillie's life in which mention is made of a 'book of songs of her writing when [in Utrecht]; many of them interrupted, half writ, some broke off in the middle of a sentence' (Murray, 49-50). Joanna Baillie's story of Grisell Baillie in *Metrical Legends* (1821) led to the publication of Lady Murray's *Memoirs* in 1822, but the manuscript poems by that time had disappeared. 'Were ne my Hearts light I wad Dye' and a shorter poem, 'Absence', first printed in 1839 in a broadsheet with music by Charles Sharpe, 'the words by Lady Grizell Baillie' (rpt. with two additional verses by Lady John Scot in Margaret Warrender, *Marchmont and the Humes of Polwarth*, 1894) have, however, been traditionally attributed to Grisell Baillie.

'Were ne my Hearts light' is equal to anything thrown up by the Scottish ballad revival, and, according to Robert Chambers (310) was the first important example of an 'aristocratic' poet being 'sensible to the beauty of national melodies'. If ever Grisell Baillie's song book were to be found, a reassessment of the history and the nature of the tradition might well have to follow.

LADY GRISELL BAILLIE

Were ne my Hearts light I wad Dye
1
There was an a May and she lo'ed na men,
She Bigged her bonny Bow'r down in yon Glen,
But now she cryes dale and a-well-a-day,
Come down the Green gate and come here away.
2
5   When bonny young *Johnny* came o'er ye sea,
He said he saw nathing so bonny as me,
He haight me baith Rings and mony bra things,
And were ne my Hearts light I wad dye.
3
He had a wee Titty that lo'ed na me,
10   Because I was twice as bonny as she,
She rais'd sick a Pother twixt him & his mother,
That were ne my Hearts light I wad dye.
4
The day it was set and the Bridal to be,
The wife took a Dwalm and lay down to dye,
15   She main'd and she grain'd out of Dollor & Pain,
Till he vow'd that he ne'er wou'd see me again.
5
His Kin was for ane of a higher degree,
Said what had he do with the likes of me,
Appose I was bonny I was ne for *Johnny*,
20   And were my Hearts light I wad dye.
6
They said I had neither Cow nor Calf,
Nor drops of drink runs thro' the drawf,
Nor Pickles of Meal runs thro' the mill Eye,
And were my Hearts light I wad Dye.
7
25   The maiden she was baith wylly and slye,
She spyed me as I came o'er the Lee,
And then she ran in and made sick a din,
Beleive your ain Een and ye trow ne me.
8
His bonnet stood ay fu' round on his Brow,
30   His auld ane lookt ay as well as his new,
But now he lets't gang ony gate it will hing,
And casts himsell down on the Corn bing.

9

And now he gaes drooping about the Dykes,
And a' he dow do is to hund the Tykes,
35   The live lang night he ne'er bows his Eye,
And were my Hearts light I wad dye.

10

But young for thee as I ha' been,
We shou'd ha' been galloping down in yon Green,
And linking out o'er yon lilly white Lee,
40   And wow gin I were young for thee.

From *Orpheus Caledonius or a Collection of the best Scotch Songs set to Music by W. Thomson* (1726). This is the earliest printed version; Grisell Baillie, her brother and her two daughters were subscribers to the volume. The song was printed again, without revision, with its music in the 1733 edition of *Orpheus Caledonius* and again in *Dale's Collection of Sixty Favourite Scotch Songs Adapted for the Voice and Piano-forte or Harpsichord:... Taken from the Original Manuscripts of the most Celebrated Scotch Authors & Composers* (London, 1795). Allan Ramsay published the song in several editions of *The Tea-Table Miscellany* (1723-1727). None of the early editors attributed the poem to Grisell Baillie. Over the years a number of significant variants crept into the text, indicating perhaps that the song was being popularly sung and collected anew, as well as printed.

19 Appose / Albeit Ramsay, 1788   22 drops / dribbles Ramsay, 1788
35 bows / steeks Ramsay, 1788   37 But young / Were I young Ramsay, 1788

1 *May*: maid
2 *Bigged*: built
3-4 the third and fourth lines of every stanza are to be repeated as the refrain.
4 *gate*: way, path
7 *haight*: promised; *bra*: splendid, showy
9 *Titty*: sister
11 *sick*: such; *Pother*: tumult, uproar
14 *Dwalm*: fainting fit
22 *drawf*: draff, the refuse or grains of malt after brewing or distilling
23 *Pickles of Meal*: small amounts of the edible parts of the grain; *mill Eye*: opening in the mill machinery through which the meal escapes
28 *trow*: believe
31 *hing*: hang; *Corn bing*: corn bin
34 *hund the Tykes*: set the dogs on a chase
39 *linking*: running arm in arm
40 *wow gin*: a Scottish exclamation of sorrow

SARAH FYGE

Sarah Fyge was born in London in 1670 to Mary Beacham of Seaton, Rutland and Thomas Fyge, physician and city councilman (Woodhead, 74). When 'scarce fourteen years' old she undertook to answer Robert Gould's misogynist satire, *Love Given O're or, a Satyr against the Pride, Lust and Inconstancy, &c. of Woman* (1682), 'and in less time than fourteen days 'twas done'. Although she claims that it was written 'without design of Publication', *The Female Advocate* was published anonymously in 1686 with a preface signed 'S. F'. It appeared amidst a series of responses and counter-responses by Gould himself and fellow satirist, Richard Ames, sometimes posing as women. A second expanded edition of *The Female Advocate* (1687) was revised according to 'the Censures of the World', as Fyge says in her address to the reader, again signed simply 'S. F.' At about this time Fyge was sent by her disapproving father to live with relatives in Shenley in Buckinghamshire. She was soon married to Edward Field, an attorney, unwillingly, by her own account (Medoff, 1982, 155 ff.).

Field died by the mid-1690s, leaving Sarah childless and well-to-do. Although she was infatuated with her deceased husband's 'once dearest Friend', an attorney's clerk, Henry Pierce (called 'Alexis' in her poems). Fyge then married a much older second cousin, the Reverend Thomas Egerton, of Adstock, Buckinghamshire. Despite her marriage, Sarah continued to pursue her beloved 'Alexis' in fact and in verse, telling the story of her misfortunes in *Poems on Several Occasions* ([1703]; reissued in 1706). In *A Letter from the Dead Thomas Brown, to the Living Heraclitus* (1704), 'Madam F-l-d' is described as having been 'forc'd to part with her Foot-boy, on Account of the great Expence she had put her self to in Publishing a Book of Poems that was like to stick upon her Hands, without the Custom of the Tobacconists, Cooks, and Grocers' (10). In the same year the poems were published Fyge sued Egerton for divorce on the grounds of cruelty and Egerton sued Sarah and her father in Chancery for the estate left to her by Field. In his defence, Egerton claimed that she had taken some of his money, run off to London with Pierce, a married man, and told Egerton he was a 'Rascal, knave, villain and pittifull Priest', who was laughed at for being a cuckold (Lambeth Palace Library, Court of Arches Records, Volume Ee8, f.242ᵛ; Ferguson, 153). The sordid details of their marital conflicts were recorded by her friend, Delariviere Manley in *The New Atalantis* (1709), in which Fyge is shown throwing a hot apple pie in her husband's face (I, 161).

Apparently the divorce suit was unsuccessful, the Egertons remaining married until his death in 1720.

Fyge's ode on Dryden's death appeared in *Luctus Britannici: or the Tears of the British Muses* (1700) and she contributed three poems to Manley's *The Nine Muses, or, Poems on the Death of the Late Famous John Dryden, Esq.* (1700). She was known as 'Mrs. Field' or 'Clarinda' to a number of literary women, including Manley, Mary Pix, Susannah Centlivre, and Elizabeth Thomas. In John Froud's *The Grove: or, the Rival Muses* (1701) to which she contributed some lines, Fyge is praised for her 'soft rural Lays': 'Not *Behn* herself with all her softest Art / So well could talk of Love, or touch the Heart' (12). The last known composition by Sarah Fyge is the unpublished poem, 'The Essay, address'd to the Illustrious prince and Duke of Marlbrow after the long Campaigne', written in 1708 (HL MS EL 8796). She died on 13 February 1723, leaving some silver plate to the parish church of Winslow, where she is buried with her ancestors, and bequeathing £1 per year to the poor, though this money was lost through the abuse of her executor, Thomas Alderige, a mercer. Her monument inscription depicts Fyge as a victim of Fate, an image she often elaborated in her poetry:

> in vain I strive to be with quiet blest;
> Various sorrows wreck't my destin'd brest,
> And I could only in the grave find rest. (Clear, 65)

The Liberty.

Shall I be one, of those obsequious Fools,
That square there lives, by Customs scanty Rules;
Condemn'd for ever, to the puny Curse,
Of Precepts taught, at Boarding-school, or Nurse,
5   That all the business of my Life must be,
Foolish, dull Trifling, Formality.
Confin'd to a strict Magick complaisance,
And round a Circle, of nice visits Dance,
Nor for my Life beyond the Chalk advance:
10 The Devil Censure, stands to guard the same,
One step awry, he tears my ventrous Fame.
So when my Friends, in a facetious Vein,
With Mirth and Wit, a while can entertain;
Tho' ne'er so pleasant, yet I must not stay,
15 If a commanding Clock, bids me away:
But with a sudden start, as in a Fright,
I must be gone indeed, 'tis after Eight.
Sure these restraints, with such regret we bear,
That dreaded Censure, can't be more severe,

20   Which has no Terror, if we did not fear;
     But let the Bug-bear, timerous Infants fright,
     I'll not be scar'd, from Innocent delight:
     Whatever is not vicious, I dare do,
     I'll never to the Idol Custom bow,
25   Unless it suits with my own Humour too.
     Some boast their Fetters, of Formality,
     Fancy they ornamental Bracelets be,
     I'm sure their Gyves, and Manacles to me.
     To their dull fulsome Rules, I'd not be ty'd,
30   For all the Flattery that exalts their Pride:
     My Sex forbids, I should my Silence break,
     I lose my Jest, cause Women must not speak.
     Mysteries must not be, with my search Prophan'd,
     My Closet not with Books, but Sweat-meats cram'd
35   A little *China*, to advance the show,
     My *Prayer Book*, and seven *Champions*, or so.
     My pen if ever us'd imploy'd must be,
     In lofty Themes of useful Houswifery,
     Transcribing old Receipts of Cookery:
40   And what is necessary 'mongst the rest,
     Good Cures for Agues, and a cancer'd Breast,
     But I can't here, write my *Probatum est.*
     My daring Pen, will bolder Sallies make,
     And like myself, an uncheck'd freedom take;
45   Not chain'd to the nice Order of my Sex,
     And with restraints my wishing Soul perplex:
     I'll blush at Sin, and not what some call Shame,
     Secure my Virtue, slight precarious Fame.
     This Courage speaks me, Brave, 'tis surely worse,
50   To keep those Rules, which privately we Curse:
     And I'll appeal, to all the formal Saints,
     With what reluctance they indure restraints.

From *Poems On Several Occasions, Together with a Pastoral. By Mrs. S.F.*
London: Printed, and are to be sold by J. Nutt, near Stationers-Hall.
[1703], 19-21.
1-9 The references are to conjuring and to the necromantic practice
of confining the subject within a chalk circle drawn on the floor so as
to show apparitions outside it. Sarah Fyge may have learned about
occult matters from the works of her father's friend and neighbour,
John Heydon, an astrologer and attorney, who wrote on
Rosicrucianism and the Cabala (*DNB*). His *Advice to a Daughter*

(1658), a 'defence' of women written in order to attack Francis Osborne's *Advice to a Son* (1656), may have influenced Fyge's *The Female Advocate* (1686), her own rejoinder to a misogynist work. Mary Astell uses Custom's chalk circle in a different context in *A Serious Proposal to the Ladies*, I:

> For shame let's abandon that *Old*, and therefore one wou'd think, unfashionable employment of pursuing Butter-flies and Trifles! No longer drudge on in the dull beaten road of Vanity and Folly which so many have gone before us, but dare to break the enchanted Circle that custom has plac'd us in, and scorn the Vulgar way of imitating all the Impertinencies of our Neighbours. (12)

11 *ventrous*: adventurous
21 *Bug-bear*: an imaginary being invoked by nurses to frighten children; bogeyman
28 *Gyves*: shackles or fetters
29 *fulsome*: disgustingly over-elaborated
32 *lose my Jest*: may not make my joke
34 *Closet*: a small room of one's own – not a cupboard
36 *seven Champions*: a old romance, *The Seven Champions of Christendom* (c.1597), typical of the kind of harmless reading in which semi-educated women might indulge without compromising morals or decorum.
41 *Cures for... a cancer'd Breast*: poultices for breast tumours
42 *Probatum est*: a phrase used in prescriptions to mean that the remedy has been tried and proven.
51-52 Fyge challenges 'the formal Saints', i.e. those who remain 'chain'd to the nice Order of my Sex', to admit their own reluctant compliance. These final lines echo the concluding couplet of Orinda's 'To the truly competent Judge of Honour, Lucasia, upon a scandalous Libel made by J.J.': 'Yet I'll appeal unto the knowing few / Who dare be just, and rip my heart to you.'

On my leaving London, June the 29.

What cross impetuous Planets govern me,
That I'm thus hurry'd on to Misery;
I thought I had been bles'd, a while ago,
But one quick push, plung'd me all o'er in Woe.
5   My cruel Fate, doth act the Tyrant's part,
And doth Torment me, with a lingering smart;
To make me sensible of greater Pain,
Lets me take Breath, then screws the Rack again:
Ah! where's the Joy, of such precarious Bliss,
10 That for one smiling short Parenthesis;
I must such tedious horrid Pangs indure,
And neither State, will either kill or cure.
With all Submission, I my Fate implore,

SARAH FYGE

Destroy me quite, or else Torment no more;
15 At least let not one glimps of Joy appear,
It only makes my Sufferings more severe.
No, here I'll Rule, not sue to you for this,
You cannot tantalize me now with Bliss;
For when you took, my Father's love away,
20 Perverse as you, I'd not let others stay:
I was not so insensibly undone,
To hoord up Counters, when my Gold was gone.
Plunder'd of all, I now forsake the Place,
Where all my Joys, and all my Treasure was,
25 Ah do not now, my wandering Footsteeps Trace;
I left the Town, and all Divertisement,
And in a lonely Village am content.
Nor do I ask to be remov'd from hence,
Tho' Man and Beast, are both of equal Sense:
30 I had not fled, but strongly forc'd by you,
In hast bid Mother, Sisters sad adieu.
I saw them last of all I knew in Town,
Yet all alike to me are Strangers grown;
I almost have forgot I e'er was there,
35 And the sad Accidents that brought me here.
Ah Fate! pursue me not in this Retreat,
Let me be quiet in this humble Seat:
Let not my Friends know where to send to me,
Lest I grow pleas'd with their Civility.
40 I'd fain live unconcern'd, not pleas'd nor cross'd,
And be to all the busy World as lost.

From *Poems on Several Occasions*... [1703], 23-24.
2 *Misery*: in 'To the Lady Cambell, with a Female Advocate', also
published in *Poems on Several Occasions*, Fyge enlarges on the
difficulties brought on by the publication of *The Female Advocate*:

> But ah! my Poetry, did fatal prove,
> And robb'd me of a tender Father's Love;
> (I thought that only Men, who writ for Fame,
> Or sung lewd Stories, of unlawful Flame,
> Were punish'd for, their proud or wanton Crime.
> But Children too, must suffer if they'll Rhyme:)
> The Present is but mean, which you receive,
> Yet cost me more, than all the World can give,
> That which I would, with Life itself retrieve.(14-22)

10 *Parenthesis*: an interval, interlude, or hiatus
17 *sue*: to petition to be allowed, to seek to do or to be something

19 *my father's love*: Thomas Fyge (or Fydge or Fagge or Frye) was the son of Valentine Fage, an apothecary, prominent Presbyterian, and, as city councilman, one of Pepys's major sources of information on London politics (Latham and Matthews, I, 9ff.). Thomas Fyge was a member of the Common Council for Bishopsgate Without in the 1680s, Master of the Society of Apothecaries in 1690, and a deputy alderman from 1699 to 1705. Following his death in 1705, his personal estate was assessed at £9,279.
21 *insensibly*: unconsciously
26-27 Fyge's parents were living in London, at the sign of the Sugar Loaf in the busy commercial area of Bishopsgate.

On a Sermon preach'd Sept. *the 6th, 1697. on these Words,*
You have sold your selves for Nought.

    With *Grotius* on *New-Testament* yo've done,
    And chose Authentick *Coke* and *Littleton*;
    The latters Tenures did inspire your Brain,
    To vent your self in legislative Strain:
5   Where you each nice Distinction did pursue,
    The Bargain, Sale, and the *habendum* too.
    It was not done by Lease or Mortgage then,
    To be redeem'd as you told how and when;
    By Deed of Feoffment we had passed away,
10   For nothing too our Tenement of Clay;
    And that the Devil who the Purchase bought,
    He nothing gave nor nothing had he got.
    On this you Cant (awhile) at last recal,
    Cum Pertinentiis, he had gotten all;
15   When of the Gospel you make Law take Place,
    Statues may well get upper-hand of Grace:
    Sure you the Primitive design have mist,
    Joshua must yield to an Evangelist.
    But *Littleton* in you has got the start,
20   Did'st know if thou in church or Temple were't?
    Tho' you so Zealously the *Non-cons* hate,
    Methinks too like the *Pro* and *Cons* you Prate,
    The Sermon is at best but a Debate:
    Instead of Proofs you bring us Presidents,
25   Need more the Judges than the Saints consents.
    You Declare, Plead, Join Issue or Demur,
    Then sell at last with (*come ceo Sur;*)
    Fatal Defeazance, for if you Preach so,

Your Hearers may remain in *Statu quo*:
30 So far you on the legal rights intrench,
We scarcely know your Pulpit from the Bench.

From *Poems on Several Occasions...* [1703], 64-65.
Title: Psalms 44:12. This sermon may have been preached by Fyge's
second husband, Thomas Egerton. The poem, in dwelling on the
legal considerations of land holdings, rents and leases, may have
been meant as a chastisement to Egerton, whose interest in Fyge's
property, inherited from her first husband, was a bone of
contention in their divorce case. 'On ----- being tax'd with Symony',
another poem in her collection, also attacks an anonymous minister.
1 *Grotius*: Hugo Grotius (1583-1645), author of *De veritate religionis
Christianae* (1627), a popular work that emphasised the common
ground of all Christian sects. It became an important text in
Protestant colleges, and was used for missionary purposes.
2 *Authentick*: in addition to 'authoritative', from the fifteenth to the
eighteenth centuries authentic also meant legally qualified or
licensed.
2 *Coke and Littleton*: Sir Thomas Littleton wrote a treatise on tenure
in the fifteenth century, which was studied by all beginning law
students in Sir Edward Coke's heavily annotated version, *The First
Part of the Institutes of the Laws of England* (1628), known as 'Coke
upon Littleton'.
3 *Tenures*: systems of landholding
6 *habendum*: from *habendum et tenendum*, a legal term meaning 'to
have and to hold'; the part of a deed that defines what estate or
interest is granted.
9 *Deed of Feoffment*: a written document which transfers inherited
property to another party
10 *Tenement of Clay*: the body, Job 10:9, 13:12, and 14:19. Fyge is
here punning on 'tenement' as a legal term referring to the holding
of land and the buildings on it.
14 *Cum Pertinentiis*: with reference to which
16 *Statues*: presumably 'statutes', meaning laws
18 *Joshua*: in the Apocrypha, 1 Macc. 2:55, Joshua is cited specifically
for his adherence to the law and is made a judge. In Joshua
14:1-19:51, he distributes land among the tribes of Israel.
20 *Temple*: the Middle and Inner Temples are courts of law in
London. Fyge may here be punning on 'temple' as a place of
worship for Dissenters.
21 *Non-cons*: abbreviation for non-conformists, those who refused
to conform to the Church of England, especially after the passing of
the Act of Uniformity in 1662. Egerton, like most of the lower
clergy of this time, was probably a 'high-flying' Tory, objecting to
the Toleration Act of 1689, which allowed Dissenters the right to
worship. Fyge herself was most likely a Whig, like her father.

24 *Proofs... Presidents*: Fyge is using legal terms to say that instead of providing actual evidence, the minister is simply citing previous cases.

26 *Declare...Demur*: Fyge is here listing the steps in presenting a legal case. *Declare*: to make a statement of claim as plaintiff in a legal action. *Plead*: to argue the case. *Join Issue*: jointly to submit a point in question for a decision. *Demur*: to admit that the facts stated by one's opponent are true, but questioning the legality of the opponent's claim.

27 *come ceo Sur*: we have not succeeded in unscrambling this tag.

28 *Defeazance*: ruin, undoing; in legal terms, a defeasance is a deed which can render a previously existing right or deed null and void.

29 *in Statu quo*: in the same state

On my wedding Day.

Abandon'd Day, why dost thou now appear?
Thou must no more thy wonted Glories wear;
Oh! Rend thy self out of the circling Year.
With me thou'rt stript of all thy pompous Pride,
5   Art now no festival Cause, I no Bride:
In thee no more must the glad Musick sound,
Nor pleasing Healths in chearful Bowls go round,
But with sad Cypress dress'd, not Mirtle crown'd;
Ne'er grac'd again with joyful Pageantry:
10   The once glad Youth that did so honour thee
Is now no more; with him thy Triumph's lost,
He always own'd thee worthy of his Boast.
Such Adorations he still thought thy due,
I learn'd at last to celebrate thee too;
15   Tho' it was long e'er I could be content,
To yield you more than formal Complement;
If my first Offering had been Free-Will,
I then perhaps might have enjoy'd thee still:
But now thou'rt kept like the first mystick Day,
20   When my reluctant Soul did Fate obey,
And trembling Tongue with the sad Rites comply'd,
With timerous Hand th' amazing Knot I ty'd,
While Vows and Duty check'd the doubting Bride.
At length my reconcil'd and conquer'd Heart,
25   When 'twas almost too late own'd thy Desert,
And wishes thou wast still, not that thou never wer't;
Wishes thee still that celebrated Day,

SARAH FYGE

I lately kept with sympathizing Joy.
But Ah! thou canst be no more to me,
30   Than the sad Relick of Solemnity;
To my griev'd Soul may'st thou no more appear,
Be blotted out of Fate's strict Calender.
May the Sun's Rays ne'er be to thee allow'd,
But let him double every thick wrought Cloud,
35   And wrap himself in a retiring Shroud;
Let unmixt Darkness shade the gloomy Air,
Till all our sable Horizon appear,
Dismale as I, black as the Weeds I wear;
With me thy abdicated State deplore,
40   And be like me, that's by thy self no more.

From *Poems on Several Occasions* [1703], 70-72.
8 *Cypress*: a light, black fabric worn for mourning. *Mirtle*: the myrtle,
sacred to Venus, represented love.
22 *amazing*: terrifying

JANE BARKER

Jane Barker was baptised on 17 May 1652, in Blatherwicke in Northamptonshire, the daughter of Thomas Barker, formerly a Royalist soldier and agent for a local squire, and his wife Anne, of a Cornish family named Connock (NRO 34 P/1 and Clayton 16). When Jane was ten years old the family moved to Wilsthorpe in Lincolnshire where her father held a lease on the manor house and a substantial amount of land owned by the Earl of Essex (NRO S [T] 674; Medoff, 1983). There, according to her autobiographical novels, she learned the art of simpling (herbal medicine) and was instructed in Latin and medicine by her elder brother, Edward, a student at Oxford.

By the 1680s Barker's father and brother were dead, and she appears to have been living in London with her mother, who died in 1685. Her poems were first published in 1688 as the first half of *Poetical Recreations*; the second part consisted of verses by Cambridge scholars and the publisher himself, Benjamin Crayle, who praises Barker, as 'Galaecia' or 'Cosmelia', for her poetical and medical skills. Crayle was in the process of publishing Barker's romance, 'Scipina', at this time, but the work did not actually appear in print until 1715, published by Edmund Curll as *Exilius: or, The Banish'd Roman*.

During the reign of James II Barker converted to Roman Catholicism; soon after the Revolution of 1688 she followed the Stuarts into exile in France. Her Connock cousins, with whom she maintained a close relationship throughout her life, were members of the Jacobite peerage. In 1700 she made a fair copy of some poems 'refering to the times', intended as a gift for the 'Prince of Wales', i.e. James Stuart, the Old Pretender, who was then twelve years old (BL Add. MS 21,621). A larger manuscript, also in Barker's hand, includes as its first part the same extraordinary poetic autobiography, expressed mostly in dialogues voicing Barker's strong political and religious beliefs (Magdalen MS 343; Spencer, 1983, 179-180; Spencer, 1986, 63). The second part consists of collected occasional poems she wrote for the exiled court (c.1692-1701), and the third, her emended versions of the unauthorised *Poetical Recreations* poems. In her preface she asks consideration for her work as that of a 'blind person'; she later explains that her cataracts were 'couched', i.e. pierced with a needle and moved below the axis of vision (Medoff, 1983).

By 1713 Barker was back in England, overseeing the land at Wilsthorpe, for which she paid a sizable annual rent of £47.10s. As a

Roman Catholic, she was compelled to register an 'annual valuation' of her estate after the Jacobite uprising of 1715 (LAO Kesteven Quarter Sessions. Papists' Estates. Rolls; Cosin, 68). At this late stage in her life, probably in an attempt to keep the Wilsthorpe household going, she began to write for profit. Her first published novel, *Love Intrigues: or, The History of the Amours of Bosvil and Galesia* (1713), is described as 'written by a young lady'; Barker was then sixty-one. In that novel and in *A Patch-Work Screen for the Ladies* (1723), Galesia describes her early disappointments in love and the solace her studies and poetry bring her: 'I was dropp'd into a Labyrinth of Poetry, which has ever since interlac'd all the Actions of my Life' (*Patch-Work Screen*, 3). At the time of publication of *A Patch-Work Screen*, she was living in Richmond. In *The Lining of the Patch-Work Screen* (1726) an older Galesia, now living in London, narrates a string of odd adventure tales and ghost stories, and pays homage, in a dream vision, to her idol, Katherine Philips. *Exilius* (translated into German in 1721) and a revised version of *Love Intrigues* were published together as *The Entertaining Novels of Mrs. Jane Barker of Wilsthorp* (1719) which continued to be published until well into the mid-century.

Barker remained devoted to the Roman Catholic Church and to the Jacobite cause, publishing a religious treatise, *The Christian Pilgrimage* (1718), and contributing to the movement of French and Anglo-Catholics to canonise James II, by testifying that a rag dipped in the King's blood had cured her of breast cancer (Royal Archives, Stuart Papers, [M] 208 / 129). In spite of the moderate success of her novels, Barker continued on the periphery of English society, an unmarried woman dependent on the companionship of her relatives and her pen, steadfast but cautious in her commitment to her studies: 'But let the World confine, or enlarge Learning as they please, I care not; I do not regret the time I bestow'd in its Company, its having been my good Friend... though I am not so generous, by way of Return, to pass my word for its good Behaviour in our Sex always, and in all Persons' (*Love Intrigues*, 52-53).

Fidelia arguing with her self
on the difficulty of finding the true Religion.

Oh wretched World, but wretched above all,
Man, man's the most unhappy animal,
Not knowing to what state he shall belong,
He tuggs the heavy chain of life along.
5   So many ages pass, yet no experience shows,
From whence man comes, nor after where he goes.
We are instructed of a future state,
Of just rewards, and punishments in that,

But ignorant how, where, or when, or what.
10   I'm shew'd a book, in which such things are writ,
And by all hands assur'd all's true in it;
But in this book, such Misterys I find,
That 'stead of healing oft corrodes the mind.
Sometimes our faith must be our only guide,
15   Our sences and our reason layd aside.
Again to reason, we our faith submit,
This spurs, that checks, we curvet, champ the bitt,
And make our future hopes uneasie sit.
Now faith, now reason, now good works doe all,
20   Betwixt these opposits, our vertues fall,
Each calling each, false and Hereticall.
And after all what rule have we to show,
Whether these writings sacred be or no?
If we allege the truths that we find there,
25   Are to themselves a testimony clear,
By the same rule such good Romances are.
Then sure some living witness there must bee,
To hand this down to all posterity,
And with their blood avouch the verity.
30   Such is the Church, not that wherein I live,
For that can no such Testimony give,
But quite contrary it's new doctrins look,
Denying things affirmed in this book:
And for her to pretend to judge in this,
35   Is to discribe to Adam Paradice,
For he must better know, who lived there
And so must they, who the first teachers were.
For us to deem our selves the Church, to me
Seems like a feather which the bird will be,
40   Or a lop'd branch, which needs will be the tree.
Now from this cant I think I ought to go,
But shame and interest still whisper no.
Beside respect to my first mother due,
I'm not assur'd this other is the true.
45   When e'er I go, I go a poor forlorn,
Into a Church by persecutions torn,
And to my friends become a general scorn.
These thoughts perhaps are sent from Heav'n
expres,

To keep me from a dangerous precipice;

50   But how know I, they do not come from Hell,
     To stop the current of my doing well.
     Thus I by doubts, and hopes, and fears am toss'd,
     And in the labrinth of disputes am lost;
     Unhappy, who with any doubts are curss'd,
55   But of all doubts, Religious doubts are worst.
     Wou'd I were dead, or wou'd I had no soul,
     Or ne'er been born, or els been born a fool:
     Then future fears wou'd not my thoughts anoy,
     But use what's truly ours, the present joy.
60   Ah happy brutes! I envy much your state,
     Whome nature one day shall annihilate;
     Compar'd to which, wretched is human fate.
     But where my God, oh wither do I run!
     Without thy check, I stop not till undone;
65   What insolence for me a thing so bad,
     To quarrel why I thus or thus am made?
     A pot-sherd is a better thing by far,
     For it against it's maker, makes no war.
     Forgive me God, forgive me but this once,
70   And I'll forever my whole self renounce;
     In testimony here I prostrate fall
     And take thee for my God, my life my all.
        Now now I feell th' effect of Heav'nly love,
     That nothing e'er my constancy can move.
75   Sure pleasant are the repasts of the just.
     Since in this tast I find so great a gust.
     Hence then all wordly joys I might persue,
     With Benit's sons, I will go bid adue,
     In pennance my baptismal vows renew.

From Magdalen MS 343, 'Poems on Several Occasions, in Three
Parts', Part I, 'part the first Poems Refering to the times Occasionly
writ according to the different circumstance Of time and place',
8-11. The poem also appears in *A Patch-Work Screen for the Ladies*
(1723). Substantive variants are listed below.

Title On the Difficulties of Religion 1723   2 Man, man's / Is Man 1723
10 such / these 1723   13 that 'stead / Instead 1723
19 doe / does 1723   26 good Romances / all good Morals 1723
27-51 omitted in 1723   52 Thus we by Doubts, & Hopes, & Fears, are tost, 1723
53 am/are 1723   57 Or ne'er / Had ne'er 1723
59 But / I'd 1723; ours / mine 1723   63-79 omitted in 1723
77 wordly / 'human' struck out in MS

1-4 Cf. Rochester's 'Satire against Mankind' (1680):

> I'd be a *Dog*, a *Monkey*, or a *Bear*.
> Or any thing but that vain *Animal*,
> Who is so proud of being rational. (5-7)

In a note to *A Patch-work Screen for the Ladies* Barker identifies 'Against Mankind' as the model for Galesia's poem 'On the Follies of Human Life', in which she again compares man's struggle with reason and passion to the more logical ways of animals:

> No *Animals* such *Bubbles* are, as *Man*;
> They strive to save *themselves* in all *they* can
> But *we* in *our own* Snares, our selves trapan. (112)

Though Barker herself may have been well aquainted with the philosophical tradition of praising animals' more rational existence, her persona, Galesia, describes Rochester as her only fellow traveller in these 'strange, unfrequented Desarts' (113-114).

5-9 Cf. Rochester, 'On Nothing':

> Eer time and place were, time and place were not,
> When primitive *Nothing* something streight begot,
> Then all proceeded from the great united--What. (4-6)

In *Love Intrigues* (1713), Barker refers to the conclusion of Rochester's poem:

behold, I say, what all this came to, even just as much as the Lord *Rochester* says of Court Promises, and Whores Vows, which all *End in Nothing*. (57)

10-13 *a book*: the Bible. By demonstrating her difficulties in interpreting the 'Misterys' of the Bible, Barker introduces some of the central issues of debate between English Protestants and Roman Catholics in her time. Catholics relied on the Bible as interpreted by the Church of Rome, through the Pope and the Church Fathers, as their 'rule of faith'. Protestants held that the Bible as understood by human reason or by the private spirit illuminated by God was in itself sufficient, though the Anglican Church did accept, to a lesser degree, the teaching of the Church Fathers. The 'rule of faith' was one of the major topics in the religious controversy.

14-21 Dryden addresses the same problem of the struggle between faith and reason in *The Hind and the Panther* (1687):

> God thus asserted: man is to believe
> Beyond what sense and reason can conceive.
> And for mysterious things of faith rely
> On the Proponent, heav'ns authority.
> If then our faith we for our guide admit,
> Vain is the farther search of humane wit, ...
> Rest then, my soul, from endless anguish freed;
> Nor sciences thy guide, nor sense thy creed,
> Faith is the best insurer of thy bliss;
> The Bank above must fail before the venture miss. (I, 118-123, 146-149)

In her dedication to the 'Prince of Wales' Barker compares her own writing on personal conversion to Dryden's:

that learned and great wit, on the occasion of his Hine and Panthar was so raild at, and ridicul'd, as if he had layd down wit and sence, when he took up Religion, and Holy

life; where as both were refind, not above their capacity to understand, but their
conveniency to approve: Now if it far'd thus with this great man, what must become of
me an insect scribler... (Magdalen MS 343, ff.3ᵛ-4)

17 *curvet*: leap or frisk about; Barker compares faith dominated by
reason to a horse given contradictory commands from its rider. In
The Hind and the Panther Dryden uses the image to depict Luther
and Calvin:

> Or like wild horses sev'ral ways have whirl'd
> The Tortur'd Text about the Christian World;
> Each *Jehu* lashing on with furious force,
> That *Turk* or *Jew* cou'd not have us'd it worse. (II, 118-121)

22-23 Barker is pointing to what she considers to be the Protestant
lack of an authoritative church, the neglect of 'tradition', i.e. the
intermediating authority of the Apostles, Popes, and early general
councils. Dryden's Hind explains:

> A guide was therefore needfull, therefore made,
> And if appointed, sure to be obey'd.
> Thus, with due rev'rence, to th' Apostles writ,
> By which my sons are taught, to which, submit;
> I think, those truths their sacred works contain,
> The church alone can certainly explain,
> That following ages, leaning on the past,
> May rest upon the Primitive at last.
> Nor wou'd I thence the word no rule infer,
> But none without the church interpreter.
> Because, as I have urg'd before, 'tis mute,
> And is it self the subject of dispute. (II, 349-360)

24-26 Dryden's Roman Catholic Hind also attacks Protestant
reliance on individual interpretation: 'All who can read, Interpreters may be' (II, 110).
27-29 Barker adduces that the history of martyrdom is relevant to
the existence of the eternal church. Testimony was an essential
point for Catholic writers in the controversy raging at this time.
This part of the poem and the ensuing lines, up to 52, which
describe her inclination towards the Roman Catholic Church, as
well as the last seventeen lines of the poem, depicting the resolution
of her doubts, were omitted from the version in *A Patch-Work Screen*
(1723). The jibe at 'good Romances' was diplomatically revised to
'all good Morals' for the novel's version.
30 *the Church... where in I live*: Barker was born into the Church of
England.
37 *the first teachers*: the Church Fathers
47 *general scorn*: Barker composed a series of poems in which her
persona, 'Fidelia', engages a male friend in what was then called a
'conference', i.e. a debate between Roman Catholic and Protestant,
like the dialogue of the Hind and Panther, each trying to convert
the other. The 'friend' accuses Fidelia of converting 'to be in the
court mode', indicating that Barker's conversion took place in
England during James II's reign, and predicts, 'Great Miserys shall

on your life attend' (Magdalen MS I, 24).

67-68 Isaiah 45:9

73 *Now now I feell*: Barker's struggle is suddenly ended when she is given the actual grace of conversion by direct heavenly intervention.

78 *Benit's Sons*: Benedictine monks. Since 1662, the time of Charles II's marriage to Catherine of Braganza, Benedictine monks served the chapel royal. Soon after James became king he installed sixteen Benedictine monks in the convent at St James that had been established for Henrietta Maria's Portuguese chaplains. In 1687 a second Benedictine priory was founded near Clerkenwell. Barker's may have been one of the many conversions for which the Benedictines were well known; Dryden was converted by Dom Corker. The poem immediately following this one in the autograph manuscripts describes the 'Convent at St. James's' as a 'terrestial Paradice' (Magdalen MS 343, I, 12). During the revolution of 1688, many of the monks fled to the monastery of St Edmund's in Paris, and were instrumental in efforts to canonise James (Morey, 273-274; Scott, 1984, 1-3; Weldon, 226).

79 In the Catholic liturgy at Baptism the infant through the sponsor vows to renounce Satan and espouse the true faith; these vows are renewed by the adult on occasions of special solemnity. Barker has decided to go into what Catholics nowadays call retreat under the spiritual direction of the Benedictines. She would be expected to make a general confession ('pennance') and renew her baptismal vows.

A Virgin life

Since gracious Heven, you have bestow'd on me
So great a kindness for verginity,
Suffer me not, to fall into the power,
Of mans, allmost omnipotent amour.
5   But in this happy state, let me remain,
And in chast verse, my chaster thoughts explain.
Fearless of twenty-five and all its rage,
When Time and beauty endless wars ingage,
And Fearless of the antiquated name,   old maid
10 Which oft makes happy maid turn helpless dame,
The scorn fix'd to that name our sex betray,
And often makes us fling our selves away.
Like harmless kids which are pursu'd by men,
For safty run into a Lyons den.
15 Ah lovely state how strange it is to see,
What mad conceptions, some have made of thee.

360

As if thy being was all wretchedness,
Or foul deformity ith' ugliest dress,
Whereas thy beauty's pure, celestial,
20   Thy thoughts divine, thy words Angelical:
And such ought all thy votaries to be,
Or else they'r so, but for necessity
A virgin bears the impress of all good,
Under that name, all vertue's understood.
25   To equal all her looks her mein, her dress
That nought but modesty, seems in excess.
When virgins any treats or visits make,
Tis not for tattle, but for friendship sake,
The neighboring poor are her adopted heirs,
30   And less she cares, for her own good than theirs.
And by obedience testifies she can
Be's good a subject as the stoutest man.
She to her church, such filial duty pays,
That one wou'd think she'd live'd ith' pristine days.
35   Her whole lives business, she drives to these ends,
To serve her god, her neighbour, and her friends.

From Magdalen MS 343, Part III, 'These following poems, are taken out of a book of Miscellany poems, and writ by the same author as the former, But without her consent, were printed in the year 1688: now corrected by her own hand, which makes the third part of this Collection', 8-8ᵛ. This poem appears in both *Poetical Recreations* (1688) and *A Patch-Work Screen for the Ladies* (1723). We have listed only substantive variants. A comparison between *Poetical Recreations* and the manuscript version (c.1701), may reflect authorial emendations of Barker's original as printed in *Poetical Recreations* or her restoration of an original altered by other hands for publication or both.

1 gracious Heven, you / O ye Pow'rs ye 1688 / O good Heavens! you 1723
3 power / Pow'rs 1688 / Powers 1723
4 mans / Mens 1688; amour / Amours 1688 and 1723
5 But in this happy Life, let me remain, 1688 / But let me in this happy state remain
1723   6 omitted in 1688   7 rage / train 1688
Instead of ll.8-12 Of slights or scorns, or being call'd Old Maid,
               Those Goblings which so many have betray'd: 1688
And in 1723   When once *that Clock has struck*, all Hearts retire,
               Like *Elves*, from *Day-break*, or like Beasts from Fire,
               'Tis Beauty's *Passing-Bell*; no more are slain;
               But dying Lovers all revive again.
               Then every Day some new Contempt we find,
               As if the Scorn and Lumber of Mankind.
               These frightful Prospects, oft our Sex betray;
               Which to avoid, some fling themselves away;

13 which are / that are 1688 / who when 1723   15 lovely / happy 1723
17 if / though 1688   18 ith'ugliest / in vilest 1723
24 Under that name / In that dread name 1688
25 To / So 1688 and 1723   26 seems/is 1723
Instead of 27-36 And when she any treats or visits make,
                'Tis not for tattle, but for Friendship's sake;
                Her Neighb'ring Poor she do's adopt her Heirs,
                And less she cares for her own good than theirs;
                And by Obedience testifies she can
                Be's good a Subject as the stoutest Man.
                She to her Church such filial duty pays,
                That one would think she'd liv'd i'th' pristine days.
                Her Closet, where she do's much time bestow,
                Is both her Library and Chappel too,
                Where she enjoys society alone,
                I'th' Great Three-One----
                She drives her whole Lives business to these Ends,
                To serve her God, enjoy her Books and Friends. 1688
Instead of 27-34
                The Business of her Life to this extends,
                To serve her God, her Neighbour and her Friends. 1723

Title: Although praise of the single life is common in women's literature, Barker here seems to be emulating the theme and sentiments of 'The Virgin' by her favourite poet, Katherine Philips:

> The things that make a Virgin please,
> She that seeks, will find them these;
> A Beauty, not to Art in debt,
> Rather agreeable than great;
> An Eye, wherein at once do meet,
> The beams of kindness, and of wit;
> An undissembled Innocence,
> Apt not to give, nor take offense:
> A Conversation, at once, free
> From Passion, and from Subtlety;
> A Face that's modest, yet serene,
> A sober, and yet lively Meen;
> The vertue which does her adorn,
> By honour guarded, not by scorn;
> With such wise lowliness indu'd,
> As never can be mean, or rude;
> That prudent negligence enrich,
> And Time's her silence and her speech;
> Whose equal mind does alwaies move,
> Neither a foe, nor slave to Love;
> And whose Religion's strong and plain,
> Not superstitious, nor profane.

Cf. Philips's juvenile work, 'A marryd state affords but little Ease', 7-16 (see p.189). In *A Serious Proposal for the Ladies* I, Mary Astell describes the plight of the 'superannuated Virgin':

quite terrified with the dreadful Name of *Old Maid*, which yet none but Fools will reproach her with, nor any wise Woman be afraid of; to avoid this terrible *Mormo* [Greek for 'bugbear'], and the scoffs that are thrown on superanuated Virgins, she flies to some dishonourable Match as her last, tho' much mistaken Refuge, to the disgrace of her Family and her own irreparable Ruin. (132-133)

35-36 These lines echo Katherine Philips's 'A Resvery':

> Who dares not keep that Life that he can spend,
> To serve his God, his Country, and his Friend. (49-50)

Cf. Sir John Denham's 'Friendship and Single Life Against Love and Marriage' (1668):

> How happy he that loves not, lives!
> Him neither Hope nor Fear deceives,
> To Fortune who no Hostage gives....
> Secure from low, and private Ends,
> His Life, his Zeal, his Wealth attends
> His Prince, his Country, and his Friends. (16-18;22-24)

She begining to study phisick, takes her leave of poetry, so falls into a long degression on anatomy.

Far^e well fare well, kind poetry my friend,
For I no longer can thy charmes attend,
On new acquaintance now I must dispence,
What I receiv'd from thy bright influence,
5   Wise Aristotle, and Hippocrates,
Gallen^{us} and the most wise Socrates.
Æsculapius whom first I shou'd have nam'd
With all Apolo's younger sons so fam'd
Are they with whome I must acquaintance make
10 Who will no doubt receive me for his sake
From whom they justly did expect to see,
new lights to search natures obscurity.
now Bartholine the first of all this row,
Does to me natures architecture show,
15 How the foundation first of earth is layd
And how the pillars of strong bones are made,
How th' walls consist of carneous parts within,
The outsid pinguid overlayd with skin,
The fretwork muscles arteries and veins
20 With their implexures, and how from the brains
The nerves decend, and how 'tis they dispence,
To every member, motive power and sence.
He shews what windows in this structure's fix'd,
How trebly glaz'd, how curtains drawn betwixt,
25 Them and earths objects, all which proves in vain,
To keep out lust, or innocence retain.
For 'twas the eye that first decern'd the food

As pleasing to it self, for eating good,
Then was perswaded that it wou'd refine,
30   The half wise soul, and make it all divine
But ah how dearly wisdom's bought with sin,
Which shuts out grace, lets death and darkness in
An^d cause our sex precipitated first
To pains and ignorance we'r most accurss'd
35   Desire of knowledge cost so very dear,
That ignorance must be our only share,
And allways move ith' low obedient sphere,
But as I was inlarging on this theam,
Willis and Harvey bid me follow them.
40   They brought me to the first and largest court
Of all this building, where as to a port,
All necessaries are brought from afar,
For sustentation both in peace and war,
For war, this common wealth does of infest,
45   Which pillages one part and storms the rest.
We view'd the kitching call'd ventriculus,
Then pass'd we through the space call'd pylorus.
Then came we to the dining room at last,
Where the lacteans take their sweet repast.
50   From then^ce we to a drawing room did pass
And came where jecur very busie was.
Sanguificating the whole mass of chyle
And severing the cruoral parts from bile,
And when she's made it tollerably good
55   She pours it forth to mix with other blood.
This and much more we saw, from thence we went
Into the next court by a small ascent,
Bless me said I, what raritys are here,
A fountain like a furnace did appear,
60   Still boyling o'er and runing out so fast,
That one shou'd think its eflux cou'd not last,
Yet it sustain'd no loss as I cou'd see,
Which made me think it a strange prodigie,
Come on, says Harvey, don't stand gazing here,
65   But follow me, and I thy doubts will clear,
Then we began our journy with the blood,
Trac'd the Meanders of its purple flood.
Thus we through many Labyrinths did pass,
In such, I'm sure, old Daedalus ne'er was.

70 Sometimes ith'out works, sometimes i th' first court
Sometimes ith' third these winding streams wou'd
sport.
Such raritys we found in this third place,
As puts ev'n comprehension to disgrace,
Here's cavitys says one, Behold says he
75 The seat of fancy, judgment memory:
Here says an other, is the fertile womb,
From whence the spirits animal do come,
Which are misteriously ingender'd here,
Of spirits from arterious blood and air.
80 Here said a third, life made her first approach,
Moving the wheels of her triumphant coach:
But Harvey that hipotheses deny'd,
Say'ng 'twas ith' deaf-ear on the dexter side.
Then there arose, a trivial small dispute,
85 Which he by fact, and reason did confute:
Which being ended, we began again,
Our former journy, and forsook the brain:
And after some small traverses about,
We came to the place where we at first set out
90 Then I perceiv'd how all this magick stood,
By th' circles of the circulating blood.
As fountains have their water from the sea,
To which again, they do themselves conveigh.
And here we found great Lower by his art,
95 Surveighing the whole structure of the heart,
Welcome said he, dear cousin are you here,
Sister to him, whose worth we all revere,
But ah alas, so cruell was his fate,
As makes us since allmost our practice hate
100 Since we cou'd find out nought in all our art
That cou'd prolong the motion of his heart.

From Magdalen MS 343, Part III, 43-45ᵛ. Substantive variants from
the printed versions in *Poetical Recreations* (1688) and *A Patch-Work
Screen* (1723) are listed below. The *Patch-Work Screen* version begins
with what is line 13 in the Magdalen Manuscript. Both printed
versions are more heavily punctuated, probably by the editors.

Title: A Farewell to Poetry, With A Long Digression on Anatomy 1688 /
Anatomy 1723
1-2 Farewell my gentle Friend, kind *Poetry*,
For we no longer must Acquaintance be;

Though sweet and charming to me as thou art,
Yet I must dispossess thee of my Heart. 1688
8 And all *Apollo*'s younger brood so fam'd, 1688
10-11 Who will, no doubt, receive me for the sake
Of *Him* (b), from whom they did expect to see 1688
(the note (b) in *Poetical Recreations* reads: *My Brother*)   13 row / Crew 1688
15-16 He tells me how th' Foundation first is laid Of Earth;
how Pillars of strong *Bones* are made; 1688
16 Then, how the *Pillars* of *Strong-Bones* are made. 1723
17 How th' / The 1723   21 'tis they dispence / they do dispence 1688
23 what / the 1723
24 how / and 1723   25 proves / prove 1723   26 or / and 1688
28-29 As pleasing to it self, then thought it good
To *eat*, as b'ing inform'd it wou'd refine 1688   31 ah / O 1723
33-39 And because we *precipitated* first,
To Pains and Ignorance are most accurs'd;
Ev'n by our *Counter-parts,* who that they may
Exalt themselves, insultingly will say,
Women know little, and they practise less;
But Pride and Sloth they glory to profess.
But as we were *expatiating* thus,
Walaeus and *Harvey* cry'd, Madam, follow us, 1688
34-37 To Pains, and Ignorance *we* since are curs'd.
Desire of *Knowledge*, cost *us* very dear;
For *Ignorance*, e'er since, became our Share.
line 37 is omitted 1723
42 afar / far 1688   44 does of / doth oft 1723   45 one / this 1688
48 And to the Dining-Room we came at last, 1688 and 1723   50 to / thro' 1728
51 And came where Madam *Jecur* busie was; 1688
72-73 Themselves; but here methought I needs must stay,
And listen next to what the *Artists* say: 1688
73 puts / put 1723   74 behold / and 1688 / and here 1723 ('and here' in MS struck out)
75 The / Is th' 1723   79 arterious / arterial 1723
82-83 Hold there, said *Harvey*, that must be deny'd,
'Twas in the deaf Ear on the *dexter* side. 1688
83 ith' / the 1723   86 which / This 1723   87 journy / Progress, 1723
89-90 Came to the Place where we before set out:
Then I perceiv'd, how Harvey all made good, 1723
92 water / Waters 1688   94 And / But 1688 ; by his / with much 1723
96 dear / sweet 1688   97 But ah, alas! So short was his Life's Date, 1723

Title *anatomy*: seventeenth-century women as a matter of course collected 'receipts' for cures to administer to their families and 'the neighbouring poor'; it was far less common for women to study anatomy and medicine, though 'doctresses' were not unheard of. Elizabeth Walker learned 'Physick and Chyrurgery' from her brother-in-law, a doctor at London College, and passed her 'Secrets as well in Medecine as in Pastry and Seasoning' on to her daughters. Elizabeth Bury studied anatomy and medicine and 'understood a Human Carcase and the Materia Medica better than most of her sex'. In 1681 Margaret Page (alias Woolfe) took Sarah Sanders as an apprentice in 'the art and business of Doctress and Chirurgy' (Gardiner, 1929, 263-264; 299). Women rarely prescribed through an apothecary, hindered by their inability to write Latin. In 'On the Apothecarys filing my bills amongst the Doctors', Barker boasts,

I hope I shan't be blam'd if I am proud

That I'm admitted in this learned croud,....
The sturdy gout, which all male power withstands,
Is overcome by my soft female hands
Not Deb'ra, Judith, or Semiramis,
Can boast of conquests half so great as this,
More than they slew, I save in this diseas. (Magdalen MS 343, Part III,16)

Cf. Anne Bradstreet, 'Of the Four Humours in Man's Constitution', particularly the section entitled 'Blood'.

4 *thy bright influence*: **having learnt latin by reading the latin poets** [Barker's own annotations appear in bold]

5 Aristotle's biological studies include *Inquiry into Animals*, *On the Parts of Animals*, and *On the Progression of Animals*. *Hippocrates*: (fl.400 BC) traditionally, the father of medicine, author of the Hippocratic Oath, the ethical code for physicians

6 *Gallenus*: (c.130-c.200), after Hippocrates, the most distinguished physician of the Ancients

7 *Æsculapius*: god of medicine, son of Apollo and Coronis

11 *from whom*: **her brother a phisician**

13 *Bartholine*: Caspar Bartholin (1585-1629) author of *Anatomicae Institutiones Corporis Humani* (1611), one of the most widely read Renaissance manuals of anatomy.

18 *pinguid*: fat

20 *implexures*: entwinings

23 *windows*: **the three humers of the eye, and its several tunicks.** Thomas Blount's *Glossographia* (second edition, 1661), provides the following definition: *Tunick*... a skin or coat that covers the eye, whereof there are four sorts (*OED*).

27 *the food*: the apple on the Tree of Knowledge

31-37 On the subject of Eve, cf. Alice Sutcliffe, 'Of our losse by Adam', 30 (see p.91).

39 *Willis*: Thomas Willis (1621-1675), one of the early fellows of the Royal Society, was known for his work on the nervous system and diabetes. Barker probably had in mind his essay *De Sanguinis Ascensione* (1670). Although '*Walaeus*' appears in *Poetical Recreations* (1688), in the Magdalen manuscript and in *A Patch-Work Screen* (1723) Barker names 'Willis'. Joannes Walaeus, or John de Wale, was a distinguished professor at Leyden, and an advocate of William Harvey (1578-1657), discoverer of the circulation of the blood. Harvey's observations were published in *De Circulatione Sanguinis* (1649), translated into English in 1653.

40 *first and largest court*: **ad infimum ventrem,** meaning to the hypogastrium, defined in the seventeenth century as the outermost part of the abdomen between the hypochondres (liver, gall bladder, and spleen) and the navel.

43 *sustentation*: maintenance or preservation of human life

44 *war*: **morbi in infimo ventre, diarrhea &c,** meaning diseases of the intestines; *of*: oft

46 *ventriculus*: **the stomake,** alternative form of 'ventricle', which

was often used in the seventeenth century for stomach.

47 *pylorus*: the opening from the stomach into the small intestine

49 *lacteans*: **venae lacteae,** lymphatic glands originating in the small intestine. They carry chyle, a milky white fluid, to the thoracic duct through which it is then conveyed to the blood.

51 **secundum opinionem Galenist; contra receptacum comune,** according to Galen's opinion; contrary to common belief; *jecur*: the liver (from the Latin). Galen considered the liver to be a kind of 'first heart' or ante-heart, manufacturing and distributing a specific type of blood. Harvey refuted this idea in his essays on the circulation of the blood.

52 *sanguificating*: forming into blood

53 *cruoral*: of the blood; *bile*: a fluid secreted by the liver and poured into the small intestine as an aid to the digestive process

57 *next court*: the heart; *a small ascent*: **per diaphragma,** through the diaphragm.

61 *eflux*: out-pouring

69 *Daedalus*: designer of the labyrinth at Minos and the father of Icarus

70-71 *out works*: the members; *third [court]*: the brain

72-85 Barker is here outlining a history of scientific theories on the brain. Harvey proved that the heart, and not the liver, as was believed by Galen, was the dynamic starting point of blood, therefore it is the place where 'life made her first approach'. The 'trivial small dispute' probably refers to the controversial responses to Harvey's discovery by Dr James Primrose, Aemylius Parisanus and Caspar Hoffman of Nuremberg.

77 *spirits animal*: it was formerly believed that there were three 'spirits' in the human body: animal, vital and natural. The animal spirits, meant to designate sensation and voluntary motion, the action of the nerves, were located in the brain, and were said to derive from pure blood. Harvey questioned this theory:

Smatterers, not knowing what causes to assign to a happening, promptly say that the spirits are responsible and introduce them as general *factota*. And, like bad poets, they call this *deus ex machina* on to their stage to explain their plot and catastrophe. (Harvey, 37)

In mentioning the spirits and presenting Galen's idea on the function of the liver (l.51), Barker appears to be hedging her bets.

79 *arterious blood and air*: before Galen, it was believed that the arteries carried air through the body, hence their name. Galen discovered that the arteries carried blood, but he believed they also transported vital air or spirit.

83 *deaf-ear on the dexter side*: the right auricle

94 *Lower*: Richard Lower (1631-1691) was the most noted physician in London in the 1670s until his political opinions affected his career (he supported the Whigs in the Titus Oates scandal). The work to which Barker refers is his *Tractatus de Corde* (1669).

95 *whole structure*: **de cordis structura**

96 *dear cousin*: Barker and Lower, who was Cornish, were related through their mothers.

97 *him*: **her deceas'd brother**. Jane Barker's brother, Edward (1650-1675), was a generation behind the noted Oxford scientists Robert Boyle, Richard Lower, Thomas Willis, and John Wallis who formed the Royal Society. He matriculated at St John's College, Oxford in 1668, just two years after Lower left Oxford for London. He graduated BA in 1672, MA from Christ Church in 1675, and died of fever in the same year (*Alumni Oxoniensis*, I, 70; *Poetical Recreations*, I, 48). In *A Patch-Work Screen* (1723) Galesia's brother instructs her in '*Anatomy* and *Simpling*' to help her recover from heart-break, and she boasts of making 'such progress in *Anatomy*, as to understand *Harvey*'s Circulation of the Blood, and *Lower*'s Motion of the Heart' (10).

101 *motion*: **de motu cordis**

'A YOUNG LADY'

Maria to Henric And Henric to Maria: Or, The Queen to the King In Holland And His Majesty's Answer, Two Heroical Epistles In Imitation of the Stile and Manner of Ovid. Written by a Young Lady, was published as a pamphlet in London in 1691. George Turberville's 1567 translation of *Ovid's Heroides* was still in print in 1605. Wye Saltonstall's translation (1636), dedicated to 'the vertuous ladies and gentlewomen of Great Britaine', was reprinted throughout the century. Three years after Saltonstall, John Sherburne brought out another translation. In 1680, Jacob Tonson invited Dryden to write the Preface to a volume of translations and paraphrases of Ovid's epistles he had collected from Dryden himself, Behn, Rymer, and other eminent hands, which was in its fourth revised edition by 1691.

In 1597 Michael Drayton had adapted the form using figures from English history in *England's Heroicall Epistles* with such popular success that the work went through five editions in as many years; in 1689 Drayton's work was republished in response to renewed interest in the Ovidian epistle. The unknown young lady who wrote the heroic epistles of Henric and Maria took the unusual step of employing as her personae the reigning monarchs, William III (whose middle name was Henric) and Mary II. Like Penelope or Dido writing to an absent beloved, Queen Mary spent long periods governing England alone while William was engaged in Ireland or on the Continent. The genuineness of the Queen's Protestantism made her admired as her father, James II, and his Italian wife had never been, and her wifely loyalty was a focus for the revulsion now felt toward the libertinage of the Restoration. It was publicly known that during William's absence in Ireland from June to September, 1690, Mary wrote to him every day; these letters were subsequently published.

MARIA to HENRIC

Minutes grow tedious, Time too slowly moves,
While *Henric*'s absent, and *Maria* loves.
Each Hour's a Week, and ev'ry Day a Year,
And ev'ry of *Maria*'s Thoughts a Fear:
5   Not for Thy Faith, my Fears are all for Thee,
For that dear Heart that nothing holds but me.

May I demand, if Love e'er taught Thee yet,
To look on lazy Moments with Regret?
If Love has taught Thee his Account of Time?
10 If *Henric*'s Love be such a Love as mine?
If so, my Sighs are justify'd by thine;
If so, you cannot frown, and cannot chuse,
But all I sigh, and all I say excuse;
And wish, and speak, and doubt, and act with me,
15 If Love like mine in a Male Breast can be.
Female our Souls, all Masculine our Love,
Strong is your Sense, feebly your Passions move.
Here shrunk my Soul, till my kind careless Pen
Run on to *Henric*'s Name---- I liv'd agen.
20 *Henric* more Noble than the rest of Men!
O happy Thought! O blest *Maria*'s Fate!
He loves, does all above the common Rate.

You busy'd yet with all those great Affairs,
Counsels, Debates, and Policy of Wars;
25 Safety of Kingdoms, all the Mighty Things,
Worthy my *Henric*, fit alone for Kings.
This some relief to painful Absence gives,
Diverts the Pangs wherewith *Maria* strives.

While You the foaming untam'd *Gallia* chase,
30 And all Your Snares around the Tigress place;
Pleas'd thus to see her all at Your Command,
Whene'er You please to move Your Conqu'ring
Hand:
Suffer not fond *Maria* to complain,
That You forget Your own dear am'rous Chain.
35 On unfledg'd Vict'ries in the Nest You smile,
And great Designs Your Love and Hours beguile:
Alone my business, and my all is You,
My self, my Wishes, all I have to do;
Your Name alone perswades me to endure;
40 That gives the Wound, and that applies the Cure:
But there's no Balsom priz'd by me above
The bright Idea of Your Noble Love.

But if Your Love (pardon the dubious Thought)
If You the gen'rous Flame from *Belgia* brought;

371

45 Why could it not perswade You to delay?
Why could not parting Tears induce Your stay?
How cruel short the pleasing Interview!
Short as 'twas sweet, as short disgustful too.
Why was I born so Great, or You so Brave?
50 Were You less so, or were I but a Slave?
My servile Consort I in view might have?
Nor think he's now engag'd, a Conqu'rour now,
Dying, perhaps, with Vict'ry on his Brow,
Wounded, or sick, or e'en I know not how.

55 Lost *Mons*, the worthy Cause, and *British* Isle,
Forgive the Queen, that on Your Loss could smile;
Th' unwelcome News no sooner reach'd my Ear,
But straight I knew my *Henric* was not there:
No Towns are ever lost when he's too near.
60 You often come indeed too near Your Foes,
Your Breast too oft, too daringly expose;
You are too much a Conquerour for me,
I love You better than the Victory:
Yet I love Conquest, and can wish it too;
65 But why, methinks, must all be done by You?
Let others take the Danger; Let them stake
Their Lives, and let them *Henric*'s Glory take ---
Ha! What! ---- What would my fondling Passion do?
Oh, that it might be Great! as Great as now;
70 And yet incapable to wrong You too!

What's State, Respect, or what's a Crown to me?
Poor Joys! ---- How poor's a Queen depriv'd of Thee?
My very Dreams, the softest Bliss I knew,
My Thoughts, my Dreams, are still employ'd with
You,
75 Pleasing at first, now serve t'afflict me too.
My Bed I with sad Apprehensions shake,
With sudden Shrieks and Cries I start, and wake:
Attendants and officious Guards rush in,
When nothing but her *Henric* wants the Queen;
80 Shipwrack'd with Doubts, and almost sunk by fear,
Least swelling *Neptune* so embrace my Dear,
E'en You that took of me so little Care:

372

You that expos'd in a small Shallop lay,
Defying *Boreas* and a Raging Sea;
85 By cruel, deadly Sheets of Ice enclos'd;
Hunger, and bold obtruding Death oppos'd:
Yet Your Prophetic Valour could inspire
Your glowing Breast with such Heroic Fire;
The Shell, that *Caesar and his Fortunes* bore,
90 Was destin'd to attain, and reach'd the Shore;
Can You suppose with me to perish more?

Cease not to fear (said You) but blush to think,
That *Henric and his Fortunes* here must sink.
Ye Gods!---- The Gods were with Thee, and they saw:
95 These words were follow'd with a sudden Thaw:
And kind Heav'n cast Thee on thy Native Shore,
When nothing less was hop'd, You wish'd no more.

If I, of more cow'rdly Sex, had seen
What mighty Perils shut my *Henric* in;
100 Away had flown my hasty tim'rous Soul:
Nor could that Prophecie, so spoke, recall
My fleeting Breath, restoring as it was,
'T had been, to dying me, of little Force.
The fearful Tale, e'en while I knew You safe,
105 A strange cold shivering to my Senses gave,
Methought, and wrapt me in a chilly Wave.
Be kind, my Love, make haste--- Be rather slow,
And be my kinder Love in being so.
Be kind, and cautious, let me not sustain
110 Those Dyings, and those Agonies again.
While I implore soft Winds, entreat the Sea
To be as gentle as my Sighs for Thee,
And careful as *Maria*'s Thoughts can be;
Safe as Thy Arms, serene as those You give
115 Your great Protection to, and wish to live.
Live you *Maria*'s, she that lives for You.
All Yours---- Adieu, my Royal Love, Adieu.

From *Maria to Henric And Henric to Maria: Or, The Queen to the King In Holland And His Majesty's Answer, Two Heroical Epistles In Imitation of the Stile and Manner of Ovid. Written by a Young Lady.* London: Printed for *Joseph Knight,* at the *Pope*'s *Head,* in the Lower Walk of the *New Exchange*, 1691.

Title: Mary Stuart (1662-1694), the daughter of James II, was married in 1677 to her Dutch cousin, William, Prince of Orange (1650-1702). After the deposition of James II they were summoned to England from Holland and crowned in 1689.

1-6 Cf. Anne Wharton, 'Penelope to Ulysses', 1-13 (see p.291).

2 *Henric's absent*: William left for Holland on 6 January 1691, returned in mid-April, only to depart again on 1 May, and remain until 18 October.

5-6 Cf. Mary to William in Ireland, 19 June 1690:

> You will be weary of seeing every day a letter from me, it may be; yet being apt to flatter myself, I will hope you will be as willing to read as I to write. And indeed it is the only comfort I have in this world, besides that of trust in God. I have nothing to say to you at present that is worth writing, and I think it unreasonable to trouble you with my grief, which I must continue while you are absent, though I trust every post to hear some good news or other from you; therefore I shall make this very short,...I cannot enough thank God for your being so well past the dangers of the sea; I beseech him in his mercy still to preserve you so, and send us once more a happy meeting upon earth. I long to hear again from you how the air of Ireland agrees with you, for I must own I am not without my fears for that, loving you so entirely as I do, and shall till death. (Dalrymple, II, ii, 114)

29 *Gallia*: France
44 *Belgia*: Belgium
55 *Mons*: in mid-March, Louis XIV caught William and his allies off guard by attacking Mons. William hurried to Halle to assemble an army, but discovered that Spain had not sent its promised military assistance. On 9 April Mons capitulated to the French, as William stood helpless.
83 *shallop*: a small boat or 'cockleshell'. The entry in Queen Mary's memoirs dated 1691 begins:

> This year began with preparations for the kings journey into Holland as the last ended. The 6th day he went away, but came back the 9th, having been no further then Canterbury; the 16th he went for good, and tho' I lookt on the journey, as it was in it self, only going about necessary bussiness, yet considering the danger of the seas at the time of the year and season so far advanced that I feard he might go to the campaign and not come back at all, I was more troubled to part with him then I could expect. My fears were prophetick. For he was not only in great danger by his impatience to be a shore, which made him expose himself in a little boat where he was all night, tho' by the mercy of God escaped only with a cold, but when he was ready to come away, was called to the army to relieve Mons then beseiged; where tho' he could not get things together time enough to venture or hazard his person, yet the endeavours he used made me almost out of my wits for fear, coming so unexpected. For the yachts were gone for him, and I in daily expectation of seeing him, when this news came. It pleased God by that surprise to shew me my own weackness; and such a mortification as the kings seeing the town taken before his face was necessary to humble us all. (Doebner, 35)

84 *Boreas*: the north wind
89 *Caesar*: William; cf. *Mercurius Reformatus: or the New Observator*, 31 January 1691, where Dr James Welwood (1652-1727), superintendent of the surgeons of the fleet, compares the King's voyage to Holland to Caesar's 'passage betwixt *Otranto* and *Brundusium*':

To be amidst an Ocean of Ice, in a small Shalop, open to the Cold, and to all the Inconveniencs [sic] of the Weather, without view of Land, and not knowing where to find it; and all this accompanied with the horror of a dark Night; to be expos'd at once to die for Hunger, to perish for Cold, to be drown'd at every stroak his small Pinnace made against the Ice, and to be in danger of being taken Prisoner by every wandering Pyrate, and a Prisoner with whom the Fate of so great a part of the World was to be enchain'd...

Narcissus Luttrell recorded the event as early as 26 January, saying that the Queen had received 'an expresse' about the King's safe arrival in Holland after he and his men had been lost in a fog among great flakes of ice 'in a small chaloup or two' (II, 165).

98 *of more cow'rdly Sex*: cf. Mary to William in Ireland, July 1, 1690:

I am so little afraid, that I begin to fear I have not sense enough to apprehend the danger; for whether it threatens Ireland, or this place, to me 'tis much at one, as to the fear; for as much a coward as you think me, I fear more for your dear person than my poor carcass. I know who is most necessary in the world. What I fear most at present is not hearing from you. Love me whatever happens, and be assured I am ever intirely yours till death. (Dalrymple, II, Part II, 118)

111-115 In *An Ode, Occasion'd by the Death Of Her Sacred Majesty. By a Young Lady*, the spirit of Britannia, rather than 'entreating', commands the Nereids to protect William:

> I charge you *Nymphs*, when he shall please,
> On naked Shoulders rock him o're these Seas,
>   Secure with Pomp and Ease;
>   Ah then Beware,
>   For then my single All's your care.
> Bear him from each proud wave, each ruining shelf,
> Through Paths by none more trac'd than by my self; (11)

The ode was one of many poems on the death of Queen Mary, 28 December 1694. Similarities in tone and diction suggest that the two poems may be by the same 'Young Lady'.

ALICIA D'ANVERS

According to manuscript notes in Anthony à Wood's copy of *Academia* (Bod. Wood 517, Pamphlet 6), Alicia D'Anvers was the daughter of Samuel Clarke, a 'sometimes superior Beadle of Law' in Oxfordshire, and the wife of Knightley Danvers, a 'sometimes scholar of Trinity College'. Clarke, originally from Brackley, Northamptonshire, also served the University as its first *architypographus* or director of printing. He was celebrated for his knowledge of Hebrew, Arabic, Farsi and Latin, and for his part in helping to prepare Brian Walton's polyglot Bible (1657); his portrait, donated by his daughter, is in the Bodleian Library (Poole, 55). Of his marriage nothing is known except that a daughter Alice was christened in Holy Cross Church at Holywell on 5 January 1668. Clarke died barely two years later.

Knightley Danvers (b.1670) was the son of Daniel Danvers, an Oxford graduate practising as a physician in Banbury. He matriculated at Oxford in 1685, studied law at the Inner Temple, and was admitted to the Bar in 1696. Alicia Clarke married him some time before 3 December 1690 when her first publication was licensed with the name 'M$^{rs.}$ D'Anvers'.

Alicia D'Anvers's burial 'in woollen' as required by the Act passed in 1666 for the encouragement of the wool-trade was certified at Holywell Parish on 19 July 1725 by Mary Wilkinson. Her husband became deputy recorder of Northamptonshire where he died in 1740.

Alicia D'Anvers's first known work is *A Poem upon His Sacred Majesty, His Voyage for Holland: By Way of a Dialogue Between Belgia and Britannia*, published in London by Thomas Bever in 1691 and dedicated to Queen Mary. It is written with the aim of enlisting support for William's policies as presented to the anti-French allies at a meeting at The Hague in January 1691 and is as dull as might be expected. Nothing is known of how or why such a commission should have been executed by Alicia D'Anvers; as it is, there can be no doubt that she existed and had some claim to be a poet, for royal dedications were not to be trifled with.

It is the more surprising then that D'Anvers's next poem should be a burlesque caricaturing university life at Oxford. The narrator of *Academia: Or the Humours Of The University of Oxford* is a town servant, who uses the case of the country bumpkin, John Blunder, to attack the current state of the university and the indiscipline, coarseness and dissipation of those *in statu pupillari*. D'Anvers's intimate knowledge of the university community, its customs,

ALICIA D'ANVERS

usages and tricks of nomenclature is displayed in her 1411 lines of robust colloquial iambic tetrameters, called hudibrastics. The form, popularised by Samuel Butler's *Hudibras* (1663-1678), is characterised by comic feminine rhymes, and the use of slang and dialect words in contriving them. In 1693 D'Anvers published *The Oxford-Act: A Poem*, another burlesque dealing with the four days of ceremonial that accompanied the presentation of degree candidates' theses. Her narrator in this poem assumes the pose of a pilgrim to a holy shrine, where the most arcane and solemn ritual is a lecture on male midwifery.

To the University

Hail peaceful Shade, whose sacred verdant side
Bold *Thamesis* salutes, hail Noble Tide;
Hail *Learning's* Mother, hail *Great Brittains* Pride.
Hail to thy lovely Groves, and Bowers, wherein
5 Thy Heav'n begotten Darlings sit, and sing;
Thy *First-born* Sons, who shall in After-Story
Share thy loud Fame, as now they bring thee Glory.

Arriv'd at such a rich Maturity,
Those who spell Man so well, would blush to be
10 Took at the Mothers Breast, or Nurses Knee;
Much more in filth to wallow Shoulder high,
In *Tears*, till his kind Nurse had laid him dry.

Actions that give no blush of Guilt, or Shame,
To those so young, that yet they want a Name,
15 (I've heard that Brute, and Infant are the same.)
Then beauteous Matron, frown not on me for't.
Tho at the triflings of your younger sort,
I smile so much; since all I hope to do,
Is but to raise your Smiles, and others too,
20 And please my self, if pardon'd first by you.

From the introductory address from *Academia: Or, The Humours Of The University of Oxford. In Burlesque Verse. By Mrs. Alicia D'Anvers.* London: Printed and sold by Randal Taylor near Stationers Hall, 1691. *Academia* was reissued anonymously by J. Morphew in 1716. The notes to Wood's copy say the poem 'First app[ea]red to sale at Oxon. 14. Mar. 1690 [Old Style]'.
1 *Hail peaceful Shade*: D'Anvers's beginning, mimicking the epic invocation and quickly collapsing into bathos, is typical of the

377

speeches of the *terrae filii* ('bastards') of the Oxford Act and the 'prevaricators' of Trinity College, Dublin and Cambridge *Tripos*. Since the sixteenth century all three universities had by statute included among their graduation ceremonies the appearance of an academic jester who, for the benefit of the audience (particularly townspeople and 'the ladies') broke the monotony of the formal Latin disputations presented publicly at final examinations with outrageous travesties of them and mockery of the university system. The tradition endured at Oxford even during the Interregnum; Alicia D'Anvers's father-in-law was *terrae filius* in 1657 (Clark, II, 563). By the Restoration the speeches had begun to resemble comic theatre and were often written by a committee of undergraduates. Few of these speeches survive because university authorities in the late seventeenth century sought to protect themselves by demanding copies either before or after the performance; the authors, who were sometimes expelled for their writing, would therefore try to keep evidence to a minimum by keeping only one script and relying heavily upon improvisation.

2 *Thamesis*: the Thames

From *Academia: Or, the Humours Of The University of Oxford*.

     Now being arrived at his *Colledge*,
60   The place of *Learning*, and of *Knowledge*,
     A while he'll leer about, and snivel ye,
     And doff his Hat to all most civilly,
     Being told at home that a shame Face too,
     Was a great sign he had some *Grace* too,
65   He'l speak to none, alas! for he's
     Amaz'd at every Man he sees:
     May-hap this lasts a *Week*, or two,
     Till some *Scab* laughs him out on't, so
     That when most you'd expect his mending,
70   His Breeding's ended, and not ending:
     Now he dares walk abroad, and dare ye,
     Hat on, in People *Faces* stare ye,
     Thinks what a *Fool* he was before, to
     Pull off his Hat, which he'd no more do;
75   But that the *Devil* shites *Disasters*,
     So that he's forc'd to cap the *Masters*,
     He might have nail'd it to his *Head*, else,
     And wore it *Night*, and *Day* a *Bed*, else,

And then de'e see, for I'de have you mind it,
80   He had always known where to find it;

59 The speaker is a town servant sneering at the antics of the newly
arrived scholar John Blunder.
68 *Scab*: rascal or scoundrel
76 *cap the Masters*: Oxford slang for doffing one's cap to senior
members of the University.

135   The next, who 'as leave to domineer,
Adds Gentleman to Commoner,
Most dearly tender'd by his Mother,
Who loves him better than his Brother;
So she at home, a good while keeps him,
140   In White-broath, and Canary steeps him,
And tho his Noddle's somewhat empty,
His Guts are stuft with Sweet-meats plent[y]:
Madam's most sadly tosticated,
Knowing her Boy but empty-pated,
145   Lest the soft *Squire might starved be*,
When e're he's sent to th' *Versity*;
Which to prevent, and to befriend him,
A Pye, or Cake, she'll quickly send him,
Directed for her loving Son,
150   *Living i'th Colledge in* Oxford *Town;*
Charging her Man to let him know,
That they're all well, and hope he's so:
But what his Mother sent up with him,
Being much more than now she gives him;
155   And all consum'd; he thinks it best
To hide, and eat by himself the rest:
His will at home (Sir,) always having,
But made his Stomach, the more craving;
May hap they'd twenty hundred *Dishes*,
160   And twenty thousand sort of *Fishes*,
Of which, when but a little Elf,
He'd eat the greatest part himself;
De'e think then 'twould not make the *young Lad*
At a *Three half pence* Meat become *sad*,
165   Which at the *Colledge*, you must know, Man's
No more, nor less; than one *Boys* Commons?
And then, they make a hideous clutter
For a *Farth'n Drink, Bread, Cheese*, or *Butter*;

And would that pay, now, in your thinking,
170   For washing of the *Pot* they drink in?
Yet for all this, his *Tutor* cryes ye,
Sufficient 'tis, and may suffice ye;
Knowing from being *bred a Schollar*,
Much *eating* breeds both *Flegm*, and *Coller*,
175   Much *praying* him, does much advise it,
If he loves *Learning*, to despise it:
Glutt'ony (thinks *Soph*,) who e're abhorr'd it,
That had wherewith, and could afford it?
Tho' like a *Log* he stands, he's thinking,
180   He lives by *eating*, and by *drinking*,
And finds it so unreasonable,
He mayn't *eat* all that comes to Table;

136 *Adds Gentleman to Commoner*: gentlemen commoners were distinguished from ordinary commoners in seventeenth-century Oxford by special dress, separate dining tables and academic immunities; they also paid higher fees. The gentleman commoner follows the 'Young *Farmer*, or young *Farrier*' and the 'Commoner' in the narrator's catalogue of Oxford scholars.
140 *White-broath*: pot liquor
Canary: a light, sweet wine from the Canary Islands
143 *tosticated*: originally a mispronunciation of 'intoxicated', later used to mean tossed about, distracted, perplexed; a common dialect term used from West Yorkshire to Somersetshire. Alicia D'Anvers's use of this term is cited in the *OED*.
174 *Flegm, and Coller*: two of the four humours; phlegm was believed to cause apathy, choler or bile, irascibility.
177 *Soph*: abbreviation for 'Sophister', a student in his second or third year. Alicia D'Anvers's use is cited in the *OED*.

427   I ask'd a *young Youth* what it mean'd,
That all them *Conjuring Books are chain'd*:
Hoa said they being full of *Cunning*,
430   It seems would else have *been for running,   * Or Stolen.
Before they had them *Chains*, they say,
A number of them run away.
There's such an *Oceant* still, I wonder'd,
How they could miss a *thousand hunder'd*.
435   But that indeed again is something,
They can know all things by the *round thing*.

As I went on, the *Folk that reads,   * students disturbed.

Would many times *pop up their Heads*.
And douck 'um down (may hap) again,
440 And these are call'd the Learned Men.
And look for all the World as frighted,
But were I to be *hang'd, or knighted*,
I can't imagine what mought ail'd 'um,
For could they think one wou'd a *steal'd 'um;*
445 Well, by and by, there's one comes to me,
I thought the Fellow might have knew me,
Hoa said, I must not make a *stomping*,
And that it was no place to *jump* in;
Whop Sir, thought I, and what ado's here,
450 About the Nails that in ones Shoes are;
Hoa told me that the Men were earning,
A world of something by their Learning,
And that a Noise might put them out,
So that they ne're could bring't about.

427 *I ask'd a young Youth*: John Blunder is telling his story 'Of where,
and how, and what hea'd seen, / And in what Colleges hea'd been'
(ll.277-278) to the servants at home. Here, he is loose in Duke
Humfrey's Library, a part of the Bodleian.
428 *Conjuring Books*: in l.385 'Conjuring' is side-noted as '*Astronomy*';
chain'd: When Thomas Bodley built the new library for Oxford
students in 1597, unlabelled books and manuscript volumes on the
open shelves were fastened to hanging chains that were connected
to rods locked to the bookcases; lists of the book titles were posted at
the end of each bookcase (Jeaffreson, II, 188).
436 *round thing*: a globe

There's some are *fat*, and some are *lean*,
And some are *Boys* and some are *Men*,
But what I'me sure will make you stare,
660 They all stand in their **Shirts* I swear;   * surplioce.
Here *Susan* blush'd, and *John* beseeches,
To tell, if these all wore no *Breeches*.
Cries *John*, that one can hardly know,
They wear their *Linnen* things so low;
665 Each one when they come in, stand still,
Bowing, and wrigling at the Sill;
I look'd a while, and mark'd one *Noddy*,
*Something he bow'd to, but no *Body*,   * The Altar
For these and other things as *apish*,

381

670   The *Town-folks* term the *Scollards* Papish;
       The *Organs* set up with a *ding*,
       The *White-men* roar, and *White-Boys* sing,
       *Rum, Rum,*the *Organs* go, and *zlid,*
       Sometimes they *squeek* out like a *Pig,*
675   Then *gobble* like a *Turky Hen,*
       And then to *Rum, Rum, Rum* again:
       What with the *Organs, Men,* and *Boys,*
       It makes ye up a *dismal Noise;*
       All being over as I wiss,
680   Out come they like a *Flock* of *Geese.*

657 *There's some are fat*: John Blunder is describing a college chapel service.
660 *surplioce*: on holy days members of a college wore ankle-length white surplices in chapel.
661 *Susan*: one of the servants at John Blunder's home
666 *Sill*: a doorstep
667 *Noddy*: fool
672 *White-men... White-Boys*: choristers. D'Anvers's use is cited in the *OED*.
673 *zlid*: a contraction of 'God's life'
679 *I wiss*: a corruption of the middle English adverb 'iwisse', meaning certainly. It came to mean 'I know', having been confused with 'I wit'.

ELIZABETH SINGER

Elizabeth Singer was born in 1674, the eldest of three daughters of a dissenting minister, Walter Singer, and Elizabeth Portnell. Her mother died when Elizabeth was about sixteen, and Singer moved his family from Ilchester in Somersetshire to Agford, near Frome, where his daughter spent most of her life. She began to write poetry at twelve and at twenty was brought to the notice of Henry Thynne, son of Viscount Weymouth, who instructed her in French and Italian. The non-conformist bishop, Thomas Ken, resident chaplain at Longleat, gave her her first poetic commission, charging her to provide a paraphrase of Job 38 (T. Rowe, I, xvii).

A curious story is told of her relationship with one of her sisters, who was immoderately fond of her. Thought to be on her deathbed, Elizabeth confessed to her sister that she was not certain of her salvation, whereupon her sister was thrown into such grief that she became ill and died (Stecher, *passim*).

At nineteen, of her own accord and without her father's knowledge, Singer began a correspondence with John Dunton, bookseller and founder of the Athenian Society. From October 1693 to January 1696, she was the principal contributor of verses to *The Athenian Mercury* (1691-1697), a journal which responded to anonymous inquiries on a wide range of subjects. In 1696, John Dunton, who called her 'the Pindarick Lady' and the 'richest genius of her sex', published *Poems on Several Occasions by Philomela*. The preface, written by an Elizabeth Johnson, is remarkable for its defence of women, 'over-rul'd by the *Tyranny* of the *Prouder Sex*'. Johnson claims that she and Dunton ('Philaret') were responsible for persuading Singer, 'whose Name had been prefix'd, had not her own *Modesty* absolutely forbidden it', to publish.

Dunton conducted a Platonic flirtation with 'Philomela'; within weeks of the death of his wife Elizabeth Annesley or 'Iris' in 1697, he proposed to Singer and was rejected (Dunton, *Athenianism*, 48). The Reverend Benjamin Colman was an acknowledged suitor, favoured by The Reverend Singer ('Argos'), but he returned to Boston, Massachusetts, in 1699 without entering into any engagement. Isaac Watts and Matthew Prior were also admirers. In 1710, Singer married Thomas Rowe, thirteen years younger than she, with whom she lived in London until his death from tuberculosis in 1715. Her passionate elegy, 'On the Death of Mr. Thomas Rowe', was the inspiration of Pope's *Eloisa to Abelard*. She never remarried, retiring to Frome where she lived with her father (both sisters having died in their youth) until his death in 1719.

Mrs Rowe spent the rest of her life on the estate she had inherited from her father, where she corresponded with the literary figures of the day and enjoyed a widespread reputation as a writer of exemplary piety and virtue. Her devotional prose and verse remained popular, particularly in America and Germany, well into the nineteenth century. She died of apoplexy on 20 February 1737 and is buried alongside her father in Frome.

Most of Singer's career belongs to the eighteenth century. We are here concerned only with her juvenile production.

Cant. 5. 6 &c.

Oh! How his *Pointed Language*, like a Dart,
Sticks to the *softest Fibres* of my Heart,
Quite through my Soul the charming Accents slide,
That from his Life inspiring Portals glide;
5 And whilst I the inchanting sound admire,
My melting Vitals in a Trance expire.
Oh Son of *Venus*, Mourn thy baffled Arts,
For I defye the proudest of thy Darts:
Undazled now, *I* thy weak Taper View,
10 And find no fatal influence accrue;
Nor would *fond Child* thy feebler Lamp appear,
Should my bright *Sun* deign to approach more near;
Canst thou his Rival then pretend to prove?
Thou a false Idol, he the God of Love;
15 Lovely beyond Conception, he is all
Reason, or Fancy amiable call,
All that the most exerted thoughts can reach,
When sublimated to its utmost stretch.
Oh! altogether Charming, why in thee
20 Do the vain World no Form or Beauty see?
Why do they Idolize a dusty clod,
And yet refuse their Homage to a God?
Why from a *beautious* flowing Fountain turn,
For the Dead Puddle of a narrow *Urn*?
25 Oh Carnal Madness! sure we falsly call
So dull a thing as Man is, rational;
Alas, my shining Love, what can there be
On Earth so splendid to *out-glitter thee?*
In whom the brightness of a God-head Shines,
30 With all its lovely and endearing Lines;
Thee with whose sight Mortallity once blest,

Would throw off its dark Veil to be possest;
Then altogether Lovely, why in thee
Do the vain World no Form or Beauty see.

From *The Athenian Mercury*, Vol.17, No.23, Tuesday, 18 June 1695. This poem and four others compose the entire publication; as Dunton explained:

We thought we could not more oblige our *Readers* than by Printing *all together* in one *Mercury*, the following Poems, they being all written by the ingenious *Pindarick Lady*, and printed *Verbatim*, as we receiv'd 'em from her.

All were included in *Poems On Several Occasions. Written By Philomela*. London, Printed for John Dunton at the Raven in Jewen-street, 1696, without significant changes. Dunton almost certainly edited the poems to some extent, despite his disclaimer. The 'Life' of Mrs Rowe prefaced to *The Miscellaneous Works in Prose and Verse Of Mrs. Elizabeth Singer Rowe. The Greater part now first published, by her order, from her original manuscripts* (1739), edited by her brother-in-law, Theophilus Rowe, noticeably omits any mention of Dunton or *The Athenian Mercury*, revealing only that the 1696 *Poems on Several Occasions* 'was published at the desire of two of her friends' (xv-xvi). Clearly it was the intention of Rowe's editor, and perhaps Rowe herself, to play down if not to belie her earlier career. None of the poems in *The Athenian Mercury* or in *Poems on Several Occasions* appears in the 1739 *Works*, although many had been available earlier in the century through *The Athenian Oracle*, a republication of most of the material in *The Athenian Mercury* (four volumes in various editions from 1703 to 1728) and through *A Collection of Divine Hymns and Poems on Several Occasions* (1709).

Title: Canticles, i.e. Song of Solomon 5:6: 'I opened to my beloved; but my beloved had withdrawn himself, and was gone: my soul failed when he spake: I sought him, but I could not find him; I called him, but he gave me no answer.' In the fifth chapter of the Song of Solomon, a male lover calls out to the speaker. She rises to 'open to' him and finds him gone (verses 1-6). Seeking him 'about the city', she is accosted by watchmen (verse 7). She then engages in a dialogue with the 'daughters of Jerusalem' in which she describes her beloved's physical beauty (verses 8-16). Biblical commentaries explicate this chapter as Christ calling to the Church, the Church hearing his voice, confessing her nakedness and praising Christ, her bridegroom. The Song of Solomon, like the Psalms, was a popular text for seventeenth-century imitations, explications and expositions. In his preface to Mrs Rowe's *Devout Exercises of the Heart* (1738), Isaac Watts excuses her 'pathetick and tender Expressions' which 'may be perversely profaned by an unholy Construction' by noting:

it was much the Fashion, even among some Divines of Eminence in former years, to express the Fervours of devout Love of our Savior in the Style of the *Song of Solomon*...

and by claiming that 'early Impressions of Piety [were] made on [Singer's] Heart by devout Writings of this Kind' (xii-xiii).

1-6 Cf. 'Eliza', 'The Dart' (see p.142). Three days after the first publication of Singer's poetry in *The Athenian Mercury*, 'the Poetical Lady' requested a list of 'Books of Poetry' for 'one that's Young' (24 October 1693). For devotional verse, along with works by Cowley, Sir John Davies, Herbert, Crashaw and Milton, the Athenians recommended George Sandys's and Samuel Woodford's versions of the Psalms, and the paraphrase of the Canticles by John Lloyd (1672-1717), Vicar of Holy Rood, Southampton. Lloyd's *Shir-ha-shirim, or, The Song of Songs* (1682), like Singer's poem, expands on 'my soul failed when he spake':

> Oh! how I trembling stood!
> No tongue can tell the smart
> That seiz'd my Heart
> Under the swift recoylment of the blood. (20)

For other paraphrases by women of Canticles 5:6 see An Collins, 'A Song expressing their happiness who have Communion with Christ' and Anna Trapnel, *Voice for the King of Saints and Nations* (1658) more or less *passim*.

4 *Portals*: figuratively, the mouth

7-34 *Son of Venus*: Eros, or Cupid. In the course of her career, Singer produced four paraphrases of this chapter, the other three adhering more closely to the Biblical text. Unlike other imitations of Canticles 5, including her own, Singer's here substitutes apostrophes to Cupid (7-18) and Christ (19-34) for the dialogue between the speaker and the daughters of Jerusalem (verses 8-16) and omits the attack by the night watch altogether (verse 7), replacing vivid description of the beloved's person, as can be found in 'Eliza', 'The Lover' (see p.146), with rhetorical questions on the blindness of the 'vain World' and exhortations against 'Carnal Madness'. Of her four imitations, it is the least likely to be 'perversely profaned by an unholy Construction'. In her earliest imitation, as in the two late versions, Singer does provide a sensuous depiction of the beloved's attributes. She interprets verse 13, 'His cheeks are as a bed of spices, as sweet flowers: his lips like lillies, dropping sweet smelling myrrh' as:

> His rosy *Cheeks* of such a *lucent Dy*,
> As *Sol* ne're *gilded* on the *morning Sky*...
> He *breaths* more *sweetness* than the *Infant morn*,
> When *heavenly Dews* the *flowery Plains* adorn.
> The fragrant *Drops* of rich *Arabian Gumes*,
> Burnt on the *Altar* yield not such *Perfumes*. (*The Athenian Mercury*, 5 June 1694; *Poems on Several Occasions* (1696), Part 1, 51)

9-12 Singer uses the proverbial expression, 'to set forth the sun with a candle', in contrasting Eros's 'weak taper', earthly love, to the 'bright *Sun*' of Christ; cf. Singer, 'A Farewell to Love', 46 (see p.394), and Piers, 'To my much esteemed Friend on her Play call'd

Fatal-Friendship', 10 (see p.447).

Fatal-Friendship', 10 (see p.447).

A Pindarick, to the Athenian Society.

I

I've toucht *each string*, each muse I have invok't,
    Yet still the mighty theam,
    Copes my unequal praise;
    Perhaps, the *God of Numbers* is provok't.
5   I grasp a Subject fit for none but him,
Or *Drydens* sweeter lays;
Dryden! A name I ne're could yet rehearse,
But straight my thoughts *were all transform'd to verse.*

II

And now methinks I rise;
10   But still the *lofty subject* baulks my flight,
And still my *muse* despairs to do great *Athens* right;
Yet take the *Zealous Tribute* which I bring,
The early products of a Female muse;
Untill *the God*, into my breast shall *mightier thoughts*
                       infuse.
15 When I with more Command, and *prouder voice* shall
                       sing;
But how shall I describe the matchless men?
I'me lost in the *bright labirinth* agen.

III

When the *lewd age*, as Ignorant as accurst,
Arriv'd in vice and error to the worst,
20 And like *Astrea* banisht from the stage,
Virtue and Truth were ready *stretcht for flight*;
Their numerous foes,
Scarce one of eithers Champions ventur'd to oppose;
Scarce one *brave mind,* durst openly engage,
25 To do them right.
Till prompted with a Generous rage;
You cop't with all th' abuses of the age;
Unmaskt and *challeng'd* its abhorred crimes,
Nor fear'd to *lash* the darling vices of the times.

IV

30 *Successfully go on,*
T' inform and bless mankind as you've begun,
Till like your selves they see;
The frantick world's imagin'd Joys to be,

Unmanly, sensual and effemenate,
35 Till they with such exalted thoughts possest;
As you've inspir'd into my *willing Breast,*
Are *charm'd*, like me, from the impending fate.

V

For ah! *Forgive me Heaven*, I blush to say't,
I with the vulgar world thought *Irreligion great,*
40 *Tho fine my breeding, and my Notions high;*
Tho train'd in the *bright* tracts of strictest piety,
I' like my *splendid tempters* soon grew vain,
And laid my slighted innocense aside;
Yet oft my nobler thoughts I have bely'd,
45 And to be ill was *even reduc'd to feign.*

VI

Until by you,
With more Heroick sentiments inspir'd,
I turn'd and *stood* the vigorous torrent too,
And at my former *weak retreat admir'd;*
50 So much was I by your *example fir'd,*
So much the *heavenly form* did win:
Which to my eyes *you'd painted vertue in.*

VII

Oh, could my verse;
With *equal flights*, to after times rehearse,
55 Your *fame*: It should as bright and Death-less be;
As that immortal flame you've rais'd in me.
A flame which time:
And Death it self, wants power to controul,
Not more sublime,
60 Is the *divine composure of my Soul;*
A friendship so exalted and immense,
A *female breast* did ne're before commence.

From *The Athenian Mercury*, Vol.17, No.29, Tuesday, 9 July 1695.
The issues on the first Tuesday of every month were devoted
particularly to women. This poem and two others by Singer were
introduced with Dunton's usual eulogies:

All the *Poems* written by the ingenious *Pindarick Lady*, having a peculiar Delicacy of
Stile and Majesty of *Verse*, as does sufficiently distinguish 'em from all others, and we
having *gratified* many of our *Querists*, by inserting in our *Mercuries*, those *Poems* she
lately sent us, we are willing to oblige 'em once more with the *following Pindarick Poem*,
which we have here Printed word for word, as we this week receiv'd it from her.

The poem also appears in *Poems on Several Occasions* (1696), with a few minor variants. In the year of Mrs Rowe's death, Edmund Curll brought out a 'second edition' of the 1696 *Poems*, entitled *Philomela: or, Poems By Mrs. Elizabeth Singer [Now Rowe,]* (1737), calling attention to the rarity of the collection in his poem 'On Reprinting Philomela's Poems Forty Years after their first Publication', 'Philomela long Dead, / Now re-warbles her Throat, again lifts up her Head' [xix]. He prefaced the publication with a letter dated 30 August 1736 from Mrs Rowe to a Mr R—, thanking him for his concern for her character, and saying that she would not dispute Curll's right to print her poems, if he would make clear that he was moved by his own 'partiality' to her work, rather than her 'vanity' [xx]. According to the 'Life' prefixed to *Miscellaneous Works* (1739), Mrs Rowe felt 'guilt' and 'remorse' for the 'harmless gayeties of a youthful muse... aton'd for [by] more serious and instructive compositions':

> Tho' many of these poems are of the religious kind, and all of them consistent with the strictest regard to the rules of virtue, yet some things in them gave her no little uneasiness in advanced life. To a mind that had so entirely subdued its passions, or devoted them to the honour of its maker, and indued with the tenderest *moral sense*, what she could not absolutely approve, appear'd unpardonable; and, not satisfied to have done nothing that injur'd the sacred cause of virtue, she was displeas'd with her self for having writ any thing that did not directly promote it. (xvi-xvii)

In a fifteen-page dedication to Pope, in which he explained the history of the Athenian Society and related the story of Mrs Rowe's marriage, Curll said of her '*First-Fruits*': 'They are faithfully Re-printed from the Copy published in 1696, except a little *Reformation* in the *Numbers* of some of them, and the *Addition* of a few *later* Compositions substituted in the Room of *others*, which the Writer's *friends* were desirous of having omitted, as favouring of *Party-Reflection* and the *Heat* of *Youth*, since *cooled* by a stricter *judgment*...' (xvii). The imitation of Canticles 5 included in the present collection appears in Curll's publication with no significant alterations (19-20). Curll's 'reformations' of 'A Pindarick, to the Athenian Society' are listed below:

1 I've toucht each string / Each String I've touch'd, 1737   18 the / this 1737
38 For / But 1737   45 reduc'd / forc'd 1737

Title *the Athenian Society*: the name used by John Dunton and his fellow editors of *The Athenian Gazette*, later called *The Athenian Mercury* (1691-1697). The two other 'members' were Dunton's brothers-in-law, the Rev. Samuel Wesley (1662-1735), father of John Wesley, founder of the Methodist Church, and Richard Sault (1660?-1702), a mathematician. John Norris of Bemerton, the philosopher, also occasionally contributed. Dunton tried relentlessly to strengthen his association with Singer; the fifteenth volume of *The Athenian Mercury* was dedicated to 'the Pindarical Lady'. In that volume, on 10 November 1694, Dunton announced the projected publication of *The Challenge... Or, The Female War* (1697), inviting the 'Pindarick Lady', among other female contributors to

The Athenian Mercury, to 'come in *Volunteers* to this Litteral War, in which all the *Dresses*, *Customs*, *Honours* and *Priviledges*, &c. belonging to the Fair Sex, will be vigorously attackt' by male writers, the women responding in their sex's defence. Singer did not contribute to *The Challenge*; in the preface 'Philaret' expresses the hope that she, along with 'Madam *D'acier* of *France*, Madam *Daunoy* (Author of the *Travels into Spain*), the Lady *Manley*', and 'Madam *Pix*' would join 'Madam Godfrey' in contributing to an anticipated (but never published) second volume. The unknown 'Madam Godfrey' was author of many of the women's responses in *The Challenge*, since 'there were not enough of her own *Sex* came in to *help her*' (Sig. [A2^{v}-A3^{v}]). Seven years later, another collection of male–female correspondence, *The Athenian Spy: Discovering the Secret Letters Which were sent to the Athenian Society by the Most Ingenious Ladies of the Three kingdoms* (1704, 1709) was dedicated to Singer. Dunton used her real name and that of her good friend, Lady Weymouth, and asked that she 'be contented for once to sit at the upper end of the Table, and *Grace the Feast* tho you did not honour us so far as to be one of our Clubb' (Sig. A3^{v}). Singer is a prominent figure in Dunton's autobiography, *The Life and Errors of John Dunton* (1705), appearing as 'The Pindarick Lady in the *West*, *Alias Philomela*, *Alias*, *Madam Singer*' (245). The 'Life' in her *Miscellaneous Works* claims that her 'indifference to glory' and the 'modesty of her conduct' were such that she 'would not, indeed, so much as allow her name to be prefixed to any of [her works] except for some few poems in the earlier part of her life', locating the last poems identified as Singer's 'by her consent' in Jacob Tonson's *Poetical Miscellanies: the Fifth Part* (1704) (T. Rowe, I, lxix). In fact, Singer's name also appears in *A Collection of Divine Hymns and Poems on Several Occasions* (1709). After 1710, when she became Mrs Rowe, her name was not used in her publications, but her reputation as a pious writer was well established. By 1718 Dunton had gone too far in making use of the name of his favourite poet. He was sent a letter by a Mr J. W. demanding that he never use her name in print again (Dunton, 1818, xxix).

3 *Copes*: figuratively, closes up the mouth, makes silent, taken from the practice of sewing up the mouths of ferrets to prevent them from biting rabbits as they drive them from their warrens.

4 *God of Numbers*: Apollo

6 Cf. Elizabeth Thomas, 'The Dream. An Epistle to Mr. Dryden', (see p.435), and Lady Sarah Piers, 'Urania: The Divine Muse. On the Death of John Dryden, Esq.' (see p.448).

7 *rehearse*: mention

9-17 This stanza is quoted in *The Life and Errors of John Dunton* (1705) as one of the many panegyrics addressed to the Athenians by 'The *Pindarick Lady*', Defoe, Swift, Nahum Tate, and others (260).

20 *Astraea*: cf. 'A Pindarick To Mrs. Behn on her Poem on the Coronation' (see p.261). Singer may be referring to 'Astraea' Behn's

last years when she wrote mostly prose and poetry rather than plays, or to the myth of Astraea or to both. An anonymous poem prefaced to *Poems on Several Occasions* (1696) compares Singer, 'Known only by *Report*, and by her Works', to Behn and Philips: '*Sappho* and *Behn reform'd*, in thee revive, / In thee we see the *Chast Orinda* live'. Curll identifies the author as Richard Gwinnett, the betrothed of Elizabeth Thomas (see p.429) (*Philomela*, xiv).

27 *cop't*: contended with

27-29 A few months before this poem was published, on 8 January 1695, the Athenians called for 'a new *Face of things* in our *once virtuous* and *religious Island*. For the *Relaxation* of *Discipline* must needs cause a prodigious increase to all *Debauchery* and mischief...' Attributing this malaise to a neglect of the teaching of the Church of England and to corruption in the ecclesiastical courts, the Athenians found it 'no wonder... that some Gentlemen who care for no *Yoke*, but are for a *Virtuoso* sort of Religion, serve God or let it alone, shou'd be willing and earnest to get this *Rod burnt*, which one time or another may happen to make 'em *smart* for their *Lewdness*...'

38-45 Here Singer confesses to having once adopted the 'irreligion' of free-thinking, would-be Rod-burners. In his edition of Rowe's *Devout Exercises of the Heart*, Isaac Watts claimed that Rowe 'was never tempted away from our common Christianity into the fashionable Apostasies of the Age' [xx].

41 *strictest piety*: Singer was born into a family of dedicated Dissenters. Her father was imprisoned in Ilchester for non-conformity; there he met Elizabeth Portnell, who was visiting the prisoners, and later married her.

42 *splendid tempters*: possibly the libertine sceptics of the previous generation. A six-line address to Sir Charles Sedley (1639?-1701) in *Poems* (1696) declares her 'Infant-muse' unfit to praise his 'Coelestial lays' (Part I, 16). In the 24 October 1693 *Athenian Mercury* Singer suggested to the Athenians that a person responsible for plunging 'a Mind less fortified' into vice through the liberties taken in his discourse and behaviour was morally obliged to 'make 'em Restitution as far as they can by a stricter Example and Friendly Advice, and to let 'em know the Pleasure and Serenity inseparable from Virtue and Innocence'.

54 *Rehearse*: to describe at length

61-62 In his *Life and Errors* (1705) Dunton claims to have carried on a correspondence with 'Madam Singer' who was 'fully satisfy'd there was nothing but Innocence (or a *Platonick Courtship*) design'd'. According to Dunton, Singer wrote to his first wife in 1695, saying, 'you need not be Jealous' (265). Earlier in the book Dunton praised her talent and her person:

She knows the purity of our Tongue and converses with all the Briskness and the Gayety that she writes. Her *Stil* is noble and flowing, and her *Images* are very vivid and shining. To finish her Character, she's as Beautiful as she's Witty. (245)

To *Mutius*

I

A thousand great resolves, as great
   As reason could inspire,
I have commenc'd; but ah how soon
   The daring thoughts expire!

II

5   *Honour and Pride* I've often rouz'd,
   And bid 'em bravely stand,
But e're my charming foe appears
   They cowardly disband.

III

One dart from his *insulting eyes*,
10   Eyes I'm undone to meet,
Throws all my boasting faculties
   At the lov'd Tyrant's feet.

IV

In vain alas, 'tis all in vain,
   To struggle with my fate,
15   I'm sure I ne're shall cease to love,
   How much less can I hate!

V

Against relentless destiny,
   Hopeless to overcome,
Not *Sisiphus* more sadly strives
20   With his Eternal Doom.

From *The Athenian Mercury*, Vol.19, No.17, Tuesday, 24 December 1695.

To Mutius / The Female Passion 1696 & 1737   16 can I / can e'er I 1737

Title *Mutius*: the name suggests changeability. This may be another name for the 'faithless lover', Theron, of 'A Farewell to Love' and other poems in *Poems on Several Occasions* (1696), who is determined to become a military hero by following the 'dangerous steps of Honour'.
19 *Sisiphus*: legendary king of Corinth, eternally condemned to roll to the top of a hill a boulder which would, upon reaching the summit, roll down again.

A Farewel to Love.

Well, since in spight of all that Love can do,
The dangerous steps of Honour thoul't pursue,

I'll just grow Wise and Philosophick too:
I'll bid these tender silly things Farewel;
5 And Love, with thy great Antidote, expel:
I'll tread the same Ambitious Paths with thee,
And Glory too shall be my Deity.
And now I'll once release my Train of Fools,
In *Sheer good* Nature to the Loving Souls;
10 For Pity's-sake at last I'll set at rights
The vain conceits of the presumptuous Wights:
For tho' I shake off *Therons* Chains, yet he
Is all that e'er deserv'd a Smile from me.
But he's unjust, and false; and I a part
15 Would not accept, tho' of *a Monarch's* heart.
And therefore flattering hopes, and wishes too,
With all Loves soft Concomitants, adieu:
No more to its Imperious Yoke I'll bow;
Pride and Resentment fortify me now.
20 My Inclinations are reverst; nor can
I but abhor the Slavery of Man,
How e'er the *empty Lords of Nature boast*
O're me, their Fond Prerogative is lost:
For, Uncontroul'd, I thus resolve to rove,
25 And hear no more of *Hymen,* or of *Love*:
No more such Wild Fantastick things shall Charm:
My Breast; nor these Serener Thoughts Alarm.
No more for Farce; I'll make a Lover Creep,
And look as Scurvy as if he had bit a Sheep.
30 Nor with Dissembled Smiles indulge the Fops,
In pure Revenge to their Audacious hopes;
Tho' at my Feet a thousand Victims lay,
I'd proudly spurn the Whining Slaves away.
Deaf, as the Winds, or *Theron*, would I prove,
35 *And hear no more of* Hymen, *or of* Love.
Like bright *Diana* now I'll range the Woods,
And haunt the silent Shades and silver Floods.
I'll find out the Remotest Paths I can,
To shun th'Offensive, Hated Face of Man.
40 Where I'll Indulge my Liberty and Bliss,
And no *Endimyon* shall obtain a Kiss.
Now, *Cupid, Mourn;* the inlargement of my fate,
Thou'st lost a Politician in thy State:
I could have taught thee, hadst thou lost thy Arms,

45 To fool the World with more delusive Charms:
I could have made thy Taper burn more bright,
And wing thy Shafts with an unerring flight:
'Twas I directed that successful dart,
That found its way to the *Great* ------'s *heart*:
50 'Twas I that made the lovely *Fl-----n* bow,
A proud contemner of thy Laws, till now;
I sung thy Power, and Inspir'd the Swains,
Or thou hadst been no Deity on the Plains,
Yet think no more my freedom to surprize,
55 Which nothing can controul but *Theron*'s *eyes*;
And every flattering Smile, and every Grace,
With all the Air of that Bewitching Face,
My Pride and Resolutions may deface:
For from those eyes for ever I'll remove,
60 To shun the Sight of what I would not love:
And then, tho every *Cyclop* stretcht his Art,
To form the little angry God a dart,
I'll yet defy his rage to touch my Heart:
For tho my years compel me to disdain,
65 Of the false Charmer meanly to complain;
'Tis yet some satisfaction to my Mind,
I for his sake abandon all Mankind.
My Prouder Muse, to love no more a slave,
Shall Sing the Gust, the Fortunate and Brave,
70 And twine her *Promis'd Wreaths* for *Theron*'s *Brow*,
The *Hero*, not the faithless *Lover* now.
More Blooming Glories mayst thou still acquire,
And urge my Breast with a more active fire.
May New Successes wait upon thy Sword,
75 And deathless Honour all thy Acts record.
May all thou dost thy Character compleat;
And, like thy self, be loyal still and great:
Whilst in an equal Orb as free I move,
And think no more of *Hymen*, or of *Love*.

From *Poems on Several Occasions. Written by Philomela.* (1696) II, 65-69. This is one of more than twenty poems here printed for the first time.

8 And now I'll once / I'll therefore now 1737   9 Sheer / Pure 1737   10 at / to 1737
16 And therefore flattering / Therefore ye flatt'ring 1737   27 these / my 1737
28 Farce / Sport 1737   29 as Scurvy as if he had / like silly wretch who 1737

ELIZABETH SINGER

49 That / which 1737; ------/ *Strephon's* 1737   50 *Fl-----n* / *Flatman* 1737
59 For from / From whom 1737   64 me to / me, in 1737   69 Gust / Just 1737

2 A series of poems concluding *Poems On Several Occasions* express concern for a lover '*gone* the bright way that his honour directs him', soon to become a 'great *Hero* Victorious' (Part II, 44).

5 *thy great Antidote*: the speaker resolves to 'expel' Love, as if it were a poison, with the same 'Antidote' that her abandoning lover uses, ambition for 'Glory'.

11 *Wights*: a term for persons or human beings, implying commiseration.

23 *their Fond Prerogative is lost*: cf. Singer's early poem, 'To Celinda':

> I Can't, *Celinda*, say, I love,
>   But rather I adore,
> When with transported eyes I view
> Your *shining* merits o're....
> Then let's my dear *Celinda* thus
> Blest in our selves contemn
> The treacherous and deluding Arts,
> Of those *base things call'd men*. (*The Athenian Mercury*, 28 September, 1695;
>   *Poems on Several Occasions*, Part II, 27)

25 *Hymen*: god of marriage; cf. Katherine Philips, 'A marryd state affords but little ease' (see p.188).

36 *Diana*: goddess of the moon and chastity. Singer's predilection for celestial imagery is satirised, along with the 'artless sounds' of other women poets, in *Bibliotecha: a poem, Occasion'd by the sight of a modern library* (1712) by Thomas Newcomb (1682?-1765), chaplain to the second Duke of Richmond:

> Singer, by name and nature made
> For music and the rhyming trade,
> For her weak genius soar'd too high,
> And lost her Muse above the sky;
> A flaming sun, a radiant light,
> In every verse, distract our sight,
> Diffuse their dazzling beams from far,
> And not one line without a star!
> Through streams of light we seem to rove,
> And tread on shining orbs above. (rpt. Nichols, *A Select
>   Collection of Poems*, III, 44)

41 *Endimyon*: Endymion, most beautiful of all men, was loved by the moon, who descended every night to embrace him in his sleep.

50 *Fl-----n*: identified in the Curll edition as 'Flatman'. It seems unlikely that Thomas Flatman (1637-1688), poet and miniature painter, is meant, since Singer was only fourteen when he died; besides the context implies that this F-----n is female.

61 *Cyclop*: the Cyclops were assistants to Hephaestus, blacksmith to the gods.

69 *Gust*: misprint for 'Just'

DELARIVIERE MANLEY

Delariviere Manley was born in about 1670, probably in Jersey where her father, Sir Roger Manley, a Royalist who had been exiled in Holland for fourteen years, was then Lieutenant-Governor (Anderson, 263-264). Her mother, a Walloon gentlewoman, died in Manley's infancy (Koster, 1977, 107). With her two sisters she was put in the charge of a governess. In 1680 the family moved to Landguard Fort, Suffolk, where Manley developed an infatuation for a young officer and actor, James Carlisle. According to Manley's autobiographical novel, *The Adventures of Rivella* (1714), she was then sent to live in the household of a Huguenot minister 'on the other side of the Sea and Country, about Eighteen Miles farther from London' where a younger brother was boarding (26). There she was educated in French. Her hopes to become a Maid of Honour to Mary of Modena were dashed by the deposition of James II. Sir Roger, author of a history of the Rebellion, died at about this time, leaving her £200 and a share in his estate. Manley, with her younger sister, was left in the care of an older cousin, John Manley, who proceeded to deceive her into a false marriage, finally abandoning her and a son, John, born 24 June 1691, to return to his legal wife. Nothing further is known about their son, although it seems he was alive in 1698 (Morgan, 47).

Thereafter, Manley lived for a time with Barbara Villiers, Duchess of Cleveland, former mistress of Charles II, who accused her of intriguing with her son. Manley then moved in 1694 to Exeter in order to live more cheaply. By 1696 she was back in London where she produced two plays: *The Lost Lover*, a comedy acted at Drury Lane, and *The Royal Mischief*, acted at Lincoln's Inn Fields, as well as *Letters Written by Mrs. Manley*, supposedly written during her stagecoach ride to Exeter. During this period she was said to be the mistress of Sir Thomas Skipwith, manager of Drury Lane, and later, on her own admission, of John Tilly, warden of the Fleet. In the 1690s Manley was closely associated with fellow playwrights Catharine Trotter (later Cockburn) and Mary Pix, who supported each other in their theatrical efforts by writing epilogues and commendatory verses. The three were satirised in *The Female Wits* (acted 1696; published 1704). As Marsilia, 'a Poetess, that admires her own Works, and a great Lover of Flattery', Manley took the brunt of the satire; *The Royal Mischief* was parodied as a bombastic, ranting piece.

Soon after Manley organised the publication of *The Nine Muses* (1700), a collection of elegies on Dryden's death with contributions from Trotter, Pix and Sarah Fyge, she quarrelled with all three women. When Fyge testified against Manley and her friend Mary Thompson in their attempt to defraud the estate of Thompson's lover, Manley lost an anticipated £100. For this, she reported the lurid details of Fyge's divorce case in *The New Atalantis* (1709), taking the husband's side, and vilified Sarah as 'shockingly ugly' in *Memoirs of Europe* (I, 290). In *The New Atalantis* Pix is depicted as a 'very lazy' poet who solicited Manley to compose some pastoral elegies, promised to share the profits, and then 'defrauded the poor Labourer of [her] Hire' (I, 90). Catharine Trotter particularly seems to have been a favourite target. In *The Adventures of Rivella* (Rivella is a partial anagram of Delariviere), Trotter is presented as the former mistress of John Tilly ('Cleander'), 'Calista', who prudishly denies the relationship (64-66, 101-102). In *Memoirs of Europe* (1710) Manley describes the charms of Trotter ('Lais') as 'the Leavings of the Multitude'(I, 289). As 'Daphne' in *The New Atalantis* Trotter is seen as a religious hypocrite who has an unusual attachment for a fellow woman writer (see Piers, p.445). When Manley was chastised for her treatment of Trotter (by then Mrs Cockburn), she promised to apologise in person, but never actually did (Birch, I, xlvii-xlviii).

Although she wrote two more plays, *Almyna, or the Arabian Vow* (1707) and *Lucius, the First Christian King of Britain* (1717), with a prologue by Steele and an epilogue by Prior, Manley began to concentrate on scandalous *romans à clef* like *The Secret History of Queen Zarah and the Zarazians* (1705), *Memoirs of Europe*, dedicated to her friend Steele, and *The Lady's Pacquet of Letters* (1707, reissued in 1711 as *Court Intrigues*). Five months after the publication of her most famous work, *Secret Memoirs and Manners of Several Persons of Quality, of both Sexes. From the New Atalantis* (1709), Manley was arrested, along with the printer and publishers, and charged with publishing a scandalous work. For four months she steadfastly refused to reveal her sources, and her case was finally dropped.

Manley produced a number of political pamphlets in support of the Tory faction, established a periodical, *The Female Tatler*, and succeeded Swift as editor of *The Examiner* in 1711. In his *Journal to Stella*, 28 January 1712, he described her at this time as ill with dropsy and a sore leg, 'she is about forty, very homely, and very fat'. She was then spending winters with John Barber, an illiterate Tory printer and alderman (later Lord Mayor of London) and summers at her house in Oxfordshire.

In the last decade of her life Manley published more letters, a fictional work, *The Power of Love, in Seven Novels* (1720), and in the same year, some verses in Anthony Hammond's *New Miscellany of Original Poems*. In that collection, Manley presents herself primarily as a writer of prose in a poem to the Countess of Bristol:

> Long had my Mind, unknowing how to Soar,
> In humble Prose been train'd, nor aim'd at more:

Near the fam'd Sisters, never durst aspire
To Sound a Verse, or Touch the tuneful Lyre (1-4)

for which the Earl of Bristol paid her twenty guineas (Anderson, 276).

She died at Barber's printing-house on 11 July 1724 and was buried at St. Benet's, in London. Her will, dated 6 October 1723, described Manley as weak and daily decaying in strength and mentioned 'her much honoured friend, the Dean of St. Patrick, Dr. Swift' (*DNB*). In her typically immodest fashion, Manley had one of the characters in *The Adventures of Rivella* say of her: '[She is] the only Person of her Sex that knows how to *Live*' (120).

To the Author of Agnes de Castro.

Orinda, and the Fair *Astrea* gone,
Not one was found to fill the Vacant Throne:
Aspiring Man had quite regain'd the Sway,
Again had Taught us humbly to Obey;
5 Till you (Natures third start, in favour of our Kind)
With stronger Arms, their Empire have disjoyn'd,
And snatcht a Lawrel which they thought their Prize,
Thus Conqu'ror, with your Wit, as with your Eyes.
Fired by the bold Example, I would try
10 To turn our Sexes weaker Destiny.
O! How I long in the Poetick Race,
To loose the Reins, and give their Glory Chase;
For thus Encourag'd, and thus led by you,
Methinks we might more Crowns than theirs Subdue.
Dela Manley.

From *Agnes de Castro, A Tragedy. As it is Acted at the Theatre Royal, By His Majesty's Servants. Written by a Young Lady.* London: H. Rhodes, R. Parker, S. Briscoe, 1696, [Sig. A2ᵛ].
Title: *Author of Agnes de Castro*: Catharine Trotter (see p.406).
1-4 Cf. 'An Elegy Upon the Death of Mrs. A. Behn' (see p.267). Verbal echoes suggest that Manley may be the anonymous author of the elegy.
9-14 In her preface to *The Lost Lover* Manley wrote, 'They [her critics] Object the Verses wrote by me before *Agnes de Castro*, where, with Poetick Vanity I seemed to think my self a Champion of our Sex...'
Dela: short for Delariviere. Manley also used the name 'Delia'.

DELARIVIERE MANLEY

Prologue from *The Lost Lover*,
Spoken by Mr. *Horden*

The first Adventurer for her fame I stand,
The Curtain's drawn now by a Lady's Hand,
The very Name you'd cry boads Impotence,
To Fringe and Tea they shou'd confine their Sence,
5   And not outstrip the bounds of Providence.
I hope then Criticks, since the Case is so,
You'l scorn to Arm against a Worthless Foe,
But curb your Spleen and gall, and trial make,
How our fair Warriour gives her first Attack.
10   Now all ye chattering Insects straight be dumb,
The Men of Wit and Sense are hither come,
Ask not this Mask to Sup, nor that to show
Some Face more ugly than a Fifty Beau,
Who, if our Play succeeds, will surely say,
15   Some private Lover helpt her on her way,
As Female Wit were barren like the Moon,
That borrows all her influence from the Sun.
The Sparks and Beaus will surely prove our Friends,
For their good breeding must make them commend
20   What Billet Deux so e're a Lady sends.
She knew old Thread-bare Topicks would not do,
But Beaus a species thinks it self still new,
And therefore she resolved to Coppy you.

From *The Lost Lover; or, the Jealous Husband: A Comedy. As it is Acted at the Theatre Royal By His Majesty's Servants. Written by Mrs. Manley.* London: R. Bentley, F. Saunders, J. Knapton, and R. Wellington, 1696, Sig.B.

The Lost Lover was not a success. Manley admitted in her preface:

to confess my Faults, I own it an unpardonable one to expose after two years reflection, the Follies of seven days, (so barely in that time this Play was wrought) and myself so great a stranger to the Stage, that I had lived buried in the Countrey, and in the six foregoing Years, had actually been but twice at the House... My design in Writing was onely to pass some tedious Country hours, not imagining I should be so severely repay'd. I now know my Faults, and will promise to mend them by the surest way, not attempting to repeat them. After all, I think my Treatment much severer than I deserved; I am satisfied the bare Name of being a Woman's Play damn'd it beyond its own want of Merit...

Title *Mr. Horden*: according to Colley Cibber, Hildebrand Horden, who played Wildman in *The Lost Lover*, was a handsome young man who was 'every day rising in public favour'. Two months after this production he was killed in a quarrel at the Rose Tavern, a popular resort of the Drury Lane company. 'Before he was bury'd... several of the Fair Sex, well dress'd, came in Masks... to visit this Theatrical Heroe in his Shrowd' (Highfill, 7, 415).

7 *Arm against a Worthless Foe*: appealing to the audience by calling attention to the author's sex was by now a convention in prologues and epilogues to women's plays; cf. the epilogue to Pix's *Ibrahim*, produced in the same year as *The Lost Lover*, 1696:

> By the great Rules of Honour all Men know
> They must not Arm on a Defenceless Foe.
> The Author on her weakness, not her strength relies,
> And from your Justice to your Mercy flies. (5-8)

12 *Mask*: women often attended the theatre in a mask, in the pursuit of amorous intrigue; see Congreve's *The Way of the World* V.v.

13 *a Fifty Beau*: an over-aged fop

15 *some private Lover*: according to *The Adventures of Rivella*, Manley was involved at this time with Sir Thomas Skipwith, manager of Drury Lane, where *The Lost Lover* was produced. She acknowledged his 'Civility, his Native Generosity, and Gallantry of Temper' in her preface to the printed play.

18-23 In her concluding appeal to gallantry, the 'good breeding' of 'Sparks and Beaus', Manley parodies the female playwright's typical stance in the 1690s; cf. Behn's attack on coxcomb 'half wits' in the epilogue to *Sir Patient Fancy* (1677), spoken by Nell Gwyn:

> But for you half Wits, you unthinking Tribe,
> We'll let you see, what e'er besides we doe,
> How Artfully we Copy some of you:
> And if you're drawn to th' life, pray tell me then
> Why Women should not write as well as Men. (40-44)

A Song from *The Lost Lover*
Written by Mrs. Manley

Ah Dangerous Swain, tell me no more,
Thy Happy Nymph you Worship and Adore;
When thy fill'd Eyes are sparkling at her Name,
I raving wish that mine had caus'd the Flame.

5   If by your fire to her you can impart
Diffusive heat to warm another's heart:
Ah dangerous Swain, what wou'd the ruine be,
Shou'd you but once persuade you burn for me.

From *The Lost Lover*, 4.
This song appears in *The Adventures of Rivella* (1714). According to the autobiographical novel, Manley read a letter from a Mrs Pym, her rival for the affections of Sir Thomas Skipwith, complaining of his attentions to Manley. Growing tired of Skipwith's 'talking

incessantly of his Mistress', Manley composed this poem as a response to that letter. The poem made Skipwith 'perfectly drunk with Vanity and Joy'; he had the words set to music and sang them around the town, which earned him the nickname 'The Dangerous Swain' (49-52).

1 tell me / tell, tell me 1714   2 Thy Happy Nymph / of the blest Nymph 1714
5 to her / for her 1714

Prologue from *The Royal Mischief*

> Criticks, ye are grown so much unkind of late,
> Who dares to write runs on their certain Fate;
> If to *Parnassus* once they miss their way,
> Once chance to glimmer out a feeble ray,
> 5 Condemn 'em always by such light to stray;
> That Poets floating betwixt hopes and fears,
> Now dread you more than Merchants Privateers.
> Fain ours wou'd bribe you high to let her live,
> At least mayn't mercy stretch to a reprieve;
> 10 So may the Statesmans Policy increase,
> And Traders have their wisht desires for Peace;
> So may the Levite, with no doubts perplext,
> E'en as dear Interest leads, explain his Text;
> So may the *Beaus* be sparkish as they can,
> 15 All Wig and Dress, no matter for the Man;
> The Souldier paid his money without fighting,
> And Poets there's in that worse Combat, Writing
> The Vizards Mask it to their Friends unknown,
> Fool most themselves in fooling of the Town:
> 20 My last kind Wishes Ladies are for you,
> Espouse your Sexes Cause, and bravely too,
> So may you still be fair, your Lovers ever true.

From *The Royal Mischief. A Tragedy. As it is Acted By His Majesties Servants. By Mrs. Manley.* London: R. Bentley, F. Saunders, and J. Knapton, 1696, Sig. [A4].
1-5 These lines probably refer to the critical response to Manley's unsuccessful first play, *The Lost Lover*; cf. the preface to *The Lost Lover*:

Once more, my Offended Judges, I am to appear before you, once more in possibility of giving you the like Damning Satisfaction; there is a Tragedy of mine Rehearsing, [*The Royal Mischief*] which 'tis too late to recall, I consent it meet with the same Fortune: 'Twill for ever rid me of a Vanity too Natural to our Sex...

A dedicatory epistle to Manley's *Letters* (1696) by 'J. H.' describes 'the Town' as 'big to see what a Genius so proportionate can produce... Sir *Thomas Skipwith* and Mr. *Betterton* are eagerly contending, who shall first bring you upon the Stage, and which shall be most applauded, your Tragick or Comick strain' (Sig. A2).

12 *the Levite*: in this play on words, Manley is using the term 'Levite' as both a contemptuous term for a clergyman, and, in conjunction with 'Interest', as an aspersion on Jews (members of the tribe of Levi), who were associated with usury.

18 *the Vizards*: prostitutes. See Etherege's *The Man of Mode* I.i.

20-23 Manley's preface echoes this appeal to women in particular:

I should not have given my self and the Town the trouble of a Preface, if the aspersions of my Enemies had not made it necessary. I am sorry those of my own Sex are influenced by them, and receive any Character of a Play upon Trust, without distinguishing Ill nature, Envy and Detraction in the Representor... I shou'd think it but an indifferent Commendation to have it said she writes like a Woman.

Manley was defending herself against complaints about the 'warmth' of the seduction scene between her villainess/heroine, Homais, and her beloved, Levan Dadian. She cites similar characters and passages in Dryden's plays as evidence that her scenes are considered unacceptable only because they are written by a woman and adds:

I do not doubt when the Ladies have given themselves the trouble of reading and comparing it with others, they'll find the prejudice against our Sex, and not refuse me the satisfaction of entertaining them...

Cf. Aphra Behn's preface to *The Lucky Chance* (1687):

All I ask, is the Priviledge for my Masculine Part the Poet in me, (if any such you will allow me) to tread in those successful Paths my Predecessors have so long thriv'd in, to take those Measures that both the Ancient and Modern Writers have set me, and by which they have pleas'd the World so well: If I must not, because of my Sex, have this Freedom, but that you will usurp all to your selves; I lay down my Quill... for I am not content to write for a Third day only. I value Fame as much as if I had been born a *Hero*... (Summers, III, 187)

Manley was supported by her friend Charles Gildon in *The Lives and Characters of the English Dramatick Poets* (1699):

This Lady has very happily distinguish'd her self from the rest of her *Sex*, and gives us a living Proof of what we might reasonably expect from Womankind, if they had the Benefit of those artificial Improvements of Learning the Men have, when by the meer Force of Nature they so much excell... There is a Force and Fire in her Tragedy, that is the Soul that gives it Life... (90)

Bevil Higgons, in 'Written in the Blank Leaf of Mrs. Manley's Tragedy, call'd The Royal Mischief', praises her 'warm lines' (Hammond, 228).

From *The Royal Mischief*, Act III, Scene I

    Hom. What to conceal desire, when every
30 Attom of me trembles with it, I'le strip
    My Passion naked of such Guile, lay it

Undresst, and panting at his feet, then try
If all his Temper can resist it.
But heark the Sign, the Prince is coming, [*Musick*
flourish.

35 My Love distracts me, where shall I run,
That I may gather Strength to stem this Tide
Of Joy, shou'd he now take my Senses in
Their hurry, the Rage my Passion gives, wou'd
Make my Fate more sudden, than severest
40 Disappointments: Coward Heart, dar'st thou not
Stand the Enjoyment of thy own Desires;
Must I then grant thee time, to Reason with.
Thy weakness, be gone, and see thou do not
Trifle Moments, more rich than all the
45 Blooming Years thou hast past...

Lev. By Heav'n, a greater Miracle than Heav'n can
show
Not the bright Empress of the Sky
90 Can boast such Majesty, no artist cou'd
Define such Beauty, see how the dazling
Form gives on, she cuts the yielding Air, and
Fills the space with Glory, Respect shou'd carry
Me to Hers, but Admiration here has
95 Fixt my Feet unable to move.
Hom. Where shall I turn my guilty Eyes------
I cou'd call on Mountains now to sink my Shame,
Or hide me in the clefts of untried Rocks,
Where roaring Billows shou'd outbeat Remembrance.
100 Love which gave Courage, till the Trial came,
That led me on to this Extravagance,
Proves much more Coward than the Heart he fills,
And like false Friends in this Extremity,
Thrusts me all Naked on to meet a Foe.
105 Whose sight I have not Courage to abide.

From *The Royal Mischief*, 20-21.
The passionate Princess Homais has given a sleeping potion to her
impotent old husband, known as 'The Protector'. She has fallen in
love with his nephew, the virtuous Levan Dadian, by gazing on his
portrait. Her eunuch cautions Homais, as she prepares to seduce
the prince with the help of her ex-lover, Ismael, not to be 'vicious'.

KISSING THE ROD

From *The Royal Mischief* Act V, Scene I

Enter an Officer.
Offic Your Orders, Sir, are punctually obey'd
The Visier went undaunted to his Fate,
Nor at the horrid manner was concern'd,
285 But cry'd, 'twas glorious all he underwent
For *Bassima*, then as the Orders ran,
Alive we cram'd him in the Fatal Canon,
Which in a moment was discharg'd in Air,
His Carcass shattering in a thousand pieces.
290 Now dread and Horrour fell on all the Crowd,
At so unhear'd, and unimagin'd Death...
Enter an Officer.
Offi. My Lord, the Princess *Selima*, distracted
With her Griefs, ranges the fatal Plain,
365 Gathering the smoaking Relicks of her Lord,
Which singes, as she grasps them; now on the
Horrid Pile, her self had heap'd, I left her
Stretcht along, bestowing burning Kisses
And Embraces on every fatal piece.

From *The Royal Mischief*, 44-46.
1 *Your orders*: The Chief Visier, married to The Protector's sister,
Selima, has been caught trying to seduce the virtuous Bassima, wife
of Levan Dadian, as she lies dying on a couch. His punishment is to
be shot alive from a cannon.

Epilogue from *The Royal Mischief*
Spoken by Miss *Bradshaw*.

Our Poet tells me I am very pretty,
Have Youth and Innocence to move your pity:
A few Years hence perhaps you may be kind,
The Tallest Trees bend to the rustling Wind;
5 Then spare me for the good which I may do,
Early bespeak me, either Friend or Foe:
Nor think those Youthful Joys I have in store,
Far distant Promises, unripen'd Oar,
Meer Fairy Treasure, which you can't Explore:
10 The *Play-House* is a Hot-Bed to young Plants,
Early supplies your Longings and your Wants.

Then let your Sun-shine send such lively Heat,
May stamp our Poet's work, and Nature's too
Compleat.

From *The Royal Mischief*, 48.
Title *Miss Bradshaw*: a child actress at the time she delivered this
epilogue, Lucretia Bradshaw continued to appear on the stage until
1714, when she married Martin Folkes (1690-1754), a wealthy
antiquary and scientist. His mother, upon hearing of her son's
marriage to an actress, threw herself out of a window, and broke an
arm.
7-11 Racy prologues and epilogues written for young girls were a
sub-genre of the 'She-Prologue' specifically written for female
actresses (Wiley, 1940, 82-83, 237; Wiley, 1933, 1073). One of the
first was written for Aphra Behn's *Abdelazer* (1676), probably by
Otway. The lubricious reference to the onset of the menarche is
typical of the sleaziness of Restoration kiddieporn. 'Little Mrs Ariell'
was required to say:

> Your last applauses, like refreshing Showers,
> Made me spring up and bud like early Flow'rs;
> Since then I'm grown at least an inch in height,
> And shall ere long be full-blown for delight.

By 1682, according to Shadwell, this kind of stuff had lost whatever
appeal it had:

> Our Prologue-Wit grows flat, the Nap's worn off;
> And howsoe're we turn, and trim the Stuff,
> The Gloss is Gone, that look'd at first so gaudy;
> 'Tis now no Jest to hear young Girls talk Bawdy. ('A Lenten Prologue Refus'd
> by the Players', 1-4)

Our women playwrights revived the tradition, Manley here in 1696,
Pix in *The Deceiver Deceived* (1698) and *The Beau Defeated* (1700).
Trotter's epilogue for Pix's *Queen Catharine* (1698) (see p.411), is less
offensive.

CATHARINE TROTTER

Catharine Trotter was born in London on 16 August 1679 to David Trotter, a naval commander, and Sarah Ballenden (*DNB*). Captain Trotter died of the plague in Turkey when Catharine was four; she and her mother and sister lived for a short time on an Admiralty pension but after Charles II's death, relied on the charity of relations, and later, the support of Bishop Burnet (Birch, I, iii-iv). Although the pension was restored to the family in the reign of Queen Anne, Trotter found it necessary to work as a companion to an ailing woman in Surrey. She was largely self-educated, mastering French on her own, and receiving only some tutoring in Latin and logic. Physical descriptions of Trotter as a young woman refer to her bright eyes and small stature.

When she was fourteen Trotter composed some verses addressed to Bevil Higgons, Jacobite poet and later historian. In the same year, 1693, her epistolary novel, *Olinda's Adventures, or, the Amours of a Young Lady* was published anonymously in *Letters of Love and Gallantry and Several Other Subjects*. Apparently autobiographical, *Olinda's Adventures* depicts the romantic predicaments of an impoverished widow's attractive but entirely virtuous young daughter. The plot of Trotter's novel is retold in Delariviere Manley's famous *roman à clef*, *The New Atalantis* (1709), but in Manley's version, the young heroine does succumb to the advances of her suitors, beginning with a character supposed to be John Churchill, later the Duke of Marlborough (II, 52-53). In 1695 Trotter's novel was translated into French and in December of that year, her first play, *Agnes de Castro*, was produced at Drury Lane. The blank verse tragedy, dedicated to the Earl of Dorset and Middlesex, was published anonymously in 1696 with a prologue by Wycherly and a commendatory poem by Manley. The play was successful and the young author's identity well known. Shortly thereafter she, Manley, and Mary Pix were parodied in *The Female Wits*, a play that satirised her as 'Calista', a pretentious pedant.

In 1697 her most successful play, *The Fatal Friendship*, was produced at Lincoln's Inn Fields, where Congreve presided as chief playwright. Trotter composed an epistolary verse for his play, *The Mourning Bride* (1697). Congreve responded with a gracious letter explaining that the poem had arrived too late to be published with his play. The correspondence thus begun continued for ten years. Though a complete stranger, Farquhar was so impressed with Trotter's talent that he sent her a copy of his first play *Love and a Bottle* (1699), claiming that his passions 'were wrought so high' by

CATHARINE TROTTER

The Fatal Friendship (Birch, I, viii). During this period Charles Gildon praised Trotter for 'two things rarely found together, Wit and Beauty; and with these a Penetration very uncommon in the Sex'. He declared himself 'transported' by *The Fatal Friendship* (*Lives and Characters*, 179).

In 1700 Trotter contributed to *The Nine Muses*, a collection of poetic eulogies on Dryden. In the next few years, three more plays were produced, but her interests began to shift to philosophy and religion. In 1702 she published an anonymous defence of Locke, who, on being told about Trotter by Elizabeth Burnet, wife of the Bishop, warmly acknowledged her support with a gift of books. She continued to publish philosophical treatises and corresponded with Malebranche, Leibnitz, Madame Dacier, and John Norris of Bemerton, among many others. At some early date Trotter had converted to Roman Catholicism (the Ballendens were a well-known Scots Catholic family), but her doctor cautioned against continuing to impair her health by excessive fasting on holy days. Her personal letters of this period mention weakened strength and poor eyesight (BL Add. MS 4264, f.99ff.). In 1707 she returned to the Church of England, publishing an explanation of her decision in two letters.

In 1708 she married a non-abjuring Scots minister, Patrick Cockburn (1678-1749), who was forced to teach Latin until 1726, when he took the oath of abjuration and was appointed minister of St Paul's Cathedral in Aberdeen (*DNB*). She wrote of this period in her life, during which she undertook no new work:

Being married in 1708, I bid adieu to the muses, and so wholly gave myself up to the cares of a family, and the education of my children, that I scarce knew there was any such thing as books, plays, or poems stirring in Great Britain. (Birch, I, xi)

From 1726 until her death in 1749, she resumed her work in philosophy. During this period she was engaged in publishing her collected works, edited by Thomas Birch (1751). Four of the five plays, some of her poems, and the novel were omitted from the *Works*, in an attempt to play down her racier youthful connections. She is buried at Long Horsley, near Morpeth, in Northumberland, where the family had moved in 1737. Trotter's literary reputation did not survive her for long. In a 1789 letter the poet and philosopher James Beattie wrote,

She lived many years (between 1726 and 1737) in Aberdeen; and yet I have never heard any person there speak of her, though I have often heard her husband spoken of by those who must have known both. (Forbes,II, 243-244).

From *Agnes de Castro* Act I, Scene II

Princess. Ah! She who told me of my Husband's Heart,
Is all a Charm, to plead for his excuse;

407

Young, Beautiful, Discreet, and Chast, as Fair;
By Nature form'd to captive ev'ry Heart,
130 My Reason must approve the Prince's choice,
For I my self, prefer her to my self,
And love her too, as tenderly as he,
Agnes. Who can this Angel be?
Princess. Are there so many merit more than I,
135 Thou can'st not guess among 'em?
Agnes. Indeed I know not one deserves like you;
And therefore cannot guess.
Princess. Have you so long been privy to my
Thoughts,
Yet know not her who is so dear to me?
140 Who with the Prince shares my divided Heart
So equally, I cannot tell my self
To which I have given most; know you not her?
For if you know my Friend, you know my Rival.
Agnes. How very Miserable must I be
145 When I'm reduc'd to wish, you did not love me!
Those marks, of that peculiar, dear affection,
Which ev'ry day your partial kindness gave,
Are Witness which I wou'd disbelieve;
Oh! Let me think your Friendship was divided,
150 Tell me you have another, nearer Friend,
For I had rather lose your Love forever,
Than be the wretched Cause of your misfortune;
Rather be hated by you, than deserve it;
Oh ease my cruel fears, and name some other.
155 *Princess.* Too sure, alas, the Prince does love thee,
Agnes
And I'm so vain to think that only thou,
Cou'd gain a Heart, to which I laid a claim.
Read from his Hand, the sad, amazing truth.

·

From *Agnes de Castro, A Tragedy. As it is Acted at the Theatre Royal, Written by a Young Lady.* London: H. Rhodes, R. Parker, S. Briscoe, 1696, 6.
A few weeks after the production and publication of *Agnes de Castro* Trotter received a letter from a rather aggressive admirer, one Thomas Chambers, which attests her budding reputation, despite her anonymity:

Fynding the Play (I have here Returnd) in The Roome Beneath Where you are pleas'd to favour wth yor Being, And (if I'm not much mistaken in the Person) Apprehending yor self to be the Author,... I made bold to borrow it... 'Tis True I was in the Pitt, the Third Night Agnes de Castro was brought to publick View, But Being Surrounded, By A more than ordinary Number of Velvet faces, I was continually troubled from all sides, with Thunder-Claps of noisy Prattle, during the whole Play, soe That I was utterly depriv'd of the satisfaction of Observeing what past upon the Stage, which made me the more desirous of perusing yor Book... (BL Add. MS 4264, f.271)

The Princess Constantia, wife of Don Pedro, Prince of Portugal, here reveals to her dearest friend and companion, Agnes de Castro, the recent discovery that her husband has written amatory verses to Agnes.

126-127 Trotter's play is an adaptation of Aphra Behn's novel *Agnes de Castro: or, The Force of Generous Love* (1688), a translation of Jean-Baptiste de Brilhac's *Agnes de Castro, nouvelle portugaise*. The quality of Trotter's blank verse can best be assessed by a comparison with the prose on which it is based:

My dear *Agnes*, interrupted *Constantia*, Sighing, she who robs me of my Husband's Heart, has but too many Charms, to plead his Excuse...(13)

158 The following lines, which represent Don Pedro's love poem, were taken directly from the Behn novel:

1
In Vain, Oh Sacred Duty you oppose,
In Vain your Nuptial tye you plead,
Those forc'd devoirs Love overthrows,
And breaks the Vows he never made.
2
Fair Princess, you to whom my Faith is due,
Pardon the Destiny that drags me on,
'Tis not my fault my Hearts untrue,
I am compell'd to be undone.

Trotter reduced Behn's six-line stanza to four lines, taming the poem by omitting references to burning, languishing, and the Prince's complaint, 'But my Fidelity I can't command' (8). About a month before *Agnes de Castro* was produced, Thomas Southerne presented his adaptation of Behn's *Oroonoko* at the same theatre, a year after his *The Fatal Marriage: or, The Innocent Adultery*, taken from Behn's *The History of the Nun: Or, The Fair Vow-Breaker* (1689). Each time Southerne acknowledged his source; Trotter, who was sixteen when her first play was produced, did not. No explanatory preface was printed with the play; in her dedication she described herself as 'one who Conceals her Name, to shun that of Poetress', but two years later she signed the dedication of *Fatal Friendship* (1698) to Princess Anne. In a copy of a letter to Thomas Birch, dated May 1739, Mrs Cockburn gives her opinion on the theatre in her heyday:

I was always so bent upon doing my part towards reforming the abuses of the Stage, that it must have been by some strange oversight if I contributed anything to it, tho' I might not think much in the heat of writing of putting some levities in the mouths of disapprov'd characters. 'Tis faults of another nature that have made plays in general so much run down; comedies especially were for a long time vicious in their very foundation, the fine gentlemen are Debauchees, intrigues of married people are the business of the Play, & coming off with success in deceiving a good natur'd or jealous Husband, the happy Event. (BL Add. MS 4265, 85b)

To Mrs. *Manley.*
By the Author of *Agnes de Castro.*

> Th' Attempt was brave, how happy your success,
> The Men with shame our Sex with Pride confess;
> For us you've vanquisht, though the toyl was yours,
> You were our Champion, and the Glory ours.
> 5   Well you've maintain'd our equal right in Fame,
> To which vain Man had quite engrost the claim:
> I knew my force too weak, and but assay'd
> The Borders of their Empire to invade,
> I incite a greater genius to my aid:
> 10 The War begun you generously pursu'd,
> With double Arms you every way subdu'd;
> Our Title clear'd, nor can a doubt remain,
> Unless in which you'll greater Conquest gain,
> The Comick, or the loftier Tragick strain.
> 15   The Men always o'ercome will quit the Field,
> Where they have lost their hearts, the Lawrel yield.

From *The Royal Mischief. A Tragedy. As it is Acted By His Majesties Servants. By Mrs Manley.* London: R. Bentley, F. Saunders, and J. Knapton, 1696, Sig. [A3ᵛ].

In the 1690s, Delariviere Manley, Catharine Trotter and Mary Pix gave each other encouragement and support. Manley wrote a commendatory poem for Trotter's *Agnes de Castro* (1696) (see p. 398). Both Trotter and Pix contributed commendatory verses to Manley's *The Royal Mischief* (1696) (see p.414), and Trotter wrote an epilogue for Pix's *Queen Catharine* (1698) (see p.411). Within a few years, however, Manley would include Pix and Trotter as targets in her scandalous novels. An undated letter from 'E. B.', possibly Elizabeth Berkeley (later the wife of Bishop Burnet), to Trotter discusses the merits of their plays:

I have not yet been able to see Mʳˢ Manleys [*The Lost Lover*]but I hear tis such a one, that if you write in praise of it, you must not pretend to be my Namesake (yᵉ Plain Dealer) her Tragedy [*The Royal Mischief*] they say is something better, Wherefore if you think your self oblig'd to make her a Complement – I suppose you'd place it there – I did not indeed suspect she should ever prove a Rivall to You who I'm sure for what You have already done, may dispute the Laurells with some of the most noted of Our Sex, and doubt not but Your next Work may be compared with the best of its Kind...(BL Add. MS 4264, f.265)

CATHARINE TROTTER

Epilogue to *Queen Catharine, or the Ruines of Love*
Written by Mrs. *Trotter*. Spoken by Miss *Porter*.

What Epilogues are made, for who can tell,
'Twere worth the pains to write and speak 'em well.
If they cou'd gain your favour for bad Plays,
But by their merits you'll condemn or praise:
5   'Tis but a form, no matter then by whom,
Or what is said, and therefore I am come.
I, who no partial Voice can hope t'engage,
No graces of my own, nor of the Stage:
But tho' I cannot yet expect to move,
10   Or merit either your applause or love:
Sure practising so young I may improve.
    That's all I come for: what's the Play to me,
    And since I'm here, I think I'll let you see,
    What you're to hope, I may hereafter be.
15   Come, a short taste of some Heroick now?
But do not trust me, no, for if you do,
By all the furies and the flames of Love:
By Love, which is the hottest burning Hell,
I'll set you both on fire to blaze for ever.
20   How was that done, I'll swear it pleases me,
    And tho' I came careless of your decree,
        If favouring, or against our Tragedy,
Methinks I'm now grown tender of its fate,
Who knows but I may come to act Queen *Kate*.

From *Queen Catharine, Or The Ruines of Love. A Tragedy. As it is Acted at the New Theatre in Little-Lincons-Inn-Fields By His Majesty's Servants. Written by Mrs Pix.* London: William Turner and Richard Basset, 1698, Sig. [A3ᵛ].

Trotter and Pix, for whom she composed this epilogue, were both writing for the company at Lincoln's Inn Fields. They were parodied in a poem prefacing *Animadversions on Mr. Congreve's Late Answer to Mr. Collier* (1698):

Or could I write like the two Female things
With *Muse Pen-feather'd*, guiltless yet of Wings;
And yet, it strives to Fly, and thinks it Sings.
Just like the Dames themselves, who flant in Town,
And flutter loosely, but to tumble down.
The last that writ, of these presuming two,
(For that Queen Ca------ne is no Play 'tis true)
And yet to Spell is more than she can do,
Told a High Princess, she from Men had torn

411

Those *Bays* which they had long engros'd and worn.
But when she offers at our Sex thus Fair,
With four fine Copies to her Play, ---O Rare!
If she feels Manhood shoot--'tis I know where.
Let them scrawl on, and Loll, and Wish at ease,
(A Feather oft does Woman's Fancy please.)
Till by their Muse (more jilt than they) accurst,
We know (if possible) which writes the worst.
Beneath these Pictures, sure there needs no name,
Nor will I give what they ne'er got in Fame. ([A4v]-[A5])

Title *Miss Porter*: Miss Porter began her career in the theatre as attendant to Elizabeth Barry, who played Queen Catharine, and eventually succeeded to the senior actress's roles. The epilogue to *Queen Catharine* appears to have been her first part. Despite a crippling accident in 1731, she continued on the stage until 1742.

11 *practising so young*: cf. Manley, 'Epilogue from *The Royal Mischief*', note to 7-11 (see p.405).

MARY PIX

Mary Pix was born in 1666 in Nettlebed in Oxfordshire, daughter of the vicar, Roger Griffith, and Lucy Berriman, a relation of John Wallis, the well-known mathematician and scholar. In the dedication of her second play *The Spanish Wives* (1696) to Colonel Tipping of Whitfield, she mentions having last seen him at Soundess House, near Nettlebed, the home of some of the Wallis family, and refers to her early 'Inclinations to Poetry'. On 25 July 1684, shortly after her father's death, she was married in the London parish of St Benet Fink to George Pix (1660- ?), a merchant tailor (P. Barbour, 1975, 3-4). They had one child, buried at Hawkhurst, Kent in 1690 (*DNB*).

Pix made her debut as playwright with a blank-verse tragedy, *Ibrahim, the Thirteenth Emperour of the Turks*, produced at Drury Lane in May, 1696. Charles Gildon claimed that the distress of the raped heroine, Morena, 'never fail'd to bring Tears into the Eyes of the Audience' (*Lives and Characters*, 111). In the 1695-1696 season six new plays by women were staged, including Pix's successful farce, *The Spanish Wives*, Delariviere Manley's *The Lost Lover* and *The Royal Mischief*, Catharine Trotter's *Agnes de Castro*, and the anonymous Ariadne's *She Ventures and He Wins*. In the next year Pix and Catharine Trotter moved from Drury Lane to join Thomas Betterton's newly formed rival company at Lincoln's Inn Fields where Pix's comedy, *The Innocent Mistress*, was well received, followed by the unsuccessful *The Deceiver Deceived* (1698). *Queen Catharine: or the Ruines of Love* (1698), a blank-verse tragedy, was published with an epilogue by Trotter, followed by a tragedy, *The False Friend, or the Fate of Disobedience* in 1699 and a comedy, *The Beau Defeated: or, the Lucky Younger Brother* in 1700. Pix wrote at least five more plays which were published anonymously in the early eighteenth century.

In the anonymous play, *The Female Wits*, produced at Drury Lane in 1696 (published 1704), which satirised the women playwrights, Pix appears as 'Mrs. Wellfed... a fat, female Author, a good, sociable, well-natur'd Companion, that will not suffer martyrdom rather than take off three Bumpers in a Hand' (Sig. [A4]). The play is laden with references to Pix's appreciation for food and drink. After their defection to Lincoln's Inn Fields, Pix and Trotter were attacked in *Animadversions on Mr. Congreve's Late Answer to Mr. Collier* (1698), probably written by rival playwright George Powell. The satirist complained of Pix's 'insufferable Dullness' and insinuated that Pix and Trotter were loose women (14). In 1703 Pix was parodied by Joseph Trapp in *The Players turn'd Academicks* as 'A Tool of a Scribe, and a Poetress great, / Who is said to *Write* well, because well she could *Treat*' and was said to have written her husband into debt (3).

With Manley and Trotter, Pix's women friends included the great Restoration actress, Elizabeth Barry, who appeared in seven of her plays; Sarah Fyge, for whom Pix composed a commendatory verse to *Poems on Several Occasions* [1703], and Susannah Centlivre, in whose most popular play, *The Busie Body* (1709), Pix may have had a hand. The dedications of Pix's plays become increasingly more ambitious, addressing successively a gentleman, a colonel, a knight, a countess, and a duchess. In her dedication of *The Deceiver Deceived*, she boasts of the encouragement of 'her Royal Highness', Princess Anne, the dedicatee of Pix's novel *The Inhumane Cardinal* (1696).

In addition to her plays and novel, Pix contributed an elegy on Dryden to *The Nine Muses* (1700) and published two poems, *To the right honourable the Earl of Kent*, a panegyric published as a broadsheet [1700] and *Violenta, or the Rewards of Virtue, turn'd from Boccace into Verse* (1704).

The Post-Boy for 26-28 May 1709 advertised a performance of *The Busie Body* as a 'benefit for the family of Mrs. Mary Pix, deceas'd' (Bowyer, 94). Two years later Richard Steele in *The Spectator*, 28 April 1711, found 'The Lady who wrote *Ibrahim*', the author of *The Rover* [Aphra Behn], and other unmentioned 'Poetesses of the Age' to be 'the Writers of the least Learning... best skill'd in the luscious Way'.

To Mrs. *Manley*, upon her Tragedy call'd
The Royal Mischief.

    As when some mighty Hero first appears,
    And in each act excells his wanting years;
    All Eyes are fixt on him, each busy Tongue
    Is employ'd in the triumphant Song:
5   Even pale Envy hangs her dusky Wings,
    Or joins with brighter Fame, and hoarsely sings;
    So you the unequal'd wonder of the Age,
    Pride of our Sex, and Glory of the Stage;
    Have charm'd our hearts with your immortal lays,
10   And tun'd us all with Everlasting Praise.
    You snatch Lawrels with undisputed right,
    And conquer when you but begin to fight;
    Your infant strokes have such *Herculean* force,
    Your self must strive to keep the rapid course;
15   Like *Sappho* Charming, like *Afra* Eloquent,

MARY PIX

Like Chast *Orinda*, sweetly Innocent:
But no more, to stop the Reader were a sin,
Whilst trifles keep from the rich store within.

M. Pix.

From *The Royal Mischief. A Tragedy. As it is Acted By His Majesties Servants. By Mrs Manley.* London: R. Bentley, F. Saunders, and J. Knapton, 1696, [Sig. A3ᵛ].

8 *Pride of our Sex*: in Pix's commendatory poem to Sarah Fyge's *Poems on Several Occasions* [1703], she again praises a sister poet as an example to all women:

> To these Triumphant Lays, let each repair,
> A sacred Sanction to the writing Fair;
> Mankind has long upheld the Learned Sway,
> And tyrant Custom forc'd us to obey.
> Thought Art and Science to them belong,
> And to assert our selves was deem'd a Wrong,
> But we are justify'd by thy immortal Song:...
> To idle Gayeties true Wit prefer,
> Strive all ye thinking Fair, to Copy her. (5-11; 18-19)

13 *infant strokes*: since Manley was probably least twenty-four at the time of publication, Pix must be referring to Manley's status as beginning playwright.

A Song from *The Spanish Wives*
Betwixt Mr. *Leveridge* a *Spaniard*, and Mrs. *Cross*
an *English* Lady.

He. Fairest Nymph that ever bless'd our Shore,
Let me those charming Eyes adore,
And fly no more, and fly no more.

She. Spaniard, thy Suit is all in vain;
5   I was born where Women reign,
And cannot brook the Laws of *Spain*.

He. For thee my Native Customs I'll forgo,
Cut my black Locks, and turn a Beau.

She. E're I submit to be your Wife,
10   Listen to an *English* Husband's life;
With Sparks abroad I'm every day,
Gracing the Gardens, Park, or Play;
Hearing all the pretty things they say;
Give and take Presents, and when that's done,

15   You thank the Beaux when I come home.

He. Oh! I now my Temper fear.
She. Oh! sigh not yet, there's more to hear:
At my Levy crowding Adorers stand,
Fix'd on my Eyes, and grasping my white Hand;
20   All their Courts and Oglings bent on me,
Not one regardful Look towards thee:
At this thou must be pleas'd, or else not see.

He. Then we must part, and I must die.
She. If thou art such a Fool, what care I?
25   *He*. I cannot share thee, so I am undone.
She. A wiser will supply thy Room.

Chorus. Then we must part, *&c*.
If thou art such a Fool, *&c*.
I cannot share thee, *&c*.
30   A wiser will supply, *&c*.

From *The Spanish Wives. A Farce, as it was Acted by His Majesty's Servants, At The Theatre in Dorset-Garden*. London: R. Wellington, 1696, 19-20. The songs in *The Spanish Wives* were set to music by Daniel Purcell (d.1717), brother of Henry. Another song from this play, 'Alas! When charming Sylvia's gone!' was published separately in single-sheet folio and appeared anonymously nearly one hundred years later in Joseph Ritson's *Scotish Songs in Two Volumes* (1794, I, 52), along with Mrs [Catharine Trotter] Cockburn's 'The Vain Advice' (I, 66-67).

According to Gildon's *Lives and Characters of the English Dramatick Poets* (1699) *The Spanish Wives* 'had the good fortune to please' (112). The play was performed a number of times in the early eighteenth century. The Governor of Barcellona, 'a merry old Lord, that has travl'd, and gives his Wife more Liberty than is usual in *Spain*', catches his 'brisk and airy' wife carrying on with a handsome English colonel. The Governor forgives her, and she swears to remain faithful. In the sub-plot, a 'jealous Lord' loses his young wife to her true love, to whom she had been previously contracted. In contrasting the well-travelled Governor, who is not as possessive as Spanish men are understood to be, with the insufferable, dominating Marquess in the sub-plot, *The Spanish Wives* is actually making a case for English wives. Pix's English colonel observes, 'To us who have been bred otherwise it seems a Miracle, That men can be so barbarous to the Fair Sex' (11) and the Governor declares the less dominating Englishmen to be 'the happiest Husbands' (2).

Title *Mrs. Cross*: in her teens Letitia Cross (c.1677-1737) was known for her singing, dancing, and hoydenish roles. She spoke the prologue to Pix's *Ibrahim* (1696), the epilogue to Manley's *The Lost Lover* (1696), and played herself in *The Female Wits* (produced in 1696). According to Manley's *The New Atalantis*, she was pursued by a 'widow' (identified in the key as Susan Howard, Lady Effingham) who, having seen her in a breeches role, 'acting the Part of a young *Lover* and a *Libertine*', fell in love with her, took her to her villa, and then abandoned her when the young actress displayed too much interest in 'the other Sex' (II, 207-209). Five years after running off to France with a baronet, she returned to Drury Lane, continuing her acting career until 1724.

Mr. Leveridge: Richard Leveridge (1670?-1758) was a bass vocalist, song-writer and composer. His performance in this farce was one of his first on the London stage; he continued to sing professionally until the age of eighty-one.

5 *where Women reign*: England, where women were thought by foreigners to have extraordinary freedom. The English lady here boasts of her mobility and independence in contrast to her sisters on the Continent. A foreigner's view of English womanhood is recorded in Misson de Valbourg's *Memoirs*: 'They pay great Honour to the Women in England, and they enjoy very great and very commendable Liberties' (364). Englishmen themselves agreed; in *The New Help To Discourse* (third ed., 1684) William Winstanley answered the question 'In what Country is it that woman have the greatest Prerogative?'

In England, where they are not kept so severly submiss as the *French*, nor so jealously guarded as the *Italians*, as being, as of a finer mould, as of a better temper than to yield to an inordinate servility, or incontinency, which makes them endued with so many priviledges amongst us, that *England* is termed by Foreigners *The Paradise of Women*, as it is by some accounted *The Hell of Horses*, and *Purgatory of Servants*. And it is a common by-word among the *Italians*, that if there were a bridge built over the Narrow Seas, all the women in *Europe* would run into *England*; they having here the upper hand in the streets, the uppermost place at the Table, the Thirds of their Husbands Estates and their equal shares in all Lands, yea, even such as are holden in nights service; priviledges wherewith women of other Countrys are not acquainted. So that we see it as well a *Paradise for woman*, by reason of their priviledges, as *a Paradise of women*, by reason of their unmatchable perfections. (60)

18 *Levy*: levee, or reception of visitors upon rising from bed

A Song by Mrs. P-- from *The Innocent Mistress*, Sung by Mr. *Hodgson*.

When I languish'd, and wish'd you wou'd something
                            bestow,
   You bad me to give it a Name;
But, by Heaven, I know it as little as you,
   Tho' my ignorance passes for Shame:

5   You take for Devotion each passionate Glance,
      And think the dull Fool is sincere,
    But never believe that I speak in Romance
      On purpose to tickle your Ear.
    To please me then more, think still I am true,
10   And hug each Apocryphal Text:
    Tho' I practice a thousand false Doctrines on you,
      I shall still have enough for the next.

From *The Innocent Mistress. A Comedy. As it was Acted, by His Majesty's Servants, At The Theatre in Little-Lincolns-Inn-Fields. Written by Mrs. Mary Pix*. London, J. Orme, for R. Basset, and F. Cogan. 1697, 21-22.

Gildon describes *The Innocent Mistress* as 'a diverting Play, and met with good Success, tho' acted in the hot Season of the Year' (111). This song appears in the third volume of the second edition of *Wit and Mirth: or, Pills to Purge Melancholy* (1707) as having been sung by Mrs Hodgson, and set to music by Mr John Eccles. It was also published as a broadsheet.

Title *Mr. Hodgson*: John Hodgson (fl. 1689-1741?), a member of the theatre company at Lincoln's Inn Fields, played Beaumont, 'an honest country gentleman'. He also acted in Pix's *The False Friend* (1699) and played Ismael in Manley's *The Royal Mischief* (1696).

Prologue from *The Deceiver Deceived*,
spoken by Mr. *Bowen*.

Deceiv'd Deceiver, and Imposter cheated!
    An Audience and the Devil too defeated!
All trick and cheat! Pshaw, 'tis the Devil and all,
I'll warr'nt ye we shall now have Cups and Ball;
5   No, Gallants, we those tricks don't understand;
'Tis t'other House best shows the slight of hand:
Hey Jingo, Sirs, what's this! their Comedy?
Presto be gone, 'tis now our Farce you see.
By neat conveyance you have seen and know it
10   They can transform an Actor to a Poet.
With empty Dishes they'll set out a Treat,
Whole Seas of Broth, but a small Isle of Meat:
With Powderle-Pimp of Dance, Machine and Song,
They'll spin ye out short Nonsense four hours long:
15   With Fountains, Groves, Bombast and airy Fancies
Larded with *Cynthias*, little Loves and Dances:

Which put together, makes it hard to say,
If Poet, Painter, or Fidler made the Play.
But hold, my business lies another way.
20   Not to bespeak your praise by kind perswasions,
But to desire the favour of your patience.
      Our case is thus:
Our Authoress, like true Women, shew'd her Play
To some, who, like true Wits, stole't half away.
25   We've Fee'd no Councel yet, tho some advise us
T'indite the Plagiaries at *Apollo*'s Sizes?
But ah, how they'd out face a Damsel civil:
Who've impudence enough to out face the Devil:
Besides, shoud they be cast by prosecution,
30   'Tis now too late to think of restitution;
And faith, I hear, that some do shrewdly opine
They Trade with other Muses than the nine.
      I name no names, but you may easily guess,
They that can cheat the Devil can cheat the Flesh.
35   Therefore to you kind Sirs, as to the Laws
Of Justice she submits her self and Cause,
For to whom else shou'd a wrong'd Poet sue,
There's no appeal to any Court but you.

From *The Deceiver Deceived: A Comedy, As 'tis now Acted by His Majesty's Servants, At The Theatre in Little-Lincolns-Inn-Fields.* London: R. Basset, 1698, Sig. [A3].
Title *Mr. Bowen*: William Bowen (1666-1718) played Gervatio, a cunning servant who masterminds the various intrigues in this comedy. Born in Ireland, Bowen, 'an actor of spirit', was known for his strong voice. He was killed in a sword fight which he initiated after hearing a rival actor's performance praised above his own.
1-2 George Powell's *The Imposture Defeated* was presented at Drury Lane in September 1697, two months before Pix's *The Deceiver Deceived* was produced at Lincoln's Inn Fields. His preface declares, 'I stand impeacht (at least the Publick Cry is loud upon that Subject) that I have stolen a Character from a Comedy of Mrs. *P-----t's.*' Powell then claims that he got the idea from a novel, and that he'd never read Pix's play. However, he admits that Pix had asked him to try to get *The Deceiver Deceived* produced at Drury Lane, before deciding to take it to the rival theatre. Pix responded in her dedication of *The Deceiver Deceived*, 'I look upon those that endeavour'd to discountenance this Play as Enemys to me' and stated that Powell 'has printed so great a falshood, it deserves no Answer'. Neither the production nor the publication of Pix's play

was a success; it was reissued as *The French Beau* in 1699, with a new title-page and prologue, and omitting the signed dedication (Thorn-Drury, 1930, 316-318). In *Animadversions on Mr. Congreve's Late Answer to Mr. Collier*, the author, very likely Powell himself, describes Congreve's attempt, with the aid of Pix, Catharine Trotter and members of the Lincoln's Inn company to 'clap down' his play:

he was seen very gravely with his Hat over his Eyes among his chief Actors, and Actresses, together with the two She Things, call'd *Poetesses*, which Write for his House, as 'tis nobly call'd; thus seated in State among those and some other of his Ingenious critical Friends, they fell all together upon a full cry of Damnation, but when they found the malicious Hiss would not take, this very generous, obliging Mr. *Congreve* was heard to say, *We'll find out a New way for this Spark, take my word there is a way of clapping of a Play down.* (34-35)

Powell had appeared in Trotter's *Agnes de Castro*, Pix's first play, *Ibrahim, Thirteenth Emperour of the Turks*, Manley's *The Lost Lover*, and *The Female Wits* (all produced in 1696) and later in Susannah Centlivre's *The Beau's Duel* and *The Stolen Heiress* (both 1702). He was respected as a tragedian, but seems to have quarrelled with Pix, Colley Cibber and Thomas Betterton, amongst others. He has gone down in history as 'a churlish, ill-conditioned man' whose 'life was debauched' (*DNB*). A character in *The Female Wits* says of Powell, 'Honest George regards neither times nor seasons in drinking' (13).

4 *Cups and Ball*: a reference to the old trick of the pea and thimble, known in America as the shell game.

6 *t'other House*: Drury Lane. Pix's play was produced at Lincoln's Inn Fields.

13-18: Powell's play, *Imposture Defeated*, includes such stage directions as 'a Simphony of Musick, as it is playing the Scene Changes to a Beautiful Garden with Orange Trees of Each Side, and at the end little Cyprus Trees' (4) and 'a Dance between a Lawyer and a poor Clyent, a Courtier and a Lame Soldier, a Userer and a Prodigal, a Physician and a Fool' (7). Feeling the effects of competition from public concerts and other forms of entertainment, both theatre companies began to make their productions more spectacular, importing foreign singers and dancers and bringing rope dancers, tumblers and vaulters on to the stage.

13 *Powderle-Pimp*: the magical powder conjurers pretend to use when changing one thing for another or making it 'disappear'.

26 *Apollo's Sizes*: Apollo is the God of poetry; 'Sizes' (assizes) are the sessions held periodically in each county of England by judges acting under special commissions.

32 *Other Muses than the nine*: Pix implies that her rival receives his poetic inspiration from alcohol and other vices, cf. 'The Emulation', 82-85 (see p.312).

From *Queen Catharine* Act the First, Scene the First

Glou. Work on my brain, help every faculty;

245   And thou invention stretch, till thou hast wound me
      Into the bottom of my Brothers Councils:
      Then give destruction power, a Crown alone
      Can safely shrou'd those foul deformities.
      Those glorious rays wou'd dazle mocking Gazers;
250   Then amongst the crowd no sawcy Slave,
      Wou'd dare in whispers to pronounce me monstrous.
      The Ladie's too, caught with unbounded sway:
      The Royal Purple to this uncouth trunk
      Gives form, and vigour to this sapless Limb.
255   By Heaven, nature sent me
      Here in spite to plague her upright Race.
      'Twas her design! nor shall she lose her end,
      A Real Foe, and deep dissembling Friend:
      Near the Crown, but not near enough ally'd,
260   *Tho Seas of Blood my Title do divide,*
      Cruel and bold I'll wade the Kindred tide.

From *Queen Catharine Or, The Ruines of Love. A Tragedy. As it is Acted at the New Theatre in Little-Lincolns-Inn-Fields By His Majesty's Servants. Written by Mrs Pix.* London: William Turner and Richard Basset, 1698, 6-7.

The heroine of this blank verse tragedy is Catherine of Valois (1401-1437), the widow of Henry V, a 'warlike queen who wealds herself the sword'. Edward IV, a rejected suitor, and the Duke of Gloucester (later Richard III), murder Catherine's second husband, Owen Tudor. Actually, Tudor, though sent to Newgate, survived Catherine by twenty-four years. The queen's devoted ward, Isabella, is tricked into betraying her by Gloucester and his brother Clarence, Isabella's beloved. When told of Isabella's death, Catharine declares, 'Love was her only crime.' Thomas Betterton (1635?-1710), the best known actor of his time, played Owen Tudor opposite Elizabeth Barry's Queen Catharine. In this scene, which we include as an example of Pix's control of dramatic blank verse, not often attempted by women, Malavill, the Duke of Gloucester's henchman, has just reported on their plans to surprise Queen Catharine and Owen Tudor, and to gain Sir James Thyrrold as an ally in their scheme to 'sink' Clarence.

244 *Glou.*: the character of the Duke of Gloucester was played by a Mr Arnold (fl. 1696-1702), a minor member of Betterton's company who usually played villains and old men.

ELIZABETH TIPPER

The Pilgrim's Viaticum: or, the Destitute, but not Forlorn. Being A Divine Poem, Digested from Meditations upon the Holy Scripture contains the only account we have of the life of its author. When she wrote, Elizabeth Tipper was a poor schoolteacher, dependent upon the charity of friends. One of the first poems in her book, '*Some* Experimental Passages *of my* Life, with Reflections *upon Jacob's Words,* Few and Evil have the days of the years of my Life Been' (19-21), records the story of a youthful five-year 'banishment' for an unnamed sin, and a period of happiness spent in a poor village where two of her greatest wants, 'Imployment and Society', were supplied. The book offers little more information other than the names of her dead friends, Madam Mary Carter (70), Robert Harding (67), and a Madam Mary Fountayn who had loved Tipper's mother 'to the end' (64).

In 1698 when her *Viaticum* was published Elizabeth Tipper had apparently suffered another crisis and was seeking the patronage of the pious and philanthropic Anne, Countess of Coventry. Her dedication to Lady Anne quickly dispenses with praise of her patron's virtues to plead 'for Sanctuary, knowing that... my humble Endeavors can meet with no securer Harbor than under your Ladyship's Protection' (Sig. A2).

The name 'Viaticum' signifies provision for a journey; Tipper announces her intention to 'repair / to a City, try the *Smiles of Fortune* there' (21). Lady Anne, the third daughter of Henry Somerset, Duke of Beaufort, was already in 1698 a supporter of a charity school near her family home in Badminton, Gloucestershire; with her friends Lady Elizabeth Hastings, Lady Catherine Jones and Mary Astell she became active in the movement to establish a network of charity schools throughout England. Tipper may have been a teacher in Lady Anne's village school (the Greater Badminton parish register records the marriage of a Robert Tipper and Mary Davis in 1641 – Gloucestershire Parish Registers, XIII 27), and have been hoping through the Countess's influence to be appointed to a school in London. There, under the guidance of the Society for the Propagation of Christian Knowledge (officially founded in 1699 by wealthy patrons, clergymen and dedicated educators), the salaries of elementary teachers were far better than they were in the country, and the teachers themselves were, for the first time, being granted professional status.

Whether Elizabeth Tipper became a teacher in a city charity

school is not known. Her name appears with that of the 'tutress' Mary Astell in a list of marriageable women published in Letter XLI of *The Athenian Spy* (1704) where the 'True Widow' Tipper is offered up as a suitably 'ingenious wife... for any *Dean* or *Prebend*' (*18ᵛ). She and her poetry were known to at least one editor of a popular London magazine: John Dunton, calling Tipper 'a philosopher, a poet, and a good Christian' (*Life and Errors*, 1818, 292), claims to have published her work in his *Athenian Mercury* (1691-1697). In one of her poems Tipper seems to be disavowing any association with another publisher, one John Tipper. John was a Coventry school teacher and poet who in 1704 began *The Ladies Diary*, an almanac filled with astrological charts and mnemonic verses. In 'On *Directions* to know how to Act *Fortunately*' (40-42) Elizabeth Tipper compares 'Babling Fortune-Teller's Skill' unfavourably with 'Divine Direction' and prays to 'manage all [her] *Days* That unto [God she] may direct [her] Ways'.

The poetry of *The Pilgrim's Viaticum* is conventionally devout, expressing deep regret for past sins and great faith in the Anglican Church. It earned Elizabeth Tipper praise from 'W.P., Gent.', 'A.L., Esquire', 'E.S., Gent', E. Steele, Joseph Perkins (the self-styled 'White Poet' who wrote an elegy to Anne Coventry's father), John Torbuck, a Wiltshire minister, and John Hallum, who wrote '*Phillips* and *Behn*, whose Praise Fame still rehearse, / In all their *Works* don't parallel thy verse' (14).

A Satyr

As *Dungeons* are for *Criminals* prepar'd,
Tyburn and *Gyves* too is their just Reward;
So *Satyr*'s *Lash* dipt, poison'd in *Disgrace*,
Is fit to scourge the *Vice* of *Human Race*.
5   Did not the *Lamb of God*, with *Sacred Terror*,
Reprove all *Pharisaic Sins* and *Error*?
Where's then my *Muse*? Does my *Poetick Vein*!
Want *Skill* or *Courage* for this useful strain?
Baptismal Vows engage *Heroic Minds*,
10 *Women* are *valiant*, tho' of *different Kinds*,
And tho' my *Sex* is weak, my *Heart*'s not so:
Lead on my *Chief*, I fear not where I go.
Instruct me Lord, I wait for *thy Command*,
Without *it* I dare stir not Foot or Hand.
15 I begg'd again, and then my Lord reply'd,
My Precepts *and* Example *be your* Guide;
Go follow them. Strait then I call'd to mind
His *Golden Rule*, propitious left behind:
First *cast away* the *Beam* that hides the *Light*

423

20   Of thine own *Eye*, deluded Hypocrite;
     Which, once *remov'd*, thou *better* may'st *discern*
     The *little Mote* thy *Brother* does *concern*,
     And with more reason ask to pull it out,
     When thy *clear Light* dispels his *darker Doubt*:
25   But if *black Vice* thy *Life* it self betray,
     And thou pretend'st to *Guide* the *perfect Way*,
     'Tis like a *blind Man* raving in a *Heat*,
     Inspir'd by some *ridiculous Conceit*,
     He's able to lead all that go astray;
30   His *Tongue* crys out, his *Feet* quite miss the way;
     Sometimes his *Steps* are *right*, but rarely so;
     Still with *invective* Bawls, *you falsly go*.
     Should this his *Conduct* be by *Prudence* try'd,
     Would he be thought a *Madman* or a *Guide*?
35   Our *Savior*, e're such Work he did begin,
     Ask'd, *Which of you convinces me of Sin?*
     And must his *spotless Life* a Pattern be
     Imitable for such a *Worm* as me?
     The great *Example* I can never reach,
40   Alas! I want time more to *Watch* than *Preach*.
     My *Self* is *Task* sufficient to look o're,
     I find no *Moment* where I need *explore*
     The *Faults* of *others*, but my *own deplore*.
     And now I *beg*, since my *Design* has mist,
45   *Make me true* Christian, *tho' no* Satyrist.

From *The Pilgrim's Viaticum: or, the Destitute, but not Forlorn. Being A Divine Poem, Digested from Meditations upon the Holy Scripture. By Eliz. Tipper.* /Oh how I love thy Law/ It is my Meditation all the Day. Psalm 119. Ver 97./ London: Printed by J. *Wilkins*, near Fleet-Street; and Sold by the Booksellers of *London* and *Westminster*, 1698, 71-72.
2 *Tyburn*: London's place of execution until 1783; *gyves*: leg-irons
3 *Satyr's Lash*: a commonplace of the tragic satire modelled on Persius and Juvenal. The satirist sees himself as *flagellum dei* scourging vices in the name of righteousness. Tipper's satire actually argues that she has no call to be chastising the vices of others when she herself is in need of reformation, thus rejecting the invective verse of Dryden as unchristian.
9 *Baptismal vows engage Heroick minds*: see Barker, p.360, note to 1.79; the Church of England liturgy had inherited baptismal vows from the Roman liturgy. Since the Restoration, Presbyterians within the established church had been pressuring for reform of the ritual to purge Romish elements; in 1689, taking courage from the

Calvinism of William III, a commission sat to review the prayer book, amid a storm of pamphlet controversy meant to influence the outcome. The 'liturgy of comprehension' devised by the commission was never adopted (Fawcett, *passim*).

18 *Golden Rule*: Matthew 7:12
19-23 Matthew 7:3-5
36 John 8:46
40 Mark 14:38
40-43 In her *Meditations and Reflections* (1707) the Countess of Coventry writes: 'One Hour spent in serious Retirement from Worldly Affairs, to consider our Latter End, ought to be preferr'd before a Thousand Days conversation with those that are accounted the most pleasant and agreeable Company' (3). The desire for 'Hours in *dear Devotion* spent' (22) is a constantly reiterated theme in the *Viaticum*, for example in 'On Sunday' (39):

> The *other* Days with loaded *Care* abound,
> *Earth's Service* drives the heavy circle round,
> And dully fix their *Aspect* on the *Ground*.

To a Young Lady that desired a Verse of my being *Servant* one *Day*, and *Mistress* another

More than a King's my *Word* dos rule to day,
His Subjects *His*, my Betters *Mine* obey;
Quality, Fortune, Beauty, Virtue, Wit,
Do *Govern* others, but to me Submit:
5   *To morrow from this *Dignity* I fall,
And am a *Servant* at each *Beck* and *Call*:
Next Day I'me *free* in *Liberty* and *Power*,
And, as before, a *Mistress* every Hour.

      Changeable is my *State*, and yet not strange,
10   When *Day* to *Night*, and *Light* to *Darkness* change:
Yet *Fate* I cannot blame, but justly own,
She, in this *Difference, Evenness* hath shown;
For when I'me *Mistress*, none I can Command,
When *Servant, curb'd* by no imperious *Hand*:
15   This is a *Riddle*, yet here wonder why,
When all the *World's* a *Riddle*, why not I?

From *The Pilgrim's Viaticum*, 1698, 34-35.
5 ***I teach Ladies Writing and Accompts one day, and keep Shop-Books the other day, in which Business I am a hired Servant.** (Elizabeth Tipper's note.) Unlike city schools which were full-time, country schools often operated part-time, as the children had often

to work. From the use of the word 'ladies' which was not applied to women of inferior social class, it seems unlikely that Tipper is here describing service in a charity school or dame-school, but rather in a merchant's house where she combined the duties of governess and book-keeper. Tipper's curriculum is, moreover, unusual for a provincial school; according to M.G. Jones, 'few women teachers taught writing, fewer still arithmetic' (Jones, 98). With the establishment of the SPCK, notice was sent out that London teachers should be in class, teaching, from eight to twelve in the morning and one to four in the afternoon; summer hours started at seven a.m. For this, male teachers received the healthy salary of £30 per year, women anywhere up to £24 per year. Tipper's *Viaticum* reads much like a *curriculum vitae* for such a post; her verses demonstrate that she is qualified to be headmistress of a typical charity school, which required:

1. That she be a member of the Church of England and of a sober life and conversation.
2. One that has frequented the Communion once a month (at least) for some years.
3. One that keeps good orders in her family (if she have one).
4. One that hath command of her passions.
5. One that is of an ingenious mind, willing to learn and apt to teach.
6. That she be solidly grounded in the true Principles and Practice of Christianity so as to give a good account thereof to the Minister of the Parish upon examination.
7. One that is sufficiently grounded in the English Tongue so as to be able to teach her scholars to read, and also one who understands knitting, writing, plane work so as to be able to instruct her scholars in the same, in order to fit them either for Service or Apprenticeship. (St. Martins in the Fields School, 1700, rpt. in Jones, 99)

Observations on the Life of Epictetus

Poor *Epictetus*, born the Slave of *Fate*,
Unparallel'd, for abject mean Estate,
Rapt in a Cloud of unkind *Fortune*'s Jars,
And *Destiny* that seem'd to have no *Stars*:
5   *Dark* as the *Eye* of *Chance*, which some call *blind*,
Obscure from *Light* in all things but his *Mind*,
Which was enricht with *Faculties* could reach
The rarest things *Philosophy* did teach;
Yet by *Laborious Burthens* bath'd in *Sweats*,
10 He every Day must *Earn* the *Bread* he eats;
But he the *Envy* of his *Fate* beguiles,
And for her *rigorous Frowns* gives *pleasing Smiles*,
Contentment plain'd and smooth'd, each step was *rough*
And in his *Wants* till made him rich enough,
15 Set him above the *Top* of *Fame's Renown*,

ELIZABETH TIPPER

And higher than the *Envy* of a *Crown*,
More happy than the *Miser*, whose *proud Share*
Of *Wealth* is equall'd with a *Load* of *Care*:
Thus liv'd he *free*, *brisk*, *satisfi'd* and *gay*,
20 As if, for *Earth*, he scorn'd to throw away
A single *Wish*; and, as he studied said,
My thoughts, just now my present State have laid
In view, and, as I look, this I behold,
In my Condition I am Poor *and* Old,
25 *And* Happy *therefore, knowing* 'tis *the best,*
Because the GODS *have chose* it *from the rest.*
To give it *me; their* Wisdom *cannot err,*
And I the Gift *before all things preferr.*
O wondrous Vertue in a *Heathen* Man!
30 With what *Impatience*, with what *Face* then can
A *Christian murmur, sorrow* or *repine,*
That reads this vast *Humility* of thine?
But who, alas! retains a *peaceful Thought,*
More than by *Heaven's Diviner Hand* is wrought?
35 *Heaven* is the *Giver* and *Preserver* too
Of every *spark* of *good* we *think* or *do*.

From *The Pilgrim's Viaticum*, 49-55.
1 *Epictetus*: (c. AD 60-140) Stoic philosopher, born lame and a slave.
His *Diatribai* and *Enchiridion* preach that suffering can be overcome
by endurance and self-denial. *The Life and Philosophy of Epictetus:*
with the Embleme of Human Life by Cebes, translated from Boileau by
John Davies, appeared in 1670. Ellis Walker's *Epicteti Enchiridion*
made English in a Poetical Paraphrase (London, 1692) entered a
second edition in 1695; George Stanhope's *Epictetus his morals, with*
Simplicius his comment was published in 1694. Ruth Perry's catalogue
of the libraries of Anne Coventry (Perry, 1986, 339-354) shows the
Countess to have possessed a copy of 'Epictetus'. (Tipper's *Viaticum*
is not listed.)
    Elizabeth Berkeley (later Burnet) told Catharine Trotter in a
letter (BL Add. MS 4264, ff.266-267) 'I find I have lent Epictetus...'
Epictetus continued to be presented as a proper subject for
women's writing during the eighteenth century. Attached to *The*
Porch and Academy Opened, or Epictetus's Manual (1707) by 'J. W.' is
the 'Table of Cebes [another Stoic] by a Lady'; in 1710 Bishop
Burnet encouraged and corrected Mary Wortley Montagu's
translation of the *Enchiridion*; Elizabeth Carter's translation, begun
in 1749 under the guidance of Catherine Talbot's guardian Bishop
Secker, was published in 1758 and went into four editions.

427

19 Cf. Davies: 'that of all the ancient Philosophers, he had the best opinions concerning the Deity, and the greatest insight into our Mysteries' (33).

ELIZABETH THOMAS

One of Sir Walter Scott's less admired historical fictions says of Elizabeth Thomas (1675-1731), 'her person, as well as her writings, seems to have been dedicated to the service of the public' (Scott-Saintsbury, XVIII, 163). She has gone down in literary history as the unprincipled mistress of Pope's friend Henry Cromwell, who gave her some letters Pope had written to him at the beginning of his career. Years later, in desperation, she sold the letters for ten guineas to the bookseller Edmund Curll, who promptly published them in *Miscellanea* (1727). Pope then accused her of theft and vilified her in 1728 as 'Curll's Corinna' (*Dunciad*, II, 69-72).

Elizabeth's father, Emmanuel Thomas of the Inner Temple, died when she was two, leaving her mother, Elizabeth Osborne, in financial difficulties (*DNB*). Thomas spent most of her life with her mother and maternal grandmother in lodgings in London. Several translations from French appear in her *Miscellany Poems on Several Subjects* (1722, republished as *Poems on Several Occasions. By a Lady*, 1726, 1727). According to the 'Life of Corinna' prefixed to *Pylades and Corinna* (1731-1732), a collection of her letters, she had read the Bible three times before she was five, and she had about nine months tutoring in Latin, writing, mathematics, pharmacy and chemistry from a 'Dr. Quibus'. Curll claimed that the 'Life' was an autobiography, written in the third person; it has been proven, however, to be a mixture of fact and fiction (Malone, I, ii, 347ff.).

In the summer of 1699 Thomas initiated a correspondence with Dryden by sending him two poems to criticise. He responded in November 1699, paying her the ultimate compliment: 'your *Verses* were, I thought, too good to be a Woman's.' He continued:

'Tis not over gallant to say this of the fair Sex; but most certain it is, that they generally write with more Softness than Strength. On the contrary, you want neither Vigour in your Thoughts, nor Force in your Expressions, nor Harmony in your Numbers and methinks I find much of Orinda in your Manner (to whom I had the Honour to be related, and also to be known). (*Miscellanea*, I, 149)

He then gave her the name Corinna, after the great poet of ancient Thebes.

In the year of Dryden's death, Thomas contributed as 'a Young Lady' to *Luctus Britannici* (1700), a collection of elegies in his honour. This prompted the attentions of Richard Gwinnett, the Pylades of *Pylades and Corinna* (*DNB*). They were engaged for about seventeen years, their marriage delayed by his consumption and her mother's breast cancer. Gwinnett died in 1717. After a law suit

429

that lasted eight years, Thomas was able to obtain only £213 of the £600 he had bequeathed to her. Her mother died in January 1719, leaving her in debt. A number of Thomas's poems refer to her own illness, as well as her mother's and grandmother's. In 1711 Thomas had swallowed 'the middle Bone of the Wing of a large Fowl' which caused her to fall 'into a most violent bloody Flux, attended with a continual Pain in the Pit of her Stomach, Convulsions and swooning Fits'. A few months later 'she was seized with a malignant Fever and... crowed like a *Cock*, and barked like a *Dog*'. Dr Samuel Garth treated her with mercury and in 1713 sent her to Bath for 'Relief by Pumping' ('The surprizing *Case* of Mrs. *Thomas*, as it was given in, to the College of *Physicians*, 1730' in *Pylades and Corinna*, II, 93-96).

From her letters and poems we know that Thomas relied on the friendship of Lady Mary Chudleigh (1656-1710), the author of *The Ladies' Defence* (1701), whom Thomas calls 'Marissa', together with a Mrs Diana Bridgeman (Musidora), Anne, Lady Dowager De La Warr (Sulpitia), and Lady Hester Pakington, the wife of the prominent politician Sir John Pakington (1671-1727), all of whom were dead by 1722. Lady Chudleigh had suggested that Thomas might be 'a better Champion' for women than she was herself (*Pylades and Corinna*, II, 247). Thomas took the suggestion seriously, paraphrasing parts of Chudleigh's *Ladies' Defence* in her own poetry, which criticises the institution of marriage and advocates women's education. In this, she was clearly influenced by Mary Astell, who eventually snubbed Thomas for being 'too much a *Williamite*' (*Pylades and Corinna*, I, 104). Both Thomas and Chudleigh wrote poems to Astell as 'Almystrea' (Perry, 1986, 107, 111), Thomas praising Astell for showing her sex's 'Aptitude and Worth' and asking her 'to set us free / From the false Brand of *Incapacity*' (*Miscellany Poems*, 219). She also may have known Sarah Fyge, her fellow contributor in *Luctus Britannici* (Medoff, 1982, 170-171).

In 1727 she was sent to Fleet prison for debt. She wrote to Cromwell in June 1727, shortly after the appearance of the Pope–Cromwell letters:

So when I found myself plunged into unforeseen and unavoidable Ruin, I retreated from the World, and in a Manner buried myself in a dismal Place, where I knew none, nor none knew me... In this dull unthinking way, I have protracted a lingering Death (for Life it cannot be called) ever since you saw me, sequestered from Company, deprived of my Books, and nothing left to converse with but the Letters of my dead or absent Friends... (*Letters of Mr. Pope*, iii)

During her incarceration she collaborated with Curll on *Codrus, or the Dunciad Dissected* (1729), published Dryden's letters in the same volume with the Pope–Cromwell correspondence, and provided Curll with a fabricated account of Dryden's funeral (*Memoirs of Congreve*, 1730). Although a warrant for her release was issued in 1729, she could not pay her jailer's fees, and remained in prison until July 1730. Her poem, *The Metamorphoses of the Town; or a View of the present fashions. A Tale, after the manner of Fontaine* was published that year with Swift's *Journal of a Modern Lady*. Thomas died destitute and alone in lodgings on Fleet Street in February 1731. Lady Margaret, wife of John West, fifteenth Baron De La Warr, paid for her burial in the churchyard of St Bride's. Eight years later, Catharine Trotter Cockburn said of Thomas:

Her case is indeed extremely pitiable, and may afford matter of submission, and even gratitude to providence, under many uneasy dispensations, when we reflect how unhappy some have been, who seem to have deserved much better than ourselves. (Birch, II, 297)

A Midnight Thought, (on the Death of Mrs. *E. H.* and Her little Daughter, cast away under *London-Bridge*, Aug. 5. 1699.) *ending with an Address to Clemena.*

Oh sacred *Time*! how soon thou'rt gone!
How swift thy circling Minutes run!
Oh *Time*! our chiefest worldly Good,
If we emply *Thee* as we shou'd!
5   And yet how few thy Value know,
But think thee troublesome and slow!
(motion and Rest fill up our Time,
And little, Oh my *Soul*, is thine!)
We *eat*, we *drink*, we *sleep*, and then
10   We rise-- to do the same again:
And thus like *Fairies* daily tread,
The same dull Round our Predecessors led.

Young *Lydia* prudent was and fair,
Was all that virtuous Women are;
15   And yet how soon her Glass was run,
How short her fatal Thread was spun!
How know we our appointed *Fate*,
Whether ordain'd us soon or late?
Health is uncertain, *Death* is more;
20   And much we have to do before.

Ah then, my *Friend*, let us be wise;
No more the precious Gift despise;
But use it for the End 'twas giv'n,
And prove we're *candidates* of Heaven.
25   Let others to the Play repair,
Be courted and reputed fair:

Whole Winter-Nights at *Ombre* play
To pass the Drug of Time away.
While we our better Parts employ,
30 And placidly our Souls enjoy:
Praising that *Pow'r* did us create;
But more the *Love* redeem'd our Fate.
Then with th' illustrious *Dead* converse,
And sometimes with a Friend in *Verse*.
35 Thus in the Culture of the Mind,
Improve those Hours by Fate assign'd:
So shall we from superfluous Time be free:
'Tis Want of Sense makes *Superfluity*.

From *Miscellany Poems on Several Subjects*. London: Tho. Combes, 1722, 115-117.
Title *Clemena*: Anne Osborne, daughter of Richard Osborne, Thomas's uncle on her mother's side. She is the subject of a number of Thomas's poems. Apparently, the women grew apart when Osborne married, moved out of London, and 'for *Misanthropy* condemn'd the Muse' (*Miscellany Poems*, 174).
21-38 In her concern about 'the Culture of the Mind' and the proper use of women's time, Thomas is a disciple of Astell, whose proposed seminary for women would dispense with frivolous activities:

Here will be no impertinent Visits, no foolish Amours, no idle Amusements to distract our Thoughts and waste our precious time; a very little of which is spent in Dressing, that grand devourer and its concomitants, and no more than necessity requires in sleep and eating; so that here's a vast Treasure gain'd, which for ought I know may purchase an happy Eternity. (*A Serious Proposal* I, 86-87)

The triple League to Mrs. Susan Dove

Pensive *Eliza* lately sate,
Bewailing her unhappy Fate;
Careless her Dress, and wild her Air,
Her self an *Emblem* of Despair:
5 Upon her Hand, she lean'd her Head,
And sighing first, these Words she said:
Ye *Fates*! why am I thus perplex'd,
And why thus daily teaz'd and vex'd?
Each Hour, new Troubles you prepare,
10 And I am born but to despair.

The first dear Friendship I profest,
Center'd in noble *Celia*'s Breast!

432

Her Soul was great! her *Friendship* true!
Her *Conversation* always new:
15 But ravish'd hence, ah me! she's gone,
And left me here to mourn alone.

   No not alone *Clemena* said,
That fair! but ah forgetful Maid;
There still is one, will prove as true
20 As e'er bright *Celia* did to you;
See where *Clemena* does attend,
And willingly wou'd be your Friend
Why shou'd you then your Grief pursue,
She loves! and is related too.

25   Thus *Phoenix* like, she did disclose,
And out of Celia's Ashes rose:
Fair *Iris* too bestow'd a Part
Of her majestick gen'rous Heart:
'Twas then of all I wish'd possess'd,
30 Was poor *Eliza*, more than bless'd.

   But this too happy was to last,
And much I fear my Joys are past;
To rural Shades, *Clemena's* gone,
And I no more am thought upon:
35 Unkindly thus she leaves her Friend,
And now will neither come nor send.

   Direct me now, ye sacred Nine,
Whilst here I for *Clemena* pine,
Will not dear *Iris* thus conclude,
40 *Eliza's* either false, or rude?
She paus'd---
When straight there shin'd a glorious Ray,
The gloomy Grott was bright as Day;
A fragrent Scent her Spirits cheer'd,
45 And whilst these *Omens* she rever'd,
Young *Cupids* came, and wanton'd there,
And gentle *Zephirs* fann'd the Air:
Room! Room! for her whom we adore!
A *Cupid* cry'd, and said no more:

50   But as she spoke there came along
       Most beauteous *Iris*, fair and young;
       So fine, so gay, so wond'rous Bright,
       As was the first created Light:
       Yet *she* both kind, and good appears,
55   And quite disperses all my Fears.

       As when, in Dead of Night alone,
       A poor Unhappy! makes his Moan,
       Dismal Horror, silent Care,
       Sighs, and Groans, and deep Despair,
60   Do this poor Mortal quite surround,
       And's little Stock of Sense confound:
       But if an Angel pity take,
       And to's Relief a Tour doth make,
       Soon as the heaven'ly Beams appear,
65   So soon is vanish'd all his Fear.

       Such you, my *Lovely Angel*, came,
       Expell'd my Doubts, and clear'd her Fame;
       You did ev'n all a Friend cou'd do,
       And for some Hours, you gave me you.

70   But say, sweet *Nymph*, can you forgive,
       The *Slights* you did that Day receive?
       If so: Pray send me in a Line,
       That charming *Iris* still is mine.

From *Miscellany Poems on Several Subjects...* 1722, 234-238. This poem is one of two Thomas sent to Dryden for his evaluation, telling him that she was attempting to imitate Aphra Behn. Dryden responded by cautioning her against

the Licenses which Mrs. Behn allowed her self, of writing loosely, and giving, (if I may have leave to say so) *some Scandal to the Modesty of her Sex.* I confess, I am the last Man who ought, in Justice to arraign her, who have been myself too much a Libertine in most of my Poems, which I should be well contented *I had time either to purge or to see them fairly burned.* (*Miscellanea*, I, 151)

In a 1727 letter to Curll prefaced to the collection of Dryden's letters, Thomas repeated that the poems were written in imitation of Behn's 'Numbers': 'I own I was pleased with the Cadence of her Verse, tho' at the same Time I no ways approved the Licentiousness of her Morals' (*Miscellanea*, I, Sig. [A4]). In her first line at least, Thomas may have had in mind Behn's 'Love in fantastic triumph sate'.

ELIZABETH THOMAS

Title *Mrs. Susan Dove* may be Susan, daughter of Henry Dove (1640-1695), Archdeacon of Richmond and chaplain to Charles II, James II, and William and Mary, born sometime before 1680.

12 *Celia's Breast*: Cecilia Bew, who died in the Autumn of 1697, was the subject of the pastoral elegy Thomas sent to Dryden.

21-24 In an undated letter to 'Clemena', Thomas professed her love:

> our Friendship is too strongly cemented to be dissolved by any of those little Punctilioes that many times separate meer Relations; there are stronger Ties that unite us, than Interest or Consanguinity, and an Affection so pure as ours, may teach the mercenary World (what is now almost extinguished) a true Love of Benevolence. I am not ashamed to own my self thus far a *Platonick*, and can tell you without Panegyric, that I loved you at first for a Sincerity which is not common, a Generosity of Temper, that could distinguish and pay a Respect to Virtue, tho' in Rags, and a Soul which abhorred Flattery, and was beyond Dissimulation... (*Pylades and Corinna*, I, 253)

27 *Iris*: Susan Dove

36 *neither come nor send*: Thomas's poem 'To Clemena' expresses her dismay that her cousin has come to town and not told her (*Miscellany Poems*, 250-252).

The Dream. An Epistle to Mr. Dryden.

When yet a Child, I read great *Virgil* o'er,
And sigh'd, to see the barb'rous Dress he wore;
The Phrase how awkward, how abstruse the Sense!
And how remote from *Roman* Eloquence!
5 And mov'd, to see his lofty Epick Rhymes
By murd'ring Pens debas'd, to doggerel Chimes;
Ye, sacred Maids, cried I, How long? and why
Must *Virgil* under *English* Rubbish lye?
He, who can charm in this Exotick Dress,
10 What Beauties must his native Tongue express?
Ah barren Isle! not One, one gen'rous Quill,
To give Him whole, will non exert their skill,
But who translate incorrigibly ill?

Then pausing here, I fell into a Dream,
15 If I may call it such? and this the Theam.
Methoughts I did the *Delphick Fane* behold,
The Doors, and Roof, were all of burnish'd Gold,
The Floor, and Walls of *Parian* Stone were built,
And these, with ductile Gold, were finely gilt.
20 Above three Hundred Lamps shone in the Place,
And twice six Altars, did the Temple grace;

A golden Tripos, in the Midst arose;
But O! what Pen it's Lustre can disclose?
So nicely grav'd, so lively ev'ry Part,
25 Nature her self was here out done by Art.
The meanest Basis was of costly Wood,
And, on it's Summit, bright *Apollo* stood:
An azure Mantle did his Arms invest,
His golden Lyre, he held before his Brest.
30 A Silver Bow was on his Shoulder bound,
And with chaste *Daphne*'s Leaves, his Head was
                                        crowned.
Ruddy his Cheeks, and flowing was his Hair,
All dazling bright he look'd, and exquisitly Fair.
Around him, sage *Memoria's* Daughters sat;
35 And all the Graces at his right Hand wait.
Then up *Calliope* arose, who sings
Of mighty Poets; and of mighty Kings:
Her lovely Breast, with her fair Hand she stroke,
And after due Obeisance, thus she spoke.

40   Thou *Great Director* of our triple Trine!
Thou, who instructed us, and made us thine!
Hast thou forgotten? when my first born Son,
My dearest *Orpheus, Pluto's* Favour won;
And how, for too much Kindness to his Wife,
45 He was by *Bacchannals* depriv'd of Life;
Who tore his Limbs, in *Hebrus* cast his Head,
Which sweetly sang his Elogy tho' Dead?
'Twas then, you chear'd me, bid me dry my Eyes,
And said, from me, another Swan should rise:
50 When *Virgil*'s born, he shall thy Joys restore,
And, for thy *Orpheus*, thou shalt weep no more.
'Twas said! 'tis done! and *Virgil* calm'd my Breast,
With *Eagles* Wings, he soar'd above the Rest;
And *Orpheus* Spirit, doubly he possest.
55 But now twelve Cent'ries past, I've cause to mourn
To see my *Virgil*'s Works thus maul'd and torn,
By *French, Dutch, English*, and each stupid Drone,
Burlesq'd, obscur'd, and in Travesty shown.
Poor mercenary Pens attempt for Gain,
60 And hungry Wits his sacred Lines profane;
'Tis thus they sully, thus disgrace his Name;

And not one gen'rous Bard, is left to clear his Fame.
Hold! he reply'd, there's one has Sense and Truth,
That is my Creature, he shall right the Youth,
65 New polish *Maro; Maro's* soul express;
And cloath him in a more becoming Dress.
And thou bold Girl! (to me) hast done amiss,
To call that barren where my *Dryden* is;
He whom I have ordain'd, by certain Doom,
70 To honour *Britain*, more, than *Virgil Rome*:
And with the self same voice, Eternal Fame,
Dryden and *Virgil's* glory shall proclaim.

The grateful Muse, profoundly bow'd her Head,
And I still trembling, wak'd, at what was said:
75 *Dryden* cried I! ev'n then, I knew your Name;
(For who was Ignorant of *Dryden's* Fame?)
'Tis he! 'tis only he the Work must do,
Then in some Years I found the Vision true,
And swiftly caught the Blessing as it flew.
80 The Death of Friends, first gave my Muse a Birth,
But you, Sir, rais'd her grov'ling from the Earth:
You taught her Numbers; and you gave her Feet;
And you set Rules, to bound Poetick Heat:
If there is ought in me deserves that Name,
85 The Spark was light at mighty *Dryden's* Flame:
But ne'er yet blest with my great Master's Sight.
I fear you'll think it Impudence to write.
Forgive me *Sir*, I long'd to let you know
How much your Pupil to your Works does owe;
90 Her Muse is yours, and is at your Command,
But envies those that in your presence stand.

From *Miscellany Poems On Several Subjects...* 1722, 18-22. This verse epistle was probably part of the Thomas–Dryden correspondence of 1699. Dryden's Virgil was published by joint-stock subscription in 1697; 101 subscribers paid five guineas for a de luxe copy with engravings, and 252 paid two guineas; Pope understood, probably from Tonson who published both, that Dryden had earned altogether more than £1,200 from the translation, unheard-of wealth for any writer of the time. In her elegy on Dryden in *Luctus Britannici*, Thomas depicts him rescuing Homer too from previous translators, 'Redeem'd his injur'd Sire, and set him free / From *Chapman*, *Hobb*'s and mangling *Ogilby*' (14).

2 *barbarous dress*: a translation into heroic verse was published by John Ogilby in 1649, and reprinted as a sumptuous illustrated folio in 1654. Although Ogilby's translation was much ridiculed it was also much read: it is the first book listed in the 'Ladies Library' described in *The Spectator*, and very much closer to Virgil's sense than Dryden. Dryden attacked Ogilby for his bad poetry and translations in *Mac Flecknoe* (1684), and in the prefaces to *Sylvae* (1685) and the *Fables* (1700).

5 *Epick Rhymes*: Virgil wrote in unrhymed dactylic hexameters.

10 *What beauties must...*: Thomas makes clear that she could not herself read Latin.

16 *Delphick Fane*: Apollo's temple at Delphi

18 *Parian Stone*: white marble from the island of Paros, prized by the ancients for sculpture

22 *Tripos*: tripod, the three-legged stool on which Apollo's priestess sat when she delivered his oracles

27 Thomas here seems to be conflating two classical images; Apollo at the summit of Parnassus, surrounded by the Muses, and his oracle at the temple at Delphi

31 *Daphne's Leaves*: bay leaves, sacred to Apollo

34 *Memoria's Daughters*: the Muses, daughters of Mnemosyne, personification of memory

35 *Graces*: the three Graces, personifications of beauty

36 *Calliope*: muse of epic poetry and mother of Orpheus

40 *triple Trine*: the nine muses

45-47 When Orpheus was torn apart by the Maenads, his head, thrown into the Hebrus river, continued to sing.

65 *Maro*: Virgil

77 Cf. Thomas's poem to Dryden 'On his Translation of Virgil', 'And none but Dryden, Virgil could translate' (*Miscellany Poems*, 23). Dryden considered another poem on his translation of Virgil, written by Lady Mary Chudleigh, to be 'better than any which are printed before the book' (Scott-Saintsbury, XVIII, 139). The poem was later published in Lady Chudleigh's *Poems on Several Occasions* (1703), 25-28.

78 *Then in some years*: Thomas claims the role of child sybil, here foretelling Dryden's translation before the event.

80 *The Death of Friends*: both poems Thomas sent to Dryden dealt with the death of her friend, Cecilia Bew. She may also be referring to 'A Midnight Thought'.

82-83 A claim by Thomas to have been taught by Dryden in any but the most general sense would be stretching a point; amid the flattery he did occasionally utter a word of caution as in November 1699:

If you have any considerable Faults, they consist chiefly in the Choice of Words, and the placing them so as to make the Verse run smoothly... (*Miscellanea*, I, 152)

'A LADY OF HONOUR'

We do not know who the 'Lady of Honour' was who wrote *The Golden Island* to encourage support for a Scottish settlement in Panama. In 1695 in response to agitation to set up a rival to the East India Company, an act of the Scots Parliament established 'The Company of Scotland trading to Africa and the Indies'. King William had sent his own representative, Lord Tweeddale, to assist them in drawing up the charter which gave them a monopoly of Scotch trade with Asia, Africa and America for thirty-one years and authorised them to take possession of uninhabited territories. When subscriptions were opened in London, £300,000 worth of stock was subscribed in nine days; in answer to pressure from the powerful East India Company, the English Parliament ordered trading to cease. King William dismissed Tweeddale. In Scotland, stock in the company realised £219,000 (J. Barbour, 22). Departure of the first expedition was delayed by mismanagement; in November 1698, 1,200 Scots arrived in Panama, then known as Darien, and renamed it New Caledonia.

The stock issue had been publicised in Scotland by a series of pamphlets and broadsides; *The Golden Island* belongs to a second wave of propaganda designed to encourage investment in a follow-up expedition. When it arrived in November 1699 the original settlers had left, their numbers decimated by illness. The second and the third expeditions ran into armed Spanish opposition and were obliged to capitulate in March 1700.

The poet had never seen Darien; her imagery is culled from the contemporary accounts that proliferated during the short life of the Scottish empire in the New World.

The Golden Island or the Darian Song

> Some slumbring thoughts possess'd my brain,
>   ['T]was Prophecied of Old,
> That Albanie should Thrissels spread,
>   o're all the *Indian Gold*.
> 5 Me thought I heard the Valiant *Scots*,
>   beneath the *Northern* Poll,
> Rejoycing of their Prosperous Voyage,
>   which *England* did Control.

The Heavens did Favour them so Fair,
10 they were into Deaths Jaws,
And *Neptune* bowed the loftie Seas,
  and humbled all her Waves,
Untill the Ransomed should pass
  that ventured on the Main.
15 The *English* Great, then ventured twice,
  and were beat back again.
Sol, Luna, Mars, and *Jupiter,*
  Heavens Canopie did keep.
Be sure some Angel stier'd our Helm,
20 when some were faln a sleep:
To guide us to that Noble place,
  was promis'd us before,
That will Enrich brave Albanie,
  which Fame does still adore:
25 It is ordain'd in Holy Write,
  Death pay'd our Sacrifice;
The *Thristle* and the *Reed Lyon*
  will Crush our Enemies.
We're Antipods to *England* now,
30 win by a pleasant Toil:
We've saild the Gulph against the Tyde,
  come to a Fruitfull Soil.
Who can express what we expect,
  since we are favoured so,
35 The Lord has thought upon our flight;
  some thought to make us low.
All Men that has put in some Stock,
  to us where we are gone;
They may expect our Saviors words
40 a Hundered reap for One;
For to Encourage every One
  that ventures on the Main,
Come cast thy Bread on Waters great,
  thou'lt get it back again.
45 The World durst never *Scotland* Brag,
  for Valour and Renown:
Go pass the Line surrownd the Glob,
  not such an Ancient Crown.
What One has slighted us before,
50 not want of Honour sure:

440

Brave Noble Spirits, in Ancient Land,
  onlie is called Poor.
Our Enemies has the Sun shine
  so well we know our Foes?
55 But the *Thrissel* in the *Lyons* hand,
  'gainst *Leopards* and *Rose*;
The Lord will mend the *Broken* Reed,
  and will not *quench the spark*:
Our Enemies shall all fall down,
60   as *Dagon* before the Ark.
Fortune put on her Gilded Sails,
  went to the Antipods:
Heathens receiv'd us with a Grace,
  as if we had been Gods.
65 The Gales blew sweet, we Bless the Lord,
  for all our sails were full,
King William did Encourage us,
  against the *English* will.
His Words is like a Statly Oak,
70   will neither Bow nor Break;
We'll venture Life and Fortune both,
  for *Scotland* and his sake,
For he has done such valiant Acts,
  what Pen can him express?
75 Lay down your Crowns and Battens all,
  that came by *Adams* Race.
What will be said in future times
  when Vertue yields her Flowers,
The Babes unborn will then cry out,
80   no Parent's like to Ours.
This great Attempt is carried on,
  by Mortals that has breath,
It seems the Lord does mind to send
  Christs Gospel through the Earth:
85 To writ the parts of these brave Men,
  that has sent us away:
The Vialactia smiles to see,
  Scotlands new Nuptial day.
The Harp play'd us a pleasant spring,
90   and *Neptune* took a dance,
Made *Monsiur Flower-de-luce* to fall,
  into a deadly Trance.

441

When we were on the *Darian Main,*
    and viewed the Noble Land,
95 The Trees joyn'd hands and bowed low,
    for Honour of *Scotland.*
Young Native Babes that never spake,
    Dame Nature bad them cry,
And utter forth some joyfull Notes,
100   to welcome Albanie!
Refreshing spring and Rivolats
    when we were Landed there,
Came glidding with her jumbling Notes,
    invits us to take share;
105 The chearming birds, that haunts the Woods,
    Meavis, Peacock, and *Dow,*
Brought Presents in their mouths, and sang
    we pay Tribute to you.
We went in Boats, and come to Land,
110   which banisht all our fears.
The Seas did mourn for want of us,
    each Oar was droping Tears.
The Woulf, the Lyon, and the Boar,
    the Wyld Tigger and Fox,
115 did fill their Claws with Golden Dust,
    salutes us from the Rocks.
The Tortels in the *Indian Seas,*
    left Eggs upon the Land
And came to see that Noble Fleet,
120   was come from Old *Scotland.*
The Hurtchon came out of the Woods,
    her prickels Load with Fruit,
She mumbled, but she could not speak,
    ye're welcome all come eat.
125 The Balmie Grass, and blooming Flowers,
    were all covered with dew;
Then *Phoebus* did bid them give a smell,
    and that would pay their due.
The Seas began to roar for joy;
130   when we were all past through,
And Neptune with's great *Harry Kains,*
    to us was like a Loach;
And still we bless the Lord of Hoasts,
    and all our Benefactors,

135   And drank a health to Albanie,
      for all our Brave Directors.
    Nilus Banks did Overflow
      only but *Egypts* land:
    But your Fame will the World Ov'rspread,
140   And Banks of Heathen sand.
    We have another Fleet to sail,
      the Lord will Reik them fast;
    It will be wonderful to see,
      the *Sun rise in the West*!
145   If I should name each One concerned,
      according to their station,
    Ten Quair of paper would not do,
      its known by true Relation:
    For some are Noble, All are Great,
150   Lord bless your Companie,
    And let your Fame in *Scotlands* Name
      O'respread both Land and Sea.

The Golden Island or the Darian Song. In Commendation of All Concerned in that Noble Enterprize Of the Valiant Scots. By a Lady of Honour. Edinburgh... 1699. From *Various Pieces of Fugitive Scotish Poetry; Principally of the Seventeenth Century.* [David Laing, ed.] Edinburgh: Printed for W. & D. Laing, [1825]. The ballad is written in fourteeners, split after the fourth foot, into alternating lines of unrhymed tetrameter and rhymed trimeter, a metre more commonly associated with poetry of a much earlier period.
Title *Golden Island*: a small island off the coast of Panama; *Darian*: Panama
2 The line as many others is corrupt; the text may represent a transcription of a Scots original.
3 *Albanie*: King William, who had among his many titles that of Duke of Albany; *Thrissels*: Scots dialect for thistles, the heraldic emblem of Scotland
4 *Indian Gold*: the settlers panned for gold in the Panamanian rivers.
6 *Northern Poll*: North Pole
8 *Control*: challenge, censure, object to
10 *they were into Deaths Jaws*: 'were' may originally have been the Scots dialect word 'quirm' or 'whirm', meaning to disappear into, to vanish suddenly.
13 *the Ransomed*: the redeemed, the delivered
14 *Main*: the open sea
15 *the English Great, then ventured twice*: presumably this refers to an English fleet. The journal of Hugh Rose, a member of the first expedition, records that the settlers originally considered the Golden Island itself for settlement but that they 'might be attacked

by the greatest either from Eastward or Westward, for they can come in both ways'. The Scots finally settled on a narrow peninsula four miles east of the Golden Island (Burton, 63; 66).

27 *Reed Lyon*: the red lion is part of the royal emblem of Scotland.

29 *Antipods*: places on the earth's surface directly opposite to each other

40 Matthew 13:8 and 13:23

43-44 Ecclesiastes 11:1

45 *Brag*: speak ill of

47 *the Line surrownd the Glob*: the equator

55 *Thrissel in the Lyons hand*: a lion rampant appears on the bearings of William III as Prince of Orange, and the Thistle is one of the heraldic emblems for Scotland. The image thus refers to the co-operation of the King and the Scots.

56 *Leopards and Rose*: heraldic emblems for England

57 *Broken Reed*: 2 Kings 19-21 and Isaiah 36:6

60 *Dagon*: In 1 Samuel 5:2-7, the statue of Dagon, chief god of the Philistines, falls before the ark of the Lord.

63-64 Hugh Rose reported that the natives unstrung their bows as a token of friendship and asked the Scots to live with them (Burton, 63-68).

67-68 Although King William had instructed the Marquis of Tweeddale to gratify the Scots as far as possible, both houses of the English Parliament, in conjunction with the East India Company, pressured the King to withdraw his support of English subscriptions to the newly formed Scots company.

75 *Crowns and Battens*: crowns and sceptres (batons)

87 *Vialactia*: Milky Way

91 *Monsiur Flower-de-luce*: sometime after the arrival of the first Scots expedition to Darian, a French ship arrived, stayed for a short while in the bay, and was shipwrecked when trying to move out to sea again (Borland, 20).

93 *Darian Main*: main here means mainland

106 *Meavis*: blackbird; *Dow*: dove

117 *tortel*: turtle

121 *Hurtchon*: our author may have misinterpreted the settlers' descriptions of prickle palms full of little kernels to mean a hurtchon (or urchin), which is a hedgehog:

There is a *Prickle Palm*, so call'd because it is infinitly full of *Prickles* from the Root to the *Leaves* ;... as thick as the Bristles of an *Hedg-Hogg*. (*A Letter, giving a Description of... Darian*, 1699)

131 *Harry Kains*: hurricanes

132 *Loach*: a small fish

142 *Reik*: or reek; Scots, equip or make ready

144 *the Sun rise in the West*: the leading ship of the second expedition was called the *Rising Sun*. A rising sun was part of the Company's coat of arms.

147 *Quair*: a quire is twenty-four sheets of writing paper.

LADY SARAH PIERS

Lady Sarah Piers, daughter of Matthew Roydon, originally of Roydon in Yorkshire, was the wife of Sir George Piers (1670-1720) of Stonepit, near Seal in Kent, an army captain and Clerk of the Privy Seal (Noble, III, 447-448; HMC, *13th Report*, App.II, 176). On the encouragement of her good friend Catharine Trotter she contributed to *The Nine Muses* (1700), a collection of elegies on Dryden's death, writing as 'Urania', the Divine Muse. Trotter dedicated her comedy *Love at a Loss* (1701) to Lady Piers in effusive language, praising her as wife, mother, and 'a Person, so capable, of so distinguishing a Genius' who 'knows how to relish the noblest things' [a2ᵛ]. Piers in turn wrote a commendatory poem for the publication of *Love at a Loss*.

Their friendship was attacked by Delariviere Manley in the second volume of *The New Atalantis* (1709). Manley includes 'Daphne', or Catharine Trotter, in a 'cabal' of women who may have carried their female friendships 'beyond what *Nature* design'd' and given 'their *Husbands* but a second place in their *Affections* and *Cares*'. Trotter is introduced into the cabal by one 'Zara', 'a Writer... whose Poetical Genius did not much lead her to the better *Oeconomy* of her *Family*'. Manley says of 'Daphne' and 'Zara', 'they seem'd to live only for each other', describing 'Zara' as 'cross'd' when 'Daphne' married a 'Priest', moved to the country, and devoted herself to the religion she had once abandoned but again professed (II, 50-56).

A contemporary key to *The New Atalantis* identifies 'Zara', with her doting husband 'Chevalier Pierro', as the Countess of Dorchester, formerly Catherine Sedley, mistress of James II, wife of David Colyear, first Earl of Portmore (Doble, II, 389). It is more likely that 'Daphne's' devoted woman friend is Lady Sarah Piers. Manley writes that 'Zara's' admiration for *Senior Mompellier* (Samuel Garth) was expressed in 'Printed *Heroicks*' shortly after he had 'newly become the Fashion' with 'his very just and admirable Poem'. The first edition of Garth's *The Dispensary* was published in 1699; Piers's poem in heroic couplets praising Garth appeared in *The Nine Muses* the following year. Nothing on Garth by the Countess of Dorchester is known. Manley says that 'Chevalier Pierro... made an admirable Husband' and thought 'that his Wife was never in the *wrong*, nor himself in the *right*, but when she said so', acting more like a lover than a husband. Trotter makes a similar assessment of Sir George Piers, in more sincere terms, in her dedication of *Love at a Loss*. 'Zara's' husband 'put himself into the Army, and Campaigns abroad' out of financial need. There is no indication that the

Countess of Dorchester suffered economic problems; her husband was said to have gained a 'great estate' by marrying her (*DNB*).

Although Thomas Birch described the Trotter–Piers relationship as a 'most intimate and unreserved friendship' (Birch, I, x) and Piers called Trotter 'the idol of all my Noblest Sentiments' (BL Add. MS 4264, f.295), in the Trotter correspondence, published and unpublished, Piers does not appear to be unduly possessive. A letter from Trotter to Cockburn written before she married him claims rather that Piers advised Trotter in the matter of her marriage (Birch, I, 239). In her later letters to Mrs Cockburn Piers refers to Patrick Cockburn as 'your valuable Dear man' (BL Add. MS 4264, f.305).

Piers's elder son died in the summer of 1707. Her letters of the period mention her husband returning from the campaign in Flanders with open wounds, and her own personal illness and need to 'take the waters'. She often stayed in Southborough near Tunbridge Wells, or at Hammersmith, associating with fashionable women of the time. A two-page broadsheet poem (title and publication date missing), 'by Lady P---', published for the bookseller Richard Standfast in Tunbridge Walks and Westminster Hall, appears in the midst of the Trotter–Piers correspondence in Birch's manuscript collection (BL Add. MS 4264, ff. 312-312ᵛ). Written in 1708, it pays homage in eighty-four lines to the various beauties that frequented Tunbridge Wells, including Susan Howard, Lady Effingham, another member of the 'cabal' who according to Manley, fell in love with the actress Letitia Cross (see p.417), and Piers's close friend, Elizabeth Smith, whose son, Sir Sidney Stafford Smith, hung Piers's portrait next to his mother's at the family seat near Tunbridge (BL Add. MS 5276 E (5), f.26).

Piers's only other known published work is a verse panegyric, *George for Britain* (1714). Both she and her remaining son died before her husband George, who was buried at Seal on 20 May 1720 (G.E.C., *The Complete Peerage*, II, 432).

To my much Esteemed Friend
On her Play call'd Fatal-Friendship

> With what Concern I sat and heard your Play,
> None else can Judge, but such a Friend sure may.
> The *Indian* Mother cou'd not feel more pain,
> Whose Newborn Babe's thrown headlong in the
> Main,
> 5   To prove him lawful: at whose welcome Rise
> (Her fears disperst) Joy gushes at her Eyes.
> Were I but Judge enough I'd do thee Right,
> Though yet much more, I want Poetick flight,

And 'twere his folly to repeat a new
10 Who light a taper the bright Sun to shew,
Shou'd I attempt your Praise, but as a Friend,
T'Express my thoughts, is all that I intend.
Your fable's clear, no rule you have transgrest,
Chast all your thoughts, yet Nature still exprest,
15 Your numbers flow, as if the Muses all
Consulted nothing, but their Rise, and fall,
Your Characters are just, and with such art
Your Passions rais'd, they gain th' unwary heart,
And what you feign, effectually Create,
20 Who was unmov'd, at sad *Felicia*'s Fate?
Scarce cou'd the stubbornest deny their Tears,
All felt your Heroes miseries, as theirs,
But as a faithful Friend, he touch'd me most;
By life's most noble, best of blessings, lost;
25 O Heaven, this my fondest wish Decree!
Our mutual Friendship, may ne'er Fatal be.

From *Fatal Friendship. A Tragedy. As it is Acted at the New-Theatre in Little-Lincolns-Inn-Fields.* London: Printed for Francis Saunders at the Blue-Anchor. in the Lower-Walk of the New-Exchange, 1698, [Sig. A4].
10 Proverbial, 'to set forth the sun with a candle'. In her commendatory verse to Trotter's *The Unhappy Penitent* (1701), Piers again compares Trotter to 'bright *Phoebus*': 'Like him bright Maid thy great Perfections shine, / As awful, as resplendent, as divine'(20-21), and to Katharine Philips and Aphra Behn:

> Thus like the Morning Star *Orinda* rose
> A Champion for her Sex, and wisely chose,
> Conscious of Female Weakness, humble wais
> T' insinuate for applause, not storm the Bays.
> Next gay *Astrea* briskly won the Prize,
> Yet left a spacious room to Criticize. (7-12)

She then holds Trotter up as a reformer of the stage,

> By thy judicious Rules the Hero learns
> To vanquish Fate, and weild his Conq'ring Arms;
> The bashful Virgin to defend her heart,
> The prudent Wife to scorn dishonest Art,
> The Friend sincerity; temp'rance the Youth,
> The Lover Chastity, and Statesman Truth. (33-38)

20 *Felicia's Fate*: the heroine of *The Fatal Friendship* is secretly married. In the last act, Gramont, her husband, kills himself after accidentally causing his best friend's death and Felicia swoons.

KISSING THE ROD

Urania: *The Divine Muse.*
On the Death of John Dryden, *Esq.*
By the Honourable the Lady P----

When through the Universe with Horrour spread,
   A sacred Voice pronounc'd Great *Pan* was dead,
All Nature trembled at the direful Fate,
And *Atlas* sunk beneath his pond'rous weight;
5   The mournful Muses hung their heads with woe,
While ev'ry Deity regrets the Blow,
And to the holy Oracles, deny
All farther Inspects of futurity;
The Earth did under strong Convulsions groan,
10 And Heaven did eccho back the dreadful moan:

   With no less grief, with no less pain opprest,
Britania felt the wound within her Breast,
When through the murmuring Croud sad Accents
                              bore
The fatal News, that *Dryden* was no more:
15 No more, to charm the list'ning World with Lays,
But fled to sing his great Creator's praise:
No more with artful Numbers, to bestow
An universal Influence below:
No more with all discerning Truth, to tell
20 How they shou'd act, and how distinguish well,
But Summon'd by *Apollo*'s sacred Lyre,
Now chaunts his Raptures in the Heav'nly Choir.

   Loud were the Clamours, and the moving Cries,
Which cut the yielding Air, and pierc'd the Skies;
25 While on *Parnassus*, 'twas the Muses care
Fresh Garlands for their Darling to prepare;
I search'd the Treasures of the Pow'rs above,
And form'd an Anthem on Seraphick Love:
New Themes we chose, not more polite than he
30 Has left already to Posterity;
But those for which the Island does repine,
For which they still invoke his awful Shrine,
And with transported Sorrow loudly cry,
Virgil, the *Roman* Eagles taught to fly,
35 But *Dryden* mounts their Pinions to the Sky!

448

To him proud *Greece* and *Italy* must bow,
And his sublime Authority allow,
Who by his never-dying Works, we see
Merits, and gives an Immortality.
40 Oh give us *Homer* yet, thou glorious Bard;
But if this last Petition can't be heard,
Yet like that Prophet, wing'd by strong desire,
Who broke from Earth, wrapt in Celestial fire,
Confer thy Spirit on the blooming Son,
45 And bless the Progress he so well begun;
Let *Garth* inherit all thy generous Flame,
Garth, who alone can justify the Claim.
He, whom the God of Wisdom did fore-doom,
And stock with Eloquence to pay thy Tomb,
50 The most triumphant Rites of ancient *Rome*.

'Tis this that fills *Urania*'s Eyes with Tears.
'Tis this ungrateful Sound that racks my Ears,
Who now to thee, *Melpomene*, repair,
To mix my Sorrows with thy anxious care;
55 Unite us all within thy gloomy Breast,
Where downy Peace, and Pleasure find no rest;
There let us drink the Floods thou shed'st, and then
A deluge of Despair pour out again.
What if our Tears shou'd drown the World a new,
60 The Sacrifice were to his *Manes* due.
Who now of Heroes, or of Gods can sing!
Who their Credentials from *Apollo* bring!
Where shall *Urania* now bestow her aid!
Or who great *Dryden*'s Province dare invade!
65 Ah none such lofty Subjects can pursue;
The Muses have, alas! no more to do,
Than sing his Elogies, and so expire,
In the cold Urn of his extinguish'd Fire.

But stay, a sudden Thought does now revive
70 My drooping heart, and keep my hopes alive;
Behold in *Albion* lately did appear
A learned Bard, to *Escalapius* dear,
Well knowing in the Secrets of his Skill,
And surely foster'd on *Parnassus*'s Hill,
75 Nor does the Chrystal *Helicon* bestow

449

A clearer Stream, than from his Numbers flow:
On him already all the Graces smile,
In him survive new Trophies for the Isle;
More I'le not urge, but know our Wishes can
80 No higher Soar, since *Garth*'s the Glorious Man;
Him let us Constitute in *Dryden*'s stead,
Let Laurels ever flourish on his head,
And let us to *Apollo* make our Pray'r
To Nominate him his Vice-regent, there;
85 By this *Britannia* shall her Joys retreive,
Nor find that *Dryden*'s dead, while *Garth* does live.

From *The Nine Muses, Or, Poems Written By Nine Severall Ladies Upon the Death of the late Famous John Dryden, Esq;...* London: Printed for Richard Basset, at the Mitre in Fleetstreet, 1700, 3-5.

Inspired by the publication of *Luctus Britannici* (1700), a volume of elegies on Dryden's death which included the work of Sarah Fyge and Elizabeth Thomas, Delariviere Manley organised the publication of a similar volume, *The Nine Muses* (1700), with her own poems and those of Pix, Fyge, Susannah Carroll (later Centlivre), Trotter, and Piers. In a letter to Trotter, Piers expressed hestitation:

I think I must own my self oblig'd to Mistress Manly for her gentile complement, yet at the same time she has put it out of my power to gratify her request, I had much rather she (as the greatest judge) shou'd be of the opinion she is of, then undeceive her by any peice of mine unworthy to joyn with hers, beside I have not the partiality of friendship to excuse me with her, as I have with you, and I doubt the tears of the musess will not have a force equal to those of Britannici, unless they have more languishing hearts than mine, I may sacrifice to Clio, or Melpomany, but know but one way to inspire me, and that I dare not think on, 'tis possible you can make me weep yet I woud not find the experiment, I do not perfectly apprehend how Mistress Manly, has fixt her thought til I have spoke with you, my time in town you know is short, but if it wou'd not interrupt one pleasant moment, I might make an esay t'wards a tryal of my self, but doe not depend on it, nor decline a better pen than that of your intire friend, & Ser^{tt}. Sar: Piers.

Lady Piers then requested a copy of *Luctus Britannici*, 'if not in latin' (BL Add. MS 4264, f.324; Medoff, 1982, 171). The book was a collection of poems in English.

Title *Urania*: the Muse of astronomy

35 *Pinions*: wings. The ancient Romans customarily sent an eagle flying from an emperor's funeral pyre, to represent his ascending spirit. Dryden referred to this custom in his 'Heroic Stanzas' to Oliver Cromwell.

35 Dryden's translation of Virgil (1697) was recognised as a great literary achievement. See Elizabeth Thomas, 'The Dream' (p.435).

40 Dryden's *Fables*, which included the first book of Homer's *Iliad*, was published in 1700, shortly before his death.

42 *that Prophet*: Elijah. II Kings 2:1-15

46 *Garth*: Sir Samuel Garth (1661-1719), physician and poet, best

known in his own time for the mock-heroic poem 'The Dispensary' (1699), influenced by Boileau and Dryden. He is remembered today as a member of the Kit-Cat Club and as a good friend of Pope.

49-50 Garth arranged for Dryden's body to lie in state at the College of Physicians. He made a Latin oration in praise of Dryden, accompanied the remains to Westminster Abbey, and in the same year, 1700, translated the 'Life of Ortho' in the fifth volume of Dryden's *Plutarch*.

53 *Melpomene*: the muse of tragedy

60 *Manes*: the spirit of a dead person, to be propitiated by reverence or revenge

72 *Esculapius*: Greek god of medicine, son of Apollo and Coronis

81 Trotter may have been responding specifically to this suggestion by Piers/Urania when she states in her own *Nine Muses* poem, 'Yet you my happier Sisters, still enflame / Some favourite Bard, who will invoke your name' (13-14).

WORKS CITED

[Agrippa, Henricus Cornelius], *A Treatise of the Nobilitie and excellencye of woman kynde*, David Clapham, trans., [n.p.] T. Bertheleti, 1542

——, *The Glory of Women. Or, A Treatise declaring the excellency and preheminence of Women above Men, which is proved both by Scripture, Law, Reason, and Authority, Divine, and Humane. Written First in Latine by Henricus Cornelius Agrippa knight, and Doctor both of Law and Physicke. And Presented to Margaret Augusta, Queen of the Austrians and Burgundians. And Now translated into English, for the Vertuous and Beautifull Female Sex of the Commonwealth of England. By Edward Fleetwood, Gent.* London, Robert Ibbetson, 1652

——, *The Glory of Women: Or A Looking-Glasse for Ladies: Wherein they may behold their own Excellency and Preheminence, proved to be greater then mans, by Scripture, Law, Reason & Authority, divine & human. Written first in Latine, by Henricus Cornelius Agrippa, Knight and Doctor both of Law and Physick. Afterwards Translated into English Prose, but now turned into Heroicall Verse. By H. C. Gent.* London, T. H. for Francis Coles, 1652

——, *Female Pre-eminence: Or The Dignity and Excellency of that Sex, above the Male. An Ingenious Discourse: Written Originally in latine, by Henry Cornelius Agrippa, Knight, Doctor of both Laws, and Privy-Counsellor to the Emperour Charles the Fifth. Done into English, with Additional Advantages. By H[enry].C[are].* London, T. R. and M. D. [for] Henry Million, 1670

'A Lady', *Six Familiar Essays upon Marriage, Crosses in Love, Sickness, Death, Loyalty, and Friendship, Written by a Lady*, London, Tho. Bennet, 1696

Allen, Thomas, *History of the County of Lincoln*, London and Lincoln, J. Saunders Jr, 1834

[Allestree, Richard], *The Ladies Calling*, Oxford, Richard Allestree, 1673

Anderson, Paul Bunyan, 'Mistress Delariviere Manley's Biography', *Modern Philology*, 33 (1936), 261-278

Animadversions on Mr. Congreve's Late Answer to Mr. Collier, London, John Nutt, 1698

Arber, Edward, ed., *The Dryden Anthology. 1675-1700*, London, Henry Frowde, 1899

'Ariadne', *She Ventures and He Wins. A Comedy... Writen by a Young Lady*, London, H. Rhodes, J. Harris, S. Briscoe, 1696

Armstrong, John, *Miscellanies*, London, T. Cadell, 1770

Aspelin, Gunnar, 'Ralph Cudworth's Interpretation of Greek

452

WORKS CITED

Philosophy', *Acta Universitatis Gotoburgensis, Goteborgs, Hogskolas Arsskrift*, 49 (1943), 1-47

Astell, Mary, *A Serious Proposal to the Ladies, For the Advancement of their true and greatest Interest. By a Lover of Her Sex... The Second Edition Corrected*, London, R. Wilkin, 1695

——, and John Norris, *Letters Concerning the Love of God, Between the Author of the Proposal to the Ladies and Mr. John Norris*, London, Samuel Manship and Richard Wilkin, 1695

——, *A Serious Proposal to the Ladies, Part II. Wherein a Method is offer'd for the Improvement of their Minds*, London, Richard Wilkin, 1697

——, *The Christian Religion as Professed by a Daughter of the Church of England*, London, S.H. for R. Wilkin, 1705

——, *Reflections Upon Marriage. Occasion'd by the Duke and Dutchess of Mazarine's Case; which is also consider'd. The Third Edition. To which is added a Preface, in Answer to some Objections*, London, John Nutt, 1706

Athenae Oxoniensis, by Anthony à Wood, ed. Philip Bliss, London, 1813, etc.

Atwood, William, *The Idea of Christian Love Being a Translation at the Instance of Mr. Waller of a Latin Sermon Upon John XIII. 34, 35. Preached by Mr. Edward Young, Prebend of Salisbury. With a large Paraphrase on Mr. Waller's Poem of Divine Love. To which are added some Copies of Verses from that Excellent Poetess Mrs. Wharton with Others to her*, London, Jonathan Robinson, 1688

'A Young Lady', *An Ode, Occasion'd by the Death of Her Sacred Majesty. By a Young Lady*. Licensed, January 9th, 1694/5. D. Poplar, London, Richard Cumberland, 1695

'A Young Lady', *The Unnatural Mother. The Scene in the Kingdom of Siam. As it is now Acted at the New Theatre in Lincolns-Inn-Fields, By His Majesty's Servants. Written by a Young Lady*, London, J.O. for R. Basset, 1698

'A Young Lady of Quality', *An Elegy upon the Death of Mrs. A. Behn; The Incomparable Astrea. By a Young Lady of Quality*, London, Printed by E.J., 1689. Broadside, Houghton Library, Harvard University, shelfmark *pEB65.A100.689e3

Baillie, Joanna, *Metrical Legends of Exalted Characters*, London, Longman, 1821

Barbour, James Samuel, *A History of William Paterson and the Darian Company*, Edinburgh and London, W. Blackwood, 1907

Barbour, Paula L., 'A Critical Edition of Mary Pix's *The Spanish Wives* (1696), with Introduction and Notes', Ph.D. dissertation, Yale University, December, 1975

——, ed., *An Essay to Revive the Antient Education of Gentlewomen (1673)* [Bathsua Makin], The Augustan Reprint Society, No. 202, William Andrews Clark Memorial Library, University of California at Los Angeles, 1980

Barker, Jane, *Poetical Recreations: Consisting of Original Poems, Songs,*

Odes, &c. With several New Translations. In Two Parts. Part I. Occasionally Written by Mrs. Jane Barker. Part II. By several Gentlemen of the Universities, and Others, London, Benjamin Crayle, 1688

[Barlow, Francis], *Aesops Fables With His Life In English, French, And Latin. Newly Translated. Illustrated by... Francis Barlow*, London, H. Hills jun. for Francis Barlow, 1687

The Bay Psalm Book, A Facsimile Reprint of the First Edition of 1640, Chicago, University of Chicago Press, 1956

[Behn, Aphra], ed., *Covent Garden Drolery... Collected by A. B.*, London, James Magnes, 1672

————, *The Rover, Or, The Banish't Cavaliers. As it is acted at His Royal Highness the Duke's Theatre*, London, John Amery, 1677

————, *Sir Patient Fancy: A Comedy. As it is Acted at the Duke's Theatre. Written by Mrs. A. Behn, the Author of the Rover*. Licenced Jan. 28. 1678. Roger L'Estrange, London, E. Flesher for Richard Tonson and Jacob Tonson, 1678

————, *Poems upon Several Occasions: With a Voyage to the Island of Love*, London, J. Tonson, 1684

————, *A Pindarick On The Death Of Our Late Sovereign: With An Ancient Prophecy On His Present Majesty*, London, J. Playford for Henry Playford, 1685

————, *A Poem Humbly Dedicated To the Great Pattern of Piety and Virtue Catherine Queen Dowager. On The Death Of Her Dear Lord and Husband King Charles II*, London, Printed by J. Playford for Henry Playford, 1685

————, *A Pindarick Poem on the Happy Coronation of His Most Sacred Majesty James II and his Illustrious Consort, Queen Mary*, London, J. Playford for Henry Playford, 1685

————, ed., *Miscellany. Being A Collection of Poems By several Hands. Together with Reflections on Morality or Seneca Unmasqued*, London, J. Hindmarsh, 1685

————, *La Montre: or the Lover's Watch*, London, W. Canning, 1686

————, *Lycidus: Or The Lover in Fashion... From the French. By the same Author of the Voyage to the Isle of Love. Together with a Miscellany of New Poems. By Several Hands*, London, J. Knight and F. Saunders, 1688

————, *Three Histories. Viz. I. Oroonoko: Or, The Royal Slave. II. The Fair Jilt: Or, Tarquin and Miranda. III. Agnes de Castro: Or, The Force of Generous Love. By Mrs. A. Behn*, London, W. Canning, 1688

————, *The History of the Nun: Or, The Fair Vow-Breaker. Written by Mrs. A. Behn*. Licensed, Octob. 22, 1688. Ric. Pocock, London, A. Baskervile, 1689

————, *A Congratulatory Poem To Her Sacred Majesty Queen Mary, Upon Her Arrival in England*, London, R.E. for R. Bentley and W. Canning, 1689

————, *The Younger Brother: Or, The Amorous Jilt. A Comedy. Acted at* the Theatre Royal By His Majesty's Servants. Written by the late Ingenious Mrs. A Behn. With Some Account of her Life, London, J. Harris for R. Baldwin, 1696

————, The Histories and Novels of the Late Ingenious M[rs] Behn... Together with the Life and Memoirs of Mrs. Behn. Written by One of the Fair Sex, London, S. Briscoe, 1696

————, All The Histories And Novels Written by the Late Ingenious M[rs] Behn, Entire in One Volume... Together with The History of the Life and Memoirs of Mrs. Behn. Never before Printed. By one of the Fair Sex. Intermix'd with Pleasant Love-Letters that pass'd betwixt her and Minheer Van Bruin, a Dutch Merchant; with her Character of the Country and Lover: And her Love-Letters to a Gentleman in England. The Third Edition, with Large Additions, London, Samuel Briscoe, 1698

Benger, Sophia Elizabeth Ogilvie, Memoirs of Elizabeth Stuart, Queen of Bohemia, daughter of King James the First. Including sketches of the state of society in Holland and Germany in the 17th century, London, Longman and Co., 1825

Bibliotheca Fanatica: or the Phanatique Library: Being a Catalogue of Such Books as have been lately made and by the Authors presented to the College of Bedlam, London, 1660

Birch, Thomas, ed., The Works of Mrs. Catharine Cockburn, Theological, Moral, Dramatic, and Poetical. Several of them now first printed. Revised and Published, With an Account of the Life of the Author, London, J. and P. Knapton, 1751

Blomefield, Francis, An Essay towards a topographical history of the County of Norfolk, London, W. Miller, 1805-1810

Blunt, J. H., ed., The Annotated Book of Common Prayer being an Historical, Ritual and Theological Commentary on the Devotional System of the Church of England, London, New York and Bombay, 1903

[Borland, Francis], Memoirs of Darien... Written mostly in the year 1700. While the Author was in the American Regions... Glasgow, H. Brown, 1715

Bowyer, John Wilson, The Celebrated Mrs. Centlivre, Durham, North Carolina, Duke University Press, 1952

Boyle, Robert, Some Motives and Incentives to the Love of God, pathetically discours'd of in a letter to a friend, London, Henry Herringman, 1659

Bradbrook, M.C., Review of The Paradise of Women: Writings by English Women of the Renaissance, compiled and edited by Betty Travitsky, Tulsa Studies in Women's Literature, 1, (Spring, 1982), 89-93

Braithwaite, William C., The Beginnings of Quakerism, Cambridge, Cambridge University Press, 1955

Bray, William, ed., Diary and Correspondence of John Evelyn, London, Henry G. Bohn, 1818; rpt. 1859

Burke, John, A Genealogical and Heraldic History of the Extinct and

Dormant Baronetcies of England, Ireland, and Scotland, Second edition, London, John Russell Smith, 1844

Burton, John H., ed., *The Darien Papers: being a Selection of Original Letters and Official Documents relating to the Establishment of a Colony at Darien by the Company of Scotland Trading to Africa and the Indies. 1695-1700*, Edinburgh, T. Constable, 1849

Butt, John, 'Izaak Walton's Collections for Fulman's Life of John Hales', *Modern Language Review*, XXIX (January, 1934), 267-273

Camden, Carroll, *The Elizabethan Woman*, London, Elsevier, 1952

Camden, William, *Annales rerum Anglicarum, Et Hibernicarum Regnante Elizabetha, Ad Annum Salutis MDLXXXIX. Londini: Typis Guilielmi Stansbij, Impensensis Simonis Watersoni, ad insigne Coronae in Coemeterio Paulino MDCXV*

Camm, Dom Bede, O.S.B., *The Life of Father John Wall, the Martyr of Harvington Hall*, Harvington, The Committee of Management of Harvington Hall, 1932

Capp, B. S., *The Fifth Monarchy Men – A Study in Seventeenth Century English Millenarianism*, London, Faber and Faber, 1972

Carnicelli, D. D., ed., *Lord Morley's* Tryumphes *of Fraunces Petrarke: The First English Translation of the* Trionfi, Cambridge, Massachusetts, Harvard University Press, 1971

Cartwright, William, *Comedies, Tragi-Comedies, With Other Poems, By Mr William Cartwright, late Student of Christ-church in Oxford, and Proctor of the University*, London, Humphrey Moseley, 1651

Cary, Elizabeth, Lady Falkland, *The Reply of the Most Illustrious Cardinall of Perron to the Answeare of the Most Excellent King of Great Britaine. The First Tome. Translated into English*, Douay, Martin Bogart, 1630

[Cary, Elizabeth, Lady Falkland?], *The History of the Life, Reign and Death of Edward II, King of England and Lord of Ireland. With the Rise and Fall of his great favourites, Gaveston and the Spencers. Written by E.F. in the year 1627. And printed verbatim from the Original*, London, J.C. for Charles Harper, Samuel Crouch and Thomas Fox, 1680

Cavendish, Margaret, Duchess of Newcastle, *The Philosophicall and Physical Opinions, Written by her Excellency, the Lady Marchioness of Newcastle*, London, J. Martin and J. Allestrye, 1655

————, *The Worlds Olio. Written by the Most Excellent Lady the Lady M. of Newcastle*, London, J. Martin and J. Allestrye, 1655

————, *Philosophical Letters: or, Modest Reflections upon some Opinions in Natural Philosophy, maintained by several famous and learned Authors of this Age, expressed by way of Letters: By the thrice Noble, Illustrious, and Excellent Princess, the Lady Marchioness of Newcastle*, London, 1664

Chambers, Robert, ed., *The Songs of Scotland Prior to Burns. With the Tunes*, Edinburgh and London, W. & R. Chambers, 1862

Channel, Elinor, *A Message from God*, [London], 1654

Chapman, George, trans., *The Crowne of all Homers Worckes*, J. Bill, 1624

WORKS CITED

————, *Ovids Banquet of Sence. A Coronet for his mistresse philosophie, and his amorous zodiacke*, J. R[oberts] for R. Smith, 1595

Chudleigh, Lady Mary, *The Ladies' Defence: or, The Bride-Woman's Counsellor Answer'd: a poem. In a Dialogue between Sir John Brute, Sir William Loveall, Melissa and a Parson*, London, John Deeve, 1701

————, *Poems on Several Occasions. Together with the Song of the Three Children Paraphras'd*, London, W.B. for Bernard Lintott, 1703

Clark, Andrew, ed., *The Life and Times of Anthony Wood*, Oxford, Clarendon Press, 1892-1900

Clayton, Thomas, ed., *The Works of John Suckling*, Oxford, Clarendon Press, 1971

Clear, Arthur, *The King's Village in Desmesne: or, A Thousand Years of Winslow Life*, Winslow, 1894

Clifford, Arthur, ed., *Tixall Letters, or The Correspondence of the Aston Family and Their Friends during the Seventeenth Century*, London, Longman [etc.], 1815

C[ogan], H[enry], *The History of Diodorus Siculus. Containing all that is Most Memorable and of greatest Antiquity in the first Ages of the World Until the War of Troy. Done into English by H. C. Gent*, London, John Macock for Giles Calvert, 1653

Cole, William, ed., *The Lyrics, Ballads, Idyls and Epics of Love – Classical to Contemporary*, New York, Random House, 1963

A Collection of Divine Hymns and Poems on Several Occasions: By the E. of Roscommon, Mr. Dryden, Mr. Dennis, Mr. Norris, Mrs. Kath. Philips, Philomela, and others. Most of them never before Printed, London, J. Baker, 1709

A Collection of Poems By Several Hands. Most of them Written by Persons of Eminent Quality, London, Frances Saunders, 1693

[Collins, Arthur], *The Baronettage of England*, London, W. Taylor [etc.], 1720

Coote, Edmund, *The English Scholemaister: Teaching all his Schollers...* London, Printed by The Widow Orwin for R. Jackson and R. Dexter, 1896

Corneille, Pierre, *La Mort de Pompee*, Paris, 1642

————, *Pompey the Great, translated out of French by Certain Persons of Honour*, London, Henry Herringman, 1664

Cosin, [James], *The Names of the Roman Catholics, Nonjurors, and Others, who refus'd to take the Oaths To his Majesty King George Together with their Title, Additions, and Places of Abode... after the Unnatural Rebellion in the North, in the Year 1715*, 1745; rpt. London, John Russell Smith, 1862

Cotton, Charles, trans., *Essays of Michael Seigneur de Montaigne*, London, T. Basset, M. Gilliflower, and W. Hensman, 1685-1686

Coventry, Anne, *The Right Honourable Anne Countess of Coventry's Meditations and Reflections, Moral and Divine*, London, B. Aylmer, 1707

Cowell, Pattie, *Women Poets in Pre-Revolutionary America 1650-1775. An Anthology*, Troy, New York, Whitson, 1981

————, and Ann Stanford, eds., *Critical Essays on Anne Bradstreet*, Boston, Mass., G.K. Hall, 1983

Cowley, Abraham, *The Second and Third Parts of the Works of Mr Abraham Cowley... The Third containing His Six Books of Plants, Never Before Published in English*, London, Charles Harper, 1689

Crawford, Patricia, 'Women's published writings 1600-1700', in *Women in English Society 1500-1800*, ed. Mary Prior, New York, Methuen, 1985

[Creech, Thomas], *T. Lucretius Carus The Epicurean Philosopher, His Six Books De Natura Rerum Done into English Verse, with Notes*, Oxford, L. Lichfield for Anthony Stevens, 1682

————, *T. Lucretius Carus. The Epicurean Philosopher, His Six Books De Natura Rerum, Done into English Verse, With Notes. The Second Edition, Corrected and Enlarged*, Oxford, L. Lichfield for Anthony Stevens, 1683

————, *The Odes, Satyrs, and Epistles of Horace*, London, for Jacob Tonson, 1684

Cressy, David, *Literacy and the Social Order: Reading and Writing in Tudor and Stuart England*, Cambridge, Cambridge University Press, 1980

Croft, P.J., ed., *The Poems of Robert Sidney*, Oxford, Clarendon Press, 1984

[Crouch, Nathaniel], *Female Excellency, or the Ladies Glory by R. B.*, London, Nathaniel Crouch, 1688

Crum, Margaret, ed., *The Poems of Henry King*, Oxford, Clarendon Press, 1965

————, ed., *First-Line Index of English Poetry 1500-1800 In Manuscripts of the Bodleian Library Oxford*, Oxford, Clarendon Press, 1969

Cudworth, Ralph, *The True Intellectual System of the Universe*, London, Richard Royston, 1678

[Curll, Edmund], ed., *Miscellanea. In Two Volumes.... Viz I Familiar Letters Written to Henry Cromwell Esq; by Mr. Pope... III Letters from Mr. Dryden, to a Lady, in the Year 1699*, London, E. Curll, 1727

————, *Memoirs Of the Life, Writings, and Amours Of William Congreve Esq;... Also Some very Curious Memoirs of Mr. Dryden and his Family, with a Character of Him and his Writings, by Mr. Congreve*, London, E. Curll, 1730

D., D., 'Governor Thomas Dudley's Library', *New England Historical and Genealogical Register* XII (October, 1858), 355-356

Dalrymple, Sir John, *Memoirs of Great Britain and Ireland*, Edinburgh and London, W. Strahan, 1771-1773

D'Anvers, Alicia, *A Poem upon His Sacred Majesty, His Voyage for Holland: By Way of A Dialogue Between Belgia and Brittania. By Mrs. D'Anvers*, London, Thomas Bever, 1691

Darcie, Abraham, trans., *Annales. The True and Royall History of the famous Elizabeth Queene of England France and Ireland &c. True faiths defendresse of Divine renowne and happy Memory*, London, Benjamin Fisher, 1625

WORKS CITED

Davies, John, of Hereford, *The Muses Sacrifice or Divine Meditations*, London, T.S. for George Norton, 1612

Davies, John, *The Life and Philosophy of Epictetus: With the Embleme of Human Life, by Cebes Rendered into English by John Davies of Kidwelly*, London, John Martyn, 1670

Davis, Harold and Irvin Ehrenpreis, eds., *The Prose Works of Jonathan Swift*, Oxford, Blackwell, 1939-1968

De Beer, E. S., ed., *The Correspondence of John Locke*, Oxford, Clarendon Press, 1976

———, ed., *The Diary of John Evelyn. IV. Kalendarium 1673-1689*, Oxford, Clarendon Press, 1955

De Bellegent, P., trans., *Annales Des Choses Qui Sont Passes en Angleterre Et Irlande Soubs Le Regne De Elizabeth: Jusques A L'An De Salut M. D. LXXXIX*, London, Richard Field, 1624

De Blegny, [Nicholas], *New and Curious Observations On the Art of Curing the Venereal Disease... with the motions, actions and effects of Mercury, and its other Remedies*, Trans. by Walter Harris, London, For Tho. Dring and Tho. Burrel, 1676

De Lafontaine, H.C., ed., *The King's Musick: A Transcript of Records Relating to Music and Musicians (1460-1700)*, London, 1909

De Sales, Francis, *An Introduction to a Devoute Life Composed in Frenche by the R. Father in God Frances Sales... Translated... by I. Y.... The last edition*, Paris, Mistrise Blangeart, 1637

Descartes, Rene, *The Passions of the Soule In three Books. The first, Treating of the Passions in Generall, and occasionally of the whole nature of man. The second, of the Number, and order of the Passions, and the explication of the six Primitive ones. The third, Of Particular Passions. By R. des Cartes. And Translated out of French into English*, London, J. Martin and J. Ridley, 1650

Dobbie, B. Willmott, 'An Attempt to Estimate the True Rate of Maternal Mortality in the Sixteenth to Eighteenth Centuries', *Medical History* XXVI (1982) 79-90

Doble, C.E., ed., *Remarks and Collections of Thomas Hearne*, Oxford, 1888

Doebner, Richard, ed., *Memoirs of Mary, Queen of England (1689-1693) Together with her Letters and those of Kings James II and William III to the Electress Sophia of Hanover*, Leipzig and London, 1886

Douglas, Lady Eleanor, *Strange and Wonderful Prophecies*, London, Robert Ibbitson, 1649

Drayton, Michael, *England's Heroicall Epistles*, London, J.R. for N. Ling, 1597

[Dryden, John], *Ovid's Epistles, Translated by Several Hands*, London, Jacob Tonson, 1680

———, *The Works of Virgil: Containing his Pastorals, Georgics, and Aeneis. Translated into English Verse; By Mr. Dryden. Adorn'd with a Hundred Sculptures*, London, Jacob Tonson, 1697

Du Bosc, Jacques, *The Compleat Woman. Written in French by Monsieur*

Du-Bosq, and by him after severall Editions reviewed, corrected, and amended: And now faithfully Translated into English, By N.N, London, Thomas Harper and Richard Hodgkinson, 1639

Duffy, Maureen, *The Passionate Shepherdess: Aphra Behn 1640-89*, London, Jonathan Cape, 1977

[Dunton, John], *The Ladies Dictionary; Being a General Entertainment for the Fair Sex: A Work Never Attempted Before in English*, London, John Dunton, 1694

————, 'Some Account of my Conversation in Ireland. In a Letter to an Honourable Lady. With Her Answer to it', in *The Dublin Scuffle*, London, 1699; rpt. New York, Garland, 1974

————, *The Athenian Oracle: being an entire collection of all the valuable questions and answers in the old Athenian Mercuries. Intermix'd with many cases in divinity history, philosophy, mathematics, love, poetry, never before published. To which is added, an alphabetical table for the speedy finding of any questions. By a member of the Athenian Society*, London, Andrew Bell, Vols. I, II, 1703; Vol. III, 1704; Vol. IV, 1710

————, *The Athenian Spy: Discovering the Secret Letters Which were sent to the Athenian Society By the Most Ingenious Ladies of the Three Kingdoms*, London, R. Halsey, 1704

————, *Athenianism: or, the new projects of Mr. John Dunton, author of the essay entitl'd, The Hazard of a Death-Bed-Repentence. Being, six hundred distinct treatises... To which is added, Dunton's farewell to printing*, London, Tho. Darrack for J. Morphew, 1710

————, *The Challenge, Sent by a Young Lady To Sir Thomas---&c. Or, The Female War. Wherein the Present Dresses and Humours, &c. of the Fair Sex Are Vigorously attackt by Men of Quality, and as Bravely defended by Madam Godfrey, and other Ingenious Ladies, who set their Names to every Challenge. The Whole Encounter consists of Six Hundred Letters, Pro and Con, on all the Disputable Points relating to Women. And is The First Battle of this Nature that ever was fought in England*, London, E. Whitlock, 1697

————, *The Life and Errors of John Dunton Late citizen of London; Written by Himself in Solitude. With an idea of a New Life*, London, S. Malthus, 1705

————, *The Life and Errors of John Dunton, Citizen of London; with the lives and characters of more than a thousand contemporary divines, and other persons of literary eminence*, London, J. Nichols, Son, and Bentley, 1818

D'Urfey, Thomas, *Love for Money, or the Boarding School*, London, J. Hindmarsh, Abel Roper, for Randal Taylor, 1691

Eccles, Audrey, *Obstetrics and Gynaecology in Tudor and Stuart England*, London and Canberra, Croom Helm, 1982

'Eliza', *Eliza's Babes: or the Virgins-Offering. Being Divine Poems, and Meditations. Written by a Lady, who onely desires to advance the glory of God, and not her own*, London, M.S. for Laurence Blaiklock, 1652

Ellis, John Harvard, ed., *The Works of Anne Bradstreet in Prose and*

Verse, New York, 1867; rpt. Gloucester, Massachusetts, Peter Smith, 1962

[Ephelia], *A Poem To His Sacred Majesty on the Plot. Written by a Gentlewoman*, London, Henry Brome, licensed Nov. 23, 1678, broadside

——, *Advice to His Grace*, [London, c. 1681-1682], broadside

Evelyn, John, *The Life of Mrs. Godolphin By John Evelyn of Wooton Esq. Now first published and edited by Samuel Lord Bishop of Oxford*, London, William Pickering, 1848

——, *Essay on the First Book of T. Lucretius Carus De Rerum Natura*, Gabriel Bedle and Thomas Collins, 1656

——, 'Kalendarium Hortense; or The Gardner's Almanac', in *Sylva, or A Discourse of Forest-trees, and the Propagation of Timber in His Majesties Dominions*, London, J. Martyn and J. Allestry, 1664

Examen Miscellaneum. Consisting of Verse and Prose. Of Verse, By the Most Honourable the Marquis of Normanby. The Late Lord Rochester. Mr. Waller. Mrs. Wharton. Mr. Wolseley, London, Printed for B. L[intot], 1702

Fage, Mary, *Fames Roule; Or, the names of our dread Soveraigne Lord King Charles, his Royall Queen Mary, and his most hopefull Posterity; Together with, The names of the Dukes, Marquesses, Earles, Viscounts, Bishops, Barons, Privie Counsellors, Knights of the Garter, and Judges. Of his three renowned Kingdomes, England, Scotland and Ireland: Anagrammatiz'd and expressed by acrosticke lines on their names*, London, R. Oulton [for J. Crouch], 1637

Faulkner, Thomas, *An historical and topographical description of Chelsea and its environs*, Chelsea, T. Faulkner [etc.], 1829

Fawcett, Timothy J., *The Liturgy of Comprehension*, 1689; rpt. Alcuin Club Collections, No. 54, Mayhew-McCrimmon, Southend-on-Sea, 1973

Fea, Allan, ed., *Memoirs of Count Grammont*, by Anthony Hamilton, London, Bickers and Son, 1906

Ferguson, Moira, *First Feminists: British Women Writers 1578-1799*, Bloomington / Old Westbury, N. Y.: Indiana University Press / Feminist Press, 1985.

Feuillerat, Albert, *The Prose Works of Sir Philip Sidney*, Cambridge, Cambridge University Press, 1965

Finch, Anne, *Miscellany Poems on Several Occasions, Written by a Lady*, London, B. Tooke, W. Taylor, J. Round, 1713

Firth, C. H., ed., *The Life of William Cavendish Duke of Newcastle To Which is Added the True Relation of my Birth Breeding and Life, by Margaret Cavendish, Duchess of Newcastle*, London, Routledge, [1907]

Fleischmann, Wolfgang B., *Lucretius and English Literature 1680-1740*, Paris, A. G. Nizet, 1964

Forbes, William, *An Account of the Life and Writings of James Beattie*, Edinburgh, Archibald Constable, 1806

Foster, Joseph, ed., *London Marriage Licences 1521-1869*, Bernard Quaritch, London, 1887

Fraser, Antonia, *The Weaker Vessel: Woman's lot in seventeenth-century England*, London, Weidenfeld and Nicolson, 1984

Froud, John, *The Grove: or, the Rival Muses, A Poem*, London, 1701

F[yge], S[arah], *The Female Advocate: Or, An Answer To A Late Satyr Against The Pride, Lust, and Inconstancy of Woman. Written by a Lady in Vindication of her Sex*, London, H. C. for John Taylor, 1687

F[yge] E[gerton], S[arah], *Poems on Several Occasions, Together with a Pastoral*, London, [1703]

G. E. C., *The Complete Peerage by G. E. C., New Edition... edited by the Hon. Vicary Gibbs*, London, St Catherine Press, 1910-1940

———, *Complete Baronetage*, Exeter, Pollard and Co., 1900-1909

Gardiner, Dorothy, *English Girlhood at School: A Study of Women's Education through twelve centuries*, Oxford, 1929

[Gildon, Charles], *The Lives and Characters of the English Dramatick Poets. First begun by Mr. Langbain, improv'd and continued down to this Time, by a careful hand*, London, Tho. Leigh and Wiliam Turner, [1699]

———, *Chorus Poetarum: Poems On Several Occasions...* London, Benjamin Bragg, 1694

———, *Miscellany Poems Upon Several Occasions: Consisting of Original Poems By the late Duke of Buckingham*, London, Peter Buck, 1692

Goreau, Angeline, *Reconstructing Aphra: A Social Biography of Aphra Behn*, New York, Dial, 1980

Gosse, Edmund, *Seventeenth-Century Studies*, London, Kegan Paul, Trench & Co., 1883

Gough, Richard, *Antiquities and Memoirs of the parish of Myddle... written by Richard Gough, A.D. 1700*, Shrewsbury, Adnit & Naughton, 1875

Gould, Robert, *Love Given O're: Or, A Satyr Against The Pride, Lust, and Inconstancy, &c. Of Woman*, London, Andrew Green, 1682

———, 'The Play-house. A Satyr', in *Poems Chiefly Consisting of Satyrs and Satyrical Epistles*, London, 1689

Grant, Douglas, ed., *The Phanseys of William Cavendish Marquis of Newcastle addressed to Margaret Lucas and her Letters in reply*, London, Nonesuch Press, 1956

Gray, G. J., 'The Diary of Jeffrey Boys of Gray's Inn, 1671', *Notes and Queries* 27 (December 1930), 456

Grosart, Alexander B., ed., *The Complete Works of John Davies of Hereford*, [Edinburgh], [T. & A. Constable], 1878

———, *The Complete Works of Joshua Sylvester*, 1880; rpt., New York, AMS Press, 1967

Grymeston, Elizabeth, *Miscelanea, Meditations, Memoratives*, London, Melch. Bradwood for Felix Norton, 1604

Guffy, George, 'Aphra Behn's *Oroonoko*: Occasion and Accomplishment', in *Two English Novelists*, Los Angeles, William Andrews Clark Memorial Library, 1975

Halkett, Samuel and Catherine Laing, *Dictionary of Anonymous and Pseudonymous Literature*, Edinburgh, W. Paterson, 1882-1888

WORKS CITED

Haller, William, *Foxe's Book of Martyrs and the Elect Nation*, London, Jonathan Cape, 1963

[Hammond, Anthony, ed.], *A New Miscellany of Original Poems*, London, T. Jauncy, 1720

Hannah, Reverend J., ed., *Poems and Psalms by Henry King*, Oxford and London, 1843

Haraszti, Zoltan, *The Enigma of the Bay Psalm Book*, Chicago, University of Chicago Press, 1956

Harlow, V.J., *Colonizing Expeditions in the West Indies and Guiana, 1623-1667*, Hakluyt Society, 2nd series, 56, London, 1923

Harris, Brice, 'Aphra Behn's "Bajazet to Gloriana" ', *TLS* 9 February 1933:92

Harvey, William, *The Circulation of the Blood: Two Anatomical Essays by William Harvey*, Kenneth J. Franklin, trans., Oxford, 1958

Heber, Reverend Reginald, ed., *The Whole Works of the Right Reverend Jeremy Taylor, D.D.*, London, Longman [etc.], 1854

Herbert, Mary, Countess of Pembroke, *The Tragedie of Antonie, 1595*
————, *A Poem on Our Saviour's Passion By Mary Sidney, Countess of Pembroke. From an Unpublished MS. in the British Museum*, R. G. B., ed., London, John Wilson, 1857

Herford, C. H., Percy and Evelyn Simpson, eds., *The Works of Ben Jonson*, Oxford, Clarendon Press, 1962

Herrick, Robert, *The Poetical Works*, ed. L. C. Marten, Oxford, Clarendon Press, 1968

Highfill, Philip H., Jr., *et al.*, *A Biographical Dictionary of Actors, Actresses, Musicians, Dancers, Managers And Other Stage Personnel in London, 1660-1800*, 10 vols. (incomplete), Carbondale and Edwardsville, 1973-

Hill, Christopher, *Intellectual Origins of the English Revolution*, Oxford, Clarendon Press, 1966
————, *The Century of Revolution 1603-1714*, Wokingham, Van Nostrand Reinhold, 1984

Hindle, C. J., 'A Bibliography of the Printed Pamphlets and Broadsides of Lady Eleanor Douglas, the 17th Century Prophetess', *Papers of the Edinburgh Bibliographical Society*, XV, ii (October, 1934)

Hiscock, W. G., *John Evelyn and his Family Circle*, London, Routledge & Kegan Paul, 1955

Hodgetts, Michael, 'John Wall at Harvington?', *Recusant History*, 8 (1965- 1966), 123-132

Hole, Christina, *The English Housewife in the Seventeenth Century*, London, Chatto and Windus, 1953

Houston, R. A., *Scottish Literacy and the Scottish Identity: Illiteracy and Society in Scotland and Northern England 1600-1800*, Cambridge, 1985

Howell, James, *Epistolae Ho-Elianae. Familiar Letters domestic and forren... Fourth edition*, London, T. Guy, 1673

Hughes, Ann, ed., *Seventeenth-century England: A Changing Culture:*

Volume I, Primary Sources, London, Ward Lock Educational, 1984

Hughey, Ruth, ed., *The Arundel Harington Manuscript of Tudor Poetry*, Columbus, Ohio State University Press, 1960

———, and Philip Hereford, 'Elizabeth Grymeston And Her Miscelanea', *The Library*, XV (1934), 61-91

Hume, Alexander, *Hymnes, or Sacred Songs, wherein the right use of Poesie may be espied*, Edinburgh, Robert Walde-grave, 1599

Hume, Anna, *The Triumphs of Love: Chastity: Death: Translated Out Of Petrarch By M^{ris} Anna Hume*, Edinburgh, Evan Tyler, 1644

Hume, David, *The History of the House and Race of Douglas and Angus*, Edinburgh, Evan Tyler, 1644

Hutchinson, Lucy, *Memoirs of the Life of Colonel Hutchinson, Governor of Nottingham Castle and Town... Written By His Widow Lucy, now first published from the original manuscript by the Rev. Julius Hutchinson... to which is prefixed The Life of Mrs. Hutchinson, written by herself, a fragment*, London, Longman [etc.], 1806

Irving, David, *The History of Scottish Poetry*, ed. John Aiken Carlyle, Edinburgh, Edmonston and Douglas, 1861

Isham, Sir Giles, ed., *The Correspondence of Bishop Brian Duppa and Sir Justinian Isham*, Publications of the Northampton Record Society 17, Lamport Hall, 1955

Isham, Thomas, *The Diary of Thomas Isham of Lamport (1658-81)*, London, Gregg International Publishers, 1971

Jeaffreson, John Cordy, *Annals of Oxford*, London, Hurst and Blackett, 1871

Joceline, Elizabeth, *The Mothers Legacie, To her unborne Childe. By Elizabeth Joceline*, London, John Haviland for William Barret, 1624

Johnson, Richard, *A Crowne-Garland of Goulden Roses Gathered out of Englands royall garden... Set forth in many pleasant new songs and sonetts never before imprinted*, London, 1612

Jones, M.G., *The Charity School Movement: A Study of the Eighteenth Century in Action*, London, Frank Cass and Co., 1964

Kenyon, J. P., *Stuart England*, Harmondsworth, Penguin, 1978

Keynes, Geoffrey, *John Evelyn: A Study in Bibliophily with A Bibliography of his Writings*, Oxford, Clarendon Press, 1968

Killigrew, Anne, *Poems by Mrs Anne Killigrew....Licensed to be Published, Sept. 30. 1685*. Ro. L'Estrange, London, Samuel Lowndes, 1686

Killigrew, Thomas, *Comedies, and Tragedies. Written by Thomas Killigrew, Page of Honour to King Charles the First. And Groom of the Bed-Chamber to King Charles the Second*, London, Henry Herringman, 1664

[King, Henry], *Poems, Elegies, Paradoxes, and Sonnets*, London, Printed by J. G. for Richard Marriot and Henry Herringman, 1657

Koster, Patricia, ed., *The Novels of Mary Delariviere Manley*, Gainesville, Florida, Scholars' Facsimiles & Reprints, 1971

————, 'Delariviere Manley and the DNB: A Cautionary Tale about Following Black Sheep, with a Challenge to Cataloguers', *Eighteenth Century Life* 3 (1977) 106-111

Kuhl, Ernest, 'Shakespere's "Lead Apes In Hell" And The Ballad Of "The Maid And The Palmer" ', *Studies in Philology*, 22 (1925), 453-466

Lachrymae Musarum: the Tears of the Muses; Written By divers persons of Nobility and Worth, Upon the death of the most hopefull, Henry Lord Hastings, London, Tho. Newcomb, 1649

Laing, David, ed., *Various Pieces of Fugitive Scots Poetry: Principally of the Seventeenth Century*, Edinburgh, W. & D. Laing, [1823]

————, *Early Metrical Tales, Including the History of Sir Egeir, Sir Gryme, and Sir Grey-St. Steill*, Edinburgh, W. & D. Laing, 1826

Langbaine, Gerard, *Momus Triumphans: Or the Plagiaries of the English Stage*, London, Samuel Holford, 1688

Lanyer, Aemilia, *Salve Deus Rex Judaeorum. Containing, 1 The Passion of Christ. 2 Eves Apologie in defence of Women. 3 The Teares of the Daughters of Jerusalem. 4 The Salutation and Sorrow of the Virgine Marie. With divers other things not unfit to be read. Written by Mistris Aemilia Lanyer, Wife to Captaine Alfonso Lanyer, Servant to the Kings Majestie*, London, Valentine Simmes for Richard Bonian, 1611

Latham, Robert and William Matthews, eds., *The Diary of Samuel Pepys*, London, Bell & Hyman, 1970-1983

Lawes, Henry, *Ayres, and Dialogues,... The First Book*, T. H. for John Playford, 1653

————, *The Second Book of Ayres and Dialogues, For One, Two and Three Voyces. By Henry Lawes Servant to his late Matie. in his publick and private Musick*, London, T.H. for John Playford, 1655

————, *Ayres, and Dialogues, For One, Two, and Three Voyces: The Third Booke*, W. Godbid for John Playford, 1658

Leigh, Dorothy, *The Mothers Blessing. Or the godly counsaile of a Gentlewoman not long since deceased, left behind her for her Children: Containing many good exhortations, and godly admonitions, profitable for all Parents to leave as a Legacy to their Children, but especially for those, who by reason of their young yeeres stand most in need of Instruction. By Mris. Dorothy Leigh*, London, John Budge, 1616

Lelen, J.M., ed., *Introduction to a Devout Life from the French of St. Francis De Sales*, New York, Catholic Publishing Co., 1946

A Letter from the Dead Thomas Brown, to the Living Heraclitus:...To which is added, the Last Will and Testament of Mr Thomas Brown, London, 1704

A Letter, giving a Description of the Isthmus of Darian: (Where the Scots Colonie is Settled;) From a Gentleman who lives there at present. With an Account of the Fertilness of the Soil, The Quality of the Air, The Manners of the Inhabitants, And the Nature of the Plants, and Animals, Edinburgh, John Mackie and James Wardlaw, 1699

Letters of Love and Gallantry and Several Other Subjects. All Written by Ladies, London, Samuel Briscoe, 1693

Lewalski, Barbara, *Protestant Poetics and the Seventeenth-Century Religious Lyric*, Princeton, Princeton University Press, 1979
———, 'Of God and Good Women: The Poems of Aemilia Lanyer', in *Silent but for the Word: Tudor Women as Patrons, Translators, and Writers of Religious Works*, ed. Margaret P. Hannay, Kent, Ohio, Kent State University Press, 1985, 203-224
Link, Frederick, *Aphra Behn*, New York, Twayne, 1968
Livingstone, John, *Memorable Characters and Remarkable Passages of Divine Providence Exemplified in the Lives of a considerable Number of the most eminent Divines and Private Christians who lived in Scotland during the first Century after the Reformation collected by the famous Mr. John Livingstone*, Glasgow, Andrew Stevenson, 1759
Lloyd, John, *Shir ha-shirim, or, The Song of Songs; being a paraphrase upon the most excellent Canticles of Solomon in a Pindarick Poem*, London, H. H. for H. Faithorne & J. Kersey, 1682
Lockley, Ronald, *Orielton: The Human and Natural History of a Welsh Manor*, London, 1977
Lockyer, Roger, *Tudor and Stuart Britain 1471-1714*, London, Longman, 1985
Lodge, Thomas, *The Famous and Memorable Workes of Josephus, A Man of Much Honour and Learning Among the Jewes, Faithfully translated out of the Latine and French, by Thomas Lodge, Doctor in Physicke*, London, G. Bishop, S. Waterson, D. Short, and Thomas Adams, 1602
Lomas, S. C., ed., *Lives of the Princesses of England From the Norman Conquest*, by Mary Anne Everett Green [Wood], London, Methuen, 1909
Long, Philip, *Summary Catalogue of the Lovelace Collection of the Papers of John Locke in the Bodleian Library*, 8, Oxford, Bibliographical Society, n.s., 1956
Lower, Richard, *Dr. Lower's and Several Other Eminent Physicians Receipts*, London, John Nutt, 1700
Luctus Britannici: Or, The Tears of the British Muses; For the death of John Dryden, Esq; Late poet Laureate to Their Majesties, K. Charles and K. James the Second. Written by the most Eminent Hands in the two Famous Universities, and by several Others, London, Printed for Henry Playford and Abel Roper and sold by John Nutt, 1700
Luttrell, Narcissus, *A Brief Historical Relation of State Affairs from September 1678 to April 1714*, Oxford, University Press, 1857
M., W., *The Female Wits; or, The Triumvirate of Poets at Rehearsal....Written by Mr. W. M.*, London, W. Turner [etc.], 1704
McDonald, James, and Brown, Nancy, eds., *The Poems of Robert Southwell, S.J.*, Oxford, Clarendon Press, 1967
McDonald, Michael, *Mystical Bedlam. Madness, Anxiety and Healing in Seventeenth Century England*, Cambridge, University Press, 1981
McElrath, Jr., Joseph R., and Allan P. Robb, eds., *The Complete Works of Anne Bradstreet*, Boston, Twayne, 1981
Mack, Phyllis, 'Women as Prophets during the English Civil War', in

WORKS CITED

The Origins of Anglo-American Radicalism, eds. Margaret Jacob and James Jacob, London, George Allen and Unwin, 1984

Mahl, Mary R. and Helene Koon, eds., *The Female Spectator: English Women Writers Before 1800,* Bloomington and London: Indiana University Press/Old Westbury, NY, The Feminist Press, 1977

Major, Elizabeth, *Honey on the Rod: Or a comfortable Contemplation For One in Affliction; with sundry Poems on several Subjects. By the unworthiest of the servants of the Lord Jesus Christ, Elizabeth Major,* London, Thomas Maxey, 1656

Makin, Bathsua, *An Essay to Revive the Antient Education of Gentlewomen,* London, Thomas Parkhurst, 1673

Malcolm, J. P., ed., *Letters between the Rev. James Granger, M. A... Composing a Copious History and Illustration of His Biographical History of England,* London, Longman [etc.], 1805

Malone, Edmund, ed., *The Critical and Miscellaneous Prose Works of John Dryden,* 4 parts in 3 vols., London, 1800

Manley, Delariviere, *Letters Written by Mrs. Manley, to Which is Added a letter from a Suppos'd Nun in Portugal,* London, R. Bentley, 1696

———, *The Lost Lover; Or, The Jealous Husband: A Comedy,* London, R. Bentley, J. Knapton, and R. Wellington, 1696

———, *The Royal Mischief. A Tragedy,* London, R. Bentley, F. Saunders, and J. Knapton, 1696

———, *The Secret History, of Queen Zarah, and the Zarazians; Being a Looking-glass For——— In the Kingdom of Albigion. Faithfully Translated from the Italian Copy now lodg'd in the Vatican at Rome, and never before Printed in any Language. Albigion, Printed in the Year 1705*

———, *Secret Memoirs and Manners of Several persons of Quality, of Both Sexes from the New Atalantis, an Island in the Mediterranean,* London, John Morphew & J. Woodward, 1709

———, *Memoirs of Europe, towards the Close of the Eighth Century. Written by Eginardus, Secretary and Favourite to Charlemagne; And done into English by the Translator of the New Atalantis,* London, John Morphew, 1710

———, *The Adventures of Rivella; Or, The History of the Author of the Atalantis. With Secret Memoirs and Characters of several considerable Persons her Contemporaries. Deliver'd in a Conversation to the Young Chevalier D'Aumont in Somerset-House Garden, by Sir Charles Lovemore, Done into English from the French,* London, 1714

M[arkham], G[ervase], *Country Contentments, or the Husbandmans Recreations,* 4th ed., London, N. Okes for J. Harison, 1631

[Masham, Damaris], *A Discourse Concerning the Love of God,* London, for Awnsham and John Churchill, 1696

———, *Occasional Thoughts in Reference to a Vertuous or Christian Life,* London, for A. and J. Churchill, 1705

Mather, Cotton, *Magnalia Christi Americana: Or the Ecclesiastical History of New England, From Its First Planting in the Year 1620. First American Edition, from the London Edition of 1702,* Volume I, Hartford, Connecticut, Silas Andrus, 1820

Mayhew, George, 'Swift and the Tripos Tradition', *Philogogical Quarterly*, XLV, 85-100

Medoff, Jeslyn, 'New Light on Sarah Fyge (Field, Egerton)', *Tulsa Studies in Women's Literature*, 1, 2 (Fall, 1982), 155-175

———, 'A Voice from the Periphery: Jane Barker, Poet, Novelist, "Spinster" and Jacobite', paper read at the annual meeting of the Northeast American Society for Eighteenth Century Studies, Syracuse University, October, 1983

Melville, James, *A Spiritual Propine of A Pastor to his People*, Edinburgh, R. Waldegrave, 1589 [1598]

Milhouse, Judith and Robert D. Hume, eds., *The Frolics or the Lawyer Cheated (1671)* by Elizabeth Polwhele, Cornell University Press, 1977

Millar, A., ed., *Works of Milton. Historical, Political and Miscellaneous*, Volume I, London, 1753

Miller, Perry and Thomas H. Johnson, eds., *The Puritans*, New York, American Book Company, 1938

Miscellanea Sacra: Or, Poems on Divine and Moral Subjects. Collected by N. Tate, London, Henry Playford, Vol. I, 1696. Vol. II, 1698

Misson de Valbourg, H., *M. Misson's Memoirs And Observations In His Travels Over England. With some Account of Scotland and Ireland. Dispos'd in Alphabetical Order. Written Originally in French, and translated by Mr. Ozell*, London, D. Browne [etc.], 1719

Mordaunt, Elizabeth, Viscountess, *The Private Diarie of Elizabeth, Viscountess Mordaunt*, ed. Robert Jocelyn, Earl of Roden, Duncairn, 1856

Morey, Dom Adrian, O.S.B., 'The English Benedictines' in David Mathew, *Catholicism in England, 1535-1935. Portrait of a Minority: Its Culture and Tradition*, London, Longmans, Green and Co., 1936

Morgan, Fidelis, *A Woman of No Character: An Autobiography of Mrs. Manley*, London, Faber and Faber, 1986

Mulvihill, Maureen, 'Makin[s], Bathsua [Pell]' in *A Dictionary of British and American Women Writers 1660-1800*, ed. Janet Todd, London, Methuen, 1984

Munda, Constantia (pseud.), *The Worming of a mad Dogge: or, a Soppe for Cerberus the Jaylor of Hell. No Confutation but a sharpe Redargution of the bayter of Women*, London, [G. Purslowe] for L. Hayes, 1617

Murray, Lady Grisell, *Memoirs of the Lives and Characters of the Right Honourable George Baillie of Jerviswood, and of Lady Grisell Baillie. By Their Daughter Lady Grisell Murray of Stanhope*, Edinburgh, 1822

Myddelton, W.M., *Chirk Castle Accounts A.D. 1605-1666*, Privately Printed, 1908.

Nash, Treadway, *Collections for the History of Worcestershire*, London, Oxford, and Worcestershire, 1781-1782

Nevinson, J.L., ed., *Mundus Muliebris or The Ladies Dressing-Room Unlock'd by Mary Evelyn Prepared for the Press by Her Father John*

WORKS CITED

Evelyn 1690, London, The Costume Society, 1977

Nichols, John, ed., *A Select Collection of Poems: With Notes, Biographical and Historical*, London, John Nichols, 1780-1782

———, *The Progresses and Public Processions of Queen Elizabeth*, London, John Nichols, 1823

The Nine Muses. Or, Poems Written by Nine severall Ladies Upon the death of the late Famous John Dryden, Esq;... London, Richard Basset, 1700

Noake, John, *Worcester Sects; or a History of the Roman Catholics and Dissenters of Worcester*, London, Longman [etc.], 1861

Noble, Reverend Mark, *A Biographical History of England, from the Revolution to the End of George I's Reign; Being a Continuation of the Rev. J. Granger's Work*, London, 1806

Norris, James, *Haec et Hic*, Jo. Harefinch for James Norris, 1683

Norris, John, *A Collection of Miscellanies: Consisting of Poems, Essays, Discourses and Letters*, 1687

———, *Practical Discourses Upon Several Divine Subjects*, London, Samuel Manship, 1691-1693

———, *The Theory and Regulation of Love*, London, Samuel Manship, 1688

———, *Reflections upon the Conduct of Human Life... In a letter to the excellent lady, the Lady Masham*, London, Samuel Manship, 1690

North, Sir Thomas, trans., *The Lives of the Nobles Grecians and Romanes, compared*, (translation of Plutarch's *Vitae*) London, J. Wight, 1579

N[orton], R[obert], trans., *The Historie of the Most Renowned and Victorious Princesse Elizabeth, Late Queene of England. Contayning all the Important and Remarkable Passages of State both at Home and Abroad, during her long and Prosperous Raigne. Composed by Way of Annals Never heretofore so faithfully and fully Published in English*, London, Benjamin Fisher, 1630

O'Donnell, Mary Ann, *Aphra Behn: An Annotated Bibliography of Primary and Secondary Sources*, New York & London, Garland, 1986

O'Donnell, Sheryl, 'Mr. Locke and the Ladies', *Studies in Eighteenth-Century Culture* 8 (1978), 151-164

———, ' "My Idea in Your Mind": John Locke and Lady Damaris Cudworth Masham', in *Mothering the Mind: Twelve Studies of Writers and Their Silent Partners*, eds. Ruth Perry and Martine Watson Brownley, London and New York, Holmes & Meier, 1984, 26-46

Osborne, Francis, *Advice to a Son*, Oxford, Henry Hall for Thomas Robinson, 1656

Palmer, George Herbert, ed., *The English Works of George Herbert*, Boston and New York, Houghton, 1905

Park, Thomas, ed., *The Harleian Miscellany: A Collection of Scarce, Curious and Entertaining Pamphlets and Tracts...* London, J. White and J. Murray, 1808-1813

Patrick, J. Max, ed., *The Complete Poetry of Robert Herrick*, New York, Anchor, 1963

Patrides, C. A., ed., *Sir Walter Raleigh: The History of the World*, Philadelphia, Temple University Press, 1971

Perry, Ruth, ed., *Memoirs of Several Ladies of Great Britain Who Have Been Celebrated for Their Writings or Skill in the Learned Languages, Arts and Sciences by George Ballard of Magdalen College, Oxford*, Detroit, Wayne State University Press, 1985

——, *The Celebrated Mary Astell*, Chicago and London, University of Chicago, 1986

Philips, Katherine, *Letters from Orinda to Poliarchus*, London, W.B. for Bernard Lintott, 1705

——, *Poems. By the Incomparable, Mrs. K.P*, London, J.G. for Richard Marriott, 1664

——, *Poems By the most deservedly Admired M^rs. Katherine Philips the matchless Orinda. To which is added Monsieur Corneille's Pompey & Horace, Tragedies. With Several other Translations out of French*, London, J.M. for H. Herringman, 1667

——, *Pompey. A Tragoedy. Acted with Great Applause*, London, John Crooke, 1663

P[hillips], E[dward], *Theatrum Poetarum: or a Compleat Collection of the Poets of all Ages*, London, Charles Smith, 1675

Pix, Mary, *The Innocent Mistress. A Comedy*, London, J. Orme for R. Basset and F. Cogan, 1697

——, *The Deceiver Deceived, A Comedy*, London, R. Basset, 1698

——, *Queen Catharine Or, The Ruines of Love, A Tragedy*, London, William Turner and Richard Basset, 1698

——, *The False Friend, Or, the Fate of Disobedience, A Tragedy*, London, Richard Basset, 1699

——, *The Beau Defeated: Or, The Lucky Younger Brother. A Comedy*, London, W. Turner and R. Basset, [1700]

Platt, Jr., Harrison Gray, 'Astrea and Celadon: An Untouched Portrait of Aphra Behn', *PMLA* 49 (1934):544-559

Poems on Affairs of State: From the Time of Oliver Cromwell, to the Abdication of K. James the Second, London, 1697

Pollen, J.H., ed., *A Briefe Historie of the Glorious Martyrdom of Twelve Reverend Priests/Father Edmund Campion & His Companions/ By William Cardinal Allen/ With Contemporary Verses by the Venerable Henry Walpole, & the Earliest Engravings of the Martyrdom/ Reprinted from the (probably unique) Copy in the British Museum*, London, Burns & Oates, 1908

Poole, Reginald Lane, *Catalogue of Portraits in the Possession of the University, Colleges, City and County of Oxford*, Oxford, Clarendon Press, 1912

Pope, Alexander, *Letters of Mr. Pope, and Several Eminent Persons. From the Year 1705 to 1735*, London, 1735

[Poulain de la Barre, Francois], *The Woman As Good as the Man: Or, The Equallity of Both Sexes. Written Originally in French, And*

WORKS CITED

Translated into English by A. L., London, T. M. for N. Brooks, 1677

Powell, George, *Imposture Defeated; or, A Trick to Cheat the Devil*, London, Richard Wellington, 1698

Primrose, Diana, *A Chaine of Pearle. Or, a memoriall of the peerles Graces, and Heroick Vertues of Queen Elizabeth of Glorious Memory. Composed by the Noble Lady, Diana Primrose*, London, Printed for Thomas Paine, to be sold by Philip Waterhouse, 1630

Prior, Roger, 'Jewish Musicians at the Tudor Court', *The Musical Quarterly*, LXIX (1983), 253-265

Quaintance, Richard E., 'French Sources of the Restoration "Imperfect Enjoyment" Poem', *Philological Quarterly*, 2,2 (April 1963), 190-199

Quarles, Francis, *Emblemes*, Cambridge, Francis Eglesfield, 1643

——, *Sions Sonnets Sung by Solomon the King and periphras'd by F. Quarles*, London, 1625

Radcliffe, Alexander, *The Ramble: an Anti-Heroick Poem Together with some Terrestrial Hymns and Carnal Ejaculations*, London, for the author, to be sold by Walter Davis, 1682

Rait, R. S., ed., *Five Stuart Princesses: Margaret of Scotland, Elizabeth of Bohemia, Mary of Orange, Henrietta of Orleans, Sophia of Hanover*, Westminster, Archibald Constable, 1902

Raleigh, Sir Walter, *The Historie of the World. In Five Books... By Sir Walter Raleigh, Knight*, London, [Dorothy Jaggard?] for G. Lathum and R. Young, 1634

Ramsay, Allen, *The Tea-Table Miscellany: A Collection of Choice Songs, Scots and English in Two Volumes, By Allan Ramsay*, The Seventeenth Edition, Kilmarnock, J. Wilson, 1788

Reynolds, Myra, ed., *The Poems of Anne, Countess of Winchelsea, from the original edition of 1713 and from unpublished manuscripts*, Chicago, University of Chicago Press, 1903

Ringler, William A., ed., *The Poems of Sir Philip Sidney*, Oxford, Clarendon Press, 1962

Roberts, Josephine A., 'The Biographical Problem of *Pamphilia to Amphilanthus*', *Tulsa Studies in Women's Literature*, 1,1 (Spring, 1982) 43-53

——, ed., *The Poems of Lady Mary Wroth*, Baton Rouge and London, Louisiana State University Press, 1983

Rollins, Hyder, ed., *The Pepys Ballads*, Cambridge, Massachusetts, Harvard University Press, 1931

Rowe, Theophilus, ed., *The Miscellaneous Works in Prose and Verse of Mrs. Elizabeth Rowe. The Greater Part now first published, by her order, from her Original Manuscripts, by Mr. Theophilus Rowe*, London, R. Hett and R. Dodsley, 1739

Rowse, A. L., *The Case Books of Simon Forman: Sex and Society in Shakespeare's Age*, London, Picador, 1976

——, ed., *The Poems of Shakespeare's Dark Lady*, London, Jonathan Cape, 1978

Sackville-West, Vita, ed., *The Diary of the Lady Anne Clifford*, London,

W. Heineman, 1923

Saltmarsh, John, *Poemata Sacra*, Cambridge, T. Buck for R. Daniel, 1636

S[altonstall], W[ye], *Ovids Heroicall Epistles; Englished by W.S.*, London, R.B. for M. Sparke, 1636

A Satyrical Epistle to the Female Author of a Poem call'd Silvia's Revenge &c. By the author of the Satyr against Women, London, R. Bentley, 1961

Savile, George, Marquis of Halifax, *The ladies New-Years gift*, Second Edition, London, Randal Taylor, 1688

Scott, Dom Geoffrey, O.S.B., *'Sacredness of Majesty': The English Benedictines and the Cult of King James II*, Huntingdon, The Royal Stuart Society, 1984

Scott, Sir Walter, *The Works of John Dryden*, revised by George Saintsbury, Edinburgh, W. Paterson, 1882-1893

Scott-Montcrieff, Robert, ed., *The Household Book of Lady Griselle Baillie 1692-1733*, Edinburgh, Scottish History Society, 1911

[Shadwell, Thomas], *The 'Tory Poets'. A Satyr*, London, R. Johnson, 1682

Shafer, Robert, *The English Ode to 1660. An Essay in Literary History*, New York, Gordian Press, 1966

Shapiro, Arlene Iris, 'Elizabeth Cary: Her Life, Letters, and Art', Ph.D. Dissertation, State University of New York at Stony Brook, 1984

Sharpe, Joane, see Sowernam, Ester.

Sherburne, John, *Ovids Heroicall Epistles, Englished by J. Sherburne, Gent.*, London, E.G. for W. Cooke, 1639

Shirley, John, *The Illustrious History of Women, or a Compendium of the many virtues that adorn that fair sex*, London, J. Harris, 1686

Simpson, Richard, ed., *The Lady Falkland, her Life, from a MS in the Imperial Archives at Lille, France*, London, Catholic Publishing and Bookselling Co., 1861

Singer Rowe, Elizabeth, *Devout Exercises of the Heart in Meditation and Soliloquy and Praise... Reviewed and Published at her Request by I. Watts, D.D....* London, R. Hett, 1738

———, *Philomela: Or, Poems by Mrs. Elizabeth Singer [now Rowe], Of Frome in Somersetshire... The Second Edition*, London, E. Curll, 1737

———, *Poems on Several Occasions. Written by Philomela*, London, John Dunton, 1696

Smith, G. C. Moore, ed., *The Letters of Dorothy Osborne to William Temple*, Oxford, Clarendon Press, 1928; rpt. Oxford, Clarendon Press, 1968

Souers, Philip Webster, *The Matchless Orinda*, Harvard Studies in English, 5, Cambridge, Massachusetts, Harvard University Press, 1931

Southerne, Thomas, *The Fatal Marriage; or, The Innocent Adultery*, London, Jacob Tonson, 1694

———, *Oroonoko: A Tragedy*, London, H. Playford, B. Tooke, and S.

WORKS CITED

Buckley, 1696

Sowernam, Ester (pseud.), *Ester hath hang'd Haman; or, An Answere To a lewd Pamphlet, entituled, The Arraignment of Women. With the arraignment of lewd, idle, froward, and unconstant men, and Husbands. Divided into two Parts. The first proveth the dignity and worthinesse of Women, out of divine Testimonies. The second shewing the estimation of the Foeminine Sexe, in ancient and Pagan times; all which is acknowledged by men themselves in their daily actions. Written by Ester Sowernam, neither Maide, Wife nor Widdowe, yet really all, and therefore experienced to defend all*, London, [T. Snodham] for N. Bourne, 1617

Speght, Rachel, *Mortalities Memorandum, with a Dreame Prefixed, imaginarie in manner; reall in matter*, London, E. Griffen for J. Bloome, 1621

————, *A Mouzell for Melastomus, the Cynical Bayter of, and foule mouthed Barker against Evah's sex. Or an apologeticall Answere to that Irreligious and Illiterate Pamphlet made by Jo. Sw. and by him Intituled, the Arraignment of Women*, London, N. Okes for T. Archer, 1617

Spencer, Jane, 'Creating the Woman Writer: The Autobiographical Works of Jane Barker', *Tulsa Studies in Women's Literature*, 2,2 (Fall, 1983), 165-181

————, *The Rise of the Woman Novelist, from Aphra Behn to Jane Austen*, London, Basil Blackwell, 1986

Spufford, Margaret, 'First steps in literacy: the reading and writing experiences of the humblest seventeenth century spiritual autobiographers', *Social History*, 4 (1979), 407-435

Stanford, Ann, *Anne Bradstreet: The Worldly Puritan. An Introduction to Her Poetry*, New York, Burt Franklin, 1974

Starr, Nathan Comfort, '*The Concealed Fansyes*: A Play by Lady Jane Cavendish and Lady Elizabeth Brackley', *PMLA* 46 (1931), 802-838

Stauffer, Donald A., 'A Deep and Sad Passion', in *The Parrott Presentation Volume*, Ed. Hardin Craig, New York, Russell and Russell, 1967

Stecher, Henry F., *Elizabeth Singer Rowe, the Poetess of Frome: A Study in Eighteenth-Century English Pietism*, Bern and Frankfurt, Lang, 1973

Steeholm, Clara and Hardy, *James I of England: The Wisest Fool in Christendom*, New York, Covici Friede Publishers, 1938

Stewart, Stanley, *The Enclosed Garden: The Tradition and the Image in Seventeenth-Century Poetry*, Madison, University of Wisconsin Press, 1966

Stone, Lawrence, *The Family, Sex and Marriage in England, 1500-1800*, London, Abridged Edition, Penguin Books, 1982

Summers, Montague, ed., *The Works of Aphra Behn*, London, William Heineman, 1915

[Swetnam, Joseph], *The Arraignment of Lewde, idle, froward, and unconstant women: Or the vanitie of them, choose you whether. With a*

Commendacion of wise, vertuous and honest Women. Pleasant for married Men, profitable for young Men, and hurtfull to none, London, E. Alde for T. Archer, 1615

Sylvester, Joshua, trans., *Bartas: His Devine Weekes & Workes Translated and Dedicated to the Kings most excellent Majestie*, London, Humphrey Lownes, 1611 (third edition)

Tate, Nahum, *Poems by Several Hands, And On Several Occasions. Collected by N. Tate*, London, J. Hindmarsh, 1685

'Tattlewell, Mary' and 'Ioane Hit-him-home', *The women's sharpe revenge: Or an answer to Sir Sel dome Sober that writ those railing Pamphlets called the Iuniper and Crab-tree Lecture, &c. Being a sound Reply and a full confutation of those Bookes: with an Apology in this case for the defence of us women. Performed by Mary Tattle-well, and Ioane Hit-him-home, Spinsters*, London, Ia. Becket, 1640

The Ten Pleasures of Marriage, 1682; rpt. Navarre Society, 1922

Thomas, Elizabeth and Richard Gwinnet, *Pylades and Corinna: or, Memoirs of the Lives, Amours, and Writings of Richard Gwinnet Esq; Of Great Shurdington in Gloucestershire; and Mrs. Elizabeth Thomas Jun*, London, [Edmund Curll], 1731-1732

Thomas, Reverend Patrick H.B., 'An Edition of the Poems and Letters of Katherine Philips, 1632-1664', Ph.D. thesis, University College of Wales, Aberystwyth

Thomson, W., *Orpheus Caledonius or a Collection of the best Scotch Songs set to Music by W. Thomson*, London, Engrav'd & Printed for the Author at his house in Leicester Fields, 1726

Thorn-Drury, George, 'An Unrecorded Play-Title', *Review of English Studies* 6 (July, 1930), 316-318

Thornton, Alice, *The Autobiography of Mrs. Alice Thornton, of East Newton, Co. York*, Publications of the Surtees Society, Vol. 62, Durham, [London], and Edinburgh, 1875

Thorpe, James, *The Poems of Sir George Etherege*, Princeton, Princeton University Press, 1963

Tipper, Elizabeth, *The Pilgrim's Viaticum: or, the Destitute, but not forlorn. Being a Divine Poem, Digested from Meditations upon the Holy Scripture*, London, J. Wilkins, 1698

Tonson, Jacob, ed., *Poetical Miscellanies: The Fifth Part. Containing a Collection of Original Poems, With Several New Translations. By the most Eminent Hands*, London, Jacob Tonson, 1704

Traill, H.D., ed., *Social England*, London, Cassell, 1909

Trapnel, Anna, *Anna Trapnel's Report and Plea. or, a Narrative Of her Journey from London into Cornwal, the occasion of it, the Lord's encouragements to it... Whereto is annexed A Defiance Against... scandalous reports*, London, Thomas Brewster, 1654

————, *The Cry of a Stone or a Relation of Something spoken at Whitehall, by Anna Trapnel*, London, 1654

————, *A Legacy for Saints; Being Several Experiences of the dealings of God with Anna Trapnel, In, and after her Conversion, (written some years since with her own hand) and now coming to the sight of some friends, they have judged them worthy of publike view: Together with some Letters of a latter date, sent to the Congregation with whom she walks in the fellowship of the Gospel, and to some other Friends,* London, T. Brewster, 1654

[Trapp, Joseph], *The Players turn'd Academicks; or, A Description (In Merry Metre) of their Translation from the Theatre in Little Lincolns-Inn-Field, to the Tennis-Court in Oxford,* London, 1703

Trevor-Roper, H. R., *Religion, the Reformation and Social Change,* London, MacMillan, 1967

Triumphs Of Female Wit, In some Pindarick Odes. Or, The Emulation. Together With an Answer to an Objector against Female Ingenuity, and Capacity of Learning. Also, A preface to the Masculine Sex, by a Young Lady, London, T. Malthus and J. Waltho, 1583

[Trotter, Catharine], *Agnes de Castro, a Tragedy,* London, H. Rhodes, R. Parker, and S. Briscoe, 1696

————, *Love at a Loss, or, Most Votes Carry It,* London, William Turner, 1701

————, *The Unhappy Penitent,* London, William Turner and John Nutt, 1701

Trotter, David, *The Poetry of Abraham Cowley,* London, MacMillan, 1979

Tryon, Thomas, *The Way to Health, Long Life and Happiness, or, A Discourse of temperance and The particular nature of all things requisit for the Life of Man,* London, Andrew Sowle, 1683

Turberville, George, *The Booke of Faulconrie or Hawking... Collected out of the best Authors,* London, Andrew Sowle, 1583

————, trans., *The Heroicall Epistles of the Learned poet Publius Ovidius Naso, in Englishe Verse,* London, H. Denham, 1567

Tusser, Thomas, *Five Hundreth Pointes of Good Husbandry united to as many of good huswiferie, nowe lately augmented,* H. Denham for R. Tottil, 1573

Tweedie, William K., ed., *Select Biographies edited for the Wodrow Society, chiefly from manuscripts in the Library of the Faculty of Advocates,* Edinburgh, Wodrow Society, 1845

Van Lennep, William, Emmet L. Avery and Arthur H. Scouten, eds., *The London Stage 1660-1800: A Calendar of Plays, Entertainments & Afterpieces. Together with Casts, Box-Receipts and Contemporary Comment. Compiled from the Playbills, Newspapers and Theatrical Diaries of the Period,* Carbondale, Southern Illinois University Press, 1960-1968

Van Schurman, Anna Maria, *The Learned Maid; or, Whether a Maid may be a Scholar? A Logic Exercise. Written in Latine by that incomparable Virgin Anna Maria a Schurman of Utrecht,* Clement Barksdale, trans., London, John Redmayne, 1659

Vann, Richard T., *The Social Development of English Quakerism 1655-1755,* Cambridge, Massachusetts, Harvard University Press, 1969

Vaughan, Henry, *Silex Scintillans: or Sacred Poems and Private Ejaculations. By Henry Vaughan Silurist*, London, H. Blunden, 1650

———, *Olor Iscanus. A Collection of Some Select Poems, And Translations, Formerly written by Mr. Henry Vaughn Silurist*, London, T. W. for Humphrey Moseley, 1651

Vieth, David M., ed., *The Complete Poems of John Wilmot, Earl of Rochester*, New Haven, Yale University Press, 1968

———, *Attributions in Restoration Poetry: A Study of Rochester's Poems of 1680*, London & New Haven, Yale University Press, 1963

Walker, A., *The Holy Life of Mrs. Elizabeth Walker, late Wife of A. W. D. D. Rector of Fyfield in Essex. Giving a modest and short Account of her Exemplary Piety and Charity. Published for the Glory of God, and provoking others to the like Graces and Vertues. Chiefly designed to be given to her Friends, who can abundantly testifie to the Truth of what is here related. With some usefull Papers and Letters writ by her on several Occasions*, London, John Leake, for the Author, 1690

Walker, Keith, ed., *The Poems of John Wilmot, Earl of Rochester*, Oxford, Basil Blackwell, 1984

Waller, G. F., ed., *The Triumph of Death and Other Unpublished and Uncollected Poems by Mary Sidney, Countess of Pembroke (1561-1621)*, Salzburg, Salzburg Studies in English Literature, 1977

———, *Mary Sidney, Countess of Pembroke: A Critical Study of her Writing and Literary Milieu*, Salzburg, Austria, Institut für Anglistik und Amerikanistik, 1979

Walsh, Elizabeth, and Richard Jeffree, *'The Excellent Mrs Mary Beale'*, Exhibition Catalogue, Inner London Education Authority, 1975

Warburg, Ingrid, *Lucy Hutchinson: Das Bild einer Puritanerin*, Hamburg, 1937

Warrender, Margaret, *Marchmont and Humes of Polwarth by one of their descendants*, Edinburgh and London, William Blackwood & Sons, 1894

Watson, Foster, *De Vives and the Renascence Education of Women*, New York, Longmans Green, 1912

Weamys, Anna, *A Continuation of Sir Philip Sidney's Arcadia: Wherein is handled the Loves of Amphialus and Helena Queen of Corinth, Prince Plangus and Erona. With the Historie of the Loves of Old Glaius and Young Strephon to Urania*, London, Thomas Heath, 1651

Weldon, Dom Benet, O. S. B., *A Chronicle of the English Benedictine Monks From the Renewing of their Congregation in the Days of Queen Mary, to the Death of King James II*, ed. G. Dolan, Worcester, Stanbrook Abbey, 1881

Welwood, James, *Mercurius Reformatus: or the New Observator. Containing Reflexions upon the most Remarkable Events, Falling out from Time to Time in Europe, and more particularly in England*, 1689-1691

Wentworth, Anne, *A Vindication of Anne Wentworth. Published*

WORKS CITED

according to the Will of God and Direction of Charity. By Anne Wentworth, London, 1677

White, Elizabeth Wade, *Anne Bradstreet: The Tenth Muse*, New York, Oxford University Press, 1971

White, Helen C., *Tudor Books of Saints and Martyrs*, Madison, University of Wisconsin Press, 1963

Wiley, Autrey Nell, 'Female Prologues and Epilogues in English Plays', *PMLA*, 48 (1933), 1060-1079

———, *Rare Prologues and Epilogues 1642-1700*, London, George Allen and Unwin, 1940

Williams, Harold, ed., *The Poems of Jonathan Swift*, Second edition, Oxford, Clarendon Press, 1958

[Wilmot, John, Earl of Rochester], *Poems on Several Occasions*. By the Right Honourable, the E. of R---, Printed at Antwerp, 1680

———, *Poems &c. on Several Occasions: With Valentinian, a Tragedy*, London, Jacob Tonson, 1691

W[instanley], W[illiam], *The New Help To Discourse: Or, Wit, Mirth and Jollity, Intermixt With more Serious Matters... The Third Edition, with many new Additions*, London, H. C. [for] P. Parker, 1684

Wit and Mirth: or, Pills to Purge Melancholy:... The Second Edition... Carefully Corrected, London, W. Pearson, 1707

Woodbridge, Linda, *Women and the English Renaissance: Literature and the Nature of Womankind, 1540-1620*, Urbana and Chicago, University of Illinois Press, 1984

Woodcock, George, *The Incomparable Aphra*, London, T.V. Boardman, 1948

Woodford, Samuel, *A Paraphrase Upon The Psalms Of David*, London, R. White for Octavian Pullein, 1667

Woodhead, John R., *The Rulers of London: 1660-1689; a Biographical Record of the Aldermen and Common Councilmen of the City of London*, London, London and Middlesex Archaeological Society, 1965

Woolf, Virginia, *Collected Essays*, London, Hogarth, 1967

Woolley, Hannah, *The Gentlewomans Companion; or a Guide to the Female Sex, with Letters and Discourses Upon All Occasions*, London, 1673

Yates, Frances A., *Astraea: The Imperial Theme in the Sixteenth Century*, London and Boston, Routledge & Kegan Paul, 1975